Poet and Orator

Trends in Classics – Supplementary Volumes

Edited by
Franco Montanari and Antonios Rengakos

Associate Editors
Evangelos Karakasis · Fausto Montana · Lara Pagani
Serena Perrone · Evina Sistakou · Christos Tsagalis

Scientific Committee
Alberto Bernabé · Margarethe Billerbeck
Claude Calame · Jonas Grethlein · Philip R. Hardie
Stephen J. Harrison · Richard Hunter · Christina Kraus
Giuseppe Mastromarco · Gregory Nagy
Theodore D. Papanghelis · Giusto Picone
Tim Whitmarsh · Bernhard Zimmermann

Volume 74

Poet and Orator

A Symbiotic Relationship in Democratic Athens

Edited by
Andreas Markantonatos and Eleni Volonaki

DE GRUYTER

ISBN 978-3-11-073689-2
e-ISBN (PDF) 978-3-11-062972-9
e-ISBN (EPUB) 978-3-11-062698-8
ISSN 1868-4785

Library of Congress Control Number: 2019931704

Bibliographic information published by the Deutsche Nationalbibliothek
The Deutsche Nationalbibliothek lists this publication in the Deutsche Nationalbibliografie;
detailed bibliographic data are available on the Internet at http://dnb.dnb.de.

© 2020 Walter de Gruyter GmbH, Berlin/Boston
This volume is text- and page-identical with the hardback published in 2019.
Editorial Office: Alessia Ferreccio and Katerina Zianna
Logo: Christopher Schneider, Laufen
Printing and binding: CPI books GmbH, Leck

www.degruyter.com

Preface

In October 2015 the Department of Philology at the University of the Peloponnese, together with the Centre for Ancient Rhetoric and Drama (C.A.R.D.), organized the First Attic Drama and Oratory International Conference with the theme: *Poet and Orator: A Symbiotic Relationship in Democratic Athens*. This four-day conference, as well as marking the inauguration of the Centre for Ancient Rhetoric and Drama (C.A.R.D.) and the 10-year anniversary of the Department of Philology, University of the Peloponnese, aimed to explore the close and interdependent relationship between the dramatist and the orator in the context of Athenian democracy by bringing together a great number of scholars with expertise on different aspects of ancient Greek theatre and Attic rhetoric.

This volume of proceedings provides an opportunity for readers to engage with a wide selection of refereed papers that were presented during the First Attic Drama and Oratory International Conference at Kalamata. In the conference we sought to raise crucial questions about how tragic and comic plays composed in the classical and postclassical periods respond to the materiality of political conflict as this is eloquently and vehemently expressed in Attic speech-making. It is perhaps not surprising that the striking interdependence in interests and motivations of Athenian dramatists and orators should take centre stage in this wide-ranging debate about the special ways in which Greek drama of the fifth and fourth centuries BCE was widely cross-fertilized not only by figures of language and rhetorical tropes but also by the social and political significance of oratory and rhetoric.

More than that, this international gathering of both worldwide acclaimed classicists and acute younger Hellenists was envisaged as part of the general effort, almost unanimously acknowledged as valid and productive, to explore the impact of formalized speech and craftsmanship rhetoric in general upon Attic drama as a moral and educational force in the Athenian city-state. Our contention was then and remains unchanged ever since that both poet and orator seek to deepen the central tensions of their work and to enlarge the main themes of their texts to even broader terms by investing in the art of rhetoric, whilst at the same time, through a skilful handling of events, evaluating the past and establishing standards or ideology. This conference, therefore, as well as bringing into clearer focus the notion of drama and oratory as important media of public inquiry and critique, aimed to generate significant attention to the unified intentions of the dramatist and the orator to establish favourable conditions of internal stability in democratic Athens. We hope that readers both enjoy and find valuable their engagement with these ideas and beliefs regarding the indissoluble bond between oratorical expertise and dramatic artistry.

In order to improve the readability of this collection of erudite articles every effort has been made to ensure that the book stays consistent, while at the same time retaining each author's stylistic intent and special preferences. On a personal note, we wish to express our immense gratitude to Professors Franco Montanari and Antonios Rengakos, chief-editors of the *Trends in Classics* series of academic monographs, for their sustaining patience and wise advice, as well as to the two anonymous readers for their useful recommendations. Last but not least we are deeply indebted to Ms Theodora Kourkoulou for aid in the preparation of the manuscript.

Andreas Markantonatos
Eleni Volonaki
Kalamata, May 2018

Contents

Preface —— V

Part I: Rhetoric in Attic Drama

Guido Avezzù
Hecuba's Rhetoric —— 3

Andreas Fountoulakis
The Rhetoric of *Erôs* in Menander's *Samia* —— 33

Edith Hall
Competitive Vocal Performance in Aristophanes' *Knights* —— 71

Ioanna Karamanou
**Fragments of Euripidean Rhetoric:
The Trial-Debate in Euripides' *Alexandros*** —— 83

Marcel Lysgaard Lech
Praise, Past and Ponytails: The Funeral Oration and Democratic Ideology in the Parabasis of Aristophanes' *Knights* —— 101

Andreas Markantonatos
**Greek Tragedy and Attic Oratory:
The *Agôn*-Scenes in Euripides' *Alcestis*** —— 123

Andrea Rodighiero
'Do you see this, natives of this land?': Formalized Speech, Rhetoric, and Character in Sophocles' *Oedipus at Colonus* 728–1043 —— 153

Adele C. Scafuro
**Justifying Murder and Rejecting Revenge:
Hypothetical Arguments and Imaginary Lawcourts in the Oresteian Tragedies
(Aeschylus *Oresteia*; Sophocles *Electra*; Euripides *Electra* and *Orestes*)** —— 181

Part II: Politics, Rhetoric and Poetry

Chris Carey
Drama and Democracy —— 233

Ioannis N. Perysinakis
**From the Ancient Quarrel Between Philosophy and Poetry:
Archaic Moral Values and Political Behaviour in Aristophanes'** *Frogs* —— 249

Margarita Sotiriou
Aspects of Epinician Rhetoric and the Democratic *polis***:
Bacchylides** *Ep.* **10 Sn.-M.** —— 269

Eleni Volonaki
Performing the Past in Lycurgus' Speech *Against Leocrates* —— 281

Part III: Drama in Attic Oratory

Evangelos Alexiou
Rhetoric, Poetry and the *agelaioi sophistai***: The Innovative Isocrates** —— 305

Mike Edwards
The Orators and Greek Drama —— 329

Lázló Horváth
Dramatic Elements as Rhetorical Means in Hyperides' *Timandrus* —— 339

Andreas Seraphim
Thespians in the Law-Court: Sincerity, Community and Persuasion in Selected Speeches of Forensic Oratory —— 347

Part IV: Society, Law and Drama

Penelope Frangakis
The Reception of Rhetoric in Greek Drama of the Fifth Century BCE: The Use of Rhetorical Techniques in the Art of Euripides —— 365

Brenda Griffith-Williams
Families and Family Relationships in the Speeches of Isaios and in Middle and New Comedy —— 375

Edward M. Harris
Aeschylus' *Eumenides*: The Role of the Areopagus, The Rule of Law and Political Discourse in Attic Tragedy —— 389

List of Contributors —— 421
General Index —— 425
Index Locorum —— 435
Index of Greek Words —— 453

Part I: **Rhetoric in Attic Drama**

Guido Avezzù
Hecuba's Rhetoric

In her study of Euripides' *Hecuba* (1995), Judith Mossman carried out a thorough analysis of the rhetoric of the protagonist, delving into its function in both Hecuba's and her interlocutors' characterization, as well as in the play's overall dramaturgical structure. In a subsequent contribution about Electra and Clytemnestra in Euripides' *Electra*, she convincingly argued that 'the Greek tragedians did try to make their female characters sound, not like *real women*, but at least like *tragic women*, as opposed to tragic men'. In her view, 'characterization can be put to so many different purposes, but usually, in one way or another, made them considerably more complex and challenging'.[1] Therefore, 'the whole range of extrinsic factors', such as 'the conventions of tragic language and tragic performance, the peculiar characteristics of Greek, the discourse structure of the dramatic mode [...] that always has to be taken into account when interpreting Greek drama, [...] sketch for us a tentative reconstruction of how what is in the text might match up to the expectations and preconceptions of the audience'. Moving from these premises, my contribution wishes to respond to Mossman's suggestive question on 'what features of tragic speech, especially [in] trimeter speech as opposed to lyrics', we might 'be able to identify as making a character sound like a woman'. I shall argue that Hecuba's subversive appropriation of a 'male' rhetoric and its revision in lyrical terms in two distinct plays pivoting on the power of her eloquence provides one such feature, 'making a character sound like a woman'. In particular, I wish to cope with two distinct moments in which Hecuba plays a relevant tragic role, and more precisely: (a) in the tragedy bearing her name, which, as is well known, dates back to 425–421, if we take into account the resolutions of its iambic trimeters, or instead to a period before 423, as suggested by the plausible allusions contained in Aristophanes' *Clouds*;[2] (b) in *The Trojan Women*, a play which, according to Aelianus' *Varia Historia* 2.8, was performed in 415. In both, Hecuba is indisputably the protagonist. My purpose is to bring into focus her peculiar interlacing of two argumentative lines, conceptually distinct and yet potentially integrated in the performance: (1) a specific forensic strategy of persuasion followed by a gestural rhetoric involving her own bodily parts as equivalents of the 'constituent parts' (μόρια, μέρη) mentioned in the late

---

1 Mossman 2001, 375 (my emphasis).
2 Collard 1991, 34f., but see also Bain 1977, 16 n. 1.

https://doi.org/10.1515/9783110629729-001

fifth-century rhetorical theories; (2) an apt use of *ekphrasis* as a descriptive strategy of those same bodily parts which she exhibits gesturally, while exploiting the expressive power of chanting and singing. These two lines form an integrated performance in the latter play, as if they were two voices of one and the same performative score.

I will begin with an analysis of the old Queen's rhetorical strategies in *Hec.* 736–836, following her initially problematic approach to Agamemnon; I will then move on to a discussion of 837–840 where she performs a 'Daedalean disarticulation' of her own body into several different 'speakers' as her ultimate persuasive resource, after acknowledging the failure of her previous tactics. Next, I will consider Hecuba's analogous disarticulation of her own body in *The Trojan Women*, 98–196, where she progresses from the recitative to the monody, and from the monody to the lyrical-responsorial structure of the *Parodos*. My contribution thus provides a commentary on the rhetorical and performative import of the two above-mentioned sequences from *Hecuba* and *The Trojan Women*.

1 *Hec.* 736–845

I will investigate Hecuba's (H.) ingenious rhetoric in her exchange with Agamemnon (A.), starting from her 'aside' (1.1: 736–786) and then proceeding to her subsequent appeal to *nomos* (1.2: 798–805). In Hecuba's rhetorical manipulation, progressing through failures and successive new attempts, persuasion replaces the Law. This is manifest first in her effort to provoke A. to consider the human condition 'from afar' (1.3: 806–813, 'stand back like a painter...'), then in her recourse to *Peitho* and Aphrodite (1.4: 814–835), and, finally, once having realized the inefficacy of both, in her devising a 'Daedalic' rhetoric involving the expressiveness of her own body (1.5: 835–840).

1.1 736–786: *Hecuba's* 'aside' and her dialogue with Agamemnon

As is well known, H.'s plea against Polymestor (787–845) is preceded by a 'dialogic prelude', 'one of the most striking pieces of stage action to be found in Greek tragedy', as David Bain has described it (1977, 13). It has often been contended that the text of *Hec.* 756–759 might be corrupted; however, I believe that these lines, in the order in which they have been transmitted in one branch of the manuscript tradition, are genuine precisely because they make sense with no need for tampering with the text, as will soon be seen – for more details on the text see *Appendix*, 24–25.

H.'s plea is introduced by
(a) what appears to be a dialogue between H. and A. (736–751): a regular, albeit 'open', distichomythia:[3] A./H. – A./H. – A. (739–748), preceded and followed by two groups of three lines, both performed by H. (736–738 and 749–751);
(b) a concise *prothesis* of H.'s case, divided in two phases: (I) a brief 'open' distichomythia: H. – A./H. (752–757), and then (II) a single line spoken by A. and H. (758–759);
(c) a *diegesis* concerning Polydoros' murder, cast in stichomythic form, this too seemingly 'open': H./A. ... H/A. – H. (760–782);
(d) A.'s show of compassion, and H.'s own comment, again in stichomythic form (783–786). Within this last sequence, 786 is only seemingly the first line of H's *rhesis*, since in fact it closes the dialogue,[4] and H. starts off her *rhesis* at 787. On the distribution and dramaturgical characterization of 736–786 see *Appendix*, 25–26.

As Mastronarde has rightly remarked, at 736–751 H.'s '[a]bsorption in a self-directed debate allows [her] to ignore A.'s attempt to engage her in dialogue'.[5] It should be recalled that at his entrance on stage (726), A. asks her questions (739–748), but receives no direct reply, since the Queen is speaking to herself, bent over Polydoros' corpse. A. hears her lament (740), but cannot find out its cause, because, although he sees the dead body in front of his own tent (733–735, cf. 761), he does not recognize it as being H.'s son. Thus, despite watching the scene from the same standpoint as the audience's, he shows his inability to comprehend it fully. Indeed, he understands her words less clearly than the audience themselves, who have heard her first desperate cry at 681 and know the reason of her despair. Consequently, A.'s manifest incomprehension on stage clashes with the audience's understanding of what is going on as they watch the scene's dynamic unfolding with sufficient knowledge of the facts. H.'s lines, which, therefore, might be considered as a kind of aside, open with H.'s address to herself and her misfortune (736–737a), but soon focus upon the choice she has to make (τί δράσω; 737b etc.): whether to implore her enemy, whom she does not perceive as

---

[3] 'Open' in the sense that their dialogue does not symmetrically end with an equal number of lines of the other interlocutor. However, as we shall see about 760–782, this asymmetry is quite specious.
[4] 785–786: ΑΓ. [...] τίς οὕτω δυστυχὴς ἔφυ γυνή; / ΕΚ. Οὐκ ἔστιν, εἰ μὴ κτλ.
[5] Mastronarde 1979, 78.

far away from herself (738: Ἀγαμέμνονος τοῦδε, 746: τοῦδε), or to keep silent, two options which she will debate with herself until the final τί στρέφω τάδε; (750: 'why do I keep pondering this question?').[6] However, it should be noticed that, as Schadewaldt already acknowledged in 1926, this distichomythia is 'not at all a sheer aside' (30),[7] since H.'s posture prevents A. from seeing rather than hearing: starting from 737–738 (H.'s πότερα ... ἤ) he begins to perceive that she is making up her mind about something, but he does not know what has happened (739–740: τί μοι [...] τὸ πραχθὲν δ' οὐ λέγεις),[8] and, '[being] no diviner', he is also unable to 'search out the path of [her] intentions'.[9] Bain offers a good interpretation of the visual scene: 'A. is supposed to hear something of what H. is saying, but not to be able properly to make out its meaning. [...] All this is different from the type of aside where the other character is quite unaware that the aside-speaker is speaking at all' (1977, 15).[10] This continuously interrupted aside, diffracted between A. on stage and the off-stage audience, unfolds exclusively for the latter, who understand that H. is debating with herself whether she should ask the King to avenge her on Polymestor or not. It has been noticed that H.'s is a 'refusal of contact', as Mastronarde put it (1979, 78–79), and that she shows that she is oblivious of 'the increasing irritation of A.' (Gregory 1999,132). Nevertheless, her self-muttering could also be interpreted as the dramatic development of a rhetorical 'reply by anticipation', or *prokatalepsis*,[11] aimed at prompting A. to come closer to her both physically and emotionally. In fact, it is precisely her communicative reticence allowing for fragments of her own self-talk to be heard

---

6 Transl. Kovacs 1995. This question will eventually solve the previous one raised at 737b.
7 'The obvious way to describe H.'s utterances at 736–738, 741–742, 745–746, and 749–751 is to call them 'asides' and most scholars agree in using the term here. Admittedly, H.'s remarks do not constitute what might be considered the purest form of aside', Bain 1977, 15.
8 Where δ[έ] should be understood as a 'connective' rather than as an 'adversative'.
9 743–744: οὔτοι πέφυκα μάντις, ὥστε μὴ κλύων / ἐξιστορῆσαι σῶν ὁδὸν βουλευμάτων, transl. Collard 1991.
10 Likewise, '[740] δύρῃ [...] need not necessarily imply that A. has heard anything', Bain 1977, 15 n. 1, and '737–738 [...] is the utterance of H. that A. characterized or most probably characterized [...] as lamentation' (*ibid.*, n. 2).
11 Anaximenes Lamps. *Rhet. ad Alexandrum* 18 (1432b11–14): Προκατάληψις μὲν οὖν ἐστι, δι' ἧς τά τε τῶν ἀκουόντων ἐπιτιμήματα καὶ τοὺς τῶν ἀντιλέγειν μελλόντων λόγους προκαταλαμβάνοντες ὑπεξαιρήσομεν τὰς ἐπιφερομένας δυσχερείας ('Anticipation is the method by which we shall counteract the ill-feeling which is felt against us by anticipating the adverse criticisms of our audience and the arguments of those who are going to speak against us', transl. Forster 1924. On this technique of anticipation in Attic drama see Sansone 2012, 180–184, 192–204. Other examples of *prokatalepsis* in *Hec.* are pointed out by Sansone at 258–263 (H. to Odysseus) and 1201–125 (H. to A.) (*ibid.*, 183 n. 42).

that eventually succeeds in gaining the King's attention. We do not know what he actually grasps, but for sure the end of 745–746 emphatically voice her own doubts on his presumed hostility (see the epiphoric δυσμενής / δυσμενοῦς), which, if heard, might have an impact upon A.'s next move.[12] Whether the King catches these last words or not, H.'s mumbling does prompt him to break through the impasse, and himself to counterattack: 'Indeed, if you do want me to know nothing of these things, you and I have come to the same conclusion, because I likewise have no desire to hear' (747–748). H.'s sudden awareness of her imminent failure (749: 'I would not be able to avenge my children without him', transl. Collard 1991) in turn spurs her on to make an all-out effort (750–751), and finally leave her in communicative isolation to formulate her request (752–753). Her plea is again cunningly delayed through reticence, which thus appears as H.'s main strategy, that now leads A. to misinterpret her request as one for freedom. He shows himself to be ready to accommodate it (754–755), and for the second time H. receives a promise of safety which does not coincide with her own actual request (the first was Odysseus' at 301–302).[13]

All this seems to suggest that in this sequence it is possible to read the equivalent of a real oratorical *prooimion*, first and foremost aimed at gaining the addressee's favour. With reference to Aristotle's definition,[14] it could be called a 'medical treatment' (ἰάτρευμα) meant to heal 'the infirmities of the hearer(s)' ([ἡ] τοῦ ἀκροατοῦ μοχθηρί[α]). Here it proves efficacious also and perhaps precisely because it is applied by way of 'subtraction', as she will later do in summarizing her own request of vengeance (*prothesis*), already anticipated at 749 (τιμωρεῖν) and 756 (τιμωρουμένη). H.'s approach to her interlocutor is radically different from her previous one in her fruitless dialogue with Odysseus in the First Episode, where she had tried to solicit his benevolence by reminding him that she had

---

12 This aspect, although endowed with an inverted function, is shared by H.'s and Odysseus' oratorical performances in the First Episode: 300–301 (O.) 'Ἑκάβη [...] μηδὲ τῷ θυμουμένῳ / τὸν εὖ λέγοντα δυμενῆ ποιοῦ φρενί ('H., [...] in your heart's anger do not make an enemy of one who speaks for the best', transl. Collard 1991). Later, I will linger on ἐξιστορῆσαι at 236 (O.) ~ 744 (H.) and, more importantly, on the parallel between Odysseus' and H.'s exordia at 321 and 788, respectively. As regards Odysseus' *captatio benevolentiae* carried out through the negation of his ill feeling, compare e.g. *Trojan Women* 914–915, where Helen addresses Menelaos by saying ἴσως με, κἂν εὖ κἂν κακῶς δόξω λέγειν, / οὐκ ἀνταμείψῃ πολεμίαν ἡγούμενος ('[i]t may be that, whether I seem to be talking sense or not, you will make no reply to me since you consider me an enemy', transl. Kovacs 1999).
13 301–2: ἐγὼ τὸ μὲν σὸν σῶμ(α) [...] / σῴζειν ἕτοιμος εἰμι κοὐκ ἄλλως λέγω ('I am myself ready to save your own life [...] and I do not say this vainly', transl. Collard 1991).
14 *Rhet.* 3.1415a24–25 and 1403b34–35.

saved him on the occasion of his *ptocheia* (239–250; cf. 301 and *Od.* 4.244–246). Furthermore, as his benefactress (251–252), she had implicitly considered herself as one of his *philoi* (256). Instead of having instilled 'uncertainty' in her,[15] her earlier failure now seems to have taught her a lesson. Thus, if with Odysseus she had begun her speech by calling herself a 'slave', and then had moved on to a *captatio benevolentiae* in order to be allowed to 'ask him questions'[16] which should neither cause him pain nor bite his heart (234–236), now she chooses to catch A.'s attention by showing indifference towards him. This is even more surprising because she is physically located between the omnipotent conqueror's pressing presence on stage and his tent, which represents the symbolic space of her own slavery. Likewise, if in her previous plea she had tried to appease her addressee, now she wishes to arouse A.'s indignation against her absent opponent, Polymestor. Also in this case she demonstrates that she possesses an inborn rhetorical capacity pivoting on two crucial procedures selected by Aristotle among those to be used, and possibly combined, in forensic proems: to 'conciliate' the addressee with the speaker and 'to incite anger in' him against the opponent.[17] H.'s following step is to rely upon A. as the one who will carry out her revenge, because, being her owner, he is entitled to represent her as plaintiff.[18] Consequently, after focusing upon her own status of 'slave and enemy' (δούλη πολεμία) at 741, and acknowledging that A. is indispensable for her vengeance at 749–50, before proceeding to present her plaint in the stichomythic *diegesis* of 760–782,[19] at 756–757 H. declares her readiness to live her whole life as a slave if only she gains retribution. It should not be forgotten that her slavery is known to the audience beginning with the prologue, when she comes out from A.'s tent at 53 and Polydoros' Ghost complains about his mother's 'day of slavery' (56: δούλειον ἦμαρ). Lines 756–757 ('If I avenge myself on evil men, I am willing to be a slave for my whole lifetime')[20] contain not only, nor even mainly, an undoubtedly heroic 'belle réponse' (Weil

---

15 Gregory 1999, 135.
16 A. will use the same word (ἐξιστορῆσαι) at 744: 'search out the path (ἐξιστορῆσαι ... ὁδὸν) of your thoughts'.
17 *Rhet.* 1415a35s.: τὰ δὲ πρὸς τὸν ἀκροατὴν ἔκ τε τοῦ εὔνουν ποιῆσαι καὶ ἐκ τοῦ ὀργίσαι ('the topics of the *prooimion* which are addressed to the hearer are derived from the conciliation of his good will and irritating him' (*scil.* against the opponent) [transl. Cope/Sandys 1877].
18 See, e.g., Lanni 2006, 34.
19 The definitions 'narrative stichomythiai' (*Erzählstichomythien*) and, in particular, 'goal-directed narrative' (*zielgerichtete Erzählung*) are offered by Schwinge 1968, 193–267 (on *Hec.* 760–86 see pp. 193–198).
20 (Εκ.) [...] τοὺς κακοὺς δὲ τιμωρουμένη / αἰῶνα τὸν σύμπαντα δουλεύειν θέλω (transl. Collard 1991).

1868, 264), but also establish a connection between H.'s servile condition and the possibility for her to wreak revenge precisely because of her dependency on A., which is the only means she has to achieve her aim.

The dialogic form of the stichomythia has the effect of enlivening H.'s narrative, allowing A. to interpolate his own deduction (781: ὡς ἔοικεν, 'as it seems') of Polymestor's offence to Polydoros' dead body thrown into the sea, as well as his own sympathetic comments on her infinite woes (783, 785). The dialogue also emphasizes the tendency of forensic oratory to '[exchange] the periodic style' of the *diegesis* 'for a more simple style in which [...] short sentences become more numerous', as illustrated by Carey[21] with reference to Lysias 32.4–18.[22]

Hecuba's following monologue (787–845), which in Gordon Kirkwood's opinion is 'the link that gives the play a logical unity' (1947, 64), is skillfully structured on four argumentative lines (798–805; 806–813; 814–835; 835–840), which I will consider separately.

1.2 798–805: Hecuba's address to *nomos*

After the stichomythic narrative regarding Polydoros' murder, H.'s introduction at 788–789 echoes the mood of the very beginning of the *peroratio* by which Odysseus had grounded his apology for Polyxena's sacrifice on Greek *nomos*:[23]

> εἰ μὲν ὅσιά σοι παθεῖν δοκῶ, στέργοιμ' ἄν. (788–789)
>
> [i]f you think the treatment I have received is such as the gods approve, I will bear it.
> (transl. Kovacs 1995)

> εἰ δ' οἰκτρὰ πάσχειν φῄς, τάδ'ἀντάκουέ μου...
> ἡμεῖς δ', εἰ κακῶς νομίζομεν
> τιμᾶν τὸν ἐσθλόν, ἀμαθίαν ὀφλήσομεν. (321, 326–327)
>
> [i]f you say that your suffering is pitiful, hear my rejoinder ... As for us, if our practice of honouring the brave [warrior] is wrong, we shall be charged with folly.
> (transl. Collard 1991 modified)

---

21 Carey 1989, 210–212.
22 About the dramatization of *diegesis* in Lysias' speeches, see Eleni Volonaki's contribution in this volume.
23 As will emerge from my following discussion, I agree with Mossman's critique of the interpretation of *Hec.* 800 (1995, 182) proposed by Reckford 1985, 120 and Nussbaum 2001, 400 and n. *, which reduces *nomos* (twice at 800) to the notion of 'convention' or 'human artifact'.

Odysseus' words εἰ κακῶς νομίζομεν convey both the notion of 'custom'[24] and the idea of enacting it, albeit without the fully deliberative meaning it would have if the tense were aorist. In this respect it should be noticed that 'honouring the brave warrior' specifies the abstract and generic 'honouring of the dead' belonging to universally shared principles, independent of honour bestowed upon individual behaviours.[25] On the contrary, 'to perform human sacrifice at a tomb' (260–261, [H.] ἀνθρωποσφαγεῖν πρὸς τύμβον, transl. Kovacs 1995) belongs to the sphere of positive law, and in fact Odysseus will later include it in the Greeks' nomic production (326).[26] To this sphere also belongs the *nomos* that H. had appealed to in entreating Odysseus (291–292):

> νόμος δ' ἐν ὑμῖν τοῖς τ' ἐλευθέροις ἴσος
> καὶ τοῖσι δούλοις αἵματος κεῖται πέρι.[27]

> 'Moreover in your country there is a law laid down, the same for free men and slaves, concerning the shedding of blood'.
> (transl. Kovacs 1995)

In a different fashion from what happens in the First Episode, where both Odysseus and H. refer to a principle adopted by a specific community, which distinguishes it from other communities, in the Third Episode the Queen will ground her first attempt to approach A. on an appeal to a cosmic and absolute principle (799–801):

> ἡμεῖς μὲν οὖν δοῦλοί τε κἀσθενεῖς ἴσως·
> ἀλλ' οἱ θεοὶ σθένουσι χὠ κείνων κρατῶν
> νόμος· νόμῳ γὰρ τοὺς θεοὺς ἡγούμεθα   800
> καὶ ζῶμεν ἄδικα καὶ δίκαι' ὡρισμένοι.

---

[24] Cf., e.g., *Helen* 1065–1066: (ΕΛ.) ἀλλ' οὐ νομίζειν φήσομεν καθ' Ἑλλάδα / χέρσῳ καλύπτειν τοὺς θανόντας ἐναλίους ('But I'll make out that it isn't the Greek custom / to bury ashore those who were lost at sea', transl. Michie/Leach 1981).

[25] Suffice it to mention Herodotus, 3.38 and Antiphon Soph. fr. 44(a) D.-K. (on the latter see the conclusive assessment by Riesbeck 2011).

[26] As pointed out by Kirkwood 1947, 65, 'Odysseus says "if", but he is sure that the principle is a right one; it is, indeed, a mark that distinguishes Greek from barbarian; it contributes to the success of Greece, the lack of it to the failure of the barbarians (328–331)'.

[27] As is well known, this is an anachronistic reference to a fifth-century Athenian law, showing that H.'s appeal is precisely to positive law, cf. MacDowell 1963, 104–111.

We may be both slave and lacking in strength, but the gods do have strength, as does the Law that has power over them. So, in virtue of the Law we believe in the gods and are living beings who determine for themselves what is right and wrong.[28]

This *nomos* is different from the cultural elaboration of a people, and, therefore, also from positive rule, in that it is a right (δίκαιον) not 'conventional' (νομικόν) but 'natural' or 'native' (φυσικόν),[29] concerning, in this case, the relation between hospitality and the right of burial.

The definition of what *hosion* is depends upon this principle, which 'rules over the gods' (799–800).[30] Nonetheless, at least in this *rhesis*, its definition is given by negation, either implicitly, as at 788, where H.'s woes are to be interpreted as appearing to her *(an)hosia*, or explicitly, as at 790 and 792, where H. labels Polymestor *anhosiotatos* and his crime *anhosiotaton*. H. identifies a progression from *nomos*, that 'has strength' (σθένει, implicit at 799), to the gods who 'have strength' (σθένουσι, at the same line), but are subordinate to *nomos* (799–800), and eventually to men, who 'to some degree' (798: ἴσως, on whose interpretation see below) are 'weak' (798: ἀσθενεῖς): since they rely upon *nomos*, they both believe in the gods and define what is right and what is wrong (800–801). As a consequence of this progression, as far as H.'s argumentation is concerned, the *hosia* are neither merely 'sanctioned by the gods', nor 'holy' (if by this we mean 'divine'), as they are instead generally interpreted when these lines from *Hecuba* are translated.[31] If the foundation of the *hosia* transcends the gods also, it is true that, at least as regards H., the gods attribute their own strength (*sthenos*) to the *sthenos* of *nomos*. This makes the latter cogent both directly (as the Law presiding over both gods and men) and indirectly (since men recognize the gods

---

28 Cf. Lysias 2,19: ἀνθρώποις ... προσήκει νόμῳ ... ὁρίσαι τὸ δίκαιον (if authentic, surely later than *Hec.*). It is worth considering that the scholium to *Hec.* 801 underlines the use of ζῶμεν instead of βιοῦμεν.
29 Aristotle, *EN* 5.1134b18–21: τοῦ δὲ πολιτικοῦ δικαίου τὸ μὲν φυσικόν ἐστι τὸ δὲ νομικόν, φυσικὸν μὲν τὸ πανταχοῦ τὴν αὐτὴν ἔχον δύναμιν, καὶ οὐ τῷ δοκεῖν ἢ μή, νομικὸν δὲ ὃ ἐξ ἀρχῆς μὲν οὐδὲν διαφέρει οὕτως ἢ ἄλλως, ὅταν δὲ θῶνται, διαφέρει ('Political justice is of two kinds, one natural, the other conventional. A rule of justice is natural that has the same validity everywhere and does not depend on our accepting it or not. A rule is conventional that in the first instance may be settled in one way or the other indifferently, though having once been settled it is not indifferent', transl. Rackham 1934).
30 [ὁ] κείνων (sci θεῶν) κρατῶν νόμος is an objective genitive, and this has not been questioned by the interpreters (see Weil 1879, 267; Heinimann 1945, 121; Heath 1987, 67; Collard 1991; Kovacs 1995; Mossman 1995, 125; Gregory 1999, 138; Matthiessen 2010, 189, 355–356).
31 'Holy' for 788 ὅσια; and 'most impious' or 'most unholy' for 790 ξένος ἀνοσιώτατος and 792 ἔργον ἀνοσιώτατον. See Collard 1991 and Kovacs 1995.

'thanks to the *nomos*'). Thus, this allows the pursuit of equality in the context of social practice[32] thanks to both man's perception of what *hosios*, or better, *an-hosios*, is, and his own capacity to define (*horizein*) what is right and what is wrong (801). We are dealing with a conception which appears systematic only insofar as it responds to H.'s argumentative purpose, while always being oriented towards neatly distinguishing the superior principle from the political and 'cultural' legislation. Heinimann remarked on the following occurrence of *nomos* (800: νόμῳ γὰρ τοὺς θεοὺς ἡγούμεθα)[33] that, to the audience, it could sound like an allusion to the 'Protagoras-Archelaos line', 'albeit foreign to H.'s meaning of *nomos*' (1945, 121–122, my transl.). Yet, not only does it not undermine the interpretation of the former occurrence as 'refer[ring] to the universal law that Pindar describes as binding on both men and gods, [...] fr. 169.1–2',[34] but also leaves open the question raised by γὰρ. This confirmatory particle suggests the same concept of *nomos* in the two occurrences connected by the expressive polyptoton *nomos, nomo(i)*. Therefore, it does not authorize the conclusion that men 'by convention' believe in the gods,[35] not only because 'it would be rhetorically disastrous for H. [...] to undercut her argument by hinting at the purely conventional authority of *nomos*' (Gregory 1999, 139, and see Kovacs 1987, 101; Heath 1987, 67), but also because men would actually 'rule over the gods' precisely through that *nomos*/convention and in spite of their weakness, weather individual, as in H.'s case, or universal. On the contrary, to acknowledge the *nomos* that allows man to tell 'right from wrong' (800–801)[36] allows one to achieve a fideistic knowledge of the gods. In sum, this 'native right' that exerts its power also upon the gods is analogous neither to the Athenian homicide law mentioned at 291–292, nor to the 'written laws' (νόμων γραφαί) to which H. will ascribe the coercion of individual judgement at 866–867. Both the patrimony of customs and positive legislation,

---

32 802–805 [H.] ὅς (as suggested by the scholium: ὁ νόμος) [...] εἰ διαφθαρήσεται / οὐκ ἔστιν οὐδὲν τῶν ἐν ἀνθρώποις ἴσον ('if this law [...] is set at naught [...] then there is no equality in rights among men' (transl. Kovacs 1995, slightly modified; for the text of 805 see Collard 1991, 171).
33 '[I]t is by virtue of law that we believe in the gods' (transl. Kovacs 1995).
34 Gregory 1999, 138.
35 As maintained by Reckford 1985, 120 and Nussbaum 2001, 400 n. *.
36 (H.) νόμῳ ... / ζῶμεν ἄδικα καὶ δίκαι' ὡρισμένοι ('in virtue of the Law [...] we are living beings [it is worth considering that here the scholium underlines the use of ζῶμεν instead of βιοῦμεν] who determine for themselves what is right and wrong').

on the one hand, and the possibility itself of a social order in which men participate on equal terms, on the other, derive from this *nomos*: 'if this law [...] is set at naught [...] then there is no more justice among men' (802–805):[37]

> H. expresses a principle according to which both gods and men belong to the same system and, albeit in different positions, are equally subjected to a sovereign principle. On its basis the former, whether heavenly or chthonic, will give rules to the latter, and these will derive from those rules implementing regulations, specifications, detailed rules.[38]

In H.'s perspective this principle, superior even to the gods, assimilates her to her interlocutor. In fact, her own condition of being a nerveless slave is unknown only to the gods and the 'Law that has power over them'. As Collard (1991) justly underlined, the antithesis between ἡμεῖς (at first glance a pluralis maiestatis) and ἀλλ' οἱ θεοὶ 'suggests rather' that 'we' is to be understood as "we mortals' in a generalization' (170).[39] On the contrary, the parenthetic ἴσως ('it may be', or rather 'to some degree') focuses on both H.'s present condition as opposed to her past one (cf. e.g. 55–56), and, perhaps with an ironical nuance, on the uncertain condition shared by everyone – cf. 282–283, to which I will soon return.

1.3 806–813: 'stand back like a painter...'

Thus, H. approaches A. not only as a suppliant, but also as one who shares with him the same human condition of subjection to a common principle which inspires both their belief in the gods, and their distinction between right and wrong. Her unlimited misfortunes (*ponoi*, *kaká*) make her stand out even compared to that Lady (Mis)Fortune to whom she had hyperbolically likened herself in the last part of the stichomythia (783–786):

> Εκ. ὄλωλα κοὐδὲν λοιπόν, Ἀγάμεμνον, κακῶν.
> Αγ. φεῦ φεῦ· τίς οὕτω δυστυχὴς ἔφυ γυνή;   785
> Εκ. οὐκ ἔστιν, εἰ μὴ τὴν Τύχην αὐτὴν λέγοις.

---

[37] ὅς (as interpreted by the scholium: τουτέστιν ὁ νόμος) [...] εἰ διαφθαρήσεται / οὐκ ἔστιν οὐδὲν τῶν ἐν ἀνθρώποις ἴσον. Transl. Kovacs 1995; Collard 1991, 171 more accurately translates ἴσον into 'equality in law'.
[38] Carlo Pelloso *per litteras* (my translation).
[39] As rightly observed also by Matthiessen 2010, 355, '[m]an könnte meinen, dass Hekabe nicht nur von sich selbst spricht, sondern von den Menschen allgemein'.

(H.) I am destroyed, Agamemnon; there can be no suffering left to come. / (A.) Ouch ['What tragedy' Collard]! What woman was born to such ill-fortune? / (H.) There is none – unless you named Lady Fortune herself.

(transl. Collard 1991)

Her misfortunes acquire objectivity and can be grasped if looked at 'from afar', as H. suggests that A. should do (807–808): once she was a queen but now she is a slave, once she was blessed with children but now she is old and childless, her city has been destroyed and herself deserted, and now she is the most wretched of all mortals. The vision Hippolytus has in mind when he regrets not having stood 'opposite' himself so as to look at his own misfortune (*Hipp.* 1078–1079) is similar to this one, although implying a sort of self-split.[40] But what counts here is the way at 806–811 H. urges A. to have an overall view of herself:

> ταῦτ' οὖν ἐν αἰσχρῷ θέμενος αἰδέσθητί με,
> οἴκτιρον ἡμᾶς, ὡς γραφεύς τ' ἀποσταθεὶς
> ἰδοῦ με κἀνάθρησον οἷ' ἔχω κακά.
> τύραννος ἦ ποτ' ἀλλὰ νῦν δούλη σέθεν,
> εὔπαις ποτ' οὖσα, νῦν δὲ γραῦς ἄπαις θ' ἅμα,   810
> ἄπολις ἔρημος ἀθλιωτάτη βροτῶν.

[T]ake pity on me; stand back like a painter to look at me, and study the nature of my misery. I was queen once, but now I am your slave; blessed with children once, but now old and childless too; without city, desolate, the most abject of mankind.

(transl. Collard 1991)

Zeitlin's literal interpretation of these lines is well known:

> [T]he aged queen likewise views herself in the painter's idiom, [...] as an object to be gazed at from afar so she may be apprehended in the totality of her physical bearing. [...] The emotive power of the image, the formal perspective of distance, and the reference to the painter's technique as he works to perfect his art are projected on to the other as spectator. But the comparison depends on the prior objectivisation of a self, who must first imagine herself in the picture in order to elicit the empathetic response to her psychological distress that she so intensely desires.[41]

Contrary to this reading, I will argue that H.'s reference to the painter's spatial distance is not to be taken literally, but figuratively. It is a fitting trope for H.'s

---

40 εἴθ' ἦν ἐμαυτὸν προσβλέπειν ἐναντίον / στάνθ', ὡς ἐδάκρυσ' οἷα πάσχομεν κακά ('if I could have stood opposite myself and looked at me, how I would have wept for the misery I suffer', transl. Collard 1991, 171).
41 Zeitlin 1994, 141.

own verbal, not visual, distancing from the scene when at 809–811 she offers her interlocutor a short self-presentation based on the opposition between her recent past (ποτ[ε] bis) and her present (νῦν bis). This emerges quite clearly if we look at the passage more closely. As noted by Mossman, H.'s 'emphasis on former wealth is not only pathetic, but the connotation here of over-confidence and arrogance contributes to the important theme of the destructive nature of the wealth of Troy which runs through the play'.[42] It should also be pointed out that the enumeration of the present *kaká* as opposed to the past ones is paradigmatic of the overthrows she has experienced at the hands of fortune, and actually coincides with the personification of Fortune herself, evoked at 786. τύραννος ἦ ποτ(ε) (809) will be echoed by the same Euripides in *Troades* 100 (βασιλῆς ἐσμεν Τροίας 'I am no longer queen of Troy'), in the same context of a reflection upon *tyche*, the 'changing god' (μεταβαλλόμενος δαίμων: 101) par excellence. However, there is a radical difference between the two situations: in *Tr.*, after Poseidon and Athena have disappeared at 97 and before the Chorus' entrance at 153, H. is alone, whereas in *Hec.* her focus on *metabolé* is meant to have an impact upon the present and actual king, from whom she demands satisfaction and sympathetic respect. The King is endowed with that *kratos* which, as H. had warned Odysseus at 282–283, 'ought not to be exercised wrongfully', since those 'who have power should not think that they will be fortunate forever'.[43] Differing from her dialogue with Odysseus (on which see Mossman 1995, esp. 113–119), in her dialogue with A. 'H.'s use of herself as an example', anyway 'motivated by insight born of bitter experience',[44] produces A.'s unexpected emotional detachment, which translates into a gesture rather than verbal rhetoric. This detachment seems to correspond kinetically to her invitation to look at her from a distance, 'like a painter', and yet H.'s invitation should not be viewed as implying a decreased contact between the two characters. True, H.'s self-pity, stressed by the assonance εὔπαις ... ἄπαις ... / ἄπολις, and, subsequently, by the typically Euripidean *tricolon* ἄπολις ἔρημος ἀθλιωτάτη βροτῶν, might suggest that her speech is no longer accompanied by gestures involving physical contact. And yet, A.'s actual stepping back (812) will be perceived by H. as the failure of her own strategy, which until then had never caused loss of contact. This contradiction revolving around H.'s disappointment with A. the moment he does what she had suggested that he should do (stepping back), prompts us to interrogate the real meaning of H.'s invitation to look at her from afar. We should consider that H.'s mention of the common image of the

---

42 Mossman 1995, 111.
43 οὐ τοὺς κρατοῦντας χρὴ κρατεῖν ἃ μὴ χρεών / οὐδ' εὐτυχοῦντας εὖ δοκεῖν πράξειν ἀεί.
44 Mossman 1995, 115.

painter's distance might not be meant to be understood literally, but figuratively. Nor may H. add other visual aspects to her own image of a mother reclined over the scorned body of her murdered son whom A. has had before his eyes since his entrance onto the stage, and whose implication he has long comprehended. Rather, the simile seems to refer to a mental distance allowing A. to understand not only her narration, which implies a time span schematically ranging from 'once' to 'now', but also the universal exemplarity of her fate. Her awareness of the weakness shared by all humans, as expressed at 798, is in line with her previous consideration addressed to Odysseus at 282–283. H. will again rhetorically exhibit her misfortunes at a subsequent turning point of her oratorical strategy (821–813), which I will examine in due course.

In conclusion, what H. suggests at 807–808 is only a mental distance, and, precisely because it is exclusively mental, that distance should not be understood as a physical one necessary to better contemplate her piteous appearance. She is not chanting a lament; rather, she is enunciating a maxim synthesizing her own destiny as well as that of all human beings. If it were a visual distance it would be located in space; on the contrary, it is projected back in time, into the past drawn by her brief narrative and into the time span comprised between 'once' and 'now', conveying an awareness that *metabole* undercuts all expectation of a lasting fortune. Therefore I believe that H. does not seem to portray herself first and foremost as though in a painting to prompt A. to pull back, which would carry a consequent pathetic effect. What she wants to elicit from him, instead, is a rational reaction to her own narrative. This is why she objectivizes herself: in order to provide not so much the visual focus of A.'s contemplation on her own dismal apperance, but as the narrative focus of a sorrowful yet exemplary story testifying to the levelling action of what in *The Trojan Women* will be called the 'changing god'. Still ritually embracing his knees as a suppliant, the former Queen asks the present King to share with her the vision of the changes produced by fortune: it is at this point that his involvement in her own narrative reaches its climax, he being always a potential part of that narrative, and this is why he now withdraws from her as if to deny that common fate:

οἴμοι τάλαινα, ποῖ μ' ὑπεξάγεις πόδα;   812
ἔοικα πράξειν οὐδέν· ὦ τάλαιν' ἐγώ.

Oh, misery! What I endure! You turn away from me — where to?
It seems I shall achieve nothing. Misery! What I endure!

(transl. Collard 1991)

Consequently, while H.s' request that A. stand away contained no specific performative indication (ἀποσταθείς: 'standing away'), thus recalling the generic dislocation of space in Hippolytus' 'double self' (ἐναντίο[ς] στά[ς]), now A.'s actual pulling back acquires the visual evidence of a real movement (ποῖ) accompanied by a particular gesture (ὑπεξάγεις πόδα: literally 'you are carrying your foot from under the burden of my body'). The burden of his own sharing in human destiny is to A. so unbearable that he rejects both physical and mental contact, in sharp contrast with the attention and favour shown to the old Queen so far. Having moved away from her, A. will address H. only at 850, after a not-purely-formal intervention of the Chorus-leader (846–849), at that point demonstrating clarity of mind both ethically and politically (850–863).

1.4 814–835: The arts of Persuasion and Aphrodite

A.'s withdrawing motivates H.'s new recourse to the power of rhetoric. In her further persuasive attempt (814–820), she tries to recover her contact with A. by adopting strategies typical of oratorical exordia, starting with the use of humility – her inadequate rhetorical knowledge. This is a new beginning:

> τί δῆτα θνητοὶ τἄλλα μὲν μαθήματα
> μοχθοῦμεν ὡς χρὴ πάντα καὶ ματεύομεν, 815
> πειθὼ δὲ τὴν τύραννον ἀνθρώποις μόνην
> οὐδέν τι μᾶλλον ἐς τέλος σπουδάζομεν
> μισθοὺς διδόντες μανθάνειν, ἵν' ἦν ποτε
> πείθειν ἅ τις βούλοιτο τυγχάνειν θ' ἅμα;

> Why the do we mortals labour in search of all other kinds of knowledge as we ought, but make no further effort, by paying fees, to learn persuasion thoroughly, the only sovereign of men, so that it might sometimes have been possible to be persuasive about one's wishes, and gain them too?
>
> (transl. Collard 1991)

Her implied, but clearly deducible claim is that she is alien to the domain whose sovereign is Persuasion.[45] It can be easily compared with other proemial or conclusive pieces of judicial speeches, such as the one uttered by the client of Lysias' *On the Property of Aristophanes*:

> Πολλήν μοι ἀπορίαν παρέχει ὁ ἀγὼν οὑτοσί, ὦ ἄνδρες δικασταί, ὅταν ἐνθυμηθῶ ὅτι, ἂν ἐγὼ μὲν μὴ νῦν εὖ εἴπω, οὐ μόνον ἐγὼ ἀλλὰ καὶ ὁ πατὴρ δόξει ἄδικος εἶναι καὶ τῶν ὄντων

---

[45] At the same time H. seems to prove 'that instruction in what we would now call 'rhetoric' may have been quite a recent addition to the curriculum' – for an in-depth analysis of this topic, see Sansone 2012, 121–122.

ἁπάντων στερήσομαι· ἀνάγκη οὖν, εἰ καὶ μὴ δεινὸς πρὸς ταῦτα πέφυκα, βοηθεῖν τῷ πατρὶ καὶ ἐμαυτῷ οὕτως ὅπως ἂν δύνωμαι.

> I find myself greatly embarrassed by this trial, gentlemen of the jury, when I consider that if I fail to speak with effect today not only I but my father besides will be held to be guilty, and I shall be deprived of the whole of my possessions. It is necessary therefore, even if I have no natural aptitude for the task, to defend my father and myself as best I can.
> (transl. Lamb 1930)

Many other examples of 'litigants denying [rhetorical skills] in themselves' are quoted in this respect by Carey in his commentary on Lysias 7.43 (1989). Indeed, this is precisely a show of rhetorical skill, whose mastery H. will confirm later, at 1195–1196, at the beginning of her counter-defence against Polymestor (1187–1237).[46] At that point she will prove fully aware of the terminology and rules of *techne*, and in fact within her speech (1137–1237) 'lines 1195–6 constitute the sort of headline which is more usually found at the beginning of a speech' (Mossman 1995, 135):

καί μοι τὸ μὲν σὸν ὧδε φροιμίοις ἔχει·   1195
πρὸς τόνδε δ' εἶμι καὶ λόγοις ἀμείψομαι·

> What I have to say to you is there in my preamble; now I'll come to his man here [Polymestor] and answer him with arguments.
> (transl. Collard 1991, 135)

As mentioned above, H.'s admission of lacking the techniques of Persuasion is at the same time aimed at *captatio benevolentiae* towards her addressee and dictated by her foreboding her impending rhetorical failure. After voicing her despair at 820,[47] with a peculiar argumentative 'jump from 819' (see Mossman 1995, 127), at 821–823 'H. returns to her own sufferings and the mutability of Fortune via her desperation over the problems of persuasion which she is experiencing' (Mossman 1995, 127):

οἱ μὲν γὰρ ὄντες παῖδες οὐκέτ' εἰσί μοι,   821
αὐτὴ δ' ἐπ' αἰσχροῖς αἰχμάλωτος οἴχομαι,
καπνὸν δὲ πόλεως τόνδ' ὑπερθρῴσκονθ' ὁρῶ.

---

46 For a full analysis of this speech and especially of its *prooimion*, see Collard 1991, 194–196; Euripides' *Suppliants* 517–518 and *Trojan Women* 916–917 are the most appropriate parallels (see also Matthiessen 2010, 406–407). Mossman 1995, 133–137 examines H.'s overall characterization, also in the light of her argumentative technique.

47 τί οὖν ἔτ' ἄν τις ἐλπίσαι πράξειν καλῶς; ('So what hope can there still be for one's success?', transl. Collard 1991).

The children I have living are alive no longer: I myself am lost, a captive in debasing slavery, and I see the smoke here leaping above my city.

(transl. Collard 1991)

At 824–830, though, H. will develop an argument that is far from being endowed with the conceptual and discursive structure recommended by the masters of rhetoric. On the contrary, it is manifestly a deliberate violation of its rules, even if it is almost predictable that, after praising Peitho, 'the only sovereign of men', H. tries to force A.'s decision by evoking the amorous bond between A. and Polydoros' sister, Cassandra (824–830). The same H. is aware that her argument may appear tenuous (κενόν), and yet she uses it.[48] All this suggests that her mention of the goddess of Persuasion is not primarily a 'conventional tribute' to the 'mythologising personification' of the 'secular persuasion'.[49] Rather, it is a clue to understand the choice H. is making to compensate for her lack of knowledge of formal rhetoric by resorting to the seductive rhetoric of Aphrodite/Peitho.[50]

And yet, this argument too is doomed to failure: A. will admit that Polydoros is his *philos* because he is the brother of his concubine Cassandra, but he will also distinguish between individual *philia* and *philia* shared by the whole army, as in Polymestor's case.[51]

1.5 835–840: The 'Daedalic' rhetoric of the body

Aware of the failure of the 'diegetic' strategy displayed at 806–813, and still uncertain about the effect of her pathetic rhetoric upon A. at 814–835, now H. decides to use a mimetic rhetoric based on the evocative power of words to describe her own body. Having discarded both mental distance (aimed at the contemplation of human *metabolai* from afar) and emotional proximity (the evocation of A.'s love for Cassandra), she now turns her own body into a multivocal performer,

---

48 824–825: [...] ἴσως μὲν τοῦ λόγου κενὸν τόδε, / Κύπριν προβάλλειν, ἀλλ' ὅμως εἰρήσεται ('perhaps this part of the argument, to bring forward Aphrodite, is empty, but it shall nonetheless be said', and see Collard 1991, 172; at 824 I do not see why Nauck's emendation ξένον should be adopted instead of κενὸν which is found in the manuscripts).
49 Cf. Collard 1991, 172, with relevant bibliography.
50 Regarding the association between Peitho e Aphrodite, suffice it to refer to Paus. 1.22.3 (Theseus establishes the cults of Aphrodite Pandemios and Peitho in Athens), and 43.6 (the statue of Peitho, 'Seduction', is located next to that of Paregoros, the 'Consolation of amorous pain', in Aphrodite's temple at Megara).
51 On this phase of H.'s plea, see Mossman 1995, 127–130.

summoned to recite a choral oration addressed to her own master and 'beacon most bright' of safety for both the Greeks and herself:[52]

> ἑνός μοι μῦθος ἐνδεὴς ἔτι.   835
> εἴ μοι γένοιτο φθόγγος ἐν βραχίοσιν
> καὶ χερσὶ καὶ κόμαισι καὶ ποδῶν βάσει
> ἢ Δαιδάλου τέχναισιν ἢ θεῶν τινος,
> ὡς πάνθ' ἁμαρτῇ σῶν ἔχοιτο γουνάτων
> κλαίοντ', ἐπισκήπτοντα παντοίους λόγους.   840
> ὦ δέσποτ', ὦ μέγιστον Ἕλλησιν φάος,
> πιθοῦ, παράσχες χεῖρα τῇ πρεσβύτιδι
> τιμωρόν...

One thing is still lacking from my speech. If only I had a voice in my arms and hands and hair, and the motion of my feet, either through the craft of Daedalus or of some god, so that together they all might hold your knees, in tears, pressing all kinds of arguments upon you! Master, beacon most bright for the Greeks, be moved by me! Lend an old woman [...] your avenging hand!

(transl. Kovacs 1999)

Her polyphonic monologue foregrounds the dualism between the pathos she had meant to arouse by her narrative of the fate she embodies (814–835), and, as opposed to that, the one she now tries to convey verbally through a sort of physical self-deconstruction: she 'daedalically' mentions her own arms, hands, hair, and feet – in short, she refers to her limbs as individually endowed with life. This disarticulation is carried out, not coincidentally, in the name of rhetorical and secular *peitho* (842: πιθοῦ), and implicitly counterpoints the functional organic unity of her own rhetorically construed previous speeches. It is as if H. now wished to make up for her argumentative failure by adopting a new strategy based on the articulation of autonomously signifying and mutually coordinated parts: in other words, she avails herself of an updated rhetoric of pathos following the current doctrine of *topoi* and partition, and applies it to her own body of suppliant, turning it into a choral speech.

This 'topography' of H.'s body has often been likened to Electra's peroration in Euripides' *Electra* 333–335. However, I neither think that in this context some of these 'regions of the body'[53] possess an 'illogical' quality, nor that Hecuba

---

[52] On 'light' as 'metaphor of (potential) rescue' (Collard 1991, 173), see Fraenkel 1950 (on *Ag.* 522 and further references). Note that in Aeschylus, when coming back from Troy, Agamemnon is welcomed not as φῶς, but as φῶς ... φέρων ('he who brings light').

[53] I obviously borrow the expressions 'topography' and 'regions of the body' from Loraux 1987, 49.

means 'that her hair is (to be) shorn in mourning', nor, finally, that hers is only, or mainly, a 'desperate appeal', like Electra's:[54]

Πολλοὶ δ' ἐπιστέλλουσιν, ἑρμηνεὺς δ' ἐγώ,
αἱ χεῖρες ἡ γλῶσσ' ἡ ταλαίπωρός τε φρὴν
κάρα τ' ἐμὸν ξυρῆκες ὅ τ' ἐκεῖνον τεκών.   335

Many are the sponsors of [my message to Orestes], I its formulator – my hands, my tongue, my sorrow-laden mind, my razor-shorn head, and [his] own begetter.

(transl. Cropp 1988)

In *Hec.* the context is dominated by a focus upon *peitho* and by the Queen's rhetorical awareness. As regards Electra's speech, instead, it should be remarked that it achieves an unintentional effect, as also Iphigenia's letter does in *Iphigenia in Tauris*.[55] It is worth recalling that Electra is the only acknowledged *hermeneus* ('interpreter', 'expounder') of the *angelia* she destines for her brother, whom she believes to be far away. Her hands, which are used to humble works, and her head, shorn as a sign of mourning, are the exhibited witnesses of her own desperate condition, reminders for the foreigner that he is entrusted with a truly crucial message for Orestes. Among the witnesses listed in her 'strained'[56] rhetorical catalogue Electra also includes not only her sorrow-laden mind and the memory of Agamemnon, but also her own voice (*glossa*). The inclusion of her voice is precisely what distinguishes the bodily fragmentation suggested by Electra from the one verbalized by H.; if the two characters are the *hermeneis* of their own messages, in Electra's case her mortified body and the evidence that she lives on painful memories are not, in her intention, the direct authors of persuasion, as they are in H.'s case, where her bodily parts implore A. together with herself.[57] In *El.* they are a sort of *pisteis atechnoi* ('artless proofs' because they are not due to the author's rhetorical skills) which the foreigner will have to describe to Orestes in his own voice. The evidence they provide the real Orestes with, present and yet unrecognizable, confirms to him the desperate condition of his sister. Although she has already unveiled her own identity in her song at 115, it is only at this point that she wishes to prove who she is, supplying the foreigner with evidence based upon facts (πρὸς ἄψυχα, as Aristotle would have called them).[58]

---

54 Therefore I do not follow Collards' commentary on 836–840 (1991, 173).
55 See Aristoteles, *Poetics* 1452b3–8.
56 Denniston 1939, 90.
57 See the scholium's paraphrase of 839: ἵνα τὰ μέλη πάντα φωνὴν ἀφιέντα κατὰ ταυτὸν ἱκετεύοιέν σε 'so that all the parts of my body can beseech you with one voice'.
58 *Poetics* 1452a34–35.

2 The *Trojan Women* 98–196

Lying on the ground (κειμένη πρὸ πυλῶν, as Poseidon describes her, 37), Hecuba weeps (it is still Poseidon who informs us) or is exhausted with long crying. She is silent for the first 97 lines, and eventually leaves with the Chorus only at the end of the tragedy.

At 98 H. gradually begins to rise, and until 121 she voices her pain in a sequence of recitative anapaests. She raises her head, then straightens up her neck (ἄνα, δύσδαιμον· πεδόθεν κεφαλὴν / ἐπάειρε δέρην ‹τ(ε)›),[59] and is finally able to see; and yet she cannot orient herself: she can only follow her own destiny and be driven by her own *daimon*, as the *scholium* comments at 103.[60] Hers is a fixed gaze. A series of rhetorical questions culminate in her final 'What plaintive dirge shall I awake?': this is the cry of a tragic hero who has become aware that no possible action is possible, and in so doing she echoes the anguished cry of many other tragic heroes: τί δρᾶν; τί δράσω; ('what am I to do?'). As opposed to 'suffer' (πάσχειν), δρᾶν is precluded to the heroines of this peculiar tragedy, and perhaps also to their masters, who are mainly invisible, only mentioned in the repetitive speeches of their herald, Talthybius, and sometimes dominated by their own ominous fate.[61] H.'s self-address is similar to her own in *Hec.* 736–737 (see *supra*, 4), yet different in that that one was based upon a dialogic splitting of herself into both speaker and addressee,[62] which eventually led her to pose a question of agency ('what am I to do?'). That question opened to the choice between imploring A. or bearing her pain in silence, something which instead does not occur here. At the same time, her focalization upon her past as a queen (100), her loss of her homeland, children, husband, and the erasure of the dynasty's ancient prosperity is like the leitmotiv of *Hec.* 806–813, that is, the *metabole* of destiny:

    οὐκέτι Τροία
  τάδε καὶ βασιλῆς ἐσμεν Τροίας,   100
  μεταβαλλομένου δαίμονος ἄνσχου.

---

[59] 'Lift your head, unhappy woman, from the ground; raise up your neck; this is Troy no more'.
[60] […] ὅ ἐστιν· μὴ ἀνθίστασο τῷ δαίμονι τοῦ βίου ('do not stand opposite the *daimon* of your life').
[61] 'Departed' and properly 'vanished' (φροῦδοι) are Priam (Poseidon: 41), both 'the gods' love for Troy' and 'the sacrifices' (Chorus: 858–859 and 1071), and H.'s care for Astyanax (H.: 1188), but also Neoptolemos, the killer of Astyanax (Talthybius: 1130), as 'in one place one thing, in another another vanishes away (φροῦδον)' (Chorus: 1323–1324).
[62] 736: δύστην', ἐμαυτὴν γὰρ λέγω λέγουσα σέ ('Hapless! – it is myself I speak of when I speak of you', transl. Collard 1991).

```
...
τί γὰρ οὐ πάρα μοι μελέᾳ στενάχειν,            106
ᾗ πατρὶς ἔρρει καὶ τέκνα καὶ πόσις;
ὦ πολὺς ὄγκος συστελλόμενος
προγόνων, ὡς οὐδὲν ἄρ' ἦσθα.
```

Troy is no more, you see, nor are we Troy's rulers. Your fortune changes, so endure it. ... Me, unlucky woman, which lament cannot I utter, who have lost my country, my children, and my husband? Massive pride of my ancestors, now lowered, how slight a thing you were after all!

From 112 to 119 H. again seems to concentrate on her own body and to perceive its suffering as if distinct from herself:

```
δύστηνος ἐγὼ τῆς βαρυδαίμονος
ἄρθρων κλίσεως, ὡς διάκειμαι,
νῶτ' ἐν στερροῖς λέκτροισι ταθεῖσ'.
οἴμοι κεφαλῆς, οἴμοι κροτάφων            115
πλευρῶν θ', ὥς μοι πόθος εἱλίξαι
καὶ διαδοῦναι νῶτον ἄκανθάν τ'
εἰς ἀμφοτέρους τοίχους μελέων,
ἐπιοῦσ' αἰεὶ δακρύων ἐλέγους.
```

Ah, woe is me! the anguish I suffer lying here stretched upon this hard pallet! O my head, my temples, my side! How I long to turn over, and lie now on this, now on that, to rest my back and spine, while ceaselessly my tearful wail ascends!

(transl. Coleridge 1891)

She exhibits her body to the audience while evidently not addressing them: all the diegetic requirements typical of a prologic piece have already been met at the beginning of the play, by Poseidon's monologue and Poseidon's and Athena's dialogue. Nor have the two semi-Choruses come out of their own shelters yet. Thus, H. may talk about something else, her own bruised articulations due to her poor squatting posture, about her own head, temples, hips, and spine, and again her hips. The verbal disarticulation of her own body progresses through a detailed description – it is hard to tell whether and to what extent it was accompanied by gesture, and perhaps it was not, or only by a slow and laborious movement. This seems to further testify to the fact that, although relying on the characterization of mask and costume, *opsis* could not fully convey the shattering of the protagonist's identity carried out by her verbal dismantling of her own body. As in an icon covered with a foil of beaten silver, we can glimpse some *arthra* suggesting a body, here too we can only see some limbs, endowed by H.'s words with symbolic meaning. When she eventually stands up, after lying down from 1 to 97, she finally appears whole and complete, confined within her costume and mask. We do not need to call in Elias Canetti's *Crowds and Power* to grasp the meaning of her gesture accompanied by her recitation of a few dozen heavily rhythmical syllables. This body, hindered by physical pain, soon tries to move and H. 'long[s] to roll [her] back and spine about, listing now to this side of [her] body, now to that', as translates Kovacs 1999, but she cannot. It is not a dancing measure, nor can it be one, since its rhythm and tonality are of a lament: *elegos*, that is, a cry, such as the halcyon's (Euripides, *IT* 1091), as upsetting as all the *alyroi* harmonies, literally 'without lyra' (*Hel.* 185, *IT* 146). Furthermore, the old Queen is *dystenos* ('wretched'), and her body is broken and cannot follow any rhythm.

At 120–121 we hear: μοῦσα δὲ χαὔτε τοῖς δυστήνοις / ἄτας κελαδεῖν ἀχορεύτους: 'stricken people find music yet / in the song undanced of their wretchedness' (I follow Richmond Lattimore's translation, which significantly replaces the common 'cheerless dirge' with 'undanced song').[63] Segal (1993) rightly underlines the performative implications of these lines, which have been commented on for their metapoetic import, as well as with reference to what he defines as 'the figure of an inverted Muse', where the Muse 'sings her disasters, unchorused, to the unfortunate':

> The figure of the joyless song of lament has an intermediate status between metaphor, enacted gesture, and the ritualized expression of intense grief [...]. By transforming the celebratory lyric of choral or symposiac music into the oxymoronic form of the 'lyreless tune' or 'unmusical Muse,' the tragic poet connects his work with the traditional, communal role of the poet in archaic society, but simultaneously also stakes out his unique, problematical place within that tradition. The figure of the 'unmusical song' is all the more paradoxical because that song is actually being performed before us [...]. (17)

As a matter of fact, these lines peculiarly and unexpectedly prelude a song which does not involve echoing participants: a monody which addresses the audience with a Trojan version of the whole story. It is an entirely anapaestic song (122–152), closely connected, from a rhythmical point of view, with the recitative: a prolonged sequence of *Klaganapäste*, or threnodic anapaests, which can be found in other Euripidean plays (for instance *El.*), albeit to a lesser extent and almost only as an initial rhythmical allusion. Isabelle Torrance has properly observed that 'the sentiment that ruin (*ate*) is *achoreutos* 'unattended by choruses', i.e. 'joyless', [...] announces metatheatrically H.'s shift into song while she is still

---

[63] Lattimore 2013, 86.

unattended by the chorus' (2013, 241). Yet the metatheatrical and metapoetic import of this passage seems to concern more the various choreutic forms – both those once performed and those now performable by H. herself – than the actual absence of the Chorus. Although the text is corrupted, we can easily understand the overall meaning of this memorial song which opens with πρῷραι ναῶν, ὠκείαις / Ἴλιον ἱερὰν αἳ κῶπαις ... βαίνουσαι ('Your ships' prows, that the rapid oars swept here to blessed Ilium', transl. Lattimore 2013, 86). Its tonality is very different from the one only seemingly similar in the First Stasimon of Euripides' *El.* (432–486, κλειναὶ νᾶες, αἵ ποτ' ἔβατε Τροίαν / τοῖς ἀμετρήτοις ἐρετμοῖς etc.: 'Glorious ships, which once went Troyward on those countless oars', transl. Cropp 1988), which is a pictorial description well in tune with the 'heroic' characterization of the protagonist. H.'s use of the first person at the end of her song is almost more emphatically self-referential than her preceding use of it in the recitative anapaests:

>   δούλα δ' ἄγομαι   140
>   γραῦς ἐξ οἴκων πενθήρη
>   ...
>   μάτηρ δ' ὡσεὶ πτανοῖς κλαγγὰν   146
>   †ὄρνισιν ὅπως ἐξάρξω 'γὼ
>   μολπὰν οὐ τὰν αὐτὰν†
>   οἵαν ποτὲ δὴ
>   σκήπτρῳ Πριάμου διερειδομένου   150
>   ποδὸς ἀρχεχόρου πλαγαῖς Φρυγίους
>   εὐκόμποις ἐξῆρχον θεούς.

I am led captive from my house, an old, unhappy woman [...]. And I, as among winged birds the mother, lead out the clashing cry, the song; not that song wherein once long ago when Priam leaned on his scepter, my feet were queens of the choir and led the proud dance to the gods of Phrygia.

(transl. Lattimore 2013, 86)

Her song confirms the metapoetic and metatheatrical interpretation of the conclusion of her previous chant: the 'sharp lament' (146: κλαγγά) she begins (147: ἐξάρξω), which will follow with the participation of the two semichoruses of Trojan women, is different from the song (148: μολπά) she used to sing and dance in the past. This difference is due not only to the fact that the song is a dirge,[64] but

---

[64] It could also allude to 'the songs of joy and the all-night dances when the Trojans, deceived by the Greek stratagem, brought the wooden horse within their walls' (Segal 1993, 18), which will be recalled by the Chorus at 529–555.

also to the profusion of the performative elements: The Queen was its *exarchon* (152) and her feet guided the Chorus (151: *archechoros*, Euripidean hapax).

At the end of this second stage of H.'s self-presentation, she therefore no longer presents herself as a future 'queen of the choir', because she can no longer move 'loud-sounding' and 'proud' dancing steps. Nevertheless, she joins in the Chorus' lyrical performance, which is also the first one in *The Trojan Women*. From 153 to 196 she will participate in a melodramatic exchange, still in lyric anapaests, with the choral collective, the two semichoruses who have come out of their temporary shelters. Euripides, 'who develops and extends the use of melic anapaests far beyond the use of other dramatists [...] particularly in the form of a solo-aria' (Dale 1968, 57), here inaugurates a new pathetic mode based on the gradual intensification of a lyrical-dramatic *pathos* which will be passed down to Seneca. As regards specifically 'the expectations and preconceptions of [Euripides'] audience' (Mossman 2001, 375), this new mode is clearly at odds with what the spectators of *The Trojan Women* had previously experienced at the performance of the earlier play. There, H. was still partly conditioned by 'male' discursivity, and anyway her speech at 736–845 reflected sophistic culture; here, instead, her voicing the disarticulation of her own body no longer relies upon rhetorical and discursive emphasis, but on an expressive intensification imbued with vibrant lyricism. Her new handling of *melos* in a piece of oratory, in fact, seems to suggest an entirely original, and precisely female, reinterpretation of the rules of argumentation, eventually revised through the power of music in conjunction with a deeply effective rhetoric of bodily gesture (even when confined, in the performance, to the sole power of *logos*).

3 Appendix: The Text of *Hecuba* 756–759 and the distribution of lines from 736 to 786

Εκ. οὐ δῆτα· τοὺς κακοὺς δὲ τιμωρουμένη
     αἰῶνα τὸν σύμπαντα δουλεύειν θέλω.
Αγ. καὶ δὴ τίν' ἡμᾶς εἰς ἐπάρκεσιν καλεῖς;   758
Εκ. οὐδέν τι τούτων ὧν σὺ δοξάζεις, ἄναξ.

Π⁷: P. Oxy. 4557 (388.400 MP³, 2nd c.); Π⁸: P. Oxy. 4559 (389.100 MP³, 4th c.); Π¹²: P. Oxy. 4558 (389.010 MP³, 6th c.).

Matthiessen 2010 (some additional information is given between ‹parentheses›):
‹752–9 spatium omnino quattuor vv. habuit Π⁸   761–6 [Π⁸]› 756–9 om. Π⁷ Π¹², fortasse etiam Π⁸   756–8 om. MBOFGKPrRT², add. B²ᵐF²ᵐGᵐKᵐPrᵐTᵗᵐ : habent F (post v. 779) re ‹def. Kirchhoff 1855› : delevit Nauck   756–7 om. RfRw, add. Rfr, delevit Diggle : solum v.

756 add. R w^m 757 Hirzel post hunc v. coniecit unius versus lacunam ‹probat Mossman 1995›
758 Kirchhoff post hunc v. coniecit unius versus lacunam   759 ‹aut delendus aut cum v.
d. Anglo ante 756 collocandus censuit Nauck 1854›, v. delevit Hartung, Hirzel et Diggle
posuerunt ante v. 758 ‹probat Mossman 1995› : Hermann (1831) post hunc v. coniecit unius
versus lacunam

In short: 756–758 are omitted by MSS. M and B but added by a second hand in B and thereafter 779 by F²ᵐ. The violation of a presumed regularity in the alternation of the speakers in the di- and stichomythiae has caused textual interventions since Kirchhoff 1855 and Hirzel 1862, 51–52 (where he speaks of 'laesa stichomythia'). The publication of P. Oxy. 4557 and 4558, who omit 756–759, has granted further authority to MOR and to the *prima manus* of BFGKT. However, certain categorical assumptions are not at all convincing, as for instance: '[t]he four lines omitted in the papyrus [...] add nothing to the sense of the passage; indeed, in their absence, the verbal exchange between Hecuba and Agamemnon is more pointed and phrased with greater succintness';[65] see also: '[d]ie Verse 756–759 sind hier nicht enthalten, sind also endgültig zu tilgen'.[66] Nor can the convergence of Π⁷ with MBOPaξT² on the same correct reading, where the *maior pars* of the other *Hec.*'s MSS shows polygenetic errors (such as 747 τι instead of the correct τοι), suffices to demonstrate its superiority.[67] With reference to 746–748, which Π⁸ seems to omit,[68] it is more cautious to follow Obbink: '752–759[:] Spacing shows that no more than four of these lines can have been present in the papyrus' text. Presumably 756–759 were omitted as in [P. Oxy.] 4557–4558, corroborating the suspicion that these lines were in fact absent in at least one branch of the ancient tradition' (2001, 49; on the bifurcation of the textual transmission at 756–758 cf. Matthiessen 2010, 349).

From the textual perspective, it has already been pointed out that the *incipit* of 755/7 (αἰῶνα *bis*) and 756/9 (οὐ δῆτα / οὐδέν τι) may produce a *saut du même au même* in all phases of the manuscript tradition.[69] All the same, the text of the papyri is the cause neither of the athetesis of 756–757 nor of the inversion of

---

65 Hughes/Nodar 2001, 40.
66 Luppe 2004, 101.
67 Hughes/Nodar 2001, 44.
68 It should be remarked, however, that Π⁸, with the *eisthesis* of the iambic lines 739–773 (only 739–751 + 4 between 752 and 759 + 760 + 767–773, because 761–766 are lost), cannot be easily explained, despite Battezzato's thorough analysis (2009, 11).
69 Cf. Weil 1868, 264 on 756/9; Collard 1991, 169, while judging 'inescapable' both the inversion of 759 and 758, and the lacuna after 757 if the sequence 758–759 is preserved, defends 754–757 and thinks that it may have been 'a scribe's eye slipping'. The same Kirchhoff 1855, 385 had posited that this phenomenon had invested 756–758 *bis* in the archetype.

759/8, both adopted by Diggle 1984. Kamerbeek's energetic defence of the 'lively, dramatic dialogue' at 754–759 (1986, 100–101) has been finally echoed by Matthiessen: '[d]ie Verse bieten weder sprachlich noch inhaltlich Anstöße und stehen im Einklang mit der Charakterisierung Hekabes' (2010, 349). 756–759 are an essential part of H.'s oratorical strategy, and therefore I do not think that they should be expunged or integrated with a hypothetical missing line after 757. Mastronarde 1988, 156–157; Gregory 1999, 135, and Matthiessen 2010, 349 argued well in favour of the text transmitted by ALPaSaVaξζ, which was defended by Schwinge 1968, 194, n. 2 and retained also by Kovacs 1995. It should also be noticed that: (a) αἰῶνα τὸν σύμπαντα δουλεύειν θέλω (757) could hardly be a suture devised by an interpolator because it repeats ἐλεύθερον / αἰῶνα at 754–755, according to the usual form of (di)stichomythies; (b) 759 provides a good answer either to the preceding line or to μῶν κτλ. at 754–755, but the latter is too far off; and (c), in the dialogic progression, 759 οὐδέν τι τούτων ὧν σὺ δοξάζεις cannot refer exclusively to the granting of freedom, but presupposes a wider range of possible aids, adumbrated by the generic τίν' … εἰς ἐπάρκεσιν at 758.

A closer analysis of the dialogue between H. and A. allows us to ascertain that at least from 752 to 787 H.'s lines are cast at the same time in different dramatic forms – stichomythia, distichomythia, and rhesis – so that these forms overlap also in textual sequences whose genuinity has not been questioned, as at 756–759. These overlappings are characterized by the presence of the vocative (752), of asyndeton (760), or of adversative particles (787) at the beginning of each line. These stylistic features affect the vocal performance and may be accompanied by gestural changes:

- at 752 '[t]he vocative […] suggests that she turns face to him' and 'H. presumably suits her actions to her words' (Ἀγάμεμνον, ἱκετεύω σε τῶνδε γουνάτων / καὶ σοῦ γενείου δεξιᾶς τ' εὐδαίμονος: 'I supplicate you by your knees, your chin, and your prospering right hand', transl. Kovacs 1995) 'by assuming a supplicatory posture' (all quotations are from Gregory 1999, 134); therefore 752–753, although being the last of five lines (749–753) spoken by H. after the distichomythia at 739–748, are the first two of the shorter distichomythia 752–757.[70]
- after 759, to which Mastronarde 1988, 157 rightly attributed a 'retarding force', and which answers directly to 758, the asyndetic ὁρᾷς νεκρὸν τόνδε κτλ. at 760 starts a new stichomythia that continues to 785 with the 'regular' alternation between H. and A.: at 760 H., who at 752 turned to A., modifies

---

[70] Seidensticker 1971, 194 n. 29 too maintains that the first part of the H.–A. stichomythia ends at 751.

her supplicatory posture and points out 'this corpse' – by now behind her – to the King. As Gregory 1999, 134 annotates, '[t]he demonstratives at 760, 778, and 782 suggest, at the very least, lively hand gestures on H.'s part'. The stichomythic exchange between A. and H. at 758–759 closes the distichomythia (H.: 752–753, A.: 754–755, H.: 756–757), therefore H.'s pair of iambic trimeters 759–760 play a pivotal role between the illocutionary acts negotiated at 753–759 and the stichomythic exposition of H.'s case at 760ff.;

– after 786, where she answers A.'s rhetorical question in the preceding line, H. finally begins her *rhesis* at 787 with the inceptive and exhortative ἀλλ(ά) that breaks off the exchange at 783–786.[71]

– Finally, 736–786 (including the three overlappings mentioned above) are all dialogic unlike A.'s tristich 733–735, where he wonders about the dead man before the tent: after the King has reproached H. at 726–732 for her delay, these lines suddenly express a new focalization on A.'s part, who shifts his attention from H. to Polydoros' corpse,[72] and are lacking such illocutionary devices as second person pronouns (recurring in the seven preceding lines). Therefore, I cannot agree with Hirzel 1862, 51, nor with Weil 1868, 266, when they maintain that the two tristichs 733–735 (A.) and 736–738 (H.) belong to one and the same quasi-dialogue 733–751.

Bibliography

Bain, D. (1977), *Actors and Audience. A Study of Asides and Related Conventions in Greek Drama*, Oxford.
Battezzato, L. (2009), 'Notes and Corrections on Papyri of Euripides and Aristophanes (P. Oxy. LXVII 4557 and 4559; PSI VI 720)', in: *ZPE* 170, 9–15.
Biehl, W. (1985), 'Interpretationsprobleme in Euripides' Hekabe', in: *Hermes* 113, 257–266.
Biehl, W. (1997), *Textkritik und Formanalyse zur der Euripideischen Hekabe. Ein Beitrag zum Verständnis der Komposition*, Heidelberg.
Carey, C. (1989), *Lysias, Selected Speeches*, Cambridge.
Collard, C. (1991), *Euripides, Hecuba*, Warminster.
Coleridge, E.P. (transl.) (1891), *The Plays of Euripides*, I, London.

---

[71] See ἀλλά II. (1), (4), and (8) in Denniston 1950, from which I quote. Already Hirzel 1862, 52, who was firmly convinced of the symmetry in Euripides' *diverbia*, implicitly admitted that 786, the first line of H.'s *rhesis*, is in fact the last line of the perfectly symmetric stichomythia starting at 760.

[72] As Mossman 1995, 63 remarks, 'Agamemnon's start of surprise at 733 is an effective way of keeping [Polydoros' corpse] in the forefront of our minds'.

Coles, R.A. et al. (2001), *The Oxyrhynchus Papyri*, Publ. for the British Academy by the Egypt Exploration Society, Vol. 67, London.
Cope, E.M./Sandys, J.E. (1877), *The Rhetoric of Aristotle*, Cambridge.
Cropp, M.J. (1988), *Euripides, Electra*, Warminster.
Dale, A.M. [1948] (1968), *The Lyric Metres of Greek Drama*, Cambridge.
Denniston, J.D. (ed.) (1939), *Euripides, Electra*, Oxford.
Denniston, J.D. (1950), *The Greek Particles*, Oxford.
Diggle, J. (ed.) (1984), *Euripidis Fabulae*, Oxford.
Forster, E.S. (1924), See Ross (1924).
Fraenkel, E. (1950), *Aeschylus, Agamemnon*, Oxford.
Gregory, J. (1999), *Euripides, Hecuba*, Atlanta/New York/Oxford.
Heath, M. (1987), '"Jure principem locum tenet": Euripides' *Hecuba*', in: *BICS* 34, 40–68.
Heinimann, F. (1945), *Nomos und Physis. Herkunft und Bedeutung einer Antithese im griechischen Denken des 5. Jahrhunderts*, Basel.
Hirzel, H. (1862), *De Euripidis in componendis diverbiis arte, comm. philo [...] una cum sententiis controversis*, Bonn.
Hughes, D./Nodar, A. (2001), '4557. Euripides, Hec. 651–69, 710–38, 742–73 (desunt 756–9)', in: Coles et al., 39–44.
Jens, W. (ed.) (1971), *Die Bauformen der griechischen Tragödie*, Munich.
Kamerbeek, J.C. (1986), 'Rereading Euripides in the New Oxford Text (Tom. I)', in: *Mnemosyne* 39, 92–101.
Kirchhoff, A. (ed.) (1855), *Euripidis fabulae*, I, Berlin.
Kirkwood, G.M. (1947), 'Hecuba and Nomos', in: *TAPhA* 78, 61–68.
Kovacs, D. (1987), *The Heroic Muse. Studies in the Hippolytus and Hecuba of Euripides*, Baltimore/London.
Kovacs, D. (ed.) (1995), *Euripides, Children of Heracles, Hippolytus, Andromache, Hecuba*, Cambridge MA/London.
Kovacs, D. (ed.) (1999), *Euripides, Trojan Women, Iphigenia among the Taurians, Ion*, Cambridge MA/London.
Lamb, W.R.M. (1930), *Lysias*, Cambridge MA/London.
Lanni, A. (2006), *Law and Justice in the Courts of Classical Age*, Cambridge.
Lattimore, R. [1958] (2013), *The Trojan Women*, in: M. Griffith/G.W. Most (eds.) *The Complete Greek Tragedies: Euripides III*, Chicago/London, 81–132.
Loraux, N. (1987), *Tragic Ways of Killing a Woman*, Cambridge MA/London.
Luppe, W. (2004), 'Review of Hughes and Nodar 2001', in: *Gnomon* 76.2, 100–104.
MacDowell, D.M. (1963), *Athenian Homicide Law in the Age of the Orators*, Manchester.
Mastronarde, D.J. (1979), *Contact and Discontinuity. Some Conventions of Speech and Action on the Greek Tragic Stage*, Berkeley/Los Angeles/London.
Mastronarde, D.J. (1988), 'Review of Diggle 1984', in: *Classical Philology* 83, 151–160.
Matthiessen, K. (2010), *Euripides, Hekabe*, Berlin/New York.
Michie, J./Leach, C. (transl.) (1981), *Euripides, Helen*, New York/Oxford.
Mossman, J. (1995), *Wild Justice. A Study of Euripides' Hecuba*, Oxford.
Mossman, J. (2001), 'Women's Speech in Greek Tragedy: The Case of Electra and Clytemnestra in Euripides' *Electra*', in: *CQ* 51, 374–384.
Murray, G. (ed.) (1902), *Euripidis Fabulae*, I, Oxonii.
Nodar, A. (2001), '4558. Euripides, Hec. 709–22, 746–61 (desunt 756–9), 782–94, 816–27', in: Coles et al. (2001) 44–47.

Nussbaum, M.C. [1986] (2001), *The Fragility of Goodness*, Cambridge.
Obbink, D. (2001), '4559. Euripides, Hec. 739–51 [sic], 768–87', in: Coles *et al.*, 47–49.
Prinz, R./Wecklein, N. (eds.) (1902), *Euripidis Hec.*, ed. R. P., editio altera quam curavit N. W., Lipsiae in aedibus B.G. Teubneri p. 62 (coniecturae minus probabiles).
Reckford, K.J. (1985), 'Concepts of Demoralization in the *Hecuba*', in: P. Burian (ed.), *Directions in Euripidean Criticism. A Collection of Essays*, Durham NC, 112–128.
Riesbeck, D.J. (2011), 'Nature, Normativity, and nomos in Antiphon, fr. 44', in: *Phoenix* 65, 268–287.
Ross, W.D. (1924), *The Works of Aristotle Translated into English: Rhetorica, De Rhetorica ad Alexandrum, Poetica*, XI, Oxford.
Sansone, D. (2012), *Greek Drama and the Invention of Rhetoric*, Oxford.
Schadewaldt, W. (1926), *Monolog und Selbstgespräch*, Berlin.
Schwinge, E.-R. (1968), *Die Verwendung der Stichomythie in den Dramen des Euripides*, Heidelberg.
Segal, C. (1993), *Euripides and the Poetics of Sorrow*, Durham NC.
Seidensticker, B. (1971), 'Die Stichomythie', in: Jens (1971) 183–220.
Torrance, I. (2013), *Metapoetry in Euripides*, Oxford.
Weil, H. (ed.) (1868), *Sept tragédies d'Euripide*, Paris.
Zeitlin, F.I. (1994), 'The Artful Eye: Vision, Ecphrasis and Spectacle in Euripidean Theatre', in: S. Goldhill/R. Osborne (eds.), *Art and Text in Ancient Greek Culture*, Cambridge, 138–198.

Andreas Fountoulakis
The Rhetoric of *Erôs* in Menander's *Samia*

For Professor P.E. Easterling

In Plutarch's praise of Menander's comedies, the former refers to some of their thematic features which are supposed to have a moralizing aspect. Citing Diogenianus of Pergamon, Plutarch mentions the absence of pederastic themes, the depiction of heterosexual relationships leading to marriage even when the affairs began as seductions or rapes of free-borne girls, and the presentation of relationships with *hetairai* in a way that would not turn out to be morally harmful for the audience:[1]

> ἔχει δὲ καὶ τὰ ἐρωτικὰ παρ' αὐτῷ καιρὸν πεπωκόσιν ἀνθρώποις, καὶ ἀναπαυσομένοις μετὰ μικρὸν ἀπιοῦσι παρὰ τὰς ἑαυτῶν γυναῖκας· οὔτε <γὰρ> παιδὸς ἔρως ἄρρενός ἐστιν ἐν τοσούτοις δράμασιν, αἵ τε φθοραὶ τῶν παρθένων εἰς γάμον ἐπιεικῶς καταστρέφουσι· τὰ δὲ πρὸς τὰς ἑταίρας, ἂν μὲν ὦσιν ἰταμαὶ καὶ θρασεῖαι, διακόπτεται σωφρονισμοῖς τισιν ἢ μετανοίαις τῶν νέων, ταῖς δὲ χρησταῖς καὶ ἀντερώσαις ἢ πατήρ τις ἀνευρίσκεται γνήσιος, ἢ χρόνος τις ἐπιμετρεῖται τῷ ἔρωτι, συμπεριφορὰν αἰδοῦς ἔχων φιλάνθρωπον. ταῦτα δ' ἀνθρώποις ἄλλο μέν τι πράττουσιν ἴσως οὐδεμιᾶς σπουδῆς ἄξιά ἐστιν· ἐν δὲ τῷ πίνειν οὐ θαυμάσαιμ' ἄν, εἰ τὸ τερπνὸν αὐτῶν καὶ γλαφυρὸν ἅμα καὶ πλάσιν τινὰ καὶ κατακόσμησιν ἐπιφέρει, συνεξομοιοῦσαν τὰ ἤθη τοῖς ἐπιεικέσι καὶ φιλανθρώποις.

> Even the erotic element in Menander is appropriate for men who after their wine will soon be leaving to repose with their wives; for in all these plays there is no one enamoured of a boy. Moreover, when virgins are seduced, the play usually ends with a marriage; while affairs with casual women, if these are aggressive and shameless, are cut short by some chastening experience or repentance on the young man's part, and good girls who give love for love either find again a father with legitimate status or get a further dispensation of time for their romance – an accommodation of conscience that is but charitable. For men who are occupied with some other business, all this is perhaps not worth serious attention; but over the wine-cups, I cannot regard it as surprising that Menander's polished charm exercises a reshaping and reforming influence that helps to raise morals to a higher standard of fairness and kindness.
>
> (transl. E.L. Minar, Jr.)

The extant plays of Menander or of the *palliatae* do not always confirm the accuracy of these comments.[2] It is nevertheless worth noting that Plutarch manages

---

1 Plut. *Mor.* (*Quaest. Conv.*) 7.8.712 c–d (= Men. Test. 104 K.–A.). All comic fragments and *testimonia* are from Kassel/Austin 1983– (abbreviated as K.–A.).
2 Cf. Gilula 1987, 511–516.

https://doi.org/10.1515/9783110629729-002

to single out an important pattern of most Menandrean plots: their thematic focusing upon the desire of a – usually wealthy – young man for a girl.[3] The couple encounters many difficulties and misunderstandings due to the social tensions produced by the rape or seduction of a free-borne girl, or even by the girl's actual or assumed social status as a *hetaira* or the daughter of a non-citizen. This happens until the moment of their wedding which is the conventional happy outcome of the affair as well as of the play's plot.[4] Considering Menander's plots through the filter of later interests in the *paideia* offered to elite audiences, Plutarch sees in them an opportunity to project in a formative manner a morality of personal integrity capable of leading to marriage and sustaining the *oikos*.[5]

The structure of Menander's *Samia* is determined by this kind of plot development – typical of a play of New Comedy –, which may reflect similar thematic interests in plays of Middle Comedy as well as in plays such as Aristophanes' *Kokalos* or Euripides' *Helen*.[6] In this play Moschion, a wealthy young man, impregnates Plangon, a poor neighbour's daughter, who gives birth to their child. After a series of adventures, concealments, revelations and misunderstandings, Moschion marries the girl, presenting as a driving force his love for her and, at the same time, managing to maintain her honour. While love in the form of a strong emotional and physical desire for a person, which in Greek is described by the word ἔρως (*erôs*) and its cognates, appears to hold such an important role in the play's plot, closer inspection may reveal a very different conception and function of Moschion's emotional disposition. In this paper the assumption that the depiction of *erôs* in the *Samia* may be related to its conception as a complex, irrational and divinely inspired emotional force, which was prevalent in Greek culture, or

---

[3] The preoccupation of Menander's plays with the theme of love is also noted by Ovid, *Trist.* 2.369 (= Men. Test. 92 K.–A.): *fabula iucundi nulla est sive amore Menandri* [no plot of playful Menander's is free of love], (transl. A.S. Kline). For a similar comment attributed to Plutarch, see Stobaeus 4.20a 34 (= Men. Test. 107 K.–A.).

[4] For variations on this plot development in Menander, see e.g. Men. *Dyskolos*, *Samia*, *Georgos*, *Aspis*, *Plokion*, *Heros*; cf. Wilamowitz-Moellendorff 1919, 59; Wehrli 1936, 30; Webster 1970², 74; Anderson 1984, 124–134; Wiles 1989, 31–32; Brown 1990, 241–243; Konstan 1995, 93–106 (for *erôs* in the *Dyskolos*); Masaracchia 1998, 405–436; Rosivach 1998, 1–2, 13–42.

[5] For the appreciation of Menander's comedies within the boundaries of the ethical concerns of authors such as Plutarch in the context of an elite symposium evolving around the demands of *paideia*, see Hunter 2014, 379–384.

[6] In addition to Aristophanes' *Kokalos* and Euripides' *Helen*, for the plays of Middle Comedy, see e.g. Alexis, *Agonis* fr. 2 K.–A., *Apokoptomenos* fr. 20 K.–A., *Syntrechontes* fr. 217 K.–A., *Traumatias* fr. 236 K.–A.; Wehrli 1936, 30, 40–42; Webster 1970², 7–8, 63–64, 74–78; Henry 1988², 36–39; Nesselrath 1990, 281–282, 318–321; Konstantakos 2002, 143–151, although it is very difficult, if not impossible, to draw firm conclusions out of scanty and fragmentary evidence.

even as a kind of 'romantic love', as some scholars tend to think,⁷ will be brought into question. Considering the emotional overtones of *erôs* in various contexts, as well as its contribution to the unfolding of the play's plot, *erôs* in the *Samia* will rather be shown to be a rhetorical device explaining human action and motivation.

This complies with the 'forensic disposition' which has been detected by Adele Scafuro with respect to the delineation of many characters of New Comedy and their subsequent action and motivation. These characters are entangled in situations which demand the assistance of the law and the use of reasoning and argumentation similar to those attested in the texts of the Attic orators.⁸ As Chris Carey notes, this happens to such an extent that rhetoric has become part of the conventions of the genre.⁹ In light of the emergence of a 'performance culture' dominating the social, political and cultural life of fifth- and fourth-century Athens,¹⁰ it comes as no surprise that, as Susan Lape argues, both oratory and Menandrean comedy betray a similar interest in the discourse of gender, sexuality, identity and citizenship, which was crucial to the identity and the ideology of the Athenian *polis*.¹¹ As regards the *Samia*, in particular, Lape rightly notes that the action of both Moschion and Demeas is often presented through forensic reasoning and argumentation aimed at the establishment of social order.¹² This is not alien to the moralizing effect attributed to Menander's plays by Plutarch. Examined from such a perspective, *erôs* will turn out to have a far more complex function within the play's plot and the formation of its ideological load, which is closely related to its cultural context.

When in his opening expository monologue Moschion refers for the first time to his affair with Plangon,¹³ the audience is informed about the girl's impregnation one night during the festival of the Adonia. Instead of mentioning *erôs*, Moschion refers at 3 to something painful he has done, which is regarded as *hamartia* (ὀδ]υνηρόν ἐστιν· ἡμάρτηκα γάρ). The fact that he considers himself at 12 to be ἀθλιώτερος may indicate his sense of guilt for his deeds. He also refers twice, quite emphatically, at 47 and 48, to his shame for what he did, although it is not

---

7 See Rudd 1981; Walcot 1987; Wiles 1989; Brown 1993.
8 Scafuro 1997, 25.
9 Carey 2011, 454–455.
10 See Goldhill 1999, 1–29.
11 Lape 2004, 68–109.
12 Lape 2004, 141–147.
13 Men. *Sam.* 35–56.

made clear whether the girl was raped or seduced.[14] This creates a frame surrounding, and to a certain extent explaining, Moschion's action. Driven by a sense of duty, he promises her mother to marry Plangon as soon as his foster father Demeas and the latter's friend Nikeratos, who is also the girl's father, come back from their trip to the Pontos, while at 53 he says that he took an oath to do so:[15]

> ὀκν]ῶ λέγειν τὰ λοίπ'' ἴσως δ' αἰσχύνομαι
> ὅτ'] οὐδὲν ὄφελος· ἀλλ' ὅμως αἰσχύνομαι.
> ἐκύ]ησεν ἡ παῖς· τοῦτο γὰρ φράσας λέγω
> καὶ] τὴν πρὸ τούτου πρᾶξιν. οὐκ ἠρνησάμην   50
> τὴν] αἰτίαν σχών, ἀλλὰ πρότερος ἐνέτυχον
> τῇ] μητρὶ τῆς κόρης· ὑπεσχόμην γαμεῖν
> καὶ ν]ῦν, ἐπὰν ἔλθῃ ποθ' ὁ πατήρ· ὤμοσα.

> I hesitate to say what happened next –
> perhaps I'm ashamed when there is no good being ashamed;
> even so, I'm ashamed.
> The girl became pregnant. By telling you this, I am also
> saying what happened before. I did not deny that I was to   50
> blame. I went first to the girl's mother and promised to
> marry the girl if ever my father returned with his companion.
> I swore an oath.

(transl. D.M. Bain)

---

14 Bearing in mind that in New Comedy rape is more common than seduction in such contexts, it appears more likely that Plangon was raped. It would have also been more appropriate for a decent Athenian girl, who would later become the wife of an Athenian citizen so as to have with him legitimate children, to be raped rather than to exhibit lust and indulge in her desires without paying any attention to the consequences. For the rape motif in Menander, see, in addition to the *Samia*, *Georgos*, *Epitrepontes*, *Kitharistes*, *Plokion*, *Phasma* and *Fabula Incerta* 1.23–24 Arnott. Cf. Gomme/Sandbach 1973, 33; Cohen 1991; Brown 1993, 196–197; Konstan 1995, 141–152; Scafuro 1997, 238–278; Rosivach 1998, 20–23, 30–33, 35–42, 146–148; Leisner-Jensen 2002, 179; Fountoulakis 2004, 126; Lape 2004, 92–93.
15 Men. *Sam.* 47–53. The text of Menander's plays which appears in this paper is that of Arnott 1979–2000.

It is noteworthy that, as happens with the young man of Menander's *Georgos* 15–16[16] or with Aeschinus in Terence's *Adelphoe* 333ff. and 470ff.,[17] Moschion's action after the girl's impregnation is presented as if it stems from a consideration of his deeds in terms of a set of socially produced norms or rules, which have been internalized as a set of moral standards, and the subsequent realization that his acts were far from the morality imposed by those norms or rules. The pain caused by his actions is therefore thought at 2–3 to be inflicted upon his father and his father's sense of honour, and not upon the girl. His own sense of shame apparently derives not only from the dishonour inflicted upon Plangon, but also from the fact that he fathered an illegitimate child.[18] Social necessity, external and internal standards, self-contempt and guilt are the main elements that shape his attitude towards the pregnant girl. His sexual incontinence, the insult against the girl's honour, and his subsequent remorse determine the antecedent circumstances that shape his action throughout the play.[19] It is for this reason that he subsequently decides to give, even temporarily, her baby to Chrysis, his father's Samian concubine who lives in their house. This would prevent a free-borne unmarried girl like Plangon from being publicly dishonoured. Such a solution suggests that his primary concern is the protection of the girl's social integrity and status, and his own good reputation as a well as of social order and morality. No reference to the symptoms of his emotional state or his feelings for Plangon has yet been made, although the possibility that he might have mentioned his love for her in the lost part of his monologue cannot be ruled out.[20]

The first reference to Moschion's love for Plangon is made not by him, but by Chrysis, and occurs at 81–82 when the latter compares his love for the girl to that of Demeas for her: ἐρᾷ γάρ, ὦ βέλτιστε, κἀκεῖνος κακῶς, / οὐχ ἧττον ἢ σύ [He's in love, dear, and in a bad way, just like you], (transl. D.M. Bain). From the κακῶς, as well as her comment concerning Demeas' love at 82–83, to which we will re-

---

16 In the fragmentary monologue preserved in *P. Geneva* 155 the young man explains at *Georg.* 15–16 that his actions result from his intention not to do wrong to the girl he left pregnant: τὴν φιλτάτην / οὐδ'] ἄν ποτ' ἀδικήσαιμ' ἄν· οὐ γὰρ εὐσεβές [I could (never) wrong my darling, that would be immoral], (transl. W.G. Arnott). Although she is called φιλτάτη, what appears more important is not to do wrong to her because of his moral standards. In a lost part of the same monologue he may refer in greater detail to his sense of duty before the girl.
17 Cf. Bain 1983, 114; Masaracchia 1998, 418–426.
18 Cf. Konstan 1995, 141–152, for a discussion of such issues in the *Epitrepontes*.
19 Cf. Zagagi 1995, 116, who refers to 'the powerful bourgeois emotions he displays, as an individual and as a citizen'.
20 Cf. Brown 1993, 195–196.

turn later, it may be inferred that Moschion's feelings are quite intense and perhaps tormenting. Yet the κακῶς is only a passing descriptive comment which does not allow a more detailed exploration of his emotional state or even of the symptomatology of his *erôs*.

In the second act Demeas, pleased with his son's decision to marry the girl he had already arranged with her father to give him as a wife, assumes that Moschion is already in love with her (165–166): ἐγὼ γὰρ οὐκ εἰδὼς ἔχον[τα τουτονὶ / ἐρωτικῶς [Not knowing Moschion was in love, I ...], (transl. D.M. Bain). This is nevertheless only an assumption which is temporarily belied in the third act. Thinking that Moschion is the father of Chrysis' child, he attempts to shed light on his adopted son's motivation as if his son had been formally accused of adultery and Demeas was delivering a forensic speech in his son's defence. Demeas appears to believe at 335–338 that he was wrong when he assumed that love had made his son want to marry Plangon; the young man's supposed intentions of getting away from Chrysis now seem more likely:

> οὐκ ἐρῶν γάρ, ὡς ἐγὼ
> τότ' ᾠόμην, ἔσπευδεν, ἀλλὰ τὴν ἐμὴν
> Ἑλένην φυγεῖν βουλόμενος ἔνδοθέν ποτε·
> αὕτη γάρ ἐστιν αἰτία τοῦ γεγονότος.

> His readiness was not, as I thought then,
> the product of love. He wants to get away from my house
> and my Helen. She is responsible for what has happened.

(transl. D.M. Bain)

Moschion's mild response to his father rules out the possibility that he might have been, among other things, in love with his father's concubine (κεκνισμένος ἔρωτι at 330–331). This type of detection of the motivation that may lead to an act presented as a criminal offence, which will subsequently reveal the person who is guilty for the committed crime, betrays the development of a reasoning expected in a forensic speech aiming at a person's acquittal or conviction. Demeas' speech is, after all, permeated by a complex argumentation with philosophical and rhetorical overtones pertaining to the permanent features of a human character being κόσμιος and σώφρων (344): a character capable of doing wrong only accidentally and not on purpose (328, 351). Earlier in the play Moschion himself had constructed his opening monologue as a forensic defence speech in which he referred to his service to the community (13–16) and the fact that he had always been κόσμιος (18). Similar references to liturgies found in forensic speeches normally aim at the favourable stance of the judges.[21] It is for this reason that such characters – and Moschion is presented as one of them – are supposed to deserve forgiveness when they commit an act which could otherwise be characterized as criminal. In their case, such acts may be considered as ἀτυχήματα.[22] Interestingly enough, *erôs* becomes part of the arguments which may be developed in such a speech with respect to the motivation that may be behind a person's criminal acts.

The reference to Helen as a mythological and literary paradigm of a notorious adulterer relating to Chrysis is inapt. Although Chrysis is ironically referred to as γαμετή at 130, she is only Demeas' concubine and not his wedded wife, and can therefore hardly be considered an adulterer, even though in Lysias 1.31 the penalty for a concubine who has been unfaithful to the man she lives with is the same as that for an adulterous wife who has been unfaithful to her husband.[23] The reference to Helen might, in fact, point towards the sphere of rhetorical argumentation in which *erôs* could be regarded as the driving force behind a person's transgressive behaviour. In Gorgias' *Helen erôs* is regarded, along with divine will and intervention, violence and persuasion, as one of the probable reasons that led her to Troy: ἢ γὰρ Τύχης βουλήμασι καὶ θεῶν βουλεύμασι καὶ Ἀνάγκης ψηφίσμασιν ἔπραξεν ἃ ἔπραξεν, ἢ βίᾳ ἁρπασθεῖσα, ἢ λόγοις πεισθεῖσα, <ἢ ἔρωτι ἁλοῦσα> [For either it was by the will of Fate or the wishes of the Gods and the votes of Necessity that she did what she did, or by force reduced or by words seduced <or by love possessed>], (transl. J. Dillon/T. Gergel).[24] As regards *erôs*, in particular, this is linked in Gorgias with vision and is, for this reason, regarded as an external force which may modify her will. The same happens if one considers *erôs* as a divinely sent emotion or as a human disease related to the ignorance of the soul. Her actions are therefore linked neither with a flaw of character nor with a conscious choice of her mind and soul. They are, by contrast, considered a kind of unfortunate incident (ἀτύχημα) caused by an external factor.[25] It is for this reason that she cannot be held responsible for her actions: εἰ οὖν τῷ τοῦ Ἀλεξάνδρου σώματι τὸ τῆς Ἑλένης ὄμμα ἡσθὲν προθυμίαν καὶ ἅμιλλαν ἔρωτος τῇ ψυχῇ παρέδωκε, τί θαυμαστόν; ὃς εἰ μὲν θεὸς <ὢν ἔχει> θεῶν θείαν δύναμιν, πῶς ἂν ὁ ἥσσων εἴη

---

[21] See e.g. Lys. 18.23, 20.31, 21.15, 25.12–13; Lape 2004, 142–146.
[22] Cf. Fountoulakis 2004, 157–166; Dedoussi 2006, 183–190; Fountoulakis 2011b, 92–95; Kiritsi 2013, 94–96; Sommerstein 2013, 205–211.
[23] Cf. Scafuro 1997, 474–479.
[24] Gorg. *Hel.* 6 D.–K.
[25] Cf. McComiskey 2002, 41–43, 140.

τοῦτον ἀπώσασθαι καὶ ἀμύνασθαι δυνατός; εἰ δ' ἐστὶν ἀνθρώπινον νόσημα καὶ ψυχῆς ἀγνόημα, οὐχ ὡς ἁμάρτημα μεμπτέον ἀλλ' ὡς ἀτύχημα νομιστέον· ἦλθε γάρ, ὡς ἦλθε, τύχης ἀγρεύμασιν, οὐ γνώμης βουλεύμασι, καὶ ἔρωτος ἀνάγκαις, οὐ τέχνης παρασκευαῖς [If, therefore, the eye of Helen, pleased by the body of Alexander, presented to her soul eager desire and contest of love, what is wonderful in that? If, being a god, love has the divine power of the gods, how could a lesser being reject and refuse it? But if it is a disease (*nosêma*) of human origin and a blind-spot (*agnoêma*) in the soul, it should not be condemned as a sin (*hamartêma*), but considered a misfortune (*atykhêma*); for she came – as she did come – by the snares of fate (*tykhês agreumasin*) not by the counsels of reason (*gnômês bouleumasin*), and by the constraints of love (*erôtos anangkais*), not by the devices of art (*teknês paraskeuais*)], (transl. J. Dillon/T. Gergel).[26] The rhetorical argumentation concerning *erôs*, which is developed in Gorgias' *Helen*, soon becomes a rhetorical *topos* relating to, and explaining, human motivation in speeches such as Lysias' *Against Teisis* or Hypereides' *Against Athenogenes*.[27] In these cases, the emphasis is placed not on the exploration of the potential manifestation and function of *erôs* with respect to human character, but on its emergence in rhetorical argumentation as a *topos* designating an external force which may only influence and explain human action. Although Demeas does not consider *erôs* to be a force leading to the supposed relationship between Moschion and Chrysis, his words betray an awareness of the function of such rhetorical references to *erôs*, which are nevertheless further exploited throughout the *Samia* in attempts to explain the attitude and behaviour of characters such as Moschion and Demeas.

It is only in the fifth act that Moschion's feelings for Plangon are explicitly acknowledged. At 616ff. Moschion feels insulted by his father's false assumptions. He says at 623–627 that he would leave as a mercenary for Bactra or Caria, if everything concerning the girl was alright and if he was not a slave to his oath, his desire for her, time, or their relationship:

εἰ μὲν καλῶς οὖν εἶχε τὰ περὶ τὴν κόρην
καὶ μὴ τοσαῦτ' ἦν ἐμποδών, ὅρκος, πόθος,
χρόνος, συνήθει', οἷς ἐδουλούμην ἐγώ,
οὐκ ἂν παρόντα γ' αὖθις ᾐτιάσατο
αὐτόν με τοιοῦτ' οὐδέν.

---

26 Gorg. *Hel.* 19 D.–K.
27 Cf. Bons 2007, 41–45; Carey 2013, 170–172.

> If there was no problem about the girl
> and there weren't so many obstacles in the way, the oath
> I swore, my love, the time that has gone by, our relationship,
> to all of which I am a slave, he would never make such a charge
> against me again, face to face.

(transl. D.M. Bain)

It is worth noting that here Moschion references his desire (πόθος) rather than his *erôs*, which is a more profound and multi-dimensional emotion. The fact that it is mentioned along with other factors contributing to his decision to marry Plangon, and after his oath, suggests that it was neither his only motive nor the most important. Social obligation deriving from a sense of shame and leading to his oath, which is mentioned first, appears to be more important. The word πόθος may suggest his erotic feelings towards her, but is rather oriented towards a carnal desire capable of leading to her pregnancy and not towards a more complex emotion manifested through specific symptoms, dominating his mind and soul, and transforming his behaviour.

At 630 631 he declares that he will not proceed to any act of bravery because of Plangon, who is described at 630 as 'most beloved' or 'dearest' (φιλτάτη). His emotional disposition towards her appears thus to be dominated by a profound affection designated as *philia*, which may come because of the factors mentioned at 624–625 (his oath, his desire, time, and their relationship),[28] but is not necessarily linked with *erôs*. It is not unreasonable to suppose that *philia*, rather than *erôs*, was in social contexts not alien to family bonds and that this provides a hint concerning the kind of the relationship that is going to be developed between Moschion and Plangon.[29]

In the following lines (631–632) it is suggested by Moschion that he could not leave Athens not only because of his sense of duty towards the girl, but also because Eros does not let him do so: οὐδ' ἐᾷ / ὁ τῆς ἐμῆς νῦν κύριος γνώμης, Ἔρως [Nor does Love, the master of my will, allow it], (transl. D.M. Bain). It should nevertheless be stressed that no reference is made to the emotion of *erôs* itself, but rather to the god Eros.[30] This takes the emphasis of these lines away from the rel-

---

28 Cf. Kiritsi 2013, 96.
29 Cf. Brown 1993, 200–201, where he also notes that New Comedy provides various examples of *philia* in marital or erotic relationships. For *philia* in contexts relating to kinship and marriage, see Konstan 2006, 169–184 and esp. 179–180.
30 Despite Brown 1993, 195, it is likely that at 632 reference is made to the god whose power can render him the κύριος of a human being and not to the emotion that may appear as a κύριος only

evant emotion and places it on the externally imposed power of the god, as happens in Gorgias, *Helen* 19 D.-K., where the theme of Eros' divine intervention is turned into part of a rhetorical argument aiming at Helen's acquittal. Moreover, the god Eros is not presented as responsible for the generation of emotion, to which no attention is paid, but appears at 632 as a divine agency which has become the master of his will. Demeas' attitude towards Moschion, being under the impression that the latter is the father of Chrysis' child, may be seen as leading to a quasi-judicial process in which Moschion is being accused of deception and adultery. If this is so, then Eros emerges as the instigator of his deeds as a third party persuading Moschion to act as he did. No reference to Eros' emotional impact is made, while his influence upon Moschion's thought may lead to the latter's acquittal. The same third party now keeps Moschion in Athens, where he will only *pretend* that he is going to leave as a mercenary, in order to make Demeas reconsider his insulting attitude (633–638).

However, *erôs* in the *Samia* is not related only to the action of Moschion. It is therefore not confined to the conventional plot-pattern of the young man who falls in love with a girl until they eventually get married after a series of adventures. *Erôs* in the *Samia* is also related to Demeas and shapes his behaviour and action in a way that interferes significantly with the pervasive plot-pattern of the young man in love. When Moschion describes the circumstances under which Chrysis came to live in their house as Demeas' concubine, he refers at 21–22 to the desire felt for her by his father; this is an emotion that is considered as something humane: Σαμίας ἑταίρας εἰς ἐ<πι>θυμίαν τινὸς / ἐλθεῖν ἐκεῖνον, πρᾶγμ' ἴσως ἀνθρώπινον [It happened that he fell in love with a certain Samian courtesan. It could have happened, I think, to anyone], (transl. D.M. Bain). Demeas' relationship with Chrysis appears as a variation on the conventional dramatic pattern of a young man in love with a girl and involves a love affair with a *hetaira*. The characters of *hetairai* and the erotic relations of men with them were already popular on the comic stage from the times of Middle Comedy onwards, as may be inferred from plays such as Philetairus' *Korinthiastes*, Pherecrates' *Korianno*, Eubulus' *Kampylion*, Anaxilas' *Neottis*, Antiphanes' *Hydria* or Eunicus' *Anteia*.[31]

---

in a personification. Yet even a personification would again lead to the presence of the god Eros. Although the influence of the god on human soul results in the generation of a relevant emotional state, a reference to the god cannot be taken as equivalent to a reference to the emotion. For the presence of Eros and the emphasis on the divine power of his emotional influence here as well as in other Menandrean plays, see Masaracchia 1998, 408–409.

31 Cf. Konstantakos 2002, 145–153.

As regards Demeas, he is presented as a *senex amator*. Gathering insight from the presentation of the *senex amator* in Plautus, the character of an old man in love in New Comedy stands out not for his tender, complex or profound feelings, but for his comic ability to get away from his wife through a younger partner or for his debauchery or both.³² Despite Aristotle's observations concerning a link between youth and lack of emotional moderation especially with respect to *erôs*,³³ Demeas appears as a self-indulgent man who yields to his feelings for Chrysis, although he eventually embarks upon a loving relationship with her. It is only after he assumes that she has insulted him and violated the order of his *oikos* that he decides to keep her away from him and his household.³⁴

It is worth noting that Moschion highlights at 21 Chrysis' identity as a *hetaira* from Samos and refers to Demeas' emotional state using the word ἐπιθυμίαν. This reduces the latter's feelings for that woman to the level of carnal desire associated with pleasure and reflects a culturally specific notion of the *hetaira* as a female whose social role was to do anything she could for a man's pleasure.³⁵ The same notion occurs in a well-known passage from Apollodorus' *Against Neaira* (122), where it is noted that a *hetaira* is used for a man's pleasure, a *pallakê* for the daily care of a man's body and a wife for the acquisition of legitimate children and the protection of the household property: τὰς μὲν γὰρ ἑταίρας ἡδονῆς ἕνεκ' ἔχομεν, τὰς δὲ παλλακὰς τῆς καθ' ἡμέραν θεραπείας τοῦ σώματος, τὰς δὲ γυναῖκας τοῦ παιδοποιεῖσθαι γνησίως καὶ τῶν ἔνδον φύλακα πιστὴν ἔχειν [For we have courtesans for pleasure, and concubines for the daily service of our bodies, but wives for the production of legitimate offspring and to have reliable guardian of our household property], (transl. C. Carey).³⁶ This statement reflects social and legal distinctions of fundamental importance for the construction of the notion of Athenian citizenship which are also found in Xenophon, *Oeconomicus* 6.17 and 7.7–13, and form the basis upon which Apollodorus' rhetorical attack against the old *hetaira* Neaira is based. Such distinctions between decent women and prostitutes were already current in the Athenian legal system from the age of Solon who

---

32 See Ryder 1984, 181–189. For such characters in Menander, see Conca 1970. Cf. Zagagi 1995, 116.
33 Aristot. *EN* 1156b 1–6.
34 Cf. Kiritsi 2013, 97.
35 Cf. Traill 2008, 156–157. Although Davidson 1997, 94–95 believes that there is no reference to the sexual aspect of Demeas' relations with Chrysis even though she is a *hetaira*, the ἐπιθυμίαν may be regarded as such a reference, which is nevertheless a mild one because her position as a *pallakê* in his household involves also the emergence of roles similar to those of a wife and a mother.
36 The Greek text of *Against Neaira* appearing in this paper is from Carey 1992.

passed the relevant legislation.³⁷ Neaira makes the illegal transition from the status of a common prostitute or *hetaira* from Corinth to that of an Athenian citizen who could become the legitimate wife of another Athenian citizen and have her children married as if they were legitimate and enjoyed citizen status. It is this that enables Apollodorus to develop his arguments against her in a forensic situation associated with transgressions of status and citizenship. Bearing in mind that Chrysis was a Samian and a *hetaira*, and that Moschion was an adopted son, it becomes clear that issues relating to identity, status and citizenship within both the *oikos* and the *polis* have a central position in *Samia*'s plot.³⁸ Apollodorus' endorsement of the fundamental, socially-produced distinction between lawful wives and women who are used for pleasure and take care of a man's body – suggesting in these latter cases women used for sexual pleasure – lies underneath Chrysis' situation and is implied by the use of ἐπιθυμίαν.³⁹

At 80–83 Moschion recognizes that Demeas may be angered when he sees that his concubine has given birth to a child which is raised by her in his house. Chrysis does not seem to be worried about this because she knows that Demeas is very much in love with her. She also knows that even the most irascible man is easily tamed by *erôs*: ἐρᾷ γάρ, ὦ βέλτιστε, κἀκεῖνος κακῶς, / οὐχ ἧττον ἢ σύ. τοῦτο δ' εἰς διαλλαγὰς / ἄγει τάχιστα καὶ τὸν ὀργιλώτατον (81–83) [He's in love, dear, and in a bad way, just like you. Love leads even the most irascible of men to make up very soon after a quarrel], (transl. D.M. Bain). The rhetorical link between *erôs* and human motivation already mentioned is being again employed by Chrysis to foresee Demeas' potential reaction. Yet, as has been noted with respect to Moschion's feelings, the κακῶς may suggest intensity of emotion, but it is not being specified or exemplified, and it remains thus a passing comment. As Brown aptly observes, in these lines the emphasis is placed on *erôs* as a 'force for reconciliation'.⁴⁰ Moreover, it will become clear that in the case of Demeas it is not only *erôs*, but also sexual jealousy as well as a concern for the integrity of his *oikos* that characterize him. Chrysis does not seem to suspect that in his case *erôs* is only a small part of antecedent circumstances that create in him a sense of possession over her, and lead to his jealousy and aggression. It is for this reason that his reaction is not what she expects. It is also worth noting that the detached way in which she refers to Demeas' feelings for her at 81–83 do not contain any hint of reciprocity on her part, unlike what one might have expected from a *hetaira*,

---

37 See Pomeroy 1975, 57–60.
38 Cf. Zagagi 1995, 116–117.
39 Cf. Carey 1992, 148–149; Kapparis 1999, 422–424.
40 Brown 1993, 195.

and especially from a *bona meretrix*, in the context of New Comedy.[41] This enhances the delineation of *erôs* in this play as a rhetorical motif associated with human motivation. Chrysis appears to be more interested in the preservation of social status and familial bonds, and this sets the tone for the play's main concerns.

When Demeas refers to his own feelings for Chrysis in his attempt to persuade himself that she should be expelled from his house, he soliloquizes at 350 to the effect that he ought to forget his desire for her as well as his *erôs*: ἐπιλαθοῦ τοῦ πόθου, πέπαυσ' ἐρῶν [Forget your passion. Stop loving her!], (transl. D.M. Bain). If the ἐπιλαθοῦ τοῦ πόθου and the πέπαυσ' ἐρῶν are taken as synonymous phrases, then *erôs* may be thought of as having carnal overtones. Even if the two phrases are taken as denoting different aspects of his feelings for her, his *erôs* may be thought to be deriving from *pothos*, constraining again his *erôs* within the boundaries of physical attraction.

It has been shown so far that *erôs* may be presented as an emotion which directs the action of both Moschion and Demeas, pervading thus the *Samia*'s plot, but is in fact a rhetorical device put forward by the play's characters to explain their behaviour or make assumptions about it. Other determinants of their personality such as a sense of shame and duty or jealousy are, by contrast, far more important in the shaping of their action, which is oriented towards the preservation of morality as well as of familial and social order. It is worth observing that the references to *erôs* are in most cases superficial comments used in arguments pertinent to those characters' motivation as if in a speech focused on the explanation of the behaviour of someone charged with a serious crime. They do not contribute to a profound exploration of the emotion of *erôs* in relation to human character as one might expect, bearing in mind the importance which is supposed to be attached to that emotion throughout the play's plot as well as the treatment of *erôs* in other literary and non-literary Greek texts.

Although it is hard to provide a concise overview of literary representations relating to *erôs* in those texts, it should be stressed that the gods Eros and Aphrodite are often presented in them as powerful divine agents inspiring mortals and immortals with desire capable of dominating their minds and bodies. From Homer onwards *erôs* is described as possessing a devastating limb-loosening power,[42] while Greek lyric often explores the multifaceted impact of *erôs* on human beings. In Sappho, for instance, *erôs* is considered a major, divinely inspired, emotional force capable of offering both pleasure and sorrow, and for this

---

41 Cf. Konstan 1994, 147–148.
42 Hom. *Il.* 13.412; *Od.* 14.69, 18.212 and 238; Hes. *Th.* 120–122. Cf. Thornton 1997, 26–28.

reason it is referred to not only as 'limb-loosening', but also as a 'bittersweet reptile' that may dissolve reason.[43] Various aspects of the profound effects of *erôs* upon the soul, the mind and the body of the man or the woman in love become obvious in early Greek poets such as Alcman, Ibycus, Alcaeus and Anacreon. Tragic texts such as Euripides' *Hippolytus* and *Medea* provide detailed explorations of the emotional breadth of *erôs* in connection with a system of values pertaining to honour, shame, pride, transgression or social integration, which contributes to the formation of the tragic self. In comedies, such as Aristophanes' *Lysistrata*, aspects of *erôs* relating to desire and sensual pleasure emerge as a driving force of human action, both male and female, affecting even the domain of politics. Dramatic patterns relating to love, which are similar to those known from Menander, already emerge in Aristophanes' *Ecclesiazusae* 877–1111 and must have been used in mythological comic plays such as Eubulus' *Danae* and *Lakones* or *Leda*, Anaxandrides' *Io* and Sophilus' *Tyndareos* or *Leda*. It appears that the plots of Middle Comedy adopted similar motifs, albeit with no elaboration on an emotional level.[44] Philosophical enquiries relating to the nature *erôs*, such as those of Plato's *Symposium* and *Phaedrus*, betray an attempt to fit it into specific modes of thought and philosophical patterns. Plato's conception of the soul or the world of ideas imagines wider, culturally-determined perceptions of *erôs* as a divinely inspired force which led to the creation of the world and affected the human soul. These perceptions of *erôs* as a major cosmogonic force, which is associated with the immense power of the deified Eros, are attested in Hesiod and Alcman as well as in Orphic myth and cult. A focus on *erôs* becomes apparent in Hellenistic poetry. As may be inferred from Apollonius' *Argonautica*, Hellenistic epic brought the exploration of *erôs* and related emotions to the foreground of narrative along with the heroic ideals of archaic Greek epic. A similar focus on *erôs* is attested in Theocritus' *Idylls*, where the expression of emotion often provides the circumstances which enable the formulation and development of bucolic song. As may be inferred from the epigrams of the fifth and the twelfth books of the *Greek Anthology*, Greek epigram developed an interest in the depiction of *erôs*, which often determined the thematic conventions of the subgenres of erotic epigram either heterosexual or pederastic. The Greek novel is another genre which embodied various explorations of *erôs* and turned them into parts of broader narrative patterns which dominate the novel's plots within an atmosphere of emotional reciprocity between male and female lovers. In New Comedy *erôs* is, by contrast, an emotion which characterizes not women, but men, who

---

[43] Sapph. fr. 130 Voigt. Cf. Calame 1992, 14–19; Thornton 1997, 27.
[44] Cf. Konstantakos 2002, 143–155, 157.

exhibit thus a somehow vulnerable and effeminate countenance. Yet their behaviour is, in fact, governed not by emotion, but by morality and conformity to social norm and convention.[45]

Most of those texts elucidate various aspects of *erôs* by drawing attention to a relevant symptomatology. As may be inferred, for example, from texts such as Euripides, *Hippolytus* 176ff., Plato, *Phaedrus* 251e or Longus 1.13–14, love, and especially unrequited or unfulfilled love, often manifests itself through the symptoms of a disease that harms the mental capacities as well as the body of the person in love. Insomnia, sweating, grief, loss of appetite and inability to think reasonably or appear happy are some of its main symptoms. This perception of *erôs* is also found in non-literary texts reflecting social experience such as the Greek magical papyri, in which a polarization between erotic suffering and pleasure, the conception of *erôs* as a disease or madness, and the extraordinary influence of *erôs* upon the bodies and the souls of the persons affected by it are attested. The symptoms of *erôs*, which are mentioned in the Greek magical papyri, are strikingly similar to those found in literary representations and this suggests the existence of wider cultural perceptions of *erôs* as a major emotional force, which attracted a great deal of interest and was often analyzed in detail and from various perspectives in Greek literature and beyond.[46]

As Christophe Cusset has shown, melancholy sometimes appears as the main symptom of *erôs* in Menander and this betrays a culturally determined perception of the symptoms of this emotion, which is very close to those emerging from relevant literary and non-literary representations.[47] Yet in the case of the *Samia* melancholy is only what Parmenon thinks that characterizes Moschion in the play's fifth act. Being under the impression that Moschion's erotic despair has led him into depression, Parmenon says at 672: διὰ κενῆς σαυτὸν ταράττεις εἰς ἀθυμίαν τ' ἄγεις [you're putting yourself into unnecessary confusion and bringing yourself to despair], (transl. D.M. Bain). In fact, melancholy has nothing to do with Moschion's actual state. It is only a quasi-theatrical device, which exploits popular perceptions of erotic sorrow and sad lovers in order to make Demeas beg for Moschion's forgiveness under the impression that his adopted son is ready to leave

---

[45] For more specific references and discussions of those texts see, among others, Padel 1992, 115–120, 126–128; Calame 1992, 19–23, 56–62, 178–191; Konstan 1994, *passim* and esp. 178–184; Sanders *et al.* 2013.
[46] Cf. e.g. *PGM* IV.356ff, IV.2444, IV.1426ff., IV.1510ff., XII.14–95, XXXVI.134–160; Dover 1974, 210–212; Winkler 1990, 87–91; Petropoulos 1997, 112–114; Fountoulakis 1999, 197–199; Faraone 1999, 43–55.
[47] See Cusset 2014, 170–177 with respect to Men. *Phasma* 9–28, 82–85 and *Epitr.* 878–900.

Athens as a mercenary.⁴⁸ Compared to the complex perceptions and representations of *erôs* in Greek culture, *erôs* in Menander's *Samia* is presented in a rather superficial manner and this is quite surprising if the importance attached to it throughout its plot is taken into consideration.

Modern scholars often appear ready to associate the presence of *erôs* in New Comedy with the notion of 'romantic love'. In an examination of the love motif in New Comedy and beyond, Peter Walcot uses the term 'romantic love' so as to describe a profound emotion leading to a long-term union of two individuals beyond the boundaries of lust and sexual relations. He nevertheless notes the paradox resulting from the link of such an emotion with marriage when in social contexts marriage was a bond between individuals of similar civic – and often social or financial – status for the acquisition of legitimate children,⁴⁹ as is also echoed in the plays of New Comedy. As he points out, this does not exclude the possibility of the development of a deeper affection or even love between husband and wife.⁵⁰ On the other hand, Niall Rudd argues that the notion of 'romantic love' was not a medieval invention but existed also in ancient times. New Comedy and the presentation of Sostratos' feelings in Menander's *Dyskolos*, in particular, are considered by him to be relevant evidence.⁵¹ Moreover, David Wiles notes the emergence of erotic reciprocity in the comedies of Menander, draws attention to the 'romantic' character of the relevant emotions, and observes that in these plays one finds depicted the action of characters in love, but not the verbal expression of their feelings.⁵² This is a right observation which is nevertheless inadequately explained. Rather than supposing that the comic theatre presents the action imposed by new moral and emotional attitudes, but has not yet found a way of expressing verbally the relevant emotions, it may be argued that this happens deliberately since other genres, such as lyric or tragedy, had already found a way of verbally expressing and exploring erotic emotions. This silence may well be an indication of the marginal position of those emotions as such within the comic plots, especially when their presentation is compared to the presentation of other topics.

---

48 See Cusset 2014, 177–178.
49 Cf. Pomeroy 1975, 63–68.
50 Walcot 1987, 5–6, 8, 26–33.
51 Rudd 1981, 144–145, 151. Rudd 1981, 151, realizing perhaps that Menander's plays do not fit into the pattern of the depiction of 'romantic love', notes that 'because of the scarcity of material we cannot adduce much evidence'. However, one ought to wonder whether the inability to adduce relevant evidence is indeed due to that reason.
52 Wiles 1989, 31–48.

Peter Brown, being in broad agreement with Rudd, refers to the following four criteria Rudd sets for the consideration of love in New Comedy as 'romantic' and notes that Sostratos in the *Dyskolos* satisfies most of them: i) 'love at first sight', ii) 'idealization of the beloved', iii) 'emotional preoccupation', and iv) 'desire for long-term attachment'.[53] As a matter of fact, Rudd also refers to two more criteria: i) 'vivid expression of the emotions of the person in love', and ii) 'postponement of physical fulfilment' or 'early separation soon after the physical fulfilment'.[54]

Are these criteria satisfied in the case of Moschion and Plangon? About the criterion of 'love at first sight', nothing is mentioned in the course of the *Samia*. Bearing in mind, however, that their houses were close to each-other, and that their fathers as well as Chrysis and Plangon's mother were friends and traveled together or exchanged visits, it is possible that they knew each-other quite well from an early age. The license promoted during the festival of the Adonia only provided them with the opportunity to have sexual intercourse.[55] As for the criteria of the 'idealization of the beloved' or the 'emotional preoccupation', it is worth remembering that the girl's name is not even mentioned until line 630[56] and that Moschion's thoughts are hardly focused upon Plangon or upon his feelings for her. Moreover, no reference is made to any attempt on the part of Moschion to ask for her forgiveness for what he has done to her.[57] He rather appears concerned with the moral and social implications of his deeds and the reaction of his father. Far from being idealized, Plangon is in the eyes of Moschion only the innocent victim of his sexual violence. That is why he must make up for that violence and the dishonour inflicted upon her. Considering that the references relating to Moschion's feelings in the extant parts of the play are scanty and superficial, neither the criterion of 'emotional preoccupation' nor that of the 'vivid expression of the emotions of the person in love' is satisfied as there is no reference to a relevant symptomatology. As regards the criterion of the 'postponement of physical fulfilment' or the 'early separation soon after the physical fulfilment', physical fulfilment is the actual starting point of their affair, while the fact that they live in neighbouring houses can hardly be considered as separation. If Plangon was indeed raped, rape could not be considered as the 'physical fuflifment' expected in a romantic relationship. Moreover, rape may come because of uncontrolled physical attraction, but can hardly be related to the complex emotional preoccupation

---

53 Brown 1993, 196.
54 Rudd 1981, 144–145.
55 See Men. *Sam.* 30–50.
56 Cf. Rosivach 1998, 21.
57 See Gutzwiller 2012, 67.

and attachment described as *erôs*. As David Konstan notes, in the New Comedy plots that include the motif of rape this is presented as a violent assault induced by drink during a night dominated by wanton passion and not by *erôs*.[58] As one might expect from a genre interested in the dramatic rendering of a social reality as well as in the depiction of a character's moral integrity, no attention is paid to Plangon's feelings for Moschion.[59] A relevant reference, which would give an impression of emotional symmetry, might seem unrealistic to Menander's spectators, who did not normally witness such symmetrical relationships in social contexts. Moreover, if Plangon was subject to emotion and erotic incontinence, this would have been a major moral flaw that would have rendered her unsuitable for marriage.[60] Only the criterion of the 'desire for long-term attachment' seems to be satisfied since even from the beginning of the play Moschion declares his intentions of marrying her. Yet, as has been pointed out, his decision to do so is associated with his sense of shame for his deeds as well as with his sense of duty to restore the honour of the free girl he has insulted rather than from an inner desire to be with her for the rest of his life. In his opening monologue, which resembles a rhetorical apology of a man charged with a serious crime, he mentions twice that he felt ashamed (αἰσχύνομαι at 47 and 48), he admitted his guilt (οὐκ ἠρνησάμην / τὴν] αἰτίαν σχών at 50–51) and promised – by giving a vow – to marry her, thereby making up for his shameful deeds (ὑπεσχόμην γαμεῖν and ὤμοσα at 52 and 53). As if he was delivering a forensic speech aimed at his acquittal, he admits his crime, shows remorse, and provides compensation for the committed injustice.

On similar grounds, Demeas' *erôs* for Chrysis can hardly be considered 'romantic love' according to the criteria set by Rudd. Although at 21–22 it is said that Demeas felt desire for a Samian *hetaira* (Σαμίας ἑταίρας εἰς ἐ<πι>θυμίαν τινὸς / ἐλθεῖν ἐκεῖνον), it is not mentioned whether this happened 'at first sight' or whether his desire was so strong that it led to 'emotional preoccupation'. The sexual overtones of the ἐπιθυμίαν as well as the fact that Chrysis was a *hetaira* could hardly have resulted in her 'idealization'. 'Physical fulfilment' must therefore have been a central issue in their relationship and was not postponed. As regards the expression of his emotions, this happens when he feels deceived and suspects the probable collapse of his *oikos*. Moreover, the emotions expressed by him are not his *erôs*, but his anger and jealousy, which may in some respects only be related to his *erôs*. Considering that Chrysis lived in Demeas' house as a *pallakê*,

---

[58] See Konstan 1994, 144.
[59] Cf. Brown 1993, 198.
[60] Cf. Konstan, 1994, 145–147; Dutsch/Konstan 2011, 60, 68; Kiritsi 2013, 85.

only the criterion of the 'desire for long-term attachment' is satisfied. And this happens as a necessary requirement for the development of the play's plot. About Chrysis' feelings for Demeas, it can hardly be argued that there is an emotional symmetry between the two. Her concern, however, for Moschion's position within the house of Demeas and his relationship with his father as well as for Plangon's honour and status betray the adoption of a role and the development of a social bond that would resemble those of a married wife, who would not be much interested in emotional attachment.

Far from being profoundly explored as a multi-dimensional emotion, *erôs* in the *Samia* is in fact a structural element of quasi-rhetorical arguments contributing to the construction of the play's plot and the articulation of its ideological load. Demeas' desire for Chrysis explains thus her presence in his house. At 17ff. Moschion says that, driven by a sense of gratitude for what Demeas had done for him, he had decided in return to do something for his father. Knowing that the latter had fallen in love with a Samian *hetaira* and that he was feeling shame for that, he had urged Demeas to bring her to their house so that he would not feel embarrassed because of the younger rivals who were around her. As has been noted, Demeas' feelings for Chrysis are significantly enough described as *epithymia* rather than *erôs* and this confines them within the limits of a mostly carnal desire.

Demeas' feelings for the woman from Samos form also an element that helps her and Moschion set in motion the plan of Demeas' deception, which leads to the series of misunderstandings and false pretensions that dominate the second, the third, and part of the fourth act. Those feelings result in a disposition on the part of Demeas which creates the antecedent circumstances exploited by Moschion and Chrysis to achieve their goals. Their actions and his subsequent reactions could not have occurred without it. When at 80 Moschion observes that Demeas might be angry with Chrysis, if he will be told that she has given birth to a child, she notes at 80–83 that he will tolerate this because he is in love with her (ἐρᾷ γὰρ at 81). This is the first time his feelings are explicitly described as *erôs*. Yet this *erôs* is treated as a means of persuasion which, as is often presented in oratory, will calm him down and persuade him to admit the child in his house. That is how they decide to present Plangon's baby as Chrysis' offspring.

At 283–356 Demeas' extreme anger and his decision to drive Chrysis out of his house stem from the jealousy he feels, because of the assumption that the woman he is in love with has had an affair with his stepson. When at 330–331, trying to explain Moschion's attitude, he assumes that his stepson might have fallen in love with Chrysis, Demeas projects upon him his own feelings. The sense that he had lost his power and exclusive possession of his concubine, the realization that she was ungrateful for what he had offered her, his wounded pride, and his subsequent anger result not only in the scene of Chrysis' violent eviction – the most spectacular scene of the play which is apparently for this reason depicted in the famous Mytilene mosaics[61] – but also in the gradual revelation of the truth. The pattern into which Demeas' action fits is a complex psychological pattern of sexual jealousy felt when a man loses or fears that he might lose possession over a female partner after the latter's sexual infidelity. In this psychological pattern, which is discernible in Demeas' action, *erôs* may stand as only part of the antecedent circumstances which lead to the development of his jealousy and his jealous outburst. What is central in this pattern is a sense of possession of his partner as well as feelings of loss, envy, deprivation of power, wounded pride, and marginalization. Grief, hatred for the partner or her new lover, and violence form the usual results of such feelings.[62] Seen from an evolutionary perspective, this psychological pattern is linked with the inner fear that the deceived male partner might raise somebody else's child.[63]

Such concerns run through Lysias, *On the Murder of Eratosthenes*. In this speech Euphiletus deliberately presents himself as a man naïve and overridden by anger because of his wife's sexual infidelity. But these features of character and attitude also fit well into a major legal pattern that justified homicide in the case of a wife's seduction.[64] Thus Euphiletus claims that the murder of his wife's lover complies with the law[65] which considers adultery as a major crime because it involved the wife's alienation from her husband, the fall of the husband's household into the seducer's hands, and the uncertainty over the legitimacy of the children acquired: τοὺς δὲ πείσαντας οὕτως αὐτῶν τὰς ψυχὰς διαφθείρειν, ὥστ' οἰκειοτέρας αὐτοῖς ποιεῖν τὰς ἀλλοτρίας γυναῖκας ἢ τοῖς ἀνδράσι, καὶ πᾶσαν ἐπ' ἐκείνοις τὴν οἰκίαν γεγονέναι, καὶ τοὺς παῖδας ἀδήλους εἶναι ὁποτέρων τυγχάνουσιν ὄντες, τῶν ἀνδρῶν ἢ τῶν μοιχῶν [those who act by seduction corrupt the minds of their victims in such a way that they make other people's wives more closely related to themselves than to their husbands. The victim's whole household becomes the adulterer's, and as for the children, it is unclear whose children they are, the husband's or the seducer's], (transl. S.C. Todd).[66] In this

---

[61] See Charitonidis/Kahil/Ginouvès 1970, 38ff.
[62] See Ben-Ze'ev 2000, 49–78, 289–290, 301; Buss 2000, 1–128; Kristjánsson 2002, 141–144.
[63] See Wilson/Daly 1996; Buss 2013, 165–166.
[64] See e.g. Lys. 1.8–13 and 24–26.
[65] Lys. 1.26.
[66] Lys. 1.33. The Greek text is that of Carey 1989.

pattern *erôs* plays only a marginal role. What matters most is an interest in possession, property, and legitimacy.⁶⁷ Moreover, in the same speech punishment for adultery is considered not as a private matter, but as something that takes place on behalf of the *polis*: οὐκ ἰδίαν ὑπὲρ ἐμαυτοῦ νομίζω ταύτην γενέσθαι τὴν τιμωρίαν, ἀλλ' ὑπὲρ τῆς πόλεως ἁπάσης [I do not accept that this redress was exacted privately on my own behalf, but rather for the sake of the whole city], (transl. S.C. Todd).⁶⁸ Despite the differences, both Euphiletus in Lysias' *On the Murder of Eratosthenes* and Demeas in the *Samia* are driven not only by their jealousy, but also by their intention of keeping their *oikos* intact against any intruder who might threaten its stability and the acquisition of legitimate children, which is crucial to the notion of citizenship and the structure of the *polis'* citizen-body. In a significant contribution to the understanding of *erôs* in Menander, Stavroula Kiritsi has persuasively shown that the lack of emotional moderation brought about by *erôs* enables Menander's characters to put forward an Aristotelian morality as well as to display both positive and negative qualities. These should nevertheless be dominated by reason and a system of values based on reason and moderation, which are important to both the *oikos* and the *polis*.⁶⁹

Yet unlike what one might have expected according to the relevant psychological pattern endorsed or the course of action reflected in Lysias' speech, Demeas does not attack his sexual antagonist. Following a quasi-judicial procedure addressed to himself, he delivers in the form of a monologue a quasi-forensic speech at 328–356 accusing his partner of being a wanton and ungrateful woman who seduced his stepson. As Scafuro observes, the play depicts the responses of the main characters to two sexual acts: an actual one which is related to Plangon and an assumed one which is related to Chrysis. Through these responses emphasis is placed on the father-son relationship.⁷⁰ Although Chrysis was not married with Demeas, she is described as a 'Helen' (337), a notorious adulteress of the mythological as well as of the epic and tragic traditions and is thought to have seduced Moschion while he was drunk (339–442). Moreover, she is equated to a common prostitute with dirty character when she is called χαμαιτύπη and ὄλεθρος (348). Demeas evokes socially produced stereotypes concerning the evil character of grasping and lecherous *hetairai* or common prostitutes in order to build, as if in a forensic speech, his argumentation against her.⁷¹ At the same time, it is worth

---

67 Cf. Carey 1989, 80; Todd 2007, 133–134.
68 Lys. 1.47.
69 Kiritsi 2013.
70 See Scafuro 1997, 259–265.
71 Cf. Lape 2004, 159–167.

noting that the play makes use of conventional dramatic representations of *hetairai* as well as of erotic affairs with *hetairai* in earlier comedy, which are centred on the types of the good, honest, and tender *hetaira*, on the one hand, and the bad, lecherous, and grasping *hetaira*, on the other.[72]

Demeas' *erôs* for Chrysis and his subsequent wounded pride and sexual jealousy might have triggered his emotional outburst. Yet this outburst is part of a major rhetorical strategy, while his *erôs* is only a marginal feeling compared to his jealousy and the concern for his *oikos*. The references to the audience at 330 (ἄνδρες) and 488 (παρόντων) may be considered as echoes of the references to judges and witnesses in judicial processes.[73] If Demeas' monologue is seen as a forensic speech directed against a person who has committed *hybris*,[74] then those negative characterizations may be regarded as a kind of *diabolê* and *loidoria* so often used in oratory as a means of 'character assassination' aimed at an opponent. According to Aristotle, *Rhetoric* 1354a 11ff. this was a means of stirring the judges' emotions at court so as to influence their judgment against an opponent and was used instead of evidence and solid argumentation.[75] It is exactly for this reason that in Apollodorus' *Against Neaira* 33–34 emphasis is placed not on evidence against Stephanus, but on rumours concerning Neaira's sexual conduct. The Corinthian *hetaira* is thus presented as having sex in public with Phrynion, while reference is made to an evening at the house of Chabrias, during which Neaira got drunk and had sex with many men including Chabrias' servants. She is thus described as a common prostitute whose wantonness turned her into an object of sexual exploitation even by the house's male slaves. These allegations must, in fact, be rhetorical exaggerations or even fabrications aiming at the negative colouring of her character for emotional effect. The negative emotions of the judges caused by this threat against their morality worked toward her conviction.[76] In a similar manner, Chrysis' 'character assassination' leads to her condemnation, not through evidence or argumentation, but through emotion. This results in her conviction and her eviction from Demeas' house, as well as in Moschion's acquittal.

---

72 See Alexis, *Isostasion* fr. 103 K.–A.; Anaxilas, *Neottis* frr. 21–22 K.–A.; Antiphanes, *Hydria* fr. 210 K.–A.; Eubulus, *Kampylion* frr. 40–41 K.–A.; Philetairus, *Korinthiastes* fr. 5 K.–A., *Kynagis* fr. 8 K.–A.; Konstantakos 2002, 145–153.
73 See Bain 1988, 9–10; Scafuro 1997, 42–50, 261, 264–265.
74 Cf. Nikeratos considers Chrysis' supposed actions as *hybris* and a kind of murder in Men. *Sam.* 507–514.
75 See Hunter 1990; Carey 2004.
76 Cf. Carey 1992, 102–103; Davidson 1997, 100–102, 105–106; Kapparis 1999, 240; Alexiou 2016, 154–161.

Demeas' decision is grounded on common moral principles as well as on relevant legal restrictions concerning the marginal role of foreigners and prostitutes within the *polis* and the fact that such women should never acquire the status of a wife in the *oikos* of an Athenian citizen (390–398). According to Pericles' citizenship law of 451/450 BCE, which often determines the development of Menander's plots, a man and a woman in Athens could get married, if they were both free-born Athenians. Only if their parents, that is, were Athenian citizens could they be united as husband and wife, and have legitimate children who could acquire citizen status like themselves.[77] Demeas' erotic feelings for Chrysis give way to reasoning that serves to safeguard his *oikos*, which now appears to him as more important than pleasure or emotional fulfilment. The fact that his judgment turns out to be wrong is due not to his principles or reasoning, but to the fact that he ignores the entire truth about Chrysis, Moschion, and Plangon.[78] This discourse of sex, status, and citizenship pervades also Apollodorus' *Against Neaira*, and is put forward when the judges are asked to convict Neaira for being illegally married to an Athenian citizen and for enjoying all the privileges of an Athenian wife, including the participation to the religious activities of the *polis* or giving her daughter in marriage as if she enjoyed citizen status, even though she was a foreigner and no better than a prostitute. Neaira's conviction is demanded by the judges, because her conduct is considered as a threat against the morality preserving the *oikos* as well as the *polis*.[79] It is the same discourse of sex, status, and citizenship that shapes Demeas' rhetoric and results in his verdict.

Chrysis is a *hetaira* who most probably becomes Demeas' *pallakê*,[80] but certainly not his wedded wife. Although in Athens the status of a *pallakê* was higher than that of a hired *hetaira*, since the former could live with a man and take care of him and his household as if she were his wife, it was not equated with that of

---

77 See Patterson 1981, *passim*; Pomeroy 1975, 62–68; Vérilhac/Vial 1998, 56–68, 78–79, 232–247.
78 Cf. Kiritsi 2013, 97–98.
79 [Dem.] 59.110–111. See also [Dem.] 59.112 where a potential acquittal of Neaira is considered an abolition of the *polis*' laws and their replacement by the power of *hetairai*: καὶ οἱ μὲν νόμοι ἄκυροι ὑμῖν ἔσονται, οἱ δὲ τρόποι τῶν ἑταιρῶν κύριοι ὅ τι ἂν βούλωνται διαπράττεσθαι [and your laws will be invalid, while the characters of courtesans will have the power to achieve whatever they wish], (transl. C. Carey). Cf. Pomeroy 1975, 67–68, 91–92; Glazebrook 2006, 129–130; Alexiou 2016, 159–161.
80 Chrysis is described as a *pallakê* by Nikeratos in Men. *Sam.* 508. It is nevertheless quite uncertain that Nikeratos' description reflects her real status which has features peculiar to the status of a wife, a mother, a companion and a prostitute. See further Henry 1988², 73; Krieter-Spiro 1997, 43–44, 47–49, 127–132.

a legitimate wife who enjoyed a much more secure, respected, and recognized social status.⁸¹ These socially informed distinctions emerge also in the *Samia*.⁸² The interplay between those roles in the *Samia* becomes apparent when Demeas declares his intention of expelling Chrysis from his house under the impression that she has given birth to an illegitimate child who threatens the stability of his *oikos*. Chrysis is sarcastically described by him at 130 as γαμετὴν ἑταίραν.⁸³ The irony generated by this reference stems from a rhetorical antithesis – designed to surprise and therefore attract the attention of the audience – between the status of the wedded wife (γαμετήν) and the *hetaira*. And, of course, as is suggested by the distinctions drawn in Apollodorus' *Against Neaira* 122, Chrysis, a foreigner who had the status of a *hetaira*, could not become the lawful wedded wife of an Athenian citizen even if she had managed to live in his house as a concubine (*pallakê*).⁸⁴

Rhetorical appropriations of desire, pleasure, and a woman's status in relation to the *oikos*, which echo relevant legal distinctions, are thus employed as important elements of the play's plot. It is, in fact, Chrysis' precarious status in Demeas' household that enables him to throw her out of his house at 369ff. after having first persuaded himself in the monologue of 328–356, which, as has been pointed out, is uttered as if he was delivering a forensic speech at a court, that it was Chrysis who seduced Moschion.⁸⁵ Being cruel with her, Demeas reminds her at 390–398 of her status as a *hetaira* and the hard life many *hetairai* have for a few drachmas. Considering his *oikos* more important than his desire for that woman,⁸⁶ it is easier for him to expel from it the female intruder rather than the son and heir who can safeguard its stability and continuity. The fact that Moschion is an adopted son makes their relationship more fragile and in need of protection. This is another reason why his love for Chrysis is less important to him.⁸⁷

---

81 Cf. Konstan 1995, 121–122.
82 See Traill 2008, 86–87, 156–160; Sommerstein 2014, 11–15, 19–21.
83 Cf. Dedoussi 2006, 136–137; Sommerstein 2013, 144, noting the 'sarcastic oxymoron' of this reference.
84 The γαμετήν may also imply the actual, and yet not formal, position and role of Chrysis in Demeas' household, who can nevertheless become only a *pallakê* because she is a non-Athenian as well as a *hetaira*. In Menander's *Perikeiromene*, it is when the Athenian origin of Glykera, Polemon's *pallakê*, is being revealed, that she can be married to Polemon. Cf. Walcot, 1987, 14; Lape 2004, 149–150.
85 Nikeratos' statement at 508–509 that Chrysis should be sold as a slave for her supposed misconduct may be seen only as an exaggeration since she was in fact a free woman. Cf. Krieter-Spiro 1997, 44 n. 4.
86 Cf. Lape 2004, 140–141 and 150–156 (for the rhetorical argumentation of Demeas).
87 Cf. Masaracchia 1998, 431–432.

After her eviction, Chrysis finds refuge in Nikeratos' house. When Nikeratos catches his daughter in the act of breastfeeding the baby, he realizes that Plangon is the child's mother and discusses this fact with Demeas at 532–536, verifying thus Moschion's confession of the truth to his father at 520–532. The ambiguities concerning Chrysis' status within Demeas' *oikos*, which spans from that of a *hetaira* to that of a *pallakê* or even to that of a wife (*gametê*),[88] invest her with an otherness that highlights the importance of the *oikos* and its constituents. It is a female otherness opposed to the male order of the *oikos* as well as an otherness pertaining to social status and citizenship which is opposed to a sense of Athenian identity associated with both the *oikos* and the *polis*.

Although at the moment of her expulsion from Demeas' house she is regarded as an outsider and a threat against the *oikos*, she eventually manages to integrate herself into it not only through the role of the *pallakê* who could act as a *gametê*,[89] but also through her action during the play. Her offer to act temporarily as the mother of Plangon's baby prevents its exposure, contributes to the preservation of Plangon's honour, and provides Moschion and Plangon with the time and circumstances they need to get married. She is thus the key character, whose action leads to the preservation of social order as well as to the order and continuation of Demeas' *oikos*. It is for this reason, and not because of Demeas' *erôs*, that at 730–732 her leading role in this *oikos* as *gametê* has already been restored and she appears in charge of the wedding preparations as the mistress of the household.[90] The importance of her presence with respect to the play's plot and ideological load is reflected in the fact that the epithet denoting her place of origin appears in the play's title. It is nevertheless important to note that, despite his unjust and violent attitude towards her, Demeas never asks for her forgiveness even though he is supposed to be in love with her.[91]

An even more important structural element of the play's plot appears to be Moschion's erotic disposition towards Plangon. Although in what survives from the play's opening monologue no explicit reference is made to Moschion's feelings for Plangon prior to her impregnation, it is reasonable to suppose that her

---

88 Cf. Henry 1988², 73.
89 In the *Samia* as well as in social contexts the role of a *pallakê* within the *oikos* was not much different from that of a wife, despite their differences in terms of status. Cf. Konstan 1995, 121–122. Chrysis' willingness to participate in Demeas' deception may thus be related not only to her good intentions towards Moschion and Plangon, but also to her plan to acquire a more stable status within Demeas' household. Cf. Krieter-Spiro 1997, 47–52, 117–120.
90 Cf. Krieter-Spiro 1997, 113–114, 127–132; Rosivach 1998, 113–115; Traill 2008, 157–169.
91 Cf. Gutzwiller 2012, 68, where she aptly observes that Chrysis' return to his house may be due to her need for economic security and not to affection.

seduction or, more probably, her rape was the result of his desire for her. Yet the fact that he was physically attracted to her does not necessarily mean that he experienced more profound emotions, especially when in the *Samia* there is no reference to a relevant symptomatology even though at 631–632 he declares that it is the god Eros who governs his will and does not let him leave for Bactra or Caria. As is made obvious at various points throughout the play,[92] emphasis is laid on the fact that Moschion is a decent and virtuous character who errs but tries to make up for his deeds. As has been noted, the fact that Eros may, as the master of his will, force him to take a morally wrong direction, turns Moschion's feelings into part of a rhetorical argument used to persuade his audience, either within or outside of the play's plot and illusory world, about his motivation. At the same time, these feelings become a structural element of the plot that leads him to successive conflicts with his own moral standards as well as with Demeas. They also give him the opportunity to challenge, prove, and establish his morality. This emerges as more important than his emotional disposition, which rather functions so as to support his argumentation concerning his motives.

Considering his action from the perspective of plot construction, Moschion's desire for Plangon leads to her impregnation and the birth of their child outside a marriage context. This birth leads to his plan to temporarily deceive Demeas and Nikeratos, and the series of misunderstandings that form an essential element of the turbulent action of the second, third, and fourth act. When at the beginning of the fifth act Moschion appears insulted by his father's false accusations, he declares himself ready to leave as a mercenary for Bactra or Caria. As he points out at 623–638, it is his desire for Plangon and the god Eros himself (πόθος at 624 and Ἔρως at 632) which, among other things, keep him in Athens and make him only pretend that he is about to leave. Wearing a cloak and taking a sword in his hand he encounters Demeas and becomes director and actor of the play within a play that dominates the fifth act and aims at the retrieval of his honour, the prevention of a similarly insulting attitude on the part of Demeas in the future, and the re-affirmation of both his own morality and their relationship.[93] If the clash between Moschion and Demeas is seen as a rhetorical dispute in a quasi-judicial procedure concerning sexual offences, then their reconciliation may be seen as the reconciliation expected in actual judicial processes of a similar kind,

---

92 See Men. *Sam.* 3, 13–18, 47–48, 50–53, 272–274, 344.
93 Cf. Keuls 1973, 20.

as often happens in New Comedy.⁹⁴ In this plot development his feelings for Plangon are used only in order to explain the course of his action. The focal point of that action may be the establishment of his proven moral integrity in his father's consciousness and the re-affirmation of his relationship with him, but the aim and result of such a re-affirmation is the preservation of their *oikos*.

Erôs is also presented as a significant force leading to the marriage of Moschion and Plangon. From the beginning of the play, when the spectators hear about the girl's impregnation and the birth of their child, the play's action is directed towards their marriage.⁹⁵ At 50–53 Moschion mentions that he gave an oath promising Plangon's mother to marry the girl as soon as Demeas comes back from the Pontos. When at 145–166 Moschion says to his adoptive father that he wants to marry Plangon, Demeas notes at 165–166 his son's attitude towards the girl, which is supposed to be dominated by *erôs*, and decides at 169–204 to proceed to the wedding on the same day. It should nevertheless be noted that Demeas and Nikeratos had already decided to have their children married to each other without knowing that emotional or sexual bonds between them had already been developed. This suggests that *erôs* is a secondary element that comes as an addition to Demeas' initial intentions of arranging his son's marriage and securing the continuation of his *oikos*. This is what at this stage is more important to him.⁹⁶ The actions that follow are marked by false knowledge and misapprehension and are directed either to the couple's wedding or to its cancellation. At 444–450 Demeas, thinking that Moschion's marriage with Plangon will keep him away from Chrysis, prays for it to Apollo. Yet at 477–505 Nikeratos cancels the wedding, thinking that Moschion is the father of Chrysis' child and that for this reason he is morally unsuitable for his daughter. When at 588–615 Nikeratos finds out that it was his daughter who had given birth to Moschion's child, he is eager to consent to their marriage. This happens not only because Moschion's innocence with respect to his suspected illicit relationship with Chrysis becomes apparent, but also, and perhaps mainly, because such a marriage will restore Plangon's honour. This is what lies behind the rhetorical references to Moschion's loving feelings towards the girl. As has already been noted, at 624–632 Moschion's intentions of marrying Plangon are clearly, and yet only rhetorically, related to – among other things – his desire for the girl (πόθος) and the god Eros, who is supposed to be acting as the master of his will. The wedding takes place at 722–733,

---

94 Cf. Scafuro 1997, 181–192. For the importance of forgiveness and reconciliation in the *Samia*'s plot as it emerges in the play's fifth act, see Gutzwiller 2012, 64–68.
95 Cf. Lape 2004, 137.
96 Cf. Brown 1993, 190.

providing the play's action with a conventional ending. The theme of marriage is so important that in antiquity an alternative title of the play was, according to a conjecture endorsed by, among others, Hugh Lloyd-Jones, Κηδεία, which means 'connection by marriage'.[97]

Considering the play's action in the light of the actantial model developed by Greimas,[98] one may distinguish the function of the plot's elements that have been detected so far in the play's narrative substructure.[99] Moschion has accordingly the role of the subject, while the girl he wishes to marry is the object. Chrysis has the role of the helper, which is also at times assumed by Demeas. False assumptions and misunderstanding function as opponents. Moschion's *erôs* for Plangon is, along with his sense of duty before the damaged girl, one of the senders that appear to instigate his action and push him towards the achievement of his goal. The receiver, that is the element which benefits from his marriage with Plangon, is the institution of the *oikos* and the community in which they live.

Erôs and marriage are linked with the institution of the *oikos* in more than one way. In the first place, the marriage of Moschion and Plangon will lead to the creation of a new *oikos* and the consideration of their child as legitimate. Yet this new household is in fact the continuation of Demeas' household and that is why Demeas' rhetoric is developed so as to protect Moschion and help him marry Plangon. Their marriage will also prevent the collapse of Nikeratos' household since it will lead to the maintenance of his daughter's honour. When in the characters' reasoning and argumentation *erôs* is dissociated from marriage and the *oikos*, it appears extremely weak. Demeas thus throws Chrysis out of his house, even though he is supposed to be in love with her, when he thinks that she is Moschion's mistress and that she has given birth to his child. Such an affair could lead to a conflict with Moschion that would affect in a disastrous manner the survival of his *oikos*.[100] What is more important to him is his *oikos* and not his *erôs* for Chrysis.

Although according to the anonymous *Vita* of Aristophanes it was not Menander, but Aristophanes the poet who introduced in the comic plots through his *Kokalos* rapes and recognitions and all those relevant elements which pervade

---

97 See Lloyd-Jones 1990, 33. See also Gomme/Sandbach 1973, 539–540; Lamagna 1998, 78; Dedoussi 2006, 6*–7*; Sommerstein 2013, 56–57.
98 See Greimas 1983, 202–207.
99 For an application of Greimas' model to the study of Menandrean comedy, although not exactly in the way that this is done in this paper, see Wiles 1991, 27–31.
100 Cf. Zagagi 1995, 116–119; Fountoulakis 2004, 152, 158–159.

the plays of Menander and New Comedy,¹⁰¹ it appears that the dramatic link between *erôs* and marriage is not an Aristophanic but a later innovation which may have been developed in the plays of Middle and New Comedy. This happens even if fifth-century tragedy provides instances of erotic emotions with a romantic colouring in conjugal relations.¹⁰² Even in Menander's time the presence of the connection between *erôs* and marriage in an Athenian play intended for performance would appear paradoxical, if it is considered in the light of the play's social context and the Athenian legal framework concerning marriage as well as in the light of the play's potential reception by its Athenian audience. In classical times *erôs* and sensual pleasure were normally expected to be found outside a marriage context. As has been pointed out, marriage in Athens aimed at the birth of legitimate children and the formation of a new *oikos* which functioned as an essential unit of the city-state. The birth of legitimate children, who would later become citizens, was stressed as a main aim of marriage during the *engyê* ceremony. The same ceremony, in which emphasis is laid upon that aim, is dramatized at the end of the *Samia* (725ff.) where it is explicitly and formulaically stated by Nikeratos as he hands over Plangon to Moschion that μαρτύρων ἐναντίον σοι τήνδ' ἐγὼ δίδωμ' ἔχειν / γνησίων παίδων ἐπ' ἀρότῳ [Before witnesses I give you this girl to keep for the production of a crop of legitimate children], (transl. D.M. Bain).¹⁰³ It appears also in Menandrean plays such as the *Aspis*, the *Dyskolos* and the *Perikeiromene*.¹⁰⁴ In the case of the *Samia* marriage would also eliminate the social and economic gap between the rich Demeas and the poor Nikeratos. As for the new *oikos*, it is amply attested by authors such as Xenophon, Plato, and Aristotle that in the Greek world, and in classical Athens in particular, its proper function was considered extremely significant for the survival and prosperity of both the individual and, perhaps more importantly, the city-state.¹⁰⁵

---

101 Anon. *Vit. Aristoph.* XVIII.50–58 Koster (= Aristoph. Test. 1 K.–A.). Note that according to the Suda (α 1982) plots based on the themes of love and the rape of girls were invented by Anaxandrides. See Konstantakos 2002, 143–144.
102 See e.g. the case of Pelops and Hippodameia from Sophocles' *Oenomaus* or that of Perseus and Andromeda from Euripides' *Andromeda*. Cf. Walcot 1987, 8–11. Considering the wider links between Menandrean comedy and fifth-century tragedy, it would not be unreasonable to assume that such tragic elements found their way into New Comedy especially if such elements were appreciated by an audience living under circumstances in which the individual and the *oikos* gained considerable attention compared to the *polis*.
103 Men. *Sam.* 726–727.
104 See Men. *Aspis* 540–544, *Dyskolos* 842–844, *Perikeiromene* 1013–1014; Patterson 1981, 56 n. 64; Vérilhac/Vial 1998, 232–247; Fountoulakis 2011a, 191 with n. 335.
105 See Xen. *Oecon.* 5.5–25, 9.14–15; Pl. *Laws* 679b, *Rep.* 369c; *Meno* 73a–b; Arist. *Pol.* 1252b9–16, 1253b1–1260b24. Cf. Lacey 1968, 15–32; Nagle 2006, *passim*.

The element of mutual desire and affection in a symmetrical relationship between husband and wife was extremely rare. When, for instance, in Xenophon, *Symposium* 8.3, Nikeratos is said to be in love with his wife and his wife equally in love with him (ἀλλὰ μὴν καὶ ὁ Νικήρατος, ὡς ἐγὼ ἀκούω, ἐρῶν τῆς γυναικὸς ἀντερᾶται), this reference reflects something uncommon which could stand as a possibility, but was certainly not what normally happened. As is noted in Apollodorus, *Against Neaira* 122, the role of wives in classical Athens was to give birth to legitimate children and keep the household in order. It is for this reason that, as may be inferred from Lysias' *On the Murder of Eratosthenes*, a wife ought to be faithful to her husband,[106] whereas there were no such restrictions for husbands. This does not mean that a deeper affection or even love between a man and a woman within a marriage context was unthinkable in classical times, especially when such cases occur in Menander and reflect a relevant conception of marital bonds in Menandrean comedy and beyond.[107] Xenophon's reference in *Symp.* 8.3 may suggest the emergence of similar, emotionally coloured marital relationships in Athenian society.

Yet, as has been shown by scholars studying the historical development of ideas relating to marriage, status, emotion, and sexuality, such as Michel Foucault, it is from the second century BCE onwards that there is a growing interest in the relation between the *oikos* and the individual in preference to the relation between the *oikos* and the city-state. Within the boundaries of such an interest, marriage tends also to be considered as a symmetrical relationship based on mutual feelings such as affection, love, understanding, and compassion. This is made obvious in various treatises on love and marriage written by authors such as Antipater, Musonius Rufus, and Plutarch[108] as well as in literary genres such as the Greek novel, in which a young man and a girl fall in love with each-other and after many adventures are reunited in a stable and long-lasting relationship characterized by affection, symmetry, and fidelity.[109] In Stoic texts of the first two centuries CE there are similar associations between love and marriage, as well as an emphasis on the significance of monogamy and concrete and stable family bonds. These elements function as the foundation of a strong *oikos* capable of safeguarding the interests of the individual and the community in which one

---

[106] For restrictions imposed specifically on wives in the relevant law, see Lys. 1.30–34.
[107] Cf. the cases of Charisios and Pamphile in the *Epitrepontes* as well as of *P. Antinoopolis* 15 and *P. Didot* I (if this indeed belongs to Menander); Walcot 1987, 26–27.
[108] See Stobaeus, *Flor.* 21–22; Musonius Rufus 13–14; Plutarch, *Mor.* (*Coniugalia praecepta*) 142 e–143 a, 144 c–d; *Mor.* (*Amatorius*) 697c–771d; *Mor.* (*Amatoriae narrationes*) 796f.
[109] See Konstan 1994, 14–98.

lives.[110] Christianity paid even more attention to the elements of mutual affection and symmetry between husband and wife. These were considered as equally important individuals who respected and loved each-other. Their bonds were safeguarded by a profound belief in the value of virginity, chastity, fidelity, and monogamous relationships.[111]

Peter Brown notes the affinities between love and marriage in the comedies of Menander as well as the deviation of this interrelationship from relevant ideas prevailing in classical Athens. At the same time, he thinks that marrying for love in Menander's times is not only a comic motif, which would reflect the dreams of a middle-class audience, as Préaux would have put it,[112] but also the dramatization of actual social practice (at least potentially).[113] This is certainly a possibility which could not be easily denied. Susan Lape, focusing upon the *engyê* ceremony, draws attention to the political implications of marriage with respect to the union of two citizens and the acquisition of legitimate children within the democratic *polis*. She subsequently sees in Menandrean plays, such as the *Samia*, the staging of a culture of democratic citizenship.[114] If the Menandrean dramatization of Pericles' citizenship law is considered in the light of the significance of that law for the structure and the identity of the citizen body of fifth- and fourth-century Athens and subsequently for the quality of fifth- and fourth-century Athenian democracy, then this dramatization may indeed be seen as an echo of Athenian society and culture. Yet the citizenship prerequisites of the Periclean citizenship law are directly linked not with the quality or the nature of the Athenian democracy, but only with some of the features of the citizen body. The relevant Menandrean representations could after all function as a nostalgic recollection of the more representative democratic culture of Athens during the fifth century.

Despite Lape, who considers Menander's plays a staging of 'the culture of democratic citizenship',[115] the prerequisites of Pericles' law have wider and more complex connotations pertaining to autochthony, ethnic and cultural identity, religious and familial order, or social formation, layering, and cohesion. The fact that in Lysias, *On the Murder of Eratosthenes* 2 adultery appears to be regarded as a serious crime in democratic as well as in oligarchic regimes suggests that its

---

110 See e.g. Dio Chrys. 7; Seneca, *Consol. to Marc.* 24.
111 For a discussion of the development of those ideas from the second century BCE onwards, see Foucault 1990, 72–80, 147–185; Foucault 1992, 143–184. Cf. Pomeroy 1975, 131–136; Goldhill 1995, 144–161.
112 Préaux 1957.
113 Brown 1993, 201–203 and *passim*. Cf. Dover 1974, 211.
114 Lape 2004, 13–17, 99–109.
115 Lape 2004, 16.

repercussions concerning property and children were not restricted to a potential violation of the right to democratic citizenship. It should be borne in mind that Lape's approach pays little attention to the unusual or unnecessary in social contexts link between *erôs* and marriage which is attested in Menander's comedies, but is regarded as only a 'romantic arrangement' used for a projection of democratic ideology.[116] Moreover, it pays little attention to the implications of the fact that these plays were created in an era marked by the decline of the autonomy and representative democracy of the Athenian *polis*, which coincides with the transition from the Classical to the Hellenistic world.

If the connections between *erôs*, marriage and the *oikos* that emerge from the *Samia* are seen from the historical perspective of the development of relevant ideas from the end of the classical period until late antiquity under new social, political, and cultural circumstances, the conclusions that may be drawn will be quite different. The reference to the mutual erotic feelings between a husband and his wife in Xenophon, *Symposium* 8.3 may after all reflect a similar development of such ideas in a social context. According to Wiles, marrying for love epitomizes the emergence of the individual beyond the traditional tensions between the *oikos* and the *polis* in a historical setting marked by the gradual decline of the city-state.[117] Wiles' observations are in the right direction, but they do not adequately explain the associations between *erôs* and the *oikos* often projected by many dramatic characters in plays such as the *Samia*. Moreover, a concern for the individual is not irrelevant to issues relating to the *polis*.[118]

The relations between *erôs*, marriage, and the *oikos*, which are attested in the *Samia*, may be seen as a tentative and premature attempt on the part of Menander to project upon his plays and through his characters the wider fantasies, fears, wishes, and mentalities of his audience, which in later eras formed mainstream ideals pertinent to conjugal relationships.[119] It was the same people living in the performance culture of late fourth-century Athens who were familiar with a discourse concerning sexuality, social order, and citizenship apparent in oratory, and faced the transition from the world of the autonomous and democratically

---

116 Lape 2004, 17.
117 Wiles 1991, 39–31. Cf. Wiles 1989, 31–48.
118 Cf. Lape 2004, 96–99.
119 Whether this was a conscious attempt is an open question. Bearing in mind that Menander lived in the same cultural ambience as his audience, it would not be unreasonable to assume that he shared most of the fantasies, fears, wishes, and mentalities of his spectators. On the other hand, it may be argued that the agonistic context of comic performance would make inevitable for the success of his plays the emergence of ideological patterns that would comply with his audience's fantasies, fears, wishes, and mentalities.

governed *polis* to a world of far less powerful cities and communities that formed parts of the Hellenistic kingdoms. This is perhaps the meaning of the observations attributed to Aristophanes of Byzantium who appears to wonder whether Menander imitated life or life imitated Menander (ὦ Μένανδρε καὶ βίε, / πότερος ἄρ' ὑμῶν πότερον ἀπεμιμήσατο;).[120]

Patterns of thought occurring in post-Aristotelian discourses concerning marrying for love and the *oikos* emerge in Menander as reflections of a wider cultural ambience marked by bold social and political developments. This is a hitherto unnoticed development in the history of ancient sexuality. Menander's time was an era in which the Athenian citizens were confronted with an increasing gap between the rich and the poor, a less representative democracy in which citizen rights were confined to a small number of relatively wealthy citizens, a series of destructive wars, the rising power of the Hellenistic kingdoms, foreign intervention, and, most importantly, the decline of the institution of a powerful and independent *polis*, whose affairs could not always be affected only by its citizens. In such a cosmopolitan and yet precarious world it comes as no surprise that there is a growing interest in the *oikos*, which replaced to some extent the classical *polis* as a means of protection of individual prosperity and security.[121] It was such a context that often affected the shaping and manipulation of emotions such as *erôs*, while marrying for love was accordingly a means of strengthening the institution of the *oikos*. The interrelationship between *erôs*, marriage, and the *oikos* in Menander, far from reflecting social reality,[122] functions as the rhetorical projection of wider goals set by contemporary society with respect to the importance of the *oikos*. In Menander, *Dyskolos* 786–790 it is explicitly stated that a young man has to marry the girl he is in love with or even that he has to be in love with the girl he is going to marry, because *erôs* makes the marriage bonds stronger: ἧς ἐρᾷς σε λαμβάνειν / καὶ βούλομαι καί φημι δεῖν ... νέῳ γάμος βέβαιος οὕτω γίνετ[αι / ἐὰν δι' ἔρωτα τοῦτο συμπεισθῇ ποε[ῖν [I want you to get married

---

[120] See Syrian. *On Hermog. de Stas.* 1 (= Test. 83 K.–A.). Cf. Test. 116 K.–A. For a consideration of Menander's alleged 'realism' in an examination of his depiction of *erôs*, see Masaracchia 1998, 415–416.

[121] Cf. Masaracchia 1998, 426–427; Fountoulakis 2004, 85–89, 93–101, 2009, *passim* and esp. 112–117.

[122] Despite the alleged realism of Menander's comedies, taking them as evidence for social practice is a rather naïve approach which does not take into account the function of comic inversion and the fictional aims of the comic plot.

to the girl you love, I say you must! ... when you're young, it adds stability to marriage if it's love that prompts the bridegroom], (transl. W.G. Arnott).[123] What appears thus to matter most is not the fulfilment of *erôs*, but the ways in which the path leading to marriage, marriage itself and, as a result, the institution of the *oikos* may become even more secure and stable. This is an idea which is discernible in the dramatic context of the *Samia*, but forms part of major ideological concerns and developments pertaining to the needs of a new era.[124]

Bibliography

Alexiou, E.B. (2016), *Η Ρητορική του 4ου αι. π.Χ.: Το Ελιξίριο της Δημοκρατίας και η Ατομικότητα*, Athens.
Anderson, W.S. (1984), 'Love Plots in Menander and his Roman Adapters', in: *Ramus* 13, 124–134.
Arnott, W.G. (ed.) (1979–2000), *Menander*, vols. I–III, Cambridge MA/London.
Bain, D.M. (ed.) (1983), *Menander, Samia*, Warminster.
Bain, D.M. (1988), 'ΤΩΝ ΠΑΡΟΝΤΩΝ in Menander, Samia 488', in: *ZPE* 71, 9–10.
Ben-Ze'ev, A. (2000), *The Subtlety of Emotions*, Cambridge MA/London.
Bons, J.A.E. (2007), 'Gorgias the Sophist and Early Rhetoric', in: I. Worthington (ed.), *A Companion to Greek Rhetoric*, Malden MA/Oxford, 37–46.
Brown, P.G. McC. (1990), 'Plots and Prostitutes in Greek New Comedy', in: *PLLS* 6, 241–266.
Brown, P.G. McC. (1993), 'Love and Marriage in Greek New Comedy', in: *CQ* n.s. 43, 189–205.
Buss, D.M. (2000), *The Dangerous Passion: Why Jealousy is as Necessary as Love and Sex*, New York.
Buss, D.M. (2013), 'Sexual Jealousy', in: *Psychological Topics*, 22.2, 155–182.
Calame, C. (1992), *The Poetics of Eros in Ancient Greece*, transl. J. Lloyd of *I Greci e l'Eros: Simboli, Pratiche e Luoghi*, Princeton NJ.
Carey, C. (ed.) (1989), *Lysias, Selected Speeches*, Cambridge.
Carey, C. (ed.) (1992), *Apollodoros, Against Neaira: [Demosthenes] 59*, Warminster.
Carey, C. (2004), 'The Rhetoric of *Diabole*', in: http://discovery.ucl.ac.uk/3281/1/3281.pdf.
Carey, C. (2011), 'Η Ρητορική στον (Άλλον) Μένανδρο', in: Th.P. Pappas/A.G. Markantonatos (eds.), *Αττική Κωμῳδία: Πρόσωπα και Προσεγγίσεις*, Athens, 435–455.
Carey, C. (2013), 'Pimps in Court', in: E.M. Harris/D.F. Leão/P.J. Rhodes (eds.), *Law and Drama in Ancient Greece*, repr., London, 169–183.

---

[123] Note, however, that, as David Konstan observes, this link between *erôs* and marriage is unusual in the world of Greek comedy, whose plots often focus on the conflict between a young man interested in the fulfilment of his desire for a girl, and a father concerned with the union of his son with a girl of equal status, which could safeguard the continuity of his *oikos*. See Konstan 1994, 143–144.
[124] See Fountoulakis 2009 and 2011a, 180–193.

Charitonidis, S./Kahil, L./Ginouvès, R. (1970), *Les mosaïques de la maison du Ménandre à Mytilène*, Bern.
Conca, F. (1970), 'Il Motivo del Vecchio Inamorato in Menandro', in: *Acme* 23, 81–80.
Cohen, D. (1991), 'Sexuality, Violence, and the Athenian Law of *Hubris*', in: *G&R* 38, 171–188.
Cusset, C. (2014), 'Melancholic Lovers in Menander', in: A.H. Sommerstein (ed.), *Menander in Contexts*, New York/London, 167–179.
Davidson, J. (1997), *Courtesans and Fishcakes: The Consuming Passions of Classical Athens*, London.
Dedoussi, C.B. (ed.) (2006), *Μενάνδρου Σαμία*, Athens.
Dover, K.J. (1974), *Greek Popular Morality in the Time of Plato and Aristotle*, Oxford.
Dutsch, D./Konstan, D. (2011), 'Women's Emotions in New Comedy', in: D. Munteanu (ed.), *Emotion, Genre and Gender in Ancient Greece*, London, 57–88.
Faraone, C.A. (1999), *Ancient Greek Love Magic*, Cambridge MA/London.
Foucault, M. (1990), *The Care of the Self: The History of Sexuality*. Volume 3, transl. R. Hurley of *Le souci de soi*, London.
Foucault, M. (1992), *The Use of Pleasure: The History of Sexuality*. Volume 2, transl. R. Hurley of *L'usage des plaisirs*, London.
Fountoulakis, A. (1999), 'Οὐσία in Euripides, *Hippolytus* 514 and the Greek Magical Papyri', in: *Maia* n.s. 51.2, 193–204.
Fountoulakis, A. (2004), *Αναζητώντας τον Διδακτικό Μένανδρο: Μια Προσέγγιση της Κωμωδίας του Μενάνδρου και μια Διερεύνηση της Σαμίας*, Athens.
Fountoulakis, A. (2009), 'Going beyond the Athenian *Polis*: A Reappraisal of Menander, *Samia* 96–118', in: *QUCC* 93, 97–117.
Fountoulakis, A. (2011a), 'Δραματικοί Αντικατοπτρισμοί: Ο Μένανδρος και το Κλασικό Δράμα στο Κατώφλι του Ελληνιστικού Κόσμου', in: Th.P. Pappas/A.G. Markantonatos (eds.), *Αττική Κωμωδία: Πρόσωπα και Προσεγγίσεις*, Athens, 103–193.
Fountoulakis, A. (2011b), 'Playing with the Dramatic Conventions: Demeas' Invocations in Menander, *Samia* 325–26', in: *C&M* 62, 81–98.
Gilula, D. (1987), 'Menander's Comedies Best with Dessert and Wine (Plut. *Mor.* 712 e)', in: *Athenaeum* 65, 511–516.
Glazebrook, A. (2006), 'The Bad Girls of Athens: The Image and Function of *Hetairai* in Judicial Oratory', in: C.A. Faraone/L.K. McClure (eds.), *Prostitutes and Courtesans in the Ancient World*, Madison, 125–138.
Goldhill, S. (1995), *Foucault's Virginity: Ancient Erotic Fiction and the History of Sexuality*, Cambridge.
Goldhill, S. (1999), 'Programme Notes', in: S. Goldhill/R. Osborne (eds.), *Performance Culture and Athenian Democracy*, Cambridge, 1–29.
Gomme, A.W./Sandbach, F.H. (1973), *Menander: A Commentary*, Oxford.
Greimas, A.J. (1983), *Structural Semantics: An Attempt at a Method*, transl. D. McDowell/ R. Schleifer/A. Velie of *Sémantique Structurale*, Lincoln NE/London.
Gutzwiller, K. (2012), 'All in the Family: Forgiveness and Reconciliation in New Comedy', in: C.L. Griswold/D. Konstan (eds.), *Ancient Forgiveness: Classical, Judaic, and Christian*, Cambridge, 48–75.
Henry, M.M. (1988[2]), *Menander's Courtesans and the Greek Comic Tradition*, Frankfurt am Main.
Hunter, V. (1990), 'Gossip and the Politics of Reputation in Classical Athens', in: *Phoenix* 44, 299–325.

Hunter, R. (2014), 'Attic Comedy in the Rhetorical and Moralising Traditions', in: M. Revermann (ed.), *The Cambridge Companion to Greek Comedy*, Cambridge, 373–386.
Kapparis, K.A. (ed.) (1999), *Apollodoros: 'Against Neaira' [D. 59]*, Berlin/New York.
Kassel, R./Austin, C. (eds.) (1983–), *Poetae Comici Graeci*, Berlin/New York.
Keuls, E. (1973), 'The Samia of Menander: An Interpretation of its Plot and Theme', in: *ZPE* 10, 1–20.
Kiritsi, St. (2013), '*Erôs* in Menander: Three Studies in Male Character', in: E. Sanders (ed.), *Erôs and the Polis: Love in Context*, London, *BICS* Suppl. 119, 85–100.
Konstan, D. (1994), *Sexual Symmetry: Love in the Ancient Novel and Related Genres*, Princeton NJ.
Konstan, D. (1995), *Greek Comedy and Ideology*, Oxford.
Konstan, D. (2006), *The Emotions of the Ancient Greeks: Studies in Aristotle and Classical Literature*, Toronto/Buffalo/London.
Konstantakos, I.M. (2002), 'Towards a Literary History of Comic Love', in: *C&M* 53, 141–172.
Krieter-Spiro, M. (1997), *Sklaven, Köche und Hetären. Das Dienstpersonal bei Menander. Stellung, Rolle, Komik und Sprache*, Stuttgart/Leipzig.
Kristjánsson, K. (2002), *Justifying Emotions: Pride and Jealousy*, London.
Lacey, W.K. (1968), *The Family in Classical Greece*, London.
Lamagna, M. (ed.) (1998), *Menandro, La Donna di Samo*, Naples.
Lape, S. (2004), *Reproducing Athens: Menander's Comedy, Democratic Culture, and the Hellenistic City*, Princeton NJ/Oxford.
Leisner-Jensen, M. (2002), '*Vis Comica*: Consummated Rape in Greek and Roman New Comedy', in: *C&M* 53, 173–196.
Lloyd-Jones, H. (1990), 'Menander's *Samia* in the Light of the New Evidence', in: H. Lloyd-Jones, *Greek Comedy, Hellenistic Literature, Greek Religion, and Miscellanea: The Academic Papers of Sir Hugh Lloyd-Jones*, Oxford, 31–52 (= *YCS* 22 [1972], 119–144).
Masaracchia, A. (1998), 'La Tematica Amorosa in Menandro', in: A. Masaracchia, *Rifflessioni sull'Antico. Studi sulla Cultura Greca*, a cura di G. D'Anna/M. Di Marco, Pisa/Roma, 405–436 (= A. Masaracchia [1981], *Letterature Comparate. Problemi e Metodo. Studi in Onore di E. Paratore*, Bologna, 213–238).
McComiskey, B. (2002), *Gorgias and the New Sophistic Rhetoric*, Carbondale/Edwardsville.
Nagle, D.B. (2006), *Household and City in the Writings of Aristotle*, Cambridge.
Nesselrath, H.-D. (1990), *Die attische Mittlere Komödie*, Berlin/New York.
Padel, R. (1992), *In and Out of the Mind: Greek Images of the Tragic Self*, Princeton NJ.
Patterson, C.B. (1981), *Pericles' Citizenship Law of 451–50 B.C.*, New York.
Petropoulos, J.C.B. (1997), 'Συμπτώματα Έρωτος στους Ερωτικούς Μαγικούς Παπύρους', in: A.F. Christidis/D. Jordan (eds.), *Γλώσσα και Μαγεία: Κείμενα από την Αρχαιότητα*, Athens, 104–119.
Pomeroy, S.B. (1975), *Goddesses, Whores, Wives, and Slaves: Women in Classical Antiquity*, New York.
Préaux, C. (1957), 'Ménandre et la société athénienne', in: *CÉ* 32, 84–100.
Preisendanz, K. (ed.) (1973–1974²), *Papyri Graecae Magicae: Die griechischen Zauberpapyri*, I–II, 2nd ed. by A. Henrichs, Stuttgart.
Rosivach, V.J. (1998), *When a Young Man Falls in Love: The Sexual Exploitation of Women in New Comedy*, London/New York.
Rudd, N. (1981), 'Romantic Love in Classical Times?', in: *Ramus* 10, 140–158.
Ryder, K.C. (1984), 'The *Senex Amator* in Plautus', in: *G&R* 31, 181–189.

Sanders, E./Thumiger, C./Carey, C./Lowe, N.J. (2013), *Erôs in Ancient Greece*, Oxford.
Scafuro, A.C. (1997), *The Forensic Stage: Settling Disputes in Graeco-Roman New Comedy*, Cambridge.
Sommerstein, A.H. (ed.) (2013), *Menander, Samia*, Cambridge.
Sommerstein, A.H. (2014), 'Menander and the *Pallake*', in: A.H. Sommerstein (ed.), *Menander in Contexts*, New York/London, 11–23.
Thornton, B.S. (1997), *Eros: The Myth of Ancient Greek Sexuality*, Boulder/Oxford.
Todd, S.C. (2007), *A Commentary on Lysias, Speeches* 1–11, Oxford.
Traill, A. (2008), *Women and the Comic Plot in Menander*, Cambridge.
Vérilhac, A.-M./Vial, C. (1998), *Le mariage grec du VIe siècle av. J.-C. à l'époque d'Auguste*, Athens.
Walcot, P. (1987), 'Romantic Love and True Love: Greek Attitudes to Marriage', in: *Ancient Society* 18, 5–33.
Webster, T.B.L. (1970[2]), *Studies in Later Greek Comedy*, Manchester.
Wehrli, F. (1936), *Motivstudien zur griechischen Komödie*, Zurich/Leipzig.
Wilamowitz-Moellendorff, U. von (1919), 'Lesefrüchte', in: *Hermes* 54, 59.
Wiles, D. (1989), 'Marriage and Prostitution in Classical New Comedy', in: J. Redmond (ed.), *Themes in Drama. 11: Women in Theatre*, Cambridge, 31–48.
Wiles, D. (1991), *The Masks of Menander: Sign and Meaning in Greek and Roman Performance*, Cambridge.
Wilson, M./Daly, M. (1996), 'Male Sexual Proprietariness and Violence against Women', in: *Current Directions in Psychological Science*, 5, 2–7.
Winkler, J.J. (1990), *The Constraints of Desire: The Anthropology of Sex and Gender in Ancient Greece*, New York/London.
Zagagi, N. (1995), *The Comedy of Menander: Convention, Variation and Originality*, Bloomington/Indianapolis.

Edith Hall
Competitive Vocal Performance in Aristophanes' *Knights*

Drama is often our best evidence for the actual performative practice of ancient oratory. Aristophanes' smash hit of 424 BCE, *Hippeis* or *Knights*, provides the most immediate picture we possess of the way in which Athenian orators confronted one another verbally in the Assembly, even if that picture is versified and comically distorted. Rhetors often debated, not in long set-piece orations, but in rapid-fire spontaneous or semi-spontaneous exchanges, punctuated by the audience's noisy responses or *thorubos*, as elucidated in a famous article by Victor Bers.[1] The text of *Knights* contains fascinating information about the Athenian political soundscape—the live aural experience of Athenian democratic political debates and their assessment by different social strata constituting the demos.

Knights is the sole surviving ancient Greek play of which the *central* topic is political rhetoric and its relationship to the democratic government of Athens. Scholars have of course acknowledged that scrutiny of the vocal performance of public speakers was a concern of Old Comedy, in *Acharnians*, and *Ecclesiazusae* as well as *Knights*. Some have been interested in the analogies Aristophanes suggests in order to illustrate the nature of the *agon* specifically in *Knights* – it is framed not only an athletics event but a sea-battle, a struggle between elements during a thunderstorm, or a cooking contest.[2] Yet commentators on *Knights* have routinely downplayed the centrality of the theme of the demagogues' actual voices. They have preferred to focus on their rhetorical strategies and the relationship of these to the ideological agendas of different factions on the post-Periclean political scene; these strategies and agendas are then customarily illustrated from Thucydides.[3]

But there is, I think, much more we can learn from *Knights*. Aristophanes subjects the agonistic political debates of the mid-420s to a rigorous analysis. It encompasses form (one-or-two-sentence-long addresses and castigations of the opponent or the demos, replete with imperatives and interrogatives). It encompasses content – Cleon's alleged strategies of controlling the men of Athens through self-promotion, threats, flattery, offers of rewards, and the recitation of oracles. But even without the added dimension of live performance by virtuoso

---
1 Bers 1985; see also Hall 2006, 353–392.
2 For a perceptive discussion of the play's metaphors and politics, see Tsoumpra 2012.
3 Woodhead 1960; Edmunds 1987; Lind 1990; Atkinson 1992; Lafargue 2013; Burns 2014.

comedians, it is clear from the transmitted text that the most important running joke is the vocal quality – especially the immense volume, *megalophōnia* – as part of the delivery style of Cleon and his processed-meat-selling Nemesis from the agora, the Sausage-Seller. Aristophanes gave his actors internal cues to the vocal fireworks he required by the wide range of linguistic terms for 'bawling' and 'shouting down' (*kataboē, phōnē miarē*), many of which are associated with the inarticulate noises made by animals, used to describe the actual sounds they make (*kraugē* and *krazein* (suggestive of dogs and ravens), *gruzein* (used elsewhere of pigs and dogs), *lalein* (elsewhere used of frogs and birds), *thrulein* (elsewhere used of frogs) and *larungizein* (elsewhere used of crows). The actors' command of variations in timbre and tonality must have been considerable.

Most of the play consists of adversarial word-fights between Paphlagon, who is of course a thinly disguised Cleon, and the Sausage-Seller. The setting of the play, on the Pnyx Hill, the open-air venue for Assembly oratory, consists of separate rounds in a blistering agon of vituperation between Paphlagon and the Sausage-Seller whom Nicias and Demosthenes persuade to challenge Cleon's supremacy. As the chorus of Knights says to Paphlagon, 'victory in yelling' also means victory overall (276). And at the end of the comedy, the victorious Sausage-Seller is named Agorakritos, 'Pick of the Agora', since he is the best at the speech-acts which gave the *agora*, or 'place to speak', its name. The Pnyx Hill word-fights take place outside the home of the personified Demos, and may indeed be understood as in some sense comic versions of the debates which took place in the Assembly. Another debate between the same two demagogues takes place offstage in the Council, and this is described in a long speech by the Sausage-Seller which includes *oratio recta* delivered both by himself and by his rival.

The oratorical power of Cleon of the central Athenian deme of Cydathenaeum – a deme he shared with Aristophanes – was legendary in his own day. This is to judge not only from Aristophanes but the explicit remarks of Thucydides that he was 'the most violent of the citizens and at that time wielding by far the most influence with the *dēmos*' (βιαιότατος τῶν πολιτῶν τῷ τε δήμῳ παρὰ πολὺ ἐν τῷ τότε πιθανώτατος, 2.36.6). But since we don't have a single word of any speech that we can be sure exactly reflects anything actually said by Cleon, it is difficult to appreciate what made his rhetoric such an influential – indeed instrumental – factor in Athenian politics. Elsewhere, in a Festschrift for Paul Cartledge, I publish an article arguing that scholars since antiquity have been far too swift to adopt, uncritically, the judgement of Cleon as a man, democrat and indeed general passed on him by Thucydides and Aristophanes.[4] The historian

---

4 Hall 2018; Morley 1997 made a similar argument, albeit much more briefly.

and the comic poet both seem to have loathed him both as an individual and as a representative of the poorer Athenian masses. There is, however, one piece of evidence that Cleon was actually admired and popular amongst respectable Athenian families as well as by the roughest segment of the urban poor. A speech by one Mantitheus in a fourth-century inheritance dispute, claiming that his mother had indeed had a dowry, argues as follows ([Dem.] 40.24):

> ...my mother is shown to have been first given in marriage to Cleomedon, whose father Cleon, we are told, commanded troops among whom were your ancestors, and captured alive a large number of Lacedaemonians in Pylos, and won greater renown than any other man in the state; so it was not fitting that the son of that famous man should wed my mother without a dowry...

This alternative view of Cleon needs keeping in mind if we are not to adopt without some scepticism the biased view of his opponents. The absence of vilification of Cleon in Plato's works may also be telling.[5] In this article, however, I am less interested in whether Aristophanes and Thucydides were right about Cleon's malign social, moral and behavioural influence on Athenian politics, and more interested in whether *Knights* can help us to understand a little better the nature and impact of his rhetorical performances. Are there any distinctive traits or qualities to his language or rhetorical style? Are there any clues as to the precise constituents of his delivery which made it seem both violent and persuasive?

First, a clue from the other play in which a character with a speaking – or barking – part is transparently Cleon *manqué*, and that is *Wasps*. Two years after the success of *Knights*, which won Aristophanes his first solo success and really made his name and reputation, he returned to the Cleon theme with a view to repeating his triumph. I like to call Cleon in *Wasps* 'the Cur of Cydathenaeum' in order to retain the alliteration in the Greek of ὁ Κυδαθηναιεὺς κύων. This alliteration of 'k' sounds is not conveyed in English by calling him a 'hound' or 'dog'. The Cur of Cydathenaeum is prosecuting the other dog, Labes, for theft. When Bdelycleon asks if the prosecuting dog is in attendance, the Cleon-cur simply says/barks '*au, au*.' For Bdleycleon this is quite enough proof: 'πάρεστιν οὗτος', is his response, delivered presumably in a knowing way calling attention to the precise form of words – or barking noises – Cleon had made. Philocleon then interjects, 'Ἕτερος οὗτος αὖ Λάβης.', allowing the Philocleon actor as well as the dog-actor to render the word '*au*'. This seems to me to be a running joke about a particular verbal quirk of Cleon's – the indignant *au*, 'yet *again*', which it is easy to see, or rather hear, could be pronounced in a way that likened it to the noise of a dog howling.

---

[5] Calder 1961; Anderson 2005; Monoson 2014.

Bearing this passage in *Wasps* in mind, the first altercation between Paphlagon and the Sausage-Seller in *Knights* can, I believe be illuminated. The Paphlagonian repeats the question, 'Won't you let me speak?', οὐκ αὖ μ' ἐάσεις? at both 336 and 338; both times the Sausage-seller jumps in, interrupts him, breaking even his iambic trimeter off with the use of aggressive *antilabe*.

What else can we learn about Cleon and Assembly debates in the mid-420s from the text of *Knights*? That the dominant theme is to be voices is established at the outset. The two slaves representing Demosthenes and Nicias begin the action with paratragic rendition of sounds of misery – ἰατταταιὰξ τῶν κακῶν, ἰατταταῖ. (line 1, Demosthenes); they are in such a plight, oppressed by their new head slave Paphlagon, that Demosthenes suggests that they sob to the tune of the Olympian nome. Together they do so, 'μυμῦ μυμῦ μυμῦ μυμῦ μυμῦ μυμῦ' (10). Within a few lines they have decided to 'tell the spectators' about their plight (τὸ πρᾶγμα τοῖς θεαταῖσιν), in a formula sometimes used by men presenting themselves as victims in the lawcourts.

Demosthenes' account of the Paphlagon's arrival at Demos' house (40–72) begins by telling us that Demos is himself brutal, bad-tempered and half-deaf (ὑπόκωφον), a sure cue that there is to be a great deal of multi-decibel shouting in the play. The Paphlagonian leather-tanner whom Demos has recently purchased as a slave is a scoundrel and, in a wonderful superlative adjective, called 'most slanderous' (45, διαβολώτατόν). The *type* of speeches which he makes, laying foul allegations against other people, is thus already established. We then have a list of verbs describing his various ways of speaking to Demos, in the asyndeton beloved of orators desirous of emotional emphasis (47–49; see Aristotle, *Rhetoric* 3.12.14):

> ὁ βυρσοπαφλαγών, ὑποπεσὼν τὸν δεσπότην
> ᾔκαλλ' ἐθώπευ' ἐκολάκευ' ἐξηπάτα
> κοσκυλματίοις ἄκροισι τοιαυτὶ λέγων:
>
> The leather-man grovels before the master;
> he acts like a fawning dog, cajoles him, flatters him and cons him
> with little leather titbits...

These verbs are fascinating: *aikallein* means to fawn or wheedle but has an association particularly with dogs. This plays into the popular characterisation of Cleon as the Cur of Cydathenaeum which he will become two years later in *Wasps*. Certainly, the canine theme returns in the first confrontation between Cleon and the Sausage vendor in *Knights* 415–416, when Cleon accuses his rival of eating pieces of bread

> ...ὥσπερ κύων; ὦ παμπόνηρε πῶς οὖν
> κυνὸς βορὰν σιτούμενος μαχεῖ σὺ κυνοκεφάλλῳ;

> ...like a dog! Ah! wretch! you have the nature of a dog and you dare to fight a dog-headed ape?

Demosthenes' next verb in asyndeton, *thōpeuein* (fawn, flatter, soothe or wheedle), is also sometimes used of dogs or of humans patting horses to calm them down. *kolakeuein* simply means, 'to be a flatterer', and the last phrase, 'he deceives him with little leather-scraps' introduces the analogy, which will recur in the play, between fraudulent practises used by leather manufacturers and those used by statesman and orators.

Next, however, 'Demosthenes' quotes the Paphlagonian in *oratio recta*, meaning that this comic actor provides the first of what are going to be several impersonations of Cleon's speaking style in the play by different characters. The sort of thing that Cleon says to Demos is this (50–51):

> ὦ Δῆμε λοῦσαι πρῶτον ἐκδικάσας μίαν,
> ἔνθου ῥόφησον ἔντραγ' ἔχε τριώβολον.

> Dear Demos, first try just one case and then
> stuff yourself, slurp, eat dessert—take three obols.

Cleon-as-impersonated-by-Demosthenes apostrophises Demos formally, and then himself uses that asyndeton to describe the insertion, gobbling up and devouring of the three obols' worth of food which he will earn by trying a single case. He wards off other orators with a leather strap and sings oracles to him (ᾄδει δὲ χρησμούς), before piling up false allegations against the other members of the household, who are whipped. Now Demosthenes once again uses direct speech to impersonate what Paphlagon says (67–68):

> ὁρᾶτε τὸν Ὕλαν δι' ἐμὲ μαστιγούμενον;
> εἰ μή μ' ἀναπείσετ', ἀποθανεῖσθε τήμερον.

> You see how I have had Hylas beaten!
> Do what I say or die at once!

These two lines consists of nicely balanced end-rhymed *isocola*, with alliteration of '*h*' and '*m*' sounds and chiasmus in the first line; note also the Gorgianic chiasmus and play on *anapeiset'/apothaneisthe*) in the internal near-rhyme of the second.[6]

Paphlagon appears at the time of the parodos. Pursued by the Knights, he calls for aid from his elderly heliastic supporters, 'whom I feed by bawling both just and unjust things, come to my aid!'—an imperative (255–257):

> ὦ γέροντες ἡλιασταί, φράτερες τριωβόλου,
> οὓς ἐγὼ βόσκω κεκραγὼς καὶ δίκαια κἄδικα,
> παραβοηθεῖθ', ὡς ὑπ' ἀνδρῶν τύπτομαι ξυνωμοτῶν.

The third line here begins with the imperative *paraboetheith*', and Paphlagon does seem to be fond of imperatives and apostrophes with an explosive 'p' sound at the beginning, for example (ὦ πόλις καὶ δῆμ' ὑφ' οἵων θηρίων γαστρίζομαι, 273).

The first confrontation with the Sausage-Seller soon breaks down into single-line stichomythia. Paphlagon/Cleon implies that he always made sure he spoke first (340), and another that he would actually gloat about his pre-eminence in the art of speaking by demanding to know why his interlocutors *dared* to speak to his face (341); this demand includes the strong and indignant phrase *pros tōn theōn* (plural, 'by the gods'). There is also a hint at metarhetoric. Cleon in Thucydides, in the Mytilenean debate, notoriously discusses the citizens' responses to *other* speakers (3.37–38). In *Knights* his metarhetoric takes the form of making fun of his rival's incompetence as a speaker (344–352);

> ἰδοὺ λέγειν. καλῶς γ' ἂν οὖν σὺ πρᾶγμα προσπεσόν σοι
> ὠμοσπάρακτον παραλαβὼν μεταχειρίσαιο χρηστῶς.
> ἀλλ' οἶσθ' ὅπερ πεπονθέναι δοκεῖς; ὅπερ τὸ πλῆθος.
> εἴ που δικίδιον εἶπας εὖ κατὰ ξένου μετοίκου,
> τὴν νύκτα θρυλῶν καὶ λαλῶν ἐν ταῖς ὁδοῖς σεαυτῷ,
> ὕδωρ τε πίνων κἀπιδεικνὺς τοὺς φίλους τ' ἀνιῶν,
> ᾤου δυνατὸς εἶναι λέγειν. ὦ μῶρε τῆς ἀνοίας.

Look at him talk! For sure, if some business opportunity fell your way, you'd really know how to grab it, take it to pieces and eat it alive! Do you realise what's happened to you? Just like everyone else. Let's say you've got some trivial lawsuit against a resident alien. Did you croak and squawk it all night to yourself in the streets, drinking only water, showing it off and boring your friends? And you reckon that qualifies you as an orator? You stupid idiot.

---

[6] On the Gorgianic features of Paphlagon's speech, see also Gurd 2016, 51–53.

This attack also contains an accumulation of direct questions to his rival – triple *hypophora*. We can also note that there are two lines with long *omega* plus *n* sounds proliferating, as Paphlagon/Cleon himself impersonates the sausage-seller in rehearsal:

> τὴν νύκτα θρυλῶν καὶ λαλῶν ἐν ταῖς ὁδοῖς σεαυτῷ,
> ὕδωρ τε πίνων κἀπιδεικνὺς τοὺς φίλους τ' ἀνιῶν,,,
>
> Did you murmur and mutter it all night long in the streets,
> drinking water and boring your friends by showing it off to them...?

Other features of the Paphlagonian's script in the first confrontation include an abundance of threats in the future tense in antilabe (368–374), and of Gorgianic rhyming final syllables – isoteleuton – for singsong emphasis (395–396):

> οὐ δέδοιχ' ὑμᾶς, ἕως ἂν ζῇ τὸ βουλευ**τήριον**
>   καὶ τὸ τοῦ δήμου πρόσωπον μακκοᾷ καθ**ήμενον**.
>
> I'm not afraid of you as long as there is still the Council there
> and the people sit gaping stupidly there.

Paphlagon/Cleon enjoys strong metaphors and similes concerning his own powers, at 429–431 likening himself to a great storm unleashed against his opponents:

> ἐγώ σε παύσω τοῦ θράσους, οἶμαι δὲ μᾶλλον ἄμφω.
> ἔξειμι γάρ σοι λαμπρὸς ἤδη καὶ μέγας καθιείς,
> ὁμοῦ ταράττων τήν τε γῆν καὶ τὴν θάλατταν εἰκῇ.
>
> I will stop your insolence, or rather the insolence of both of you. I will throw myself upon you like a terrible hurricane ravaging both land and sea at the will of its fury.

Here the chiasmus of *exeimi lampros ... megas kathieis* in the middle line, and especially the Gorgianic aural correspondence *tarratōn/thalattan* in the last line,[7] are verse-like techniques to support and enhance the acoustic emphasis. Paphlagon/Cleon is here responding to 'both' the Sausage-Seller and the chorus. For the Knights have contracted the Cleon-bug and begun to speak like the famous orator themselves, with a tongue-twister of alliterative of *p*, *k* and *s* sounds, constituting a showstopping but untranslatable obscene proverb (428):

---

[7] On the recurrence of the verb *tarattein* in relation to Paphlagon, see Edmunds 1987.

ὁτιὴ 'πιώρκεις θ' ἡρπακὼς καὶ κρέας ὁ πρωκτὸς εἶχεν.

Perjury and thievery ensure that the anus gets fed.

Oaths, too, are frequent – the two exchange and build on the others – By Zeus!, By Poseidon! (338–339). In the first altercation alone, Paphlagon/Cleon swears by Zeus, Poseidon, Demeter and Heracles. He departs to denounce the Sausage-Seller to the Council, closing his aural performance with a triple anaphora of *kai* connecting the different charges he will lay against his opponent, after a pointed antithesis of the pronouns 'I' and 'you (475–479):

ἐγὼ μὲν οὖν αὐτίκα μάλ' ἐς βουλὴν ἰὼν
ὑμῶν ἁπάντων τὰς ξυνωμοσίας ἐρῶ,
καὶ τὰς ξυνόδους τὰς νυκτερινὰς τὰς ἐν πόλει,
καὶ πάνθ' ἃ Μήδοις καὶ βασιλεῖ ξυνόμνυτε,
καὶ τἀκ Βοιωτῶν ταῦτα συντυρούμενα.

I, then, will hurry to the Council to reveal everything
you've plotted against me:
and your nightly conspiracies in the city,
and your collaborations with the Medes and with the Great King,
and your scavengings in Boeotia.
It is exhausting but exhilarating to hear.

At 611 the Sausage-Seller returns from the Council. His report requires that he impersonate Cleon—or rather, impersonate the other actor's impersonation of Cleon (658–682). The actors playing three characters and the chorus have all now been required by the script to impersonate Cleon directly. The Sausage-Seller first uses a torrent of extravagant metaphors to describe Paphlagon/Cleon, who had reached the Council before him, 'letting loose the storm, unchaining the lightning, crushing the Knights beneath huge mountains of calumnies heaped together and having all the air of truth'. Sausage-Seller responded by coming up with the good news of a price cut in anchovies. But the Paphlagonian counter-responded with a higher-value bribe which Sausage-Seller quotes in direct speech (654–656):

Men, I am now resolved
in recognition of this happy event,
to offer one hundred oxen to the goddess.

ἄνδρες, ἤδη μοι δοκεῖ
ἐπὶ συμφοραῖς ἀγαθαῖσιν εἰσηγγελμέναις
εὐαγγέλια θύειν ἑκατὸν βοῦς τῇ θεῷ.

Here we have jingling play on the stem *aggel-* and with the string of three feminine plural datives. But we get no more of Paphlagon/Cleon in the form of direct speech here – he is dragged from the rostrum, and the Sausage-Seller's anchovies prevail.

The report of the Sausage-Seller reminds us of the *similarity* between the two rivals for Demos's affections. How far were the two actors' performances intended to *contrast* with or to *resemble* each other like an echo-chamber in a non-stop display of Girardian, mimetic violence in the vocal sphere? I suspect that the Sausage-Seller, at least initially before learning through combat with Paphlagon/Cleon, sounded like an uncouth, semi-literate tradesman hawking his wares in the marketplace. The question is whether Cleon, whose diction is of a higher register, more akin to tragic diction than his interlocutor's,[8] was played as a reasonably well-educated middle-class man, who had adopted street language and manners in order to cosy up to the Piraeus thetes. The issue of the level of Cleon's education, combined with the tendency to associate Cleon as vocal performer with an animal or bird, provides Aristophanes with one of his better puns at the demagogue's expense: the chorus sing (985–996),

> I also marvel at his pig's education (ὑομουσία). His school-mates say he was always tuning his lyre to the Dorian mode and would learn no other; his music-master got angry and sent him away, saying, 'This one will only learn the Dorian because it is akin to bribery (Dōrodokisti)'.

But Cleon's rhetorical education, it seems, has been far from that of a pig's; his style is emotive and fluent and wordy and therefore could not be further from what was traditionally defined as the Doric style of Laconic speech.

Aristophanes suggests that Cleon's talismanic power as a speaker was inseparable from his Pnyx Hill performances. He loses the debate with the Sausage-Seller before the five-hundred-strong Council, under a roofed colonnade. But when it comes to addressing the thousands-strong Assembly, in the open air, the Sausage-Seller confesses he is terrified to go against Cleon (752–755).[9] This may reflect the speaking styles which work in different venues. Cleon's volume will have triumphed in the Assembly but may have been less attractive in a venue more like a modern lecture hall. Many great outdoor orators fell by the wayside

---

8 See O'Sullivan 1992, a fine study proposing that in such Aristophanic speakers we can see the origins of Greek rhetorical theories of the several 'styles'.
9 McGlew 1996, 350, by incorrectly stating that the reported altercation took place in the Assembly, misunderstands this point.

with the invention of audio and video recordings in the late 19th and 20th centuries.

The long third altercation is won by the Sausage-Seller for six reasons. First, he succeeds in making his overall self-characterisation conspiratorial, knowing, and collusive with the audience, Demos and the chorus, while isolating Paphlagon who has chosen *indignatio* as his primary register. Second, the Sausage-Seller takes the initiative (he is the first to introduce new agonistic strategies involving clothes or bodily care procedures). Third, he repeatedly employs brutal bathos to puncture high-flown language. Fourth, he is given all the scatological jokes, vital instruments in achieving that bathos. Fifth, Aristophanes writes for him a dazzling piece of *autoschediasmos* with his spontaneous invention of the oracles of Glanis (1000–1050).

But sixth, and most important, he everywhere 'out-Cleons' Cleon. He performs in exactly the same way as Paphlagon, but more successfully. Riposte after riposte flattens Paphlagon's interventions but by using Paphlagon's techniques, thus hoisting Cleon with his own petard. This even extends to the aural shape of their respective utterances in stichomythia. A fascinating acoustic pattern entails the Sausage-Seller responding to Paphlagon in ways which acoustically mimic the total sound effect. This implies that the Sausage-Seller actor was using Cleontic tricks and exaggeration of the 'real' Cleon-actor's speech in order to win the argument. Thus at 748–749, they exchange threats. Paphlagon says 'I will drag out your entrails with my claws', and the Sausage-Seller responds that he will claw away his meals in the prytaneion. In *Knights*, the threat in the first person singular future indicative has already become a standard way of opening a line. But listen to the noise correspondence:

Κλέων: ἐξαρπάσομαί σου τοῖς ὄνυξι τἄντερα.
Ἀλλαντοπώλης: ἀπονυχιῶ σου τἀν πρυτανείῳ σιτία.

There are many other examples of these aural rallies, where the Sausage-Seller wins because his actual syntax and sounds echo back, harder and with homoioteleuton, the crashing noise of the volley which Paphlagon had smashed over the net at him.

In the event, of course, the fears of the Sausage-Seller about the Pnyx prove unfounded. One reason, I believe, is that he takes the focus off actual speechmaking by introducing the sub-competitions in providing clothing and toiletries. He never lets Paphlagon/Cleon get launched into a rhesis that lasts more than a line or two: he uses diversions of an inherently theatrical nature to disrupt the agonistic form. And here I would like to make one other suggestion. Cleon and Aristophanes are in 424 BCE the two most famous men from Cydathenaeum in democratic Athens. One has made his name as an orator; the other is trying to establish his name as star comic dramatist. In the third altercation of *Knights*, we begin to see that the Sausage-Seller stands for comedy in opposition, as a literary genre, to political rhetoric—there is a sense in which Aristophanes himself lurks behind the Sausage-Seller. Comic theatre is staking a claim to be more use to the demos than politics itself. Cleon is enduring trial by comedy. Of course he *did* endure, and indeed survived it, was re-elected general a few months later, and rode high in the popularity stakes until his death at Amphipolis. But Aristophanes did very well out of it too. I have even wondered whether the two boys from Cydathenaeum weren't actually in secret league with one another to enhance each other's careers. Stranger relationships between politicians and theatre professionals have been known even in our own time.

In *Knights*, therefore, the man who defeats the Cleon-representative is an alternative comic avatar of Cleon himself: although I agree with Zumbrunnen that *Knights* celebrates lower-class Athenians' intelligence, it is too crude to say that it does so by showing 'an ordinary citizen standing up to demagogues'.[10] Aristophanes' polarising comic imagination has attributed to Paphlagon all the vices of which Cleon's enemies accused him, and to Agorakritos all the virtues which Cleon's own supporters admired. In Agorakritos, Aristophanes' experience of Cleon and the other non-aristocratic new politicians such as Lysicles allowed him to produce the most radical—even though fictional—political figure in ancient literature. *Knights* staged 'a fantastic journey that simultaneously lampooned and celebrated the Athenians and their democracy',[11] but it is also a 'Cleon-Fest'. Almost all the performers are required to impersonate Cleon, whose oratorical brilliance, with all the rich imagery, emotional power and acoustic effects of which *Knights* suggests he was absolute master, must often have given his Pnyx audiences exactly their 'pleasure in listening' to which the Thucydidean Cleon caustically refers (ἀκοῆς ἡδονῇ 3.38.7). And its conclusion puts on the stage a lowlife leader, from the bottom rung of the ladder of Athenian citizen society: 'I too, was bred in the agora', he says with some pride when Paphlagon/Cleon challenges him to a face-off (293). Cleon's commitment to the poorer citizens and effectiveness in pursuing their interests prompted the comic invention of a more perfect democracy than was ever actually achieved in Athens. In *Knights* he was sub-

---

10 Zumbrunnen 2004, 669, whose position reflects much German scholarship and is similar to that of Lind 1990, 211.
11 McGlew 1996, 358.

jected to brutal trial by comedy, a prime instrument of accountability in that democracy, and with his subsequent election as general showed he had passed his comedic *euthuna* with flying colours.

Bibliography

Anderson, M. (2005), 'Socrates as hoplite', in: *Ancient Philosophy* 25, 273–289.
Atkinson, J.E. (1992), 'Curbing the Comedians: Cleon versus Aristophanes and Syracosius' Decree', in: *CQ* 42, 56–64.
Bers, V. (1985), 'Dikastic thorubos', in: P. Cartledge/D. Harvey (eds.), *Crux: Essays in Greek History Presented to G.E.M. de Ste. Croix*, Exeter, 1–15.
Burns, T.W. (2014), 'Anger in Thcydides and Aristophanes: The Case of Cleon', in: J.M. Mhire/B.-P. Frost (eds.), *The Political Theory of Aristophanes: Explorations in Poetic Wisdom*, Albany, 229–258.
Calder, W.M. (1961), 'Socrates at Amphipolis (Ap. 28e)', in: *Phronesis* 6, 83–85.
Edmunds, L. (1987), 'The Aristophanic Cleon's 'Disturbance' of Athens', in: *AJP* 108, 233–263.
Gurd, S.A. (2016), *Dissonance: Auditory Aesthetics in Ancient Greece*, Oxford.
Hall, E. (2006), *The Theatrical Cast of Athens*, Oxford.
Hall, E. (2018), 'The Boys from Cydathenaeum: How to do things with Cleon and Aristophanes' *Knights*', in: D. Allen/P. Christesen (eds.), *How to Do Things with History*, Cambridge, 339–364.
Lafargue, P. (2013), *Cléon: Le Guerrier d'Athéna*, Paris.
Lind, H. (1990), *Der Gerber Kleon in den 'Rittern' des Aristophanes: Studien zur Demagogenkomödie*, Frankfurt am Main/New York.
McGlew, J. (1996), "Everybody Wants to Make a Speech': Cleon and Aristophanes on Politics and Fantasy', in: *Arethusa* 29, 339–361.
Monoson, S.S. (2014), 'Socrates in combat: trauma and resilience in Plato's political thought', in: P. Meineck/D. Konstan (eds.), *Combat Trauma and the Ancient Greeks*, New York, 131–162.
Morley, N. (1997), 'Cleon the misunderstood?', in: *Omnibus* 35, 4–6.
O'Sullivan, N. (1992), *Alcidamas, Aristophanes, and the Beginnings of Greek Stylistic Theory*, Stuttgart.
Tsoumpra, N. (2012), 'Who is to blame? Political leaders and Demos in Aristophanes' *Knights*', in: http://athensdialogues.chs.harvard.edu/cgi-bin/WebObjects/athensdialogues.woa/wa/dist?dis=100.
Woodhead, A.G. (1960), 'Thucydides' portrait of Cleon', in: *Mnemosyne*, 13, 289–317.
Zumbrunnen, J. (2004), 'Elite Domination and the Clever Citizen: Aristophanes' *Acharnians* and *Knights*', in: *Political Theory* 32, 656–677.

Ioanna Karamanou
Fragments of Euripidean Rhetoric
The Trial-Debate in Euripides' *Alexandros*

This article seeks to investigate Euripides' use of agonistic rhetoric through a case study of the less explored trial-debate in the fragmentarily preserved *Alexandros*. It will be argued that the group of fragments coming from this formal debate could yield insight not only into the dramatic situation, but also into the agonistic opposition of ideas which pervades late fifth-century Athenian culture with its use of tragic rhetoric including style, notions, and forms of argument.

The *Alexandros* was produced in 415 BCE alongside *Palamedes*, the *Trojan Women*, and the satyr-play *Sisyphos*.[1] Research on the *Alexandros* has benefited enormously from papyrus-finds preserving many fragments (P. Stras. 2342–44) and a major part of the narrative hypothesis of this play (P.Oxy. 3650, col. i). The hypothesis reports that when Alexandros was born, Hecabe had him exposed due to an ill-omened dream, according to which he would bring disaster to Troy. The child was raised by a herdsman, who named him Paris. Hecabe, still grieving over his exposure, persuaded Priam to establish funeral athletic games in his memory. When twenty years had passed, the boy excelled among his fellow herdsmen, who brought him bound in front of Priam, accusing him of arrogance. Based on schol. vet. E. *Hipp*. 58 (Schwartz), we know that Alexandros' fellow herdsmen formed a secondary chorus. The hypothesis goes on to mention that after defending himself before the king, Alexandros was granted permission to participate in his own funeral games. Having been crowned winner, he infuriated his brother Deiphobos and his companions who, realizing that they had been defeated by a slave, demanded that Hecabe should kill him. The hypothesis then reports that Cassandra recognized him while she was in a state of prophetic frenzy foretelling the forthcoming disaster, and that Hecabe was prevented from killing him. His foster-father arrived, and, because of the danger, he was compelled to tell the truth. Alexandros thus returned to the Trojan palace.

I am much indebted to Professors Chris Carey, Christopher Collard, Martin Cropp, and Mike Edwards for valuable comments. This paper has already been published in Quijada Sagredo/Encinas Reguero 2017, 161–176. For more detail, see also Karamanou 2017, 182–199.

1 Schol. vet. Ar. *Vesp*. 1326b (Koster), Ael. *VH* 2.8.

The *Alexandros* comprises two agon scenes. The first agon, which is the focus of the present study, is a trial-debate in which Alexandros defends himself before Priam as a judge, on the basis of the hypothesis (P.Oxy. 3650, col. i, 15–21) and the fragmentary evidence referring to this dramatic situation (frr. 48, 50, 56, 60, 61 Kannicht, henceforth abbreviated as K.). In an earlier publication I argued that the play also contains a second agon, which is held between Hector and Deiphobos in front of their mother Hecabe as a judge (frr. 62a–b K.). In that agon Deiphobos expresses his resentment at his defeat by the herdsman Alexandros and tries to persuade his brother Hector to plot against him and have him eliminated.[2] It is noteworthy that the *Alexandros* and the *Andromache* (147–273, 547–746) provide the two attested cases of Euripidean tragedies where one finds two formal debates within the same play, thus indicating the dramatist's penchant for agonistic rhetoric.

To identify the ideological context of Euripidean formal debates, it is worth bearing in mind that rhetoric was an essential part of Athenian culture from the second half of the fifth century BCE onwards. Rhetorical discourse was at the core of Athenian civic and forensic processes and was a means of evaluating political conduct and citizenly behaviour.[3] Euripides' agonistic rhetoric in particular is imbued with the notion of competition, which is an inherent feature of Greek culture[4] and shares the formality of sophistic *antilogiai*.[5] Rhetorical drama or 'the drama of *logos*', to quote Simon Goldhill,[6] thus constitutes an integral part of the audience's experience of theatre and is most eloquently articulated in the rhetorical contests of Euripidean tragedy.

In the first formal debate of the play, according to the hypothesis, Alexandros' fellow herdsmen brought him bound before Priam to accuse him of haughty behaviour. Alexandros defended himself in front of the king and was allowed to participate in the games held in his memory. A group of fragments refers to the hostility aroused by the arrogant behaviour of a slave (fr. 48 K.) and by his fondness for the noble class (fr. 50 K.), including comments on the rhetorical capacities of the speakers (frr. 56, 61 K.) and Priam's decision to allow the unknown herdsman Alexandros to compete in the athletic contest (fr. 60 K.). The trial-scene

---

[2] Karamanou 2011.
[3] See Hall 1995, 39–58; Mastronarde 2010, 207–245; Goldhill 1986, esp. 1–3, 75–78; Pelling 2005, 83–85; Rosenbloom 2009, 194–198 and most recently Quijada Sagredo/Encinas Reguero 2013.
[4] On the pivotal role of competition in Greek thought and culture, see, for instance, Fisher/van Wees 2011; Hawhee 2004, 15–64; Poulakos 1995, 32–39.
[5] See Conacher 1998, ch. 4; Lloyd 1992, 23–24; Collard 1975, 63; Guthrie 1962–1981, III 50–51, 127–129; Kerferd 1981, 83–91; Froleyks 1973, 264–274.
[6] Goldhill 1986, 3.

attested in the hypothesis, in conjunction with the rhetorical elaboration and contrasting argumentation of these fragments, indicates a trial-debate held between Alexandros as the defendant and a prosecutor accusing him of arrogance before Priam as judge. This has been widely accepted ever since the publication of the hypothesis, which revealed the objective and location of the trial-debate within the dramatic plot, as well as the hostility of the subsidiary chorus of herdsmen towards Alexandros.[7]

This type of trial-debate held between two dramatic characters in front of a third person as judge ('Abrechnungsagon vor einem Richter', following Dubischar's categorization[8]) recurs in the next two tragedies of this trilogy. In the *Trojan Women* Helen is the defendant and Hecabe is the plaintiff before Menelaos (*Tr.* 860–1059), while in the *Palamedes* the title-character is accused of treachery by Odysseus in front of Agamemnon (frr. 580–581, 583–585 K.).[9] It is also noteworthy that the defendants in all three debates are regarded as enemies of the community. The first agon in the *Alexandros* presents the clash of the royal son, who has been raised as a herdsman, with his fellow herdsmen. Subsequently, Palamedes is falsely regarded as a betrayer of the Greek army, while Helen is held responsible for communal damage.

Euripidean trial-debates seem to reflect the practice of forensic oratory and lawcourt procedure. According to this practice, Alexandros is likely to speak second,[10] defending himself against his opponent's accusations. It is also noteworthy that unlike most formal debates, which tend to remain unresolved,[11] the outcome of this agon serves to promote the dramatic plot: Alexandros is granted permission by Priam to enter the games to prove his worth, and thus becomes actively involved in the dramatic events.

A crucial question concerns the identity of Alexandros' prosecutor in this debate. Most scholars have so far assigned the role of the plaintiff to Hecabe or Deiphobos in view of their subsequent hostility towards Alexandros and because they inferred that the prosecutor is high-born based on a group of fragments expressing prejudice against slaves (frr. 49, 51, 59 K.) and counter-argumentation

---

[7] See Coles 1974, 14–15, 24–25; Scodel 1980, 28–31, 83–90; Jouan/van Looy 1998, 49–50; Kannicht 2004, I 186; Collard/Cropp/Gibert 2004, 36, 38–39; Collard/Cropp 2008, I 35–36.
[8] Dubischar 2001, 96–97, 125–126.
[9] See Collard *et al.* 2004, 95.
[10] For the order of speakers in Euripidean agones, see Schlesinger 1937, 69–70; Collard 1975, 62 and for only few exceptions, see Lloyd 1992, 101.
[11] For this feature of Euripidean debates, see Strohm 1957, 37–38, 45–46; Collard 1975, 62; Mastronarde 1986, 205–206; Lloyd 1992, 16–17.

against wealth (fr. 55 K.).[12] These fragments, however, may well belong to the second agon of the play, which revolves around the antithesis between nobility and slavery, as Deiphobos disparages Alexandros' lowly status because of his resentment at his being defeated by a slave (fr. 62a.9–10, fr. 62b.33–34 K.). Moreover, it is worth considering the fact that the hypothesis clearly states that the accusation against Alexandros concerns his arrogance (P.Oxy. 3650, col. i, 15.16: διὰ τὴν ὑπερήφανον cυμβίωcιν) and not his status as a slave *per se*. Accordingly, the trial-debate seems to have focused on the theme of his haughty behaviour and incompatibility with his social context of fellow herdsmen (frr. 48, 50 K.), as well as on the question of his usefulness and worth (raised in frr. 48, 60, 61 K.).

Considering also that Deiphobos is Hector's opponent in the second agon of this play, it is highly improbable that he participated in both formal debates of the same tragedy. In addition, Deiphobos' appearance along with Hector later in the plot, in the course of the second agon, is signposted with the conventional announcement: καὶ μὴν ὁρῶ τόν]δ᾽ Ἕκτορ᾽ ἐξ ἀγωνίω[ν / cτείχοντα μό]χθων cύγγονόν τε, παῖδε cώ, / [Δηίφοβον·] ('And now I see] Hector [here] / [coming] from the toils of the games and his brother, / [Deiphobos,] your two sons').[13] This formulaic announcement is regularly employed by Euripides to designate the entry of a new character,[14] which entails that Deiphobos is very unlikely to have appeared onstage before, and so to have held the role of the plaintiff in the trial-debate.

Hecabe remains an appealing candidate for this role, though there is no obvious reason why she would have such a grievance against Alexandros at this early stage of the plot, so as to get involved in the quarrel of the herdsmen. Nevertheless, as Professor Christopher Collard has pointed out to me, it would be powerful drama for her to have lost the argument about Alexandros in the trial-debate and then to lose – and yet win – when Alexandros survives the attack

---

12 In favour of Deiphobos, see Coles 1974, 24; Scodel 1980, 30–31, 82; Jouan/van Looy 1998, 50. In favour of Hecabe, see Collard *et al.* 2004, 39; Collard/Cropp 2008, I 36 and Di Giuseppe 2012, 80–81.

13 [Δηίφοβον] is Diggle's plausible supplement (Diggle 1997, 99) fitting the approximate space of ca. 7–8 letters. Deiphobos' name needs to be clearly stated along with Hector's, given that Hecabe has a considerable number of sons (as Di Giuseppe 2012, 134 reasonably points out).

14 Cf. *Alc.* 611–612 (and Parker 2007, 161); *Hipp.* 1151–1152, *Andr.* 545–546; see Jacob 1976, esp. 340; Hamilton 1978, 63–65 and n. 1; Hourmouziades 1965, 142–144; Mannsperger 1971, 145; Belardinelli 1994, 130.

against him and is subsequently identified. Such a possibility would serve to underscore the idea of human self-delusion, which is a key notion of this trilogy, brought into prominence in the *Trojan Women*.[15]

Still, the fragmentary material requires that every possibility should be explored, and a close reading of the hypothesis could alternatively hint at another possible candidate for the role of Alexandros' opponent in the debate. The hypothesis (P.Oxy. 3650, col. i, 15–17) reports that the other herdsmen brought Alexandros bound before Priam: οἱ δ' ἄλλοι νομεῖς διὰ τ]ὴν ὑπερήφανον συμ-βίωσιν δ]ήσαντες ἐπ[ὶ] Πρίαμον ἀνήγαγον αὐτόν. The verb ἀνάγω can be used in the judicial sense of 'bringing s.o. to justice' (*VdLG*[2]: 'condurre in giudizio'), which would be consistent with the context of a trial. The characters accusing Alexandros of arrogance are none other than his fellow herdsmen asking Priam to undertake arbitration of this matter. Two lines below (hyp. 18–21) Alexandros' accusers are again referred to in the plural: τοὺς διαβάλλοντας ἑκάϲτ[ο]υϲ ἔλαβε καὶ τῶν ἐπ' αὐτῷ τελ[ο]υμέν[ων] ἀγώνων εἰάθη μετασχεῖν. Considering that οἱ διαβάλλοντες are mentioned in the hypothesis as a group of people needing no further specification, while there is no reference to any other dramatic character disparaging Alexandros in this debate, the reasonable inference is that the characters implied here are the herdsmen attested to bring Alexandros to trial two lines above. If so, this group can be no other than the subsidiary chorus of herdsmen perhaps rebuking Alexandros in a lyric song, while someone, conceivably a herdsman, is speaking on their behalf and participating in the agon as plaintiff. In Euripidean tragedies the *exarchos* of the secondary chorus is a dramatic character, such as Hippolytos in *Hipp*. 58–72, Dirce in the *Antiope* (as attested in schol. *Hipp*. 58 Schwartz) and Merops in *Phaethon* fr. 781.218, 227–244 K.;[16] considering that Alexandros cannot assume this role due to his overt hostility with the shepherds, it is worth raising the question whether Alexandros' opponent in the debate might have been the *exarchos* of this subsidiary chorus conveying the accusations of his fellow herdsmen.

The participation of a minor character, such as a herdsman, in a Euripidean agon would not be unprecedented. Eloquent parallels are provided in *Heracl*. 134–287 and *Supp*. 381–597, which present heralds as participating in formal debates.[17] Moreover, in the fragmentarily preserved *Alope* an agon seems to have

---

15 On this dominant idea, see Murray 1946, 127–148; Scodel 1980, 105–121; Cropp 2004, 47–48; Di Giuseppe 2012, 192–193.
16 On the subsidiary chorus of the *Antiope*, see Kambitsis 1972, xv; Collard *et al*. 2004, 263; on that of the *Phaethon*, see Diggle 1970, 144.
17 For such anonymous characters, see, for instance, Yoon 2012, 107–111.

been held between two herdsmen before Alope's father as judge.[18] The possible involvement of a herdsman as Alexandros' prosecutor in this trial-debate could serve to illustrate Alexandros' clash with his foster environment in the first agon, which would be mirrored in the hostility felt by his natal family towards him in the second formal debate of this play.

The *agones* of Euripides are clearly defined scenes displaying formal markers. In the ensuing discussion I shall investigate the rhetorical terms, notions and devices which formally signpost this scene as an agon and constitute indicators of the Athenian rhetorical culture.

Fr. 50 K.:
δούλων ὅσοι φιλοῦσι δεσποτῶν γένος,
πρὸς τῶν ὁμοίων πόλεμον αἴρονται μέγαν.

Slaves who are fond of their masters' class
arouse much hostility from their own kind.

This fragment refers to the hostility felt by slaves against those of them who are attached to the class of the masters and presumably would wish to belong to their rank. The hypothesis stresses Alexandros' natural inclination towards the noble class (P.Oxy. 3650, col. i, 13–14), which is the reason why his fellow herdsmen accuse him of arrogance. The rather neutral and generalizing tone of this remark makes it likely for it to have been a distich comment by the chorus-leader after the prosecutor's speech and before Alexandros' *rhēsis*, considering that set-speeches are formally separated by means of brief comments made by the chorus-leader on each preceding speech.[19] Alternatively, this fragment may have belonged to the plaintiff's speech expressing the hostility aroused against Alexandros by his fellow herdsmen because of his haughty behaviour towards them; or perhaps it was made by Alexandros himself in an attempt to gain the favour of his master (i.e. Priam) by appealing to his fondness for the class of his masters.[20]

Stylistically speaking, δούλων is emphatically placed first in the colon, drawing an antithesis with δεσποτῶν. A similar contrast between slaves and masters occurs in fr. 51 K. of this play, probably alluding to Alexandros' proven superiority over the royal sons in the athletic games. Parallel instances of this antithesis

---

18 Hyg. *fab*. 187: see Jouan/van Looy 1998, 141–142; Collard/Cropp 2008, I 115–117; Duchemin 1968², 83; Karamanou 2003, 30–31, 35.
19 On the brief comments of the chorus-leader in formal debates, see Duchemin 1968², 152; Collard 1975, 60; Graf 1950, 165; Lloyd 1992, 5.
20 See Scodel 1980, 30.

include *Andr.* 30, *Hel.* 1630, 1640, *El.* 899, *Ion* 837f., *Arch.* fr. 261 K. In addition, the notions of class-distinction and status are underscored through the reference to γένος.

Πόλεμον...μέγαν is a case of *hyperbaton*.[21] The adjective μέγας tends to be emphatically placed at the end of the colon mostly by Euripides and often by means of a *hyperbaton*; see *Hel.* 55: συνάψαι πόλεμον Ἕλλησιν μέγαν, *Heracl.* 504: κίνδυνον ἡμῶν οὕνεκ᾽ αἴρεσθαι μέγαν, *Hec.* 244: μεμνήμεθ᾽ ἐς κίνδυνον ἐλθόντες μέγαν.

> Fr. 56 K.:
> ἄναξ, διαβολαὶ δεινὸν ἀνθρώποις κακόν·
> ἀγλωσσίᾳ δὲ πολλάκις ληφθεὶς ἀνήρ
> δίκαια λέξας ἧσσον εὐγλώσσου φέρει.
>
> My lord, slander is a horrible vice for people.
> Frequently, one seized by ineloquence,
> even if one has spoken justly, is less effective than an eloquent speaker.

The speaker of these lines is addressing king Priam (l. 1: ἄναξ) and is expressing the need to refute the argumentation of an eloquent and slanderous opponent. This fragment is likely to have been the *exordium* of Alexandros' defence-speech,[22] since it displays certain typical features of rhetorical proems in formal debates, such as the initial address to the judge of the agon aimed at obtaining the *captatio benevolentiae* (cf. similarly *Heracl.* 181, *Hec.* 1187),[23] which is also attained through the appeal to a common type of rhetorical *aporia* (ll. 2–3), as it will be further discussed below. These elements, in combination with the rhetorical elaboration of these lines, which comprise an antithesis and a cross-arrangement (ll. 2–3), as well as a *hyperbaton* (in l. 1), are suggestive of the formality of this proem.

---

21 See Devine/Stephens 2000, esp. 112–115; Dik 2007, 24–25, 61, 100, 241–242; Lausberg 1998, 318–319; Slings 1997, 174–175.
22 See also Huys 1986, 35; Jouan/van Looy 1998, 50; Collard *et al.* 2004, 75; Collard/Cropp 2008, I, 36; Di Giuseppe 2012, 91.
23 On the *captatio benevolentiae* as one of the aims of the *exordium*, see [Arist.] *Rh. Al.* 29, Cic. *Inv.* 1.16.21, *De Or.* 1.119, [Cic.] *Rhet. Her.* 1.4.6, Quint. *Inst.* 4.1. Cf. also Duchemin 1968², 169 and n. 5; Lloyd 1992, 25–27; Carey 1994, 27–28.

Attic law prohibited slander and abusive language. The reference to the slander employed by the adversary is a *topos* in oratory.²⁴ Lysias describes it in a similar way in 19.6: πάντων δεινότατόν ἐστι διαβολή. Isocrates regards it as a *μέγιστον κακόν* (15.18) and Antiphon as *ἀδικώτατον* [...] *τῶν ἐν ἀνθρώποις* (6.7). In *Hipp*. 932–933 Hippolytos as defendant in the trial-debate protests against slander: ἀλλ' ἤ τις ἐς σὸν οὖς με διαβαλὼν ἔχει / φίλων, νοσοῦμεν δ' οὐδὲν ὄντες αἴτιοι. Likewise, Socrates states that he aims at refuting *διαβολή* at the *prothesis* of his speech in the *Apology* (18e.5–19a.2). The idea that slander undermines justice is also brought forward in *Supp*. 415–416: εἶτα διαβολαῖς νέαις / κλέψας τὰ πρόσθε σφάλματ' ἐξέδυ δίκης; Alexandros is expressing here a rhetorical *aporia* aiming at achieving the *captatio benevolentiae;* he is appealing to a feigned helplessness and presents himself as disadvantaged because of the slander employed by his eloquent adversary, with the purpose of predisposing the judge of the agon to look favourably on his case. The rhetorical device of *aporia* is regularly employed in Euripidean formal debates (*Hipp*. 986–991, *Andr*. 186–191, *Or*. 544–550).²⁵

Alexandros' speech opens with a gnome, as Andromache's in *Andr*. 183–185 and Eteocles' speech in *Ph*. 499–500. The antithesis drawn in ll. 2–3 between an eloquent, effective but unjust speaker and an ineloquent, ineffective but truthful one is elaborately articulated through the framing function of the first (ἀγλωσσίᾳ) and the last element (εὐγλώσσου).

The attack on unprincipled rhetoric is a *topos* in Euripides²⁶ and pervades all three trial-debates of the production of 415 BCE: see *Palamedes* fr. 583 K. (cf. Falcetto 2002, 129–130 and n. 6): ὅστις λέγει μὲν εὖ, τὰ δ' ἔργ' ἐφ' οἷς λέγει / αἴσχρ' ἐστί, τούτου τὸ σοφὸν οὐκ αἰνῶ ποτέ and *Tr*. 967–968 (cf. Lee 1976, *ad loc*.): πειθὼ διαφθείρουσα τῆσδ', ἐπεὶ λέγει / καλῶς κακοῦργος οὖσα· δεινὸν οὖν τόδε.²⁷ The similarities of these passages with the present fragment may be even closer in view of their particular emphasis on the inverse relation between eloquence and

---

24 See MacDowell 1978, 126–129; Carey 1994, 31–32; Loomis 2003, 287–300; Wallace 1994, 109–124; Csapo/Slater 1994, 168–171.
25 Cf. also Antiphon 1.2, 3.2.1, Lys. 8.2, 17.1, 19.1, 32.1 (and Carey 1989, *ad loc*.), Isoc. 12.22, D.H. *Lys*. 24. See Usher 2008, 33, 41, 213; Lausberg 1998, 343–344; Too 1995, 134–135.
26 Cf. *Med*. 576–578 (and Mastronarde 2002, *ad loc*.), *Hipp*. 486–489, 503, 1038–1040, *Hec*. 1187–1191 (with Collard 1991, *ad loc*.), *Supp*. 426, *Ph*. 526–527 (and Mastronarde 1994, *ad loc*.), *IA* 333, 1115–1116, *Ba*. 266–271 (and Dodds 1960², *ad loc*.), *Antiope* fr. 206.4–6 K. (and Kambitsis 1972, 80–81), *Arch*. fr. 253 K. (and Harder 1985, *ad loc*.), *Hipp.Cal*. fr. 439 K., *Meleagros* fr. 528.2 K., fr. inc. 928b K. See also Collard *et al*. 2004, 76; Scodel 1999–2000, 134–139; Dover 1994², 25–26; Jouan 1984, 7–13; Lloyd 1992, 26, 51; Buxton 1982, 181–182.
27 See also Scodel 1980, 114.

justice. The terms εὔγλωσσος and εὐγλωσσία are also employed in fr. inc. 928b.2 K. and *Antiope* fr. 206.4 K. respectively to criticize the eloquence of an unjust speaker. A character's articulacy is further described with phrases such as εὔτροχον στόμα (*Hipp.Cal.* fr. 439.3 K.), εὔτροχος γλῶσσα (*Ba.* 268), γλώσσῃ εὖ περιστελεῖν (*Med.* 582), λέγειν δεινός (*Med.* 585, *Hipp.Cal.* fr. 439.2 K.), εὖ κοσμεῖν λόγους (*Med.* 576), κομψός and its derivatives. Eloquence is presented as intrinsically interwoven with persuasion in Isoc. 15.230–236, Ar. *Nub.* 1397–1398, *Eq.* 836–840.[28]

The opposite term ἀγλωσσία in the sense of 'ineloquence' is very rare in fifth-century literature and occurs also in Antiphon 87 B97 D.-K. (see Pendrick 2002, 350–351). The adjective ἄγλωσσος denoting 'ineloquent' is employed in Pi. *N.* 8.24 and Ar. fr. inc. 756 K.-A.: Ἀριστοφάνης δὲ ἄγλωττον τὸν εἰπεῖν ἀδύνατον ἔφη.[29] The literal meaning of ἄγλωσσος is 'tongueless' and is attested in Eub. *Sfingokarion* fr. 106.1, 7 K.-A., *A.P.* 7.191.5, 7.641.2, 9.439.2, 16.153, Eudem. Περὶ λέξεων ῥητορικῶν s.v ἄγλωσσος and Suda α 271 (Adler): ἀγλωττία· ἡσυχία, σιωπή. καὶ ἄγλωσσος, ὁ ἄναυδος, ὁ ἄφωνος. In metaphorical terms the epithet may also mean 'barbarian' (S. *Tr.* 1060, Hesych. α 626 Latte).

The phrase ἧσσον φέρει seems to involve an agonistic metaphor. The meaning of φέρω as 'win in a contest' (*VdLG*²: 'conseguire, guadagnare, guadagnarsi, spec. di vittorie o premi') suits the competitive and agonistic context of this scene.

Fr. 61 K.:
†μισῶ σοφὸν ἐν λόγοισιν, ἐς δ' ὄνησιν οὐ σοφόν†

μισῶ σοφὸν {ἐν} λόγοισιν, ἐς δ' ὄνησιν οὐ {σοφόν} Cobet *Novae Lectiones*, p. 293: μισῶ / σοφὸν <μὲν> ἐν λόγοισιν-οὐ {σοφόν} Wagner *Poetarum Tragicorum Graecorum Fragmenta*, Vol. II, p. 33: μισῶ <δ' ἐγώ> / σοφὸν {ἐν} λόγοισιν-οὐ σοφόν Schneidewin: μισῶ σοφόν / <ὄντ'> ἐν λόγοισιν-οὐ σοφόν Meineke: μισῶ <δ' ἐγώ> / <τὸν> σοφὸν <μὲν> ἐν λόγοισιν-οὐ σοφόν Headlam *JPh* 23 (1895) 273

I detest someone skilled in speech but not in service.

The transmitted text is unmetrical. Cobet's emendation (μισῶ σοφὸν {ἐν} λόγοισιν, ἐς δ' ὄνησιν οὐ {σοφόν}) is the most economical one, since it requires the least intervention in the text. A further merit of this proposal is that it accounts for the intrusion of σοφόν as an explanatory gloss.[30] Euripides tends to

---

28 See further Buxton 1982, 48–58; Sansone 2012, ch. 8; Rosenbloom 2009, 201–202; Roisman 1999, 114–116.
29 Cf. also Jouan/van Looy 1998, 64 n. 51 and Cropp 2004, 76.
30 For this type of textual discrepancy, see for instance West 1973, 22–23.

employ this type of structure to express emphatic antithesis. The closest parallels, both stylistically and thematically, are *Or*. 287: τοῖς μὲν λόγοις ηὔφρανε, τοῖς δ' ἔργοισιν οὔ and *Erechtheus* fr. 360.13 K.: λόγωι πολίτης ἐστί, τοῖς δ' ἔργοισιν οὔ. The antithetic force of the opposition between speech (*λόγοισιν*) and action (*ὄνησιν*) is enhanced by cross-arrangement.[31]

This line involves an aphorism against someone who is skilled in words but not in making himself useful. Scholars have assigned this fragment either to Alexandros disparaging the eloquence of his opponent, as in the previous fragment, or to his adversary rebuking Alexandros' lack of usefulness.[32] Though no definite conclusion can be drawn as to either possibility, it is worth taking into account that the question of Alexandros' usefulness (ὄνησις) is given particular prominence in this agon. In fr. 48.3–4 K., which will be discussed below, he is regarded as a useless possession for a household due to his arrogance, while in fr. 60 K. (on which, see also below) Priam declares that he awaits evidence for Alexandros' worth. Hence, considering that his usefulness and efficacy are challenged in this debate and proven in the course of the plot by means of his athletic achievement, I would be inclined to favour the possibility that this line could have been delivered by Alexandros' opponent criticizing him as useless.

This fragment highlights the dual use of *sophia* in Euripides, both as 'eloquence' and as 'prudence'. In the former sense it is employed in *Ph*. 1259–1260: ἀλλ', εἴ τιν' ἀλκὴν ἢ σοφοὺς ἔχεις λόγους / ἢ φίλτρ' ἐπωιδῶν and *Antiope* fr. 189 K.: ἐκ παντὸς ἄν τις πράγματος δισσῶν λόγων / ἀγῶνα θεῖτ' ἄν, εἰ λέγειν εἴη σοφός. Accordingly, Euripides is described as σοφώτατος in Ar. *Ra*. 774–776 in view of his elaborate rhetoric.[33] The sense of *sophia* as 'prudence' is related to the notion of *sōphrosynē*, encompassing good sense, self-control and mode-ration, which are prerequisites for a righteous conduct in the private and public sphere of action.[34] This concept is brought forward in *Autolykos* fr. 282.23–25 K.: ἄνδρας χρὴ σοφούς τε κἀγαθοὺς / φύλλοις στέφεσθαι, χὤστις ἡγεῖται πόλει / κάλ-λιστα σώφρων καὶ δίκαιος ὢν ἀνήρ, *Antiope* fr. 200 K.: γνώμαις γὰρ ἀνδρὸς εὖ μὲν οἰκοῦνται πόλεις, / εὖ δ' οἶκος, εἴς τ' αὖ πόλεμον ἰσχύει μέγα·/ σοφὸν γὰρ ἓν βούλευμα τὰς πολλὰς χέρας / νικᾷ, σὺν ὄχλῳ δ' ἀμαθία πλεῖστον κακόν and fr. 202

---

31 On cross-arrangement, see Lausberg 1998, 322–323.
32 For the former possibility, see Lefke 1936, 78; Snell 1937, 13; Jouan/van Looy 1998, 50, 64, while Collard *et al.* 2004, 76 regard both options as equally possible.
33 See Winnington-Ingram 1969, 127–128, 139–141; Hunter 2009, 12–13; Goff 1990, 24, 42–43; Buxton 1982, 170.
34 Cf. Rademaker 2005, 148–150, 161–163; Adkins 1960, 177–178, 195–198, 244–246, 1972, 104–105; North 1966, 168–170; Dover 1994², 128–129; Gill 1995, 34–38; Di Benedetto 1971, 201–205.

K. The association of *σοφία* with *ὄνησις* in this passage further underscores their significance for the good management of the household and everyday life.

The rhetorical antithesis between words and deeds regularly acquires a political nuance. This dichotomy is a distinctive feature of Periclean discourse (Thuc. 2.35.1, 2.40.1–3, 2.41.2, 2.41.4, 2.42.2, 2.43.1, 2.46.1), while actions or facts tend to be elevated above words in Thucydides' hierarchy of values, as, for instance, in the famous passage in Thuc. 2.65.9–10.[35] The use of politically charged vocabulary could be congruent with the socio-political character of the dramatic situation of Alexandros' incompatibility and clash with the community of his fellow herdsmen.

Fr. 60 K.:
χρόνος δὲ δείξει <σ'>· ᾧ τεκμηρίῳ μαθών
ἢ χρηστὸν ὄντα γνωσόμεσθά σ' ἢ κακόν.

Time will reveal you; by that proof
I shall know whether you are useful or vile.

The male speaker of these lines (to judge from the masculine participle *μαθών*) is expressing his confidence in the power of time to reveal the qualities of his addressee. This fragment has plausibly been regarded as comprising Priam's decision to grant permission to Alexandros to participate in the athletic contest.[36] The tone of these lines, which employ the concept of time as a future witness of Alexandros' qualities, is congruent with the content of a verdict in the trial-debate. The multilayered irony of this fragment is interrelated with the revealing power of time:[37] in the short run, the seemingly lowly herdsman Alexandros is going to prove his worth at the athletic games, thus subverting the position of his opponents, who challenged his usefulness. In a larger time-scale, however, the long-lost son bringing joy through his unexpected homecoming [38] will ultimately prove to be disastrous for Troy and its royal *oikos*.

The term *tekmērion* denoting 'a compelling sign that permits firm conclusions to be drawn about a particular matter'[39] is an indication that the result will

---

[35] For this contrast, see also Thgn. 1.979–982 W., Democr. 68 B53a D.-K, Gorgias 82 A27, B6, B11a.35 D.-K, Antiphon 3.3.1, 3.3.3, 5.84, 6.47, Is. 2.35, 38, 44. Cf. Price 2001, 45–51; Ober 1998, 84–86, 88–89; Parry 1981, esp. 38–51, 57–61; Michelini 1987, 156–157; Montiglio 2000, 284–286.
[36] See Snell 1937, 14; Murray 1946, 131; Webster 1967, 171; Scodel 1980, 31; Huys 1986, 34 and 1995, 354; Jouan/van Looy 1998, 66; Collard et al. 2004, 74; Di Giuseppe 2012, 101–102 and n. 123.
[37] See also Scodel 1980, 90.
[38] See especially fr. 62 K. and Collard et al. 2004, 87.
[39] Lausberg 1998, 166.

necessarily occur (as distinguished from *sēmeion*, which may be fallible[40]). The term is here employed in its forensic function and, taken in combination with the rhetorical nuance of the verb δείξει regularly employed in formal debates (*Med.* 548-549, *Andr.* 706, *HF* 173, *Tr.* 970), it is suggestive of the formality of the debate. It also occurs within the context of a trial in A. *Eum.* 447: τεκμήριον δὲ τῶνδέ σοι λέξω μέγα, 485: μαρτύριά τε καὶ τεκμήρια, 662: τεκμήριον δὲ τοῦδέ σοι δείξω λόγου.[41]

The epithet *χρηστός* here conveys the sense of 'useful', 'worthy'. In late fifth century this epithet commends a person who makes himself beneficial in private and public life. This is an outcome of the development of co-operative excellences mainly urged by democratic institutions.[42] In fr. 62i K. Alexandros describes his capacities with the similar term *τὸ χρήσιμον φρενῶν*, which is particularly associated with practical activity[43] and in that case alludes to his athletic achievement.

> Fr. 48 K.:
> σοφὸς μὲν οὖν εἶ, Πρίαμ', ὅμως δέ σοι λέγω·
> δούλου φρονοῦντος μεῖζον ἢ φρονεῖν χρεών
> οὐκ ἔστιν ἄχθος μεῖζον οὐδὲ δώμασι
> κτῆσις κακίων οὐδ' ἀνωφελεστέρα.
>
> You are indeed wise, Priam, but I am telling you:
> there is no bigger burden than a slave having a higher
> opinion of himself than he should, nor a possession
> more spiteful or worthless for a household.

---

40 See Arist. *Rh.* 1357b4-17 and Cope 1867, 160-168; Quint. *Inst.* 5.9.3.
41 See also *Danae* fr. 322.3 K. possibly deriving from a formal debate as well (cf. Karamanou 2006, 86): ἓν δέ μοι τεκμήριον, fr. inc. 898.5-6 K.: τεκμήριον δέ, μὴ λόγῳ μόνον μάθῃς, / ἔργῳ δὲ δείξω τὸ σθένος τὸ τῆς θεοῦ . For the use of this term in tragic rhetoric, see Goebel 1983, 55-73; Lloyd 1992, 22; Bers 1994, 180-181. See also Thuc. 1.34.3, 2.39.2, 3.66.1 (and Hornblower 1987, 101-104; Finley 1967, 9), Antiphon 5.61.1, Lys. 13.20.2, 19.25.1, D. 20.10.3, 23.207.1, Isoc. 19.51.1, 21.11.1.
42 See *Heracl.* 1-5 (and Allan 2001, 133; Wilkins 1993, 46), *Autolykos* fr. 282.23-28 K., S. *Ant.* 661-662 (and Griffith 1999, 237), Ar. *Pax* 910-921, *Th.* 832, *Ra.* 1455-1456 (and Dover 1993, 212), Eupolis *Dēmoi* fr. 129 K.-A. (and Storey 2003, *ad loc.*), Thuc. 2.37.1, D. 18.190, Aeschin. 1.30-31 (and Fisher 2001, *ad loc.*). Cf. Adkins 1960, 195-199; Rosenbloom 2004, 56-57 and n. 5 (with further bibliography), 63-66, 351-353; Dover 1994², 296-299; Adkins 1972, 115-127, 146; Fouchard 1997, 194-199; Bryant 1996, 151-168, 205.
43 On this sense of φρένες, see Sullivan 2000, 11-12, 16; Snell 1977, 35-37; Padel 1992, 20-23; Webster 1957, 152-153.

>   2 μεῖζον ἢ inscr. in pectore hermae aetatis Marci Aurelii (Lehmann- Hartleben ap. Lefke 73, n. 102, Richter, *The Portraits of the Greeks* I 139s., figg. 771–773), prob. Lefke 73, Huys *AC* 64 (1995) 187s. et Collard/Cropp/Gibert 56, 75, ante inscriptionem inventam coniecerat Blaydes Adversaria in Tragicorum Graecorum Fragmenta, p. 92: μᾶλλον ἢ Stob. IV 19.14, prob. Kannicht

This comment is likely to have been a reaction at Priam's decision to allow Alexandros to compete at the games. This carefully balanced statement could plausibly be assigned to the chorus-leader, as Huys argued on the basis of similar comments by chorus-leaders in agonistic contexts.[44] Alternatively, I would suggest that this comment may have anticipated Priam's verdict as an appeal addressed to the king to reach the right decision. A similar appeal is delivered by the chorus-leader to Menelaos in the trial-debate in *Tr.* 1033–1035. Another feasible speaker of these lines could be Alexandros' opponent in the debate, if the role of the plaintiff was not held by a character of lowly status, but by Hecabe, who would naturally address Priam by name.

This statement touches on the issue of the master-slave relationship and warns against allowing a slave to transcend the limits of his class. Stylistically speaking, in ll. 3–4 the slave's arrogance is emphatically juxtaposed to a group of plights, which are constructed upon a *tricolon* (οὐκ ἔστιν ... οὐδὲ ... οὐδ'...). The phrasing ὅμως δέ σοι λέγω (l. 1) recalls similar admonitions within agonistic contexts, as in *Hec.* 1232–1233: σοὶ δ' ἐγὼ λέγω, / Ἀγάμεμνον, *Ph.* 568: σοὶ μὲν τάδ' αὐδῶ. σοὶ δέ, Πολύνεικες, λέγω, *Or.* 560, 622: Μενέλαε, σοὶ δὲ τάδε λέγω.

As these lines suggest, the authority of the master over the slave defines the latter's usefulness and effectiveness and is essential for the good management of the household. Consequently, the challenge of the master's authority through the slave's arrogance bears serious implications for the administration of the *oikos*.[45] In turn, the ruling of the *oikos* affects the *polis*, as the former is a constituent part of the latter, according to Aristotle (*Pol.* 1252a.24–1253b.23). The arrogance of slaves is criticized in *Andr.* 433–434, *IA* 313, *Antiope* fr. 216 K. (cf. Collard *et al.* 2004, 324), A. *Ag.* 1039 and S. *Ant.* 478–479 (stylistically similar, though used as *hyperbole*; cf. Griffith 1999, *ad loc.*): οὐ γὰρ ἐκπέλει / φρονεῖν μέγ' ὅστις δοῦλός ἐστι τῶν πέλας.

---

44 Huys 1995, 189–190.
45 On the master-slave relationship, see Arist. *Pol.* 1255b30–40, 1277a5–11, 1278b-1279a, Pl. *Lg.* 778a; cf. Dillon 2004, 128–130; Klees 1975, 37–141; Vogt 1974, 15–23; Synodinou 1977, 61–76; Pomeroy 1989, 11–18; Du Bois 2003 196–99; Golden 2011, 135–141 and Konstan 2013, 150–151.

The evidence coming from the trial-debate in the *Alexandros*, despite its fragmentary state, showcases its rhetorical sophistication emerging from the use of rhetorical vocabulary, argumentation, forensic notions and devices in a dramatic and purposeful manner indicative of the formality of this agon. At the same time, the theme of a character's clash with the community, which permeates this trial-debate and those of the *Palamedes* and the *Trojan Women* coming from the same trilogy, bears socio-political implications. These resonances are consistent with the emphasis placed in this agon on the cardinal virtues of usefulness and prudence, which define one's conduct in the private and public spheres of action. This trial-debate may thus contribute to a more comprehensive picture of Euripides' agonistic rhetoric, contextualizing the evidence of the dramatist's extant corpus and yielding insight into the pivotal role of rhetorical discourse in shaping the Athenian self-image in the late fifth century BCE.

Bibliography

Adkins, A.W.H. (1960), *Merit and Responsibility: A Study in Greek Values*, Oxford.
Adkins, A.W.H. (1972), *Moral Values and Political Behaviour in Ancient Greece*, London.
Belardinelli, A.M. (ed.) (1994), *Menandro, Sicioni*, Bari.
Allan, W. (ed.) (2001), *Euripides, Children of Heracles*, Warminster.
Bers, V. (1994), 'Tragedy and Rhetoric', in: I. Worthington (ed.), *Persuasion: Greek Rhetoric in Action*, London/New York, 176–195.
Bryant, J.M. (1996), *Moral Codes and Social Structure in Ancient Greece*, New York.
Buxton, R.G.A. (1982), *Persuasion in Greek Tragedy: A Study of Peitho*, Cambridge.
Carey, C. (ed.) (1989), *Lysias, Selected Speeches*, Cambridge.
Carey, C. (1994), 'Rhetorical Means of Persuasion', in: I. Worthington (ed.), *Persuasion: Greek Rhetoric in Action*, London/New York, 26–45.
Coles, R.A. (1974), *A New Oxyrhynchus Papyrus: The Hypothesis to Euripides' Alexandros*, BICS Supp. 32, London.
Collard, C. (1975), 'Formal Debates in Euripides' Drama', in: *G&R* 22, 58–71.
Collard, C. (ed.) (1991), *Euripides, Hecuba*, Warminster.
Collard, C./Cropp, M.J./Gibert, J. (eds.) (2004), *Euripides, Selected Fragmentary Plays*, II, Oxford.
Collard, C./Cropp, M.J. (eds.) (2008), *Euripides, Fragments*, I–II, Cambridge MA/London.
Conacher, D.J. (1998), *Euripides and the Sophists*, London.
Cope, E.M. (1867), *An Introduction to Aristotle's Rhetoric*, London.
Csapo, E./Slater, W.J. (1994), *The Context of Ancient Drama*, Ann Arbor.
Devine, A.M./Stephens, L.D. (2000), *Discontinuous Syntax: Hyperbaton in Greek*, Oxford.
Di Benedetto, V. (1971), *Euripide, Teatro e Società*, Torino.
Diggle, J. (ed.) (1970), *Euripides, Phaethon*, Cambridge.
Diggle, J. (1997), 'Notes on Fragments of Euripides', in: *CQ* 47, 98–108.
Di Giuseppe, L. (ed.) (2012), *Euripide, Alessandro*, Lecce.

Dik, H. (2007), *Word Order in Greek Tragic Dialogue*, Oxford.
Dillon, J.M. (2004), *Morality and Custom in Ancient Greece*, Edinburgh.
Dodds, E.R. (ed.) (1960²), *Euripides, Bacchae*, Oxford.
Dover, K.J. (ed.) (1993), *Aristophanes, Frogs*, Oxford.
Dover, K.J. (1994²), *Greek Popular Morality in the Time of Plato and Aristotle*, Indianapolis/Cambridge.
Dubischar, M. (2001), *Die Agonszenen bei Euripides*, Stuttgart/Weimar.
Du Bois, P. (2003), *Slaves and Other Objects*, Chicago/London.
Duchemin, J. (1968²), *L'Agon dans la tragédie grecque*, Paris.
Falcetto, R. (2002), *Il Palamede di Euripide*, Alessandria.
Finley, M.I. (1967), *Three Essays on Thucydides*, Cambridge MA.
Fisher, N. (ed.) (2001), *Aeschines, Against Timarchos*, Oxford.
Fisher, N./Van Wees, H. (2011), *Competition in the Ancient World*, Swansea.
Fouchard, A. (1997), *Aristocratie et Démocratie*, Paris.
Froleyks, W.J. (1973), *Der Agon Logon in der antiken Literatur*, Bonn.
Gill, C. (1995), *Greek Thought*, Oxford.
Goebel, G.H. (1983), *Early Greek Rhetorical Theory and Practice: Proof and Arrangement in the Speeches of Antiphon and Euripides*, PhD Diss., University of Wisconsin, Madison.
Goff, B. (1990), *The Noose of Words: Readings of Desire, Violence and Language in Euripides' Hippolytos*, Cambridge.
Golden, M. (2011), 'Slavery and the Greek Family', in: K. Bradley/P. Cartledge (eds.), *The Cambridge World History of Slavery*, I: *The Ancient Mediterranean World*, Cambridge, 134–152.
Goldhill, S. (1986), *Reading Greek Tragedy*, Cambridge.
Graf, G. (1950), *Die Agonszenen bei Euripides*, PhD Diss., University of Göttingen.
Griffith, M. (ed.) (1999), *Sophocles, Antigone*, Cambridge.
Guthrie, W.K.C. (1962–1981), *A History of Greek Philosophy*, I–VI, Cambridge.
Hall, E. (1995), 'Lawcourt Dramas: The Power of Performance in Greek Forensic Oratory', in: *BICS* 40, 39–58.
Hamilton, R. (1978), 'Announced Entrances in Greek Tragedy', in: *HSCP* 82, 63–82.
Harder, M.A. (1985), *Euripides' Kresphontes and Archelaos*, Leiden.
Hawhee, D. (2004), *Bodily Arts: Rhetoric and Athletics in Ancient Greece*, Austin.
Hornblower, S. (1987), *Thucydides*, London.
Hourmouziades, N. (1965), *Production and Imagination in Euripides*, Athens.
Hunter, R.L. (2009), *Critical Moments in Classical Literature*, Cambridge.
Huys, M. (1986), 'The Plotting Scene in Euripides' *Alexandros*', in: *ZPE* 62, 9–36.
Huys, M. (1995) 'Euripides' *Alexandros* fr. 48 N.²', in: *AC* 64, 187–90.
Jacob, D.I. (1976), 'Δύο αποσπάσματα του 'Αλεξάνδρου του Ευριπίδη και η χρήση του ρήματος ΗΚΩ', in: *Hellenica* 29, 340–343.
Jouan, F. (1984), 'Euripide et la Rhétorique', in: *LEC* 52, 3–13.
Jouan, F./van Looy, H. (eds.) (1998), *Euripide, Les Fragments*, I, Paris.
Kambitsis, J. (ed.) (1972), *L'Antiope d' Euripide*, Athènes.
Kannicht, R. (ed.) (2004), *Tragicorum Graecorum Fragmenta (TrGF)*. V 1–2, *Euripides*, Göttingen.
Karamanou, I. (2003), 'The Myth of Alope in Greek Tragedy', in: *AC* 72, 25–40.
Karamanou, I. (ed.) (2006), *Euripides, Danae and Dictys*, Leipzig/Munich.
Karamanou, I. (2011), 'The Hektor-Deiphobos Agon in Euripides' *Alexandros* (frr. 62a-b K.: P. Stras. 2342, 2 and 2343)', in: *ZPE* 178, 35–47.

Karamanou, I. (2017), *Euripides: Alexandros*, Berlin/Boston.
Kerferd, G.B. (1981), *The Sophistic Movement*, Cambridge.
Klees, H. (1975), *Herren und Sklaven*, Wiesbaden.
Konstan, D. (2013), 'Menander's Slaves: The Banality of Violence', in: B. Akrigg/R. Tordoff (eds.), *Slaves and Slavery in Ancient Greek Comic Drama*, Cambridge, 144–158.
Lausberg, H. (1998), *Handbook of Literary Rhetoric*, transl. M.T. Bliss/A. Jansen/D.E. Orton, Leiden.
Lee, K.H. (ed.) (1976), *Euripides, Troades*, London.
Lefke, C. (1936), *De Euripidis Alexandro*, PhD Diss., University of Münster.
Lloyd, M. (1992), *The Agon in Euripides*, Oxford.
Loomis, W.T. (2003), 'Slander at Athens: A Common Law Perspective', in: G.W. Bakewell/J.P. Sickinger (eds.), *Gestures: Essays in Ancient History, Literature and Philosophy presented to A.L. Boegehold*, Oxford, 287–300.
MacDowell, D.M. (1978), *The Law in Classical Athens*, London.
Mannsperger, B. (1971), 'Die Rhesis', in: W. Jens (ed.), *Die Bauformen der griechischen Tragödie*, Munich, 143–181.
Mastronarde, D.J. (1986), 'The Optimistic Rationalist in Euripides: Theseus, Jocasta, Teiresias', in M.J. Cropp/E. Fantham/S.E. Scully (eds.), *Greek Tragedy and its Legacy: Essays presented to D.J. Conacher*, Calgary, 201–211.
Mastronarde, D.J. (ed.) (1994), *Euripides, Phoenissae*, Cambridge.
Mastronarde, D.J. (ed.) (2002), *Euripides, Medea*, Cambridge.
Mastronarde, D.J. (2010), *The Art of Euripides: Dramatic Technique and Social Context*, Cambridge.
Michelini, A.M. (1987), *Euripides and the Tragic Tradition*, Madison/London.
Montiglio, S. (2000), *Silence in the Land of Logos*, New Jersey.
Murray, G. (1946), 'Euripides' Tragedies of 415 BCE: The Deceitfulness of Life', in: *Greek Studies*, Oxford, 127–148.
North, H.F. (1966), 'Canons and Hierarchies of the Cardinal Virtues in Greek and Latin Literature', in: L. Wallach (ed.), *The Classical Tradition. Literary and Historical Studies in Honour of H. Caplan*, Ithaca, 165–186.
Ober, J. (1998), *Political Dissent in Democratic Athens: Intellectual Critics of Popular Rule*, New Jersey.
Padel, R. (1992), *In and Out of the Mind: Greek Images of the Tragic Self*, Princeton.
Parker, L.P.E. (ed.) (2007), *Euripides, Alcestis*, Oxford.
Parry, A. (1981), *Logos and Ergon in Thucydides*, New York.
Pelling, C. (2005), 'Tragedy, Rhetoric and Performance Culture', in: J. Gregory (ed.), *A Companion to Greek Tragedy*, Malden/Oxford, 83–102.
Pendrick, G.J. (ed.) (2002), *Antiphon the Sophist, The Fragments*, Cambridge.
Pomeroy, S.B. (1989), 'Slavery in the Light of Xenophon's *Oeconomicus*', in: *Index* 17, 11–18.
Poulakos, J. (1995), *Sophistical Rhetoric in Classical Greece*, Columbia.
Price, J. (2001), *Thucydides and Internal War*, Cambridge.
Quijada Sagredo, M./Encinas Reguero, M.C. (eds.) (2013), *Retórica y discurso en el teatro griego*, Madrid.
Quijada Sagredo, M./Encinas Reguero, M.C. (eds.) (2017), *Connecting Rhetoric and Attic Drama*, Bari.
Rademaker, A. (2005), *Sophrosyne and the Rhetoric of Self-Restraint*, Leiden.

Roisman, H.M. (1999), *Nothing is as it seems: The Tragedy of the Implicit in Euripides' Hippolytus*, Lanham.
Rosenbloom, D. (2004) '*Ponēroi* vs *Chrēstoi*: The Ostracism of Hyperbolos and the Struggle for Hegemony in Athens after the Death of Perikles', in: *TAPhA* 134, 55–105 (Part I) and 323–58 (Part II).
Rosenbloom, D. (2009), 'Staging Rhetoric in Classical Athens', in: E. Gunderson (ed.), *The Cambridge Companion to Ancient Rhetoric*, Cambridge, 194–211.
Sansone, D. (2012), *Greek Drama and the Invention of Rhetoric*, Malden/Oxford.
Schlesinger, A.C. (1937), 'Two Notes on Euripides', in: *CPh* 32, 67–70.
Scodel, R. (1980), *The Trojan Trilogy of Euripides*, Göttingen.
Scodel, R. (1999–2000), 'Verbal Performance and Euripidean Rhetoric', in: M.J. Cropp/K.H. Lee/D. Sansone (eds.), *Euripides and the Tragic Theatre in the Late Fifth Century*, Urbana, 129–144.
Slings, S.R. (1997), 'Figures of Speech and their Lookalikes: Two Further Exercises in the Pragmatics of the Greek Sentence', in: E.J. Bakker (ed.), *Grammar as Interpretation: Greek Literature in its Linguistic Contexts*, Leiden, 169–214.
Snell, B. (1937), *Euripides Alexandros und andere Strassburger Papyri mit Fragmenten Griechischer Dichter*, Berlin.
Snell, B. (1977), 'Φρένες-Φρόνησις', in: *Glotta* 55, 34–64.
Storey, I.C. (2003), *Eupolis: Poet of Old Comedy*, Oxford.
Strohm, H. (1957), *Euripides: Interpretationen zur dramatischen Form*, Munich.
Sullivan, S.D. (2000), *Euripides' Use of Psychological Terminology*, Montreal/Kingston/London/Ithaca.
Synodinou, K. (1977), *On the Concept of Slavery in Euripides*, Ioannina.
Too, Y.L. (1995), *The Rhetoric of Identity in Isocrates: Text, Power, Pedagogy*, Cambridge.
Usher, S. (2008), *Cicero's Speeches: The Critic in Action*, Oxford.
Vogt, J. (1974), *Ancient Slavery and the Ideal of Man*, Oxford.
Wallace, R.W. (1994), 'The Athenian Laws against Slander', in: G. Thür (ed.), *Symposion 1993*, Cologne, 109–124.
Webster, T.B.L. (1957), 'Some Psychological Terms in Greek Tragedy', in: *JHS* 77, 149–154.
Webster, T.B.L. (ed.) (1967), *The Tragedies of Euripides*, London.
West, M.L. (1973), *Textual Criticism and Editorial Technique*, Stuttgart.
Wilkins, J. (ed.) (1993), *Euripides, Heraclidae*, Oxford.
Winnington-Ingram, R.P. (1969), 'Euripides *poētēs sophos*', in: *Arethusa* 2, 127–142 (also included in: J. Mossman [ed.], *Oxford Readings in Classical Studies: Euripides*, Oxford 2003, 47–63).
Yoon, F. (2012), *The Use of Anonymous Characters in Greek Tragedy: The Shaping of Heroes*, Leiden.

Marcel Lysgaard Lech
Praise, Past and Ponytails
The Funeral Oration and Democratic Ideology in the Parabasis of Aristophanes' *Knights*

Hippês or *Knights* was staged in 424 BCE. As the title suggests, Aristophanes has for his chorus chosen the aristocracy, metonymically represented by the cavalry that in the comic (and to some extend elsewhere too) world represented a luxurious lifestyle and a cowardly manner of fighting.[1] Nonetheless, the Athenians were, of course, not always loathing their cavalry; in fact the *polis* spend a vast amount of recourses on the corps,[2] which did play a minor part in the defence of Attica and retaliation raids on the Peloponnese during the first decade of the hippic force's reformation. Not to mention, that 'the cavalry had a greater role in festal processions than other parts of the army'[3] and could be seen gallantly parading on the Parthenon Frieze.[4] Thus this chorus could be displaying its processional character rather than its military qualities, since there is not the slightest mention of any arms of any sort to be found in the text.[5]

The chorus of *Knights* has never received much attention except for the possible historical dispute between the cavalrymen of Athens and Cleon alluded to throughout the play and elsewhere.[6] The ancestry of Cleon is basically unknown

---

[1] For discussion and sources, Spence 1993, 180–216, esp. 191–210; it may perhaps have been the case as Spence argues 'that the climate of opinion was generally favourable to the cavalry' (212). I nonetheless argue that the cavalry is the object of satire in this play. As a synthesis of Spence's and my own argument, it could be argued that the cavalry is made fun of *because* of their growing popularity. See Pritchard 2013, 134–136 for a splendid discussion of the Athenian view on the cavalry's usefulness and vices. Nonetheless, a playwright of Old Attic comedy would of course focus on the vices of his artistic creations.
[2] See Pritchard 2015. Spence 2012, 123 sees the thought of the cavalry as an expensive luxury as one of the main barriers for the Athenians to have their own cavalry; perhaps we should turn the argument around and say the because of this luxury the Athenians reformed their cavalry force, to show their opponents that they had the power and money to do so.
[3] Spence 1993, 187.
[4] See Stevenson 2003.
[5] The weapons of other choruses are clearly displayed and used (e.g. *Ach*. 184, 236, 295, 341–346; *Vesp*. 225–226, 420, 1062, 1075; *Av*. 348, 364).
[6] e.g. Bugh 1988, 112–114; Henderson 2013.

but the picture we get of his family is clearly that is was well off.[7] Aristophanes thus creates an opposition between two groups of rich: the cavalrymen and the nouveau riche democratic leaders. Whether or not Cleon was the guiding hand behind the taxations in the middle of the Archidamian war,[8] it looks, at least, as if he was held responsible for them by Aristophanes (e.g. 248, 305), and that is of course (in a comic universe) a completely legitimate reason for hating him (226, 400, 510).[9] In *Knights*, taxation of the rich and of the empire is one of the political focal points connected with the character 'Paphlagon' (likewise in *Wasps* 923–926), the other being Cleon's unexpected success at Pylos. Both were apparently popular with the *demos*, but very likely quite disturbing for the more well off; being victims of Cleon's taxation, the rich may have hoped that his adventure at Pylos failed; however, when he returned, his power over the *demos* had grown, and so had the likelihood that he would continue the war and the taxations for supporting it (792–809).[10] In this paper I argue that the chorus in *Knights* uses the discourse of the democratic funeral orations wishing to inscribe their corps into the eternal glory of Athens in order to outdo the surprising glory of the capture of Pylos by Cleon. Aristophanes seems to show that neither the aristocrats of the cavalry nor the demagogue, Cleon, may hold such glory for themselves: the glory is that of democratic Athens, not particular groups or individuals.[11]

εὐλογῆσαι βουλόμεσθα τοὺς πατέρας ἡμῶν, ὅτι
ἄνδρες ἦσαν τῆσδε τῆς γῆς ἄξιοι καὶ τοῦ πέπλου,
οἵτινες πεζαῖς μάχαισιν ἔν τε ναυφάρκτῳ στρατῷ
πανταχοῦ νικῶντες ἀεὶ τήνδ' ἐκόσμησαν πόλιν·
οὐ γὰρ οὐδεὶς πώποτ' αὐτῶν τοὺς ἐναντίους ἰδὼν
ἠρίθμησεν, ἀλλ' ὁ θυμὸς εὐθὺς ἦν ἀμυνίας·
εἰ δέ που πέσοιεν εἰς τὸν ὦμον ἐν μάχῃ τινί,
τοῦτ' ἀπεψήσαντ' ἄν, εἶτ' ἠρνοῦντο μὴ πεπτωκέναι,
ἀλλὰ διεπάλαιον αὖθις. Καὶ στρατηγὸς οὐδ' ἂν εἷς

---

[7] Davies 1971, 318–320 n. 8674. MacDowell 995, 81 is too suspicious of his wealth; Cleon as rich, cf. Connor 1971, 151–2; If Ober 1989, 75 is right in arguing that 'those who ended up being ostracized were members of the elites'. *Knights* 855 implies that Cleon at least could be seen as elite.
[8] Kagan 1974, 145. On the economy of Athens during the Peloponnesian War, Pritchard 2015.
[9] Henderson 2013 discusses Aristophanes' motivations for using the cavalry as Cleon's adversary.
[10] On the costing of the war and the taxation, see Pritchard 2015.
[11] Of course, victories could be *connected* with the strategos, e.g. Cleon here in *Knights*, and celebrated (Hölscher 2003), and Cimon's stone herms (though his name was not on the herms), but it does not seem likely that the different military units were singled out, thus the chorus righteously (*pace* Henderson 2013, 292) feel bamboozled by the Paphlagon in 267–268. Regardless of military or civic status, all casualties in war were buried according to phyle in *demosia semata*, see Low 2010.

τῶν πρὸ τοῦ σίτησιν ᾔτησ' ἐρόμενος Κλεαίνετον·
νῦν δ' ἐὰν μὴ προεδρίαν φέρωσι καὶ τὰ σιτία,
οὐ μαχεῖσθαί φασιν. ἡμεῖς δ' ἀξιοῦμεν τῇ πόλει
προῖκα γενναίως ἀμύνειν καὶ θεοῖς ἐγχωρίοις.
καὶ πρὸς οὐκ αἰτοῦμεν οὐδὲν πλὴν τοσουτονὶ μόνον·
ἤν ποτ' εἰρήνη γένηται καὶ πόνων παυσώμεθα,
μὴ φθονεῖθ' ἡμῖν κομῶσι μηδ' ἀνεστλεγγισμένοις.[12]

We want to praise our fathers for being
men worthy of this land and the Robe,
who in infantry battles and naval expeditions
were always victorious everywhere and adorned our city.
For not one of them ever reckoned the enemy's numbers,
but as soon as he saw them his spirit was defiant (or of Amynias).
If in any battle they happened to fall on their shoulder,
they would slap off the dirt, deny they'd fallen,
and get back into the match. And not a single general
of yore would have applied to Cleaenetus for state subsidy;
whereas now, if they don't get front-row seats and free meals,
they refuse to fight! But we want only to fight
nobily and for free for the city and for its native gods.
We ask of nothing more, except for only this little thing:
if peace ever comes and our toils are ended,
don't begrudge us our long hair and us wearing headbands.

(565–580, transl. J. Henderson with minor adjustments)

The epirrhematic syzygy of the *parabasis* consists of two odes and two *epirrhemes* intertwined and thematically connected. The gods Poseidon and Athena are called upon in hymnic fashion, but the *epirrhemes* leave the gods aside, and turn to praise of the inhabitants of Athens – just as Olympians are not mentioned in funeral orations.[13] However, just as the praise of the former generations of comedians in the *parabasis* proper was ironic and only worked as a vehicle of buttressing the playwright's own excellence and denigration of Cratinus, this choral praise is equally ambiguous.[14]

---

12 The headbands is based on an emendation made by Van Leuween, and defended by both Sommerstein and Wilson. Cf. Imperio 2004, 243. The meaning of *stlengides* is disputed, but van Leeuwen's emendation is preferable because the whole verse would then refer to the appearance of the chorus, instead of referring to bathing which was not a privilege of the aristocracy. In *Clouds* (991), the traditional education despises baths, but the discussion at 1044–1054 implies that bathing was not something unusual.
13 Pl. *Men.* 283b; Dem. 60.30. Parker 1983, 64–65.
14 See Biles 2001, 2002 and 2010; Ruffell 2002; Bakola 2008; Teló 2014.

Since the cavalry in the contemporary Athenian discourse in martial matters was defined negatively against the fleet and the democracy[15] (though no doubt exaggeratedly by Aristophanes), there seems to be a discrepancy between the horsemen's belief in their own value and Athenian history in this play.[16] The navy and the hoplites are still the real defenders of Athens.[17] The strong hoplite ethos was during these years under pressure from the growing self-confidence of the navy (e.g. 1184–1188).[18] The cavalry, however, was consistently considered an unmanly and relatively secure way of fighting.[19] The cavalry will surely have been acting as support troops,[20] on more occasions than Thucydides cares to mention, and the presence of the cavalry at Athens in these years must have been a fact of everyday life, as it was used to harass intruders on attic soil,[21] but this does not buttress the omnipresence evoked by the chorus of cavalrymen: Solygeia was *de facto* the only major success to date where the cavalry had played an important part. This success, however, was only possible because the Corinthians had no cavalry at all (Thuc. 4.44, see discussion of this battle below):

> χρόνον μὲν οὖν πολὺν ἀντεῖχον οὐκ ἐνδιδόντες ἀλλήλοις· ἔπειτα (ἦσαν γὰρ τοῖς Ἀθηναίοις οἱ ἱππῆς ὠφέλιμοι ξυμμαχόμενοι, τῶν ἑτέρων οὐκ ἐχόντων ἵππους) ἐτράποντο οἱ Κορίνθιοι.

> So for a long while they both stood firm and did not yield to one another. Then, since the Athenians had the advantage of cavalrymen supporting, *while the others had no horses*, the Corinthians were routed.

---

15 e.g. Ar. *Eq.* 1369–1372; Lys. 14.7, 11–12, 14–15; 16.13. See Blanshard 2012, 215–218.
16 Pritchard 2013, 136 concludes: 'Cavalry service, then, serves as a clear point of comparison to the democracy's treatment of athletics. Both were publicly subsidised by the democracy and favourably assessed in its popular culture. But of these two activities only cavalry service attracted regular and substantive criticism in the democracy's public discourse'.
17 See Pritchard (forthcoming).
18 For a thorough discussion of the hoplite ethos and the cavalry in this period, see Spence 1993, 164–216 and 2012, 118, 123; Crowley 2012. For a discussion of the evolving of a more democratic mode of courage, see Ballot 2012. However, during the Archidamian war, Aristophanes seems to buttress the hoplite ethos, (e.g. *Ach.* 696–697; *Eq.* 781, 1334; *Nub.* 985–986; *Vesp.* 711). The high-status cavalry thus suffered from the same prejudice as the low-status light infantry, see Trundle 2012, 141–142.
19 See Blanshard 2012.
20 Spence 1993, 140–151.
21 Spence 1993, 127–133, see below.

Thus, while *Knights* at first seems to celebrate the cavalrymen of Athens,[22] the comic chorus continuously deconstructs the portrait, which they as 'the cavalry' paint of themselves. In the end of the *parabasis* proper, after an extensive use of nautical metaphorical expression (541–544), the coryphaeus exclaims:

       Τούτων οὖν οὕνεκα πάντων,
ὅτι σωφρονικῶς οὐκ ἀνοήτως εἰσπηδήσας ἐφλυάρει,   445
αἴρεσθ' αὐτῷ πολὺ τὸ ῥόθιον, παραπέμψατ' ἐφ' ἕνδεκα κώπαις,
θόρυβον χρηστὸν ληναΐτην,
ἵν' ὁ ποιητὴς ἀπίῃ χαίρων
κατὰ νοῦν πράξας,
φαιδρὸς λάμποντι μετώπῳ.   450

    So for all these reasons,
that he acted discreetly, and didn't leap mindlessly in and spout rubbish,
raise a big wave of applause for him, and give him an eleven-oar cheer
worthy of the Lenaea,
so that our poet may go away
happy and successful,
gleaming to the top of his shinning head!

                                               (transl. J. Henderson)

If the poet of the play will leave the theatre gloriously 'gleaming to the top of his shinning head' – apparently alluding to the real Aristophanes' baldness – this baldness sets the poet apart from the aristocratic, longhaired (580, 1121) cavalrymen, just as the extensive use of nautical imagery expressions of the navy must have done. The Coryphaius then orders the audience to join the chorus in celebrating Aristophanes' anticipated victory at this competition as a great achievement by alluding to Phormio and his eleven ships, who by their supreme skill vanquished the enemy at the battle of Naupactus,[23] alluded to through an Aeschylean echo from no other play than the *Persians*.[24] Aristophanes thus makes his own claim of poetic superiority harmonize with the self-proclaimed ideological superiority of the Athenian navy. By contrast the cavalry will in this syzygy, in

---

[22] This is basically the consensus, see e.g. Spence 1993, 211–212. There is (*pace* Slater 2002, 72) no reason at all to believe that Aristophanes had to 'tread carefully in his representation of them', since he obviously does not do so towards Cleon, even when at his highest of political power.
[23] As argued in Lech 2009.
[24] Aeschylus, *Persians* 951–952: Ἰάων ναύφαρκτος Ἄρης; 1028: ναύφρακτον ... ὅμιλον.

wordings reminiscent of the democratic public praise at the annual funeral oration – though the horsemen are of course still very much alive[25] – proclaim their own superiority be trying to harmonize their merits with that of the rest of army, the hoplites and the navy, through a widely fantastic historical narrative.

In Old Attic Comedy, the wish to praise anyone is unusual (εὐλογῆσαι βουλόμεσθα):[26] Praising someone is usually confined to the *parabasis* proper and there directed at the playwright himself (e.g. *Ach.* 633; *Pax* 738), just as the preceding anapaests of the *parabasis* show (509–510). Nonetheless, the general theme of this *parabasis* is praise and merit, though nothing has hitherto in the play been praiseworthy in the actions of the Sausage-Seller or the Paphlagon, and the question of the *parabasis* is thus whether there is anything praiseworthy in the history of the cavalry.

The fact that the cavalry of one thousand upper class citizens (225) was a rather new invention in Athens is not mentioned,[27] and that blurs the epirrhema's distinction between the aristocratic praise[28] and the democratic public praise of the annual funeral oration.[29] The passage carefully echoes such speeches[30] without denigrating Athenian history[31] – Aristophanes is balancing on a knife's edge here. We can detect the following topoi:

1) eulogy, *epainos* (e.g. Dem. 60.1-3, 10–13, 15, 33; Lys. 2.1; Thuc. 2.35.2, 36.2)
2) merit, *axiotes* or *arete* (e.g. Dem. 60.9, 30–31, 34; Lys. 2.6, 61, 80; Thuc. 2.36.2)
3) historical narrative (e.g. Lys. 2.3–66; Pl. Men. 239a-246b; Dem. 60.6–11.)
4) fathers, *progonoi* (e.g. Dem. 60.4-7, 12; Lys. 2.6, 17, 20, 23, 26, 32, 62, 69; Thuc. 2.36.1)
5) defence, *amynia* (e.g. Dem. 60.7, 31; Thuc. 2.36.4; Pl. *Men.* 241b, 244b)
6) never afraid of the numbers of enemies (e.g. Lys. 2.23, 50, 63; Pl. *Men.* 241b-c)
7) envy, *phtonos* (e.g. Thuc. 2.35; Lys. 2.80; Dem. 60.23)

---

25 On praising the dead, see Hunt 2010, 241.
26 On praise in Aristophanes, see Harriot 1986, 46–67, esp. 58–67. Contrast *Ach.* 676–677; *Nub.* 575–576; *Vesp.* 1016.
27 For the history of the cavalry, see Spence 2010, 113–123.
28 Through symposiac or epinician echoes, e.g 276–277, see Pütz 2007, 103–111 on symposiac language in *Knights*.
29 On this institution, see Loraux 2006; Low 2010; Pritchard 2010, 33–46.
30 781–785 actually refer directly to funeral orations, and it is noteworthy that both Marathon and Salamis are mentioned.
31 On the historical narrative of the funeral orations and 'historical' accuracy, see Thomas 1989, 196–237.

Beginning emphatically with praise, the chorus mentions 'our fathers' (τοὺς πατέρας ἡμῶν) and while this clearly echoes the timelessness of 'we' and 'our' in the public funeral orations,³² the pronoun ἡμῶν does not denote 'all Athenians', but correlates to the implicit subject of the verb (βουλόμεσθα):³³ our fathers are thus the former aristocrats, the 'eternal' cavalry.

The chorus continues by a spatial and thematically implication, ἄνδρες ἦσαν τῆσδε τῆς γῆς ἄξιοι καὶ τοῦ πέπλου, in which the *peplos* works as a metonymy for the Panathenaic festival and, by implication, for Athenian cultural extravagance. The presentation of the new *peplos* to the goddess was one of the major events of the great Panathenaic festival and the *peplos* was embellished with a depiction of Athena's victory in the Gigantomachy, possibly in connection with Nike (as on the eastern metope nr. 4 of the Parthenon).³⁴ Thus, the *peplos* had become a historical, ideological and spatial marker that frames this verse democratically in opposition to the fundamental aristocratic frame of the choral voice: the eulogy moves from 'we' the aristocrats to 'we' the Athenians, as in Pericles' oration, with an ideological clash erupting.³⁵

This conceptual discontinuity (or script opposition in modern humour theory)³⁶ becomes clear as the chorus continues their praise of their fathers (topos 4) (οἵτινες still syntactically correlates with τοὺς πατέρας) and alludes to Marathon and Salamis (πεζαῖς μάχαισιν ἔν τε ναυφάρκτῳ στρατῷ πανταχοῦ νικῶντες) – battles in which the Athenian cavalry played no part – in language of a higher register (see above, contrast with *Vesp.* 684–685). Marathon and Salamis were victories of the hoplite army and the navy, and by having the cavalry praising these battles, the chorus humorously undermines its own merit.

Furthermore, the spatial (πανταχοῦ) and temporal (ἀεί) deictics (both exaggerated) in connection with the poetic metaphor ἐκόσμησαν generates a mythical textual world saturated with Athenian ideology.³⁷ The phrase is ideological

---

32 Loraux 2006, 184–187.
33 *Pace* Edmunds 1987, 40ff. and thus opposed to Pericles' 'we', see Louraux 2006, 177.
34 On the imagery of the *peplos*, see Mansfield 1985; Shear 2001, 173–186.
35 I find it significant that the cavalrymen are not shown as fighting in any of the sculptures of the Parthenon, whereas unnamed hoplites are seen just below the western pediment which depicts Athena and Poseidon quarrelling over who is to be the city's patron divinity. Thus, when democratic Athens had depicted its ideology so forcefully on the Acropolis, it was easy for Aristophanes to play with the imagery. See also Blanshard 2012, 208.
36 For modern humour theory and its use in Aristophanic studies, see Robson 2006; Ruffell 2011, 54–111, on *Knights* in particular, see 65–77, 179–213.
37 An allusion to Pericles' funeral speech in Thuc. 2.41 (πανταχοῦ δὲ μνημεῖα κακῶν τε κἀγαθῶν ἀίδια) seems obvious, also at 2.42: αἱ τῶνδε καὶ τῶν τοιῶνδε ἀρεταὶ ἐκόσμησαν. See also *Frogs*

charged not only through their above-mentioned use, but also because of Cimon's famous three herms at the agora all inscribed with epigrams connecting his victory at Eion in Thrace in 479 (in the cleansing out of the Persians after their final defeat) with the only Athenian hero of the Homeric epics, Menestheus.

Plutarch has preserved the epigrams of which the two shorter, each a pair of elegiac couplets, employ epic language to describe the ordeals of the men who fought at Eion and the example they have set for the future.[38] The second epigram speaks of the εὐεργεσίης καὶ μεγάλων ἀγαθῶν of the Athenian commanders on a par with the spirit found in the funeral orations, but it also reveals the importance of the reward (ἡγεμόνεσσι δὲ μισθὸν Ἀθηναῖοι τάδ (viz. the stone herms) ἔδωκαν), which is one of the focal points of *Knights*.[39] The third epigram emphasizes the link between Cimon and Menestheus:

> ἔκ ποτε τῆσδε πόληος ἅμ' Ἀτρείδῃσι Μενεσθεὺς
> ἡγεῖτο ζάθεον Τρωικὸν ἐς πεδίον·
> ὅν ποθ' Ὅμηρος ἔφη Δαναῶν πύκα θωρηκτάων
> κοσμητῆρα μάχης ἔξοχον ὄντα μολεῖν.
> οὕτως οὐδὲν ἀεικὲς Ἀθηναίοισι καλεῖσθαι
> κοσμηταῖς πολέμου τ' ἀμφὶ καὶ ἠνορέης.

> Once from this city Menestheus, with the Sons of Atreus,
> led his men to the divine plain of Troy;
> Menestheus, whom Homer said was an outstanding kosmeter of battle
> among the well-armored Achaeans who came to Troy.
> Thus there is nothing unseemly for the Athenians about being called
> kosmetai, both of war and of manly strenght.

Consequently, the use of κοσμεῖν here, I argue, leads to a mythico-ideological frame where Menestheus[40] plays a decisive role, not as a marshal of hippic attacks (cf. H. *Il.* 2.554), but as an Athenian soldier and sailor. There is no allusion to any equine activity in our passage, and the focus is entirely on the bravery of the 'real'

1026–1027 (Aeschylus speaking): Εἶτα διδάξας Πέρσας μετὰ τοῦτ' ἐπιθυμεῖν ἐξεδίδαξα νικᾶν ἀεὶ τοὺς ἀντιπάλους, κοσμήσας ἔργον ἄριστον; Melanthius fr. 1D.
38 Plut. *Cim.* 7.4–6.
39 e.g. 1066, 1367.
40 See entry Menestheus in *LIMC*; No archaeological evidence for a cult of Menestheus has yet been unearthed, but Pausanias (1.1.2) saw a sanctified spot at the harbour of Phaleron, from whence Menestheus left for Troy, and Theseus left for Crete. This seems to buttress a naval relevance for the both of them.

army of Athens. The Athenian conceptualisation of war hardly includes hippic warfare, and not even a recent success could change that.⁴¹

Echoing topos (6), the ambiguity of how to interpret 'of them' in the phrase οὐδεὶς πώποτ' αὐτῶν anticipates the coming punch line (see below). The continuous use of unspecific temporal deictics makes local and historical specificity impossible and strengthens the idea of timelessness (see above). This timelessness is also felt in the semantics of the imperfect 'ἦν' denoting repeated actions: the θυμός (spirit, an elevated word, perhaps mirroring the prosaic equivalent, ἀρετή⁴² and/or ψυχή) was always of defiance (on *Amynías*, see below). However, there seem to be a crux of meaning here. If they really grew bold every time they saw the enemy, who is 'they' then? The reference can only be to the Athenian army in general, but the οὐδεὶς αὐτῶν correlates with οἵτινες (none of those), which clearly correlates to the chorus' fathers. And though the chorus depicts their fathers as Athenian soldiers in general, the exclusion of hippic activities generates a conceptual discord; the cavalry were *not* Athenian soldiers in general. However, the punch line of the paragraph is a pun playing on both meanings; the 'real' army and the hippic force. The pun lies in the word ἀμυνία, which plays on the meaning *defence* and the name, Amynias (meaning the defender or the like).⁴³ A certain Amynias is known, not flatteringly, from other plays, and he is conspicuously associated with hippic class, selling wheels (*Nub.* 31), being effeminate and shirking his military duty (*ibid.*, 689–692), gaming (*Vesp.* 74–75), evading πόνοι and having long hair (*ibid.*, 466):⁴⁴ all these phenomena apply to the chorus in *Knights* as well. Here the joke is generated by the obvious contradiction between this man's name and his nature: there is no defiance in him, only running away, and thus Amynias becomes the opposite of the Athenian heroes alluded to in the preceding passage. Furthermore, one script speaks of the Athenian army and navy as defiant and eternally brave, but is at the same time being juxtaposed with

---

41 Of the 21 major battles including the Athenian cavalry listed in Spence 1993, 138–139, only eight were victories, and of these eight, only Solygeia during the Archidamian War. This might explain the public reluctance to accept the cavalry, in which they indeed spend a vast amount of money each year, see above.
42 See Yoshitake 2010, 363–369.
43 On this name, see Molitor 1973.
44 cf. Imperio 2004, 241 for more sources; however, she denies a reference to a person here, buttressing her point by reference to Campagner 2001, 70–71 who argues that that the word denotes athletics. However, the frame of athletics is irrelevant at the moment and ἀμυνεῖν is perfectly normal as a military term (e.g. 577; *Vesp.* 383). An athletic frame is first generated later. Amynias was clearly well known and it seems clear to me that the neologism puns on his name and his nature.

a script conveying the idea that the cavalry runs away like girl[45] every time there is some hardship to endure (579: πόνων παυσώμεθα is a nice circumscription of this theme). Furthermore, we may detect a jibe here on the Periclean tactics of which the cavalry played an important part, but the tactics were mainly defensive, just as Hermippus (fr. 47) criticized Pericles for not taking action against the invaders.[46]

Taking up the ambiguous 'they', the chorus transforms the aristocratic frame of hippic activities and generates two opposing images of which the democratic hoplite dominates. Using the war/sports-metaphor employed in their description of Crates (540), the imagined battleground becomes the *palaistra*, instantly making it an impossible locus of hippic activities: no one falls off a horse and denies it. Falling in the dust in a wrestling match and in a real battle is more likely to be relevant here. The double perspective enhances the idea of the strong valiant hoplites, while emphasizing the role of the aristocratic: fight in the *palaistra*, that is what aristocrats do after all, this is the place where they endure πόνοι (hardship).[47] Thus, the imagery used here pin-points the paradox of sport under the Athenian democracy: though athletics were mainly elite activities, the non-elite Athenians held sport in high regard.[48]

Having then introduced the idea of aristocratic athletics, the chorus finally gets to the point of the *epirrhema*: the question of merit, repeating the '*axios*' and thus creating a sort of ring composition from their fathers worth to their own. Who will receive the honour of dinner at the Prytaneion and *prohedria* in the theatre? While the old *strategoi* (such as Cimon, Pericles and Phormio) were from aristocratic families, the new stock like Cleon had non-aristocratic origins and supposedly lesser education, but nonetheless enjoyed honours, having done nothing (766, or like the Paphlagon by stealing others merits, e.g. 52–57, 741–742, 817–819). The chorus refers vaguely to the former generals and generates a picture of the past that juxtaposes the contemporary situation of 'Cleon' who engulfs the democracy, with the former generation of Cleaenetus, Cleon's father, who did not venture to harass the *strategoi*: it was the democracy that honoured those who served it well, whereas now the Athenian democracy *is* Cleon. This has clearly

---

45 Which the chorus eventually becomes, 1300–1315.
46 Notice that also Hermippus mentions Cleon as fierce. Thucydides describes the growing disquiety of the passivity in 2.20–22; 59–65.
47 For a discussion of *ponoi*, see Pritchard 2013, 176–84, though it seems that Pritchard understands 'comparable toils' of athletes and soldiers as 'identical toils', which they were obviously not; then war would be sport, and vice versa. He understates the metaphor WAR IS SPORT/SPORT IS WAR, see e.g. Pinar Sanz 2005; Charteris-Black 2004, 114–116.
48 See Pritchard 2013.

been shown by the character and acts of his dramatic counterpart, the Paphlagon (e.g. 58–60).

It is interesting that in this part of *epirrhema* the main characters, the chorus and Cleon, are being defined with reference to their fathers and referred to through them. The picture of the aristocracy of yore, however, was shattered and it is reasonable to assume that the mentioning of Cleaenetus, besides being a slab at Cleon, is parallel; if Cleaenetus is a 'nonentity',[49] what does that imply for Cleon (perhaps verses 186–187 answers this question)? There is no suggestion here that Cleaenetus had any real powers to bestow any honours on anyone, though the reference to him here can not only be explained by his being the father of Cleon: the audience would have to know him for the verse to make sense. On the other hand, he is strongly contrasted with his son, to whom the other generals allegedly must lower themselves in order not to get beaten up (e.g. 5, 60, 64–70, 355–358, 878–880). Furthermore, and even more degrading, these generals (including Cleon) deny fighting at all unless they receive honours from the state.[50] This strongly contrasts the imagery of the *palaistra*/battlefield where both aristocrats and hoplites deny the short moment of their falling and strike back, while the new stock of generals simply refuse to fight at all, and with the inscribed text of the second stone herm on the agora:

μᾶλλόν τις τάδ' ἰδὼν καὶ ἐπεσσομένων ἐθελήσει
ἀμφὶ περὶ ξυνοῖς πράγμασι δῆριν ἔχειν.

all the more will future generations be willing
for the common cause to go to war.

The opposition between words and deeds could not be contrasted more strongly.[51] So while the Paphlagon has curtailed the Demos by giving him food (46–52, 213–218, 788), the democracy is forced to feed its generals to make them take action, which creates a spiral of democratic degeneration (766: μηδὲν δράσας of the politicians and μηδὲν δρῶντι of the People in 905 sum it up).

The members of the chorus, then, returning to their now conspicuous self-praise, describe themselves as a contrast to the modern generals and their claims

---

49 Sommerstein 1981, 175 *ad* 574.
50 Neither the slaves (representing generals? On this question, see Henderson 2003; Ruffell 2011, 182, 185) nor the chorus will in fact: both groups make the Sausage-Seller do the hard work. See also *Ach.* 593–622.
51 The fact the Cleon actually did go to war is reduced to mere theft of honour, e.g. 55–56, 353–355.

for honours and echoing the beginning of the passage, they claim concern for the city. They will defend the city and they will do it for free (576–577). They are seeking the opposite of Cleon, while associating themselves with the brave *persona* of the poet (511: γενναίως πρὸς τὸν Τυφῶ χωρεῖ – 577: γενναίως ἀμύνειν).[52] However, whereas their poet attacked (χωρεῖ) the evils, they will merely defend (ἀμύνειν) themselves against them, their spirit being only suited for defence (ὁ θυμὸς εὐθὺς ἦν ἀμυνίας) – and the orders of Pericles of course.

Their proclaimed contrast to Cleon, while echoing the times where none had to beg for honour, is shattered when the chorus proceeds to beg for nothing but a change in the ways the society looks at them (almost the entire verse emphasizes this little wish). Representing the entire aristocracy, the chorus reflects as a growing disapproval among the elite of the democratic warmongering.[53] However, this needs not to be the view Aristophanes takes – *Knights* is not a peace play – for by getting peace, the chorus wishes to have their hair long and to wear their headbands (as on parade on the Parthenon Frieze) without everyone begrudging them (showing φθόνος, topos 7). This social recognition stands in clear contrast to the visual representation of the chorus: the chorus already had long hair (also in 1121) and possibly wore the headbands as well. What the chorus in fact asks for is to continue their aristocratic lifestyle without annoying interruptions of war imposed on them by the democracy and Cleon's policies in particular. Consequently, the cavalrymen would simply confirm their stereotypicality in the eyes of the comic audience and thus they come to reflect effeminacy and cowardice, themes, which Aristophanes openly exploits in the second *parabasis* (1300–1315).[54]

The effect of the final verse is a clash between points of view within the text. The subject of μὴ φθονεῖθ' is apparently the audience, but the object of the verb is clearly embedded in the fiction, the chorus in character as cavalrymen. But the proposition of the cavalrymen is so absurd (don't begrudge us) that the spectators can only deny the possibility of it; this spectator-intrusion into the fiction thus underlines the impossibility of their wish. By negating the φθόνος, the chorus simply underlines the solidity of the social barrier of democratic Athens.[55]

---

[52] Perhaps we can even detect an echo of Pericles' words in Thuc. 2.41.5: γενναίως...μαχόμενοι ἐτελεύτησαν.
[53] Boegehold 1982.
[54] See Anderson 2003.
[55] This is a question about how the chorus frames their position. Aristophanes makes them choose the negative framing which will make it quite difficult for them to break the frame of envy, see Lakoff 2004, e.g. 4.

Antepirrhema:

Ἃ ξύνισμεν τοῖσιν ἵπποις, βουλόμεσθ' ἐπαινέσαι.
ἄξιοι δ' εἴσ' εὐλογεῖσθαι· πολλὰ γὰρ δὴ πράγματα
ξυνδιήνεγκαν μεθ' ἡμῶν, εἰσβολάς τε καὶ μάχας.
ἀλλὰ τἀν τῇ γῇ μὲν αὐτῶν οὐκ ἄγαν θαυμάζομεν,
ὡς <δ'> ὅτ' εἰς τὰς ἱππαγωγοὺς εἰσεπήδων ἀνδρικῶς,
πριάμενοι κώθωνας, οἱ δὲ καὶ σκόροδα καὶ κρόμμυα,
εἶτα τὰς κώπας λαβόντες ὥσπερ ἡμεῖς οἱ βροτοὶ
ἐμβαλόντες ἂν ἐφρυάξανθ'· «ἱππαπαῖ, τίς ἐμβαλεῖ;
ληπτέον μᾶλλον. τί δρῶμεν; οὐκ ἐλᾷς, ὦ σαμφόρα;»
ἐξεπήδων τ' εἰς Κόρινθον· εἶτα δ' οἱ νεώτατοι
ταῖς ὁπλαῖς ὤρυττον εὐνὰς καὶ μετῇσαν βρώματα·
ἤσθιον δὲ τοὺς παγούρους ἀντὶ ποίας Μηδικῆς,
εἴ τις ἐξέρποι θύραζε κἀκ βυθοῦ θηρώμενοι·
ὥστ' ἔφη Θέωρος εἰπεῖν καρκίνον Κορίνθιον·
«Δεινά γ', ὦ Πόσειδον, εἰ μηδ' ἐν βυθῷ δυνήσομαι
μήτε γῇ μήτ' ἐν θαλάττῃ διαφυγεῖν τοὺς ἱππέας.»

We want to praise what we saw our horses accomplish.
They deserve our eulogy, for they've borne us many
hardships, invasions and battles.
But we aren't too amazed at their actions on land,
considering how they jumped manfully aboard the horse transports
after buying canteens and rations of garlic and onions,
then sat to their oars like we humans,
dipped their blades, and raised a snort of 'Heave Horse!
Who'll dip his blade? Stroke harder! What are we doing? Pull harder, S-brand!'
They jumped ashore at Corinth, and the colts made
dugouts with their hooves and foraged for fodder.
Instead of Persian clover they ate crabs, whenever
any crawled ashore and even fishing them from the deep.
So Theorus claims a Corinthian crab said, 'Lord Poseidon,
it's awful if even here in the deep I cannot succeed
either by land or by sea in escaping the Knights!'

(595–610, transl. J. Henderson with minor adjustments)

Following up on the eulogy for their fathers – and ultimately themselves –, the chorus turns to their horses and creates a comic counterpoint to the praise of the forebears. There, the chorus focused on men at arms in action, trying to include themselves, but faltered by their comic need to look good and the concluding disjunction becomes relevant for the theme and overall tone of the *antepirrhema*. However, as in the *epirrhema*, the deconstruction of the narrative once again puts the cavalrymen in the centre of the actual eulogy: '*laudatores* and *laudandi* are identical'.⁵⁶

Knowing the qualities of their steeds, the cavalrymen want to celebrate the actions of their horses (τοῖσιν is a possessive pronoun here, 'our') and echoing the *epirrhema*, they state that the horses deserve a commemoration for their value to the city (βουλόμεσθ' ἐπαινέσαι. ἄξιοι δ' εἴσ' εὐλογεῖσθαι 595–596 – εὐλογῆσαι βουλόμεσθα ..., ὅτι ... ἄξιοι). Thus, the aristocratic fathers were worthy, and the cavalrymen, deeming themselves worthy too, now play with the epinician (and aristocratic) genre of praise as they turn to the medium of their alleged worth, their horses.⁵⁷ They claim that their horses have joined them at many occasions of invasions and battles. However, the language here is very ambiguous (echoing the antistrophe, 587), for not only are πολλὰ γὰρ δὴ πράγματα (596) a weak expression without any sort of notion of what these cases might be,⁵⁸ but the explanation (εἰσβολάς τε καὶ μάχας) seems to be more of an afterthought.⁵⁹ Thucydides seldom relates hippic battles on the plains of Attica (2.19; 2.22; 3.1),⁶⁰ though as Iain Spence has demonstrated more must have taken place.⁶¹ However, Thucydides describes one successful hippic battle (probably the reason for including the story in the first place). It seems that Thucydides did not go as far to criticise the cavalry, which in its form and tactics was the design of Pericles.⁶² On the other hand, the lack of references to the cavalry indicates that the historian had difficulties in finding any reasons to write about them. Imperio (2004 *ad loc.*), on the other hand, argues that the chorus is referring to the battle at Corinth the year

---

56 Harriott 1986, 64.
57 e.g. Pi. *O.* 1.18, see later in *Eq.* 1265–1266 with a clear reference to epinician lyric.
58 The particle δὴ either emphasises the πολλὰ 'many indeed' (Denniston 1959, 205: iii), or emphasises γὰρ and arrests 'attention at the opening of a narrative' (Denniston 1959, 243, 1); the latter seems more likely. If the relevance of Cimon's herms in the *epirrhema* is correct, perhaps this expression echoes ἀμφὶ περὶ ξυνοῖς πράγμασι δῆριν ἔχειν of the second herm, Plut. *Cim.* 7. 5.
59 Sommerstein 1981, 176 *ad* 597 argues that the 'invasion and battles' refer to the invasion of foreign forces on Attic soil in the beginning of the Archidamian war and that the battles refer to the defensive fights put up by the cavalrymen to protect the country. Thus the invasions have a suppressed subject (the enemy) while the battles have the cavalrymen as subject. However, such a construction seems to force the Greek. It is hard to believe that any spectator in the audience would think that the defence put up by the cavalry under the framework of Periclean tactics could be counted as εἰσβολάς τε καὶ μάχας, since the power of the cavalry was its ability to harass raiding troops.
60 At 2.19 and 22 the Athenian cavalry are routed, while at 3.1 it keeps the light infantry of the Spartans from doing any significant harm to the fields.
61 Spence 1990 and 1993, 103.
62 For an account of Pericles' tactics, see Spence 1990 and 2012.

before and thus takes 'invasions and battles' as a hendiadys. This, however, cannot be the point of the text, since the chorus makes a clear distinction between the actions on land (τὰν τῇ γῇ μὲν), and those marvels the horses performed at sea.[63] The fact that the engagement of Solygeia was a hoplite battle[64] on land is suppressed by the chorus, who depicts the incident as a raid from the seaside. Thus the audience would not yet know what actions the chorus might be talking about, and the invasion of Corinth is postponed so as to become the comic – and fantastic – point of the *antepirrhema*.

What might then be the point of the vagueness of reference to actual warfare? Like the choral endeavour in the *epirrhema* to write itself into the history of Athenian martial success, the chorus now nonchalantly assumes that the audience accepts this as true, and thus the εἰσβολάς τε καὶ μάχας should refer to the retaliation raids on the Peloponnese carried out by none else than the union of the navy and the hoplites; occasionally the cavalry did join these raids in their horse transports, but we are only explicitly told so twice; Epidaurus in 430 (Thuc. 2.56) and Solygeia 425. However, the creation and maintenance of horse transports[65] suggest that they were employed on other occasions as well, though the cavalry never was the decisive factor on the battlefield.[66] Solygeia in 425 was *de facto* the only major success of the Athenian cavalry to date, and this only because the Corinthians had no cavalry at all (see above).

It seems then that Aristophanes has constructed the *epirrhema* and the *antepirrhema* to represent a connected narrative as following:

Epirrheme, past	
progonoi, our fathers	(565)
Salamis & Marathon	(567–568)
the cavalry as a defensive force	(576–577)
Antepirrheme, present	
contemporary raids on the Peloponnese	(597)
the new victory at Solygeia	(599–610)

---

63 Wilson 2007 inserts a ὡς <δ'> ὅτ'.
64 Notice Thucydides' emphasis on close combat καὶ ἦν ἡ μάχη καρτερὰ καὶ ἐν χερσὶ πᾶσα (4.43.3.1).
65 Thuc. 2.56.1; ἦγε δ' ἐπὶ τῶν νεῶν ὁπλίτας Ἀθηναίων τετρακισχιλίους καὶ ἱππέας τριακοσίους ἐν ναυσὶν ἱππαγωγοῖς πρῶτον τότε ἐκ τῶν παλαιῶν νεῶν ποιηθείσαις·
66 e.g. with Hagnon at Poteidaia likewise in 430 (2.58; that this force included the cavalry is first acknowledged in 6.31) and obviously with Xenophon at the disastrous defeat at Spartolus (2.79) in 429. The casualty list in Thuc. 3.37 lists 300 cavalrymen on duty to die of the plague in 430–426 and renders a larger use of the cavalry abroad than we are told by the historian probable.

The obvious lack of mentioning of the victory at Pylos here is stunning, though not surprising since the choral voice despise Cleon, and thus Aristophanes enables his chorus to silence the shouting of Cleon/Paphlagon. This I believe is one of the strongest satirical attacks in the play. It will not last the play out, but it is thrown into relief among the splendours of Athens, Salamis and Marathon. But the satire is double-edged, for the Athenian cavalry's endeavour to inscribe their glory into the city's glory – like Cleon is trying to inscribe his victory into the history of Athens (see below) – is shown to be completely without justification.

The growing ambiguity about the exact value of the cavalry reflects a contemporary tension towards the expensive – but rarely decisive on the battlefield – cavalry, which Aristophanes exploits through a satirical and negative lines – to account for the victory at the Corinthian battle and, I assume, contemporary aristocratic attitudes towards the incident. Cleon's marvellous victory at Pylos was the ultimate democratic humiliation of the hoplites of Sparta: finally, the Athenian hoplites were reversing the traditional weight of Sparta's invincible phalanxes, and taken together with Phormio's naval supremacy, the democratic warmongering looked as if it would in fact carry the day. Nicias' victory at Solygeia near Corinth was a victory still, but it was not the victory of the aristocratic cavalry who joined the fleet and hoplites there, it was just another victory symbolising how the democracy now ruled both land and sea (basically the themes of the parabatic odes). Consequently, the chorus though representing the aristocracy undermines this social group by singing its own ironic praise: the more the aristocracy is ridiculed, the stronger the non-Cleonic democracy stands, a democracy that in the comic world of Aristophanes needs to be revived through magical means.

The self-praising of the aristocracy seems to be simple bragging (cf. 271, see above). To the delight of the democratic part of the audience, the chorus moves their imaginary space from land to sea by shifting from land-battles to the fleet, though this time it is not the common people of the navy who embark on the triremes, but the horses themselves. As opposed to all other martial incidents retold by the chorus this movement in space and ideology is specific, so specific that the coryphaeus quotes the actual voices of the 'rowing horses': the exaggeration is glaring.[67] The chorus now focuses entirely on one specific occasion as opposed to

---

[67] Consequently, we have a conjunction of at least three incongruous aspects: the cavalrymen representing aristocracy, the rowing signifying the labours of democracy, and the horse to connect them. This connection becomes possible through the double nature of Poseidon as Hippios and Thalassios and generates an almost mythical setting of the equine sailors (notice the use of the lyric-tragic βροτοί, 601, normally demarcating human from gods, not humans from animals).

all other martial reference in their eulogies, the Corinthian bay. The cavalrymen are proud of it and it may be a fact that the aristocratic group in Athens saw this victory as a good chance of getting to grips with the democracy and their leaders. If any Athenian aristocrat thought that the aristocracy could earn some points of goodwill because of this victory, Aristophanes, through his own aristocrats, has surely tried to make such hope obsolete.

Since the chorus has spoken mostly in dual voices, so to speak, one giving their own point of view and the other that of the democratic audience, a deliberate irony seems to rise from the ambiguity. This makes the statement of G.W. Dobrov true of comic choruses as well: 'The Aristophanic character ... is entirely on display to the point where the spectators are aware of more about him and the meaning of his words than is the character himself'.[68] For instance, as the cavalry, the comic chorus wants to celebrate the poet, but by alluding to Phormio, who represents the most democratic part of the army, the navy, the *choreutai* undermine their fictive character as aristocratic cavalrymen. On the other hand, wanting to celebrate themselves through their fathers and their steeds, the 'cavalrymen' say one thing (namely how worthy they are), while the *choreutai* say another (the exact opposite). This is not particularly strange, since the persona 'Aristophanes' often relies on an irony between what he claims and what he does (e.g. *Vesp.* 54–66; *Nub.* 534–562). Thus, as noticed, the eulogy of this passage should be taken *cum grano salis*: It is simply a means of satirical humour here. However, among the *laudandi*, Cleon conspicuously fails to be mentioned. And this I believe is the satirical point of the *parabasis*: the silence on Cleon's success.

There can be no doubt about Cleon's political success in these years (e.g. the reassessment of the taxation of the empire and several victories associated with his policies),[69] and the Pylos episode only buttressed his power over the *demos*.[70] In the *parabasis* of *Knights*, however, there are only three indirect references to Cleon (and the first is ambiguous, since it could refer to Cratinus as well): first, the imagery of the monster Typho at 511,[71] second, through his father, Cleaenetus,

---

The mythical background recalls how Poseidon once turned himself into a stallion to have sex with Demeter (Paus. 8.25.5). The offspring of Poseidon's caper was a horse called Areion who in some of the versions of the myth had the ability to speak like humans and is mentioned as early as the *Iliad* (23.346).

68 Dobrov 2001, 35.
69 See Schultz 2009, 151–154 and Kallet 2009, 105–108 for discussion and sources.
70 For the mechanisms behind inciting the Demos to desire war, see Raaflaub 2001, 218–220; Hunt 2010, 231–232.
71 In verse 75–79, Cleon is described as a monster of almost godly size, in verse 137, his voice is compared to the thunders (626) of a river (Cycloborus punning on Cyclops?), in verse 197, he is

a theme Aristophanes has touched upon on more occasions already (e.g. 180–186, 333–334, 411–428), and third, through his associate Theorus, emphasising politics, but not without a hint of corruption.⁷² These are all themes that have run through the play so far. While being silent about his adversary, Aristophanes still aims his tacit satire at him.

On the other hand, Aristophanes alludes to the victory of Phormio, one of the old sorts of soldier, and the golden *Nikai* connected with him, and, if I am right, Aristophanes also refers to Cimon's *stelai* describing the valour of Menestheus and his Athenians. These references are clearly circumscribing the success of Cleon at Pylos and his commemoration of his own feats with the Athena Nike temple. As Schultz (2009) has persuasively argued, the Northern frieze of this temple depicted the battle of the Heraclidae against Eurystheus, which should mirror the recent Athenian victories, but by alluding to Menestheus, Aristophanes plays a mythological game in the *epirrhema*; just as the *strategoi* of old were better than the new politicians, the Homeric *and* indigenous Menestheus and his historical embodiments (Cimon and Phormio in particular) stand above the migrant Heraclidae as exploited by Cleon's policies and taken to the extreme in the character Paphlagon.⁷³

Another aspect of the epirrhematic syzygy of the *parabasis* is how theology, ideology and space are interwoven in a chiastic structure that explicitly fails to recognise the space both physically and ideological of the cavalry: the first ode to Poseidon emphasises the sea and thus the navy, while the *epirrhema* centres on the battlefield and politics; next, the ode to Athena reinforces the *epirrhema* but emphasises the ideal Athenian society and turns the cavalrymen into a chorus – not in any way degraded, but not particularly martial either⁷⁴ – while the *antepirrhema* leaves the battlefields aside and turns to the sea in a structure

---

a mythic eagle (of leather, of course), in verses 223–224 everyone fears him, and in 248 he is again, firstly a violent stream, secondly, a creature of myth, Charybdis. See Teló 2014.

72 From the chorus' point of view, this Solygeian adventure shows their worth to the city and is an aristocratic counterpoint to the Cleonian democracy, of which Theorus plays a part. That the companion of Cleon, Theorus, is mentioned last in the passage (608) emphasises the competitiveness of getting the good jobs as envoys, which Theorus was accused of in *Acharnians* as well (134ff.) The scholia (VEΓΘM), I believe, are quite right when they describe the character of Theorus: ὡς μοιχὸς δὲ κωμῳδεῖται ὁ Θέωρος καὶ ἰχθυοφάγος καὶ πονηρός. περὶ Κόρινθον οὖν διέτριβεν, ἴσως διὰ τὰς ἐκεῖ πόρνας· 'Theorus is ridiculed as an adulterer, fish-glutton and wicked. He is thus hanging around in Corinth, perhaps because of the whores there'.

73 The hypothesis of Lippman et al. 2006 may be of further interest here, though it is beyond the scope of the paper.

74 Especially if joining a city chorus exempted you from military service, Macdowell 1985.

wholly opposite to the ode to Athena: the cavalry (or rather – most magically their horses) in a classic comic routine, namely the 'high-brow' as 'low-brow' sailors; a classic topsy turvy routine.

Bibliography

Anderson, C.A. (2003), 'The Gossiping Triremes in Aristophanes' *Knights*, 1300–1315', in: *CJ* 99, 1–9.
Bakola, E. (2008) 'The Drunk, The Reformer and the Teacher. Agonistic Poetics and the Construction of Persona in the Comic Poets of the Fifth Century', in: *CCJ* 54, 1–29.
Balot, R.K. (2010), 'Democratizing courage in classical Athens', in: D. Pritchard (ed.), *War, democracy and culture in classical Athens*, Cambridge, 88–108.
Biles, Z. (2001), 'Aristophanes' Victory Dance: Old Poets in the Parabasis of Knights', in: *ZPE* 136, 195–200.
Biles, Z. (2002), 'Intertextual Biography in the Rivalry of Cratinus and Aristophanes', in: *AJP* 123 (2), 169–204.
Biles, Z. (2010), *Aristophanes and the Poetics of Competition*, Cambridge.
Blanshard, A.J.L. (2010), 'War in the law-court: some Athenian discussions', in: D. Pritchard, (ed.), *War, democracy and culture in classical Athens*, Cambridge, 203–224.
Boegehold, A.L. (1982), 'A Dissent at Athens ca 424–421 B.C.', in: *GRBS* 23, 147–56.
Bugh, G.R. (1988), *The Horsemen of Athens*, Princeton.
Campagner, R. (2001), *Lessico agonistico di Aristofane*, Pisa.
Charteris-Black, J. (2004), *Corpus Approaches to Critical Metaphor Analysis*, New York.
Connor, R.W. (1971), *The New Politicians of Fifth-century Athens*, Princeton.
Davies, J.K. (1971), *Athenian Propertied Families*, Oxford.
Denniston, J.D. (1959), *The Greek Particles*, Oxford.
Dobrov, G.W. (2001), *Figures of Play*, Oxford.
Edmunds, L. (1987), *Cleon, Knights, and Aristophanes' Politics*, Lanham.
Harriott, R.M. (1986), *Aristophanes: Poet & Dramatist*, London.
Henderson, J. (2003), 'Demos, demagogue, tyrant in Attic Old Comedy', in: K.A. Morgan (ed.), *Popular Tyranny: Sovereignty and its Discontents in Ancient Greece*, Texas.
Henderson, J. (2013), 'The comic chorus and the demagogue', in: R. Gagné/M.G. Hopman (eds.), *Choral Mediations in Greek Tragedy*, Cambridge.
Hunt, P. (2010), 'Athenian militarism and recourse to war', in: D. Pritchard (ed.), *War, democracy and culture in classical Athens*, Cambridge, 225–242.
Hölscher, T. (2003), 'Images of War in Greece and Rome: Between Military Practice, Public Memory, and Cultural Symbolism', in: *JRS* 93, 1–17.
Imperio, O. (2004), *Parabasi di Aristofane*, Bari.
Kagan, D. (1974), *The Archidamian War*, New York.
Kallet, L. (2009), 'War, Plague, and Politics in Athens in the 420s B.C.', in: O. Palagia (ed.), *Art in Athens During the Peloponnesian War*, Cambridge, 94–127.
Lakoff, G. (2004), *Don't Think of an Elephant*, Vermont.
Lech, M.L. (2009), 'The Knights' Eleven Oars: In Praise of Phormio? (Ar. *Eq.* 546–7)', in: *CJ* 105,1 19–26.

Lind, H. (1990), *Der Gerber Kleon in den 'Rittern' des Aristophanes. Studien zur Demagogenkomödie*, Frankfurt am Main.
Lippman, M./Scahill, D./Schultz, P. (2006), '*Knights* 843–59, The Nike Temple Bastion, and Cleon's Shields from Pylos', in: *AJA* 110, 551–563.
Loraux, N. (2006²), *The Invention of Athens: the Funeral Oration in Classical Athens*, New York.
Low, P. (2010), 'Commemoration of the war dead in classical Athens: remembering defeat and victory', in: D. Pritchard (ed.), *War, democracy and culture in classical Athens*, Cambridge, 341–358.
MacDowell, D.M. (1995), *Aristophanes and Athens*, Oxford.
MacDowell, D.M. (1985) 'Athenian Laws about Choruses', in: *Symposium 1982*, 65–77.
Mansfield, J.M. (1985), *The Robe of Athena and the Panathenaic Peplos*, Berkeley.
Molitor, M.V. (1973), 'The Readings ΑΜΥΝΙΑΣ and ΑΜΕΙΝΙΑΣ in Aristophanes, 'Nubes' 31', in: *Mnemosyne* 26, 55–57
Ober, J. (1989), *Mass and Elite in Democratic Athens*, Princeton.
Parker, R. (1983), *Miasma: Pollution and Purification in Early Greek Religion*, Oxford.
Pinar Sanz, M.J. (2005), 'Ideological Implications of the Use of Metaphors in the Discourse of Sports News', in: J.L.O. Campo/I.N. Ferrando/B.B. Fortuño (eds.), *Cognitive and Discourse Approaches to Metaphor and Metonymy*, Castelló de la Plana.
Pritchard, D. (1998) 'The fractured imaginary: popular thinking on military matters in fifth-century Athens', in: *AH* 28, 38–61.
Pritchard, D. (2010), 'The symbiosis between democracy and war: the case of ancient Athens', in: D. Pritchard (ed.), *War, democracy and culture in classical Athens*, Cambridge, 1–62.
Pritchard, D. (2013), *Sport, Democracy and War in Classical Athens*, Cambridge.
Pritchard, D. (2015), *Public Spending and Democracy in Classical Athens*, Austin.
Pritchard, D. (forthcoming), 'Navel Matters in Old Comedy'.
Pütz, B. (2007), *The Symposium and Komos in Aristophanes*, Oxford.
Robson, J. (2006), *Humour, Obscenity and Aristophanes*, Tübingen.
Ruffell, I. (2002), 'A Total Write-Off: Aristophanes, Kratinos and the Rhetoric of Comic Competition', in: *CQ* 52, 138–163.
Ruffell, I. (2011), *Politics and Anti-Realism in Attic Old Comedy*, Oxford.
Schultz, P. (2009) 'The North Frieze of the Temple Athena Nike', in: O. Palagia (ed.), *Art in Athens During the Peloponnesian War*, Cambridge, 128–167.
Shear, J. (2001), *Polis and Panathenaia: The History and Development of Athena's Festival*, Pensylvania.
Yoshitake, S. (2010), 'Aretê and the achievements if the war dead: the logic of praise in the Athenian funeral oration', in: D. Pritchard (ed.), *War, democracy and culture in classical Athens*, Cambridge, 359–377.
Slater, N. (2002), *Spectator Politics*, Philadelphia.
Sommerstein, A.H. (ed.) (1981), *The Comedies of Aristophanes*. II, *Knights*, Warminster.
Spence, I. (1993), 'Perikles and the Defence of Attika during the Peloponnesian War', in: *JHS* 110, 91–109.
Spence, I. (1993), *The Cavalry of Classical Greece*, Oxford.
Spence, I. (2010), 'Cavalry, democracy and military thinking', in: D. Pritchard, (ed.), *War, democracy and culture in classical Athens*, Cambridge, 111–138.
Stevenson, T. (2003) 'Cavalry Uniforms on the Parthenon Frieze?', in: *AJA* 107, 629–654.
Telò, M. (2014), 'Aristophanes vs Typhon: Co(s)mic rivalry, voice and temporality in *Knights*', in: *Ramus* 43, 25–44.

Trundle, M. (2010), 'Light troops in classical Athens', in: D. Pritchard (ed.), *War, democracy and culture in classical Athens*, Cambridge, 139–160.

Wilson, N.G. (ed.) (2007), *Aristophanis Fabulae*, I, Oxford.

Andreas Markantonatos
Greek Tragedy and Attic Oratory
The *Agôn*-Scenes in Euripides' *Alcestis*

Introduction

It is reasonable to suggest that since the fifth century BCE (perhaps from the late sixth century BCE onwards) the fruitful osmosis of dramatic poetry with speech-making was recognized as a major aspect of ancient Greek tragedy and comedy in the minds of contemporary audiences.[1] Aristophanes, such a careful noticer of the political and social details of Athenian society, but also a sensitive and close observer of the monumental changes taking place during those turmoil-stricken times at the close of the fifth century BCE, firmly believed that tragic poetry must always seek to enlighten and educate citizens. In other words, as is pointed out with characteristic passion in his *Frogs*, the tragedian, and more generally the poet, has a moral duty to offer useful and sensible advice to his city (lines 1006–1012). Guided by Aristophanes' incisive observations and spurred on by current theories about the significant moralizing effect ancient performances were capable of effecting upon their viewers, modern scholarly criticism places strong emphasis on the indisputably striking similarities between Attic drama and such fundamental institutions of Athenian democracy as the Assembly and the Courts.[2]

In all those cases of communal gatherings the effective deployment of word power and impressive diction to maximize conviction – that is to say, the clear knowledge of the art of public speaking (*bene dicendi scientia*), as well as the painstaking combination of inductive, deductive, and proportional reasoning, and on the whole the meticulous employment of sound and strong arguments – manage to arouse in the souls of both listeners and viewers an extremely broad

---
[1] The edition here used for *Alcestis* is the Oxford Classical Text by James Diggle, and the translations are based on the Loeb Classical Library edition of Euripides by David Kovacs. I am particularly indebted to Chris Carey and Michael Edwards, who have looked at substantial sections of this paper in draft form and given me their valuable comments and advice. I am also most grateful to the late Daniel I. Iakov for his consistent encouragement and for countless useful alterations and corrections.
[2] See recently Markantonatos 2007, 2012a, and 2012b with extensive bibliography.

array of emotions. In Attic drama intense verbal confrontations and public expressions of opposing opinions, widely known as *agônes logôn*, are often compelling rhetorical climaxes serving as important yardsticks by which the oratorical aptness of the *dramatis personae* is always rigorously measured and evaluated.[3] Mainly in view of the evident parallels between certain aspects of dramatic performances and a wide range of speechifying techniques and rhetorical devices featuring most prominently in the context of the Athenian self-governing democratic system, in recent times several scholars of Greek tragedy have argued convincingly that with its highly stylized expressiveness and fluency tragic diction would have functioned as a powerful disseminator of democratic values and beliefs.[4]

First and foremost, the students of the Paris School, who have made a name for themselves by capably using the theoretical tools of structuralist anthropology to interpret the tragic works, have strongly asserted that, not unlike Attic oratory, Greek tragedy constantly submits the public life of the Athenian city to a strict critique, sometimes dropping acerbic hints at immoral actions, while sometimes explicitly passing judgment on shameful behaviour. Although this censure refers to mythological personages and events, they suggest that it essentially reflects historical circumstances. The Parisian approach to Greek tragedy, which, among much else, seeks to uncover the concealed political and social dimensions of the plays, encouraged several scholars to screen out the dramatic texts to identify suggestive references to time-honoured laws and principles, as well as established norms and traditions of the Athenian state. The results of this detailed research into tragedy's political and social considerations have been no less than impressive. It has already become the *communis opinio* that in the fifth century

---

3 On ancient oratory, see (e.g.): Bizzell Herzberg 1990; Bonner 1949; Clark 1957; Clarke 1962[2]; Cole 1991; Conley 1990; Dominik 1997; Edwards 2002; Enos 1993; Fuhrmann 1990[3]; Gilman/Blair/Parent 1989; Gunderson 2003; Habinek 2005; Heath 1995; Kennedy 1963, 1972, 1980, 1983, 1984, 1989, and 1994; Kinneavy 1987; Lausberg 1990[3]; Leeman 1963; Martin 1974; McComiskey 2002; Navarre 1900; Norden 1909–1958[2]; Russell 1983; Schiappa 1999; Solmsen 1931; Usher 1999; Volkmann 1885; Walker 2000; Winterbottom 1980; Wisse 1989; Wooten 1987 and 2001.

4 On tragic style and diction, as well as the expressive power of the Greek language in general, see the following scholarly works (in alphabetical order): Bagordo 2003; Battezzato 2012; Bers 1974, 1984, and 1994; Breitenbach 1934; Bruhn 1899; Budelmann 2000; Campbell 1879[2]; Clay 1958; Colvin 2004; de Jong/Rijksbaron 2006; Denniston 1952; Dover 1997; Earp 1944 and 1948; Easterling 1973 and 1999; Eicken-Iselin 1942; Goldhill 2012; Heath 1987; Kirkwood 1994[2]; Markantonatos 2009; Mastronarde 2010; McClure 1999; Moorhouse 1982; Rutherford 2010 and 2012; Willi 2002 and 2007. See further Buck 1955; Colvin 2007; Nagy 1970; Thomson 1989[2].

BCE there was indeed a mutually beneficent cross-fertilization between the rhetorical energy of Greek tragedy and the declamatory dynamism of the Athenian democratic regime.⁵

It is certainly not surprising that contemporary literary criticism focused attention upon Euripides, a tragic poet considered since ancient times to be extremely bold in his views on the ways in which mortals wield state power and Olympic gods administer divine providence often with the lamentable result that innocent human victims suffer the severe consequences coming upon them from both ends. Furthermore, it did not escape the attention of ancient and modern literary critics that Euripidean dramas observe both god and man through rhetorically coloured lenses, most frequently highlighting the collision dynamics between the terrestrial world and the heavenly sphere. There are indeed many Euripidean masterworks, in which the dialogic parts culminate in tumultuous oratorical confrontations; this is true in scenes where the principal characters engage in passionate exchanges of appeals and counter-appeals, arguments and counter-arguments. One is therefore tempted to suggest that those acrimonious debates, during which the dramatic characters struggle on the one hand to show off their incontestable arguments and on the other to shoot down any potentially incriminating thought, would have served as a helpful testing ground for developing and emerging tropes and schemes, as well as a fertile breeding ground for novel and more effective declamatory modes and rhetorical techniques in fifth-century Athens.

It is really interesting to see that the intense rhetoric of Euripidean tragedies drew scornful comments and criticisms from Aristophanes, who was always ready to scoff at Euripides' flamboyant way of words, going so far as to contemptuously call his fellow Athenian poet not more than a mere ποιητὴ ῥηματίων δικανικῶν (*Peace* 533–534, 'poet of long-winded disputations'). In the same way, but without the slightest hint of Aristophanes' typically stinging mockery, Desiderius Erasmus of Rotterdam, a distinguished Dutch scholar and theologian of the 16th century CE, in a letter addressed to the archbishop of Canterbury, William Warham, expresses his deep discontent over the great difficulties surrounding the translator of Euripidean tragic works. As he notes in the same letter, he feels challenged by the occasionally torrential eloquence and declamatory articulacy

---

5 Cf., among much else, Eden 1980; Ober/Strauss 1990; Hall 1995; Allen 2005; Rosenbloom 2009; Harris/Leão/Rhodes 2010; Wohl 2010b; Sansone 2012 with further references. See also recently Carey 2011 with extensive bibliography. On the distinctly political dimension of Athenian legal processes, see (e.g.) Allen 2002; Cohen 1995; Kelly 1994; Lanni 2006; Papakonstantinou 2008; Wohl 2010a.

of the dramatic characters – to be sure constitutive elements of the tragedies of Euripides, but highly resistant to precise and faithful rendition into a modern language (*Opus Epistolarum* 188.30–31). It is no accident that, considering at least the many surviving textual passages, numerous works of post-classical tragedy constantly advance a fascinating oratorical expressiveness, thereby displaying a wide variety of characters well versed in the art of public speaking. This should be a further proof that in fourth century BCE the poetry of Euripides made a profound impact on dramatists. Bearing witness to this post-classical tendency towards stage stylistics and declamatory pomposity, in his *Poetics* Aristotle seems to find fault with his contemporary tragedians for favouring powerful and effective language over restrained style and prudent political judgement, rather disapprovingly pointing out that 'the older poets make their characters speak the language of civic life, while the poets of my time, the language of the rhetoricians' (1450b7–8, ed. R. Kassel, transl. S.H. Butcher, οἱ μὲν γὰρ ἀρχαῖοι πολιτικῶς ἐποίουν λέγοντας, οἱ δὲ νῦν ῥητορικῶς).

The significance of powerful and effective communication in fifth-century Attic tragedy, but also the widespread influence of tragic oratorical smoothness and efficiency on later dramaturgy, did not go unnoticed by modern literary criticism. The verbal conflicts, which, as mentioned, abound in the Euripidean dramatic *corpus*, were analyzed in detail by a multitude of the ablest scholars who, based primarily on exhaustive surveys conducted by British and German classicists, brought to light the great importance of verbal confrontations and intense oral exchanges between theatrical characters. In the 19th century CE German researchers Chy Höhne and Johannes Berlage, as well as their British colleagues Thomas Miller and Douglas Thomson, raised the crucial question as to whether the Euripidean tragic works through those verbal clashes between dramatic characters rallied rhetorically-informed topics and motifs that had a distinctively political relevance to an Athenian audience. Specifically, those topics and motifs were either strongly linked to such fundamental themes and premises of democratic ideology as the so-called Athenian clemency and mildness to all weak and victimised, or closely connected with such urgent concerns as the growing fear among Athenians about the harmful influence of sophistic concepts upon traditional democratic institutions.[6] Recently the British Hellenists Christopher Collard, Desmond Conacher, Michael Lloyd, and David Sansone, as well as the French philologist Jacqueline Duchemin and the German scholar Markus Dubischar, succeeded in considerably expanding our knowledge about not only the ty-

---

[6] See Höhne 1867; Berlage 1888; Miller 1887; Thomson 1898.

pology of the ἀγὼν λόγων or ἅμιλλα λόγων but also its remarkable thematic diversity and lexical richness. They managed thereby to draw enough attention to the extraordinary dramaturgical value of those theatrical wars of words for the furtherance of tragic plots and the fuller delineation of the *dramatis personae*.[7]

Agôn-Scenes in Euripides' *Alcestis*

Keeping in mind the introductory remarks and the specialized studies mentioned therein, I shall attempt, as far as possible in the short space of an article, to broaden the debate on the decisive and purposeful role of rhetorical art, seen in the Platonic sense as πειθοῦς δημιουργὸς (Plato, *Gorgias* 453a2), in the context of Greek tragedy, taking as a case study the oldest surviving work of Euripides, the *Alcestis*, which was produced at the Great Dionysia of 438 BCE as the last play of a tetralogy in the position customarily reserved for satyr-drama.[8] There is no point here, I should think, to examine in detail the stylistic issues that may reasonably arise with regard to the likely 'satyric' character of Euripides' work, as well as crucial questions pertaining to wider problems of genre and classification. Yet in a more extensive discussion of the impressive rhetorical acrobatics and declamatory devices abounding in the Euripidean text I believe that one would benefit greatly from looking at this important generic aspect of the play.[9]

---

[7] See Collard 1975, 2005, and 2013; Conacher 1972 and 1981; Lloyd 1992; Sansone 2012; Duchemin 1945–1968²; Dubischar 2001 and 2006. Furthermore, see (in alphabetical order): Barker 2009; Buxton 1982; Castelli 2000; Croally 1994; Dorjahn 1927; Encinas Reguero 2008 and 2011; Epke 1951; Fialho 2007; Froleyks 1973; Gallagher 2003; Gödde 2000; Goebel 1983; Goldbrunner 1957; Goldhill 1986a, 1986b, 222–243, and 1997; Graf 1950; Halliwell 1997; Hamilton 1985; Hubbard 2007; Hudson-Williams 1950; Jouan 1984; Lechner 1874; Lees 1891; McDonald 2007; Meridor 2000; Murphy 1938; Nightingale 1992; Nuchelmans 1971; O'Brien 1988; O'Reagan 1992; O'Sullivan 1992; Pelling 2005; Quijada Sagredo/Encinas Reguero 2013; Riedweg 2000; Ritoré Ponce 2005; Schmalzriedt 1980; Scodel 1997 and 1999–2000; Senoner 1960; Silva 1987–1988; Tietze 1933; Várzeas 2009; Wilson 1996.
[8] It should be emphasized from the start that the bibliography on Euripides' *Alcestis* and Euripidean drama in general is extremely extensive and often not easily accessible; for this reason, in this paper an effort was made to limit bibliographical references to a minimum, in order to save readers the overwhelming feeling stemming from having to tackle long lists of specialized books and articles. For exhaustive discussions of the play's principal interpretative problems with useful bibliographical guides, see mainly Iakov 2012; Slater 2013; Markantonatos 2013. See also Roisman 2013.
[9] Cf. Iakov 2012, I.47–51; Slater 2013, 1–8; Markantonatos 2013, 88–93.

To be more specific, I shall argue that the *Rede-Agon* between the Thessalian King Admetus and his father Pheres on the occasion of the voluntary sacrifice of Queen Alcestis for the survival of her ill-fated husband is not only a remarkable example of exhilarating eloquence and oratorical grace but at the same time the culmination and the climax of a staggering verbal conflict that has its starting point – with different protagonists this time, of course – in the prologue scene, where in an acerbic altercation Apollo and Thanatos exchange verbal fire in a stormy rhetorical standoff (lines 28–76). The recognition of this strong thematic linkage between *prima facie* different and unrelated scenes in the play affords new interpretative insights into Euripides' *Alcestis*; for our better understanding of the distinctly rhetorical dimension of the text allows us to study in more depth some of the dramatic ways in which Euripides enriches his play with Athenian ideas and themes in particular and Panhellenic values and aspirations in general, while simultaneously filtering fundamental political, social, and religious questions through a broad range of individual perspectives.

The ἄμιλλα λόγων between father and son, that is to say their violent verbal confrontation in front of the dead body of Alcestis and shortly before the performance of the customary burial rites, serves as a mirror scene of the earlier rancorous debate between Apollo, the human-loving protector of the royal household, and Thanatos, Hades' ruthless enforcer. Death protests strongly and not without playful ironic banter against the deceitful daring of Apollo, who had the audacity to trick the Fates to rescue his mortal protégé and then went so far as to demand the prolongation of Alcestis' life. Similarly, Pheres disparages his son for consenting to Apollo's preposterous plan, thereby mocking with belittling insinuations and denigrating suggestions any desperate attempt by mortals to remain alive by forcing themselves to come to terms with the preposterous idea that their loved ones would very well offer themselves as propitiatory sacrifice to the merciless gods of the Underworld. On the face of this striking resemblance in word and action between those scenes, it is reasonable to argue that the controversial topics of the drama – literally and without a trace of overstatement, the ἐπίδικα of this tragedy, namely the legal issues of this play – are dealt with and analyzed thoroughly at both divine and human levels through a long series of powerful arguments, compelling pieces of evidence, convincing explanations, devastating counterarguments, and forceful rebuttals.[10] The *constitutiones* or *quaestiones* of this unimaginable concurrence of unlikely events in the Thessalian city of Pherae, that is to say, the ultimate στάσεις of a completely absurd hypothesis, so

---

[10] On the play's complex narrative structure, see Markantonatos 2013, 22–85.

brilliantly dramatized by Euripides, increase in equal measure the rhetorical reflexes of both gods and men.

It should be emphasized, however, that this truly impressive accumulation of ἔντεχναι πίστεις in those two closely interrelated oral confrontations, specifically the deployment of arguments, examples, and opinions, as well as the use of *schemata sensum* and spectacular verbal fireworks, fails to offer the desirable solution to the looming moral impasse; on the contrary, it reinforces embarrassment and gives rise to more doubt about the required course of action. It would not be overbold to argue that the more deeply the antagonistic speakers explore the aspects of the acute controversy (*res*) regarding the very intrinsic constitution of what appears to be an absolutely unthinkable situation (*in rem*), the possible similarities between the case at hand and other comparable cases (*circa rem*), and the catastrophic consequences resulting from the above (*post rem*), the more clearly emerges the total inability of both gods and men to overcome the apparent moral and practical obstacles and thereupon to refine and recalibrate the already highly convoluted grid of their mutual relations.

It is obvious that Euripides does not wish to dispel doubts and suspicions before Heracles' final decision to rescue Alcestis, which is purposely taken immediately after the fiery oral confrontation between Pheres and Admetus. His goal, I should think, is to highlight with the strongest emphasis this impossible situation through rhetorical means and dramaturgical analogies. Both divine and human realms appear deeply divided over the very idea of a reward of length of days given to mortals for their goodness, which certainly not only presupposes the fundamental restructuring of the celestial system of powers and privileges, but at the same time it involves the risk of collateral human losses. I shall argue, therefore, that the more passionately opponents verbally attack and resist, act and counteract, in order to equalize spiteful innuendoes with passionate refutations, the more helplessly verbal schemes and rhetorical devices are bent under the weight of a fruitless exploration into the unknown, the more declamatory tropes and figurative techniques suffocate under the storm of repulsive insult and unbridled empathy dominating the souls of both mortal and immortal interlocutors. It is essentially a vicious circle: on no account would the virtuous mortals, who justifiably stake a claim to prolonged life, accept as legitimate the self-chosen sacrifice of a loved one to compensate for their survival, and on the event they would have been morally devastated under the unbearable weight of so heavy a price; on the contrary, those dishonest mortals, who are by no means considered worthy of enjoying lengthened days, would have never been prevented by ethical misgivings from gleefully accepting this invaluable prerogative.[11]

In the prologue scene Apollo, clad in a magnificent garment and holding his infallible bow in hand, as befits an Olympian god and not a vengeful slayer of the Cyclopes serving a humiliating punishment as herder in the service of a mortal king, emerges from the central gate of the Thessalian palace, and, while bidding farewell to the hospitable royal house, he recounts the προγεγενημένα of the play in the form of a short flashback (lines 1–27).[12] The characteristic rhetorical dexterity of the god had already been acknowledged by the ancient commentator, who leaves no doubt about the markedly declamatory quality of Apollo's prologue-narrative: ἐξιὼν ἐκ τοῦ οἴκου τοῦ Ἀδμήτου προλογίζει ὁ Ἀπόλλων ῥητορικῶς (ed. E. Schwartz). The narrative attempts to explain in the first instance the presence of Apollo onstage. Initially the human-loving god focuses on his violent conflict with his father and ruler of the universe, Zeus (lines 1–7), and immediately after he swerves to give details about his subsequent compulsory residence as simple herder in the city of Pherae under the supervision of Admetus. The loyalty and affability of the Thessalian king were duly appreciated by the resentful Olympian. In particular, Apollo rescued Admetus from certain premature death after deceiving the Fates, an audacious undertaking resulting in a compromise agreement according to which the king's survival can only be ensured through the sacrificial offer of another mortal; Alcestis eventually consented to lay down her life in exchange for the survival for her husband, whereas the aged parents of Admetus remained indifferent to any requests for assistance (cf. lines 8–18; esp. 16).[13] Apollo's tale rounds off with an image of present action unfolding within the palace, an event serving as both a staggering narrative peak and at the same time a heartbreaking confirmation of destiny's ruthless workings: Alcestis fading in the arms of her relatives inside the palace (lines 19–21).[14] In view of the irreversible occurrence of doom, Apollo declares his intention to leave Thessaly in order to avoid pollution, but it seems that he lingers slightly as if to await the appearance of merciless Death, who actually arrives without much ado with the aim of hurriedly leading the vanishing queen to the murky dwellings of Hades (lines 22–27).

It is undoubtedly no accident that, according to Apollo's introductory précis, the play has its origin in an acute confrontation between father and son because

---

11 See also Markantonatos 2013, 134.
12 See Iakov 2012, II.13–16 and Markantonatos 2013, 23–37.
13 On the authenticity of line 16, see Markantonatos 2013, 29 n. 16 with detailed discussion.
14 Cf. Markantonatos 2013, 29 n. 17.

of the inappropriate revival of mortals through the extraordinary effect of Asclepius' miraculous medical cures. The explosive dispute between Apollo and his progenitor, Zeus, with regard to fundamental issues concerning the reformation of cosmic order, and primarily the critical dilemma about whether to approve or disapprove of the extension of human life and, if opting for the first line of action, to remorselessly encroach upon the constitutional rights of the netherworld, paves the way for the onstage heated discussion between Apollo and Death, where once again the central problem of the conflict appears to be the acceptance or exclusion of the possibility, if specific reasons arise, of granting mortals lengthened days. By extension and according to the pervading tenor of my remarks – i.e. that the two large-scale verbal confrontations of the play progressively evolve from wide-ranging metaphysical reflections on the promi-sing prospect of restructuring the human condition to a profound meditation on mortal men's strongest yearning: prolonged existence – I shall argue that even the emblematic war of words between Pheres and Admetus, father and son, originates from that fundamental conflict between Apollo and his ancestor, mighty Zeus. During this primordial quarrel, the resurrection of mortals not only gives rise to abominable acts of vengeance and retaliation, during which Asclepius and the Cyclopes fall victim to the divine wrath of Zeus and Apollo, but also results in the dishonourable punishment of the latter, who is purposely demoted to almost subhuman status.

Therefore, although the outcome of the play's verbal intensification remains indecisive and inconclusive, the bloody conflict between Zeus and Apollo is indeed the *extra drama* cause of this escalating oral feuding, wherein the thunderblasting of Asclepius and the ensuing shooting-down of the Cyclopes apparently act as powerful catalysts of vast speech material (ὕλη) accumulated over the centuries about impenetrable problems and ardent aspirations of meta-cosmic proportions. In Pherae the same verbal and thematic material is reworked and recalibrated at least twice into a clearly enhanced and refined form, while retaining all the sharply controversial and highly disconcerting primary predicaments. This leaves no room for a settlement of differences by mutual adjustment or modification of opposing claims, principles, and demands, just as the pre-dramatic bloodshed did not afford any possibility of eliminating those fierce disputes between Zeus and Apollo. Nevertheless, we must always bear in mind that the incipient friction, which eventually turns into a ghastly impasse in Thessaly, is a matter of intense murderous action, in which the unnerving disorder stemming from the celestial conflict weakens every attempt to find a provisional non-violent solution even by way of a malicious rhetorical brawl. On the contrary, in the Euripidean play, the repulsive canon of unexamined reprisals gives way to the refined aesthetics of masterfully stylized declamation – admittedly a welcome development preparatory to the play's miraculous finale, where most astoundingly homicidal retaliation is concomitant but also attenuated by the dominant, exclusively verbal aggression to the point of climaxing into a grandiose bloodless feat by large-hearted Hercules in the face of implacable netherworld forces.[15]

As we have already argued, the Euripidean *Alcestis* surveys the feverish processes, particularly with respect to long-standing disputes between Olympians and mortals, which take place from the first moment in the divine sphere – because it is hierarchically superior and inevitably inclusive of all others – and later on in the human sphere, where the constantly arising moral questions about longevity and revivification of mortals rekindle dormant passions, and above all, reawaken secret desires, fading hopes, and untold aspirations. More important still, through conflicting one-liners and thematically contrasting longer passages, verbal disputes and acrimonious debates, animated by both the friction and grinding facilitated by the art of speaking (εὖ λέγειν), highlight with decisive emphasis inescapable metaphysical questions. More than that, they underline the need for man to recognize the moral essence of his life – that is, the realization of his ethical responsibility towards his fellow humans under the shadow of the terror of death. Length of days without moral integrity, drained of the streams of compassion and affection for fellow humans, ends up transforming trust and warmth, unconditionally presupposed by human friendship, into existential deadlock and nightmarish tribulation. Ultimately, one could argue that the pivotal idea pervading the play is that the prolongation of human survival causes uncontainable moral drainage, especially when this continuation of human existence is deficient in the inspiring anticipation of posthumous fame – an important inner urge regenerative and reconstructive of life itself.

The gruesome rupture of the relations between Zeus and Apollo over the violation of principal cosmic laws is the root and matrix of the ensuing verbal conflicts between gods and men. Once Thanatos becomes aware of the presence of Apollo, he expresses his great discomfort instantaneously; for Apollo's trickery and deception of the Fates and the unexpected rescue of Admetus from early demise loom large in his memory. Not unlike Zeus, the almighty overseer of eternal universal rules and regulations, Thanatos attempts immediately to defend his widely recognized institutional role as High Priest of all manner of 'human sacrifice', here interpreted even more broadly by him as predetermined human casualties regardless of age, social status, and moral worth. Reacting to Death's stern

---

[15] See principally Markantonatos 2013, 86–130 with further bibliography.

objections, Apollo attempts to prevent the mortal blows directed against Alcestis, thereby employing elaborate rhetorical manoeuvres and influential declamatory tactics. Nonetheless, the evocation of possible reciprocations, which however lack in moral fortitude, proves sadly futile. Therefore, this emotionally charged repartee between Death and Apollo (lines 38–63) serves as an *agôn logôn*, for now embryonic and unformed, whilst at the same time introductory to more profound reflections. But when the course of the drama reaches about halfway the relentlessly vibrating atmosphere at Pherae will erupt into a series of shockingly fiery verbal contests, during which urgent will be the need for transformation of the god-given benefaction of human survival into a compelling motivation for an infinitely powerful meditation on the moral debt each human incurs in the face of destiny (lines 28–76):

Θάνατος:	ἆ ἆ· τί σὺ πρὸς μελάθροις; τί σὺ τῇδε πολεῖς,	
	Φοῖβ'; ἀδικεῖς αὖ τιμὰς ἐνέρων	30
	ἀφοριζόμενος καὶ καταπαύων;	
	οὐκ ἤρκεσέ σοι μόρον Ἀδμήτου	
	διακωλῦσαι, Μοίραις δολίῳ σφήλαντι τέχνῃ; νῦν δ' ἐπὶ τῇδ' αὖ	
	χέρα τοξήρη φρουρεῖς ὁπλίσας,	35
	ἣ τόδ' ὑπέστη, πόσιν ἐκλύσασ'	
	αὐτὴ προθανεῖν Πελίου παῖς;	
Ἀπόλλων:	θάρσει· δίκην τοι καὶ λόγους κεδνοὺς ἔχω.	
Θάνατος:	τί δῆτα τόξων ἔργον, εἰ δίκην ἔχεις;	
Ἀπόλλων:	σύνηθες αἰεὶ ταῦτα βαστάζειν ἐμοί.	40
Θάνατος:	καὶ τοῖσδέ γ' οἴκοις ἐκδίκως προσωφελεῖν.	
Ἀπόλλων:	φίλου γὰρ ἀνδρὸς συμφοραῖς βαρύνομαι.	
Θάνατος:	καὶ νοσφιεῖς με τοῦδε δευτέρου νεκροῦ;	
Ἀπόλλων:	ἀλλ' οὐδ' ἐκεῖνον πρὸς βίαν σ' ἀφειλόμην.	
Θάνατος:	πῶς οὖν ὑπὲρ γῆς ἐστι κοὐ κάτω χθονός;	45
Ἀπόλλων:	δάμαρτ' ἀμείψας, ἣν σὺ νῦν ἥκεις μέτα.	
Θάνατος:	κἀπάξομαί γε νερτέραν ὑπὸ χθόνα.	
Ἀπόλλων:	λαβὼν ἴθ'· οὐ γὰρ οἶδ' ἂν εἰ πείσαιμί σε.	
Θάνατος:	κτείνειν γ' ὃν ἂν χρῇ; τοῦτο γὰρ τετάγμεθα.	
Ἀπόλλων:	οὔκ, ἀλλὰ τοῖς μέλλουσι θάνατον ἀμβαλεῖν.	50
Θάνατος:	ἔχω λόγον δὴ καὶ προθυμίαν σέθεν.	
Ἀπόλλων:	ἔστ' οὖν ὅπως Ἄλκηστις ἐς γῆρας μόλοι;	
Θάνατος:	οὐκ ἔστι· τιμαῖς κἀμὲ τέρπεσθαι δόκει.	
Ἀπόλλων:	οὔτοι πλέον γ' ἂν ἢ μίαν ψυχὴν λάβοις.	
Θάνατος:	νέων φθινόντων μεῖζον ἄρνυμαι γέρας.	55
Ἀπόλλων:	κἂν γραῦς ὄληται, πλουσίως ταφήσεται.	
Θάνατος:	πρὸς τῶν ἐχόντων, Φοῖβε, τὸν νόμον τίθης.	
Ἀπόλλων:	πῶς εἶπας; ἀλλ' ἦ καὶ σοφὸς λέληθας ὤν;	
Θάνατος:	ὠνοῖντ' ἂν οἷς πάρεστι γηραιοὶ θανεῖν.	
Ἀπόλλων:	οὔκουν δοκεῖ σοι τήνδε μοι δοῦναι χάριν.	60

Θάνατος:	οὐ δῆτ'· ἐπίστασαι δὲ τοὺς ἐμοὺς τρόπους.
Ἀπόλλων:	ἐχθροὺς γε θνητοῖς καὶ θεοῖς στυγουμένους.
Θάνατος:	οὐκ ἂν δύναιο πάντ' ἔχειν ἃ μή σε δεῖ.
Ἀπόλλων:	ἦ μὴν σὺ παύσῃ καίπερ ὠμὸς ὢν ἄγαν·
	τοῖος Φέρητος εἶσι πρὸς δόμους ἀνὴρ 65
	Εὐρυσθέως πέμψαντος ἵππειον μετὰ
	ὄχημα Θρῄκης ἐκ τόπων δυσχειμέρων,
	ὃς δὴ ξενωθεὶς τοῖσδ' ἐν Ἀδμήτου δόμοις
	βίᾳ γυναῖκα τήνδε σ' ἐξαιρήσεται.
	κοὔθ' ἡ παρ' ἡμῶν σοι γενήσεται χάρις 70
	δράσεις θ' ὁμοίως ταῦτ', ἀπεχθήσῃ τ' ἐμοί.
Θάνατος:	πόλλ' ἂν σὺ λέξας οὐδὲν ἂν πλέον λάβοις·
	ἡ δ' οὖν γυνὴ κάτεισιν εἰς Ἅιδου δόμους.
	στείχω δ' ἐπ' αὐτὴν ὡς κατάρξωμαι ξίφει·
	ἱερὸς γὰρ οὗτος τῶν κατὰ χθονὸς θεῶν 75
	ὅτου τόδ' ἔγχος κρατὸς ἁγνίσῃ τρίχα.

Death:	Ho! What are you doing at the palace? Why do you loiter about here, [30] Phoebus? Are you engaged in more injustice, curtailing and annulling the prerogatives of the gods below? Was it not enough that you prevented the death of Admetus, tripping up the Fates by cunning trickery? Are you now [35] standing guard, bow in hand, over her, Pelias' daughter, who promised to free her husband by dying in his stead?
Apollo:	Fear not: I have nothing, I assure you, but justice and reasonable words.
Death:	If justice, then what need for your bow and arrows?
Apollo:	[40] It is my custom always to carry them.
Death:	Yes, and also to give unjust assistance to this house.
Apollo:	Certainly, since I am grieved by the misfortunes of my dear friend.
Death:	And will you rob me of a second corpse?
Apollo:	But not even the first did I take from you by force.
Death:	[45] Then how is he still on earth and not beneath the ground?
Apollo:	By giving in exchange the wife you have now come to fetch.
Death:	Yes, and I will take her down below.
Apollo:	Take her and go. For I doubt if I can persuade you.
Death:	To kill my fated victims? Yes, for those are my orders.
Apollo:	[50] No, to postpone death for the doomed.
Death:	I grasp now your purpose and your desire.
Apollo:	Is there any way Alcestis might reach old age?
Death:	There is none. I too, you must know, get pleasure from my office.
Apollo:	You will not, of course, get more than one life in any case.
Death:	[55] I win greater honor when the victims are young.
Apollo:	And yet if she dies old, she will receive a rich burial.
Death:	The law you are trying to establish, Phoebus, is to the advantage of the rich.
Apollo:	What do you mean? Can I have failed to appreciate what a thinker you are?
Death:	Those with means could buy death at an advanced age.
Apollo:	[60] You are not inclined, I take it, to grant me this favor.
Death:	No, indeed. You know my character.

Apollo:	Yes, hateful to mortals and rejected by the gods.
Death:	You may not have all that you should not have.
Apollo:	I swear to you that, ruthless as you are, you will yet cease from your hateful ways. [65] The man to make you do so is coming to the house of Pheres sent by Eurystheus to fetch the horses and chariot from the wintry land of Thrace. He, entertained as a guest in this house of Admetus, shall take the woman from you by force. [70] You shall do precisely as I have asked and yet get no gratitude from me but hatred instead.
Death:	Your plentiful talk will gain you nothing. At all events, the woman is going down to the house of Hades. I go to her to take the first sacrificial cutting of her hair. [75] For when this sword has consecrated the hair of someone's head, he is the sacred property of the gods below.

Although this shouting match, like the earlier vicious falling-out between Zeus and Apollo, leads to the renewal of latent passions and expectations, the launching of serious threats, and the ruthless use of the bludgeon of bitter invective, the fascinating rhetorical eloquence of the interlocutors, especially Thanatos' utterly unexpected articulacy, which takes Apollo by surprise (line 58), at least manage to raise specific issues of concern with regard to the turbulent relations between Olympian and Stygian divinities. Indeed, where in the past the primary rupture between powerful divine forces segued into impulsive brutal retaliation, the opening scene between Apollo and Death culminates in almost playful reproach, when in response to the highly cynical suggestion of luxury burials as an enticing policy of appeasement of the netherworld deities (line 56) comes the ironic retort that this argument introduces a shameful law in favour of the rich (line 57), because it would be expected that the wealthy mortals would be ever ready to dispose of their property in order to redeem their longevity (line 59), while obviously the destitute would be forced to succumb to their inexorable fate.

Death's remarkable display of scornful derision aims to highlight, through the most emphatic rhetorical figure of the *adynaton*, the endless absurdity that lies in the philanthropic action of Apollo, but at the same time seeks to disparage the lack of unwavering ethical criteria that would allow unconditional expansion of human life. There is always the clear and present danger that the benefit of length of days would degenerate into an object of despicable bargaining and suspicious dealing between gods and men, with the result that religious devotion and commitment will become an unprecedentedly profane and gratuitous transaction. It is more than evident that the deities of the infernal regions, who are also defenders of the cosmic order and hence of Zeus himself, are very disturbed by the possibility that the lengthening of human life may be granted at the discretion of those immortals, who, frequently driven by highly personal incentives or allured by lavish offers, would also bestow this invaluable benefit upon utterly unworthy individuals.

The sarcastic reference to the rich, who would, of necessity, dispose of all material goods to receive favourable treatment from the heavenly and infernal powers, but also more broadly the acerbic mention of the acute moral issues that would arise from an uncontrolled and unrestricted diffusion of divine benefaction, allude to the miserable death of Asclepius, as indeed this is recounted with unparalleled vividness and intensity by Pindar in his third *Pythian Ode*.[16] In this victory hymn, which serves as a consolatory epistle to Hieron, the ailing tyrant of Syracuse and time-and-again victor in Panhellenic athletic contests, the Theban bard narrates the awful end of Asclepius, who succumbed to the temptation of lavish gifts in order to bring back to life a wealthy mortal, thereby both placing strong emphasis on the inexorability of human destiny and underlining the common debt all men must pay:

ἀλλὰ κέρδει καὶ σοφία δέδεται.
ἔτραπεν καὶ κεῖνον ἀγάνορι μισθῷ
  χρυσὸς ἐν χερσὶν φανείς
ἄνδρ' ἐκ θανάτου κομίσαι
ἤδη ἁλωκότα· χερσὶ δ' ἄρα Κρονίων
  ῥίψαις δι' ἀμφοῖν ἀμπνοὰν στέρνων κάθελεν
ὠκέως, αἴθων δὲ κεραυνὸς ἐνέσκιμψεν μόρον.

(lines 54–59 ed. Snell/Maehler)

But even skill is enthralled by the love of gain. [55] Gold shining in his hand turned even that man, for a handsome price, to bring back from death a man who was already caught. And so the son of Cronus hurled his shaft with his hands through both of them, and swiftly tore the breath out of their chests; the burning thunderbolt brought death crashing down on them.

(transl. Diane Arnson Svarlien)

The striking-down of Asclepius by fire-dealing Zeus, the unyielding overseer of universal harmony and the incorruptible advocate of cosmic law, puts at least for a while an end to the chimaeric aspirations of mortals to devise ways of avoiding their destiny even by means of bountiful inducements to god-born miracle therapists. Pindar, moreover, advises Hieron to accept his mortal nature and to seek

---

[16] Cf. Iakov 2000, 210–225 with further bibliographical guidance.

out the promising prospect that his reputation will be indelibly etched in the indestructible lyrical eulogy of his triumphant athletic victories.

Ever mindful of the kindness of Admetus, Apollo wishes earnestly to pay tribute to his gracious and hospitable host, especially now that the friendly gesture of the king of Pherae is magnified by his wife's extraordinary self-sacrificing offer. It is, however, patently obvious that the gift of the Olympian god, after the deception of the gullible Fates, whom he deliberately invokes through certain fractions of *narratio* in both his prologue-speech and subsequent replies to Thanatos (lines 12–14 and 44) to indicate his intellectual superiority, poses serious risks to the cosmic order and the equality of all towards the eternal celestial rules and statutes. It is not accidental that Apollo purposely plays down the threatening prospect that the expansion of human life will seriously undermine the impartiality and fairness in the imposition of established laws and institutions regulating the worldwide dealings between gods and men; it seems that he attaches more weight to the importance of friendship that inextricably links the benevolent host with the grateful guest (line 42).[17]

Considering the above-mentioned, seemingly unbridgeable differences, one could argue that this is the first time, since the crucial question arose as to whether the exemplary record and the stainless reputation of a human being should be rewarded with longevity as opposed to those infringing moral laws and principles, that these convoluted issues relating to divine justice are subjected to detailed discussion. Much as this discussion is violent and stormy, the outcome will be catalytic for the future structure of the universe. In the meantime, however, the rhetorical energy of the two rival gods fails to culminate in some sort of mutually acceptable conciliation; but this first instance of acute verbal controversy ends with Apollo's stern reproof. In line 62, Apollo deploys the rhetorical figure of *hyperbole* (note that this rhetorical device is a highly popular way of declaiming in this play) to express his intransigent hatred of Death's despicable methods of operation before he launches a vicious attack against him. Surprisingly enough, Apollo, the god of ambiguous foretelling, offers a distinctly clear and intelligible prediction that Heracles will come to the city of Pherae and will gain victory over the netherworld (lines 65–69). Hades' outspoken envoy, by contrast, raises sarcastically a wall of defiance against Apollo's repeated requests for the salvation of Alcestis from an early demise (lines 72–76). This conflict will continue with even greater intensity during the following scenes, where a long series of recriminations and allegations will accelerate into a harshly frantic verbal quarrel following the heartrending and at the same time dramaturgically-unique

---

[17] On the theme of *philia* in the play, see the helpful discussion in Slater 2013, 41–45.

episode of the Queen breathing her last in front of the Thessalian palace and in full view of the Chorus and the audience. In general, one could argue that the prevailing reflection on the metaphysical question of the evaluation of human moral conscience against the incomprehensible and largely perplexing cosmic order continues to be present during the play through repeated rhetorical transformations of its substance into a series of extraordinary counterbalances between conflicting beliefs and assumptions. In a similar way, in the scene between Admetus and Pheres before the dead body of Alcestis, the cacophony of rival voices, which dominated the play's Prologue, does not yet result in a harmonious tune, capable enough of soothing violent feelings and passions, but instead it turns into an even more chaotic and noisy welter of opposing views and abusive *ad hominem* remarks.

The pair of divine adversaries is replaced here by a parallel pair of mortal opponents: Admetus, who as the earthly double of Apollo struggles to emerge morally intact from an impossible situation, and Pheres, who as the human *alter ego* of Pluto recalls with extreme cynicism that the power of death is essentially the emblem of life itself.[18] It is evident that the fiendish complexity of the issue at hand, namely the possibility of closer interconnection between the ethical integrity of mortals and an unprecedented exemption from human destiny in the form of a trophy revival, calls for further discussion and revision of those time-honoured principles and values moderating the relationship between gods and men. It is so improbable the unanimity between rival factions, so difficult and arbitrary the associated moral commitments, so dangerous and unpredictable the consequences of a supposed universal redeployment of Olympian and Hadean forces, that even the remarkable rhetorical mastery of the concerned parties ends in perplexing embarrassment.

Pheres brings funeral offerings to the dead Alcestis, thereby seeking to express his admiration and respect for her self-sacrificing stand (lines 614–628). Untouched by his father's gesture, Admetus goes on to pour rivers of invective upon Pheres, rekindling dormant passions and reinforcing the loathing that continues to subsist between parent and offspring from the time when Pheres and his aged wife refused to offer their lives in order to free their only son from the shackles of Hades (lines 629–672):[19]

οὔτ' ἦλθες ἐς τόνδ' ἐξ ἐμοῦ κληθεὶς τάφον
οὔτ' ἐν φίλοισι σὴν παρουσίαν λέγω.   630

---

[18] Cf. Markantonatos 2013, 114 and n. 40.
[19] Cf. Iakov 2012, I.281–318, who offers a detailed discussion of this *agôn logôn*.

κόσμον δὲ τὸν σὸν οὔποθ' ἥδ' ἐνδύσεται·
οὐ γάρ τι τῶν σῶν ἐνδεὴς ταφήσεται.
τότε ξυναλγεῖν χρῆν σ' ὅτ' ὠλλύμην ἐγώ·
σὺ δ' ἐκποδὼν στὰς καὶ παρεὶς ἄλλῳ θανεῖν
νέῳ γέρων ὤν, τόνδ' ἀποιμώξῃ νεκρόν;   635
οὐκ ἦσθ' ἄρ' ὀρθῶς τοῦδε σώματος πατήρ,
οὐδ' ἡ τεκεῖν φάσκουσα καὶ κεκλημένη
μήτηρ μ' ἔτικτε, δουλίου δ' ἀφ' αἵματος
μαστῷ γυναικὸς σῆς ὑπεβλήθην λάθρᾳ.
ἔδειξας εἰς ἔλεγχον ἐξελθὼν ὃς εἶ,   640
καί μ' οὐ νομίζω παῖδα σὸν πεφυκέναι.
ἦ τἆρα πάντων διαπρέπεις ἀψυχίᾳ,
ὃς τηλικόσδ' ὢν κἀπὶ τέρμ' ἥκων βίου
οὐκ ἠθέλησας οὐδ' ἐτόλμησας θανεῖν
τοῦ σοῦ πρὸ παιδός, ἀλλὰ τήνδ' εἰάσατε   645
γυναῖκ' ὀθνείαν, ἣν ἐγὼ καὶ μητέρα
καὶ πατέρ' ἂν ἐνδίκως ἂν ἡγοίμην μόνην.
καίτοι καλόν γ' ἂν τόνδ' ἀγῶν' ἠγωνίσω,
τοῦ σοῦ πρὸ παιδὸς κατθανών, βραχὺς δέ σοι
πάντως ὁ λοιπὸς ἦν βιώσιμος χρόνος.   650
[κἀγώ τ' ἂν ἔζων χἥδε τὸν λοιπὸν χρόνον,
κοὐκ ἂν μονωθεὶς ἔστενον κακοῖς ἐμοῖς.]
καὶ μὴν ὅσ' ἄνδρα χρὴ παθεῖν εὐδαίμονα
πέπονθας· ἥβησας μὲν ἐν τυραννίδι,
παῖς δ' ἦν ἐγώ σοι τῶνδε διάδοχος δόμων,   655
ὥστ' οὐκ ἄτεκνος κατθανὼν ἄλλοις δόμον
λείψειν ἔμελλες ὀρφανὸν διαρπάσαι.
οὐ μὴν ἐρεῖς γέ μ' ὡς ἀτιμάζοντα σὸν
γῆρας θανεῖν προύδωκας, ὅστις αἰδόφρων
πρὸς σ' ἦ μάλιστα· κἀντὶ τῶνδέ μοι χάριν   660
τοιάνδε καὶ σὺ χἠ τεκοῦσ' ἠλλαξάτην.
τοιγὰρ φυτεύων παῖδας οὐκέτ' ἂν φθάνοις,
οἳ γηροβοσκήσουσι καὶ θανόντα σε
περιστελοῦσι καὶ προθήσονται νεκρόν.
οὐ γάρ σ' ἔγωγε τῇδ' ἐμῇ θάψω χερί·   665
τέθνηκα γὰρ δὴ τοὐπὶ σ'. εἰ δ' ἄλλου τυχὼν
σωτῆρος αὐγὰς εἰσορῶ, κείνου λέγω
καὶ παῖδά μ' εἶναι καὶ φίλον γηροτρόφον.
μάτην ἄρ' οἱ γέροντες εὔχονται θανεῖν,
γῆρας ψέγοντες καὶ μακρὸν χρόνον βίου·   670
ἢν δ' ἐγγὺς ἔλθῃ θάνατος, οὐδεὶς βούλεται
θνήσκειν, τὸ γῆρας δ' οὐκέτ' ἔστ' αὐτοῖς βαρύ.

I did not invite you to this funeral, [630] nor do I count your presence here as that of a friend. As for your finery, she shall never wear it, for she needs nothing of yours for her burial. You should have shared my trouble when I was dying. You stood aside and, though you are old, [635] allowed a young person to die: and will you now come to mourn her? You were not, as it now seems clear, truly my father, nor did she who claims to have borne me and is called my mother really give me birth, but I was born of some slave and secretly put to your wife's breast. [640] When you were put to the test you showed your true nature, and I do not count myself as your son. You are, you know, truly superlative in cowardice; for though you are so old and have come to the end of your life, yet you refused and had not the courage to die [645] for your own son, but you and your wife let this woman, who was no blood relative, do so. I shall consider her with perfect justice to be both mother and father to me. And yet it would have been a noble contest to enter, dying for your son, and in any case [650] the time you had left to live was short. [And she and I would have lived for the rest of our time, and I would not be grieving for my trouble, bereft of her.]

What is more, all that is required for a man to be happy has already befallen you: you spent the prime of your life as a king, [655] and you had me as son and successor to your house, so that you were not going to die childless and leave your house behind without heirs for others to plunder. Surely you cannot say that you abandoned me to death because I dishonored you in your old age, for I have always shown you [660] every respect. And now this is the repayment you and my mother have made to me. You had better hurry, therefore, and beget other children to take care of you in old age and, when you have died, to dress you and lay you out for burial. [665] I for my part shall never bury you myself. For as far as in you lay I am dead. And if I have found another savior and still look upon the sun, I am that savior's child and fond support in old age. It seems that old men, [670] who find fault with age and length of years, pray for death insincerely. For once death comes near, none of them wishes to die, and age is no longer burdensome to them.

The torrential eloquence of Admetus becomes the vehicle for a storm of indignation and an unprecedented explosion of anger – that is, the conduit of powerful feelings, apparently stemming from a painful emotional shock. It is obvious that Admetus interprets his father's words as hypocritical because of his earlier reluctance to offer a helping hand to the struggling royal couple. This adds further force to his feelings of immense sorrow for the unfortunate loss of his beloved wife, in addition to transforming his bitter complaints against his insensitive parents into an overflowing of uncontrollable rage and bilious rebuke. It is noteworthy that the uncontainable wrath of the king of Thessaly does not entail, as is often the case in everyday life, an ungraceful and awkward oratorical style featuring an endless litany of circumlocutions, tautologies, expletives, digressions, improprieties, vulgarisms, solecisms, and mannerisms; quite the reverse, in Greek tragedy, the emotional collapse and the raging fury of the dramatic characters are the perfect reason for majestic eloquence and impressive diction. Oddly enough, wrath and indignation allow the protagonists to rise to an overwhelming rhetorical concentration. Similarly, Admetus' resentful speech, which directly aims to challenge the moral worth of his adversary – that is to say, the moral *qualitas* of the actions of his opponent – is endowed with *probationes artificiales*, chaotically contradictory rhetorical figures, evocative assonances, arresting alliterations, striking echo rhymes, fiery examples of *pollysyndeton*, absurd hyperboles, and outrageous instances of *adynaton*. All these important rhetorical devices aim to contain in a single piece a whole series of stern accusations and strong insults, which, of course, are designed to show that Pheres failed to honour, as it should, the hallowed bonds of blood kin.

The first four lines of Admetus' angry speech serve as a remarkable *exordium*. This overture paves the way to the incremental evolution of his astounding declamatory display from verbal excessiveness into clinically precise condemnatory prosecution, where a string of emphatic negations (lines 629–632, οὔτ' … οὔτ' … οὔποθ' … οὐ γάρ) creates an appropriate climate from the outset of the play, in the context of which the hostile and incriminating rhetoric against Pheres will develop slowly but surely. These successive negatives are particularly reinforced by the escalation of grammatical time, which starts from the past (line 629, ἦλθες), segues into the present (line 630, λέγω), only to take a leap into the near future (line 631, ἐνδύσεται) and then into the distant future (line 632, ταφήσεται); and they are overly accentuated by the sonorous, anticipatory *homoioteleuton* occupying the third and fourth lines of the preamble (lines 631–632, ἐνδύσεται … ταφήσεται). Additionally, in order to buttress his rhetorical probity and to shame his counterpart's stance on the issue at hand, in the following lines Admetus reveals fragments of the play's backstory by way of a carefully crafted *narratio*, which is intimately mixed with examples of *polysyndeton* featuring continual negations, diplologies, repetitions, assonances, overstatements, and rhetorical questions – that is, any manner of emphatic verbal ploy.[20]

More specifically, with the temporal pointer τότε (line 633) Admetus' *rhesis* swerves to the past, when the desperate king was faced with the disheartening refusal of his aged father in his agonizing request for survival leave; in fact, this concise narrative *analepsis* leads the way to an astounding rhetorical question (line 635). The indignation of the speaker culminates in a preposterous *reductio ad absurdum*, according to which Admetus is supposedly of low origin and hence an illegitimate child of Pheres (lines 636–641); above all, this same indignation is even more reinforced by the painful knowledge that Admetus' parents had almost run the course of their lives, while their son was still at the prime of life, as highlighted by the striking juxtaposition of νέῳ γέρων (line 635), and the emphatic *polysyndeton* of cold-hearted Pheres' strong disapprovals (lines 636, 637 & 641), further accentuated by the assonance of -ου and -ε, especially in line 640.

Correspondingly, in the aftermath of the verbal attack, Admetus deploys a broad array of oratorical devices and techniques similar to those already used, in

---

20 See further Gygli-Wyss 1966; Fehling 1969.

order to shake his adversary's credibility and moral merit by denying any blood bond with him, as well as adding to his rhetorical quiver even more powerful arrows, such as the self-referential irony of the *figura etymologica*,[21] the typological variety of the *polyptoton*, the captivating refinement of the *gnome*, the fascinating force of *prokatalepsis*, and the clarifying emphasis of *hypostasis*. The censure against Pheres takes off through a double-looping negation within the same verse (line 644), which ends again in an implausible *reductio ad absurdum* with the incredible assertion by raging Admetus that his wife must be considered both his father and mother (lines 646–647). But at the same time, the highly apologetic tone paves the way for a *figura etymologica* (line 648, ἀγῶν' ἠγωνίσω), which clearly aims to damage irreparably the trustworthiness of Pheres, who failed to live up to his principles and proved to be morally bankrupt as to family and social values and standards. The reference to the concept of ethical *agôn* certainly conceals a self-referential hint at the ongoing debate between father and son, thus acting as a transparent, intrinsic sign for the highly rhetorical framework of this scene of fierce verbal confrontation.

Subsequently, Admetus reprises variations of associated themes and images already deployed in his attempt to revile his father for his heartlessness and cruelty; in fact, once again the rhetorical figure of *polyptoton*, as well as placing strong emphasis on the concept of πάθος (lines 653–654), makes even more illustrious the narrative account of Pheres' privileged circumstances, as he was a mighty ruler fortunate enough to have a son most respectful and virtuous (lines 653–661). Further, the rhetorical device of *hypostasis*, which can most probably be detected through the masterly deployment of alliteration and *polyptoton* in lines 655–656, highlights and clarifies the threatening dangers surrounding the royal house, the δόμον, on account of the predetermined demise of the successor king Admetus; but also, in addition to illuminating afresh through fragments of rhetorical *narratio* the play's backstory, the advance response, namely the rhetorical figure of *occupatio*, to a possible counter-attack by Pheres about his son's lack of respect (lines 658–660), explicitly reveals the speaker's moral fibre and prudence.

As he thinks of his generosity towards his father, he cannot help hurling insulting overstatements and mocking hyperboles at Pheres, thereby attempting to underline the moral divide that separates him from his progenitor regarding the fulfilment of the most sacred duties of solidarity and altruism towards relatives at risk (lines 662–672). Indicative of the deepening gloominess of Admetus is his excessive statement that he is now dead to his father (line 666); similarly, through

---

21 See also van Looy 1975.

the parabolic mode of *reductio ad absurdum*, he has come to regard himself as both child and guardian of Alcestis, thus investing his dead wife with every kind of affinity that would connect him with his biological parents. It is noteworthy that his acerbic *rhesis* rounds off with an extremely ironic *gnome*, which, reinforced by the rhetorical figure of *polyptoton* juxtaposing the concepts of old age and death and underpinned by alliteration, highlights the disgrace and pretentiousness of Pheres and his elderly wife, who preferred to go against their moral values and to violate unwritten laws governing blood relations in order to remain alive for a relatively short period of time (lines 669–672).

As expected, Admetus' bilious and rancorous attack could not have given rise to a less fierce counter-attack by Pheres, although the Chorus of old men attempts to take the edge off the devastating passions engulfing the protagonists and to bring things back to peace (lines 673–674). Pheres, in turn, flies into a rage and hurls vulgar insults and abusive remarks at his son, thereby unleashing ferocious counter-arguments and flagrant affronts to offset the preceding offensive allegations about his moral failure and emotional frostiness (lines 675–705):[22]

ὦ παῖ, τίν' αὐχεῖς, πότερα Λυδὸν ἢ Φρύγα	675
κακοῖς ἐλαύνειν ἀργυρώνητον σέθεν;	
οὐκ οἶσθα Θεσσαλόν με κἀπὸ Θεσσαλοῦ	
πατρὸς γεγῶτα γνησίως ἐλεύθερον;	
ἄγαν ὑβρίζεις, καὶ νεανίας λόγους	
ῥίπτων ἐς ἡμᾶς οὐ βαλὼν οὕτως ἄπει.	680
ἐγὼ δέ σ' οἴκων δεσπότην ἐγεινάμην	
κἄθρεψ', ὀφείλω δ' οὐχ ὑπερθνῄσκειν σέθεν·	
οὐ γὰρ πατρῷον τόνδ' ἐδεξάμην νόμον,	
παίδων προθνῄσκειν πατέρας, οὐδ' Ἑλληνικόν.	
σαυτῷ γὰρ εἴτε δυστυχὴς εἴτ' εὐτυχὴς	685
ἔφυς· ἃ δ' ἡμῶν χρῆν σε τυγχάνειν ἔχεις.	
πολλῶν μὲν ἄρχεις, πολυπλέθρους δέ σοι γύας	
λείψω· πατρὸς γὰρ ταῦτ' ἐδεξάμην πάρα.	
τί δῆτά σ' ἠδίκηκα; τοῦ σ' ἀποστερῶ;	
μὴ θνῇσχ' ὑπὲρ τοῦδ' ἀνδρός, οὐδ' ἐγὼ πρὸ σοῦ.	690
χαίρεις ὁρῶν φῶς· πατέρα δ' οὐ χαίρειν δοκεῖς;	
ἦ μὴν πολύν γε τὸν κάτω λογίζομαι	
χρόνον, τὸ δὲ ζῆν σμικρὸν ἀλλ' ὅμως γλυκύ.	
σὺ γοῦν ἀναιδῶς διεμάχου τὸ μὴ θανεῖν	
καὶ ζῇς παρελθὼν τὴν πεπρωμένην τύχην,	695
ταύτην κατακτάς· εἶτ' ἐμὴν ἀψυχίαν	
ψέγεις, γυναικός, ὦ κάκισθ', ἡσσημένος,	

---

22 See Iakov 2012, I.294–298.

ἢ τοῦ καλοῦ σοῦ προύθανεν νεανίου;
σοφῶς δ' ἐφηῦρες ὥστε μὴ θανεῖν ποτε,
εἰ τὴν παροῦσαν κατθανεῖν πείσεις ἀεὶ   700
γυναῖχ' ὑπὲρ σοῦ· κᾆτ' ὀνειδίζεις φίλοις
τοῖς μὴ θέλουσι δρᾶν τάδ', αὐτὸς ὢν κακός;
σίγα: νόμιζε δ', εἰ σὺ τὴν σαυτοῦ φιλεῖς
ψυχήν, φιλεῖν ἅπαντας: εἰ δ' ἡμᾶς κακῶς
ἐρεῖς, ἀκούσῃ πολλὰ κοὐ ψευδῆ κακά.   705

Son, whom do you imagine you are berating with insults, some Lydian or Phrygian slave of yours, bought with money? Do you not know that I am a freeborn Thessalian, legitimately begotten of a Thessalian father? You go too far in insult, and since you hurl [680] brash words at me, you will not get off with impunity.
I begot you and raised you to be the master of this house, but I am not obliged to die for you. I did not inherit this as a family custom, fathers dying for sons, nor as a Greek custom either. [685] For you are happy or unhappy for yourself alone. What you should in justice have received from me you have: you rule over many subjects, and I shall leave to you many acres of land, for I received the same from my father. What injustice have I done you? Of what am I robbing you? [690] Do not die on my behalf, and I shall not die on yours. You enjoy looking on the light. Do you think your father does not? Truly I regard the time below as long and life as short but sweet for all that. At all events you have shamelessly striven to avoid death, [695] and you live beyond your fated day by killing her. Can you then reproach me for cowardice when you, consummate coward, have been bested by a woman, who died to save you, her fine young husband? You have cleverly found out a way never to die [700] by persuading each wife in turn to die on your behalf. Can you then cast in the teeth of your kin that they do not wish to do this when you yourself are so craven? Hold your tongue! Consider that if you love life, so do all men. If you continue to insult me, [705] you shall hear reproaches many and true.

Generally speaking, Pheres' verbal fire comes to complete the typical agonistic form of the large-scale oral conflict; in particular, through the two consecutive rhetorical questions and the derogatory hint at the fecklessness of the young opponent, and through the enthusiastic display of the experienced speaker's self-consciousness, thus confirming his inalienable right to oratorical display (lines 675–680), the highly technical *exordium* of this rival *rhesis* gradually prepares for the ensuing ἔντεχναι πίστεις, which depict the incremental progress of the speech from *narratio* and *probatio* into the summing-up of *peroratio*. Beyond the usual attempt to secure the favour of his audience from the very beginning of the speech, the main objective of the irate speaker is to highlight those comparable properties which he shares with his opponent. This will allow Pheres to remove Admetus from the moral high ground, on which he previously placed himself, and subsequently to divest him of any remaining ethical merit.

In the same way as in the highly investigative and sceptical prelude, impressive fragments of analeptic *narratio* regarding Admetus' effortless prosperity due to his blood relationship with the king Pheres go hand in hand with a long series of rhetorical devices: euphemistic negations brought about by the oratorical technique of *paradiastole* (lines 683–684), striking conjunctions of opposing concepts (lines 685, εἴτε δυστυχὴς εἴτ' εὐτυχὴς & 692–693), rhetorical questions (lines 689, 691 & 698), analogical arguments (lines 691 & 703–704), instances of the rhetorical figures of *anadiplosis* or *conduplicatio* (line 691, χαίρεις … χαίρειν) and *litotes* or *exadversio* (lines 694, τὸ μὴ θανεῖν & 705, κοὐ ψευδῆ), misleading arguments stretched beyond the boundaries of hyperbole (lines 694–701), resonant examples of *polyptoton* playing with the ideas of death (lines 699–700) and evil (lines 697–705), reverberations of emblematic words through the rhetorical figures of *epanodos* (line 677, Θεσσαλόν … Θεσσαλοῦ) and *antimetavole* (lines 704–705, κακῶς … κακά), as well as emphatic reiterations of the concept of friendship (line 701, φίλοις, 703, φιλεῖς & 704, φιλεῖν) through the rhetorical device of *commoratio* or *epimone*.

It should be noted here that in a gesture of intratextual self-referentiality Euripides shows Pheres posing the burning question as to whether there is a written law compelling the father to be sacrificed for his children (lines 683–684). This unambiguously reflects Death's mocking language about an alleged transcendental law in favour of rich mortals (line 57). It is more than evident that Pheres' aside is a major hint and an indication that the Prologue-scene debate is the root and matrix of the play's principal *agôn logôn*; indeed, in both cases, numerous verbal modes and rhetorical devices are employed to explore in depth an insanely difficult question regarding whether self-denial is either an externally imposed stipulation or a moral impulse stemming from personal heroism. Pheres quite cynically admits that he has no care at all about his post-mortem reputation, brandishing as powerful argument in his favour the risk of retaliation by the close relatives of Alcestis (lines 726 & 730–733). Characteristic of the abysmal chasm between Admetus and his father is without a doubt the closing section of the abovementioned statement, in which through the suggestive *enumeratio* of hypothetical interpretations and repetitive references to friendship, greatly enriched by the balancing force of the rhetorical figure of *dirimens copulatio*, the invocation of blood ties is addressed to someone who has just forever renounced his parents and elevated the non-kin's self-sacrificing choice to an infrangibly inalienable bond.

Closing Remarks

The play's impressive *agônes logôn*, although distinguished for their rhetorical dexterity and finesse, and while each speaker is sufficiently *vir bonus dicendi peritus*, lack the synthetic force that would allow definitive answers to the startling questions posed by a concourse of impossible events at Pherae. In a masterly way Euripides draws on the genre of agonistic oratory, laying much stress upon its sensitive points and weaknesses, in order to suggest that neither humans nor the gods have the power to break the mystical bonds of those age-old laws that regulate the relationship between mortals and immortals, unless a hero-god, that is, one who has a share in both human and divine spheres and is obviously blessed by the divine grace of Zeus himself, comes along to reverse the course of events.

Heracles, this prominent symbol of the titanic struggle of man with destiny, but also the celebrated recipient of the favour and protection of mighty Zeus, establishes triumphantly a new moral law, or more fittingly invites his fellow humans to reflect on the possibility that the self-sacrificial honesty of mortals could be, under certain circumstances, a path to long-term survival, renewal, and ultimately immortality.[23] It would be, however, unwise to believe that the miraculous resurrection of Alcestis fundamentally overthrows the canons and principles moderating the human condition, in view of the fact that the extraordinary revival of Alcestis is a unique episode in Greek mythological tradition. At any rate, this phenomenal event does not cease to point out that moral excellence and ethical integrity are such important virtues that they have the power to shatter even the apparently indestructible shackles of mortality in which humans are chained.

Bibliography

Allen, D.S. (2002), *The World of Prometheus: The Politics of Punishing in Democratic Athens*, Princeton.
Allen, D.S. (2005), 'Greek Tragedy and Law', in: M. Gagarin/D. Cohen (eds.), *The Cambridge Companion to Ancient Greek Law*, Cambridge, 374–393.
Bagordo, A. (2003), *Reminiszenen früher Lyrik bei den attischen Tragikern*, Munich.
Barker, E.T.E. (2009), *Entering the Agon: Dissent and Authority in Homer, Historiography and Tragedy*, Oxford.
Battezzato, L. (2012), 'The Language of Sophocles', in: A. Markantonatos (ed.), *Brill's Companion to Sophocles*, Leiden/Boston, 305–324.

---

[23] On Heracles, see the excellent discussion in Stafford 2012 with extensive bibliography.

Berlage, J. (1888), *Commentatio de Euripide Philosopho*, Leiden.
Bers, V. (1974), *Enallage and Greek Style*, Leiden.
Bers, V. (1984), *Greek Poetic Syntax in the Classical Age*, New Haven.
Bers, V. (1994), 'Tragedy and Rhetoric', in: I. Worthington (ed.), *Persuasion: Greek Rhetoric in Action*, London, 176–195.
Bizzell, P./Herzberg, B. (eds.) (1990), *The Rhetorical Tradition: Readings from Classical Times to the Present*, Boston.
Bonner, S.F. (1949), *Roman Declamation*, Liverpool.
Breitenbach, W. (1934), *Untersuchungen zur Sprache der Euripideischen Lyrik*, Stuttgart.
Bruhn, E. (1899), *Anhang*, in: F.W. Schneidewin/A. Nauck, *Sophokles*, VIII, rev. E. Bruhn/L. Radermacher, Berlin.
Buck, C.D. (1955), *The Greek Dialects*, Chicago.
Budelmann, F. (2000), *The Language of Sophocles: Communality, Communication and Involvement*, Cambridge.
Buxton, R.G.A. (1982), *Persuasion in Greek Tragedy: A Study of Peitho*, Cambridge.
Campbell, L. (1879²), 'Introductory Essay on the Language of Sophocles', in: L. Campbell (1879²), *Sophocles Edited with English Notes and Introductions*, I, Oxford, 1–107.
Carey, C. (2011), 'Ἡ Ῥητορική στον (Ἄλλον) Μένανδρο', in: Th. Pappas/A. Markantonatos (eds.), *Ἀττική Κωμῳδία. Πρόσωπα καὶ Προσεγγίσεις*, Athens, 435–455.
Castelli, C. (2000), *Μήτηρ σοφιστῶν: La tragedia nei trattati greci di retorica*, Milan.
Clark, D.L. (1957), *Rhetoric in Greco-Roman Education*, New York.
Clarke, M.L. (1962²), *Rhetoric at Rome*, London.
Clay, D.M. (1958), *A Formal Analysis of the Vocabularies of Aeschylus, Sophocles and Euripides*, Part 2, Athens.
Cohen, D. (1995), *Law, Violence, and Society in Classical Athens*, Cambridge.
Cole, T. (1991), *The Origins of Rhetoric in Ancient Greece*, Baltimore.
Collard, C. (1975), 'Formal Debates in Euripidean Drama', in: *G&R* 22, 58–71.
Collard, C. (2005), 'Colloquial Language in Tragedy: A Supplement to the Work of P.T. Stevens', in: *CQ* 55, 350–386.
Collard, C. (2013), 'Formal Debates', in: H.M. Roisman (ed.) (2013), *The Encyclopedia of Greek Tragedy*, I, Malden/Oxford, 534–536.
Colvin, S. (2004), *Dialect in Aristophanes: The Politics of Language in Ancient Greek Literature*, Oxford.
Colvin, S. (2007), *A Historical Greek Reader: Mycenaean to the Koiné*, Oxford.
Conacher, D.J. (1972), 'Some Questions of Probability and Relevance in Euripidean Drama', in: *Maia* 24, 199–207.
Conacher, D.J. (1981), 'Rhetoric and Relevance in Euripidean Drama', in: *AJPh* 102, 3–25.
Conley, T.M. (1990), *Rhetoric in the European Tradition*, New York.
Croally, N.T. (1994), *Euripidean Polemic: The Trojan Women and the Function of Tragedy*, Cambridge.
De Jong, I.J.F./Rijksbaron, A. (eds.) (2006), *Sophocles and the Greek Language: Aspects of Diction, Syntax and Pragmatics*, Leiden/Boston.
Denniston, J.D. (1952), *Greek Prose Style*, Oxford.
Dominik, W. (ed.) (1997), *Roman Eloquence: Rhetoric in Society and Literature*, New York.
Dorjahn, A.P. (1927), 'Poetry in Athenian Courts', in: *CPh* 22, 85–93.
Dover, K.J. (1997), *The Evolution of Greek Prose Style*, Oxford.

Dubischar, M. (2001), *Die Agonszenen bei Euripides: Untersuchungen zu ausgewählten Dramen*, Stuttgart.
Dubischar, M. (2006), 'Der Kommunikationsmodus der Debatte im griechischen Drama', in: *Rhetorik* 25, 14–29.
Duchemin, J. (1945–1968²), *L'ΑΓΩΝ dans la tragédie grecque*, Paris.
Earp, F.R. (1944), *The Style of Sophocles*, Cambridge.
Earp, F.R. (1948), *The Style of Aeschylus*, Cambridge.
Easterling, P.E. (1973), 'Repetition in Sophocles', in: *Hermes* 101, 14–34.
Easterling, P.E. (1999), 'Plain Words in Sophocles', in: J. Griffin (ed.) (1999), *Sophocles Revisited*, Oxford, 95–107.
Eden, K. (1980), *The Influence of Legal Procedure on the Development of Tragic Structure*, PhD Thesis, University of Stanford.
Eicken-Iselin, E. (1942), *Interpretationen und Untersuchungen zum Aufbau der Sophokleischen Rheseis*, PhD Thesis, University of Basel, Dortmund.
Encinas Reguero, M.C. (2008), *Tragedia y retórica en la Atenas clásica: la rhesis tragica como discurso formal en Sófocles*, Logroño.
Encinas Reguero, M.C. (2011), 'Exhibicionismo retórico y transformación narrative en Edipo en Colono', in: M. Quijada Sagredo (ed.), *Estudios sobre tragedia griega Eurípides, el teatro griego de finales del s. V a.C. y su influencia posterior*, Madrid, 105–130.
Enos, R.L. (1993), *Greek Rhetoric before Aristotle*, Prospect Heights.
Epke, E. (1951), *Über die Streitszenen und ihre Entwicklung in der griechischen Tragödie*, PhD Thesis, University of Hamburg.
Fehling, D. (1969), *Die Wiederholungsfiguren und ihr Gebrauch bei den Griechen vor Gorgias*, Berlin.
Fialho, M.C. (2007), 'A retórica do sofrimento no *Filoctetes* de Sófocles. O poder persuasive de *pathos* e a força ética da *philia*', in: J.V. Bañuls/F. De Martino/C. Morenilla (eds.), *El teatro Greco-latino y su recepción en la tradición occidental*, Bari, 157–171.
Froleyks, W.J. (1973), *Der ΑΓΩΝ ΛΟΓΩΝ in der antiken Literatur*, PhD Thesis, University of Bonn.
Fuhrmann, M. (1990³), *Die antike Rhetorik*, Munich/Zurich.
Gallagher, R.L. (2003), 'Making the Stronger Argument the Weaker: Euripides, *Electra* 518–44', in: *CQ* 53, 401–415.
Gilman, S.L./C. Blair/D.J. Parent (ed. & transl.) (1989), *Friedrich Nietzsche on Rhetoric and Language*, Oxford.
Gödde, S. (2000), *Das Drama der Hikesie: Ritual und Rhetorik in Aischylos' Hiketiden*, Münster.
Goebel, G.H. (1983), *Early Greek Rhetorical Theory and Practice: Proof and Arrangement in the Speeches of Antiphon and Euripides*, PhD Thesis, University of Michigan.
Goldbrunner, H. (1957), *Studien zur sophokleischen Rhesis*, PhD Thesis, University of Munich.
Goldhill, S. (1986a), 'Rhetoric and Relevance: Interpolation at Euripides *Electra* 367–400', in: *GRBS* 27, 157–171.
Goldhill, S. (1986b), *Reading Greek Tragedy*, Cambridge.
Goldhill, S. (1997), 'The Language of Tragedy: Rhetoric and Communication', in: P.E. Easterling (ed.), *The Cambridge Companion to Greek Tragedy*, Cambridge, 127–150.
Goldhill, S. (2012), *Sophocles and the Language of Tragedy*, Oxford.
Graf, G. (1950), *Die Agonszenen bei Euripides*, PhD Thesis, University of Göttingen.
Gunderson, E. (2003), *Declamation, Paternity, and Identity: Authority and the Rhetorical Self*, Cambridge.
Gygli-Wyss, B. (1966), *Das nominale Polyptoton im älteren Griechisch*, Göttingen.

Habinek, T. (2005), *Ancient Rhetoric and Oratory*, Malden/Oxford.
Hall, E. (1995), 'Lawcourt Dramas: The Power of Performance in Greek Forensic Oratory', in: *BICS* 40, 39–58.
Halliwell, S. (1997), 'Between Public and Private: Tragedy and Athenian Experience of Rhetoric', in: C.B.R. Pelling (ed.), *Greek Tragedy and the Historian*, Oxford, 121–141.
Hamilton, R. (1985), 'Slings and Arrows: The Debate with Lycus in the *Heracles*', in: *TAPA* 115, 19–25.
Harris, E.M./D.F. Leão/P.J. Rhodes (eds.) (2010), *Law and Drama in Ancient Greece*, London.
Heath, M. (1987), *The Poetics of Greek Tragedy*, Stanford.
Heath, M. (1995), *Hermogenes on Issues: Strategies of Argument in Later Greek Rhetoric*, Oxford.
Heiden, B. (1989), *Tragic Rhetoric: An Interpretation of Sophocles' Trachiniae*, New York.
Höhne, H.W.C. (1867), *Euripides und die Sophistik der Leidenschaft*, Plauen.
Hubbard, T.K. (2007), 'Attic Comedy and the Development of Theoretical Rhetoric', in: I. Worthington (ed.), *A Companion to Greek Rhetoric*, Oxford, 498–508.
Hudson-Williams, H.L. (1950), 'Conventional Forms of Debate and the Melian Dialogue', in: *AJP* 71, 156–169.
Iakov, D.I. (2000), *Πινδάρου Ἐπίνικοι, τ. Α'. Πυθιόνικοι*, Thessaloniki.
Iakov, D.I. (2012), *Εὐριπίδης, Ἄλκηστη. Ἑρμηνευτικὴ Ἔκδοση*, I–II, Athens.
Johnstone, S. (1999), *Disputes and Democracy: The Consequenses of Litigation in Ancient Athens*, Austin.
Jouan, F. (1984), 'Euripide et la rhétorique', in: *LEC* 52, 3–13.
Kelly, A. (1994), *Damaging Voice: Language of Aggression for the Athenian Trial*, PhD Thesis, University of Berkeley.
Kennedy, G.A. (1963), *The Art of Persuasion in Greece*, Princeton.
Kennedy, G.A. (1972), *The Art of Persuasion in the Roman World*, Princeton.
Kennedy, G.A. (1980), *Classical Rhetoric and Its Christian and Secular Tradition from Ancient to Modern Times*, Chapel Hill.
Kennedy, G.A. (1983), *Greek Rhetoric under Christian Emperors*, Princeton.
Kennedy, G.A. (1984), *New Testament Interpretation through Rhetorical Criticism*, Chapel Hill.
Kennedy, G.A. (ed.) (1989), *The Cambridge History of Literary Criticism*. I, *Classical Criticism*, Cambridge.
Kennedy, G.A. (1994), *A New History of Classical Rhetoric*, Princeton.
Kinneavy, J.L. (1987), *Greek Rhetorical Origins of Christian Faith*, New York.
Kirkwood, G.M. (1994²), *A Study of Sophoclean Drama. With a New Preface and Enlarged Bibliographical Note*, Ithaca, NY.
Lanni, A. (2006), *Law and Justice in the Courts of Classical Athens*, Cambridge.
Lausberg, H. (1990³), *Handbuch der literarischen Rhetorik. Eine Grundlage der Literaturwissenschaft*, Stuttgart.
Lechner, M. (1874), *De Euripide Rhetorum Discipulo*, Ansbach.
Leeman, A. (1963), *Orationis Ratio: The Stylistic Theories and Practice of the Roman Orators, Historians, and Philosophers*, II, Amsterdam.
Lees, J.T. (1891), *ΔΙΚΑΝΙΚΟΣ ΛΟΓΟΣ in Euripides*, PhD Thesis, Johns Hopkins University.
Lloyd, M. (1992), *The Agon in Euripides*, Oxford.
Markantonatos, A. (2002), *Tragic Narrative: A Narratological Study of Sophocles' Oedipus at Colonus*, Berlin/New York.
Markantonatos, A. (2007), *Oedipus at Colonus: Sophocles, Athens, and the World*, Berlin/New York.

Markantonatos, A. (2012a) [& B. Zimmermann], 'Preface', in: A. Markantonatos/B. Zimmermann (eds.), *Crisis on Stage: Tragedy and Comedy in Late Fifth-Century Athens*, Berlin/Boston, v–xi.

Markantonatos, A. (2012b), 'Leadership in Action: Wise Policy and Firm Resolve in Euripides' *Iphigenia at Aulis*', in: A. Markantonatos/B. Zimmermann (eds.) (2012), *Crisis on Stage: Tragedy and Comedy in Late Fifth-Century Athens*, Berlin/Boston, 189–218.

Markantonatos, A. (2013), *Euripides' Alcestis: Narrative, Myth, and Religion*, Berlin/Boston.

Markantonatos, G.A. (2009), *Tragic Irony in Aeschylus, Sophocles, and Euripides*, Athens.

Martin, J. (1974), *Antike Rhetorik: Technik und Methode*, Munich.

Mastronarde, D.J. (2010), *The Art of Euripides: Dramatic Technique and Social Context*, Cambridge.

McClure, L.K. (1999), *Spoken like a Woman: Speech and Gender in Athenian Drama*, Princeton.

McComiskey, B. (2002), *Gorgias and the New Sophistic Rhetoric*, Carbondale.

McDonald, M. (2007), 'Rhetoric and Tragedy: Weapons of Mass Persuasion', in: I. Worthington (ed.), *A Companion to Greek Rhetoric*, Malden/Oxford, 473–489.

Meridor, R. (2000), 'Creative Rhetoric in Euripides' *Troades*: Some Notes on Hecuba's Speech', in: *CQ* 50, 16–29.

Miller, Th. (1887), *Euripides Rhetoricus*, PhD Thesis, University of Göttingen.

Moorhouse, A.C. (1982), *The Syntax of Sophocles*, Leiden.

Murphy, C.T. (1938), 'Aristophanes and the Art of Rhetoric', in: *HSCP* 49, 69–113.

Murphy, J.J. (1974), *Rhetoric in the Middle Ages: A History of Rhetorical Theory from Saint Augustine to the Renaissance*, Berkeley.

Nagy, G. (1970), *Greek Dialects and the Transformation of an Indo-European Process*, Cambridge MA.

Navarre, O. (1900), *Essai sur la rhétorique avant Aristote*, Paris.

Nightingale, A.W. (1992), 'Plato's *Gorgias* and Euripides' *Antiope*: A Study in Generic Transformation', in: *CA* 11, 121–141.

Norden, E. (1909–1958²), *Antike Kunstprosa vom VI. Jarhunderts vor Christus bis in die Zeit der Renaissance*, II, Leipzig.

Nuchelmans, J.C.F. (1971), *De ΑΓΩΝ of ΑΜΙΛΛΑ ΛΟΓΩΝ in de Tragedies van Euripides*, Nijmegen.

O'Brien, M.J. (1988), 'Character, Action and Rhetoric in the *Agon* of the *Orestes*', in: *Filologia e forma letterarie: Studi offerti a Francesco della Corte*, Urbino, I, 183–199.

O'Reagan, D. (1992), *Rhetoric, Comedy, and the Violence of Language in Aristophanes' Clouds*, Oxford.

O'Sullivan, N. (1992), *Alcidamas, Aristophanes, and the Beginnings of Greek Stylistic Theory*, Stuttgart.

Ober, J./Strauss, B. (1990), 'Drama, Political Rhetoric, and the Discourse of Athenian Democracy', in: J.J. Winkler/F.I. Zeitlin (eds.) (1990), *Nothing to Do with Dionysos? Athenian Drama in its Social Context*, Princeton, 237–270.

Papakonstantinou, Z. (2008), *Lawmaking and Adjudication in Archaic Greece*, Bristol.

Pelling, C. (2005), 'Tragedy, Rhetoric, and Performance Culture', in: J. Gregory (ed.), *A Companion to Greek Tragedy*, Malden/Oxford, 83–102.

Quijada Sagredo, M./Encinas Reguero, M.C. (eds.) (2013), *Retórica y Discurso en el Teatro Griego*, Madrid.

Riedweg, C. (2000), 'Der Tragödiendichter als Rhetor? Redestrategien in Euripides' *Hekabe* und ihr Verhältnis zur zeitgenössischen Rhetorik-theorie', in: *RhM* 143, 1–32.

Ritoré Ponce, J. (2005), 'Tragedia y Retórica', in: M. Brioso Sánchez/A. Villarrubia Medina (eds.), *Aspectos del teatro griego antiguo*, Seville, 121–141.
Roisman, H.M. (2013), 'Euripides: *Alcestis*', in: H.M. Roisman (ed.), *The Blackwell Encyclopedia of Greek Tragedy*, London/New York, 339–345.
Rosenbloom, D. (2009), 'Staging Rhetoric in Athens', in: E. Gunderson (ed.), *The Cambridge Companion to Ancient Rhetoric*, Cambridge, 194–211.
Russell, D.A. (1983), *Greek Declamation*, Cambridge.
Rutherford, R.B. (2010), 'The Greek of Athenian Tragedy', in: E. Bakker (ed.), *A Companion to the Ancient Greek Language*, Malden/Oxford, 441–454.
Rutherford, R.B. (2012), *Greek Tragic Style: Form, Language and Interpretation*, Cambridge.
Sansone, D. (2012), *Greek Drama and the Invention of Rhetoric*, Oxford.
Schiappa, E. (1999), *The Beginnings of Rhetorical Theory in Classical Greece*, New Haven.
Schmalzriedt, E. (1980), 'Sophokles und die Rhetorik', in: *Rhetorik* 1, 89–110.
Scodel, R. (1997), 'Drama and Rhetoric', in: S.E. Porter (ed.), *Handbook of Classical Rhetoric in the Hellenistic Period (330 BCE – AD 400)*, Leiden, 489–504.
Scodel, R. (1999–2000), 'Verbal Performance and Euripidean Rhetoric', in: M. Cropp/K. Lee/D. Sansone (eds.), *Euripides and Tragic Theatre in the Late Fifth Century* [*ICS* 24–25 (1999–2000)] 129–144.
Senoner, R. (1960), *Der Rede-Agon im euripideischen Drama*, PhD Thesis, University of Vienna.
Silva, M.F. (1987–1988), 'Crítica à retórica na comédia de Aristófanes', in: *Humanitas* 39, 43–104.
Slater, N.W. (ed.) (2013), *Euripides, Alcestis*, London/New York.
Solmsen, F. (1931), *Antiphonstudien: Untersuchungen zur Entstehung der attischen Gerichtsrede*, Berlin.
Stafford, E.J. (2012), *Herakles*, London.
Thomson, A.D. (1898), *Euripides and the Attic Orators: A Comparison*, London/New York.
Tietze, F. (1933), *Die euripideischen Reden und ihre Bedeutung*, PhD Thesis, University of Breslau.
Usher, S. (1999), *Greek Oratory: Tradition and Originality*, Oxford.
Van Looy, H. (1975), 'Figura etymologica et etymologie dans l'oeuvre de Sophocle', in: *Museum Philologum Londiniense* 1, 109–119.
Várzeas, M. (2009), *A força da palavra no teatro de Sófocles: Entre retórica e poética*, Lisbon.
Volkmann, R. (1885), *Die Rhetorik der Griechen und Römer*, Leipzig.
Walker, J. (2000), *Rhetoric and Poetics in Antiquity*, Oxford.
Willi, A. (2007), *The Languages of Aristophanes*, Oxford.
Willi, A. (ed.) (2002), *The Language of Greek Comedy*, Oxford.
Wilson, P.J. (1996), 'Tragic Rhetoric: The Use of Tragedy and the Tragic in the Fourth Century', in: M.S. Silk (ed.), *Tragedy and the Tragic: Greek Theatre and Beyond*, Oxford, 310–331.
Winterbottom, M. (1980), *Roman Declamation*, Bristol.
Wisse, J. (1989), *Ethos and Pathos from Aristotle to Cicero*, Amsterdam.
Wohl, V. (2010a), *Law's Cosmos: Juridical Discourse in Athenian Forensic Oratory*, Cambridge.
Wohl, V. (2010b), 'A Tragic Case of Poisoning: Intention between Tragedy and the Law', in: *TAPA* 140, 33–70.
Wooten, C. (1987), *Hermogenes' On Types of Style*, Chapel Hill.
Wooten, C. (2001), *The Orator in Action and Theory in Greece and Rome*, Boston.
Quijada Sagredo, M./Encinas Reguero, M.C. (eds.) (2013), *Retórica y Discurso en el Teatro Griego*, Madrid, 61–90.

Andrea Rodighiero
'Do you see this, natives of this land?'

Formalized Speech, Rhetoric, and Character in Sophocles'
Oedipus at Colonus 728–1043

1 The limits of interpretation

'The highly rhetorical nature of Greek Tragedy in general'[1] has been widely recognized by critics and scholars, yet one of the main questions occupying classicists working on Greek drama is that of the genuine possibility of a formal, more than linguistic, analysis. Should tragedy be scrutinized with the same means and through the same lens as a page of Lysias or an oration of Demosthenes? Is tragic poetry *also* rhetorical?

When we read or watch a tragedy, we are dealing with something that is conceived as a fiction, partly realistic but not real.[2] The fiction of tragedy is expressed through a variety of metres, and at least three different forms of performance: recited sections and dialogues, songs, and the *parakatalogé*, or recitative. Can we find a distinct space for rhetorical analysis in this assortment of performative modes? The answer is obviously yes, but we still need to bear in mind that the shape, the syntax, and very often the vocabulary of poetic discourse are rather different from a λόγος uttered in plain prose.[3]

In a well-known passage of the *Poetics*, Aristotle states that 'when spoken dialogue was introduced, tragedy's own nature discovered the appropriate metre. For the iambic trimeter, more than any other metre, has the rhythm of speech'.[4] However, no one in Greece spoke in trimeters in his or her everyday life. In abstract terms, therefore, we should paradoxically consider choral or solo songs as

---

[1] I owe this *incipit* to Conacher 1981, 3. I would like to thank Alexander Johnston for his help with improving the English version of this paper.
[2] That rule can also be applied to a non-mythical drama such as Aeschylus' *Persians*.
[3] 'The play itself was a medley of speaking, chanting and singing in a variety of verse forms, using a type of Greek never heard in everyday use in Athens or anywhere else': Bers 1994, 176; see also Scodel 1997, 489: 'often [...] it is hard to distinguish tricks of style that genuinely come from rhetorical practice from those that belong to poetic tradition'.
[4] 'An indication of this – the philosopher continues – is that we speak many trimeters in conversation with one another, but hexameters only rarely and when diverging from the colloquial register': 1449a23–28 (transl. S. Halliwell); this opinion is confirmed in *Rhet.* 1408b33–35.

formally *more realistic* and more natural than dialogues, since it was not impossible for the community and for the average citizen to be involved in the performance of celebratory hymns, religious songs, and musical prayers as a *real* and achievable experience.

Even in the Euripidean ἀγών, which is the best place in Attic drama to detect and recognize rhetorical devices, we are not able to recreate, behind the fiction, a perfect likeness (or mirror image) of what happened in the public assemblies, in courts, and in oratorical meetings. To describe these *real* situations, tragedy makes clever use of messengers, who sometimes develop a narrative about assemblies, trials, and off-stage public decisions (the most significant being the episode related by the ἄγγελος in Euripides' *Orestes* where a group of citizens must decide whether to condemn or to release Orestes and Pylades: vv. 852–956).[5]

To end this list of misgivings, in a passage of the *Rhetoric* Aristotle claims that there is a prescriptive difference between prose and poetry: the λόγος must be provided with a rhythm, not with a metre, for in the latter case it would be a poem.[6] We will see later that this basic Aristotelian distinction could restrict (or enlarge) our vision of things.

I do not intend, in the following pages, to revisit one of the principal and most interesting issues in the field, concerning when rhetorical technique became part of the shared skills a poet could pick up to improve and embellish his poetry. The previous question has to do with the ways in which one might distinguish a natural aptitude to rhetoric and eloquence, used with the aim of persuading or praising someone (without following any fixed rules), from the formal education in learned rhetorical τέχνη and its calculated, deliberate use in a way which displays sensitivity to the audience. In recent years there has been much speculation on the origins of rhetoric (its 'archaeology', as it were), which some trace back – following the traditional interpretation – to the Sicilian school of Corax and Tisias

---

[5] See Willink 1986, 223–225 and 229–231; on the *Orestes* scene and other reported assemblies where a decision is made democratically in Greek tragedy, see Carter 2013 (with Aesch. *Supp.* 600–624, Eur. *Hec.* 107–143).
[6] *Rhet.* 1408b30–31: ῥυθμὸν δεῖ ἔχειν τὸν λόγον, μέτρον δὲ μή· ποίημα γὰρ ἔσται. For an attempt to reconcile the rhetorical development of Greek speeches and (primarily archaic) poetry as displaying rhetorical argumentation see Walker 2000 (especially pp. 139ff.), who argues against the opposition between practical (i.e. political) rhetoric and the supposedly mere aesthetic pleasure of poetic eloquence, and against the 'inauspicious declaration that poetry and rhetoric were fundamentally different, even incompatible things' (p. vii, with reference to C.S. Baldwin's preliminary statement in *Ancient Rhetoric and Poetic*, 1924).

(before Protagoras and Gorgias); others, to the primitive, spontaneous, and sometimes ineffective eloquence developed in the Homeric dialogues,[7] but also to the two main philosophers, Plato and Aristotle. It has even been assumed that tragedy was able to create or influence the shaping and formalisation of speeches and discourses, while oratory, coming later, aspired to imitate drama, bringing characters onto the rostrum rather than onto the stage.[8]

2 Characters and oratorical talent (I): Creon

The term ἐνθύμημα occurs for the first time in extant Greek literature in the *Oedipus at Colonus*.[9] This is of course not a good reason to interpret Sophocles' last tragedy as a paradigmatic model of rhetorical knowledge, or as a list of guidelines. Therefore, my perspective will remain theatrical, and my analysis of a segment of the drama will focus on the relations between tragic characters (Creon, Oedipus, and Theseus), their speeches, and the role played by the poet in the construction of different rhetorical levels. Finally, we will briefly clarify for what dramatic as well as ideological purpose – if any – those levels are designed.

Can such speeches disclose any hints of the ἦθος, the character of individual tragic *personae*, and its consistency? Or should we believe that the poet himself,

---

[7] See recently Knudsen 2014 on Homer as a master of rhetoric (and the Homeric epics as the locus of its origins) and his heroes as a gallery of skilled speakers; for a summary of ancient and modern debates, see Dentice di Accadia Ammone 2012, 1–46.
[8] On the presence or absence of advanced rhetorical theory before the death of Sophocles and Euripides see, among many others, Cole 1991 (in favour of Plato and Aristotle as the founders of a scientific language defining and analyzing rhetoric); Schiappa 1999; Gagarin 2007; Sansone 2012, 5 (and *passim*, esp. chapter 7) with further bibliography (p. 126 n. 14 in particular); Sansone believes that 'formalized rhetoric in ancient Greece is, in effect, largely an outgrowth of Athenian tragic poetry', and cf. p. 145: 'the audience member would hear one figure speaking and see a second figure processing what the first was saying, at the same time as the audience member himself was processing the words and, perhaps, anticipating the second figure's response to them. It is my belief that it was precisely in this context that we can see the origin of rhetorical theory'.
[9] Cf. v. 1199: τἀνθυμήματα ('the food for meditation' in Jebb's explanation [Jebb 1907, 188]). The word also occurs at v. 292, and in this case some critics have suggested a rhetorical nuance: according to Untersteiner 1929, 79, this is the first occurrence of the term as 'retorico' (he translates 'i tuoi ragionamenti', and cf. Kamerbeek 1984, 169), but see Guidorizzi 2008, 249: 'quelle di Edipo però non sono semplici argomentazioni, in senso dialettico, ma pensieri angosciosi'.

like a kind of λογογράφος,[10] 'writes for' them, and emphasizes the rhetorical background of the speeches at a particular moment and for a particular purpose? In the case of Creon, a good λογογράφος would have written a speech suppressing any hint of negative ἦθος. Yet what we observe is different (728–762):[11]

Κρ. ἄνδρες χθονὸς τῆσδ' **εὐγενεῖς οἰκήτορες**,
ὁρῶ τιν' ὑμᾶς ὀμμάτων εἰληφότας
φόβον νεώρη τῆς ἐμῆς ἐπεισόδου·   730
ὃν μήτ' ὀκνεῖτε μήτ' ἀφῆτ' ἔπος κακόν.
ἥκω γὰρ οὐχ ὡς δρᾶν τι βουληθείς, ἐπεὶ
γέρων μέν εἰμι, πρὸς **πόλιν** δ' ἐπίσταμαι
σθένουσαν ἥκων, **εἴ τιν' Ἑλλάδος, μέγα**.
ἀλλ' ἄνδρα τόνδε **τηλικόσδ'** ἀπεστάλην   735
πείσων ἕπεσθαι πρὸς τὸ Καδμείων πέδον,
οὐκ ἐξ ἑνὸς στείλαντος, ἀλλ' ἀστῶν ὕπο
πάντων κελευσθείς, οὕνεχ' ἧκέ μοι γένει
τὰ τοῦδε **πενθεῖν** πήματ' **εἰς πλεῖστον πόλεως**.
ἀλλ', ὦ ταλαίπωρ' Οἰδίπους, κλυών ἐμοῦ   740
ἱκοῦ πρὸς οἴκους. πᾶς σε Καδμείων λεὼς
καλεῖ δικαίως, ἐκ δὲ τῶν μάλιστ' ἐγώ·
ὅσπερ, **εἰ μὴ πλεῖστον ἀνθρώπων ἔφυν
κάκιστος**,[12] ἀλγῶ **τοῖσι σοῖς κακοῖς**, γέρον,
ὁρῶν σε τὸν **δύστηνον** ὄντα μὲν ξένον,   745
ἀεὶ δ' ἀλήτην κἀπὶ προσπόλου μιᾶς
βιοστερῆ χωροῦντα, τὴν ἐγὼ **τάλας**
οὐκ ἄν ποτ' ἐς τοσοῦτον αἰκίας πεσεῖν
ἔδοξ', ὅσον πέπτωκεν ἥδε **δύσμορος**,
ἀεί σε κηδεύουσα καὶ τὸ σὸν κάρα   750
πτωχῷ διαίτῃ, **τηλικοῦτος**, οὐ γάμων
ἔμπειρος, ἀλλὰ τοὐπιόντος ἁρπάσαι.
ἆρ' ἄθλιον τοὔνειδος, ὦ **τάλας** ἐγώ,
ὠνείδισ' ἐς σὲ κἀμὲ καὶ τὸ πᾶν γένος;

---

[10] Conacher 1981, 6–9, writing on the character of Admetus in Euripides' *Alcestis*, rightly says that he does not believe that 'Euripides like a good logographer is concerned to let the speaker *make* the best case for himself on each occasion [...]: Admetus scores so many points *against* himself' (p. 8). On Euripides as a λογογράφος see *infra*. For a general and valuable approach to the character of tragic figures see Rutherford 2012, 283–322, with further bibliography (and Goldhill 2009, 36 n. 20); on Sophocles' characters, see Easterling 1977; Blundell 1989, 16–25; Budelmann 2000, 61–91.

[11] The text, here as elsewhere, is from Lloyd-Jones and Wilson's edition (1990), the translation from H. Lloyd-Jones' Loeb version (1994).

[12] This is the text printed in the Loeb edition, following **L** (where ἀλγῶ is s.l.) as other modern editors do (e.g. Dawe 1996); in the OCT edition, Lloyd-Jones and Wilson print vv. 743–744 as follows: [ὅσπερ, εἰ μὴ πλεῖστον ἀνθρώπων ἔφυν] / μάλιστα δ' ἀλγῶ τοῖσι σοῖς κακοῖς, γέρον (743 del. Nauck, μάλιστα δ' **T**).

ἀλλ' οὐ γὰρ ἔστι τἀμφανῆ κρύπτειν, σὺ νῦν   755
πρὸς θεῶν πατρῴων, Οἰδίπους, **πεισθεὶς ἐμοὶ**
†κρύψον† θελήσας ἄστυ καὶ δόμους μολεῖν
τοὺς σοὺς πατρῴους, τήνδε τὴν πόλιν φίλως
εἰπών· ἐπαξία γάρ· ἡ δ' οἴκοι πλέον
δίκη σέβοιτ' ἄν, οὖσα σὴ πάλαι τροφός.   760
Οι. ὦ πάντα τολμῶν **κἀπὸ παντὸς** ἂν φέρων
λόγου δικαίου μηχάνημα ποικίλον,
κτλ

CREON: Men who are the noble dwellers in this land, I see in your eyes a fear newly caused by my arrival! But do not be alarmed by it, nor let fall a hostile word! For I have not come intending any action, since I am old, and I know that I have come to a city that has great power, if any has in Greece. But I set out, old as I am, to persuade this man to accompany me to the land of the Cadmeans; it is not one man only who has sent me, but all the citizens who commanded me, because family ties caused me to mourn his sorrows most in all the city.
Come, long-suffering Oedipus, listen to me and come home! The whole people of Cadmus summons you, with good reason, and I most of all inasmuch as, if I am not the very worst of men, I grieve at your sorrows, aged man, seeing that in your misery you are an exile, and ever wander in indigence with but one attendant. Never would I have thought that this poor girl could fall to such a depth of misery as that to which she has fallen, always caring for you and for your person, living like a beggar at her age, ignorant of wedlock, but at the mercy of a chance comer!
Is not the reproach bitter that I have levelled, woe is me, at you and at myself and at all our family? But since one cannot hide what is manifest, do you now, Oedipus, in the name of the gods of your fathers let me persuade you and yield, consenting to return to the town and to the home of your fathers, saying a kind farewell to this city, for she deserves it; but your home city should in justice be reverenced more, since she reared you long ago.
OEDIPUS You who would stop at nothing and would extract a cunning scheme from any just plea...

The exordium of Creon's speech seems an example of modesty[13] which could be paraphrased and shortened as follows: 'I am a harmless old man, I have arrived in a powerful city, I am here on behalf of Thebes'.

---

[13] Another wonderful example is the exordium of Hippolytus' speech in Euripides' play: 'I am unaccomplished at giving speeches before a crowd' (v. 986: ἐγὼ δ' ἄκομψος εἰς ὄχλον δοῦναι λόγον), followed by the negative evaluation of others' speeches in general – a sign of his arrogant and contemptuous character: 'for those who are inadequate in the presence of the wise are more eloquent at speaking before a crowd' (vv. 988–989: οἱ γὰρ ἐν σοφοῖς / φαῦλοι παρ' ὄχλῳ μουσικώτεροι λέγειν, transl. M.R. Halleran), cf. Conacher 1981, 15. Further bibliography on speeches and characters in Pelling 2005, 100 ('we so often see characters not making the best of their cases – Euripides' Electra and Clytemnestra, for instance – and it is precisely the ways that the rhetoric misfires which make it most interesting').

In his opening words, Creon deploys a formula that could be used by a speaker politely addressing the citizen body: ἄνδρες χθονὸς τῆσδ' εὐγενεῖς οἰκήτορες, 'men who are the noble dwellers in this land'. This can easily be read as a sign of diplomacy; that this is the case is partly betrayed by the immediate reference to his fear of the old men.[14] As Stephen Halliwell puts it, Creon 'uses rhetoric not only to give prominence to his own official status as a delegated representative of Thebes, but also to broach his business in a public manner, as though the return of Oedipus to Thebes could only be executed by a piece of interstate negotiation'.[15] This analysis is confirmed by the fact that in 'a brilliant combination of subtlety and tact' he identifies himself three times as an emissary of *all* the Thebans,[16] presenting his expedition as a diplomatic mission (vv. 735, 737–738, 741).

Following his effort to sound grieved by the fate of his kinsman, Creon addresses Oedipus directly in an affected tone and in 'an enormously long sentence [vv. 741–752], a preposterous piece of shammed emotion and false compassion' inspired by an overstated sense of dissimulation. Aristotle would have called it a case of artificial persuasion: ἔντεχνοι πίστεις.[17] We observe that in both cases the Theban displays a docile ἦθος, while endeavouring to arouse sympathy in his listeners; that is, to manipulate and direct the audience's disposition towards a sympathetic attitude.[18]

---

14 Creon adopts a similarly formal approach in his self-defence before Theseus: τέκνον Αἰγέως (v. 940). On general addresses to groups – not only ethnic – see Dickey 1996, 177–184, with the examples listed at pp. 293–305 (for a similar expression on Oedipus' lips cf. v. 1348: ἄνδρες τῆσδε δημοῦχοι χθονός).

15 Halliwell 1997, 138. See also Guidorizzi 2008, 294s.

16 See Buxton 1982, 137: 'like Odysseus (*Phil.* 1243, 1257–1258, 1294) and Menelaos and Agamemnon (e.g. *Aj.* 1136, 1242–1243; cf. 1055), he represents his own conduct as properly democratic, being in accordance not merely with the majority view but with the consensus of the entire citizen body'.

17 The quotation is from Kamerbeek 1984, 114. See Arist. *Rhet.* 1355b35–38: τῶν δὲ πίστεων αἱ μὲν ἄτεχνοί εἰσιν αἱ δ' ἔντεχνοι… ἔντεχνα δὲ ὅσα διὰ τῆς μεθόδου καὶ δι' ἡμῶν κατασκευασθῆναι δυνατόν, 'of the *pisteis* some are atechnic ('non-artistic'), some entechnic ('embodied in art, artistic'). […] and *entechnic* whatever can be prepared by method and by "us"' (transl. G.A. Kennedy).

18 See again Arist. *Rhet.* 1356a1–4: τῶν δὲ διὰ τοῦ λόγου ποριζομένων πίστεων τρία εἴδη ἔστιν· αἱ μὲν γάρ εἰσιν ἐν τῷ ἤθει τοῦ λέγοντος, αἱ δὲ ἐν τῷ τὸν ἀκροατὴν διαθεῖναί πως, αἱ δὲ ἐν αὐτῷ τῷ λόγῳ διὰ τοῦ δεικνύναι ἢ φαίνεσθαι δεικνύναι, 'of the *pisteis* provided through speech there are three species; for some are in the character of the speaker, and some in disposing the listener in some way, and some in the speech itself, by showing or seeming to show something' (transl. G.A. Kennedy).

Creon's speech is full of rhetorical virtuosity, but the excessive use of superlative formulas and flattering distinctions heightens the impression that he sounds false. We may note at least (in bold in the Greek text above):
- the adulatory εὐγενεῖς οἰκήτορες (v. 728);
- the praise of Athens as a unique πόλις in Greece, a city with great power (σθένουσαν[19]... εἴ τιν' Ἑλλάδος, μέγα: v. 734);
- Creon's position as the one who has most grieved Oedipus' sorrows, and the best person to take care of them (πενθεῖν... εἰς πλεῖστον πόλεως, v. 739, 'to mourn... most in all the city'), with the same formula employed a few lines later: εἰ μὴ πλεῖστον ἀνθρώπων ἔφυν / κάκιστος ('if I am not the very worst of men': vv. 743-744);[20]
- the disingenuous declaration that he has been moved to grief and pain (v. 744: ἀλγῶ, thus more than pity) by the unmerited suffering of Oedipus, who does not deserve his misfortune;
- the false equivalence of their wretched family status (vv. 745-753): Oedipus is δύστηνον, Antigone is δύσμορος, and Creon therefore is τάλας (twice);[21]
- the insistence on an everlasting affliction (ἀεί: vv. 746 and 750, in the same metrical position);

---

[19] The term is in enjambment and in a prominent position, as γέρων in the previous verse. 'Questo modo di procedere (con parole-chiave ambigue, spesso isolate in enjambement all'inizio di verso, quasi fossero dette con esitazione in un discorso pieno di sottintesi) ricorre con una certa frequenza nel modo di esprimersi di Creonte' (Guidorizzi 2008, 295); cf. v. 730: τιν'... / φόβον, 733: ἐπεὶ / γέρων, 734: πόλιν... / σθένουσαν, 752: οὐ γάμων / ἔμπειρος, 941: ἄβουλον ... / τοὔργον, 943: οὐδείς ... / ζῆλος, 957: ἐπεὶ / ἐρημία).

[20] 'The extravagant phrase is suggestive of his dishonesty, his faked concern': Kamerbeek 1984, 114. The adjective κακός is repeated in polyptoton in the same verse (κάκιστος ~ κακοῖς), and the emphatic double superlative (πλεῖστον / κάκιστος) seems to occur particularly in cases of dialectic stress: see e.g. Phil. 631, Eur. Alc. 790, Med. 1323.

[21] The idea of expressing pity for relatives or friends is common: see e.g. Soph. El. 1201, Phil. 806. In Sophocles' plays certain figures are of course sincerer and more genuine than Creon: compare the pity of the Chorus and Theseus towards Oedipus (vv. 254-255 [to Antigone]: σέ ... οἰκτίρομεν καὶ τόνδε, v. 461: ἐπάξιος ... κατοικτίσαι, v. 556: σ' οἰκτίσας). Well known is the compassion shown by Odysseus – the verb is ἐποικτίρω – towards his enemy Ajax in Aj. 121-124 (with Heath 1987, 168ff.); on Aristotle's definition of pity (as different from grief), see Rhet. 1386a17-24, where the feeling depends on the level of acquaintance with the suffering individual, and the undeserved nature of their suffering (cf. Konstan 2001, 49-74; Tzanetou 2005, who connects pity and power in OC). It is worth noting that according to Aristotle 'no good person would be distressed when parricides and bloodthirsty murderers meet punishment' (Rhet. 1386b28-29, transl. G.A. Kennedy): only a little later in our play Creon will use the parricide argument against Oedipus (vv. 944-945).

- the emphasis on age: he is too old, and Antigone is too young – with an undertone of reproach against Oedipus (v. 735: τηλικόσδ',²² v. 751: τηλικοῦτος, in the same metrical position);
- finally, the reference to the key-word of rhetorical argumentation in the verb πείσων at v. 736, and cf. πεισθεὶς ἐμοί at v. 756;²³ Creon has come to *persuade* his relative and fellow-citizen to return 'to the home of *his* fathers', but at v. 757 he is lying, since Oedipus will not actually be welcomed home, as is confirmed by Ismene at vv. 396–400 (and cf. 784–786).

In this first intervention, Creon astutely attempts to distribute the blame partly accusing himself and taking on a share of responsibility and reproach and embellishing this kind of self-incrimination with a highly emphatic cognate accusative construction (vv. 753–754: τοὔνειδος... ὠνείδισ'):²⁴ he has so far accepted the fact that a member of his γένος should suffer such a miserable fate, and he still considers Oedipus (but not for long) to be intimately connected to him.

3 Characters and oratorical talent (II): Oedipus

When we analyse Oedipus' reply, we immediately notice that he does not follow the same path of caution and circumspection, and that his verbal devices seem very basic. This is especially clear in his indignant condemnation of some traditional clichés of rhetorical ability, which suggests at the same time that he is entirely aware of the strategies of persuasive speech being used against him.

We should not forget that Athenian culture often displays an explicit mistrust of the danger represented by good speakers: a clever orator is to be suspected.²⁵

---

22 Brunck's correction for the τηλικόνδ' transmitted by some manuscripts (**L**: τηλίκονδ') is accepted by most editors.
23 On persuasion in *Oedipus at Colonus*, see Buxton 1982, 132–145. We look forward to the publication of the proceedings of a conference held in Cyprus in August 2015: *The Art of Persuasion across Genres and Times*.
24 Cf. similarly Soph. *Phil.* 523: τοὔνειδος ... ὀνειδίσαι, with Moorhouse 1982, 39–41. As Kamerbeek 1984, 115 rightly notes, "reproach' [ὄνειδος] is not entirely satisfactory. It is rather the 'disgrace' of all involved as manifested in Creon's description of the situation'.
25 Dem. 19.184.2–4: οἷς γάρ ἐστ' ἐν λόγοις ἡ πολιτεία, πῶς, ἂν οὗτοι μὴ ἀληθεῖς ὦσιν, ἀσφαλῶς ἔστι πολιτεύεσθαι; 'how could people whose government is based on speeches govern themselves securely unless the speeches are true?' (transl. H. Yunis), with Halliwell 1997, 121f., Pelling 2005, 84, and Bers 1994, 181f. On strength associated to a κακὸς λόγος cf. Soph. *Phil.* 407–409, Eur. *Ba.* 270–271, *Or.* 903; on the suspicion surrounding political and forensic oratory in general,

The blind man feels that in his brother-in-law's speech every word is aimed to persuade – he says – through a λόγου δικαίου μηχάνημα ποικίλον, 'a cunning scheme from any just plea' (v. 762) aimed at bad actions (v. 782). The Theban is γλώσσῃ ... δεινός (v. 806), he has a ready tongue full of verbal tricks, and he is labelled as a ὑπόβλητον στόμα, an 'untruthful mouth' (v. 794) capable of saying 'hard things in soft words' (σκληρὰ μαλθακῶς λέγων, v. 774),[26] an ἀνόσιον στόμα, an 'unholy mouth' (v. 981, along with the paronomastical στόμωσιν in the following verse and δυσστομεῖν at v. 986). Devoid of any shame, he thinks it proper to say anything: ἅπαν καλὸν / λέγειν νομίζων (vv. 1000–1001). Commentators rightly note that we are in a fully sophistic ambience,[27] yet it seems to me that Oedipus is not consciously and cleverly arousing the audience's hostility towards his opponent, but simply displaying his ἦθος.

Let us now focus our attention on v. 787 as a possible example of the irruption of Oedipus' proverbially grumpy character.[28] This verse may be taken as an example of Sophocles' rhetorical and stylistic tools; we are confronted to the rare case of an iambic trimeter made up of nine elements. This is above all a sign of tension. Rage, anger, and irritation are mounting, and the prophetic curse is ready to be fulfilled: Oedipus is going to announce that he will become an ἀλάστωρ.

In the preceding speech, Creon utters – not by accident – several verses made up of five, six, and even four elements, but never with more than eight. We may infer that he speaks calmly; frequently using long words, he avoids breaking

---

see Dover 1974, 25–28, Ostwald 1986, 257; on the political 'dangers of Rhetoric,' see Ober 1989, 165–177; for other examples in tragedy, see Halliwell 1997, 131 n. 34.

26 In *Rhet.* 1408b9–10 Aristotle considers that such a way of speaking is disadvantageous and unpersuasive (note the use of the same vocabulary as Sophocles): ἐὰν οὖν τὰ μαλακὰ σκληρῶς καὶ τὰ σκληρὰ μαλακῶς λέγηται, ἀπίθανον γίγνεται, 'but if, as a result, gentle things are said harshly and harsh things gently, the result is unpersuasive' (transl. G.A. Kennedy).

27 And cf. v. 861; 'the δεινὸς γλώσσῃ is the advocate, pupil of the sophists, who makes wrong into right by specious arguments': Kamerbeek 1984, 120 (see also Worman 2012, 338f., and *infra*, n. 73). δεινὸς λέγειν is a colloquialism used to describe someone who is particularly skilled in rhetoric. On direct accusations of 'sophism' in Attic forensic oratory with the aim of arousing hostility in the audience, see Sanders 2012, 373f. (δεινός is frequently used with this implication: see also p. 370 with n. 61, and the *iunctura* δεινὸς σοφιστής not necessarily in a negative sense at Eur. *Hipp.* 921, uncertainly in *Supp.* 903 with the related *TrGF* II F 323 [and Collard 1975a, 335]). Oedipus repeatedly criticizes Creon's use of rhetoric; cf. vv. 761–762, 794–796, and 806–809: for him, Creon is a φθέγμ' ἀναιδές, a 'shameless voice', at v. 863 (~ λῆμ' ἀναιδές at v. 960: 'we should never forget that Oedipus is blind': Kamerbeek 1984, 128). Schmalzriedt 1980, 99 n. 37, notes that two of Oedipus' most furious reactions are verbally matching: v. 761: πάντα τολμῶν ~ v. 806: γλώσσῃ σὺ δεινός, v. 761: ἀπὸ παντὸς ~ v. 807: ἐξ ἅπαντος, v. 762: δικαίου ~ v. 807: δίκαιον, v. 762: λόγου ~ v. 807: λέγει.

28 Cf. Soph. *Ant.* 471–472.

down his discourse in short words and particles (and he will do the same in his speech to Theseus).[29]

Even more interesting is the presence of what appears to be a poet's self-quotation. More precisely, Oedipus is quoting *himself*, after several years, and displaying a similarly vehement attitude (vv. 783–788):

> [Οι.] φράσω δὲ καὶ τοῖσδ', ὥς σε δηλώσω κακόν.
> ἥκεις ἔμ' ἄξων, οὐχ ἵν' ἐς δόμους ἄγῃς,
> ἀλλ' ὡς πάραυλον οἰκίσῃς, πόλις δέ σοι   785
> κακῶν ἄνατος τῆσδ' ἀπαλλαχθῇ χθονός.
> οὐκ ἔστι σοι ταῦτ', ἀλλά σοι τάδ' ἔστ', ἐκεῖ
> χώρας ἀλάστωρ οὑμὸς ἐνναίων ἀεί·

OED. And I shall explain it to these men also, so that I can prove you are a villain! You have come to fetch me, not so as to take me home, but so that you can settle me near the country, and that your city can escape the harm that threatens it from this land. You shall not have that, but you shall have this, my vengeful spirit ever dwelling here.

If we compare verse 787 to v. 370 of the *Oedipus Tyrannus*, we discover a surprising analogy. That verse is made up of ten elements, and contains a mass of figures: chiasmus, repetition, parallelism[30] (*OT* 370–371):

> Οι. ἀλλ' ἔστι, πλὴν σοί· σοὶ δὲ τοῦτ' οὐκ ἔστ', ἐπεὶ
> τυφλὸς τά τ' ὦτα τόν τε νοῦν τά τ' ὄμματ' εἶ.

there is [the strength of] truth, except for you; you are without it, since you are blind in your ears, in your mind, and in your eyes.

The similarity is clearer if we look at the two verses in synopsis. They are almost perfectly symmetrical even in the word division (in *OC* 'retrospective ταῦτ'' contrasts with prospective τάδ'', not present in *OT*):[31]

OT 370:	ἀλλ' ἔστι, πλὴν	σοί· σοὶ δὲ τοῦτ'	οὐκ ἔστ', ἐπεὶ
OC 787:	οὐκ ἔστι σοι	ταῦτ', ἀλλά σοι	τάδ' ἔστ', ἐκεῖ

---

29 The only passage in which we detect a sensible increase in the word number is at vv. 951–952, where Creon refers to the πικρὰς ... ἀράς Oedipus has put on him.
30 On the sound value, the alliterative sequence of τ, and the difficulty in translating v. 371, see Rodighiero 2011, 142–146. On the self-quotation, see Rodighiero 2017.
31 Ruijgh 2006, 154 n. 6.

In both cases there is the sign of an explosion, the violent reaction of Oedipus against Tiresias in the past, and now against Creon. This instance confirms a passage of the *Life of Sophocles*, where the anonymous author writes: 'he knows how to arrange the action with such a sense of timing that he creates an entire character out of a mere half-line or a single expression'.[32] This statement draws a bold connection between Sophocles' characters and their λέξις (though without specific reference to any of them), and might therefore be said – at least in the case of Oedipus – to restrict the extent to which a character's personal language (as a mirror of his ἦθος) can be adapted to external circumstances and various interlocutors.[33]

4 Brevity, opportunity, and formalized speech

Later, at the beginning of the stichomythic exchange, it is Creon himself who confesses his credo: rhetoric is an instrument of power, it implies political responsibilities, and is geared towards obtaining a result. When he states at v. 808 that 'speaking much is not the same as speaking rightly' (χωρὶς τό τ' εἰπεῖν πολλὰ καὶ τὸ καίρια), he is reaffirming a common principle of political and non-sophistic(ated) behaviour in Greek tragedy, namely the necessity of speaking briefly, plainly, and to the point. Oedipus' reply ironically follows the same line of reasoning (v. 809): ὡς δὴ σὺ βραχέα, ταῦτα δ' ἐν καιρῷ λέγεις, 'so you speak briefly but to the point!'.[34]

---

[32] *TrGF* IV T 1.21.90–91, οἶδε δὲ καιρὸν συμμετρῆσαι καὶ πράγματα ὥστε ἐκ μικροῦ ἡμιστιχίου ἢ λέξεως μιᾶς ὅλον ἠθοποιεῖν πρόσωπον, quoted by Easterling 1977, 123.
[33] Homer is praised for the opposite quality by the anonymous author of the *Essay on the Life and Poetry of Homer* ([Plutarchi] *De Homero* 2.164, ll. 2015–2017 Kindstrand): πολλὰ δὲ τῶν εἰσαγομένων ὑπ' αὐτοῦ προσώπων λέγοντα ποιῶν ἢ πρὸς οἰκείους ἢ φίλους ἢ ἐχθροὺς ἢ δήμους ἑκάστῳ τὸ πρέπον εἶδος τῶν λόγων ἀποδίδωσιν, 'many of the characters he introduces he causes to speak, whether to relatives or friends or enemies or to the people, and he gives to each the appropriate form of speech' (transl. J.J. Keaney and R. Lamberton: cf. Knudsen 2014, 22–23), while at the same time attributing specific modes of discourse to single characters: Nestor, Menelaus, Odysseus, Antenor (§ 172: see *infra*, n. 65).
[34] See especially Eur. *Phoe.* 469–472 and *IA* 829. The best-known example of tragic καιρός is probably Aesch. *Sept.* 1: Κάδμου πολῖται, χρὴ λέγειν τὰ καίρια, 'men of Cadmus' city, it is necessary to say what the hour demands'. See also *OC* 31–32: λέγειν, and εὔκαιρον, as 'what is convenient and appropriate' to say, and v. 569 on Oedipus' praise of Theseus' concise speech. It is well known that καιρός is a frequently attested word in oratory, see for instance Vallozza 1985; an

A second and no less important rhetorical element emerging from these verses concerns the length of speeches, for opportunity and long speeches do not suit each other. Now we need to look ahead to a passage occurring a little later in our play. At a certain point, Theseus cuts short what to him sounds like a useless flow of words: ἅλις λόγων, he says at v. 1016. His interruption displays a sudden urge to bring the conversation to an end,[35] coming only after Oedipus' excessively long response to Creon. This may sound strange to a modern reader: Theseus fulfils the role of internal audience – or an 'audience on stage', as Simon Goldhill puts it[36] – for almost 80 verses (vv. 937–1015). His manner then becomes urgent, but only after an ἀγών-like passage of completely imbalanced proportions (22 trimeters uttered by Creon in self-defence vs. 54 trimeters recited by Oedipus).

Upon closer examination, Theseus' preoccupation emerges as a real political statement stemming from the idea, common in democratic Athens, that inactivity can be dangerously filled with words, but words cannot replace action.[37] We may recall two instances of this idea. At 3.38, Thucydides reports Cleon's description of the idle Athenians as θεαταὶ ... τῶν λόγων, 'spectators of speeches' (besides, Cleon, like Theseus, stresses the fact that new speeches and new resolutions are only χρόνου διατριβή, a waste of time favouring the enemy). The second passage, from the second *Olynthiac*, conveys Demosthenes' criticism of his citizens on the grounds that they love words but are unable to transform their plans into action.[38] This point of view contradicts what we may call the 'sophistic' perspective, well illustrated by Odysseus' words in *Philoctetes*: ὁρῶ βροτοῖς / τὴν γλῶσσαν, οὐχὶ τἄργα, πάνθ' ἡγουμένην, 'I see that words, not deeds, are ever the masters among men' (98–99).[39]

---

overall study is Trédé-Boulmer 2015 (on oratory see chapter V); for its use in tragedy, see Halliwell 1997, 129 n. 28; Friis Johansen/Whittle 1980, II, 353; Race 1981, 202; Schmalzriedt 1980, 95–97 and 100–102 on *OC*.

35 See Fraenkel 1950, III, 795f.
36 Goldhill 2009.
37 Paradoxically, Oedipus confirms the principle when he says that he defends himself against actions with words (v. 873: ἔργοις πεπονθὼς ῥήμασίν σ' ἀμύνομαι).
38 The episodes narrated by the historian and Cleon's speech occur in the context of the desertion of Mytilene in 428–427 BCE (analysed in Sansone 2012, 28–32). Cf. Dem. *Ol.* 2.12: ὡς ἅπας μὲν λόγος, ἂν ἀπῇ τὰ πράγματα, μάταιόν τι φαίνεται καὶ κενόν, μάλιστα δ' ὁ παρὰ τῆς ἡμετέρας πόλεως, 'all words, apart from action, seem vain and idle, especially words from Athenian lips' (transl. J.H. Vince); see Goldhill 2009, 28, with further bibliography (for the opposition between action and words cf. also Solon, fr. 11.7–8 W.²); on tragedy, see Halliwell 1997, 133 n. 38: 'length of speech is itself a rhetorical concern: see the passages cited by Fraenkel (1950) on *Ag.* 916, and cf. e.g. Aesch. *Eum.* 585, Soph. *OC* 808–9, Eur. *IA* 378, 400, Th. 4.17.2'.
39 In R. Jebb's translation: see Goldhill 1997, 142.

Returning to Creon, the features of his language are in the final analysis nothing but conventional, and they are in no way the expression of the speaker's actual position: 'there are habits of style – as remarked by Patricia E. Easterling – that any character will use in certain circumstances'. Yet, if 'Sophocles' conception of his central [...] characters influences his choice of words and images',[40] is there a personality behind this predictable stylistic filter?

The strength of Creon's persuasion is weak, and he is unmasked by his inability to keep calm. It is not by chance that a few lines later he tries to seize Oedipus (v. 814: ἢν δ' ἕλω ποτέ... '... and if I ever catch you...'), confesses to the kidnapping of Ismene, and declares what kind of καιρός he has in mind. In this second occurrence (after that of v. 809) there is an indisputable reference to the temporal nuance of the term καιρός, as well as to the notion of 'profit' and 'opportunity': the right moment and the fitting time have arrived – Creon says – to abduct Antigone (v. 826: ὑμῖν ἂν εἴη τήνδε καιρὸς ἐξάγειν, 'it is the moment for you to take this girl away').

Adopting a more general view, if we look at the structure of the second episode – from the arrival of Creon to the second stasimon – we observe that Creon's false modesty constantly arouses antagonistic reactions, not from Theseus, but from Oedipus. In the confrontations between the two relatives we are of course not dealing with an abstract model, a case of pure ῥητορεύειν, and not even with a typical Euripidean ἀγών-scene.[41] Until the king's arrival (vv. 817–886), a rhetorical void is imposed by the presence of the stichomythic dialogue and the reiterated *antilabé* – and especially the outbreak of excited scenic movement.

At this very point, then, action[42] interrupts the flow of words, disrupting the dialogue and partly shifting the focus. What follows is a sequence of pure violence: neither mediation, nor peaceful solutions are proposed, and the speech-

---

40 Easterling 1977, 128.
41 As is elegantly noted by Halliwell 1997, 139, while in other tragic ἀγῶνες we see 'the opposing parties put forward alternative narratives to ground their claims and counter-claims, Oedipus' response to Creon compels us to notice that Oedipus has a narrative to tell *where Creon had none at all*'. On the rhetoric of the *agon* in Euripides, see among others Lloyd 1992; Dubischar 2001; Mastronarde 2010, 207–245, and Riedweg 2000 (Barker 2009 focuses more on the concept of debate in general: on tragedy, see pp. 267ff., with criticisms of Lloyd's view at p. 272 n. 24). It is probable that Plato had these tragic passages in mind in *Grg.* 502d2–3, when he says that poets seem to ῥητορεύειν in the theatre.
42 I find somewhat excessive the statement by Bers 1994, 177 that in the tragic space 'the main doings are not action, for the conventions of the Attic theatre virtually excluded the performance of action on stage, but speech about action: action announced, contemplated and judged'; more acceptable is the idea that 'a great part of that speech is rhetorical'.

making turns out to be inadequate. This seems to validate the idea that Sophocles 'incorporates agones into his plays in a [...] naturalistic way', avoiding formality and the rigidity of closed structures.[43]

Furthermore, several short and tentative, yet unproductive, sentences uttered by Creon appear to confirm the fact that he is communicating on two levels. At v. 871, following the curse, Creon in a scornful remark calls the Chorus to attention, interrupting his dialogue with Oedipus and temporarily turning away from him. He addresses them and invites them to 'see' in a way that emphasises their involvement: ὁρᾶτε ταῦτα, τῆσδε γῆς ἐγχώριοι; 'do you see this, natives of this land?' Creon's approach to persuasion is, as it were, tailored to the social status of the addressee. Yet his solemn, deictic approach strikingly diverges from the less refined exclamations of Oedipus during their struggle, at v. 838 (οὐκ ἠγόρευον ταῦτ' ἐγώ; 'did I not say it would be so?') and at v. 881 (ἀκούεθ' οἷα φθέγγεται; 'hear the words he utters').[44]

The topical element in Creon's sentence is the term ταῦτα, and ὁρᾶτε is the formula usually employed to attract attention to specific points or situations (as for instance in Demosthenes). Through this covert attempt to arouse the elders' emotions, Creon's strategy is once again exposed. Not only does he fail to display any kind of closeness towards Oedipus, but he also attempts to persuade the Chorus of the latter's insanity and misery instead of trying to deceive Oedipus in 'a perversion of intimacy' (as Stephen Halliwell rightly puts it).[45] This isolated sign of formalized speech is destined to dissolve quickly, and again contrasts with the verbal anxiety exhibited by Oedipus in the following verse, where we note the repetition of καί, the trimeter made up of seven elements, and the enjambment (v. 872: ὁρῶσι κἀμὲ καὶ σέ, καὶ φρονοῦσ' ὅτι κτλ). Yet two verses later the rhetoric misfires: the θυμός of Creon prevails upon rationality and transforms words into action (vv. 874–875):

---

[43] Lloyd 1992, 2; see also Collard 1975b, 59f., who lays similar emphasis on the fact that Sophoclean ἀγῶνες are 'less rigid in structure' and 'more naturally accommodated to episodic development'.

[44] For similar alterations of tone in certain Sophoclean dialogues, see Rodighiero 2016. On a slightly different apostrophe – that which is most commonly addressed to the speaker's opponent – as an oratorical phenomenon of the fourth century and almost absent from the earlier orators, see Usher 2010.

[45] Halliwell 1997, 131 referring to Sophocles' *Philoctetes* and Euripides' *Medea*, where 'the audience is placed in a position to follow the workings of such perversion from conception to execution'.

Κρ. οὔτοι καθέξω θυμόν, ἀλλ' ἄξω βίᾳ
κεἰ μοῦνός εἰμι τόνδε κεἰ χρόνῳ βραδύς   875

> CREON I shall no longer restrain my anger, but shall carry this man away, even if I am alone and am made slow by age!

His behaviour fluctuates between false kindness and ferocity, and suddenly the tone and words change again when Theseus returns. This continuous shifting is symptomatic of the fact that Sophocles manifestly wants his character to be self-conscious of his speechmaking and of the different rhetorical tricks by which he must abide.[46] This is confirmed by the following passage.

5 Characters and oratorical talent (III): Creon vs. Oedipus vs. Creon

Upon his return, Theseus is about to give Creon a beating, but his regal composure stops him from committing any act of violence; this marks a fundamental difference of position and disposition between the two men, and it is not surprising that Theseus' words can be shown to reflect part of the construction of Athenian propaganda in the theatre. They are the highest praise for the πόλις, since Athens is being celebrated by its mythical king, who glorifies a fundamental value of the democratic city: Creon has come into a community which practices justice and does not operate outside the law, a motif typically related to epideictic oratory (913–914):[47]

---

[46] The character of Creon could perhaps be said to provide evidence for a broader literary phenomenon: the well-known influence of Euripides on Sophocles' later work (bibliography in Rodighiero 2018, 162 n. 85). On Euripidean characters' consciousness of their own speech-making, see Pelling 2005, 85, with further bibliography (Sansone 2012, 155–158 is cautious about this idea: once more, he sees the leading figure of Aeschylus behind this process, and argues for the development of a rhetorical theory as a form of imitation of tragic practice).

[47] Cf. Thuc. 2.37, [Lys.] 2.17.2 – the spurious epitaph: περὶ τοῦ δικαίου διαμάχεσθαι, 'to fight the battles of justice'. Kamerbeek 1984, 133 quotes Dem. 21.150: πατρίδος τετυχηκὼς ἢ νόμοις τῶν ἁπασῶν πόλεων μάλιστ' οἰκεῖσθαι δοκεῖ, 'he [...] has found a fatherland which is reputed to be of all states the most firmly based upon its laws' (transl. J.H. Vince). Theseus' speech even includes praise of Thebes (vv. 929–931: σὺ δ' ἀξίαν οὐκ οὖσαν αἰσχύνεις πόλιν κτλ, 'you are disgracing your own city, which does not deserve it'), contradicting the negative judgement on the city he expresses at Eur. *Supp.* 399–462. In *Oedipus at Colonus* his attack is against a man, not against a πόλις: for a brief survey of previous critical positions on this praise, see most recently Finglass 2012, 47–52.

[Θη.] ὅστις δίκαι᾽ ἀσκοῦσαν εἰσελθὼν πόλιν
κἄνευ νόμου κραίνουσαν οὐδέν κτλ

THESEUS ... you came to a city that abides by justice and decides everything according to the law...

The tone of Creon's response does not disappoint. Analysis of the twenty trimeters constituting Creon's self-defence suggests that he is acting as if he were on trial, yet it is difficult fully to dismiss the idea that they are a piece of recited poetry (939–959):

Κρ. ἐγὼ οὔτ᾽ ἄνανδρον τήνδε τὴν πόλιν λέγω,
ὦ τέκνον Αἰγέως, οὔτ᾽ ἄβουλον, ὡς σὺ φῄς, 940
τοὔργον τόδ᾽ ἐξέπραξα, γιγνώσκων δ᾽ ὅτι
**οὐδείς ποτ᾽ αὐτοῖς τῶν ἐμῶν ἂν ἐμπέσοι
ζῆλος ξυναίμων**, ὥστ᾽ ἐμοῦ τρέφειν βίᾳ.
ἤδη δ᾽ ὁθούνεκ᾽ ἄνδρα **καὶ πατροκτόνον
κἄναγνον** οὐ δεξοίατ᾽, οὐδ᾽ ὅτῳ γάμοι 945
ξυνόντες ηὑρέθησαν ἀνοσιώτατοι.
τοιοῦτον αὐτοῖς Ἄρεος εὔβουλον πάγον
ἐγὼ ξυνῄδη χθόνιον ὄνθ᾽, ὃς οὐκ ἐᾷ
τοιούσδ᾽ ἀλήτας τῇδ᾽ ὁμοῦ ναίειν πόλει·
ᾧ πίστιν ἴσχων τήνδ᾽ ἐχειρούμην ἄγραν. 950
καὶ ταῦτ᾽ ἂν οὐκ ἔπρασσον, εἰ μή μοι πικρὰς
αὐτῷ τ᾽ ἀρὰς ἠρᾶτο καὶ τὠμῷ γένει·
ἀνθ᾽ ὧν πεπονθὼς ἠξίουν τάδ᾽ ἀντιδρᾶν.
[θυμοῦ γὰρ οὐδὲν γῆράς ἐστιν ἄλλο πλὴν
θανεῖν· θανόντων δ᾽ οὐδὲν ἄλγος ἅπτεται.] 955
πρὸς ταῦτα πράξεις οἷον ἂν θέλῃς· ἐπεὶ
ἐρημία με, κεἰ δίκαι᾽ ὅμως λέγω,
σμικρὸν τίθησι· πρὸς δὲ τὰς πράξεις ἔτι,
καὶ τηλικόσδ᾽ ὤν, ἀντιδρᾶν πειράσομαι.

CREON: I do not say your city has no men, son of Aegeus, nor was my action rash, as you say, but I knew that no desire for my relations would so fall upon your people that they would keep them here against my will. I knew, too, that they would not receive a parricide and a man impure, nor one in whose company were found the children of an unholy marriage. Such is the wisdom of the council of the hill of Ares, which I knew was in their land, one which does not permit such wanderers to live together with this city. In this knowledge I put my trust when I secured this prey; and I would not have done so, had not he called down bitter curses on me and on my family. For this treatment I thought it right to make this return. [For anger knows no old age, till death; and no pain afflicts the dead.]
In the face of that you may do what you will, since even if my plea is just, I am alone and powerless; but in response to what you do, old as I am, I shall one day attempt to act.

The first detail to be considered is the opening word of the passage (ἐγώ: repeated some verses later at v. 948). Creon's response begins in the form of a self-defence which reminds me of Solon's absolving ἐγώ-speech (fr. 36 W.²), a poem in iambic trimeters where the politician lists his main deeds and the 'ἐγώ, placed emphatically at the beginning of the verse, displays an apologetic stance'.⁴⁸ One may also note that there is a clear demarcation of the different sections: the opening praise of Athens is followed by an expression of contempt for Oedipus' lineage, and the celebration of the Areopagus is again combined with disdain; only at the end does the apparent reason of Creon's behaviour emerge: Oedipus' curse, his ἀραί.

This speech is constructed with explicit rhetorical stratagems, among which one may note:
- the symmetrical οὔτ' ἄνανδρον / οὔτ' ἄβουλον (vv. 939 and 940; the Areopagus is εὔβουλον some verses later);
- the impressive frequency of negative particles, adjectives, and pronouns;
- some internal echoes, v. 944: ᾔδη, and v. 948: ξυνῄδη;
- the *figura etymologica* at v. 952: ἀρὰς ἠρᾶτο, as well as at v. 955 if the verse is genuine: θανεῖν· θανόντων (with the alliterative theta also in the θυμοῦ of the previous verse);⁴⁹
- a recurrent use of terms related to action: v. 941 (ἐξέπραξα), v. 951 (οὐκ ἔπρασσον), v. 956 (πράξεις), v. 958 (πράξεις again); this is also implicitly evoked in the double use of ἀντιδρᾶν (vv. 953 and 959). (It is well known that the idea of reciprocity, the response to an action with a reaction, is a widespread theme in judicial oratory).

We can also detect – though only initially – a kind of general reticence in Creon's words, probably because he must weigh every single term carefully. At vv. 942–943, there is a slowing down in the syntax, and a peculiar and unclear sequence of complements which become intelligible to the audience only later: οὐδείς ποτ' αὐτοὺς τῶν ἐμῶν ἂν ἐμπέσοι / ζῆλος ξυναίμων (where ζῆλος is the first word of the line): 'I knew that no desire for my relations would so fall upon your people'. The first trimeter does not contain any noun, and only the pronoun αὐτοὺς can

---

48 Solon, fr. 36.1–2 W.² (see Noussia-Fantuzzi 2010, 460): ἐγὼ δὲ τῶν μὲν οὕνεκα ξυνήγαγον / δῆμον, τί τούτων πρὶν τυχεῖν ἐπαυσάμην; 'before achieving what of the goals for which I brought the people together did I stop?' (transl. D.E. Gerber); Mülke 2002, 368f. (among others), assumes that the poem's opening verses are lost.
49 Vv. 954–955 should be deleted, according to the OCT edition (*del.* Blaydes). An even more impressive symmetry is displayed by two verses with the same word division, strong assonances, and homeoteleuta (ἐμοῦ τρέφειν ~ ὁμοῦ ναίειν): v. 943 ζῆλος ξυναίμων, ὥστ' ἐμοῦ τρέφειν βίᾳ ~ v. 949 τοιούσδ' ἀλήτας τῇδ' ὁμοῦ ναίειν πόλει.

be referred to the Chorus and the city. Moreover, as Helma Dik has shown, τῶν ἐμῶν is preposed in the sequence possessive + noun (τῶν ἐμῶν... ξυναίμων),[50] as frequently happens in *Oedipus at Colonus* (in prose, kinship terms predominantly take postpositive possessives).[51] The emphatic word, the noun ζῆλος, comes unusually late, anticipated from afar by the heavy modifier οὐδείς which is highlighted in a hyperbaton, creating a strict connection in the prosody of the two verses. As Sir Richard Jebb noted with reference to v. 776 (τις before εἰ), Sophocles 'is sometimes bold' in his use of hyperbaton.[52]

Moreover, this singular construction forms a parallel with Creon's first intervention, where he seems similarly to accentuate some words which are marked as salient by placing them in enjambment.[53] Let us attempt to reconstruct what might have occurred during the actor's performance. We should probably assume a first delay after the ὅτι; it ends v. 941, creating a rare hiatus with the following οὐδείς (although the scheme short vowel in hiatus + enjambment occurs more frequently in late Sophocles). Secondly, we can also speculate that an additional pause was inserted after v. 942 (hyperbaton + enjambment). The word order and

---

50 See Dik 2007, 103: 'in raw numbers, preposed possessives turn out to be more frequent in my corpus than postposed ones: in *OC*, preposing is roughly twice as frequent'; τῶν ἐμῶν... ξυναίμων corresponds to type (a') in Dik's classification, and the verse is analyzed at p. 110: 'the focal elements of the noun phrase, οὐδείς and τῶν ἐμῶν, come first, and are separated by postpositives'.
51 Devine/Stephens 2000, 23f. (cf. table 1.5: the corpus is composed of Hdt., Lys., and Dem.), with Dik 2007, 107 n. 35, and p. 109 for the polyptoton at vv. 789–790: παισὶ *τοῖς ἐμοῖσι τῆς ἐμῆς* / χθονός.
52 Jebb 1907, 130. See Dik 2007, 3: 'emphatic words precede non-emphatic words in the Greek sentence'. Of particular importance is the interweaving of clause and verse: as Dik correctly says (p. 10), 'it is not so much the position in the line as the position in the clause in *combination* with that in the line that marks words as salient'; for the normal place of salient words at the beginning and not at the end of a trimeter see *ibid.*, 169ff. On discontinuous noun phrases see also Devine, Stephens 1994, 480–494; the scheme of vv. 942–943 can be described as follows: Y_1XY_2, where Y_1 (οὐδείς) is the modifier, Y_2 (ζῆλος) the head of the phrase and X the verb as the pivot element (ἐμπέσοι). The same construction can be found at vv. 729–730 (again with Creon speaking): τιν' ὑμᾶς ὀμμάτων εἰληφότας / *φόβον* νεώρη.
53 See *supra*, n. 19, for examples. On hiatus, verse-ending, and enjambment, see Battezzato 2008, 103–132 ('l'avversione per lo iato aumenta quanto più stretto è l'enjambement': p. 104, and 'Sofocle ha la proporzione più alta di enjambement e l'avversione più marcata per gli iati in enjambement', 'lo iato avrebbe portato a una interruzione del flusso ritmico dei versi che il poeta cercava di unire in maniera sempre più forte': pp. 126 and 128). 'Line end [...] is a curious animal in the Sophoclean trimeter. On the one hand, many of his line ends show the characteristics of the ideal metrical period end: *brevis in longo* and hiatus; on the other, he allows proclitics and elision at line end. It is as if in Sophocles' hands, period end was an option, not a rule, in the trimeter' (Dik 2007, 176: see also p. 193 n. 48, and pp. 217f.).

word length are necessarily subjected to the flow of the verse, and 'the difficulty of distinguishing organic link from mere coincidence is exacerbated by the poetic habit of deviating from the precise wording of the corresponding prosaic utterance';[54] nonetheless, it remains true that we can only fully understand this sentence when the subject ζῆλος is pronounced, and after the object of this attention – that is, Creon's family as expressed in the term ξυναίμων – is mentioned.

After this hesitation, Creon appears to build up strength and to become more self-confident, as suggested by the use of legal terminology against Oedipus (whom he calls πατροκτόνον and ἄναγνον),[55] and later by the completely anachronistic celebration of the Areopagus.[56] We are dealing with a distorted form of oratorical διαβολή, a violent slander or κακηγορία.[57] I use the terms 'distorted διαβολή' because Creon lists a series of accusations which are actually true: the son of Laius *is* parricidal and incestuous. Again, when Creon claims that he was merely reacting to the insults uttered by his blind brother-in-law, his defensive rhetoric betrays his hidden temper, and reveals what he really is (that is, what Sophocles wants him to be), a character caught in a continual 'relationship between surface impression and ulterior intention'.[58] Finally, we should also note the last words of the speech: even in bad times, even alone, Creon declares his intention to react, rebutting the accusations and emphasizing the *topos* of the disadvantageous position of an isolated man (vv. 956–959). Sophocles lets the rhetoric fade gradually, revealing his theatrical depiction of the character and conveying his emotions and ethics through his words and behaviour.

In his response, Oedipus uses a key-word of strong legal and moral value: he is ἄκων, that is, not guilty because unaware (he uses the term four times, at v. 964, v. 977, v. 987: ἄκων ἔγημα, φθέγγομαί τ' ἄκων τάδε). A similar if not precisely matching category of homicide – ἀκούσιος φόνος: to kill someone against one's own will – was regulated by Athenian law, and the penalty on this charge was exile.[59] Although Oedipus' homicide was not in the least unintentional, and did

---

54 Bers 1994, 181.
55 The hearer may have noticed a massive presence of the alpha privative; cf. at vv. 939–940 ἄνανδρον and ἄβουλον, and at vv. 945–946 ἀνόσιοι γάμοι. Significantly, the term ἄβουλον is echoed some verses later (v. 947), where the πάγος of Ares is called εὔβουλον by opposition.
56 I have tried elsewhere to analyse the meaning of such a precise connection between Colonus and the Areopagus: Sophocles represents an imaginary Colonus, which features some of the main characteristics of the Areopagus hill. See Rodighiero 2012.
57 The only surviving text dealing with slander laws is Lys. 10. Examples of invectives in Greek tragedy in Duchemin 1968, 206f.
58 See Halliwell 1997, 138.
59 Harris 2010, 131 and 2012, 292.

not happen by accident, he nevertheless applies to himself a *remotio criminis* when he locates the principal cause of his deeds in the gods' will (v. 964: θεοῖς γὰρ ἦν οὕτω φίλον, 'it was the pleasure of the gods').[60]

Later, Oedipus resorts to a typical form of rhetorical reasoning which is not foreign to the tragic genre, although it is used predominantly in judicial oratory: the argument from probability[61] and the postulation of an imaginary case which excludes the potential accusation both of wilful murder and of parricide. Oedipus did not have any reason – he claims – to kill his father and did it only in self-defence; hence he asks Creon how he would have behaved in a similar situation. The dramatic effect of this hypothetical meeting is also laced with sarcasm, as Oedipus calls Creon σε τὸν δίκαιον, 'you, the righteous one' at 992[62] (991–999):

[Οι.] ἓν γάρ μ' ἄμειψαι μοῦνον ὧν σ' ἀνιστορῶ·
εἴ τίς σε τὸν δίκαιον αὐτίκ' ἐνθάδε
κτείνοι παραστάς, πότερα πυνθάνοι' ἂν εἰ
πατήρ σ' ὁ καίνων, ἢ τίνοι' ἂν εὐθέως;
δοκῶ μέν, εἴπερ ζῆν φιλεῖς, τὸν αἴτιον   995
τίνοι' ἂν, οὐδὲ τοὖνδικον περιβλέποις.
τοιαῦτα μέντοι καὐτὸς εἰσέβην κακά,
θεῶν ἀγόντων· ὥστ' ἐγὼ οὐδὲ τὴν πατρὸς
ψυχὴν ἂν οἶμαι ζῶσαν ἀντειπεῖν ἐμοί.

---

60 On the supposed past divine anger against Oedipus' γένος (v. 965), see Guidorizzi 2008, 324ff.
61 According to Aristotle, the responsibility for this 'invention' lies with the Sicilian Corax (*Rhet.* 1402a3–28), whereas Plato claims that its inventor was Tisias (*Phdr.* 273a–c); however, against what has become a *lieu commun* of the critical literature see among others Sansone 2012, 5–7; Gagarin 1994 and 2007, 30–34, both starting from Cole's scepticism (Cole 1991; see also Kraus 2007 for its use in judicial oratory and further bibliography). Amongst several examples, we may mention *H. Hom. Merc.* 4.265–274 (and again at 376–377), where Hermes, in his dialogue with Apollo, resorts to an argument centred on probability, declaring that – as a new-born child – he is interested not in cattle but in sleeping and his mother's milk etc.: he does not at all look – so he says – like a cattle-thief (cf. Knudsen 2014, 112: the presence of the argument κατὰ τὸ εἰκός has also been taken as evidence to date the hymn, but see *contra* Vergados 2013, 24, 30, and in particular 138–140).
62 τὸν δίκαιον at v. 992 is said 'with a great amount of sarcasm', according to Kamerbeek 1984, 143, and at 1000 εἰ γὰρ οὐ δίκαιος is a reminder of this sarcastic tone. We can perhaps recognize an internal echo with 745: ὁρῶν σε τὸν δύστηνον (Creon addressing Oedipus) ~ v. 992, εἴ τίς σε τὸν δίκαιον, following which (v. 1000) Oedipus refers to his own sentence: σὺ δ', εἰ γὰρ οὐ δίκαιος (in all three cases the adjectives occupy the same metrical position). In this section of the drama the derivatives of δίκη are obsessively used; there are twenty occurrences in three hundred verses: 742, 760, 762, 807, 825, 831, 832 – twice – 880, 913, 920, 925, 938, 957, 971, 992, 996, 1000, 1027, 1043.

OED.: Of all my questions, answer me just one! If here and now a man stood near you, the righteous one, and tried to kill you, would you ask if the would-be killer was your father, or would you strike back at once? I think that if you value life you would strike back at the guilty one, and would not consider whether it was just or no. But this were the sorrows into which I entered, led by the gods, so that I do not think that even my father's spirit, if it came to life, could contradict me.

In legal terms, we could object that as far as we know from the *Oedipus Tyrannus*, Laius did not intend to kill Oedipus and did not strike him with a lethal weapon, but with his goad (807–809). Oedipus' reaction was simply disproportionate to the offence and dictated by his inborn anger, not by fear for his safety – although this is a minor point. More crucially, as Edward M. Harris has shown, if we consider the account provided in the *OT* as the only 'true' one, then Oedipus is guilty of deliberate homicide, whereas at Colonus he changes his previous version of events, describing himself as 'pure' (at 548 he states that he is νόμῳ ... καθαρός).

What is remarkable in our passage is that the *adynaton* imagined by Oedipus in his conditional analepsis is a radical, yet impossible justification, appealing to a testimony from a witness who happens to be the victim himself: if Laius were alive – he says – he could confirm this and share the same point of view.[63] It does not sound like a strong defence, nor is it a good reason to free Oedipus from his responsibility, and this deficiency is partly betrayed by his stumbling over the knot of words and sounds made up by τὸ δίκαιον ~ τοὖνδικον and the almost anagrammatic τίνοι' ἄν ~ τὸν αἴτιον ~ τίνοι' ἄν.

I believe that Oedipus – like other characters in tragedy – is driven to the argument from probability because it is rather difficult to prove his full innocence and to clear himself of the charge levelled against him.[64]

---

63 See Harris 2012, and particularly Harris 2010. 'L'evocare l'ombra del padre ucciso è peraltro un effetto forte, emozionante: la figura di una personificazione (prosopopea) che richiama [...] la stessa situazione di *El.* 548': Guidorizzi 2008, 327 (*Electra*'s passage sounds as follows: φαίη δ' ἂν ἡ θανοῦσά γ', εἰ φωνὴν λάβοι, 'and so would say the dead, if she could speak', transl. R. Jebb). We may also note the similarity between Oedipus' words and Antiphon's *Third Tetralogy*, where a young man justifies his murder as a case of self-defence (4.2.1–6, cf. Saïd 1978, 216–220, though it is not true that 'le récit du meurtre de Laios que fait Œdipe aux vers 800–813 d'*Œdipe Roi* s'accorde [...] parfaitement avec la version des faits qu'il donne dans *Œedipe à Colone*', p. 217: see Harris 2010, 134). For a useful analysis of the analepsis and Oedipus' retrospective narrative in this passage, see Markantonatos 2002, 49–52.

64 Cf. Scodel 1997, 491: 'tragedy quickly adapted the argument from probability. Creon in Sophocles' *Oedipus* argues that no sensible man in his position would try to overthrow the king [...] (583–602); Euripides' Hippolytus argues that he had no reason to rape Phaedra (*Hipp.* 1008–1020), especially since she was not the most beautiful of all women. Arguments from probability are oddly ironic in tragedy'.

6 A conclusion

Not all the *personae loquentes* make use of rhetorical skills at the same time and to the same extent, otherwise we would have a flat sequence of stylistic devices all through the drama.[65] But behind the skill and the linguistic quality of these figures, Sophocles adds perceptible character traits: fairness, anger, duplicity, deceit, honesty, and so on. According to Aristotle, if the ἦθος is that of an honest person (which is not always the case), then character is close to being the most authoritative form of verbal persuasion[66]. Yet in our passage, rhetoric defines characters, becomes a foil for them, and contributes to making them emerge more clearly. (And according to Plutarch, Sophocles described his mature style as 'the best and most expressive of character': ἠθικώτατον καὶ βέλτιστον).[67]

Looking back to the beginning of this paper, I must disagree in part with the point of view expressed by the great scholar A.M. Dale,[68] who considered it a peculiar trait of Greek tragedy that the poet was a kind of λογογράφος who promises

---

[65] Scodel 1999–2000, 132ff., considers Euripides' plays as 'a sort of laboratory of verbal performance. What would the social world be like if everyone were a skilled speaker, and if all situations of conflict were arenas for verbal performance?'; Scodel highlights the fact that in Euripides' rhetorical performances, characters never conceal their hidden purpose, and rhetoric is at the service of the speaker's actual position. The association between characters and different styles of speech is attested for figures as early as the Homeric heroes, as Varro testifies (in Gel. 6.14.7): *sed ea ipsa genera dicendi iam antiquitus tradita ab Homero sunt tria in tribus: magnificum in Ulixe et ubertum, subtile in Menelao et cohibitum, mixtum moderatumque in Nestore*, 'but in early days these same three styles of speaking were exemplified in three men by Homer: the grand and rich in Ulysses, the elegant and restrained in Menelaus, the middle and moderate in Nestor' (transl. J.C. Rolfe; cf. *supra*, n. 33, and Knudsen 2014, 23–36, and see also, *inter alia*, *schol. ad Il.* 3.212, p. 398, 5–12 Erbse, where the same heroes are matched with the three orators: ἀπολελυμένος Μενέλαος Λυσίας, πυκνὸς Ὀδυσσεὺς Δημοσθένης, πιθανὸς Νέστωρ Ἰσοκράτης, 'the 'free' style of Menelaus and Lysias, the close of Odysseus and Demosthenes, the persuasive of Nestor and Isocrates' [11–12, *schol.* **T**]).
[66] Arist. *Rhet.* 1356a1–13 (σχεδὸν ὡς εἰπεῖν κυριωτάτην ἔχει πίστιν τὸ ἦθος, 'character is almost, so to speak, the most authoritative form of persuasion': 13, transl. G.A. Kennedy; cf. Dow 2015, 95–99).
[67] *De prof. in virt.* 79B5 (= *TrGF* IV T 100.4).
[68] Dale 1954, xxviii, for whom (yet with special reference to *Alcestis*), the Greek actor was 'trained not in 'interpretation' but in rhetorical performance, before an audience that expected nothing less'. Dale rightly insists on the strict relation between the two verbal domains: 'rhetoric is a concept we tend to hold in some suspicion, as if in its nature there must be something slightly bogus; but we shall never properly understand Greek tragedy unless we realize how closely related were the rhetoric of Athenian life, in the assembly and law-courts and on other public occasions, and the rhetoric of the speeches in drama' (p. xxvii).

to do his best for each of his clients in turn as the situations change and succeed one another. This does not by any means exclude an interest in character; the skilful λογογράφος takes that into account in its proper place. But the dominating consideration is: What *points* could be made here?

This opinion implies a minor interest in characters. What would have happened, in the *Oedipus at Colonus*, if Theseus had hit Creon instead of renouncing physical action against him? And what if Creon had been able to manage his rhetorical skills, displaying greater self-control and mediating without yielding to anger?

To conclude, rhetoric here influences poetry in arguments and stylistic devices, and in the application of its own tactics to fictional speeches with the aim of persuading, but it is conditioned both by the speaker's nature and by the external situation. Consequently, rhetoric also contributes to bringing out the oscillations of a character (Creon) who uses the more trivial rhetorical devices as an instrument of deception, and conversely, to sanctioning Theseus' firmness and nobility (who is, according to Richard G.A. Buxton 'one of the flattest characters in the entire corpus of Greek tragedy').[69]

Oedipus remains apart: he seems to live and die in a pre-rhetorical world, where gods, religion, intricate rituals and prayers, curses and oaths, and most importantly, the truth, are more valuable than a deceitful mastery of speech. I do not mean that in his two interventions against Creon he is completely lacking in rhetorical skills. We observe quite the opposite, and critics have shown that he can organize his second speech as if it were an apology before a court[70]. We may note *inter alia* the particularly meaningful use of δίδαξον – 'explain to me' – at v. 969, an important example of technical vocabulary, and a formal marker which acquires this specialised use in late Sophocles[71]. Yet the blind man's speech is

---

69 Buxton 1982, 136, with p. 220 n. 63. 'this is perhaps inevitable: virtue is the hardest thing in the world to invest with literary life'.
70 His speech displays certain features linking it to forensic oratory, according to Untersteiner 1929, 208 (proem: 960–965; argument and refutation: 966–1009; epilogue: 1010–1013, 'uno dei luoghi comuni dell'eloquenza attica'). See also the repetition of the verb θέλω at 763, 767 (twice) and 777, the triple homeoteleuton at 761–763: φέρων ~ ποικίλον ~ δεύτερον, the alliteration of α at 764, the repetition of τέρψις at 766 and 775 (in the same metrical position) and the polyptoton of χάρις at 779, the oxymoron σκληρὰ μαλθακῶς at 774, the parallelism at 782 λόγῳ/τοῖσι δ' ἔργοισιν, ἐσθλά/κακά ('antitesi con omoioteleuto di stampo gorgiano': Guidorizzi 2008, 302), the anaphora at 784, 789, and 798–799, the chiasmus at 787, the pun between στόμα and στόμωσιν at 794–795, the use of the verb πείθω at 797.
71 Passages listed by Guidorizzi 2008, 325. According to Encinas Reguero 2007, 203, in late Sophocles 'abundan este tipo de referencias al propio lenguaje o, mejor dicho, abundan los clichés que marcan el paso de una línea de argumentación a otra y que anuncian el razonamiento que se

dictated more by the intention of unmasking the wheedling[72] Creon through the latter's own means, than by a deceptive verbal strategy in the service of καιρός. The model of the law-court is disregarded precisely in the fact that Oedipus' way of speaking does not seem to fulfil a premeditated rhetorical design conceived to persuade a judge, a court, or even a more generic audience.

It is precisely this twofold and differentiated use of rhetorical devices which makes it difficult to determine whether Sophocles intended his last drama to contain a deliberate condemnation of rhetoric as a τέχνη[73] (which is indisputable in the case of *Philoctetes*). *Oedipus at Colonus* is too complex to be reduced to a simple definition, but it is clear at least that in this drama a certain type of rhetoric is neither politically nor ethically successful.[74] The 'Good Discourse' prevails over the worse one,[75] and Sophocles' preference leans towards the less sophisticated king of Athens, and the often anti-rhetorical – or, as I said, pre-rhetorical – Oedipus. Is that a lesson for the Athenian democracy conceived by the old poet in the bad times of the war against Sparta, immediately before the final defeat?

---

va a seguir', probably due to the influence of contemporary rhetoric (cf. p. 409: 'en los pasajes de las tragedias tardías, *Electra* [352, 534, 585] y *Edipo en Colono* [969], el imperativo [δίδαξον] aparece dentro de *rheseis* argumentativas y marcando el inicio de una nueva línea argumental, es decir, articulando la argumentación', whereas in the other occurrences it is employed in stichomythic contexts; the presence of technical terminology should be interpreted as evidence of a major influence exerted by rhetoric: pp. 503ff.; cf. also Encinas Reguero 2011). For Schmalzriedt 1980, 97ff. the *Streitgespräch* between Creon and Oedipus is the most important example of the influential role played by rhetoric in late Sophocles.

72 Cf. the use of the verb θωπεύω at 1003 (Creon considers it καλόν to fawn immorally over Theseus): 'Oedipus' characterization of Kreon's attitude toward Theseus and Athens as θωπεῦσαι 'wheedling' (1003) invokes the atmosphere of the Athenian law court, in which, says Aristophanes' Philocleon, the juror can hear every kind of wheedling (θώπευμ' V. 563)' (Edmunds 1996, 135).

73 This idea is put forward by Guidorizzi 2008, 296: 'nella rappresentazione di Creonte emerge con evidenza la sua natura 'sofistica' e l'alone di biasimo di cui Sofocle la circonda; Creonte è anzi la traduzione scenica del sofista, come e più ancora che l'Odisseo del *Filottete*', with a rich list of arguments (on Odysseus' sophistic language, see Schein 2013, 22ff.).

74 Scodel 1997, 493. 'when rhetoric in tragedy of the late fifth century is successful, it is nearly always destructive'.

75 '[...] stellen die Rede [Creon's + Oedipus'] in eine Traditionslinie, die für uns vom Agon zwischen λόγος δίκαιος und λόγος ἄδικος in den Aristophanischen Wolken von 423 über die Δισσοὶ λόγοι (3) bis zum Platonischen Gorgias (bes. 462b ff.) führt': Schmalzriedt 1980, 100.

Bibliography

Barker, E.T.E. (2009), *Entering the Agon: Dissent and Authority in Homer, Historiography and Tragedy*, Oxford.
Battezzato, L. (2008), *Linguistica e retorica della tragedia greca*, Rome.
Bers, V. (1994), 'Tragedy and rhetoric', in: I. Worthington (ed.), *Persuasion. Greek Rhetoric in Action*, London/New York, 176–195.
Blundell, M.W. (1989), *Helping Friends and Harming Enemies: A Study in Sophocles and Greek Ethics*, Cambridge.
Budelmann, F. (2000), *The Language of Sophocles. Communality, Communication and Involvement*, Cambridge.
Buxton, R.G.A. (1982), *Persuasion in Greek Tragedy: A Study of Peitho*, Cambridge.
Carter, D.M. (2013), 'Reported Assembly Scenes in Greek Tragedy', in: *ICS* 38, 23–63.
Cole, T. (1991), *The Origins of Rhetoric in Ancient Greece*, Baltimore.
Collard, C. (ed.) (1975a), *Euripides, Supplices*. II, *Commentary*, Groningen.
Collard, C. (1975b), 'Formal Debates in Euripides' Drama', in: *G&R* 22, 58–71 (now in: J. Mossman [ed.] [2003], *Oxford Readings in Classical Studies: Euripides*, Oxford, 64–80).
Conacher, D.J. (1981), 'Rhetoric and Relevance in Euripidean Drama', in: *AJPh* 102, 3–25.
Dale, A.M. (ed.) (1954), *Euripides, Alcestis*, Oxford.
Dawe, R.D. (ed.) (1996), Sophocles, *Oedipus Coloneus*, tertium edidit R.D. D., Stutgardiae et Lipsiae.
Dentice di Accadia Ammone, S. (2012), *Omero e i suoi oratori: Tecniche di persuasione nell'Iliade*, Berlin/Boston.
Devine, A.M./Stephens, L.D. (1994), *The Prosody of Greek Speech*, New York/Oxford.
Devine, A.M./Stephens, L.D. (2000), *Discontinuous Syntax: Hyperbaton in Greek*, Oxford.
Dickey, E. (1996), *Greek Forms of Address. From Herodotus to Lucian*, Oxford.
Dik, H. (2007), *Word Order in Greek Tragic Dialogue*, Oxford.
Dover, K.J. (1974), *Greek Popular Morality in the Time of Plato and Aristotle*, Oxford.
Dow, J. (2015), *Passions and Persuasion in Aristotle's Rhetoric*, Oxford.
Dubischar, M. (2001), *Die Agonszenen bei Euripides: Untersuchungen zu ausgewählten Dramen*, Stuttgart/Weimar.
Duchemin, J. (1968), *L'ἀγών dans la tragédie grecque*, Paris.
Easterling, P.E. (1977), 'Character in Sophocles', in: *G&R* 24, 121–129.
Edmunds, L. (1996), *Theatrical Space and Historical Place in Sophocles' Oedipus at Colonus*, Lanham.
Encinas Reguero, M.C. (2007), *Tragedia y retórica en la Atenas clásica: la rhesis trágica como discurso formal en Sófocles*, PhD Diss., Universidad de la Rioja, Logroño.
Encinas Reguero, M.C. (2011), 'Exhibicionismo retórico y transformación narrativa en *Edipo en Colonó*, in: M. Quijada Sagredo (ed.), *Estudios sobre Tragedia Griega. Eurípides, el teatro de finales del siglo V a.C. y su influencia posterior*, Madrid, 105–130.
Finglass, P.J. (2012), 'Sophocles' Theseus', in: A. Markantonatos/B. Zimmermann (eds.), *Crisis on stage: Tragedy and Comedy in Late Fifth-Century Athens*, Berlin/Boston, 41–53.
Fraenkel, E. (ed.) (1950), *Aeschylus, Agamemnon*, I–III, Oxford.
Friis Johansen, H./Whittle, E.W. (eds.) (1980), *Aeschylus, The Suppliants*, I–III, København.
Gagarin, M. (1994), 'Probability and persuasion: Plato and early Greek rhetoric', in: I. Worthington (ed.), *Persuasion. Greek Rhetoric in Action*, London/New York, 46–68.

Gagarin, M. (2007), 'Background and Origins: Oratory and Rhetoric before the Sophists', in: I. Worthington (ed.), *A Companion to Greek Rhetoric*, Malden/Oxford, 27–36.

Goldhill, S. (1997), 'The language of tragedy: rhetoric and communication', in: P.E. Easterling (ed.), *The Cambridge Companion to Greek Tragedy*, Cambridge, 127–150.

Goldhill, S. (2009), 'The audience on stage: rhetoric, emotion, and judgement in Sophoclean theatre', in: S. Goldhill/E. Hall (eds.), *Sophocles and the Greek Tragic Tradition*, Cambridge, 27–47.

Guidorizzi, G. (2008), *Sofocle. Edipo a Colono*, introduzione e commento di G. G., testo critico a cura di G. Avezzù, traduzione di G. Cerri, Milan.

Jebb, R.C. (ed.) (1907), *Sophocles, The Plays and Fragments.* II, *The Oedipus Coloneus*, Cambridge, Reprint (Introduction by R. Rehm, General Editor P.E. Easterling) London, 2004.

Halliwell, S. (1997), 'Between Public and Private: Tragedy and Athenian Experience of Rhetoric', in: C.B.R. Pelling (ed.), *Greek Tragedy and the Historian*, Oxford, 121–141.

Harris, E.M. (2010), 'Is Oedipus Guilty? Sophocles and Athenian Homicide Law', in: E.M. Harris/ D.F. Leão /P.J. Rhodes (eds.), *Law and Drama in Ancient Greece*, London, 122–146.

Harris, E.M. (2012), 'Sophocles and Athenian Law', in: K. Ormand (ed.), *A Companion to Sophocles*, Malden/Oxford, 287–300.

Heath, M. (1987), *The Poetics of Greek Tragedy*, London.

Kamerbeek, J.C. (1984), *The Plays of Sophocles.* Commentaries, part VII, *The Oedipus Coloneus*, Leiden.

Konstan, D. (2001), *Pity Transformed*, London.

Knudsen, R.A. (2014), *Homeric Speech and the Origins of Rhetoric*, Baltimore.

Kraus, M. (2007), 'Early Greek Probability Arguments and Common Ground in Dissensus', in: H.V. Hansen et al. (eds.), *Dissensus and the Search for Common Ground*, University of Windsor, Ontario, OSSA Conference Archive 7, 1–11.

Lloyd, M. (1992), *The Agon in Euripides*, Oxford.

Lloyd-Jones, H. (ed.) (1994), *Sophocles, Antigone, The Women of Trachis, Philoctetes, Oedipus at Colonus*, Cambridge MA/London.

Lloyd-Jones, H./Wilson, N.G. (eds.) (1990), *Sophoclis fabulae*, recognoverunt breviqve adnotatione critica instruxerunt H. L.-J. et N.G. W., Oxonii.

Markantonatos, A. (2002), *Tragic Narrative: A Narratological Study of Sophocles' Oedipus at Colonus*, Berlin/New York.

Mastronarde, D.J. (2010), *The Art of Euripides: Dramatic Technique and Social Context*, Cambridge.

Moorhouse, A.C. (1982), *The Syntax of Sophocles*, Leiden.

Mülke, C. (2002), *Solons politische Elegien und Iamben (Fr. 1–13; 32–37 West)*, Einleitung, Text, Übersetzung, Kommentar, Munich/Leipzig.

Noussia-Fantuzzi, M. (ed.) (2010), *Solon the Athenian, The Poetic Fragments*, Leiden/Boston.

Ober, J. (1989), *Mass and Elite in Democratic Athens: Rhetoric, Ideology, and the Power of the People*, Princeton.

Ostwald, M. (1986), *From Popular Sovereignty to the Sovereignty of Law: Law, Society, and Politics in Fifth-Century Athens*, Berkeley.

Pelling, C. (2005), 'Tragedy, Rhetoric, and Performance Culture', in: J. Gregory (ed.), *A Companion to Greek Tragedy*, Malden, 83–102.

Race, W.H. (1981), 'The Word Καιρός in Greek Drama', in: *TAPhA* 111, 197–213.

Riedweg, C. (2000), 'Der tragödiendichter als rhetor? Redestrategien in Euripides' *Hekabe* und ihr Verhältnis zur zeitgenössischen Rhetoriktheorie', in: *RhM* 143, 1–32.

Rodighiero, A. (2011), 'Appunti sulle traduzioni da un classico: Sofocle tra Otto- e Novecento (con qualche primo sondaggio su un inedito pascoliano)', in: F. Condello/B. Pieri (eds.), *Note di traduttore. Sofocle, Euripide, Aristofane, Tucidide, Plauto, Catullo, Virgilio, Nonno*, Bologna, 135–157.

Rodighiero, A. (2012), 'The Sense of Place: *Oedipus at Colonus*, 'Political' Geography and the Defence of a Way of Life', in: A. Markantonatos/B. Zimmermann (eds.), *Crisis on stage: Tragedy and Comedy in Late Fifth-Century Athens*, Berlin/Boston, 55–80.

Rodighiero, A. (2016), 'Riprese di parola in tre sezioni dialogiche sofoclee tra lingua d'uso ed espedienti retorici', in: R. Capelli/C. Concina/M. Salgaro/T. Zanon (eds.), *Scritti in onore di A. M. Babbi*, Verona.

Rodighiero, A. (2017), 'Una (trascurata) autocitazione sofoclea', in: *QUCC* 117 (3), 57–71.

Rodighiero, A. (2018), 'How Sophocles begins: Reshaping Lyric Genres in Tragic Choruses', in: R. Andújar/T. Coward/T. Hadjimichael (eds.), *Paths of Song: Interactions between Greek Lyric and Tragedy*, Berlin/Boston, 137–162.

Ruijgh, C.J. (2006), 'The Use of the Demonstratives ὅδε, οὗτος and (ἐ)κεῖνος in Sophocles', in: I.J.F. de Jong/A. Rijksbaron (eds.), *Sophocles and the Greek Language. Aspects of Diction, Syntax and Pragmatics*, Leiden, 151–161.

Rutherford, R.B. (2012), *Greek Tragic Style. Form, Language and Interpretation*, Cambridge.

Saïd, S. (1978), *La faute tragique*, Paris.

Sanders, Ed. (2012), '"He is a Liar, a Bounder, and a Cad". The Arousal of Hostile Emotions in Attic Forensic Oratory', in: A. Chaniotis (ed.), *Unveiling Emotions: Sources and Methods for the Study of Emotions in the Greek World*, Stuttgart, 359–387.

Sansone, D. (2012), *Greek Drama and the Invention of Rhetoric*, Malden/Oxford/Chichester.

Schein, S.L. (ed.) (2013), *Sophocles, Philoctetes*, Cambridge.

Schiappa, E. (1999), *The Beginnings of Rhetorical Theory in Classical Greece*, New Haven/London.

Schmalzriedt, E. (1980), 'Sophokles und die Rhetorik', in: *Rhetorik* 1, 89–110.

Scodel, R. (1997), 'Drama and Rhetoric', in: S.E. Porter (ed.), *Handbook of Classical Rhetoric in the Hellenistic Period 330 B.C.-A.D. 400*, Leiden, 489–504.

Scodel, R. (1999–2000), 'Verbal Performance and Euripidean Rhetoric', in: *ICS* 24–25, 129–144.

Trédé-Boulmer, M. (2015), *Kairos. L'à-propos et l'occasion: Le mot et la notion, d'Homère à la fin du IVe siècle avant J.-C.*, Paris.

Tzanetou, A. (2005), 'A Generous City: Pity in Athenian Oratory and Tragedy', in: R.H. Sternberg (ed.), *Pity and Power in Ancient Athens*, New York, 98–122.

Untersteiner, M. (ed.) (1929), *Sofocle, Edipo a Colono*, Turin.

Usher, S. (2010), 'Apostrophe in Greek Oratory', in: *Rhetorica* 28, 351–362.

Vallozza, M. (1985), 'Καιρός nella retorica di Alcidamante e di Isocrate, ovvero nell'oratoria orale e scritta', in: *QUCC* n.s. 21, 119–123.

Vergados, A. (ed.) (2013), *The 'Homeric Hymn to Hermes': Introduction, Text and Commentary*, Berlin/Boston.

Walker, J. (2000), *Rhetoric and Poetics in Antiquity*, Oxford.

Willink, C.W. (ed.) (1986), *Euripides, Orestes*, Oxford.

Worman, N. (2012), 'Oedipus, Odysseus, and the Failure of Rhetoric', in: A. Markantonatos (ed.), *Brill's Companion to Sophocles*, Leiden/Boston, 325–347.

Adele C. Scafuro
Justifying Murder and Rejecting Revenge

Hypothetical arguments and imaginary lawcourts in the Oresteian tragedies (Aeschylus, *Oresteia*; Sophocles, *Electra*; Euripides, *Electra* and *Orestes*)

It is an understatement to say that Aeschylus' *Oresteia*,[1] as well as his less well-known trilogy on the Trojan War, the *Achilleis* (*Myrmidons, Nereids, Phrygians*), and other plays such as his *Iphigeneia*, left a rich and suggestive legacy for later dramatists. Indeed, they took the material and they flew with it: they might change the outlines of stories, use other sources, invent their own, tease or taunt their audiences with backward references, mock their grand predecessor for grandiloquence and sometimes for naiveté, or hold him in awe: Aeschylus was always there. Some scholars have argued for a revival of the *Oresteia* as early as the 420s that will then have ushered in the *Electras* of Sophocles and Euripides; the argument is attractive but not certain and has vigorous opponents.[2] The Aeschylean legacy extends to scholars who have interested themselves in what some might call the fifth century reception of Aeschylus, and others would call intertextuality, metatheatrics, performance history, and the politics of different times and places. The same legacy has extended to textual critics; in the case of plays that were revived for later productions in antiquity, the occasions for actors' interpolations may have been ample.

---

[1] The plays mentioned in this essay and their posited dates: Aesch. *Oresteia* 458; Soph. *Ant.* 442 or 440; *OT* 436–433; *El.* c. 420–410, *OC* 401 (posthumous); Eur. *Cretans* c. 438 (see n. 31 *infra*); *Med.* 431; *Hipp.* 428; *El.* c. 422–417 or 415–413; *Heracl., Hec., Andr.* 420s; *Erechth.* 422 (see n. 41 *infra*); *Ph.* c. 411; *Or.* 408; *IA* 405–400 (posthumous). For a succinct synthesis of scholarly arguments on the dating of the two *Electra* plays, see Roisman/Luschnig 2011, 28–32; to their bibliography, add Müller 2000, 37–45. Texts are cited from *TLG*: D.L. Page for Aeschylus; Lloyd-Jones/Wilson for Sophocles; Diggle for Euripides; Gernet for Antiphon; Carey for Lysias. In most cases, I have used the translations of the Loeb Classical Library; in the case of *Orestes*, West 1987 is used. A catalogue of the passages discussed in this essay appears at its end.

[2] E.g., supporters: Newiger 1961, 422–430, followed by more recent scholars as Mueller 2016, pp. 43 and 205 n. 6; opponents: Biles 2006–2007. For the integration of revivals of tragedy and comedy into the Dionysia in the fourth century, see Nervegna 2014, 65–66. It is an interesting coincidence that comedies are revived in 340/39, in the year following the re-performance of Euripides' *Orestes*.

Viewers, scholars, and readers have long noticed the way the characters in the two *Electra* plays look back to Aeschylean arguments, or sometimes appear to be talking against or in harmony with one another;[3] they have also noticed, on a broader scale, how Euripides' *Orestes* re-makes Aeschylus' trilogy and at the same time provides an entirely new ending. Here, I should like to consider some rhetorical formulations that are used in similar ways in the *Electra* plays and in *Orestes*. All are used either to justify a murder or reject revenge and in this respect, belong to modern discussions of the intertextuality of these plays and the Aeschylean legacy. There is, however, a noticeable departure from the norm of argumentation more generally in *Orestes* that can be seen as contingent on the political events in the aftermath of regime changes in Athens in 411/10 and in this respect, my discussion accords with political interpretations of the play over the last forty or fifty years.[4] Where I think I cut my own path in this dense forest is in the way I relate the dramatists' arguments to (imaginary) courtroom rhetoric. To set the stage, I begin with an outline of *Orestes* and I briefly consider some recent views of scholars who have situated the arguments of the play in Athenian law and lawcourts. I start here because I think *Orestes* can locate for us the *imaginary* law court for which the language of this and the other plays is designed. I then take my leave of these technical discussions and look at a particular mode of argument in six passages from the *Electras* and *Orestes*; in the end, I try to find a place for them – or outside – the history of rhetoric.

1 The emergence of Orestes

In Euripides' *Electra*, at play's *dei ex machina* ending, the divine Dioscuri send Orestes to the court of Areopagus where Ares had *already* been tried in the first homicide trial. It is a bit of a weird twist that a homicide court pre-exists in Athens but is only acknowledged at play's ending. Weirder twists come in Euripides' *Orestes* in 408: a little more than half-way through the human drama, a Messenger reports that the Argive Assembly has condemned brother and sister for murdering their mother: Orestes and Electra are to kill themselves that day (946–949). Orestes had earlier limped off to that meeting on the arm of Pylades to plead for lenient treatment; his uncle Menelaus had been no help – in fact, had not even

---

3 E.g., Zeitlin 1980; West 1987, 31–32.
4 Burkert 1974, 106–108; also, Longo 1975; Schein 1975; Euben 1986; Hall 1993. More recently, Scodel 2015 sees different characters constructing and responding to different political/historical or mythical situations.

shown up – whereas his grandfather Tyndareus, father of Clytemnestra, had provided the arguments against him. Condemned and back at the palace now, in the last moments before the enforced suicide, Pylades has devised a plan: they should kill Helen for revenge on the inactive and cowardly Menelaus (1102); the murder will satisfy Hellenes in general: 'she'll be paying the penalty on account of all Greece, those whose fathers she killed, whose children she destroyed and made brides bereft of their husbands: there'll be a hallelujah' (1134–1137); Orestes, instead of being called the 'matricide' will be known as 'the slayer of Helen the mass murderer!' (1140–1142). And in case the scheme to murder Helen fails, they'll set fire to the palace; they 'shall be famous for a glorious death or a glorious deliverance' (1152). Electra with her wonderfully 'masculine mind' (1204) adds inducement for Menelaus' eleventh hour aid: they shall take his daughter Hermione hostage and threaten to kill her unless Menelaus secures their safe escape (1191–1203). The plan first materializes off-stage: Helen is put to the sword amidst a scuffling with Phrygian slaves that leaves at least one of them dead (1486). Then onstage, on palace's rooftop, Hermione is held hostage beneath Orestes' sword (1653); Pylades and attendants stand ready with torches to burn the place down; Menelaus at the palace door quivers (1598, 1610, 1613, 1617) and calls for Argive aid (1621–1624). The human tragedy ends *in medias res* (a tableau of futility?), but now the heavenly one begins: Apollo appears in the sky with Helen, rescued from the clutches of the murderous Pylades and Orestes – and announces her new stardom. Further dispensations follow: Orestes is to go into exile for a year, then onwards to Athens to stand trial for matricide before Areopagus where three benign goddesses – the Eumenides – will oppose him, where gods as referees (βραβῆς) will divide their vote most piously, and where Orestes is fated to win (1648–1652). Moreover, he is then to return to Argos and marry Hermione, the maiden he has been holding hostage and finally, he is to rule (happily?) in Argos ever afterwards. Manly-minded Electra will marry Pylades.

Modern critics sometimes interpret this play as a major dramatic fiasco, sometimes as a dramatic tour de force, sometimes as a parody of the genre.[5] I think it rather something of the last two: terrific theatre as well as some sort of parody.

Why parody? Why the heavenly make-believe ending that is no ending at all for the human drama? Many have answered, because socio-political circumstances at the end of the fifth century made grand tragedy a thing of the past. Tragedy now, e.g., cannot have a tragic ending because it has lost its fixedness, its bearings in a world ever more controlled by Tyche where men can no longer

---

[5] For parody, see especially Burkert 1974 and Burnett 1998, 247–272.

be heroes. The Athenians are demoralized after more than two decades of war; political upheaval has had its effects not only on real persons but also on the literature that real persons produce. Burkert points (as earlier scholars had done and later scholars would repeat) to the polarization of the social classes in 415, the emergence of *hetaireai* (allegedly partisan and conspiratorial clubs), the overthrow of the democracy in 411 and its resuscitation four months later, the assassination of Phrynichus and the rewards for his killers that were inscribed on a stele in 409 (IG I³ 102), the trials of the dead Phrynichus and of Antiphon, Archeptolemus, and Onomacles, and the codification of the lawcode – including the republication of Draco's homicide law in 409/408: all in all, a period of lawbreaking and lawmaking in Athens.⁶

Political upheavals, conspiracies, and assassinations in the years 415–408 have thus come into consideration as the backdrop – and explanation – for the production of *Orestes*. And, given this backdrop, scholars have understandably not been slow to point out the fine traces of instruments of Athenian justice that appear just beneath the surface of the play. Two scenes have come into particular focus: that in which the messenger gives his report about the Argive Assembly and earlier in the play, when Tyndareus encounters his ailing grandson Orestes. Only the latter can be discussed in any detail here.

Menelaus and Orestes are onstage before the elderly man arrives. Menelaus has just now returned from Troy, bringing the beautiful Helen home. Upon arriving at Nauplia, the port for Argos, he had learned that Orestes had killed his sister-in-law Clytemnestra. After sending Helen ahead at nightfall, he has now come by daylight to the palace to greet his murderous nephew. The conversation (356–455) is brilliant: Menelaus, a prissy scientific sophist is interested, it seems, in the daily progression of Orestes' madness while the latter amidst his ailing sees Menelaus as his only chance for deliverance – for the polis will vote this day on Orestes' fate (48–50, 440, 755–758, 884–887). Menelaus, meanwhile, summarizes Orestes' situation as 'the ultimate in disaster' (447), and is prevented from further gnomic reflection by the arrival of Tyndareus. Orestes cowers (467–469). An *agon* is about to begin.

The old man addresses his entire first speech (491–541) to Menelaus except for seven lines near its end (526–533) when he turns to Orestes.⁷ Tyndareus' main theme is Orestes' stupidity – indeed, 'who has ever behaved more stupidly than he has?' he asks at the outset (493). The reason follows: 'He paid no regard to

---

6 See n. 4 *supra*. Phrynichus looms large over the events of these years. For a good reconstruction of his career and some of the events mentioned here, see Heftner 2005.
7 See Willink 1989, 166.

what was right and did not take recourse to the standard Greek procedure', (494–495, ὅστις τὸ μὲν δίκαιον οὐκ ἐσκέψατο / οὐδ' ἦλθεν ἐπὶ τὸν κοινὸν Ἑλλήνων νόμον). He continues, defining the Greek *nomos* that Orestes should have followed after Clytemnestra's murder of Agamemnon:

> He ought to have imposed a pious penalty for bloodshed (αἵματος δίκην/ὁσίαν) by pursuing (διώκοντ') her and thrown his mother out of the house. He would have got credit for sanity out of the calamity, he would be keeping to the law (or 'convention'), and he would be a righteous man (καὶ τοῦ νόμου τ' ἂν εἴχετ' εὐσεβής τ' ἂν ἦν).
> (Eur. *Orestes* 500–503, transl. West, modified)[8]

Tyndareus next spins out a hypothetical scenario of cyclical killings – how far will it extend? He rounds off this section of the speech with reference to ancestral tradition:

> Our fathers of old ordered these matters well: they were not for allowing a man who had blood on his hands to come into anyone's sight to meet them, but for rehabilitating him by banishment, not killing him in turn. Otherwise there would always be one person guilty of murder, taking over the latest pollution on his hands. As for me, I hate impure women, and first of all my daughter, who killed her husband... ; but I will defend the law (or 'convention') as far as I am able (ἀμυνῶ δ' ὅσονπερ δυνατός εἰμι τῶι νόμωι), to curb this animal butchery which is always the ruin of land and community.
> (Eur. *Orestes*, 512–519, 523–525, transl. West.)

Tyndareus ends his speech with a warning to Menelaus not to intervene in Orestes' behalf and with a final comment on his daughter Clytemnestra:

> So to make it clear to you, Menelaus, don't go against the gods by choosing to help him, but leave him to be stoned to death by the townspeople. [Or else do not set foot on Spartan soil.] My daughter in dying had her just deserts, but it was not fitting that she be killed by him. I have been a fortunate man otherwise, except as regards my daughters. In this respect I am ill-starred.
> (Eur. *Orestes* 534–541, transl. West)[9]

---

8 For the translation of αἵματος δίκην/ὁσίαν in 500/501, see Willink 1986, 169. I have translated διώκοντ' as 'by pursuing' rather than by 'by prosecuting' to suggest the ambiguity in the language: one might impose a penalty (or 'justice' or 'punishment') without necessarily taking a person to court.

9 Tyndareus repeats the warning at 536 ('leave him to be stoned to death') once again at 625 before he leaves the stage. Many editors delete ll. 536–537 because of the dublette; Diggle athetizes 537 and 625; for argument in favour of deleting 536–537, Willink 1989, 172; against deletion of 536, West 1987, 219; against deletion of 536–537, Holzhausen 2003, 29 n. 30 with reference to earlier literature.

J.R. Porter in his study of the play devotes a chapter to the *agon* and concludes that Tyndareus is neither the 'hypocrite' nor the 'reasonable old dicast' that earlier scholars have perceived; he is less a 'stern guardian of antique virtue' and 'more the sophistic rhetor.'[10] Indeed, Porter reaches these conclusions from an analysis of Tyndareus' speech as a progression of rhetorical *topoi* that can be paralleled from the Attic orators of the fifth and fourth centuries. The heart of Tyndareus' case, he claims, is his 'reliance upon *nomos*'; he continues:

> ... the key to Tyndareus' argument lies in his assuming the role of self-proclaimed champion of law and social order. This is the note he sounds in his prooemion (494–95) and it forms the cornerstone of the formal charge against Orestes (496–517): Orestes scorned the law and its provisions for dealing with malefactors (496–506) ... [11]

So pervasive is Tyndareus' concern for law and order, so saturated is his speech with anachronistic forensic *topoi* and legal terminology that in the end, Porter maintains that Euripides has recast the Aeschylean trial of Orestes as a contemporary trial that:

> assumes all of the legal mechanisms of present-day Athens and casts the audience in the role of jurors. Aeschylus' Furies have been transformed by the poet into the equally savage but more prosaic figure of Tyndareus, who develops his case as would a contemporary litigant in an Athenian courtroom, playing off the bias of the jurors, their concerns with the nature of law and its role in human society, and their more immediate concerns (particularly acute in the waning years of the war) regarding factional violence.[12]

It is but a short step from perceiving Tyndareus' case as dependent on *nomoi* and his speech as saturated with legal terminology to trying to identify what precisely those *nomoi* are. It is perhaps not surprising, then, that some scholars have seen in the αἵματος δίκη of line 500 a reference to a δίκη φόνου (a lawsuit for homicide) and have tried to identify the *nomos* that Orestes should have carried out as Draco's law on homicide (*IG* I³ 104);[13] the Athenian *boule* and *demos*, after all, had ordered that Draco's law be copied onto a stēlē and set out in the Stoa Poikile in

---

[10] Porter 1994, 103.
[11] Porter 1994, 106 with n. 17 in which he argues against Ostwald's (1969, 25) assertion that *nomos* in 503 is 'general in nature.' For an interpretation that embraces the ambiguities in Tyndaeus' speech, see Scodel 2015, 114–120.
[12] Porter 1994, 126–127 with n. 93. Porter is helped to this view by an alternative tradition (which he reports *ibid*. 102 n. 7) by which Tyndareus and Erigone prosecuted Orestes before the Areopagus: Jacoby (1950–1962) IIIb (Suppl.) ii 48 n. 8.
[13] Δίκη φόνου: Holzhausen 2003, 49–50. Draco's law: Holzhausen 2003, 63; Flashar 1997, 107–108.

the archonship of Diocles, that is, in 409/08, the very year that *Orestes* was produced. If indeed Draco's law as we have it furnished provisions for both intentional and unintentional killers, then one could conceivably maintain, as Flashar did in 1997, that Euripides anachronistically alludes to that law when Tyndareus identifies the procedure that Orestes should have followed (500–503).[14]

Nonetheless, a charge of homicide may be irrelevant to the legal scenario of the play. Recently Naiden has presented a different and more compelling scenario, treason tried by *eisangelia* (impeachment). Orestes, Naiden argues, is not charged with murder (though he says so at 756) for these reasons: (i) he is not likewise charged with the murder of Aegisthus (so we must infer a different charge); (ii) Pylades helped out with the murder and is not charged (so homicide is not an issue); (iii) there are two Assembly meetings: at the first (756, 884–887), Orestes is put under arrest but guilt and penalty are not decided until the second (unlike a trial for a *dike phonou*); (iv) he is not permitted to purify himself nor to flee into exile before the verdict is given (as in a *dike phonou*) but is kept under arrest (as in cases of *eisangelia*); (v) he is not tried by a lawcourt but by an Assembly (as in some cases of *eisangelia*); and (vi) the speeches in the Assembly do not focus on any particular charge though one (depicted by Talthybius) claims that Orestes has established laws about parents that are not good (893–893).[15] The charge is tantamount to 'taking the law into his own hands' and that is similar ('in a general sense'), argues Neiden, to the charge of treason, e.g., against Phrynichus in 410 (Lyc. 1.113).[16]

Naiden's argument for a treason trial before the Assembly as a model for the trial in *Orestes* is attractive; certainly numerous eisangeltic trials had been held in the last decade before the play was produced. The Assembly will thus have often debated proposals for arrest and trial, even though it may have have dispatched most cases to a lawcourt; few will have been heard and decided by the Assembly itself.[17] But it is one thing to identify a possible model for a dramatic

---

14 Flashar 1997, 107–108. Holzhausen in his 2003 study of the play took Flashar's casual identification of the law as Draco's so seriously that he devoted an excursus to demonstrate that Draco's law as we have it had nothing to do with intentional killers (such as Orestes) and concluded that we cannot know for certain how Draco treated them. While he nevertheless offered interesting hypothetical possibilities, there is no supporting evidence, especially for the specific regulations for kin-killing that he suggested.
15 Naiden 2010, 67–69.
16 Naiden 2010, 70.
17 See Hansen 1975, cat. nos. 1–65 and 131–138 for cases before 408 (the date of *Orestes*); only nos. 2, 3, and 66 are known to have been heard before the Assembly; in many instances, there is

legal scenario and quite another thing to claim that Euripides adhered to it in any precise way.[18] As a 'loose model', however, the undertaking of an impeachment trial would allow the playwright a great deal of flexibility in defining the offence, formulating the penalty, and delineating procedure – for that would be left in the hands of the Assemblymen. Indeed, it would be ideal for a dramatist precisely because the format is so flexible and allows for so much allusiveness – and when transferred to Argos, even moreso.[19] Consider, e.g., as lierary and historical allusive background for *Orestes*: Aeschylus' early hailing of 'the decisive hand of the People' (δήμου κρατοῦσα χείρ) when referring to the Argive Assembly in *Supplices*;[20] consider as well the impeachment for treason against Phrynichus in 410/09(?) that followed an investigation into his murder in 411/10[21]—whose assassin's accomplice Thucydides designates as an Argive;[22] consider also the Argive general who escaped the unruly and discontented Argive populace's attempt to stone him to death by fleeing to an altar in 418;[23] and consider, too, the republication of Draco's homicide law in 409/08.

The allusions are so pervasive and diverse that I am inclined to scepticism about any particular Athenian legal underpinnings in this play and I prefer to focus on the *imaginary* construction of law and lawlessness that Euripides has created here. In the first place, the drama is an imaginary construction that tries to eliminate Aeschylean foundations. That elimination had begun in *Electra* with all that shenanigans with the footprints and lock of hair at Agamemnon's tomb. In *Orestes*, on the other hand, before the divine intervention and dispatch to Athens, justice is sought and provided in Orestes' hometown by angry men rather than by the Erinyes. We are far from the *Weltanschauung* of the Aeschylean trilogy. Secondly, while the construction looks to that earlier masterpiece so as to

---

simply no information relavant to the venue of the case; in other instances, there is certain evidence for trial in a *dikasterion*.

18 Naiden 2010, 62 goes a step too far, I think, when he claims more assertively that the play 'stands as an example of a dramatic critique of a legal procedure – an entirely human procedure as opposed to the divinely sanctioned procedure found in the Eumenides.'

19 Scodel 2015, 115–116 argues that the Argive Assembly meetings are an 'historical thought experiment': insofar as Orestes in *Eumenides* leaves Argos immediately after the matricide, the Argives have had no occasion to voice their reaction; in Euripides' play, they do, and not as 'a false intrusion of democracy into the heroic past' but as a plausible scenario 'that the assembly could assert itself in the absence of a ruler'. Nonetheless, it is hard not to see a glimmer of the contemporary Argive democracy, as well as the famed Argive Assembly of Aesch. *Suppl.* 601–609.

20 Aesch. *Suppl.* 604.

21 Lys. 13.71; Thuc. 8.92; *IG* I³ 102.38–47 (see Scafuro 2009); Lyc. 1.112.

22 Thuc. 8.92.

23 Thuc. 5.60.6 and Hornblower 2008, 158.

know where to erase its traces and build anew, it also looks to Athenian law and erases that as well. If we have law and if we have lawcourts in these dramas, they are imaginary.

Rhetoric, however, abides, and Porter is right in seeing it as the rhetoric of the lawcourts; but there is no legal underpinning for it.[24] Also, there is little contemporary evidence for it: many of the rhetorical arguments he has found as parallels for Euripides come from the fourth century.[25] The rhetorical formulations I focus on in the later 'Oresteian plays' (*Orestes* and the two *Electras*) belong to the rhetoric of an imaginary lawcourt. I shall later return to the history of rhetoric in Athens; I look back now to the *Oresteia*.

2

2.1 The *Oresteia*'s legacy to rhetoric: origins of artifice

I begin with Agamemnon's dilemma: the sacrifice of Iphigenia: to execute it or not to execute it: the dilemma, as first presented in Aeschylus' play:

> ἄναξ δ' ὁ πρέσβυς τόδ' εἶπε φωνῶν·
> 'βαρεῖα μὲν κὴρ τὸ μὴ πιθέσθαι,
> βαρεῖα δ' εἰ τέκνον δαΐξω, δόμων ἄγαλμα,
> μιαίνων παρθενοσφάγοισιν
> ῥείθροις πατρῴους χέρας πέλας βω-
> μοῦ· τί τῶνδ' ἄνευ κακῶν;
> πῶς λιπόναυς γένωμαι
> ξυμμαχίας ἁμαρτών;
> παυσανέμου γὰρ θυσίας
> παρθενίου θ' αἵματος ὀρ-
> γᾷ περιόργῳ σφ' ἐπιθυ-
> μεῖν θέμις. εὖ γὰρ εἴη.'

And the senior king spoke, and said this: 'Fate will be heavy if I do not obey, heavy as well if I hew my child, the delight of my house, polluting a father's hands with streams of a slaughtered maiden's blood close by the altar. What is there without evil here? How can I

---

24 None of the occurrences of the word *nomos* in the play needs to refer to 'written statute': 429, 487, 495, 503, 523, 571, 892, 941, 1426, [1430], 1507. The play is set both in and out of myth and history.
25 Many parallels are drawn from Demosthenes, Aeschines, and Isaeus; there is no attempt to date the speeches of Lysias; indeed, there is no concern for the relative chronology of plays and speeches. See Sansone's critique (2012, 148–149).

become a deserter of the fleet, losing my alliance? That they should long with intense passion for a sacrifice to end the winds and for the blood of a maiden is quite natural. May all be well!'

(transl. Sommerstein, slightly modified)

Unforgettable words, indeed – and not forgotten by later playwrights. 'Fate will be heavy if I do not obey, heavy as well if I hew my child'. A hypothetical proposition at the outset ('z if I do X, z if I do Y') and an implicit syllogism with a morally equivocal conclusion: 'whether I do X or Y makes no difference'. Was Agamemnon's subsequent decision right? Did he have real choices? His decision certainly had consequences: the murder of Agamemnon by Clytemnestra and Aegisthus; and then the murder of Clytemnestra and Aegisthus by Orestes and Electra: were these murders right? And so there evolves, not only a series of killings, but also a rhetoric of killing in revenge, a rhetoric of justifications and rebuttals that explores the rights and wrongs of responses to the murder of kin.

Rhetorical artifice is there, too, even as Apollo sets Orestes on the road to Athens at the opening of *Eumenides*: 'There,' he says, 'we will have judges to judge these matters, and words that will charm (κἀκεῖ δικαστὰς τῶνδε καὶ θελκτηρίους |μύθους ἔχοντες μηχανὰς εὑρήσομεν)'.[26] We have an example of θελκτήριοι μῦθοι in Apollo's defence speech, namely his 'flower-pot argument' at *Eum.* 657–666:[27]

καὶ τοῦτο λέξω, καὶ μάθ᾽ ὡς ὀρθῶς ἐρῶ.
οὐκ ἔστι μήτηρ ἡ κεκλημένη τέκνου
τοκεύς, τροφεὺς δὲ κύματος νεοσπόρου·
τίκτει δ᾽ ὁ θρῴσκων, ἡ δ᾽ ἅπερ ξένῳ ξένη
ἔσωσεν ἔρνος, οἷσι μὴ βλάψῃ θεός.
τεκμήριον δὲ τοῦδέ σοι δείξω λόγου·
πατὴρ μὲν ἂν γείναιτ᾽ ἄνευ μητρός· πέλας
μάρτυς πάρεστι παῖς Ὀλυμπίου Διός,
οὐδ᾽ ἐν σκότοισι νηδύος τεθραμμένη,
ἀλλ᾽ οἷον ἔρνος οὔτις ἂν τέκοι θεά.

I will tell you that too—and mark how rightly I argue. The so-called 'mother' is not a parent of the child, only the nurse of the newly-begotten embryo. The parent is he who mounts; the female keeps the offspring safe, like a stranger on behalf of a stranger, for those in whose case this is not prevented by god. I shall give you powerful proof of this statement. A father can procreate without a mother: a witness to this is here close by us, the daughter

---

26 Aesch. *Eum.* 81–82 (transl. Sommerstein).
27 Saxonhouse 1992, 83 ascribes the use of term 'flowerpot' to unnamed others who have thus described the role that Apollo assigns to women in nurturing a child.

of Olympian Zeus, who was not even nurtured in the darkness of a womb, but is such an offspring as no female divinity could ever bring forth.

(transl. Sommerstein, slightly modified)

The argument is alluded to by Praxithea in Eur. *Erectheus* fr. 360.38 (in an Aeschylean context, cited in n. 41 *infra*) and by Orestes in the eponymous play at 552–554. In the latter passage, Orestes is addressing Tyndareus:

πατὴρ μὲν ἐφύτευσέν με, σὴ δ' ἔτικτε παῖς,
τὸ σπέρμ' ἄρουρα παραλαβοῦσ' ἄλλου πάρα.
[ἄνευ δὲ πατρὸς τέκνον οὐκ εἴη ποτ' ἄν.]
ἐλογισάμην οὖν τῷ γένους ἀρχηγέτῃ
μᾶλλόν μ' ἀμῦναι τῆς ὑποστάσης τροφάς.

(Eur. *Orestes* 552–554)

My father planted me, and your daughter bore me—ploughland taking over the seed from another: [without the father there would never be a child.] So I reckoned I should rather take the side of the author of my birth than of her who undertook the fostering.

(transl. West)

Aeschylus set in motion artifices of argument that will be picked up and developed—and sometimes mocked and eliminated—as Euripides most famously does in his *Electra* when he eliminates the 'proofs' of shorn hair, footprints, and even any suggestion of a bit of weaving.

2.2 'Hypotheticals'

With an origin for rhetorical artifice clear in the *Oresteia*, I now turn to some arguments in the Oresteian tradition in the later fifth century that justify murder or reject revenge and take the form of 'the hypothetical'. By 'hypothetical', I mean an imaginary scenario that a character depicts, often in the form of a contrafactual (i.e., a 'contrary-to-fact' or 'unreal' condition) but sometimes in the form of a future conditional. Hypothetical contrafactual statements are found in all genres of Greek literature – e.g., in epic, lyric poetry, history, tragedy, comedy, philosophy and oratory. They have been much studied, especially in the fields of history, philosophy, and linguistics.[28] For the purpose of this essay, I have borrowed and

---

[28] For 'historical contrafactuals', see Flory 1988; Hornblower 1994, 158–159; Rood 1998, 278–280. Tordoff 2014 offers a brilliant account of contrafactual arguments that were widely used

adapted the term from the 'hypotheticals' that are used in American law schools where students are asked to consider legal and ethical problems from different perspectives. These hypotheticals are formulated as 'counter factual variations on the fact pattern of an actual case'.[29] They are often posed as a series of 'what if' questions (e.g., what if x had happened, what would have been the result? Would it have been lawful? Would it have been good?'). When we look for this type of hypothetical more broadly in tragedy (and do not limit ourselves to such statements in revenge scenarios), we find that the poser of the hypothetical contemplates a set of imaginary circumstances in contrast to what happened in the past in order to endorse or reject an act – a killing, a sexual act, a marriage, a forbidden burial – to claim that it was fair or unfair, or that the doer or participant was right or wrong: there is almost always an ethical component to the hypothetical, an assessment of the act or actor.[30] Sometimes the poser will pitch the hypothetical argument to future events ('if x should happen, then y will be the consequence', or 'if A does B, then C will happen') and asks (explicitly or implicitly), 'will this be a good thing?' or 'will the doer be an upright person?'. Such 'hypotheticals' are not conveyed as contrafactuals but as future conditionals (in different degrees: less vivid, more vivid and most—the last being tantamount to a threat), but like the contrafactuals that I have identified, they look to the ethical quality of the action or actor.

Some examples will clarify. An early contrafactual appears in Eur. *Cretans* fr. 472e, which has been dated by metrical criteria to a year between 455 and 428 and

---

about the Peloponnesian War after the fall of the Athenian Empire. For philosophic contrafactuals, see Chisolm 1946; Goodman 1947; Lewis 1973; for linguistic contrafactuals, see Funk 1985; for Homeric, see de Jong 1987, 68–81. For earlier studies of contrafactuals in tragedy and oratory, see n. 34 infra.

29 Law School Pedagogy, Legal Theory Lexicon 003: Hypotheticals, online resource: http://lsolum.typepad.com/legal_theory_lexicon/law_school_pedagogy/, accessed June 1, 2017.

30 The tragic hypotheticals under discussion here differ from strictly 'historical hypotheticals' that may suggest, e.g. that a battle would have gone differently if a heavy wind had not arisen to drive the ships off-course; and they differ as well from 'deductive hypotheticals' such as Thucydides' argument (1.9.4) that Agamemnon must have had a large navy (examples in Flory 1988, 45) or Orestes' argument about the meaning of Clytemnestra's dream at *Cho*. 543–550. Contrafactuals in Aeschylus are rare: Orestes uses one at *Cho*. 994–996 but it is more rhetorical than character-assessing. Consider the more ethical shading of Eur. *Hec*. 1217–1233 where Hecuba pleads before Agamemnon after she and her companions have killed Polymestor's sons and blinded their father; addressing Polymestor, she says, 'if you had reared my son and saved his life [sc. and not have murdered him]... you would have won good repute'. By demonstrating that Polymestor is *kakos*, she also justifies her vengeful acts against him.

perhaps nearer to 438.³¹ Here, Pasiphae argues before her husband Minos that she is not responsible for her liaison with the bull:

ἐγ[ὼ] γὰρ εἰ μὲν ἀνδρὶ προύβαλον δέμας
τοὐμὸν, λαθραίαν ἐμπολωμένη Κύπριν,
ὀρθῶς ἂν ἤδη μάχ[λο]ς οὖσ' ἐφαινόμην·
νῦν δ', ἐκ θεοῦ γὰρ προσβολῆς ἐμηνάμην,
ἀλγῶ μέν, ἐστὶ δ' οὐχ ἐκο[ύσ]ιον κακόν.

(Eur. Cretans 472e, 7–11)

If I had thrown myself at a man in love's furtive commerce, I should rightly now be revealed as lascivious. As it is, because my madness was a god's onslaught, I hurt, but my trouble is not voluntary.

(transl. Collard/Cropp)

'*If I had thrown myself at a man*' – but Pasiphae had not 'thrown herself' at a man; she remains a chastely married woman who had been divinely compelled to act otherwise and so is wrongly accused; nonetheless, her husband condemns her to death by (underground?) imprisonment (*Cretans* 472e 46–49). Pasiphae's speech of defence has sometimes been compared to Hippolytus' rebuttal to Theseus (Eur. *Hipp.* 983–1035) after the latter has accused him of seducing his wife (*Hipp.* 983–1035).³² When Theseus condemns him to exile, his response is a brutal hypothetical:

καὶ σοῦ γε ταὐτὰ κάρτα θαυμάζω, πάτερ·
εἰ γὰρ σὺ μὲν παῖς ἦσθ', ἐγὼ δὲ σὸς πατήρ,
ἔκτεινά τοί σ' ἂν κοὐ φυγαῖς ἐζημίουν,
εἴπερ γυναικὸς ἠξίους ἐμῆς θιγεῖν.

(Eur. *Hipp.* 1041–1044)

I feel the same great wonder at you, father. For if you were my son and I your father, I would not have banished but killed you, if you had dared to touch my wife.

(transl. David Kovacs)

The substitution of father for son creates a fantastical marriage for the same imaginary offence as Pasiphae's (seduction); at the same time, the ratcheting up of

---

31 Cropp/Fick 1985, 70, 82; Collard/Cropp/Lee 1995, 58.
32 Lloyd 1992, 50; Gould 1978, 57. See especially the argument at *Hipp.* 1007–1012 and the contrafactual at 1021–1024, where Hippolytus pleads for his life before his father.

punishment turns into a fantastical filicide – and a proof of Hippolytus' severely moral character.

Another early and sophisticated hypothetical argument appears at Soph. *Ant.* 905–912 (cat. no. 8), a passage that famously owes a debt to Herodotus 3.119, where Darius offers to spare the life of one member of the imprisoned family of Intaphrenes, and his wife chooses to save her brother. In Sophocles' play, Antigone in her 'farewell speech' offers a justification for the burial of Polyneices, an act that will lead to her suicide (for Creon had declared a death penalty for anyone who did just that and Antigone will pre-empt him). She would not have performed such a deed, she says, for the sake of a husband if she had one (for she could remarry) nor for a child if she had borne one (for she could have one by someone else); but siblings are different, for they cannot be replaced. In an indirect way, Antigone is justifying a kin killing, her own.[33]

In the Oresteian tragedies, the persons deploying such arguments usually mean to show that a murder was or was not justified in the past. By examining these arguments as a group, with comparisons now and again to other tragic hypotheticals that do not belong to it, something of their coherence, affect, and relationship to oratory may be discovered.[34] Often the Oresteian hypotheticals are quite spectacular and the reason for this may be due to their focus on shocking kin killings. Even in tragedies that are not properly 'tragedies of revenge', the more stunning of such hypotheticals (as in the ones just mentioned from *Hippolytus* and *Cretans*) have to do with kin (or spousal) killings; thus, e.g. at Sophocles *OC* 988–999, Oedipus addresses Creon:

ἀλλ' οὐ γὰρ οὔτ' ἐν τοῖσδ' ἀκούσομαι κακὸς
γάμοισιν οὔθ' οὓς αἰὲν ἐμφορεῖς σύ μοι
φόνους πατρῴους ἐξονειδίζων πικρῶς.
ἓν γάρ μ' ἄμειψαι μοῦνον ὧν σ' ἀνιστορῶ·
εἴ τίς σε τὸν δίκαιον αὐτίκ' ἐνθάδε
κτείνοι παραστάς, πότερα πυνθάνοι' ἂν εἰ

---

[33] On the controversy over the authorship of the Soph. *Ant.* 904ff., Jebb's (1900) Appendix on 904–920 is still useful; also Page 1934, 86–90; for more recent discussion and persuasive argument of Sophoclean authorship, see Cropp 1997 and S. West 1999; and further bibliography in Burnett 2014, 217 n. 51.

[34] Hypothetical arguments in tragedy and the orators are sometimes identified differently. E.g., Lloyd 1992, 32 considers hypotheticals (which he calls 'hypothetical syllogisms') in Euripides as a 'variety of the argument of probability' and writes, 'In this type of argument, the speaker postulates a condition which would substanstiate his opponent's position. He then points out that the position was not fulfilled, so that his opponent's position collapses'. Such arguments, he continues, are frequent in Lysias.

πατήρ σ' ὁ καίνων, ἢ τίνοι' ἂν εὐθέως;
δοκῶ μέν, εἴπερ ζῆν φιλεῖς, τὸν αἴτιον
τίνοι' ἄν, οὐδὲ τοὔνδικον περιβλέποις.
τοιαῦτα μέντοι καὐτὸς εἰσέβην κακά,
θεῶν ἀγόντων· ὥστ' ἐγὼ οὐδὲ τὴν πατρὸς
ψυχὴν ἂν οἶμαι ζῶσαν ἀντειπεῖν ἐμοί.

(Soph. *OC* 988–999)

No, neither this marriage nor the killing of my father, which you never cease to cast in my teeth with bitter reproaches, shall prove me to be evil. Of all my questions, answer me just one! If here and now a man stood near you, the righteous one, and tried to kill you, would you ask if the would-be killer was your father, or would you strike back at once? I think that if you value life you would strike back at the guilty one, and would not consider whether it was just or no. But these were the sorrows into which I entered, led by the gods, so that I do not think that even my father's spirit, if it came to life, could contradict me.

(transl. H. Lloyd-Jones)

This is a valiant, even triumphant argument in defence of Oedipus' killing of his father, carried out in a hypothetical scenario: if a person's life appears to be under imminent threat, would anyone really stop and ask the identity of the alleged would-be killer?[35] The hypothetical invites a sympathetic response to Oedipus: he was right to have killed the man immediately, even though it turned out that the man he killed was his father.

2.3 Three hypotheticals in the *Electra* plays

Our first examples appear in Soph. *El.* 528–532 and 534–546; mother and daughter are debating. As in our subsequent hypotheticals, Agamemnon's motive for 'killing' Iphigenia is addressed. Clytemnestra for her part freely admits she killed Agamemnon but augments the admission with the clarification:

Hypothetical no. 1:
ἡ γὰρ Δίκη νιν εἷλεν, οὐκ ἐγὼ μόνη,
ᾗ χρῆν σ' ἀρήγειν, εἰ φρονοῦσ' ἐτύγχανες.
ἐπεὶ πατὴρ οὗτος σός, ὃν θρηνεῖς ἀεί,   530
τὴν σὴν ὅμαιμον μοῦνος Ἑλλήνων ἔτλη
θῦσαι θεοῖσιν...
εἶἑν· δίδαξον δή με <τοῦτο>· τοῦ χάριν
ἔθυσεν αὐτήν; πότερον Ἀργείων ἐρεῖς;   535

---

[35] To contextualize the episode, see Markantonatos 2007, 94–96.

ἀλλ' οὐ μετῆν αὐτοῖσι τήν γ' ἐμὴν κτανεῖν.
ἀλλ' ἀντ' ἀδελφοῦ δῆτα Μενέλεω κτανὼν
τἄμ' οὐκ ἔμελλε τῶνδέ μοι δώσειν δίκην;
πότερον ἐκείνῳ παῖδες οὐκ ἦσαν διπλοῖ,
οὓς τῆσδε μᾶλλον εἰκὸς ἦν θνῄσκειν, πατρὸς   540
καὶ μητρὸς ὄντας, ἧς ὁ πλοῦς ὅδ' ἦν χάριν;
ἢ τῶν ἐμῶν Ἅιδης τιν' ἵμερον τέκνων
ἢ τῶν ἐκείνης ἔσχε δαίσασθαι πλέον;
ἢ τῷ πανώλει πατρὶ τῶν μὲν ἐξ ἐμοῦ
παίδων πόθος παρεῖτο, Μενέλεῳ δ' ἐνῆν;

(Soph. *El.* 528–532; 534–546)

Yes, Justice was his killer, not I alone, and you would take her side, if you happened to have sense. Why, that father of yours, whom you are always lamenting, lone among the Greeks brought himself to sacrifice your sister to the gods... For whose sake did he sacrifice her? Will you say for that of the Argives? But they had no right to kill her, who was mine. But if he killed her who was mine for his brother Menelaus, was he not to pay the penalty to me? Had not Menelaus two children, who would have been put to death with more fairness than my child, since it was for the sake of their father and mother that the voyage took place? Had Hades a desire to feast on my children rather on hers? Or did your accursed father feel sorrow for the children of Menelaus, but none for mine?

(transl. H. Lloyd-Jones 1994, slightly modified)

The presentation is emotional and fast-paced, with Clytemnestra's claim that not only was she the destroyer of Agamemnon, but so was Justice–whom Electra, if she had sense, would assist (first contrafactual). She then follows up, posing suppositions of others as questions and providing the rebuttals.[36] In the first, the participle κτανών provides the protasis (in a mixed condition): 'if A. killed my daughter instead of Menalaus' children, he would have to pay for it'.[37] The apodosis of the second (a contrafactual) is embedded in the relative clause οὓς τῆσδε μᾶλλον εἰκὸς ἦν θνῄσκειν (540); spelled out, it runs: 'if M.'s children had been put to death rather than my child [but this did not happen], *it would have been more fair*'.[38] For all its abridgement, the argument remains clear: the wrong victim has

---

[36] The rhetorical shape of the questions, as Jebb 1891 nicely points out *ad loc.*, 'the first supposition is introduced by πότερον and the second by ἀλλὰ δῆτα. ... ἀλλὰ was regularly used in thus putting the imagined arguments of an adversary'. Jebb compares And. 1.148.

[37] See Smyth 2013 for the omission of ἄν in the apodosis of unreal conditions with impersonal expressions such as εἰκὸς ἦν with the infinitive.

[38] A similar argument (but situated in the present) appears in Eur. *Hec.* (see cat. no. 12); the eponymous heroine offers an 'Oresteian' argument when she learns that her daughter must be sacrificed (258–270): it is not Polyxena who should be sacrificed; it should be a bull, and if not a bull, and if Achilles wishes to revenge his murder by murdering someone else, then her daughter

been selected for sacrifice. That, of course, is a red-herring: Agamemnon was not permitted a substitute for his daughter: his was the offence and this was the penalty (and this is made clear at Aesch. *Agam.* 109–157, 184–227 and more explicitly at Soph. *El.* 566–574).

Our next hypothetical appears in Euripides' *Electra*; at this point in the play, Clytemnestra has just arrived before Electra's country cottage; she steps down from her carriage, offers an embarrassed remark to explain the presence of the Trojan slaves who help her along, and then dives into a long speech to Electra, justifying her killing of Agamemnon by suggesting what might be considered plausible motives for killing a child and arguing that Agamemnon had no plausible motive at all:

Hypothetical no. 2:
κεἰ μὲν πόλεως ἅλωσιν ἐξιώμενος
ἢ δῶμ' ὀνήσων τἄλλα τ' ἐκσῴζων τέκνα
ἔκτεινε πολλῶν μίαν ὕπερ, συγγνώστ' ἂν ἦν.
νῦν δ' οὕνεχ' Ἑλένη μάργος ἦν ὅ τ' αὖ λαβὼν
ἄλοχον κολάζειν προδότιν οὐκ ἠπίστατο,
τούτων ἕκατι παῖδ' ἐμὴν διώλεσεν.³⁹

(Eur. *Electra* 1024–1029)

Here, Clytemnestra's argument has the visible form of a contrafactual hypothetical: if Agamemnon had killed one for the sake of many, to avert the sack of a city or to benefit the house and save the children—that would have been pardonable!⁴⁰ But no, he destroyed her daughter because Helen was lewd and Menelaus

---

is not the best choice – Helen is, for she is outstanding in beauty. In *Electra*, the sacrifice/murder has already taken place; not so in *Hecuba*.
39 '... If he had killed one child for the sake of many, trying to avert the sack of our city or to benefit our house and save our other children, it would have been pardonable. But as it is, he killed her only because Helen was a whore and the man who married her did not know how to chastise the wife who betrayed him'. (transl. David Kovacs, slightly modified)
40 A similar contrafactual (arguing that 'if *x* had happened, it would have been pardonable, but ... ') appears in Eur. *Medea* (cat. no. 15a), not indeed a part of the 'Oresteian story', but nonetheless a play of revenge. At this point, Medea has announced her plan to create three corpses (Creon, his daughter, and Jason, 374–375); she has won Creon's permission to remain in Corinth one more day; and now she encounters Jason. She reminds him of her benefactions on his behalf: she betrayed her father and home and she accompanied him to Pelias' land of Iolcus. She continues, arguing that children make the difference (ll. 486–491; see cat. no. 8): 'if you were without any, the new marriage would be pardonable.' She refrains from stating the obvious antithesis and the (not so obvious) consequences: with children, his conduct is not pardonable and there-

cowardly. For Clytemnestra, numbers matter: if by Iphigenia's death, a family or a city had been saved, there would have been no need for her to impose justice, to return murder with murder.[41]

Another hypothetical appears towards the end of the same long speech, at ll. 1041–1045. The argument from 1024–1029 is here resumed and once again the motive for the murder/sacrifice is questioned. Whereas the earlier passage emphasized that the rescue of one person was not sufficient to justify the cost (the murder/sacrifice of Iphigenia), this one more directly addresses that valuation. Clytemnestra now imagines a reverse scenario in which Menelaus (and not Helen) had been abducted, and in which she herself (and not Agamemnon) had killed Orestes (and not Iphigenia).

Hypothetical no. 3:
εἰ δ' ἐκ δόμων ἥρπαστο Μενέλεως λάθραι,
κτανεῖν μ' Ὀρέστην χρῆν, κασιγνήτης πόσιν
Μενέλαον ὡς σώσαιμι· σὸς δὲ πῶς πατὴρ
ἠνέσχετ' ἂν ταῦτ'; εἶτα τὸν μὲν οὐ θανεῖν
κτείνοντα χρῆν τἄμ', ἐμὲ δὲ πρὸς κείνου παθεῖν
⟨κτείνουσαν αὐτοῦ παῖδας, οὐκ ἐλάσσονα⟩; (post 1045)

(Eur. *Electra* 1041–1045)[42]

If Menelaus had been abducted from his house in secret, would I have been right to kill Orestes in order to preserve Menelaus, my sister's husband? How would your father have

---

fore it is right that Creon and his daughter should die, and also, so it will turn out, Jason's children. Medea uses a simpler hypothetical at 586–587 to depict Jason's character in light of the new marriage (cat. no. 15b): χρῆν σ', εἴπερ ἦσθα μὴ κακός, πείσαντά με / γαμεῖν γάμον τόνδ', ἀλλὰ μὴ σιγῆι φίλων.

41 Praxithea in Eur. *Erectheus* fr. 360.13–21, 32–41 (cat. no. 17) appears to make a direct allusion to Clytemnestra's argument at Eur. *El.* 1024–1029 – except that Praxithea is a mother who says 'yes' to the sacrifice of her child. She, too, uses a 'numbers' argument, but not a 'hypothetical': 'The city as a whole has a single name, but many inhabit it: why should I destroy them when I can give one child to die for all?... This girl – not mine (in fact) except in birth – I shall offer for sacrifice to defend our land. For if the city is taken, what share in my children have I then? Shall not all, then, be saved, so far as is in my power?' (transl. Collard/Cropp). For the date of *Erectheus* (422), see Calder III 1969; Treu 1971; Clairmont 1971. For fathers who say 'no' to the sacrifice of their children, see Creon in Eur. *Phoenician Women*, 962–976 and Demophon in Eur. *Heracleidae*, 398–419; the latter uses a 'numbers' argument (cat. no. 18).
42 See Diggle 1977, 121–22 for the supplement. He assumes a lacuna after 445, on the grounds that the absolute use of παθεῖν is open to grave doubt.

put up with that? Then ought he not to have died for killing my child and I to have suffered no less at his hands for killing his child?

(transl. David Kovacs)

The scenario clearly aims to show that Agamemnon deserved death for killing Iphigenia: surely Clytemnestra would have suffered revenge at Agamemnon's hands, had she killed Orestes in order to rescue an abducted Menelaus; accordingly, it was only fair that he was put to death for his killing of Iphigenia to rescue Helen.[43] The pivot of the hypothesized situation is provided by the gender reversals and the emphasis is on the end result, the sacrificed/murdered child: not Iphigenia but Orestes. Clytemnestra's argument not only has greater force by imagining a female murderer of a son/victim because of society's uneven treatment of men and women and greater valuation for men (in this case, the son/victim), but it also allows for the irony that the son/victim whom she imagines herself killing will instead become her killer.[44]

The hypothetical arguments and the motif of sacrificial death/murder are organically combined in these plays with the dynamic of revenge. They seem also to have been so combined in *Iphigenia at Aulis*; I have included two passages from that play in the catalogue (nos. 19 and 20) at the end of this essay. The same components are less organically combined in Euripides' *Hecuba*: here the Greeks have decided that Polyxena must be sacrificed on Achilles' tomb; the revenge taken by Hecuba on Polymestor (the Thracian king) at the end of the play, however, is for the killing of her son Polydorus; the sacrifice of Polyxena and the revenge are disconnected.[45]

---

43 Earlier commentators see the gender reversal as 'grotesque'; thus Denniston 1939, 178: 'The supposition of a war waged to recover an abducted husband – that is clearly what is implied – is certainly grotesque'; nonetheless, he did not go so far as Wilamowitz (1883, 223) who deleted the lines as senseless actor's interpolation. Some have seen here evidence of Euripides' 'feminist thinking' (see Roisman/Luschnig 2011, 213, citing England 1926, 103). That is absurd: the emphasis in the hypothetical is not on gender equality or any feminist agenda but on the gender and person of the child/victim. Michelini 1987, 220 thinks '[t]he argument resembles and exaggerates the elaborate hypothetical constructs of the new rhetoric' but does not offer any parallels.
44 In Eur. *Hipp.* 1041–1044, the eponymous character uses a substitute 'victim' in a surprising contrafactual; see §IIb *supra* and cat. no. 7.
45 See n. 38 *supra* for Hecuba's 'Oresteian argument' that Helen should be substituted for Polyxena.

2.4 Three Hypotheticals in Euripides' *Orestes*

In Euripides' *Orestes*, a quite different world unfolds: at play's opening, we meet an Electra watchful over a sick Orestes as both await the decision of the Argive Assembly, whether or not they are to be stoned to death that day. Orestes, once wakened from his sleep, experiences mixed emotions, and among them, regret; thus he addresses his sister and offers a picture of his father supplicating him not to kill his mother:

> Hypothetical no. 4:
> μὴ τῶν ἐμῶν ἕκατι συντήκου κακῶν·
> σὺ μὲν γὰρ ἐπένευσας τάδ', εἴργασται δ' ἐμοὶ
> μητρῷον αἷμα· Λοξίᾳ δὲ μέμφομαι,
> ὅστις μ' ἐπάρας ἔργον ἀνοσιώτατον,
> τοῖς μὲν λόγοις ηὔφρανε, τοῖς δ' ἔργοισιν οὔ.
> οἶμαι δὲ πατέρα τὸν ἐμόν, εἰ κατ' ὄμματα
> ἐξιστόρουν νιν μητέρ' εἰ κτεῖναί με χρή,
> πολλὰς γενείου τοῦδ' ἂν ἐκτεῖναι λιτὰς
> μήποτε τεκούσης ἐς σφαγὰς ὦσαι ξίφος,
> εἰ μήτ' ἐκεῖνος ἀναλαβεῖν ἔμελλε φῶς
> ἐγώ θ' ὁ τλήμων τοιάδ' ἐκπλήσειν κακά.
>
> (Eur. *Orestes* 283–293)
>
> Don't pine on account of my ills. I mean, you agreed to this business, but it's my doing, mother's murder; and it's Loxias I blame, who put me up to a most unholy deed and encouraged me with words but not with actions. I think that if I had asked my father face to face about whether I should kill my mother, he would have reached for my chin with many an appeal never to drive my sword into the neck of her who bore me, if he was not to get his daylight back and my suffering self was to endure ills like these.
>
> (transl. M.L. West, slightly modified)

This is an imaginative little picture, a contrafactual hypothetical for sure ('I think that if I had asked my father [sc.: but I did not]... he would have ...'), but not one that is deployed to argue the fitness of a sacrifice or the justness of a killing in revenge in the same way as in the earlier plays. Orestes uses the hypothetical to express regret—not for believing in revenge ideology or for being the agent of revenge (for he puts the blame squarely on Apollo for that) but rather for its inefficacy; simply put: the murder of his mother did not work. In fact, the hypothetical takes the form of a proof of the inefficacy of revenge and in that respect, it does assess the killing.⁴⁶

The next hypothetical appears at *Orestes* 507–517. It uses a ploy familiar from the one that appeared in Eur. *El.* 1041–1045; as there, we have substitute retaliatory killers – but it is a generational bender rather than a gender bender. An infinitude of family talionic killings is suggested – the hypothetical is, in fact, an argument against private revenge killings: exile, claims Tyndareus in his address to Menelaus, was the ancestral punishment and is to be preferred.⁴⁷ To create the cycle of retaliatory killings, he begins by imagining that Orestes' (imagined) wife will murder him; thus:

Hypothetical no. 5:
ἐρήσομαι δέ, Μενέλεως, τοσόνδε σε·
εἰ τόνδ' ἀποκτείνειεν ὁμόλεκτρος γυνή,
χὠ τοῦδε παῖς αὖ μητέρ' ἀνταποκτενεῖ,
κἄπειθ' ὁ κείνου γενόμενος φόνωι φόνον
λύσει, πέρας δὴ ποῖ κακῶν προβήσεται;
καλῶς ἔθεντο ταῦτα πατέρες οἱ πάλαι·
ἐς ὀμμάτων μὲν ὄψιν οὐκ εἴων περᾶν
οὐδ' εἰς ἀπάντημ' ὅστις αἷμ' ἔχων κυροῖ,
φυγαῖσι δ' ὁσιοῦν, ἀνταποκτείνειν δὲ μή.
ἀεὶ γὰρ εἷς ἔμελλ' ἐνέξεσθαι φόνωι,
τὸ λοίσθιον μίασμα λαμβάνων χεροῖν.

(Eur. *Orestes* 507–517)

I will ask you this, Menelaus. If his wife who shared his bed were one day to kill Orestes, and his son in turn were to kill his mother, and then his son pay off that murder with another—how far will it go till the end of the troubles? Our fathers of old ordered these matters well: they were not for allowing a man who had blood on his hands to come into anyone's sight or meet them, but by restoring purity by exile, not by killing him in turn. Otherwise

---

46 Cf. Porter 1994, 311. Indeed, the hypothetical argument is surprising, Porter remarks, with 'Euripides rather mischievously standing tradition on its head: Agamemnon, who in *Choephori* is such a powerful sponsor of the matricide, here is envisioned as pathetically begging Orestes not to perform the deed'. It is not unlikely that Sophocles looked back to this argument, when he created the hypothetical (cited earlier, *ad fin.* §IIb) for Oedipus at *OC* 988–999. That hypothetical, with its ambiguous depiction of Oedipus' father, stands Sophocles' own *Oedipus at Colonus* on its head.
47 Porter 1994, 116–117 compares Tyndareus' techniques (anachronistically) with those used in [Dem.] 25.25–26. He sees Tyndareus' argument 'artificially restricted to kin murder, resulting, ultimately, in the rather strained picture of a grandson killing his father for the murder of his grandmother, with the implication that the great-grandson then will feel impelled to kill his own father in turn.'

there would always be one person guilty of homicide, taking over the latest pollution on his hands.

(transl. M.L. West, modified)

It is surprising that none of our protagonists thus far has offered such a hypothetical argument;[48] nonetheless, the infinitude of talionic killings *has* been expressed elsewhere; thus in the agonistic exchange between Electra and her mother in Eur. *El.*, the former asks the latter a series of rhetorical and to some degree, nonsensical, questions: why isn't Aegisthus in exile in requital for Orestes' exile, and why isn't Aegisthus dead in requital for her (i.e., Electra), seeing that he has killed her, while alive, twice as much as he killed her sister; and then:

εἰ δ' ἀμείψεται
φόνον δικάζων φόνος, ἀποκτενῶ σ' ἐγὼ
καὶ παῖς Ὀρέστης πατρὶ τιμωρούμενοι.
εἰ γὰρ δίκαι' ἐκεῖνα, καὶ τάδ' ἔνδικα.

(Eur. *El.* 1093–1096)

But if one deed of murder decrees another in requital, I shall kill you, I and your son Orestes, in vengeance for our father. For if what you have done is just, this too is right.

(transl. David Kovacs)

Electra refrains from distancing her thoughts away from the present by using a more artificial argument; she is perfectly comfortable using that most emphatic of all conditions, the 'emotional future' (or 'most vivid'); she is all but threatening her mother with the murder that she will help her brother execute later in the play.

Before leaving behind Tyndareus' hypothetical at 507–517 and its argument against talionic kin killings, it will be useful to consider a variant that appears in *Andromache*, a play of the 420s that takes place in Phythia. Neoptolemos is the husband of Hermione and is away from home; Andromache, his slave, has born a son to him, has concealed him in fear of Hermione, and has taken refuge at the altar of Thetis. At this point in the play, the two women have argued and Hermione, after threatening Andromache, has left the stage; now Menelaus enters along with Andromache's son and threatens to kill one or the other. Andromache argues valiantly and says:

---

48 The form of the condition is mixed here (see Smyth 2359, 2361, εἰ with the optative instead of ἐάν with the subjunctive, cf. Ant. 4 *Tetr.* 3.1,4) and is similar to that at Soph. *OT* 851–854, Jocasta, speaking to Oedipus of what the herdsman might say: εἰ δ' οὖν τι κἀκτρέποιτο τοῦ πρόσθεν λόγου, / οὔτοι ποτ', ὦναξ, τόν γε Λαΐου φόνον / φανεῖ δικαίως ὀρθόν, ὅν γε Λοξίας / διεῖπε χρῆναι παιδὸς ἐξ ἐμοῦ θανεῖν).

```
        <        > (post 333)
τέθνηκα τῆι σῆι θυγατρὶ καί μ' ἀπώλεσεν·            334
μιαιφόνον μὲν οὐκέτ' ἂν φύγοι μύσος.                335
ἐν τοῖς δὲ πολλοῖς καὶ σὺ τόνδ' ἀγωνιῆι
φόνον· τὸ συνδρῶν γάρ σ' ἀναγκάσει χρέος.
ἢν δ' οὖν ἐγὼ μὲν μὴ θανεῖν ὑπεκδράμω,
τὸν παῖδά μου κτενεῖτε; κᾆτα πῶς πατὴρ
τέκνου θανόντος ῥαιδίως ἀνέξεται;                   340
οὐχ ὧδ' ἄνανδρον αὐτὸν ἡ Τροία καλεῖ·
ἀλλ' εἶσιν οἷ χρή, Πηλέως γὰρ ἄξια
πατρός τ' Ἀχιλλέως ἔργα δρῶν φανήσεται,
ὤσει δὲ σὴν παῖδ' ἐκ δόμων· σὺ δ' ἐκδιδοὺς
ἄλλωι τί λέξεις; πότερον ὡς κακὸν πόσιν             345
φεύγει τὸ ταύτης σῶφρον; ἀλλ' οὐ πείσεται.
γαμεῖ δὲ τίς νιν; ἢ σφ' ἄνανδρον ἐν δόμοις
χήραν καθέξεις πολιόν; ὦ τλήμων ἀνήρ,
κακῶν τοσούτων οὐχ ὁρᾶις ἐπιρροάς;
πόσας ἂν εὐνὰς θυγατέρ' ἠδικημένην                  350
βούλοι' ἂν εὑρεῖν ἢ παθεῖν ἁγὼ λέγω;
```

[Kovacs deletes 330–351; Diggle 330–333 and supposes a lacuna after 333; Wilamowitz deletes 333]

(Eur. *Andromache* 334–351)

Suppose I have died at your daughter's hand and she has destroyed me. From that point on she will not escape the pollution of murder. But in the eyes of the majority you also will be on trial for this murder, for your complicity will make you so against your will. But if I escape death, will you kill my son? And then how will his father cheerfully put up with his son being killed? Troy does not call him such a coward. But he will go to all necessary lengths and will make it clear that his conduct is worthy of Peleus and of his father Achilles and will expel your daughter from the house. And if you try to marry her to another husband, what will you say? That her virtuous nature recoiled from a bad husband? But he will not believe you. Who will marry her? Or will you keep her gray-headed and without a mate in your own house? O unhappy man, do you not see what disasters are rushing upon you? How many marriage beds would you not see your daughter wronged in rather than suffer what I am describing?

(transl. David Kovacs)

Here, if l. 334 is genuine, Andromache imagines her own death at Hermione's hands – this is a first among our hypothetical scenarios.[49] She then imagines the

---

49 Stevens 1971, 138 reports he knows of no other example of a bare verb indicating imaginary realization, which is normally expressed by καὶ δή...' (e.g. Dem. 39.7–8; but also Eur. *Med.* 387); possibly a lacuna before the line (as posited by Diggle) allowed for a different collocation. The

consequences for Hermione and Menelaus: pollution and trial. Next she imagines what might happen if she escapes death: possibly Menelaus will kill her son by Neoptolemus. Like Tyndareus, she imagines the kin killing to be followed by another, for surely the boy's father will take action; but finally, instead of the endless killings suggested by Tyndareus, she suggests that an endless number of marital injuries (πόσας ἂν εὐνὰς θυγατέρ' ἠδικημένην) would be in store for Hermione, a bad deal, to be sure, but nevertheless a better lot than suffering old age alone or being tried for murder.[50] A series of retaliatory kin murders is thus to be replaced by a series of 'marital beds', witnesses for Hermione of her husband's infidelities. Revenge killings and marital injuries may be infinite in number.[51]

We return now to Orestes in his eponymous play; he answers his grandfather's charge in part with another hypothetical:

Hypothetical no. 6:
εἰ γὰρ γυναῖκες ἐς τόδ' ἥξουσιν θράσους,
ἄνδρας φονεύειν, καταφυγὰς ποιούμεναι
ἐς τέκνα, μαστοῖς τὸν ἔλεον θηρώμεναι,
παρ' οὐδὲν αὐταῖς ἦν ἂν ὀλλύναι πόσεις,
ἐπίκλημ' ἐχούσαις ὅτι τύχοι. δράσας δ' ἐγὼ
δείν', ὡς σὺ κομπεῖς, τόνδ' ἔπαυσα τὸν νόμον.

(Eur. *Orestes* 566–571)

I mean, if women are going to have the effrontery to murder their husbands, taking refuge with their children, angling for mercy with their breasts, it would cost them nothing to do

---

'bare verb ὑπακήκο' appears at Men. Dyscolus 494: πρεσβύτερός τις τ[ῇι] θύραι / ὑπακήκο'; possibly this is a comic development.

50 Stevens 1971, 140 suggests (rightly) that 'A.'s argument appears to be that if M. carries out his threats the consequences for him and his daughter will be such (as indicated in 335–45) that it would be better not merely to put up with A. as Neoptolemus' concubine but with many others in the same position'.

51 Both arguments – Tyndareus' and Andromache's, might be compared to a similarly structured argument in P. Didot 1, and known today as authored by a playwright of New Comedy, possibly but by no means certainly, Menander. For all its condemnation by Wilamowitz in 1889, 41–42 n. 82, it is nevertheless a clever re-working of a Euripidean hypothetical. The speaker argues that if her father continues his present conduct, conferring a new husband upon her to replace an unfortunate one, that conduct will lead to an endless series of husbands (cf. the hypothetical argument pitched by Helen to Aphrodite at Homer *Il.* 3.399–406, 'how many cities will you lead me to, if a mortal man is dear to you?'). Although there is no connection here with cyclical retaliatory kin killings, the form of the hypothetical argument itself, so prominently connected with kin killings in Euripides, might suggest that an infinitude of husbands is only slightly better than an infinitude of kin killings.

away with their husbands when they have a grievance of any kind; but I, by acting monstrously (as you claim), have put a stop to this practice.

(transl. M.L. West)

The hypothetical introduces Orestes' own justification for murdering his mother; he is, implicitly, the (unmarried, but for Tyndaeus' hypothetical argument) savior of that endangered species, the married man.[52] If ll. 935–937 are genuine, Orestes' justification may have been repeated in the Herald's (*Oratio Recta*) report of Orestes' speech before the Argive Assembly:

ὑμῖν ἀμύνων οὐδὲν ἧσσον ἢ πατρὶ
ἔκτεινα μητέρ'· εἰ γὰρ ἀρσένων φόνος
ἔσται γυναιξὶν ὅσιος, οὐ φθάνοιτ' ἔτ' ἂν
θνῄσκοντες, ἢ γυναιξὶ δουλεύειν χρεών.

(Eur. *Orestes* 934–337)[53]

... I was fighting for you just as much as for my father when I killed my mother. For if murder of menfolk is to be permitted to women, you had better hurry up and die or you must be slaves to women.

(transl. M.L. West, modified)

2.5 Preliminary conclusions: contrafactual arguments in tragedy

Six hypothetical arguments that have to do with kin killing within the Oresteian tradition have so far formed the basis of this study (§§IIc and d); additional 'kin-killing hypotheticals' have been adduced here and there (in §IIb and in footnotes)

---

52 Porter 1994, 150–151 compares Orestes' argument of deterrence (i.e., no longer will women betray and kill their husbands in fear of such punishment as he has exacted on his mother) with Lys. 1. 47–48 and 36. Naiden 2010, 68 with n. 55 sees the emphasis in the same lines on Orestes as 'protecting the norms of supplication, a practice that should not aid the unworthy'; that is, I think, an over-interpretation.
53 This is Diggle's text, and he does not delete 935–937; Willink 1986, 237 finds it 'hard to believe that E. wrote this', and observes, 'The logical apodosis to 'if killing of men is to be holy for women' should be 'you will all be in danger of being killed'. Instead, we have 'hurry up and die, or it is necessary to be slaves to women'. The language is as odd as the logic ...'; he singles out the 'jussive idiom' (οὐ φθάνοιτ' ἔτ' ἂν) and the following ἢ ... χρεών 'as tantamount to another sarcastic command'. As the same jussive command appears at 1551, it seems reckless to posit it as grounds for deletion here.

for comparison from tragedies outside of those designated the 'Oresteian tragedies'; hypotheticals for other tragic offences have also been adduced. Five of the original six used contrafactuals (hypotheticals nos. 1–4 and 6) in the context of kin killings, and so did three more outside the Oresteian tradition, viz., Eur. *Hipp.* 1041–1044, Soph. *Ant.* 905–912, and Soph. *OC* 988–999. To these we can add two more contrafactuals in the context of another tragic offence, seduction: Eur. *Cretans* 472e, 7–11 and *Hipp.* 1021–1024. These two instances, however, might be pushed into the 'kin-killing category', insofar as Pasiphae uses her hypothetical (cat. no. 10) in a defence to save her from a death penalty that will be imposed by her husband and Hippolytus uses his (cat. no. 11) in a defence before his father that will end in his exile and death.

Each of the arguments articulates an evaluative view of a kin killing or of an offence that could lead to a kin killing and seeks to elicit a response from an internal audience; each, moreover, stands out prominently in whatever speech it appears; that prominence suggests that the form of the argument as a contrafactual was important for conveying its content. Contrafactual arguments are more frequent in plays with revenge killings than in those with sacrificial killings; the former are reactions to killings that have already taken place (and hence past contrafactuals are useful) whereas the latter (e.g., the sacrifice of a child) would usually be underway in the course of the drama rather than be completed before it began and so subject to revenge.[54]

In any case, we may note again that the hypothetical used by Oedipus in Soph. *OC* directly confronted the question of Oedipus' responsibility for the (past) killing of his father (992–994: 'If here and now a man stood near you, the righteous one, and tried to kill you, would you ask if the would-be killer was your father, or would you strike back at once?'). Arguments about the rightness or wrongness of kin killings along with their ethical assessments of the actor or the

---

54 Cf., e.g., the use of the argument that 'numbers matter' in Eur. *El.* 1024–1029 which uses a contrafactual hypothetical and Eur. *Erectheus* fr. 360.13–21, 32–41 and *Heracl.* 398–419, which do not: the killing has already happened in Eur. *El.* whereas the sacrifices in *Erechth.* and *Heracl.* are under discussion. An argument for using a substitute in the sacrifice/murder of a particular child is made at *Hec.* 267–270 (see n. 38); unlike the argument at Soph. *El.* 528–540 which also suggested using substitute victims, Hecuba does not use a past contrafactual – for the sacrifice has not yet taken place. In cases where a kin killing has not yet taken place and nevertheless past contrafactuals are used, (as in the examples from Soph. *Ant.* and from Eur. *Hipp.* and *Cretans*), the imminence of the kin killing (Creon's sentence on Antigone, the sentences of Theseus on Hippolytus and of Minos on Pasiphae) may have been decisive for the use of the hypothetical: death was a foregone conclusion.

action, will have become associated, by iterated use, with hypotheticals in the dramatic tradition; for such content, it became the articulation of choice.

3 Contrafactual arguments in tragedy and oratory

Can we find a relationship between the 'kin-killing contrafactual arguments' of tragedy and similar arguments in oratory (e.g. contrafactuals that deal with wrongdoing, even if not kin-killing, or with kin, plain and simple)?

The plays in which kin-killing arguments appear range from 442 or 440 (Soph. *Ant.*) to 401 (Soph. *OC*);[55] the period of the 420s down to 408, by itself, will account for the *Electras, Hippolytus, Andromache, Hecuba, Heraclidae, Erechtheus,* and *Orestes*. This same period was a remarkable one for the development of rhetoric in Athens – Gorgias arrived in 427;[56] Antiphon may have circulated his *Tetralogies* at around the same time, if not a little earlier;[57] and his clients will have delivered his speeches before his death in 411.[58] Lysias' logographic speeches may have been first produced at that time or a little later but Andocides may not have delivered his first one until 399. For the purposes of this search for hypothetical contrafactual arguments of similar content in the early orators, I have limited myself to speeches and rhetorical exercises from the 420s to 399, although I have occasionally added examples from speeches (with due notation) that are later or not dateable.[59] While the dates for the plays and speeches that

---

[55] See n. 1, *supra*.
[56] Diod. Sic. 12.53.
[57] *Tetr.* 1 mentions the defendant's payments of *eisphorai* (2.2.12); Thuc. 3.19.1 (428/7) says that this was 'the first time the Athenians raised an amount as high as 200 talents by means of the *eisphora*'. Hornblower 1991, 404 interprets that 'he is *not* saying that this was the first ever *eisphora* (which would contradict the clear evidence of the Kallias decrees, as normally dated, which show that the institution existed as early as 433: ML 58B, lines 17 and 19 = Fornara 119)'. Gagarin 2002, 62 seems non-committal on the question. It now seems, however, that ML 58B (*IG* I³ 52B) should be dated to 426/5 (see Matthaiou 2016, 107–108). That would still mean that *Tetr.* 1, following Hornblower's interpretation of Thuc. 3.19.1, can be dated some years before 426 and so Gorgias' arrival in Athens and the *First Tetralogy* may be proximate in time. In any case, the *Tetralogies* are probably earlier than the lawcourt speeches (thus Gagarin 2002, 171 n. 1).
[58] Ant. 6 was delivered in 419/18; see Dover 1950, 60; Hansen 1975, cat. no. 131–3 n. 3; Gagarin 1997, 245.
[59] Thus, 420–411: Ant. *Tetralogies* and Ant. 1, 5, and 6. 410/09: Lys. 20. 403/02: Lys. 12, Lys. 21. 400?: Lys. 25. Ca. 399: And. 1, Lys. 6, Lys. 13, Lys. 30. 384/83: Lys. 10.

are compared thus have an apparent correspondence, nonetheless, speeches (forensic and deliberative) will have been delivered for decades preceding the 420s, and likewise will dramas have been performed; perhaps more importantly, even for the period for which we do have plays and speeches, our record is terribly incomplete. Any conclusions about the relationship between tragedy and oratory, that is, about the influence of one on the other and the direction of posited influence must be tentative. On the other hand, it may be possible to articulate differences of the one from the other with more clarity, especially if we find arguments that involve the killing of kin or contrafactuals that look to an ethical assessment of an offence or the character of an actor.

In Gorgias' *Encomium of Helen*, causes for Helen's departure to Troy (fate, speech, force, love) are hypothesized; each is presented in a simple conditional clause, but none as a contrafactual hypothetical; thus, regarding the use of force:

> (7) εἰ δὲ βίαι ἡρπάσθη καὶ ἀνόμως ἐβιάσθη καὶ ἀδίκως ὑβρίσθη, δῆλον ὅτι ὁ <μὲν> ἁρπάσας ὡς ὑβρίσας ἠδίκησεν, ἡ δὲ ἁρπασθεῖσα ὡς ὑβρισθεῖσα ἐδυστύχησεν.

> But if she was by violence raped and lawlessly forced and unjustly outraged it is plain that the rapist, as the outrager, did the wronging, and the raped, as the outraged, did the suffering.
> (transl. Dillon/Gergel)

Here the hypothetical circumstances are not posed so as to invite contemplation of the unjustness of the deed and an evaluation of Helen's character: Helen's innocence is assured; the simple form of the condition suffices. On the other hand, all attention is given to the artifice of the repetitive endings of verbs and participles, with due concern for the active and passive voice to match the character of the doer and the sufferer. In Gorgias' *Defence of Palamedes*, the speaker presents reasons why he could not have committed treason, but once again his articulations do not usually look for any assessment of the quality of the actions involved. A contrafactual condition, however, does appear near the opening; while it offers an assessment of character, it looks more to the preciosity of its antitheses than to a vital evaluation of consequences; thus:

> (3) εἰ μὲν οὖν ὁ κατήγορος Ὀδυσσεὺς ἢ σαφῶς ἐπιστάμενος προδιδόντα με τὴν Ἑλλάδα τοῖς βαρβάροις ἢ δοξάζων γ' ἀμῆ οὕτω ταῦτα ἔχειν ἐποιεῖτο τὴν κατηγορίαν δι' εὔνοιαν τῆς Ἑλλάδος, ἄριστος ἂν ἦν [ὁ] ἀνήρ· ἄριστος ἂν ἦν [ὁ] ἀνήρ· ... εἰ δὲ φθόνωι ἢ κακοτεχνίαι ἢ πανουργίαι συνέθηκε ταύτην τὴν αἰτίαν, ὥσπερ δι' ἐκεῖνα κράτιστος ἂν ἦν ἀνήρ, οὕτω διὰ ταῦτα κάκιστος ἀνήρ.

> If, then, the prosecutor Odysseus were bringing such an accusation because he knew for sure or conjectured that I was betraying Hellas to the barbarians, he would be the best man

on account of his good will to Hellas; ... but if he concocted this charge, just as he would have been the best man for those earlier reasons, so he would be the worst for this reason.

(transl. Adele Scafuro)

In Antiphon's *Tetralogies*, while arguments of probability may be more abundant, hypotheticals (and specifically, contrafactuals) appear frequently. Thus in *Tetr.* 2.2, 4–5, in the well-known case of the javelin thrower whose javelin hits and kills a boy, the defendant's father argues:

Εἰ μὲν γὰρ τὸ ἀκόντιον ἔξω τῶν ὅρων τῆς αὑτοῦ πορείας ἐπὶ τὸν παῖδα ἐξενεχθὲν ἔτρωσεν αὐτόν, οὐδεὶς <ἂν> ἡμῖν λόγος ὑπελείπετο μὴ φονεῦσιν εἶναι· τοῦ δὲ παιδὸς ὑπὸ τὴν τοῦ ἀκοντίου φορὰν ὑποδραμόντος καὶ τὸ σῶμα προστήσαντος, <ὁ μὲν διεκωλύθη> τοῦ σκοποῦ τυχεῖν, ὁ δὲ (5) ὑπὸ τὸ ἀκόντιον ὑπελθὼν ἐβλήθη, καὶ τὴν αἰτίαν οὐχ ἡμετέραν οὖσαν προσέβαλεν ἡμῖν ... οὐ γὰρ ἂν ἐβλήθη ἀτρεμίζων καὶ μὴ διατρέχων.

(Gernet)

Had the boy been wounded because the javelin had travelled in his direction outside the area appointed for its flight, we should be left unable to show that we had not caused his death. But he ran into the path of the javelin and placed his person in its way. Hence my son was prevented from hitting the target: while the boy, who moved into the javelin's path, was struck, thereby causing us to be blamed for what we did not do... . Had he stood still and not run across, he would not have been struck.

(transl. Maidment)

As Gagarin points out, a contrast is made between 'the hypothetical case of a throw that goes astray which would be the youth's fault' and 'the actual events in which he did nothing wrong... The contrast between the actual situation and its hypothetical opposite is the essential feature of antithesis in Hermogenes' discussion (Inv. 4.2, p. 173 Rabe).'[60] In the *Tetralogy* passage under discussion, another contrast is that between the actual case of the boy (not the 'youth') running into the path of the javelin and the hypothetical and exact opposite, viz., the boy standing still.[61] Other examples from the *Tetralogies* show the same predilection to use the hypothetical scenario as an antithesis to what really happened – sometimes piling one hypothetical on top of another, for intensifying or rhetorical effect.[62]

---

[60] Gagarin 1997, 149.
[61] Flory 1988, 46 n. 7 thinks that this hypothetical (at *Tetr.* 2.2.5, 'Had he stood still...') comes close to being a 'historical hypothetical'; the hypothetical that starts the passage is deductive.
[62] E.g., Ant. *Tetr.* 1.1,9; 1.2,13; 1.3,2 (multiple hypotheticals); *Tetr.* 2.2, 4–5; 2.3,11 (multiple); 2.4,6; *Tetr.* 3.1,6; 3.2,3–4; 3.2,6; 3.4,2. Similarly in the speeches: Ant. 1.7, 11–12 (multiple); Ant. 1.11; Ant. 5.32, 52, 74; 84; 93; Ant. 6.48. A predilection for antithesis was evident in the example cited from Gorgias' *Palamedes*.

Amongst Antiphon's hypotheticals, Solmsen designated one type of argument as 'hypothetische Rollentausch oder Umkehrung' ('hypothetical role change or reversal');[63] these often appear in *topoi* dealing with *prosklēsis* (challenge), *basanos* (examination under torture) and *martyres* (witnesses) and are thus 'procedural *topoi*'.[64] Most often they are 'deductive' hypotheticals; thus, e.g., at 5.74–75, the speaker/defendant/son takes on the role of advocate for his father and 'countrafactually' exchanges roles with his accuser:

> I must also defend my father; although, as my father, it would have been far more natural for him to be defending me ... If my accuser were on trial, and I were giving evidence against him based on hearsay instead of certain knowledge, he would protest that he was being treated monstrously; yet he sees nothing monstrous in forcing me to explain occurences for which I am far too young to be aquainted save from hearsay.
>
> (transl. Maidment)[65]

At 6.27, another speaker exchanges roles:

> Suppose that the offer had come from them. Then had I refused to hand over my servants at their request: or had I been afraid to accept some challenge, they would be claiming that those facts in themselves afforded to my detriment the strongest presumption of the truth of their charge. Instead, it was I who issued the challenge and the prosecution who evaded the test. So it surely is only fair that this same fact should afford me a presumption to their detriment that the charge which they have made against me is untrue.
>
> (transl. Maidment)[66]

While roles are reversed (father/son, accuser/defendant, the agent of a challenge/its recipient), these are far from the type of role reversals or role changes that we see, for example, when Hippolytus imagines his father as his son (Eur. *Hipp.* 1041–1044) or when Clyemnestra substitutes a son for a daughter (Eur. *El.*

---

63 Solmsen 1931, 6 (reported by Gagarin 1997, 113); Ant. 1.11 is an excellent example and similar to 6.27 cited in the text *supra*.
64 Due 1980, 21 and 27 n. 7.
65 Ant. 5.74–75: Δεῖ δέ με καὶ ὑπὲρ τοῦ πατρὸς ἀπολογήσασθαι. Καίτοι γε πολλῷ μᾶλλον εἰκὸς ἦν ἐκεῖνον ὑπὲρ ἐμοῦ ἀπολογήσασθαι πατέρα ὄντα ὁ μὲν γὰρ πολλῷ πρεσβύτερός ... Καὶ εἰ μὲν ἐγὼ τούτου ἀγωνιζομένου κατεμαρτύρουν ἃ μὴ σαφῶς ᾔδη, ἀκοῇ δὲ ἠπιστάμην, δεινὰ ἂν ἔφη πάσχειν ὑπ' ἐμοῦ· νῦν δὲ ἀναγκάζων ἐμὲ ἀπολογεῖσθαι ὧν ἐγὼ πολλῷ νεώτερός εἰμι καὶ λόγῳ οἶδα, ταῦτα οὐ δεινὰ ἡγεῖται εἰργάσθαι (Gernet).
66 Ant. 6.27: Καὶ εἰ μὲν ἐγὼ τούτων προκαλουμένων μὴ ἠθέλησα τοὺς παραγενομένους ἀποφῆναι, <ἢ> θεράποντας ἐξαιτοῦσι μὴ ἤθελον ἐκδιδόναι, ἢ ἄλλην τινὰ πρόκλησιν ἔφευγον, αὐτὰ ἂν ταῦτα μέγιστα τεκμήρια κατ' ἐμοῦ ἐποιοῦντο ὅτι ἀληθὴς ἦν ἡ αἰτία· ἐπεὶ δ' ἐμοῦ προκαλουμένου οὗτοι ἦσαν οἱ φεύγοντες τὸν ἔλεγχον, ἐμοὶ δήπου δίκαιον κατὰ τούτων τὸ αὐτὸ τοῦτο τεκμήριον γενέσθαι, ὅτι οὐκ ἀληθὴς ἦν ἡ αἰτία ἣν αἰτιῶνται κατ' ἐμοῦ (Gernet).

1041–1045 hypothetical no. 3). What is uppermost in the Antiphonian contrafactuals are their contextualization in a pattern of antitheses: the imaginary scenario becomes a mirror in which to envision procedural conduct as carried out by a different actor; then, as if by magic, the tables are turned: in reality, the speaker's hearsay evidence in the first passage (Ant. 5.74–75) is only monstrous because his accuser has compelled him to speak about what he could not possibly know first-hand; and in the second Ant. 6.27), it was the defendant who had issued the challenge and so the accuser must suffer the disapprobation for refusing it.

Once again, this is not the way tragic hypotheticals operate. In Clytemnestra's argument in Eur. *El.* 1041–1045 ('If Menelaus had been abducted from his house in secret, would I have been right to kill Orestes in order to preserve Menelaus, my sister's husband?'), the precise antithesis of Helen's abduction could not be Menelaus' abduction – rather, it would be Helen *staying at home*; and the precise antithesis of Agamemnon killing Iphigenia could not be Clytemnestra killing Orestes – it would be Agamemnon *not killing Iphigenia*. The tragic hypotheticals are not articulated for rhetorical effect with a view to creating precious and precise antitheses, but rather are more subtly nuanced to consider and assess the quality of an event or an actor. Such ethical assessments are rare in Antiphon; consider an example at *Tetr.* 2.3.11 (and another will be considered shortly) where the accuser is speaking:

> Thus, on the basis of their own defense speech, the young man shares responsibility for the killing, and it would be unjust and ungodly for you to acquit him. We have already been destroyed by their mistake; if you now convict us of murder, you would make us suffer not righteously but unrighteously. And if those who have brought us this death are not banned from the appropriate places, your acquittal would be disrespectful of the gods.
>
> (transl. Gagarin)[67]

Here, an acquittal of the young man by the judges is viewed as 'unjust and ungodly' (δικαίως οὐδὲ ὁσίως ἀπολύοιτε); such an acquittal would be tantamount to convicting the accuser and would cause suffering that was not righteous but

---

[67] Ant. Tetr. 2.3.11: Ἐκ δὲ τῆς αὐτῶν τῶν ἀπολογουμένων ἀπολογίας μετόχου τοῦ μειρακίου τοῦ φόνου ὄντος, οὐκ ἂν δικαίως οὐδὲ ὁσίως ἀπολύοιτε αὐτόν. Οὔτε γὰρ ἡμεῖς, οἱ διὰ τὴν τούτων ἁμαρτίαν διαφθαρέντες, αὐθένται καταγνωσθέντες ὅσια ἀλλ' ἀνόσι' ἂν πάθοιμεν ὑφ' ὑμῶν· οὔθ' οἱ θανατώσαντες ἡμᾶς μὴ εἰργόμενοι τῶν οὐ προσηκόντων εὐσεβοῖντ' ἂν ὑπὸ τῶν ἀπολυσάντων τοὺς ἀνοσίους. Πάσης δ' ὑπὲρ πάντων τῆς κηλῖδος εἰς ὑμᾶς ἀναφερομένης, πολλὴ εὐλάβεια ὑμῖν τούτων ποιητέα ἐστί· καταλαβόντες μὲν γὰρ αὐτὸν καὶ εἴρξαντες ὧν ὁ νόμος εἴργει καθαροὶ τῶν ἐγκλημάτων ἔσεσθε, ἀπολύσαντες δὲ ὑπαίτιοι καθίστασθε. (Text of Gernet). See Gagarin 1997, 156–157 for textual uncertainty here.

unrighteous (ὅσια ἀλλ' ἀνόσια). Attention once again is on the articulation of paradox (the accuser is condemned whereas the defendant is acquitted) and creating antithesis and polarity. Hypotheticals in Antiphon (like those in Gorgias) thus have a rhetorical shape that bask in their antithetical design; they lack the nuance and emotional vigor of tragic hypotheticals that allow Clyemnestra's passion to tear through her speech (Soph. *El.* 528–546); that fill Hecuba's careful verbal destruction of Polymestor with hatred (Eur. *Hec.* 1217–1233); and that render Andromache's anger palpable (Eur. *Andr.* 334–335).

An example from Lysias 1 (a speech that cannot be dated, except to Lysias' lifetime) exhibits a predilection for antithesis similar to the one we see in Antiphon's *Tetralogies* – except that it is more complex.[68] The speaker is here countering the accuser's charge that he had ordered the house servant to fetch his wife's lover on the fatal day:

> ἐγὼ δέ, ὦ ἄνδρες, δίκαιον μὲν ἂν ποιεῖν ἡγούμην ᾡτινιοῦν τρόπῳ τὸν τὴν γυναῖκα τὴν ἐμὴν διαφθείραντα λαμβάνων· εἰ μὲν γὰρ λόγων εἰρημένων ἔργου δὲ μηδενὸς γεγενημένου μετελθεῖν ἐκέλευον ἐκεῖνον, ἠδίκουν ἄν· εἰ δὲ ἤδη πάντων διαπεπραγμένων καὶ πολλάκις εἰσεληλυθότος εἰς τὴν οἰκίαν τὴν ἐμὴν ᾡτινιοῦν τρόπῳ ἐλάμβανον αὐτόν, σώφρον' ἂν ἐμαυτὸν ἡγούμην·

(Lysias 1.37–38)

> Gentlemen, I would have considered myself justified, using whatever means possible, provided I would have caught the man who was my wife's corruptor. For if I had bidden the girl fetch him, when words alone had been spoken and no act had been committed, I would have been in the wrong; but if, when once he had compassed all his ends, and was frequently entering my house, I had then caught him by any means possible, I would have considered myself quite in order.

(transl. Lamb)

The speaker imagines circumstances that would have cancelled any justification for the killing of the intruder, and also their opposite – circumstances that would have justified the act.[69] The two conditional clauses are perfectly balanced, with words contrasted with deeds in the two protases with an additional sub-division of words and deeds in the first (εἰ μὲν γὰρ λόγων εἰρημένων ἔργου δὲ μηδενὸς γεγενημένου and εἰ δὲ ἤδη πάντων διαπεπραγμένων καὶ πολλάκις εἰσεληλυθότος

---

[68] Lloyd 1992, 32–33 thinks that the typical Lysian form 'if ... then ... but in fact...' is frequently used by Euripides; the forms may be similar, but it is impossible to argue for priority, or influence of one from the other.
[69] Cf. Ant. Tetr. 3.2.2: Τὸν γὰρ ἄρξαντα τῆς πληγῆς, εἰ μὲν σιδήρῳ ἢ λίθῳ ἢ ξύλῳ ἠμυνάμην αὐτόν, ἠδίκουν μὲν οὐδ' οὕτως – οὐ γὰρ ταὐτὰ ἀλλὰ μείζονα καὶ πλείονα δίκαιοι οἱ ἄρχοντες ἀντιπάσχειν εἰσί –·

εἰς τὴν οἰκίαν), and with wrongness contrasted with rightness in the two apodoses (ἠδίκουν ἄν and σώφρον' ἂν ἐμαυτὸν ἡγούμην). Not unlike the contrafactuals in Gorgias and Antiphon, Lysias' are often if not always carefully constructed antitheses.⁷⁰

The Oresteian hypotheticals, on the other hand, lack this blatant joy in antithesis and are at once more dramatic and sharper in meaning; their speakers also more urgently engage with their immediate audience onstage (recall the hypothetical uttered by Pasiphae). Yet it would be wrong to assume that no such 'urgently engaging hypotheticals' appear in the early orators. One appears in Lysias 12, the speech in which he prosecutes Eratosthenes, a former member of the Thirty, (404/03) for the murder of his brother Polemarchus; thus at 12.28–29, Lysias asks:

> ἔτι δὲ τοῖς μὲν ἄλλοις Ἀθηναίοις ἱκανή μοι δοκεῖ πρόφασις εἶναι τῶν γεγενημένων εἰς τοὺς τριάκοντα ἀναφέρειντὴν αἰτίαν· αὐτοὺς δὲ τοὺς τριάκοντα, ἂν εἰς σφᾶς αὐτοὺς ἀναφέρωσι, πῶς ὑμᾶς εἰκὸς ἀποδέχεσθαι; εἰ μὲν γάρ τις ἦν ἐν τῇ πόλει ἀρχὴ ἰσχυροτέρα ταύτης, ὑφ' ἧς αὐτῷ προσετάττετο παρὰ τὸ δίκαιον ἀνθρώπους ἀπολλύναι, ἴσως ἂν εἰκότως αὐτῷ συγγνώμην εἴχετε· νῦν δὲ παρὰ τοῦ ποτε καὶ λήψεσθε δίκην, εἴπερ ἐξέσται τοῖς τριάκοντα λέγειν ὅτι τὰ ὑπὸ τῶν τριάκοντα προσταχθέντα ἐποίουν;

> Again, the rest of the Athenians have a sufficient excuse, in my opinion, for attributing to the Thirty the responsibility for what has taken place; but if the Thirty actually attribute it to themselves, how can you reasonably accept that? For had there been some stronger authority in the city, whose orders were given him to destroy people in defiance of justice, you might perhaps have some reason for pardoning him; but whom, in fact, will you ever punish, if the Thirty are to be allowed to state that they merely carried out the orders of the Thirty?
>
> (transl. Lamb)

Here, the particular formulation of the apodosis of the contrafactual (ἴσως ἂν εἰκότως αὐτῷ συγγνώμην εἴχετε) with its circumstantial pardon bears a resemblance to that in Eur. *El.* 1024–1029 (hypothetical no. 2: κεἰ μὲν πόλεως ἅλωσιν ἐξιώμενος / ἢ δῶμ' ὀνήσων τἆλλα τ' ἐκσῴζων τέκνα / ἔκτεινε πολλῶν μίαν ὕπερ, συγγνώστ' ἂν ἦν) and also to that in Eur. *Med.* 490–491 (n. 41, cat. 15a: εἰ γὰρ ἦσθ' ἄπαις ἔτι, / συγγνώστ' ἂν ἦν σοι τοῦδ' ἐρασθῆναι λέχους).⁷¹ It is tempting to think that Lysias, in a case where he is prosecuting the killing of his brother, has

---

70 410/09: Lys. 20. 4, 19, 27. 403/02: Lys. 12. 28–29, 32, 34, 47, 48, 52, 98; Lys. 21.5, 17. 400 (?): Lys. 25.5. 399: Lys. 6 (none); Lys. 13.16, 22, 36, 53, 85, 90; Lys. 30.15, 17; Lys. 32.1; 397/6: Lys. 7.19, 20–21, 22, 23, 24, 32, 36, 37. See Wilcox 1938; Bateman 1962, 168–170; Tordoff 2014, 116–119 discusses 'historical' contrafactuals appearing at Lys. 2.65; 12.98; 13.16; and 14.16.
71 Cf. Bateman 1962, 168–169 on Lys. 12.28–30.

adapted συγγνώστ' ἂν ἦν from the kin-killing hypotheticals of tragedy so as to become his ἴσως ἂν εἰκότως αὐτῷ συγγνώμην εἴχετε, the apodosis of a contrafactual.[72] In any event, he uses the hypothetical in a 'tragic way', to assess the alleged excuse offered by the killer and not (only) to show off its own antithetical dressing. Possibly, too, he uses the contrafactual to engage his (reading?) audience to contemplate the killings of the Thirty and to stir them to retaliate in court or elsewhere. A similar formulation appears in *Tetr.* 3.1.6:

> εἰ μὲν γὰρ ἄκων ἀπέκτεινε τὸν ἄνδρα, ἄξιος ἂν ἦν συγγνώμης τυχεῖν τινός· ὕβρει δὲ καὶ ἀκολασίᾳ παροινῶν εἰς ἄνδρα πρεσβύτην, τύπτων τε καὶ πνίγων ἕως τῆς ψυχῆς ἀπεστέρησεν αὐτόν, ὡς μὲν ἀποκτείνας τοῦ φόνου τοῖς ἐπιτιμίοις ἔνοχός ἐστιν, ὡς δὲ συγχέων ἅπαντα τῶν γεραιοτέρων τὰ νόμιμα οὐδενὸς ἁμαρτεῖν, οἷς οἱ τοιοῦτοι κολάζονται, δίκαιός ἐστιν.

> Had he killed his victim accidentally, he would have deserved some measure of pardon. But he wantonly committed a brutal assault upon an old man when in his cups; he struck him and throttled him until he robbed him of life. So for killing him he is liable to the penalties prescribed for murder: and for violating every right to respect enjoyed by the aged he deserves to suffer in full the punishment usual in such cases.
> (transl. Maidment, slightly modified)

The consideration of pardon shows that an assessment is in process, even if its negation is pre-judged; nonetheless the passage evinces none of the forcefulness of the Lysian one.[73] Can we posit a relationship between tragedy and oratory here? Probably not: the instances in which 'pardon' appears as part of the apodosis of a contrafactual are so rare, both in the early rhetorical record (only here in Antiphon) and in tragedy that it is probably best not to think of transposition from one genre to the other.[74]

---

[72] A personal tone may also be heard in Lys. 12.32: χρῆν δέ σε, ὦ Ἐρατόσθενες, εἴπερ ἦσθα χρηστός, πολὺ μᾶλλον τοῖς μέλλουσιν ἀδίκως ἀποθανεῖσθαι μηνυτὴν γενέσθαι ἢ τοὺς ἀδίκως ἀπολουμένους συλλαμβάνειν. νῦν δέ σου τὰ ἔργα φανερὰ γεγένηται οὐχ ὡς ἀνιωμένου ἀλλ' ὡς ἡδομένου τοῖς γιγνομένοις·

[73] In Lysias 10.2–3, a later speech (384/3), the same consideration is filled with sarcasm: ἐγὼ δ', εἰ μὲν τὸν ἑαυτοῦ με ἀπεκτονέναι ᾐτιᾶτο, συγγνώμην ἂν εἶχον αὐτῷ τῶν εἰρημένων (φαῦλον γὰρ αὐτὸν καὶ οὐδενὸς ἄξιον ἡγούμην)· οὐδ' εἴ τι ἄλλο τῶν ἀπορρήτων ἤκουσα, οὐκ ἂν ἐπεξῆλθον αὐτῷ (ἀνελευθέρου γὰρ καὶ λίαν φιλοδίκου εἶναι νομίζω κακηγορίας δικάζεσθαι)· νυνὶ δὲ αἰσχρόν μοι...

[74] A borrowing from tragedy may occur in Lys. 1.26: the speaker, as he recreates the scene of the killing of his wife's paramour, uses the *topos* that it is not he who is killing him, but the law of the city (οὐκ ἐγώ σε ἀποκτενῶ, ἀλλ' ὁ τῆς πόλεως νόμος), reminiscent of Soph. *El.* 528 (ἡ γὰρ Δίκη νιν εἷλεν, οὐκ ἐγὼ μόνη); the *topos* appears later in Ar. *Eccl.* 1055–1056 and Anaximenes 36.44 Fuhrmann. Clytemnestra in Aesch. *Agam.* 1501–1502 used a more complicated evasion to

We might look elsewhere for a reception of tragic argument in rhetoric or vice versa. The argument that 'numbers matter' (Eur. *El* 1024–1029, *Erecth.* fr. 360 and *Heracl.* 398–419) shows up in And. 1 *On the Mysteries*, a speech of 399 BCE that refers to events in 415, viz., the arrests and trials that were the aftermath of the mutilation of the Herms and the profanation of the Mysteries. Charmides, who is in prison awaiting trial along with his cousin Andocides (And. 1.48–53), begs him to inform and save lives (Andocides reports the speech *Oratio Recta*):

> ... I beg of you: if you have heard anything concerning this affair, disclose it. Save yourself: save your father, who must be dearer to you than anyone in the world: save your brother-in-law, the husband of your only sister: save all those others who are bound to you by ties of blood and family: and lastly, save me, who have never vexed you in my life and who am ever ready to do anything for you and your good.
>
> (And. 1.50, transl. Maidment)

Andocides mulls over Charmides' request and reports his private ratiocinations (likewise in *Oratio Recta*) as a soliloquy:

> Never, oh never, has a man found himself in a more terrible strait than I. Am I to look on while my own kindred perish for a crime which they have not committed... Am I to pay no heed to three hundred Athenians who are to be wrongfully put to death, to the desperate plight of Athens, to the suspicions of citizen for citizen? Or am I to reveal to my countrymen the story told me by the true criminal, Euphiletus?
>
> (And. 1.51, transl. Maidment)

In the end, Andocides decides to inform on four men:

> So I decided that it was better to cut off from their country four men who richly deserved it – men alive to-day and restored to home and property – than to let those others go to a death which they had done nothing whatever to deserve.
>
> (And. 1.53, transl. Maidment)

Numbers matter for Andocides. The argument is fundamentally similar to that in Eur. *El.* 1024–1029 but the formulation is not. The arguments may be independently derived.

---

express the agent of the murder (ὁ παλαιὸς δριμὺς ἀλάστωρ / Ἀτρέως χαλεποῦ θοινατῆρος). Additionally, Lloyd 1992, 31 sees a parallel between 'Euripides and Lysias in their use of the *reductio ad absurdum* between Orestes' evocation of the absurdity of wives being allowed to get away with killing their husbands (*Or.* 566–571) and Euphiletus' drawing-out of the consequences of adulterers not being punished (Lys. 1.36)'. The direction, however, may be from tragedy to oratory.

I have found two arguments, however, that may more persuasively suggest transpositions from drama to rhetoric. The first comes, once again, from And. 1. Here (§§ 117–119), Andocides is explaining why Callias, a kinsman of Andocides, had urged that a prosecution be brought against him. Andocides weaves a tale about a personal rivalry over two heiresses (*epiklēroi*) whom both men, Andocides and Callias, apparently wanted to marry; Andocides, however, had prevented Callias from winning either of them. He managed this lawfully through the procedure of *epidikasia* by which a court decides who is the appropriate kinsman to marry–and obtain the estate of–a woman without a father or brothers. Thus Andocides made a court claim for one of the women, and urged another kinsman named Leagros to claim the other. He reports that he arranged a meeting with this Leagros and used the following argument to persuade him to marry one of the heiresses:

> ἡμᾶς γὰρ οὐ δίκαιόν ἐστιν οὔτε χρήματα ἕτεραοῦτ' εὐτυχίαν ἀνδρὸς ἑλέσθαι, ὥστε καταφρονῆσαι τῶν Ἐπιλύκου θυγατέρων. καὶ γὰρ εἰ ἔζη Ἐπίλυκος ἢ τεθνεὼς πολλὰ κατέλιπε χρήματα, ἠξιοῦμεν ἂν γένει ὄντες ἐγγυτάτω ἔχειν τὰς παῖδας. τοιγάρτοι ἐκεῖνα μὲν δι' Ἐπίλυκον ἂν ἦν ἢ διὰ τὰ χρήματα· νῦν δὲ διὰ τὴν ἡμετέραν ἀρετὴν τάδε ἔσται. τῆς μὲν οὖν σὺ ἐπιδικάζου, τῆς δὲ ἐγώ.
>
> (And. 1. 119)

> We have no right to prefer a wealthy or successful alliance and look down upon the daughters of Epilycus,' I argued: 'for if Epilycus were alive, or if he had died a rich man, we should be claiming the girls as their next of kin. We should have married them then either because of Epilycus himself or because of his money; we will do the same now because we are men of honour. Do you obtain an order of the court for the one, and I will do the same for the other.
>
> (transl. Maidment, slightly modified)

Andocides uses the contrafactual argument to demonstrate that it is right (*dikaion*) for the men to marry the heiresses. And he uses it in the context of kin, hypothesizing how the two kinsmen would have acted had their kinsman Epilycus been alive or had died as a rich man, in order to show how they should behave now that he is dead and in fact died as a (reputedly) poor man.

A second passage, perhaps more persuasive of a connection with the tragic hypotheticals, appears in in Lys. 19, *On the property of Aristophanes*. Aristophanes, a minor politician in the 390s, had been executed and his property confiscated; the property, when sold at public auction, had yielded less money than was thought to belong to the estate; consequently, in the belief that Aristophanes' marital kin had concealed his wealth so as to preserve it from confiscation, the estate of Aristophanes' father-in-law was also confiscated, apparently to make up for the perceived difference.⁷⁵ As the father-in-law had died before trial, the estate is now defended by his son (unnamed) who is thus the brother-in-law of the deceased Aristophanes (whose property had been confiscated in the first place). The relationships are perhaps intricate, but understanding them will aid in de-coding the hypothetical argument that the speaker presents to the judges. Clearly the speaker does not expect his contemporary audience to be familiar with his cast of characters, namely: the Aristophanes whose property was confiscated and sold; Aristophanes' father-in-law, whose property is now undergoing confiscation; the widow of the dead Aristophanes (and sister of the speaker) who is now left with no material assistance from her dead husband's estate for the nurture of her children. But the speaker might very well expect the audience to be familiar with Conon, one of the most famous generals of the fourth century, and also with his son Timotheus, even though he may not have held public office yet. Here is the way the speaker explains the unfortunate events that have unfolded for Aristophanes' widow:

> φέρε πρὸς θεῶν Ὀλυμπίων· οὕτω γὰρ σκοπεῖτε, ὦ <ἄνδρες>δικασταί. εἴ τις ὑμῶν ἔτυχε δοὺς Τιμοθέῳ τῷ Κόνωνος τὴν θυγατέρα ἢ τὴν ἀδελφήν, καὶ ἐκείνου ἀποδημήσαντος καὶ ἐν διαβολῇ γενομένου ἐδημεύθη ἡ οὐσία, καὶ μὴ ἐγένετο τῇ πόλει πραθέντων ἁπάντων τέτταρα τάλαντα ἀργυρίου, διὰ τοῦτο ἠξιοῦτε ἂν καὶ τοὺς προσήκοντας τοὺς ἐκείνου ἀπολέσθαι, ὅτι οὐδὲ πολλοστὸν μέρος τῆς δόξης τῆς παρ' ὑμῖν ἐφάνη τὰ χρήματα;
>
> (Lys. 19.34)
>
> I adjure you, by the Olympian gods, gentlemen, just consider it in this way: suppose that one of you had happened to bestow his daughter or his sister on Timotheus, son of Conon, and during his absence abroad Conon was involved in some slander and his estate was confiscated, and the city received from the sale of the whole something less than four talents of silver. Would you think it right that his children and relatives should be ruined merely because the property had turned out to be but a trifling fraction of the amount at which it stood in your estimation?
>
> (transl. Lamb)

If each judge in the courtroom were to apply the hypothetical scenario to his own daughter, then she would now be married to Timotheus; Conon's estate would be confiscated and Timotheus and his imaginary wife and children would be on the verge of being financially ruined because Conon's estate, upon being auctioned, will have brought in only a trifling amount. The formulation of the hypothesis here is similar to the type used by Tyndareus at Eur. *Orestes* 507–517 (hypothetical no. 5); there Tyndareus had imagined a wife for Orestes who would one day

---

75 Todd 2000, 200–201.

kill him and a son who would one day 'pay off that murder with another'; the imaginary substitutions illustrate the current dramatic situation. A similar formulation was used by Clyemnestra at Eur. *El.* 1041–1045 (hypothetical no. 3); there she had substituted Menelaus as the person who was abducted (not Helen); in that case, she asks, would it have been right for her to kill Orestes in order to save Menelaus? Similarly in Lysias' speech: if Timotheus had been the husband and his father's estate confiscated, in that case would it have been right for Timotheus and his family to suffer? In the three cases, the hypothetical configuring of a similar scenario cast with a different set of family related characters clarifies and dramatizes the ethical situation. I would conjecture that here we see a borrowing or adaptation from the storeroom of tragic hypotheticals.

4 Some speculative conclusions

With the exception of Lysias 34, and perhaps Andocides 1, with their hypothetical arguments that exploit kinsmen to make their cases, it seems impossible to argue definitively that hypotheticals in tragedy and oratory communicate with one another, borrow from one another, or evolve from one another. Rather, while being aware of one another, they may nevertheless have developed independently and they surely flourished idiosyncratically in their own genres.[76] The particular formulations that I have focused on in the course of this essay may have experienced a blossoming in fifth century tragedies and in the 'imaginary lawcourts' and 'imaginary forensic discourse' that will have evolved there. Kin killings were especially horrid to Athenians;[77] perhaps not by coincidence, there is hardly any mention of them in historical Athens. In the fourth century, the speaker of Lysias 10 has sued Theomnestus for defamation, specifically for saying that he (the speaker) had killed

---

[76] In this respect, it is useful to consider Flory 1988 and his examination of Thucydides' hypotheses about the Peloponnesian War, in which he distinguishes (and eliminates from his study) those that did not have to do with the Peloponnesian War, those used in speeches, and 'those that are mere rhetorical flourishes or logical twists and not true hypotheses about the past' (1988, 45). What I think his essay shows is an instance of the way another genre (history) develops its own special kind of hypothetical argument (viz., the historical hypothesis: 'if x had not happened, then ...').

[77] See Parker 1983, 122–123. It remains paradoxical that so many kin-killings appear in Greek myth; Parker's appendix (pp. 375–392) 'Exile and Purification of the Killer in Greek Myth' is packed with kin-killers.

his own father; indeed, it was unlawful to make such an assertion against any person – unless, indeed, he were a parricide.[78] The speaker in this case begs the judges:

> to vote according to justice, reflecting that it is a far greater slur to be told that one has killed one's father than that one has thrown away one's shield. I, for one, would rather have cast any number of shields than entertain such thoughts regarding my father.
> (Lys. 10.21, transl. Lamb)[79]

The speaker of Isaeus 9 reports hearing (λέγεται) that Thudippus caused the death of his brother Euthycrates; the speaker can find no demesman to give evidence.[80] In Dem. 22, the speaker complains:

> if the charges that Androtion trumped up against me had been accepted in your courts, not a single living man would have opened his door to me, for he accused me of things that anyone would have shrunk from mentioning, unless he were a man of the same stamp as himself, saying that I had killed my own father.
> (Dem. 22.1–2, transl. Vince)[81]

Father-killing was reprehensible; but so, too, was any kin killing. Even to prosecute a kinsman for murder could be deemed reprehensible. So apparently it was for Euthyphro, as Plato narrates in the eponymous dialogue (*Euth.* 4d–e):

> Now my father and the rest of my relatives are angry with me, because for the sake of this murderer I am prosecuting my father for murder. For they say he did not kill him, and if he had killed him never so much, yet since the dead man was a murderer, I ought not to trouble

---

78 For discussion of this law, see Phillips 2013, 124–136.
79 Lys. 10.21: ... τὰ δίκαια ψηφίσασθαι, ἐνθυμουμένους ὅτι πολὺ μεῖζον κακόν ἐστιν ἀκοῦσαι τὸν πατέρα <ἀπεκτονέναι ἢ τὴν ἀσπίδα> ἀποβεβληκέναι. ἐγὼ γοῦν δεξαίμην ἂν πάσας τὰς ἀσπίδας ἐρριφέναι ἢ τοιαύτην γνώμην ἔχειν περὶ τὸν πατέρα.
80 For discussion of the homicides mentioned here and in Dem. 22 and 24, see Philipps 2008, 105–109 and 2013, 453.
81 Dem. 22.1–2: ἐμὲ δ᾽ οὐδ᾽ ἂν ἐδέξατο τῶν ὄντων ἀνθρώπων οὐδὲ εἷς, εἰ τὰ κατασκευασθένθ᾽ ὑπὸ τούτου παρ᾽ ὑμῖν ἐπιστεύθη. αἰτιασάμενος γάρ με ἃ καὶ λέγειν ἂν ὀκνήσειέ τις, εἰ μὴ τύχοι προσόμοιος ὢν τούτῳ, τὸν πατέρ᾽ ὡς ἀπέκτον᾽ ἐγὼ τὸν ἐμαυτοῦ. In the following section, the speaker reports that Androtion additionally brought a charge of impiety against his uncle, for associating with the alleged parricide (Dem. 22.2–3). If we give credence to the similar report in Dem. 24.7–8, then Androtion prosecuted the alleged parricide with an indictment for impiety rather than homicide.

myself about such a fellow, because it is unholy for a son to prosecute his father for murder...

(transl. Fowler)[82]

It cannot pass without notice that, in the two passages just now cited from Demosthenes and Plato, hypotheticals were used to depict the circumstances of the persons accused of murder. In both tragedy and oratory, hypotheticals may have been customarily used when speaking of kin killings for their distancing and dramatic effect. As to historical Athens, we do not know whether kinsmen would in fact have prosecuted their kinsmen. By Draco's law on homicide, only kinsmen were permitted to prosecute cases of homicide; but that same law allowed kinsmen to pardon an unintentional killer if all the kinsmen agreed and none dissented.[83] Family members may have given such pardons to a kinsman who had unintentionally killed a cousin or nephew, and they may possibly have extended such pardons to intentional kin killers as well, especially to those claiming to have killed justifiably. If kinsmen agreed, why drag their brother, cousin, nephew, father or uncle into court – especially if the exile or execution of another family member would mean a gross material loss for the remaining family?[84] If circumstances were such, then kin killings may rarely have come to trial (for surely they did occur, even if we hear so little of them), and it may have been the tragedians who developed the language and tropes for the justifications of kin killing in their imaginary lawcourts.[85] Clearly the tragedians and Euripides in particular found hypothetical arguments useful: they could be messily passionate, angry, hateful, or surgically precise. Even Sophocles in *Antigone* 905–912 may have been spurred to add quintupled contrafactuals to enlarge the horror of being

---

82 Plato *Euth.* 4d-e: οἱ ἄλλοι οἰκεῖοι, ὅτι ἐγὼ ὑπὲρ τοῦ ἀνδροφόνου τῷ πατρὶ φόνου ἐπεξέρχομαι οὔτε ἀποκτείναντι, ὥς φασιν ἐκεῖνοι, οὔτ' εἰ ὅτι μάλιστα ἀπέκτεινεν, ἀνδροφόνου γε ὄντος τοῦ ἀποθανόντος, οὐ δεῖν φροντίζειν ὑπὲρ τοῦ τοιούτου—ἀνόσιον γὰρ εἶναι τὸ ὑὸν πατρὶ φόνου ἐπεξιέναι...

83 *IG* I³104.13–20; the lines recording the procedure of pardon are restored from Dem.43.57. See Stroud 1968, 49.

84 Parker 1983, 123 with n. 75 remarks that 'the pressure towards connivance is in practice very strong' but '[P]ollution does its best to reassert the claims of the victim against those of convenience'.

85 Sansone 2014, 163–166 makes a similar argument regarding arguments of probability that pertain to marriage and sexual liaisons in tragedies such as *Hipp.*, *Andr.*, and esp. *Cretans*: these are not arguments that would be used in court 'so that one wonders why we should look to the law courts in search of Euripides' inspiration' (166).

killed by one's brother (as Antigone's brothers were), or by one's uncle and even by oneself – as she would be.[86]

5 Catalogue of Hypotheticals

A. Oresteian kin-killings

1. Soph. *El.* 528–532; 534–546 (§IIc)

> ἡ γὰρ Δίκη νιν εἷλεν, οὐκ ἐγὼ μόνη,
> ᾗ χρῆν σ' ἀρήγειν, εἰ φρονοῦσ' ἐτύγχανες.
> ἐπεὶ πατὴρ οὗτος σός, ὃν θρηνεῖς ἀεί,   530
> τὴν σὴν ὅμαιμον μοῦνος Ἑλλήνων ἔτλη
> θῦσαι θεοῖσιν...
> εἶἑν· δίδαξον δή με <τοῦτο>· τοῦ χάριν
> ἔθυσεν αὐτήν; πότερον Ἀργείων ἐρεῖς;   535
> ἀλλ' οὐ μετῆν αὐτοῖσι τήν γ' ἐμὴν κτανεῖν.
> ἀλλ' ἀντ' ἀδελφοῦ δῆτα Μενέλεω κτανὼν
> τἄμ' οὐκ ἔμελλε τῶνδέ μοι δώσειν δίκην;
> πότερον ἐκείνῳ παῖδες οὐκ ἦσαν διπλοῖ,
> οὓς τῆσδε μᾶλλον εἰκὸς ἦν θνῄσκειν, πατρὸς   540
> καὶ μητρὸς ὄντας, ἧς ὁ πλοῦς ὅδ' ἦν χάριν;
> ἢ τῶν ἐμῶν Ἅιδης τιν' ἵμερον τέκνων
> ἢ τῶν ἐκείνης ἔσχε δαίσασθαι πλέον;
> ἢ τῷ πανώλει πατρὶ τῶν μὲν ἐξ ἐμοῦ
> παίδων πόθος παρεῖτο, Μενέλεῳ δ' ἐνῆν;

2. Eur. *Electra* 1024–1029 (§IIc, 'numbers matter'; cf. cat. nos. 17 and 18)

> κεἰ μὲν πόλεως ἅλωσιν ἐξιώμενος
> ἢ δῶμ' ὀνήσων τἄλλα τ' ἐκσῴζων τέκνα
> ἔκτεινε πολλῶν μίαν ὕπερ, συγγνώστ' ἂν ἦν.
> νῦν δ' οὕνεχ' Ἑλένη μάργος ἦν ὅ τ' αὖ λαβὼν
> ἄλοχον κολάζειν προδότιν οὐκ ἠπίστατο,
> τούτων ἔκατι παῖδ' ἐμὴν διώλεσεν.

3. Eur. *Electra* 1041–1045 (§IIc)

> εἰ δ' ἐκ δόμων ἥρπαστο Μενέλεως λάθρᾳ,
> κτανεῖν μ' Ὀρέστην χρῆν, κασιγνήτης πόσιν

---

[86] See cat. no. 8.

Μενέλαον ὡς σώσαιμι; σὸς δὲ πῶς πατὴρ
ἠνέσχετ' ἂν ταῦτ'; εἶτα τὸν μὲν οὐ θανεῖν
κτείνοντα χρῆν τἄμ', ἐμὲ δὲ πρὸς κείνου παθεῖν
(κτείνουσαν αὐτοῦ παῖδας, οὐκ ἐλάσσονα); (post 1045)

[Diggle 1977: 121–22 for the supplement. He assumes a lacuna after 445, on the grounds that the absolute use of παθεῖν is open to grave doubt.]

4. Eur. *Orestes* 283–293 (§IId)

μὴ τῶν ἐμῶν ἕκατι συντήκου κακῶν·
σὺ μὲν γὰρ ἐπένευσας τάδ', εἴργασται δ' ἐμοὶ
μητρῷον αἷμα· Λοξίᾳ δὲ μέμφομαι,
ὅστις μ' ἐπάρας ἔργον ἀνοσιώτατον,
τοῖς μὲν λόγοις ηὔφρανε, τοῖς δ' ἔργοισιν οὔ.
οἶμαι δὲ πατέρα τὸν ἐμόν, εἰ κατ' ὄμματα
ἐξιστόρουν νιν μητέρ' εἰ κτεῖναί με χρή,
πολλὰς γενείου τοῦδ' ἂν ἐκτεῖναι λιτὰς
μήποτε τεκούσης ἐς σφαγὰς ὦσαι ξίφος,
εἰ μήτ' ἐκεῖνος ἀναλαβεῖν ἔμελλε φῶς
ἐγώ θ' ὁ τλήμων τοιάδ' ἐκπλήσειν κακά.

5. Eur. *Orestes* 507–517 (§IId; cf. cat. 14)

ἐρήσομαι δέ, Μενέλεως, τοσόνδε σε·
εἰ τόνδ' ἀποκτείνειεν ὁμόλεκτρος γυνή,
χὠ τοῦδε παῖς αὖ μητέρ' ἀνταποκτενεῖ,
κἄπειθ' ὁ κείνου γενόμενος φόνωι φόνον
λύσει, πέρας δὴ ποῖ κακῶν προβήσεται;
καλῶς ἔθεντο ταῦτα πατέρες οἱ πάλαι·
ἐς ὀμμάτων μὲν ὄψιν οὐκ εἴων περᾶν
οὐδ' εἰς ἀπάντημ' ὅστις αἷμ' ἔχων κυροῖ,
φυγαῖσι δ' ὁσιοῦν, ἀνταποκτείνειν δὲ μή.
ἀεὶ γὰρ εἷς ἔμελλ' ἐνέξεσθαι φόνωι,
τὸ λοίσθιον μίασμα λαμβάνων χεροῖν.

6. Eur. *Orestes* 566–571 (§IId)

εἰ γὰρ γυναῖκες ἐς τόδ' ἥξουσιν θράσους,
ἄνδρας φονεύειν, καταφυγὰς ποιούμεναι
ἐς τέκνα, μαστοῖς τὸν ἔλεον θηρώμεναι,
παρ' οὐδὲν αὐταῖς ἦν ἂν ὀλλύναι πόσεις,
ἐπίκλημ' ἐχούσαις ὅτι τύχοι. δράσας δ' ἐγὼ
δείν', ὡς σὺ κομπεῖς, τόνδ' ἔπαυσα τὸν νόμον.

(Eur. *Orestes* 566–571)

B. Non-Oresteian contrafactual kin killings

7. Eur. *Hipp.* 1041–1044 (§IIb)

> καὶ σοῦ γε ταὐτὰ κάρτα θαυμάζω, πάτερ·
> εἰ γὰρ σὺ μὲν παῖς ἦσθ', ἐγὼ δὲ σὸς πατήρ,
> ἔκτεινά τοί σ' ἂν κοὐ φυγαῖς ἐζημίουν,
> εἴπερ γυναικὸς ἠξίους ἐμῆς θιγεῖν.

Cf. *TrGF*I 70 Carcinus II F 1e (Medea)=Aristot. *Rhet.* 2.23 1400b9, along with the anon. commentator in *CAG* XXI.2 p. 146, 1–3 and also West 2007.

8. Soph. *Ant.* 905–912 (§IIb)

> οὐ γάρ ποτ' οὔτ' ἂν εἰ τέκν' ὧν μήτηρ ἔφυν
> οὔτ' εἰ πόσις μοι κατθανὼν ἐτήκετο,
> βίᾳ πολιτῶν τόνδ' ἂν ᾐρόμην πόνον.
> τίνος νόμου δὴ ταῦτα πρὸς χάριν λέγω;
> πόσις μὲν ἄν μοι κατθανόντος ἄλλος ἦν,
> καὶ παῖς ἀπ' ἄλλου φωτός, εἰ τοῦδ' ἤμπλακον,
> μητρὸς δ' ἐν Ἅιδου καὶ πατρὸς κεκευθότοιν
> οὐκ ἔστ' ἀδελφὸς ὅστις ἂν βλάστοι ποτέ.

Note: The contrafactuals (two protases appear in ll. 905 and 906, another, as a participle, in l. 909, and still another in 910) suit Antigone's situation: she has neither children nor husband; the future condition suits Intaphernes' wife who has both. Cf. Herodotus 3.119 (not a hypothetical):

> Ὦ βασιλεῦ, ἀνὴρ μέν μοι ἂν ἄλλος γένοιτο, εἰ δαίμων ἐθέλοι, καὶ τέκνα ἄλλα, εἰ ταῦτα ἀποβάλοιμι· πατρὸς δὲ καὶ μητρὸς οὐκέτι μευ ζωόντων ἀδελφεὸς ἂν ἄλλος οὐδενὶ τρόπῳ γένοιτο. ταύτῃ τῇ γνώμῃ χρεωμένη ἔλεξα ταῦτα.

9. Soph. *OC* 988–999 (§IIb)

> ἀλλ' οὐ γὰρ οὔτ' ἐν τοῖσδ' ἀκούσομαι κακὸς
> γάμοισιν οὔθ' οὓς αἰὲν ἐμφορεῖς σύ μοι
> φόνους πατρῴους ἐξονειδίζων πικρῶς.
> ἓν γάρ μ' ἄμειψαι μοῦνον ὧν σ' ἀνιστορῶ·
> εἴ τίς σε τὸν δίκαιον αὐτίκ' ἐνθάδε
> κτείνοι παραστάς, πότερα πυνθάνοι' ἂν εἰ
> πατήρ σ' ὁ καίνων, ἢ τίνοι' ἂν εὐθέως;
> δοκῶ μέν, εἴπερ ζῆν φιλεῖς, τὸν αἴτιον
> τίνοι' ἄν, οὐδὲ τοὔνδικον περιβλέποις.
> τοιαῦτα μέντοι καὐτὸς εἰσέβην κακά,

θεῶν ἀγόντων· ὥστ' ἐγὼ οὐδὲ τὴν πατρὸς
ψυχὴν ἂν οἶμαι ζῶσαν ἀντειπεῖν ἐμοί.

10. Eur. *Cretans* 472e, 7–11, Pasiphae pleads for her life before her husband (§IIb and §IIe)

  ἀρνουμένη μὲν οὐκέτ' ἂν πίθοιμί σε·   5
  πάντως γὰρ ἤδη δῆλον ὡς ἔχει τάδε.
  ἐγ[ὼ] γὰρ εἰ μὲν ἀνδρὶ προὔβαλον δέμας
  τοὐμόν, λαθραίαν ἐμπολωμένη Κύπριν,
  ὀρθῶς ἂν ἤδη μάχ[λο]ς οὖσ' ἐφαινόμην·
  νῦν δ', ἐκ θεοῦ γὰρ προσβολῆς ἐμηνάμην,   10
  ἀλγῶ μέν, ἔστι δ' οὐχ ἐκο[ύσ]ιον κακόν.

  LCL 504: P. Berlin 13217, ed. U. von Wilamowitz and W. Schubart (1907); re-ed. Page, GLP 70-7 (no. 11), Cozzoli 42–3 with Plates III, IV. The parchment was lost in 1945 and rediscovered in Warsaw in 1992.

11. Eur. *Hipp.* 1021–1024 (§IIb and n. 32)

  ἓν οὐ λέλεκται τῶν ἐμῶν, τὰ δ' ἄλλ' ἔχεις·
  εἰ μὲν γὰρ ἦν μοι μάρτυς οἷός εἰμ' ἐγὼ
  καὶ τῆσδ' ὁρώσης φέγγος ἠγωνιζόμην,
  ἔργοις ἂν εἶδες τοὺς κακοὺς διεξιών.

C. Non-Oresteian hypothetical non-kin killings

12. Eur. *Hec.* 267–270 (cf. hypothetical no. 1)

  εἰ δ' αἰχμαλώτων χρή τιν' ἔκκριτον θανεῖν
  κάλλει θ' ὑπερφέρουσαν, οὐχ ἡμῶν τόδε·
  ἡ Τυνδαρὶς γὰρ εἶδος ἐκπρεπεστάτη,
  ἀδικοῦσά θ' ἡμῶν οὐδὲν ἧσσον ηὑρέθη.

13. Eur. *Hec.* 1217–1233

  πρὸς τοῖσδε νῦν ἄκουσον ὡς φαίνῃ κακός·
  χρῆν σ', εἴπερ ἦσθα τοῖς Ἀχαιοῖσιν φίλος,
  τὸν χρυσὸν ὃν φῂς οὐ σὸν ἀλλὰ τοῦδ' ἔχειν
  δοῦναι φέροντα πενομένοις τε καὶ χρόνον   1220
  πολὺν πατρῴας γῆς ἀπεξενωμένοις·
  σὺ δ' οὐδὲ νῦν πω σῆς ἀπαλλάξαι χερὸς
  τολμᾷς, ἔχων δὲ καρτερεῖς ἔτ' ἐν δόμοις.   1223
  καὶ μὴν τρέφων μὲν ὥς σε παῖδ' ἐχρῆν τρέφειν

σώσας τε τὸν ἐμόν, εἶχες ἂν καλὸν κλέος·
ἐν τοῖς κακοῖς γὰρ ἀγαθοὶ σαφέστατοι
φίλοι· τὰ χρηστὰ δ' αὔθ' ἕκαστ' ἔχει φίλους.
εἰ δ' ἐσπάνιζες χρημάτων, ὁ δ' εὐτύχει,
θησαυρὸς ἄν σοι παῖς ὑπῆρχ' οὑμὸς μέγας·
νῦν δ' οὔτ' ἐκεῖνον ἄνδρ' ἔχεις σαυτῶι φίλον   1230
χρυσοῦ τ' ὄνησις οἴχεται παῖδές τε σοὶ
αὐτός τε πράσσεις ὧδε. σοὶ δ' ἐγὼ λέγω,
Ἀγάμεμνον· εἰ τῶιδ' ἀρκέσεις, κακὸς φανῆι·

14. Eur. *Andromache* 334–351 (§IIc)

   <   > (post 333)
τέθνηκα τῆι σῆι θυγατρὶ καί μ' ἀπώλεσεν·   334
μιαιφόνον μὲν οὐκέτ' ἂν φύγοι μύσος.   335
ἐν τοῖς δὲ πολλοῖς καὶ σὺ τόνδ' ἀγωνιῆι
φόνον· τὸ συνδρῶν γάρ σ' ἀναγκάσει χρέος.
ἢν δ' οὖν ἐγὼ μὲν μὴ θανεῖν ὑπεκδράμω,
τὸν παῖδά μου κτενεῖτε; κἆιτα πῶς πατὴρ
τέκνου θανόντος ῥαιδίως ἀνέξεται;   340
οὐχ ὧδ' ἄνανδρον αὐτὸν ἡ Τροία καλεῖ·
ἀλλ' εἶσιν οἷ χρή, Πηλέως γὰρ ἄξια
πατρός τ' Ἀχιλλέως ἔργα δρῶν φανήσεται,
ὤσει δὲ σὴν παῖδ' ἐκ δόμων· σὺ δ' ἐκδιδοὺς
ἄλλωι τί λέξεις; πότερον ὡς κακὸν πόσιν   345
φεύγει τὸ ταύτης σῶφρον; ἀλλ' οὐ πείσεται.
γαμεῖ δὲ τίς νιν; ἤ σφ' ἄνανδρον ἐν δόμοις
χήραν καθέξεις πολιόν; ὦ τλῆμον ἀνήρ,
κακῶν τοσούτων οὐχ ὁρᾶις ἐπιρροάς;
πόσας ἂν εὐνὰς θυγατέρ' ἠδικημένην   350
βούλοι' ἂν εὑρεῖν ἢ παθεῖν ἁγὼ λέγω;

[Kovacs deletes 330–351; Diggle 330–333 and supposes a lacuna after 333; Wilamowitz deletes 333]

D. Miscellaneous hypotheticals

15a. Eur. *Medea* 486–491 (see n. 41)

Πελίαν τ' ἀπέκτειν', ὥσπερ ἄλγιστον θανεῖν,
παίδων ὕπ' αὐτοῦ, πάντα τ' ἐξεῖλον δόμον.
καὶ ταῦθ' ὑφ' ἡμῶν, ὦ κάκιστ' ἀνδρῶν, παθὼν
προύδωκας ἡμᾶς, καινὰ δ' ἐκτήσω λέχη,
παίδων γεγώτων· εἰ γὰρ ἦσθ' ἄπαις ἔτι,   490
συγγνώστ' ἂν ἦν σοι τοῦδ' ἐρασθῆναι λέχους.

15b. Eur. *Medea* 586–587

> χρῆν σ', εἴπερ ἦσθα μὴ κακός, πείσαντά με
> γαμεῖν γάμον τόνδ', ἀλλὰ μὴ σιγῆι φίλων.

16. Soph. *OT* 851–854

> εἰ δ' οὖν τι κἀκτρέποιτο τοῦ πρόσθεν λόγου,
> οὔτοι ποτ', ὦναξ, τόν γε Λαΐου φόνον
> φανεῖ δικαίως ὀρθόν, ὅν γε Λοξίας
> διεῖπε χρῆναι παιδὸς ἐξ ἐμοῦ θανεῖν

E. Non-hypothetical variants

17. Eur. *Erectheus* fr. 360.32–41
Praxithea speaking; 'numbers matter' (see n. 41 in text)

> καὶ μὴν θανόντες γ' ἐν μάχῃ πολλῶν μέτα
> τύμβον τε κοινὸν ἔλαχον εὐκλειάν τ' ἴσην·
> τἠμῇ δὲ παιδὶ στέφανος εἷς μιᾷ μόνῃ
> πόλεως θανούσῃ τῆσδ' ὕπερ δοθήσεται,
> καὶ τὴν τεκοῦσαν καὶ σὲ δύο θ' ὁμοσπόρω
> σώσει· τί τούτων οὐχὶ δέξασθαι καλόν;
> τὴν οὐκ ἐμὴ <δὴ> πλὴν φύσει δώσω κόρην
> θῦσαι πρὸ γαίας. εἰ γὰρ αἱρεθήσεται
> πόλις, τί παίδων τῶν ἐμῶν μέτεστί μοι;
> οὔκουν ἅπαντα τοὖν γ' ἐμοὶ σωθήσεται;

18. Eur. *Heracleidae*, 398–419
A father who says 'no' (Demophon addressing Iolaus); the end of this speech is a 'numbers matter argument'

> καὶ τἀμὰ μέντοι πάντ' ἄραρ' ἤδη καλῶς·
> πόλις τ' ἐν ὅπλοις σφάγιά θ' ἠτοιμασμένα
> ἕστηκεν οἷς χρὴ ταῦτα τέμνεσθαι θεῶν,   400
> θυηπολεῖται δ' ἄστυ μάντεων ὕπο.
> χρησμῶν δ' ἀοιδοὺς πάντας εἰς ἓν ἁλίσας   403
> ἤλεγξα καὶ βέβηλα καὶ κεκρυμμένα
> [λόγια παλαιὰ τῇδε γῇ σωτήρια]·   405
> καὶ τῶν μὲν ἄλλων διάφορ' ἐστὶ θεσφάτοις
> πόλλ'· ἓν δὲ πᾶσι γνῶμα ταὐτὸν ἐμπρέπει·
> σφάξαι κελεύουσίν με παρθένον κόρῃ
> Δήμητρος, ἥτις ἐστὶ πατρὸς εὐγενοῦς,
> τροπαῖά τ' ἐχθρῶν καὶ πόλει σωτηρίαν.   402

```
ἐγὼ δ' ἔχω μέν, ὡς ὁρᾷς, προθυμίαν                410
τοσήνδ' ἐς ὑμᾶς· παῖδα δ' οὔτ' ἐμὴν κτενῶ
οὔτ' ἄλλον ἀστῶν τῶν ἐμῶν ἀναγκάσω
ἄκονθ'· ἑκὼν δὲ τίς κακῶς οὕτω φρονεῖ,
ἄκονθ'· ἑκὼν δὲ τίς κακῶς οὕτω φρονεῖ,
ὅστις τὰ φίλτατ' ἐκ χερῶν δώσει τέκνα;
καὶ νῦν πυκνὰς ἂν συστάσεις ἂν εἰσίδοις,         415
τῶν μὲν λεγόντων ὡς δίκαιος ἦ ξένοις
ἱκέταις ἀρήγειν, τῶν δὲ μωρίαν ἐμοῦ
κατηγορούντων· εἰ δὲ μὴ δράσω τόδε,
οἰκεῖος ἤδη πόλεμος ἐξαρτύεται.
```

19. Eur. *IA* 528–537

Agamemnon responds to Menelaus. The end of this speech is a 'numbers matter' argument.

```
οὔκουν δοκεῖς νιν στάντ' ἐν Ἀργείοις μέσοις
λέξειν ἃ Κάλχας θέσφατ' ἐξηγήσατο,
κἄμ' ὡς ὑπέστην θῦμα, κᾆτ' ἐψευδόμην
Ἀρτέμιδι θύσειν; οὐ ξυναρπάσας στρατόν,
σὲ κἄμ' ἀποκτείναντας Ἀργείους κόρην
σφάξαι κελεύσει; κἂν πρὸς Ἄργος ἐκφύγω,
ἐλθόντες αὐτοῖς τείχεσιν Κυκλωπίοις
ἀναρπάσουσι καὶ κατασκάψουσι γῆν.
τοιαῦτα τἀμὰ πήματ'· ὦ τάλας ἐγώ,
ὡς ἠπόρημαι πρὸς θεῶν τὰ νῦν τάδε.
```

20. Eur. *IA* 481–495

Menelaus addresses Agamemnon. His argument is a variant of the 'inappropriate sacrificial victim argument' as in Soph. *El.* 534–546 (cat. no. 1, hypothetical) and the similar argument in *Hec.* 258–70 (cat. no. 12). It also shares motifs with Soph. *Ant.* 905–912 and so also with Herodotus 3.119 (cat. no. 8a): Menelaus may marry again and have more children but it is unthinkable to lose a brother.

```
καί σοι παραινῶ μήτ' ἀποκτείνειν τέκνον
μήτ' ἀνθελέσθαι τοὐμόν· οὐ γὰρ ἔνδικον
σὲ μὲν στενάζειν, τἀμὰ δ' ἡδέως ἔχειν,
θνῄσκειν τε τοὺς σούς, τοὺς δ' ἐμοὺς ὁρᾶν φάος.
τί βούλομαι γάρ; οὐ γάμους ἐξαιρέτους         485
ἄλλους λάβοιμ' ἄν, εἰ γάμων ἱμείρομαι;
ἀλλ' ἀπολέσας ἀδελφόν, ὅν μ' ἥκιστ' ἐχρῆν,
Ἑλένην ἕλωμαι, τὸ κακὸν ἀντὶ τἀγαθοῦ;
ἄφρων νέος τ' ἦ, πρὶν τὰ πράγματ' ἐγγύθεν
σκοπῶν ἐσεῖδον οἷον ἦν κτείνειν τέκνα.       490
ἄλλως τέ μ' ἔλεος τῆς ταλαιπώρου κόρης
```

ἐσῆλθε, συγγένειαν ἐννοουμένωι,
ἢ τῶν ἐμῶν ἕκατι θύεσθαι γάμων
μέλλει. τί δ' Ἑλένης παρθένωι τῆι σῆι μέτα;
ἴτω στρατεία διαλυθεῖσ' ἐξ Αὐλίδος, 495

469–537, deleted by Kovacs: see *JHS* 123 (2003) 77–103; according to Diggle: *fortasse Euripidei* (see Kovacs ibid. App. B, p. 102)

Bibliography

Arnott, W.G. (ed.) (2000), *Menander*, III, Cambridge MA.
Bateman, J.J. (1962), 'Some Aspects of Lysias' Argumentation', in: *Phoenix* 16, 157–177.
Biles, Z.P. (2006–2007), 'Aeschylus' Afterlife Reperformance by Decree in 5th C. Athens?', in: *Illinois Classical Studies* 31–32, 206–241.
Burkert, W. (1974), 'Die Absurdität der Gewalt und das Ende der Tragödie: Euripides' *Orestes*', in: *Antike und Abendland* 20, 97–109.
Burnett, A.P. (1998), *Revenge in Attic and Later Tragedy*, Berkeley.
Burnett, A.P. (2014) 'The First Burial of Polyneices, "That Critical Chestnut"', in: *Phoenix* 68, 201–221.
Calder, W.M. III (1969), 'The date of Euripides' *Erechtheus*', in: *GRBS* 10, 147–56.
Chisolm, R.M. (1946), 'The Contrary-to-Fact Conditional', in: *Mind* 55, 289–307.
Clairmont, C.W. (1971), 'Euripides' *Erechtheus* and the Erechtheion', in: *GRBS* 12, 485–495.
Collard, C./Cropp, M./Lee, K.H. (eds.) (1995), *Euripides, Selected Fragmentary Plays*, I, Warminster.
Cropp, M. (1997) 'Antigone's Final Speech', in: *G&R* 44, 137–160.
Cropp, M./Fick, G. (1985), *Resolutions and Chronology in Euripides: The Fragmentary Tragedies*, Institute of Classical Studies Bulletin Supplement 43, London.
De Jong, I.J.F. (1987), *Narrators and Focalizers: The Presentation of the Story in the Iliad*, Amsterdam.
Denniston, J.D. (ed.) (1939), *Euripides, Electra*, Oxford.
Diggle, J. (1977), 'Notes on the *Electra* of Euripides', in: *Illinois Classical Studies* 2, 110–124.
Dillon, J./Gergel, T. (2003), *The Greek Sophists*, London.
Dover, K.J. (1950), 'The Chronology of Antiphon's Speeches', in: *CQ* 44, 44–60.
Due, B. (1980), *Antiphon. A Study in Argumentation*, Vol. 17 Supplementa Musei Tusculani, Copenhagen.
Euben, P. (1986), 'Political Corruption in Euripides' *Orestes*', in: P. Euben (ed.), *Greek Tragedy and Political Theory*, Berkeley, 222–251.
Flashar, H. (1997), 'Orest vor Gericht', in: W. Eder/K.-J. Hölkeskamp (eds.), *Verfassung im vorhellenistischen Griechenland*, Stuttgart, 99–111.
Flory, S. (1988), 'Thucydides' Hypotheses about the Peloponnesian War', in: *TAPA* 118, 43–56.
Funk, W.-P. (1985), 'On a Semantic Typology of Conditional Sentences', in: *Folia Linguistica* 19, 365–413.
Gagarin, M. (1981), *Drakon and Early Athenian Law*, New Haven.
Gagarin, M. (ed.) (1997), *Antiphon, The Speeches*, Cambridge.
Gagarin, M. (2002), *Antiphon the Athenian*, Austin.
Gagarin, M./MacDowell, D.M. (1998), *Antiphon and Andocides*, Austin.

Goodman, N. (1947), 'The Problem of Contrafactual Conditionals', in: *Journal of Philosophy* 44, 113–128.
Gould, J.P. (1978), 'Dramatic Character and "Human Intelligibility" in Greek Tragedy', in: *PCPS* 24, 43–67.
Hall, E. (1993), 'Political and Cosmic Turbulence in Euripides' Orestes', in: A.H. Sommerstein *et al.* (eds.), *Tragedy, Comedy, and the Polis*, Bari, 263–285.
Hansen, M.H. (1975), *Eisangelia. The Sovereignty of the People's Court on Athens in the Fourth Century BCE and the Impeachment of the Generals and Politicians*, Odense.
Heftner, H. (2005), 'Phrynichos Stratonidou Deiradiotes als Politiker und Symbolfigur der athenischen Oligarchen von 411 v. Chr.', in: U. Bultrighini (ed.), *Democrazia ed antidemocrazia nel mondo greco. Atti del Convegno internazionale di studi – Chieti, 9–11 aprile 2003*, Alessandria, 89–108.
Holzhausen, J. (2003), Euripides Politikos. Recht und Rache in 'Orestes' und 'Bakchen', in: *Beiträge zur Altertumskunde*, Munich.
Hornblower, S. (1994), 'Narratology and Narrative Techniques in Thucydides', in: S. Hornblower (ed.), *Greek Historiography*, Oxford, 131–166.
Hornblower, S. (1997), *A Commentary on Thucydides*, I, Oxford.
Hornblower, S. (2008), *A Commentary on Thucydides*, III, Oxford.
Jebb, R. (ed.) (1891), *Sophocles, Electra*, London.
Jebb, R. (ed.) (1900), *Sophocles, Antigone*, London.
Kovacs, D. (2003), 'Toward a Reconstruction of *Iphigenia Aulidensis*', in: *JHS* 123, 77–103.
Lambrinoudakis, V. *et al.* (eds.) (2016), *ΑΡΧΙΤΕΚΤΩΝ, Honorary Volume for Professor Manolis Korres*, Athens.
Lang, M. (1989), 'Unreal conditions in Homeric narrative', in: *GRBS* 30, 5–16.
Lewis, D.K. (1973), *Counterfactuals*, Cambridge MA.
Lloyd, Mi. (1992), *The Agon in Euripides*, Oxford.
Longo, O. (1975), 'Proposte di lettura per l'Oreste di Euripide', in: *Maia* 27, 265–287.
MacDowell, D.M. (2000), *Demosthenes On the False Embassy (Oration 19)*, Oxford.
Markantonatos, A. (2007), *Oedipus at Colonus: Sophocles, Athens, and the World*, Berlin/New York.
Matthaiou, A.P. (2016), 'Ὣς ἂν ὁ ἀρχιτέκτων κελεύῃι. Ο ΑΡΧΙΤΕΚΤΩΝ ΣΤΗΝ ΠΟΛΗ ΤΩΝ ΑΘΗΝΩΝ ΤΟΝ 5ο ΚΑΙ 4ο ΑΙ. π.Χ.', in: V. Lambrinoudakis *et al.* (eds.), *ΑΡΧΙΤΕΚΤΩΝ, Honorary Volume for Professor Manolis Korres*, Athens.
Michelini, A.N. (1988), *Euripides and the Tragic Tradition*, Madison.
Müller, C.W. (2000), 'Überlegungen zum zeitlichen Verhältnis der beiden Elektren', in: E. Stärk/G. Vogt-Spira (eds.), *Dramatische Wäldchen. Festschrift für Eckard Lefèvre*, Hildesheim, 37–45.
Mueller, M. (2016), *Objects as Actors. Props and the Poetics of Performance in Greek Tragedy*, Chicago.
Naiden, F.S. (2010), 'The Legal and Other Trials of Orestes', in: E.M. Harris/D. Leão/P.J. Rhodes (eds.), *Law and Drama in Ancient Greece*, London, 61–76.
Nervegna, S. (2014), 'Performing Classics: The Tragic Canon in the Fourth Century and Beyond', in: E. Csapo/H.R. Rupprecht/J.R. Green/P. Wilson (eds.), *Greek Theatre in the Fourth Century*, Berlin, 157–187.
Newiger, H.J. (1961), 'Elektra in Aristophanes Wolken', in: *Hermes* 89, 422–430.
Ostwald, M. (1969), *Nomos and the Beginnings of the Athenian Democracy*, Oxford.
Page, D.L. (1934), *Actors' Interpolations in Greek Tragedy*, Oxford.

Parker, R. (1983), *Miasma. Pollution and Purification in early Greek Religion*, Oxford.
Phillips, D.D. (2008), *Avengers of blood: Homicide in Athenian law and custom from Draco to Demosthenes*, Stuttgart.
Porter, J.R. (1994), *Studies in Euripides' Orestes*, Mnemosyne Suppl. 128, Leiden.
Roisman, H.M./Luschnig, C.A.E. (eds.) (2011), *Euripides' Electra*, Norman.
Rood, T. (1998), *Thucydides: Narrative and Explanation*, Oxford.
Sansone, D. (2012), *Greek Drama and the Invention of Rhetoric*, West Sussex.
Saxonhouse, A.W. (1992), *Fear of diversity: the birth of political science in ancient Greek thought*, Chicago.
Scafuro, A.C. (2009), 'Eudikos' Rider: *IG* I^3 38–47', in: A.A. Themos/N. Papazarkadas (eds.), *Attica Epigraphica: Studies in honour of Christian Habicht*, Athens, 47–66.
Schein, S.L. (1975), 'Mythical Illusion and historical reality in Euripides' Orestes', in: *Wiener Studien* 9, 49–66.
Scodel, R. (2012), 'Debating the past in Euripides' *Troades* and *Orestes* and in Sophocles' *Electra*', in: J. Marincola/L. Llewellyn-Jones/C. MacIver (eds.), *Greek notions of the past in the archaic and classical eras*, Edinburgh, 113–126.
Solmsen, F. (1975), *The Intellectual Experiment of the Greek Enlightenment*, Princeton.
Stevens, P.T. (ed.) (1971), *Euripides, Andromache*, Oxford.
Stroud, R.S. (1968), *Drakon's Law on Homicide*, Berkeley.
Todd, S.C. (2000), *Lysias*, Austin.
Tordoff, R. (2014) 'Counterfactual history and Thucydides', in: V. Wohl (ed.), *Probabilities, Hypotheticals, and Counterfactuals in Ancient Greek Thought*, Cambridge, 101–121.
Treu, M. (1971), 'Der Euripideische Erechtheus als Zeugnis seiner Zeit', in: *Chiron* 1, 115–131.
West, M.L. (ed.) (1987), *Euripides, Orestes*, Warminster.
West, M.L. (2007), 'A New Musical Papyrus: Carcinus, Medea', in: *ZPE* 161, 1–10.
West, S. (1999), 'Sophocles' Antigone and Herodotus Book 3', in: J. Griffin (ed.), *Sophocles Revisited: Essays Presented to Sir Hugh Lloyd-Jones*, Oxford, 91–136.
Wilamowitz-Moellendorff, U. von (1883), 'Die Beiden Elektren', in: *Hermes* 18, 214–263.
Wilamowitz-Moellendorff, U. von (ed.) (1889), *Euripides, Herakles*, Berlin.
Wilcox, S. (1938), *The Destructive Hypothetical Syllogism in Greek Logic and in Attic Oratory*, New Haven.
Willink, C.W. (ed.) (1986), *Euripides, Orestes*, Oxford.
Zeitlin, F. (1980), 'The Closet of Masks: Role-Playing and Mythmaking in the *Orestes* of Euripides', in: *Ramus* 9, 51–77.

Part II: **Politics, Rhetoric and Poetry**

Chris Carey
Drama and Democracy

This chapter looks at the institutional relationship between *bema* and *theatron*. A generation ago, in a world still heavily influenced by New Criticism, the question was lost in the long grass of outmoded scholarship. But in the wake of the New Historicism scholars have been much more sympathetic to the view that texts arise in and reflect their historical contexts, however much the reaction of the original audience may be overwritten by subsequent receptions. The last two decades have seen a renewed interest in the question of the degree to which, and the way in which, the Athenian theatre responds to its political environment.[1] This chapter does not take this debate in a new direction. With so much ink spilled, and trees felled already it cannot hope to. Rather it strives to clear some of the debris of contemporary debate and to arrive at an intelligent (I hope) synthesis between competing perspectives. Unlike most modern discussions, it also seeks to integrate both tragedy and comedy within a single synthesis. Though they reached the civic festivals at different times, tragedy and comedy inhabited the same (literal) performance and (metaphorical) political space. They evolved together and spoke to the same audiences. So, any discussion of the civic role of the theatre has to take account of both.

The world of Athenian tragedy is a remarkable fictional creation. It is (almost) invariably set in a world where the polis is ruled by a king. Yet for two hundred years or more democratic audiences sat and watched plays about kings. It is worth pausing for a moment to consider the scale of this over the period from the democratic reforms of Kleisthenes to the suppression of the democracy after the Lamian War. With three tragedies per poet per year the collective output amounts to almost 1800 plays performed over the lifetime of the democracy. And this is the figure only for the City Dionysia. We have no figure for the deme festivals where plays were performed or for the tragedies at the Lenaia; but the effect is to increase the number and stress further the paradox.

The paradox is reduced significantly when we take account of the iconic cultural status of epic and of the central role played by myth in almost all Greek poetry of any kind. There was no way of avoiding the heroic world and its political structures for anyone who wanted to write large scale poetic texts on serious

---
[1] Some of the more significant scholarship is signalled in the bibliography; I would especially single out the collection of essays edited by David Carter in 2011.

themes. But this easy route to dismissal is itself complicated by the cultural amalgam created by the tragic theatre.² For sometimes the kings inhabit a world very like that of the theatre audience. To take an obvious example, in Aischylos' *Suppliants* Danaos and his daughters arrive in Argos; they are running from Aigyptos and his sons, who wish to marry the girls against their will. The mytheme of the king receiving the exile is a typical epic motif. In Athens any decision to intervene in a foreign dispute would be referred to the Assembly. And sure enough the king in Aischylos refuses to take the responsibility for the decision; he requires the support of the people (365–369):

> Βα. οὔτοι κάθησθε δωμάτων ἐφέστιοι
> ἐμῶν. τὸ κοινὸν δ' εἰ μιαίνεται πόλις,
> ξυνῇ μελέσθω λαὸς ἐκπονεῖν ἄκη.
> ἐγὼ δ' ἂν οὐ κραίνοιμ' ὑπόσχεσιν πάρος,
> ἀστοῖς δὲ πᾶσι τῶνδε κοινώσας πέρι.

> You are not suppliants at a hearth
> of mine. If the city is publicly stained,
> let for the people together contrive to work a cure.
> I would make no promise until
> I have conferred with the citizens about this matter.

The examples could be multiplied.³ This rapprochement between the heroic world and contemporary Athens extends to the incorporation of political prac-

---

2 On this see in brief Carey 2003.
3 Closest is Euripides *Suppl.* 349–358:

> δόξαι δὲ χρῄζω καὶ πόλει πάσῃ τόδε,
> δόξει δ' ἐμοῦ θέλοντος· ἀλλὰ τοῦ λόγου
> προσδοὺς ἔχοιμ' ἂν δῆμον εὐμενέστερον.
> καὶ γὰρ κατέστησ' αὐτὸν ἐς μοναρχίαν
> ἐλευθερώσας τήνδ' ἰσόψηφον πόλιν.
> λαβὼν δ' Ἄδραστον δεῖγμα τῶν ἐμῶν λόγων
> ἐς πλῆθος ἀστῶν εἶμι· καὶ πείσας τάδε,
> λεκτοὺς ἀθροίσας δεῦρ' Ἀθηναίων κόρους
> ἥξω·

> I want the whole city to decide for this,
> and decide it will if I wish it. But by giving chance to speak
> I should have the demos more favourable.
> For I set them up as monarch,

tices familiar to the fifth century audience, such as the refusal of burial to Polyneikes as a traitor in Sophokles' *Antigone*, which (though the denial of proper funeral rites as a mode of punishment has epic antecedents)[4] is very close to Athenian punishment for those guilty of *prodosia*.[5]

Anachronism is inescapable in any creative literature which deals with the past. Sometimes it is unconscious, sometimes it is designed to remove inexplicable features and bring the play closer to its audience, sometimes it is both (like the notorious striking clock in *Julius Caesar*).[6] What continues to fascinate about the anachronisms in the theatre of Dionysos is the recurrent contemporary political colouring in a theatre dominated by alien political structures at a festival sponsored by the democratic polis. Inevitably it raises the question: what did they think they were doing?

One answer is to reject outright the contemporary political dimension of the theatre. This is (to a large extent) the line taken by Jasper Griffin,[7] who insists that tragedy like epic is interested not just in the politics of the moment but in enduring ideas and experience. Essentially this is the concept of the timelessness of the classic. It is a view with much to recommend it. Greek theatre clearly does have an appeal beyond the time and place of its first production; or we would not be reading it now. And this must in part be due to its ability to distil recurrent human experience with an extreme clarity. The problem is that the Athenian theatre does – sometimes – address issues specific to Athens and Athenian democracy. It is also true that the festivals (and probably the tragic performances) were not created by the democracy but in the sixth century, under the tyrants.[8] The point is worth making, since it reminds us that there is nothing inherently democratic about drama as a vehicle. Certainly, it allows different voices to be heard and

---

setting free this city under equal vote.
Taking Adrastos as proof of my words
I shall face the mass of citizens. And persuading them to this
I'll gather here the Athenian youth
and set out.

4 *Little Iliad* fr.3 Bernabé.
5 Briefly Carey 2003, 499.
6 Act II scene 1:
BRUTUS
Peace! Count the clock.
CASSIUS
The clock hath stricken three.
7 Griffin 1998, especially 59–60.
8 See on this Rhodes 2003, 106–107.

opens up issues to debate. But drama has flourished in many regimes which have no relation to democracy. Shakespeare's England for instance was an oppressive place; yet it produced both tragedy and comedy. And the theatre flourished, despite intermittent attacks from the authorities. Most relevant to our purpose is the active theatrical culture in Sicily, where the tyrants actively encouraged the theatre.[9] Drama always or almost always requires us to question; but the questions can vary from culture to culture and there is nothing inherently democratic (in the constitutional sense) about drama as a vehicle. But the argument from origin is not a powerful objection; since civic institutions can change as their context changes, the date of the founding of the festival is of little relevance to its function under the democracy.

But this does not take us very far. We are still left then with the question: *how* does the theatre relate to Athenian democracy?

One recent view is that the theatre is potentially at odds with the emerging democracy. The theatre audience is more conservative and so are the plays, which must appeal to this audience. The argument rests on the date of the theoric fund, which doled out money to citizens to defray the costs of theatre attendance.[10] We have no evidence that the fund existed before the end of the fifth century and it may be even later. Without the theoric fund there was no free admission to the theatre in the fifth century. So (the argument goes) the audience of tragedy are people who can pay. But it has also been noted that we do not know whether there was a charge for admission in the fifth century or what it might have been.[11] And even if we knew that the ticket price was high, with an annual festival it is entirely possible that people would save for the event. This festival was so important that the Athenians let people out of prison to attend.[12] But the composition of the audience is actually a problem for this view from another di-

---

9 For the theatre in the west, see in general the recent collection edited by Bosher 2012, and for the engagement of Athenian tragedians with non-democratic regimes, see Duncan 2011.
10 See on this Sommerstein 1997, 65–73.
11 Rhodes 2003, 111.
12 Dem. 22.68 with scholion.

rection. The recurrent figure we are offered (at least in the fourth century) for citizens rich enough to sustain the liturgy system is 1200.[13] Recent research has argued down the size of the theatre audience.[14] But we are still offered a figure of perhaps 6,000, possibly even 8,000. Unless we suppose that the audience was made up entirely of the small elite and the hoplite class together with some rich metics, this cannot be an elite group. It would also be quite remarkable for the democracy to lavish so much resource on a festival which ultimately benefited only the better off. This was of course the money of the rich through the liturgy system. But this was still money which could have been spent on other civic needs, either religious or military.

The opposite (and more influential) approach has been essentially to institutionalize the theatre. That is, to make the theatre a formal tool of the democracy by placing emphasis on the links to democratic structures, processes and personnel. This view rests on the highly political nature of some aspects of the dramatic festival context. Some of these features are inescapable. The Great Dionysia took place in spring when the seas were open; and there were many foreigners in the audience. The Athenians used the event to display the power and wealth of Athens to the Greek world. Visiting dignitaries were given seats of honour and Athenian politicians could be rewarded with front row seats for their service. In the fifth century (we're told) the Athenians displayed the tribute from their empire in the theatre.[15] It was the Athenian practice to bring up the orphans of men who died for the city at public expense. When they reached the age of eighteen, they paraded in the theatre in full armour before the Athenian people.[16] The theatre was also used to proclaim honours to benefactors of Athens.[17] This both offered a role model for those living in Athens and dramatized to the Greek world the readiness of the city to reward those who served it well. The dramatic performances are themselves largely funded by the liturgy system imposed by the democracy on members of the wealthy elite. More recently Peter Wilson has emphasized the very high participation ratio of choral activity at the Dionysia in Athens (as indeed in all Athenian choral competitions) in contrast for instance to oligarchic

---

13 The figure represents the recurrent arithmetic with reference to the *symmoriai* in fourth century sources, for which see Hansen 1991, 113–115. We cannot assume a static figure from the fifth century to the fourth, but it is difficult to believe that the number of the richest members of society was wildly different for the fifth century.
14 E.g. Goette 2007; Roselli 2011, 65; Tordoff 2013, 38. Given the cyclic nature of scholarship we can expect the figure to rise again.
15 Isokrates 8.82.
16 Aischines 3.154.
17 For the case for the origin of this practice in the fifth century, see Wilson 2011, 31.

Thebes.[18] One detail much cited in this context is the role of the generals in controlling the vote in the City Dionysia to prevent favouritism.[19] Almost all of this is inescapably true. However, recent research, especially the work of Peter Rhodes, makes a good case against the specifically democratic nature of some aspects at least of the organization of the dramatic festivals. Rhodes has pointed out that the liturgy system is not unique to Athens.[20] Our source for the involvement of the generals notes that the generals performed libations at the Dionysia. But in a culture (such as that throughout Greece) where the secular and the sacred were enmeshed, Rhodes is right to note that the generals could theoretically perform ritual acts in any polis where the role of general was an official position.[21] The involvement of the generals in the judging process was according to our source a single unique event, not part of the regular functioning of the festival. It has been suggested in favour of a theatre which is seen as exclusively democratic that the tragic chorus was formed of ephebes.[22] The evidence for this is thin. But even if one accepts all the evidence for the specifically democratic context of the theatrical performances, and some of it is very strong, all that this creates is an environment potentially friendly to the presence of democratic ideas and structures, not evidence for a systemic or systematic engagement at the level of content.

There are also problems when one looks at the internal evidence. If we tie tragedy too closely with politics, we miss the fact that many tragedies have no pronounced or even obvious political dimension. We lose the distinction between a play like Aischylos' *Eumenides*, which is deeply interested in questions of civic justice and stability at an institutional level, and a play like Euripides' *Medea*, which is not primarily interested in the organization of the state or the pursuit of state policy. So at most we can only argue that tragedy is intermittently political. We also have to beware of taking too Athenocentric an approach, when its festival points outward. The presentation of tragedy to a panhellenic audience was part of Athens' claim to be the cultural centre of Greece. As a gesture of cultural hegemony, it was remarkably successful from very early on. When Hieron the tyrant of Syracuse founded his new city of Etna in the 470s, he invited Aischylos to produce a play, possibly a trilogy, to commemorate the event. Greeks in the west

---

[18] Wilson 2011, 21–26.
[19] Plutarch *Kimon* 8.7–9; see on this Goldhill 2000, 44.
[20] Rhodes 2003, 108.
[21] Rhodes 2003, 112.
[22] Winkler 1990.

were aware of the new literary form created in Athens, and it was considered distinctive enough to add lustre to Hieron's ceremonials.[23] At the end of the fifth century we find Euripides and Agathon producing plays in Macedonia. Euripides' play for Macedon, the *Archelaos*, proved a classic and was revived in the following century. Athenian tragedy had high status as a marker of taste and culture. This immediate reception places tragedy from the start in a tradition directly in line with Homer and lyric. From Homer onward, as Gregory Nagy has stressed, poetic success depends on panhellenic acceptance.[24] This applies to Athenian tragedy also. The festival with its panhellenic audience encouraged tragedy to face outward as well as inward; and the readiness of other Greeks to import Athenian tragedy shows that tragedy could speak to Greece and not just to Athens.

But there is also a danger in dismissing too easily the interest of tragedy in issues facing democratic Athens in particular. It is true that many of the issues in tragedy are shared by democratic Athens with the various non-democratic states. But the scale and complexity of state control at Athens were probably unusual even by the standards of Greek democracies. In the case of *Antigone* scholars have stressed that some of the features of death and burial (specifically the apparent state hostility to private funeral display) which appear at first sight to be peculiar to fifth century Athens are in fact part of a larger Greek pattern. But it remains the case that as far as we know Athens appropriated the war dead to a degree unmatched by any other Greek state. It was the Athenian practice to bury the war dead in communal state graves (excavations for the Athens metro unearthed one such burial a few years ago) without patronymic or demotic, just the tribe name. At the same time private memorials almost disappear from the Kerameikos. By the late fifth century the private memorials, including memorials for those who die in war, become more common, and it looks as though the tensions between the demands of the state and the needs of the family have been resolved. Issues such as family or individual versus state are Greek issues as well as Athenian issues. But they were probably present in Athens to an unusual degree and were at their most visible at the time *Antigone* was (probably) performed.

The cases can be multiplied. I start with the *Orestes* of Euripides. The messenger speech provides an account of the trial of Orestes which like the *Eumenides* of Aischylos puts the emphasis on the political aspect of the administration

---

23 We should perhaps not put too much weight (though in an early version of this paper I did) on Plutarch's claim that after the failure of the Athenian attack on Syracuse in 413 some Athenian prisoners were liberated because of their knowledge of Euripides' songs (*Life* of Nicias, 29.2–3).
24 See especially Nagy 1979, 7ff. and 1990, 70ff.

of justice. He describes a trial which resembles a meeting of the assembly at Argos. Though the speaker is biased in Orestes' favour, at this stage in the play he is our only source, and nothing is said to contradict his version. The conduct of the assembly does not present democracy in a good light. The debate is eventually won by a ranting speaker who resembles the demagogue as presented by comedy (*Orestes* 943–945):

> ἀλλ' οὐκ ἔπειθ' ὅμιλον, εὖ δοκῶν λέγειν.
> νικᾷ δ' ἐκεῖνος ὁ κακὸς ἐν πλήθει λέγων,
> ὃς ἠγόρευσε σύγγονον σέ τε κτανεῖν.
> Yet he did not persuade the assembly, though he seemed to speak sense.
> But that rogue won the day speaking to the mob,
> the one who argued for slaying you and your brother.

Democratic debate is presented as open to abuse.

My second example is Euripides' *Trojan Women*, produced in 415, the year after the Athenian suppression of Melos. Melos was the latest in a string of ruthless Athenian actions against resistance from those they regarded as subjects. Skione and Torone had received the same treatment in 421.[25] These too formed part of the experience of members of the audience. For an audience many of whom will have been involved in the decisions, and some of whom will have done the killing, the connection between *Trojan Women* and Melos must have been an inviting one. And the invitation to look at the suffering of war through the eyes of the victims may (for those who made the link) have been uncomfortable. This is of course inference from chronology. It is an inference which has been both asserted and contested. But right or wrong it is not *just* chronological inference. When the Athenians drew back from the prospect of killing the adult male population of Mytilene and enslaving the women and children, the force sent to prevent the slaughter hastened on their way, while those charged with the massacre moved slowly because they found their task distasteful (Thuc. 3.49.4):[26]

> κατὰ τύχην δὲ πνεύματος οὐδενὸς ἐναντιωθέντος καὶ τῆς μὲν προτέρας νεὼς οὐ σπουδῇ πλεούσης ἐπὶ πρᾶγμα ἀλλόκοτον, ταύτης δὲ τοιούτῳ τρόπῳ ἐπειγομένης, ἡ μὲν ἔφθασε τοσοῦτον ὅσον Πάχητα ἀνεγνωκέναι τὸ ψήφισμα καὶ μέλλειν δράσειν τὰ δεδογμένα, ἡ δ' ὑστέρα αὐτῆς ἐπικατάγεται καὶ διεκώλυσε μὴ διαφθεῖραι.

---

[25] Thuc. 5.3, 5.32
[26] The troops sent to massacre the Mytilenaeans would have understood Zorbas: 'There was a time when I used to say: that man's a Turk, or a Bulgar, or a Greek. I've done things for my country that would make your hair stand on end, boss. I've cut people's throats, burned villages, robbed and raped women, wiped out entire families. Why? Because they were Bulgars, or Turks'.

> As it happened there was no opposing wind and since the earlier ship was sailing without enthusiasm on is distasteful mission and this one was hastening in the manner described, the first ship arrived ahead only so far that Paches had read the decree [authorizing the killing] and was about to carry out the decision, and the second ship put in just after it and prevented the slaughter.

As noted above, the Athenians had slaughtered and enslaved in the recent past. But it cannot have been any easier to massacre men and force women and children into slavery in 415 than it had been twelve years ago at Mytilene.

This takes me back to the question of the Athenian-ness of tragedy. The Spartans committed atrocities. So did the Thebans. Problems of conflicting responsibilities such as the experience of Neoptolemos in *Philoktetes* were not just Athenian. They are part of war and part of politics throughout time. But there is no other art form in any other culture in archaic or classical or Hellenistic Greece which explores social and political issues as problems before a mass audience. Where lyric deals with political issues, it is most often in the context of the symposion in the company of like-minded members of the elite. The big public lyric compositions for cult occasions or for the celebration athletic victory do not open up political questions to debate but close them off. The *status quo* is assumed to be the norm and the patrons of Pindar and Bakchylides found their political prejudices comfortably reinforced, not challenged. The songs may allude to problems, but they invariably place these problems in the city's past. They do raise profound questions about human life; but they do not question policy or structure. Some of the voices which we hear in tragedy are highly critical of democracy. And not all of the criticisms can be dismissed. The caricature demagogue who speaks for the execution of Orestes in Euripides' play is a type familiar from comedy (*Orestes* 902ff.):

> κἀπὶ τῷδ' ἀνίσταται
> ἀνήρ τις ἀθυρόγλωσσος, ἰσχύων θράσει·
> Ἀργεῖος οὐκ Ἀργεῖος, ἠναγκασμένος,
> θορύβῳ τε πίσυνος κἀμαθεῖ παρρησίᾳ,
> πιθανὸς ἔτ' αὐτοὺς περιβαλεῖν κακῷ τινι.
> ὅταν γὰρ ἡδύς τις λόγοις φρονῶν κακῶς
> πείθῃ τὸ πλῆθος, τῇ πόλει κακὸν μέγα·

> Next there rose a man
> with tongue without control, his power in impudence,
> an Argive, yet no Argive, who had forced his way in,
> putting his confidence in bluster and ignorant outspokenness,
> still persuasive enough to lead his hearers into mischief.
> For when a pleasing speaker with bad intent
> persuades the people, this is a great bane for the city.

Whatever view we take of this as a description of problems faced by Athenian democracy, the Athenians themselves would recognize the analysis, since it finds echoes both in comedy and in Thucydides.[27]

Here however we have to pause. The mythic content of tragedy means that even when tragedy comes closest to talking about Athenian experience, it is never about Athens in any literal senses. In *Orestes* we are in Argos, not Athens, even if the procedures are unambiguously Athenian; it is mythic Argos. This is an obstacle for any attempt to look for allegories; it is also a problem for any attempt to focus exclusively on the local political role of tragedy. Goldhill suggests (drawing on the work of Vidal-Naquet) that Sophokles' *Philoktetes* draws on the ritual of the Athenian ephebeia to explore problems of conflicting duty and responsibility.[28] The play may indeed suggest the ephebeia to some, perhaps many, members of the audience. But the *Philoktetes* is not about the ephebeia. The issues it raises about duty to friend and duty to principle and self as against perceived duty to country or about both the potential and the limitations of Realpolitik go far beyond a single civic institution. It has been suggested – plausibly – that Euripides' *Orestes* (produced in 408), a play in which friends band together to commit violence, was influenced by the oligarchic coup of 411, which rose out of the aristocratic clubs.[29] But the play is not about the revolution. A direct and unequivocal link between events and structures in the theatrical context and those in the theatre is always just out of reach.

It is also important to bear in mind that where it does address contemporary concerns, the theatre is not telling the Athenians anything new. I return to *Trojan Women*. Thucydides' account of Melos gives us the impression that what we see at Melos is unanimous Athenian action.[30] But the insights we get into decision making at Athens make it unlikely that any debate in the Athenian assembly was ever completely uncontentious. And Thucydides' account of the Mitylenaean debate of 427 suggests both that those proposing extreme measure will have had to persuade the demos and that there will have been alternative views, even if these were minority views. Athenian imperialism too was hotly debated, within Athens as well as outside. This is important, for it means that an audience watching *Trojan Women* in 415 will have fresh memories of animated discussion of precisely these issues. And as noted above the unscrupulous demagogue whom we meet

---

[27] Thuc. 2.65, 3.36.6, 4.21–22 (also 6.35–41). Aristophanes *Knights passim*, *Wasps* 1029–1037, *Peace* 752–760, *Ath.Pol.* 28.3.
[28] Goldhill 1987, 73 and 1990, 122.
[29] Hall 1993, 269–271.
[30] Thuc. 5.116.3–4.

in *Orestes* is not an unfamiliar figure. He is a bugbear whom we meet already in the fifth century in the Assembly in Thucydides. And he populates whole comic plays (Aristophanes' *Knights*, Eupolis' *Marikas*, Plato's *Kleophon*). These are shared concerns and they lie behind the clause in the law of eisangelia which applied to politicians who deceive the demos. The description of him (if we accept the MSS text) as a Mycenaean but not a Mycenaean reflects the endless charges of alien birth which were hurled at political opponents at political trials and echoed in the comic theatre.

No discussion of the politics of the Athenian theatre can be complete without comedy, to which I now turn briefly. In an interesting article some years ago Oliver Taplin explored the contrasting profiles of tragic and comic theatre as genres which perform distinct and complementary roles.[31] He rather overstates the firmness of the boundaries between the genres. But the position is broadly sound, and it is especially visible in the case of politics. Where tragedy relocates political issues to a mythic time and often (as scholars have emphasized) to other cities than Athens,[32] comedy is decidedly Athenocentric throughout its history. It can take its audience to Olympos or to the Underworld but the vast majority of plots are set in Athens. Athenian locations, institutions, personalities and events are a constant presence. This was probably also the case in the lost mythic comedies, where contemporary events either lurked very visible behind the literal events of the plot, as with Kratinos' lost play *Dionysalexandros*, or as passing mentions, as for instance in his *Seriphians*. This is always recognizably Athens, and Athens as we know it. And the issues which form the basis of the play are almost always large issues of public concern. This is a persistent feature of comedy throughout the history of the democracy, though the focus on the polis diminishes radically during the fourth century. In fifth century comedy the polis is almost always an important part of the plot in one way or another, and often the big contemporary political issues form the stimulus for the plot, the empire (*Babylonians*), the war (Kratinos' *Dionysalexandros*, Aristophanes' *Peace* – two plays of this name – *Lysistrata*, *Acharnians*), the quality of political leadership (Telekleides, Aristophanes' *Knights*, Eupolis' *Marikas* on Hyperbolos, the *Kleophon* of the comic poet Plato). Comedy too deals in myths, in two ways. Firstly, as satire should, it turns

---

31 Taplin 1996.
32 The classic discussion is Zeitlin 1986–1990, who views Thebes as the negative counter-image of Athens. The view has been much criticized and is highly schematic. But there is a pronounced if not uniform tendency in the tragic theatre to locate mythic crises in other Greek cities (though not exclusively Thebes) and to present Athens in ways which bear a striking resemblance to the eulogistic ideological statements of the *epitaphios logos*.

the world of Athens into a grotesque parody of itself. All politicians are corrupt and sexually deviant. The people are stupid. The Assembly is torpid and ineffectual. The courts are a place where the judges instead of giving justice indulge their worst instincts while the politicians enjoy the income from the empire. Secondly it generates large impossible narrative structures which allow ordinary Athenians to put the world right by performing superhuman acts of comic heroism. But it still stays within the political world of classical Athens. And sometimes it lectures its audience on political issues, as with Aristophanes' plea for a degree of political reconciliation in the *Frogs*.

Comedy is not of course unique to Athens. At the same time as comedy was finding a place in the Athenian civic festivals Epicharmos was active in Sicily, probably working under the tyrants. It is striking however how little evidence one can find for political themes or allusions in his fragments. Comedy also has antecedents in archaic iambos, where personal attack is one of the staple themes. But these are personal attacks. For all we know they may be grounded in political as well as personal hostility. But they remain personal. This capacity to debate contemporary political issues and criticize both the masses and the active politicians directly is at this date peculiar to Athenian comedy. And we know that this is conscious policy by the democracy, precisely because of the exceptions. An ancient note on Aristophanes' *Acharnians* suggests that around 441 BCE the Athenians banned the satirizing of individuals by name;[33] if true, and it probably is, this may be connected with the revolt of Samos, which profoundly shook the confidence of an Athens which had been expanding its power for a generation. We also have evidence for a decree by a man named Syrakosios which limited comic freedom in 415. This one is less certain, and some scholars would dismiss it altogether.[34] But even if we accept both, the rarity of such intervention points to a reluctance to intervene in the freedom of the theatre. A tragic dramatist might be taking a risk if he brought the play too close to contemporary reality (this is a grumble against Euripides which we find echoed in Aristophanes). And a comic playwright was taking a risk if he annoyed his audience too much (this may be part of the reason for the change in the treatment of the Demos in *Knights*). But what he risked was losing, if the audience didn't like the play, not prosecution or punishment. With tragedy we have the case of Phrynichos, who was fined for his *Capture of Miletos* not long after the collapse of the Ionian revolt, which distressed the Athenians by reminding them of a painful failure, but that is a specific

---

33 Schol. on Aristophanes' *Acharnians* 67.
34 Discussion in Halliwell 1991, 59–63.

and isolated example.³⁵ We never hear of another. And we know that Kleon prosecuted Aristophanes for insulting the people in front of foreigners with his treatment of the empire in *Babylonians* in 426.³⁶ But Kleon lost and Aristophanes after pretending to be scared in *Acharnians* in 425 returned to attack Kleon mercilessly in *Knights* in 424. Contrast here the British stage, where until 1968 the Lord Chamberlain could prevent a play from being staged – and in fact (as Fiona MacIntosh has discussed at some length) Sophokles' *OT* fell victim to this power in the late nineteenth and early twentieth centuries.³⁷

This disinclination to control makes sense when we reflect that criticism of aspects of the democracy in public discourse is part of Athenian democratic culture. As I have argued elsewhere, comedy in some respects departs from every model we have of Greek choral voice.³⁸ The disgruntlement which we get in the comic parabases sets the chorus against the polis in a way which we find in no other Greek choral medium. But though it may be out of step with Greek choral culture outside Athens, it is not out of step with other Athenian voices. The same is true of the poet's own voice, which readily upbraids the audience for their political failures. This agrees with the tone adopted by public speakers facing the demos either in court or in the Assembly. Thucydides complains that the successors to Perikles were subservient to the demos, where he controlled it.³⁹ He is wrong; successful politicians were always, before and after Perikles, happy to confront the demos. And specific complaints in comedy find echoes in oratory. The argument of Bdelykleon in *Wasps* for instance that politics is controlled by a clique who enjoy all the benefits of power while treating the masses as a pet find echoes throughout surviving fourth century oratory.⁴⁰ The fact that discordant views are aired in the comic and tragic theatre is itself a useful indicator of the nature of democratic politics, a register of the openness of debate.

It is time to wrap up. In looking at the relationship between the theatre and the bema it is important to bear in mind the vagueness of its link to other political structures such as the assembly. Any attempts to institutionalize the theatre in a very specific way are unhelpful. The theatre and the *Ekklesia* are civic institutions. But they are complementary. They function in different ways and are doing very different jobs. Though the festivals were governed by legislation, and paid

---

35 Herodotos 6.21.2.
36 Aristophanes' *Acharnians* 377–382, 502–503.
37 See MacIntosh 1997, 295–298.
38 Carey 2013.
39 Thuc. 2.65.10.
40 See on this Carey 2016.

for by the state, the theatre had no formal function beyond the worship of the god of the festival. Beyond that everything is undefined except (and significantly) by shared experience and expectations. The result is that for both comic and tragic drama the relationship between theatre and politics was open to renegotiation play by play. This is important in itself at a very basic level. Discussions of theatre and democracy tend to create monoliths, like most searches for a single model. But in the fifth century alone we have to reckon with about 900 tragic plays by perhaps 50 dramatists all competing against each other (not to mention satyr plays). It would be wildly optimistic to imagine that a single frame will contain all of this. All Greek plays are ultimately 'political' (*politikos*) in the sense that they are about life in the polis.[41] But in the case of tragedy not all plays are interested in issues of political structure or policy. And even comedy in the period of its most intense political engagement in the fifth century differs in the degree of its engagement with political structures and policy. So, the theatre overlaps with but is not co-extensive with the Assembly in interest. The Assembly when it met had an agenda prepared by the Council of 500. Each item required a decision. The audiences were different even if they overlapped (up 6,000 in the assembly, all male citizens, perhaps 7–8,000 in the theatre on current estimates, including metics and visiting foreigners, even without the question of women). And the Assembly had hard decisions to reach about real events; war, peace and alliance were not abstract but concrete and specific issues. The theatre only had to judge the best plays and even then the audience exercised only an indirect influence on the judges by their vocal response to what they saw and heard.[42] Politicians and comic poets can complain about the quality of current leadership and the nature of current political debate. But the demos still had to choose in the Assembly between the politicians currently active. And they needed realistic proposals to respond to. This dichotomy is a partial explanation for a fact which is often cited. In 424 the Athenians in the theatre gave first prize to Aristophanes for a savage attack on Kleon in *Knights*. Yet within weeks they elected Kleon general. This looseness of relationship is what allowed the theatre to look beyond specific events at larger issues which are more difficult to address in everyday situations. It created space for reflection and even anxiety, about demographic changes in the leadership, about political style, about duty to the polis and its limits. There is no need to find solutions. The problems are what matter. It is worth here noting how remote even comedy is in this respect from practical politics. It can draw

---

[41] Thus Rhodes 2003 and before him Macleod 1982, 132.
[42] The difference is well articulated by Heath 2011, 166–168.

attention to the offensive way in which people like Kleon conduct the city's business. It can grumble about the war and even pine for peace. But its solutions are always, and are meant to be, fantastic. Comedy very rarely offers anything remotely resembling practical advice and almost never on contentious issues. Where it does, the advice is usually inoffensive and non-partisan. The parabasis of *Knights* invites the Athenians to judge the cavalry less harshly after its excellent military service the previous year. The parabasis of *Wasps* invites the Athenians to use jury service as a kind of pension for past military service. The parabasis of *Acharnians* proposes that the age of prosecutor and defendant in court should match. How this is meant to be effected is never clear and some of it looks impractical. Only in *Frogs* does the parabasis grasp a nettle, in arguing for a limited amnesty for some of those caught up in the oligarchic movement of 411.[43] Otherwise for the most part comedy is about what is wrong, not about how to put things right.

We are left with overlapping ways of doing politics. The Pnyx and the courts share themes, values and concerns with the theatre.[44] And tragedy and comedy complement the Pnyx and the courts by offering additional space for political thinking, while tragedy and comedy complement each other not just by the different tone and register but also by working at different degrees of remove from practical politics. It is unlikely that any Athenian would have formulated it in this way. But that may not matter.

Bibliography

Bosher, K. (ed.) (2012), *Theater outside Athens: drama in Greek Sicily and South Italy*, Cambridge/New York.
Carey, C. (1994), 'Comic ridicule and democracy', in: R.G. Osborne/S. Hornblower (eds.), *Ritual, Finance, Politics*, Oxford, 71–83.
Carey, C. (2003), 'The political world of Homer and tragedy', in: *Aevum Antiquum* 3, 463–484.
Carey, C. (2013), 'Comedy and the civic chorus', in: E. Bakola/L. Prauscello/M. Telò (eds.), *Comic Interactions*, Cambridge, 155–174.

---

[43] The potentially contentious nature of the proposal is mirrored in the cautious presentation of the beneficiaries of the proposal as those 'tripped by Phrynichos' wrestling tricks' (*Frogs* 689), which explicitly excludes the ringleaders and there is no word about recalling the exiles.
[44] More accurately they *can* share themes, values and concerns with the theatre. Again we must resist the temptation to view any of these institutions as a monolith, especially the theatre, where individual writers are free to engage or not with contemporary political issues, and (where they do engage) to engage to varying degrees and in varying ways not merely from author to author but from play to play within the corpus of any individual author.

Carey, C. (2016), 'Bashing the establishment', in: E. Sanders/M. Johncock (eds.), *Emotion and persuasion in classical antiquity*, Stuttgart, 27–39.

Carter, D. (ed.) (2011), *Why Athens? A reappraisal of tragic politics*, Oxford.

Duncan, A. (2011), 'Nothing to do with Athens? Tragedians at the court of tyrants', in: D. Carter (ed.), *Why Athens? A reappraisal of tragic politics*, Oxford, 69–84.

Goette, H.R. (2007), 'An archaeological appendix', in: P. Wilson (ed.), *The Greek theatre and festivals: Documentary studies*, Oxford, 116–121.

Goldhill, S. (1987–1990), 'The Great Dionysia and civic ideology', in: *JHS* 107, 58–76, and in: J. Winckler/F. Zeitlin (eds.), *Nothing to do with Dionysos?*, Princeton.

Goldhill, S. (2000), 'Civic ideology and the problem of difference: the politics of Aeschylean tragedy, once again', in: *JHS* 120, 34–56.

Griffin, J. (1998), 'The social function of Attic tragedy', in: *CQ* 48, 39–61.

Hall, E. (1993), 'Political and cosmic turbulence in Euripides' *Orestes*', in: A. Sommerstein/ S. Halliwell/J. Henderson/B. Zimmermann (eds.), *Tragedy, comedy and the polis*, Bari, 263–285.

Halliwell, S. (1991), 'Comic satire and freedom of speech in classical Athens', in: *JHS* 111, 48–70.

Hansen, M. (1991), *The Athenian democracy in the age of Demosthenes*, Oxford/Cambridge MA.

Heath, M. (2011), 'Response to Burian, Hesk and Barker', in: D. Carter (ed.), *Why Athens? A reappraisal of tragic politics*, Oxford, 163–171.

MacIntosh, F. (1997), 'Tragedy in performance: nineteenth and twentieth century productions', in: P.E. Easterling (ed.) *The Cambridge companion to Greek tragedy*, Cambridge, 284–323.

Macleod, C. (1982), 'Politics and the Oresteia', in: *JHS* 102, 124–144.

Nagy, G. (1979), *The Best of the Achaeans*, Baltimore.

Nagy, G. (1990), *Pindar's Homer*, Baltimore.

Rhodes, P.J. (2003), 'Nothing to do with democracy: Athenian drama and the polis', in: *JHS* 123, 104–119.

Roselli, D.K. (2011), *Theater of the People: Spectators and Society in Ancient Athens*, Austin.

Sommerstein, A.H. (1997), 'The theatre audience, the demos, and the *Suppliants* of Aeschylus', in: C.B.R. Pelling (ed.), *Greek tragedy and the historian*, Oxford, 63–80.

Taplin, O. (1996), 'Fifth-century tragedy and comedy: a synkrisis', in: *JHS* 106, 163–174.

Tordoff, R. (2013), 'Introduction: slaves and slavery in ancient Greek comedy', in: B. Askrigg/ R. Tordoff (eds.), *Slaves and slavery in Ancient Greek comic drama*, Cambridge, 1–62.

Wilson P. (2011), 'The glue of democracy?', in: D. Carter (ed.), *Why Athens? A reappraisal of tragic politics*, Oxford, 19–44.

Winkler J.J. (1990), 'The Ephebes' song: tragōidia and the polis', in: J. Winckler/F. Zeitlin (eds.), *Nothing to do with Dionysos?*, Princeton, 20–62.

Zeitlin F. (1986–1990), 'Thebes: Theater of self and society in Athenian drama', in: P. Euben (ed.), *Greek tragedy and political theory*, Berkeley, 101–141, reprinted in: F. Zeitlin/J. Winkler (eds.), *Nothing to do with Dionysos? Athenian drama in its social context*, Princeton, 130–167.

Ioannis N. Perysinakis
From the Ancient Quarrel Between Philosophy and Poetry: Archaic Moral Values and Political Behaviour in Aristophanes' *Frogs*

1 The citizens and the leaders of *demos*

In the prologue of the *Frogs* Dionysus decides to descend to Hades: he declares his intention to bring Euripides back to life. He needs a sophisticated poet; however, if you seek a competent poet who could utter a lordly phrase, you won't find any left (66–67, 96–97); 'for some are gone, and those who are alive are bad' [71; cf. E. (*Oeneus*) fr. 565 K]. Dionysus is the first recorded reader in ancient Greek literature, and he chooses to read Euripides' *Andromeda* (52–53).[1]

In the parabasis (674–737) the chorus leader establishes his right to give good advice (*chresta*) and instruction to the city.[2] On account of this he was officially commended and crowned (*Life of Ar.*, test. 1.35–9 K–A). There is more advice in the speech which concludes the parabasis (the *antepirrhema*) (718–737). Introduced by a famous comparison with Athenian coinage and current circulation, the speech is not about ordinary citizens, but political leaders.[3] 'The same thing has happened to the best men, states the chorus, just like the old silver coins and the new gold ones. At this time, the Athenians had three kinds of coinage. For nearly two centuries, they had used silver coins, but in the latter part of the Peloponnesian War, when the Spartans occupied Dekeleia, they no longer had regular access to their silver mines at Laureion. So in 407/6 they melted down some gold dedications on the Acropolis to make gold coins; but even a small gold coin

---

The translation used is that of Henderson 2002; the Greek text and verse numbering follow the OCT (Hall/Geldart 1970). I am grateful to Dr Anna Fyta who read this paper and improved its English; for whatever blemishes remaining the responsibility is of course mine.

1 Woodbury 1976: this does not make us believe in a widespread literacy. Sfyroeras 2008.
2 MacDowell 1995, 286–287. This proposal echoes the proposal made six years before in *Lysistrata* (ibid. 287). Dover 1994, *ad loc.* and 73–75. Sheppard 1910, 249–256. Bremer 1993, 127–128: the poet teaches the audience what is right and wrong. Vickers (2001): *Frogs* only incidentally addresses the realm of literature.
3 Dover 1994 *ad* 718–737 and 69–70; Stanford 1958 *ad* 718; De Ste. Croix 1996, 46; Carey 1994, 81–83.

https://doi.org/10.1515/9783110629729-010

has a high value, and this currency was not of much use for daily shopping. A few months before the performance of *Frogs*, therefore, they produced some bronze coins plated with silver. These were, like most modern coins, tokens, representing a higher amount than the intrinsic value of the metal they contained. Consequently, they were unpopular while Gresham's law prevailed: the bronze coins were constantly in circulation, while the silver and gold ones disappeared'.[4] 'Bad money drives out good money'. Just like the old coinage and the new gold, the city treats shabbily and casts aside the well-born, well-behaved, outstanding men (*chrestoi*), while it selects the 'coppers', the aliens, bad people (*poneros*) of poor ancestry, the latest arrivals, whom formerly the city would not readily have used even as scapegoats. To be a scapegoat (*pharmakos*) is worse than to be *poneros*, it is the lowliest condition of human being; deformity and worthlessness stood as qualifications for one's status as scapegoat (cf. Dover *ad* 733). Even at this late hour, Athenians are summoned to change their ways and, once again, choose the good (*chrestoi*) people (727–737).

This exhortation carries a clear politics, in a way that reminds of the Old-Oligarch in his support of the traditional *agathoi* (cf. 1.4, 2.19). The traditional *agathoi* are like the old silver coins of the Athenians; the κακοί and πονηροί, who are in power as the leaders of *demos*, have to leave the posts. These political terms recur in many parts of the play. πονηρός is the opposite of ἀγαθός, as well as the opposite of κακός. And as is the case with κακός, which evinces all the behaviours inappropriate to the code of values and behaviours of the *agathoi*, πονηρός is a standard component of the comic hero. The πονηροὶ κἀκ πονηρῶν (cf. *Eq.* 336–337) is equivalent to κακοὶ κἀκ κακῶν (cf. Eur. *Andr.* 590), a notion opposed to the καλούς τε κἀγαθούς, people who come from noble birth (εὐγενεῖς 727, γενναῖος 1050, γεννάδας 738). Πονηρός is a synonym of κακός, 'one who has to work for a living', the opposite of χρηστός (725, 1456), the traditional *agathos*. This opposition is a part of the struggle between the *chrestoi* and *poneroi* in Athens at the end of the fifth century.[5] There would be no other politician save Alcibiades who

---

[4] MacDowell 1995, 287. Hubbard's 1991 analysis of the *Frogs* is entitled 'Debased Coinage' (199–219).
[5] The noun *kakotes*, with the adjective *kakos*, and its synonyms *deilos* and *poneros*, are the words of designation, Adkins 1960, 30–37 and *passim*. Dover 1974, 52–53, 64–65; Carter 1986, 11, 38; Donlan 1980, *passim*, esp. ch. Four: 'The Aristocratic Ideal in the Classical period' 113–153; Rosenbloom 2002, 300–312; Rosenbloom 2004, part I, 59–66, 78–86; 2004, part II, 326–328, 332–41; Rosen 2014, 225–230 (*poneros*). Ehreberg 1962, 95, 99, 349–350. Whitman 1964, 29–58 reads comic heroism as a form of *poneria*. By 'mimetic badness' Rosen 2008 refers to dramatic representation of bad people and bad behaviour, and by 'bad' he means 'as understood by the intended audience at the time of production'.

would be *chrestos* or καλός τε κἀγαθός par excellence: from his maternal side, he came from the Alkmaeonidae, one of the most famous families in Athens. It is impossible to avoid the conclusion that in the parabasis Aristophanes is exhorting the Athenians to recall Alcibiades.[6]

The splendour Alcibiades exhibited in providing choruses, the magnificence of his personality, and finally his victory in Olympia (416) triggered envy in his fellow-citizens (Thuc. 6.16.1–3; cf And. 4.42). In the aftermath of this victory, Hyperbolos, who bore the mark *poneros* as a fixed epithet, emerged to defend the demos as *prostates tou demou*. Ostracism could prevent Alcibiades from unrivaled political leadership. An *ostrakophoria* would challenge the class whose *arete* Alcibiades exemplified, it would cast suspicion upon the *chrestoi* as inimical to the demos, and to legitimize Hyperbolos' own leadership and that of his faction (*poneroi*). This last ostrakophoria (415) sought to resolve *stasis* between two types of leaders, and pitted the *poneroi* against the *chrestoi* in the former's bid to become a hegemonic class in Athenian society. *Poneroi* by definition have a 'fluency' that *chrestoi* lack.[7] The plan failed: the demos in alliance with the *chrestoi* and the *hetaireiai* ostracized Hyperbolos for ten years, 'because of his *poneria*' (Thuc. 8.73.3) as a *poneros* and *pharmakos*; he was assassinated at Samos (411). But stasis between the *chrestoi* and the *poneroi* persists through the affairs of the mutilations of the Herms and the profanations of the Mysteries, the oligarchic takeovers of 411 and 404, and the restoration of democracy in 403. Though the labels *chrestos* and *poneros* are non-negotiable and class-based throughout the fifth century, they become negotiable and generally applicable in the aftermath of the Thirty's *poneria*. The legal definition of the *poneros*, and the cultural acceptance of the agora as hegemonic, gradually made it possible for members of moneyed *oikoi* and *rhetores* to claim the label *chrestos* and to share in the hegemony. Hyperbolos and his faction lost this battle but their class won the war.[8]

2 The Mission of Poetry

The conversation between the two slaves (756–813) after the *parabasis* presents Dionysus' arbitration between Aeschylus and Euripides as a fortunate consequence of his arrival in the underworld, not as a means to the achievement of his

---

[6] Alcibiades had made a triumphant return to Athens in 408/7, but in 405 he was in voluntary exile, and was killed in the autumn of 404 while still in exile.
[7] Rosenbloom 2004, part I, 55–57, 60–61, 78–86, 96–97; 2002, 300, 337–339.
[8] Rosenbloom 2004, part I, 97–98; Rosenbloom 2004, part II, 323, 352–353; 2002, 337–339.

purpose. There is a custom (*nomos*) in Hades where 'the one who is best of all his fellow professionals is entitled to maintenance in the Prytaneum and a seat next to Pluto'. It is obvious that at this point a change of subjects is occurring (a reversal, περιπέτεια): Though Dionysus started to bring Euripides back to earth, now he has to arbitrate a contest between the representative of the old honoured tragedy and the representative of the modern one. So, the comedy's action is engineered not only by Dionysus' initial desire but also 'by chance' by the debate between the two poets in the underworld, a fact verified by Pluto's question (1414). From the first part of the contest (895–1098), the dialogue between Aeschylus and Euripides is of particular importance.

Adopting the Socratic method,[9] Aeschylus asks Euripides 'Why are poets admired?' Euripides readily responds, 'for their skill and good counsel, and because we make people better members of their communities' (1008–1010). This constitutes the earliest recognition that poetry has a specific didactic function. It is worth noticing here the word pun between ποιητής and ποιοῦμεν. Socrates claims that it is fair 'to inquire about the most important and noblest things of which Homer undertakes to tell concerning war and generalship and governance of cities and the education of men' (*Rep.* 599c–d, Allen; cf. *Ion* 541a). The real test of a politician is if he made the citizens better or as good as possible (*Gorg.* 513e, 515c, 521a). Through Euripides, Aristophanes voices his own views in concealed irony. But if Euripides has in fact precisely not done that, and, instead, turned decent and respectable Athenians into a miserable rabble (ἐκ χρηστῶν καὶ γενναίων μοχθηροτάτους), what reward should he receive for that? Dionysus supplies the answer τεθνάναι (1010–1012), the death sentence. Μοχθηρός is the extreme form of πονηρός. In the actual text of the *graphe asebeias* against Socrates, one of the three charges Meletus made is that he 'corrupts the youth' and that 'the penanlty demanded is death' (Diog. Laert. 2.40). Several critics assert that lines 1008–1010 constitute the most crucial moment in the play (Dover *ad loc.*, Griffith 74).[10] In addition, they derive from the skill of the Homeric speaker and the lesson of Platonic Protagoras (*Il.* 9.443, *Prot.* 318e), and they are used later in the rhetorical and moralising traditions.

---

9 Euripides uses three times the verb of the Socratic elenchus *elenchein* (894, 908, 922), as well as the verb *basanizein* (1121, repeated by Dionysus 1123). Aeschylus uses once *exelenchein* (1366), *basanizein* (1367) and *antilegein* (1007). Dionysus twice uses the verb *elenchein* (857).

10 The contest is ἀγὼν σοφίας and Griffith 2013 investigates the meaning of σοφία (91–92, 114, 215–216). Woodbury 1986, 244–246; Edwards 1990, 152–153; Hubbard 1991, 213–215; Hunter 2014, 384–385. For Aristophanes' originality himself, cf. Bremer 1993, 160–165.

The central issue, namely that poets bear heavy responsibility towards Athenian society and politics, is a familiar element dating from Aristophanes' earliest extant comedy.[11] In the parabasis of *Acharnians*, the poet says that the strangers who come to pay their tribute to the city wanted to see this great poet who had dared to speak the truth to Athens (644–645). Meanwhile the king of Persia thought Athens' military to be superior because of the poet's activity and his ability to improve his fellow citizens (650), obviously ridiculing the fact that the Greeks allowed the interference of the King in Greek politics. And he goes on to say that he will teach the city many good lessons through this justified ridicule, so as to make the Athenians truly fortunate (655–656). In both of the latter claims, Aristophanes assigns himself a role identical to that attributed to Aeschylus through Euripides (1009–1010). Aeschylus' poetic claims can be identified with Aristophanes' own (cf. 686–687).

Poets have been beneficial from the beginning of time (1031). Homer's fame is that he χρήστ'ἐδίδαξεν, namely τάξεις, ἀρετάς, ὁπλίσεις ἀνδρῶν (1035–1036). Aeschylus taught the Athenians the desire to defeat the enemy (1026), to be brave and noble and, like Ajax's shield, to have 'seven-ply oxhide' hearts (1011, 1014, 1017). His characters 'breathe' spears and helmets, and their souls are dense with the presence of things; his poetry has spirit and the spirit has substance. Aeschylus believes that the moral qualities of poetry reproduce themeslves directly in the souls of the audience, and so he approaches his single goal, to foster virtue, through a single virtuous medium; Euripides' aesthetic virtues are moral flaws by Aeschylus' standards.[12] Besides, Aeschylus subscribes himself in this tradition verifying 'from the inside' that his tragedies are τεμάχη τῶν Ὁμήρου μεγάλων δείπνων (Ἀθήναιος 8.347e). Euripides, on the contrary, made the Athenians *mochtheroi*, men who evade military service, vulgarians, and rogues (1011, 1014–1015),[13] while his supporters in the underworld are criminals (771–781). All these are labels of the *poneroi* in their conflict with the *chrestoi*. Aeschylus describes the Athenians in terms of traditional values blaming Euripides that he has 'modernized' them while vesting them with character traits inappropriate for being *agathoi*.

The battle of Marathon plays an important role in the self-definition of Athens, as shown in epideictic oratory and in funeral speeches. The fighters in the

---

11 Biles 2015, 247–248.
12 Walsh 1988, 87, 91. Cf. Konstan 1995, 72–73.
13 Cf. also 1078–1082. For young aimlessly roaming the agora, cf. ἀγάλματ' ἀγορᾶς (Ἠλέκτρα 388), πόλεως ἀγάλματα (Αὐτόλυκος fr. 282.10 K.).

battle of Marathon are the symbol of the bravery of the Athenians at war and Aristophanes refers in many plays to the 'trophy of Marathon'.[14] One of the propositions on Aristophanes is that he was conservative in his attitude both to politics and to cultural movements. For some, Aristophanes had two objects of attack, newer intellectual movements and democratic politics, or that he was an enemy only of the demagogues who misled the demos.[15]

In the same dialogue between Aeschylus and Euripides, a second literary principle is expressed. The poet does not present on stage prostitutes and women in love: 'the poet has a special duty to conceal what is wicked (πονηρόν), not stage it or teach it' (1053). This literary principle, as well as the former views on the poet's mission (1008–1010), echo Plato's *Republic*. Like Plato, Aristophanes speaks here in moral (and political) terms, not in literary terms like Aristotle. In short, what the teacher is for children, so are poets for adults (1053–1055, cf. 1421), a claim also made in the *Republic*. Hence, πάνυ δὴ δεῖ χρηστὰ λέγειν ἡμᾶς (1056). But what exactly comprises this χρηστόν is to date a debatable issue. For Aristophanes it is clearly defined by the symbolic figure of Aeschylus, expressed by his condemnation of Euripides.[16] *Chrestos*, however, is synonym of *agathos* (1011, 1035, 1055, 1057, 1455, 735, 686, 599) and has no aesthetic literary value. The subject matter in Aristophanes' poetry, as well as in Xenophanes' (1W.23), is *chreston*; and Plato is under Xenophanes' influence (cf. *Rep.* 377b–378e, *Euthphr.* 6a–c). The language of concealing the *poneron* and saying *chresta* is particularly important and forms the politics of the period.

The *chrestoi* are nobles, with landed wealth, military prominence, and aristocratic culture; they have the highest value in the moral economy of the polis, and are 'useful' to the safety of the polis; they produce food for the citizen body. In the struggle between the *poneroi/mochtheroi* and the *chrestoi*, by the end of the fifth century in Athens Aristophanes in his comedies was on the side of the *chrestoi*.[17]

---

14 Cf. Loraux 1986, 155–171; Bowie 1996, 201: 'old fighters of Marathon' (*Ach.* 181), 'the happiness you enjoy is worthy of this city, worthy of the glory of Marathon' (*Knights* 1334), enjoying the delights to which the great name of their country and the trophies of Marathon give them the right (*Wasps* 711), etc., while in the *Clouds*, the Right Logos refers to those principles by which his system of education nurtured the men who fought in Marathon (961).
15 Gomme 1996, 29–31; Bremer 1993, 129–134; De Ste Croix 1996, 63–64.
16 Kannicht 1988, 26; the noun *arete*, with the adjective *agathos*, its synonyms *esthlos* and *chrestos*, are the most powerful words of commendation, Adkins 1960, 30–37 and *passim*. Dover 1974, 63, 65, 73; Donlan 1980, 113–153 *passim*; Carter 1986, 38, 49, 187, 193; Kannicht (1988) uses *chrestos* with aesthetic value: 17–18, 24, 26.
17 Rosenbloom 2004, part I, 63–66, 56–57, 2002, 300–312; De Ste Croix 1996, 46–47.

But some scholars assume that at the end of *Frogs* Aristophanes, through the character of Dionysus, take the first steps towards formulating an aesthetic theory set out later by Plato in the *Republic* (e.g. 3.386–398). Like Dionysus, Plato was well aware of the seductive, though potentially 'amoral', allure of poetry and he has Socrates situate the aesthetic dilemma of controversial poetry as part of an 'age-old disagreement between philosophy and poetry' (*Rep.* 607b5). By doing this, he evidently refers to a broader tension between what we call 'formalism' and 'didacticism' in the interpretation of poetry.[18]

The contest itself in the first part goes through several stages or rounds. The characters of tragedy are by definition *agathoi*, members of the nobility or kings (according to Aristotle's definition of tragedy), but Euripides claims that he left no characters in idleness; he had the wife speak, and the slave just as much, and the master, and the maiden, and the old lady, and he calls this a *democratic* act (948–952). Euripides himself provides his famous definition of the notion of realism, 'by staging everyday scenes, things we're used to, things that we live with' (959). This realism and the 'democratic act' during the dramatic action constitute components coordinated with the function of poetry (1008–1010): the bad (κακοί) participate in the *mimesis* of *spoudaia* action of the noble, that is, the subject-matter of tragedy. On the other hand, Euripides made royals wear rags (1063), portrayed lustful queens in love on stage (1043–1044): the noble are abused, and behaviours of the noble which are bad (κακαί) are represented on stage. Aristophanes looks as though he 'agrees' with Aristotle in that tragedy is the representation of a serious, complete action, a notion which Euripides seems to be challenging. This 'democratic' realism is later used in the rhetorical and moralizing traditions.[19]

In fifth-century Athenian education, teachers set before the children's 'desks the works of good poets to read, and made them learn [these works] by heart; they contain a lot of exhortation, and many passages are praising and eulogizing good men of the past, so that the child will be fired with enthusiasm to imitate them' (*Prot.* 325e–26a, Taylor). Poetry is studied not for its aesthetic value, but for its moral content, as becomes absolutely clear from its detailed criticism in the second and third books of the *Republic*. The battle of the gods, which Homer created (*pepoieken*), must not be admitted into the city. 'A child cannot distinguish the allegorical sense from the literal, and the ideas he takes in at that age are likely

---

18 Rosen 2004, 315–316. The meaning of the 'ancient quarrel' may be controversial, but it is not aesthetic (see below).
19 Cf. Hunter 2014, 375–376 (on 948–950, 959); for Hunter 2009, 10–51, *Frogs* foreshadows more of the subsequent critical tradition than is often realised.

to become indelibly fixed; hence the great importance of seeing that the first stories he hears shall be designed to produce the best possible effect on his character (ὅτι κάλλιστα μεμυθολογημένα πρὸς ἀρετὴν ἀκούειν)' (*Rep.* 378d–e, Cornford; cf. 377b).

The discussion on mimesis is focused on influencing behaviour, since a great part of the poet's function is to offer patterns for the young by praising the heroes of the past. 'Poets and prose writers speak badly about what is most important for men, claiming that many men are happy but unjust, or just but wretched, and that the doing of injustice is profitable if it escapes detection, while justice is another's good and one's own loss. We shall forbid them to say this sort of thing' (*Rep.* 392b, Allen). Plato believed that one becomes the kind of person one is projecting, and this led to the conclusion that drama has a bad moral and psychological effect on performers who, in their turn, exert influence on their audience (cf. *Ion* 535d).

In the tenth book of the *Republic* Socrates and Glaucon agree that people 'praise Homer and claim that this poet has educated Greece, and deserves to be taken up and studied both for the conduct of human affairs, for education and culture, ... and concede that Homer is the most poetical and first among tragedians'. Poetry has been banished from the city according to the demands of reason. And they conclude in their defence: 'lest she accuse us of any harsh rudeness, let us further tell her that there is an ancient quarrel between philosophy and poetry' (606e–607b, Allen).

Both Aristophanes and Plato believe that the poets teach the citizens and young men. But, while Aristophanes believes that poets make people better members of their communities by teaching them traditional values and that a good poet is judged precisely based on that, Plato believes that because poets educate people in the city, the poets who do not speak well about what is most important for men must be banished from the city because their work is not conducive to justice and virtue. In the *Frogs*, Aeschylus criticizes Euripides since the poet's prerogative is to conceal what is wicked (πονηρόν). One may notice that transgression of this principle may result in the banishment of the poets in the *Republic*. But this is not true, because many passages from the criticism of poetry in the second book come from Aeschylus' tragedies. For instance, in fr. 350 Radt, the dramatist has Thetis tell how Apollo sang at her wedding and celebrated the happy fortune of her child (*Rep.* 383b). Here the theme is not about the πονηρόν, but one of the philosopher's main attitudes toward the divine: 'when someone says things of that sort about gods, we will be angry' (cf. 380a, fr.154a 15–16 Radt).

3 Alcibiades and the salvation of the city

In the second part (1119–1413) of the contest, prologues, monodies, choruses are cross-examined, and finally the verses and the words are weighed. But though the scale tips three times to the side of Aeschylus, Dionysus is not intent on judging between them; he refuses to be on bad terms with either: 'One I consider a master, the other I enjoy' (1411–1413). The god of tragedy would not want to lose either Aeschylus or Euripides.

In the third part of the contest, the questions on Alcibiades and the city (1414–1499) articulate the application of the *parabasis* and of the moral and political principles in the poet's mission (1008–1010).[20] This principle is evidently self-referential. In the prologue, Dionysus declares his decision to bring back Euripides. Facing his inability to judge on literary grounds between the two poets, Dionysus realizes that he has descended into Hades in search of a poet (1418) to save the city and ensure the continuation of its choral festivals. The poet is a means to a higher end, the continuation of the dramatic festivals, a most urgent feat for the salvation of the city. 'City saved' (1419) in 405 inevitably means 'saved from defeat and destruction from the Spartans'. The Dionysian festivals and the polis are inextricably bound together and rest in the balance.

Whichever of the two dead poets recommends something more *chreston* for the city, he will be the one to take back to the world of the living (1420–1421). Dionysus poses two questions which are not 'off theme' since they are relevant to the poet's mission in the city (1008–1010). The first question posed is their opinion of Alcibiades (who is *chrestos*), while the second asks for their proposal (*chreston*) regarding the salvation of the city. The elucidating question of what the city thinks of Alcibiades (1424) makes Aeschylus' preceding response plausible since Aeschylus does not know Alcibiades: '[the city] yearns for him, detests him, and wants to have him' (1425; Plut. *Alc*.16.2). His response, nevertheless, in Euripides' style is also an apt description of the ambivalence the Athenians held towards the politician.[21]

Euripides' answer is: 'I detest the citizen who will prove to be slow in aiding his country, quick to do her great harm, resourceful for himself, incompetent for

---

20 Cf. Dover 1994, 10–37, 369–381; MacDowell 1995, 293–297; Lada-Richards 1999, ch. 5 'Dionysus, the Poets, and the *Polis*' esp. 216–217, 220–223, 278; Griffith 2013, ch. 7, 200–219; Biles 2015, 240–256; Silk 2000, 258–259, 264, 365–337; Padilla 1992, 378–381; Woodbury 1986, 244–252; Sheppard 1910, 257–259.
21 Cf. Cornelli 2016, who names his paper after Aristophanes' verse.

the city' (1427–1429), which in a chiasmus of parallel opposite political behaviours seems to mean Alcibiades' capricious policy. The phrase recalls ironically Artabanus' view in Herodotus on the political leader: 'He is the best of men who, when he is laying his plans, dreads and reflects on everything that can happen him but is bold when he is in the thick of the action' (7.49.5 Greene; cf. 50.2, 50.3, 7.10.ζ, 7.157.3), or what Thucydides writes about Themistocles: 'he was at once the best judge in those sudden crises which admit of little or no deliberation, and the best prophet of the future, even to its most distant possibilities' (1.138.3 Livingstone; cf. Hdt. 8.60.γ).[22] Aeschylus' response, 'it is not good to rear a lion in the city. If you do raise one to maturity, then cater (ὑπηρετεῖν) to its ways' (1431–1432; Plut. *Alc*.16.2), comes into agreement with his writing style as he himself described it earlier (1058–1059), both in terms of its oracular wording and the meaning of its content. Some attribute the verses to Aeschylus. Aeschylus advises the Athenians to invite back Alcibiades even if they do not like his way of life.[23]

The verb ὑπηρετεῖν (1433), a nautical metaphor, derives from ὑπηρέτης, which is compound of ὑπὸ and ἐρε- of the verb ἐρέσσω: the rowers now became under-rowers, and the main meaning of ὑπηρετεῖν is in this context 'implicit, unquestioning service in response to another's authoritative bidding.'[24] The poet's meaning is that Alcibiades should be recalled and made virtual commander-in-chief of the Athenian forces because he is best qualified to restore the once-preeminent fortunes of Athens.

But Dionysus for a second time cannot decide: one poet spoke sagely (Aeschylus), the other clearly (Euripides), and thus he now has to pose the second question concerning the city's salvation (1435–1436). Euripides' answer is: 'the city may be saved, if we stopped trusting the citizens we now trust, and start making use of the citizens we now do not use' (1446–1448). Euripides states that if the Athenians use as leaders those out of favour, and turn out those in favour, the city could be saved. This exhortation urges a change in political leadership and offers nearly the same recommendation as that made in the last part of the parabasis, yet more concisely (734–735). Aeschylus' second elucidating question as to whether the city is making use of the good people or delights in the bad people (1455–1456) is posed in order to make his response more concurrent with Athenian reality, since he has been away for more than fifty years. This question, too, is analogous to the political exhortation in the parabasis. In Dionysus' answer

---

[22] Perysinakis 1998, 147, 232. Cf. also Euripides fr. 61 K. (*Alexander*).
[23] Cf. Griffith 2013, 203–207.
[24] Moorton 1988, 353–354; Richardson 1943, 55, 59–69.

that the city hates the good, and therefore the only alternative is the bad, Aeschylus poses the question 'then how could anyone save a city like that, if she won't wear either a cloak or a goatskin?' (1458–1459), that is, a city that follows neither the good, who wear a cloak, nor the bad, who wear a goatskin. These lines echo the current vogue in Athenian political discussion. In Megara, the people who wore tattered goatskins about their sides and lived outside this city like deer are now noble (Thgn. 55–56). Aeschylus' final reply is that the city will be saved 'when they think of the enemy's country as their own, and their own as the enemy's; and the fleet as their wealth; and their wealth as poverty' (1463–1465). Here escapes notice the unobserved etymological relation between πλοῦς and πλοῦτος. This is a serious strategic exhortation recalling the oracle for the wooden walls which will save Athens (Hdt. 7.141.3, 142.1–2) and Pericles' policy in the beginning of the Peloponnesian war, in which he advised against military warfare but supported a policy favourable to a sea-power like Athens. The second half-verse 'I opt for Aeschylus' corresponds to Euripides' second half-verse, in particular to *phren*. Nevertheless, the city's departure from this policy led to its defeat (Thuc. 1.140–144, 2.13.2, 14.2, 41.4; Old-Oligarch 2.4, 5, 14). This is placed in Pericles' legacy. Leadership after Pericles' death expressed the yearning to consolidate a power-base of the magnitude of Pericles, refashioning the verbal expression of political power. In the *Frogs* the Athenians are persuaded to choose the spirit of Pericles' policy. Aeschylus could plausibly be viewed as a mask of Pericles.[25]

Finally, Dionysus announces his decision: 'he will choose the dramatist that his soul wishes to choose' (1468). In this context, the soul is the decision-making organ and bears something in common with the soul in Plato's *Republic* (443d–e, 433d–e), even more so since such a decision is connected with temperance, good counsel (εὐβουλία) and knowledge (428b).[26] Euripides hastens to remind Dionysus that he swore to take him back, invoking the principle of 'helping friends and harming enemies' (1470). This intervention purposefully prepares Dionysus' reply, which uses in Euripidean sophistry the first half of the famous verse from Euripides' *Hippolytus* (612): 'it was my tongue that took the oath: I opt for Aeschylus' (1471). The verse is repeated with changes in 101–102 and *Th.* 275–276. The contest is ἀγὼν σοφίας (884) and the winner is Aeschylus: therefore, the notion

---

25 Cf. Vickers 2001, 188–201; Rosenbloom 2004, part I, 90–93.
26 Griffith 2013, 213–214 argues that ψυχή reminds of the eschatological dimensions of Dionysus. Halliwell 2011, 145–146; Biles 2015, 254; Woodbury 1986, 245–246; Handley 1956, 214–215: 'emotional soul'.

σοφός in previous crucial lines (1413, 1434) refers to Aeschylus. Nevertheless, Aristophanes draws great pleasure from Euripides (1413); he is a poet δεξιός. *Sophia* is Aeschylus' μεγάλαι γνῶμαι καὶ διάνοιαι (sound judgments 1059, 1502; cf. *Pax* 750). Endowed with vision is the speaker who has γνώμη (sound judgment) in Thucydides' debates; Themistocles, by his own capacity, was the best judge, and Solon praises γνωμοσύνης μέτρον (Thuc. 1.138.3; Solon 16W). 'Wisdom is one thing, to be acquainted with true judgement, how all things are steered through all' (Heraclitus B 41 DK).[27] Strepsiades in the *Clouds* (1366) also rates Aeschylus first among the poets. In his *Rhetoric*, Aristotle writes: 'Another topic can be used if there has been a previous decision, as in Euripides' reply to Hygiainon in an *antidosis* trial when, accused of impiety because he had written a line recommending perjury, he said: "My tongue swore, but my mind was unsworn"; such a man could not be trusted' (1416a 29–34, Kennedy). Dionysus exploits the skilfulness, which characterizes Euripides' poetry and repeats ironically his sophisticated half-line.

Some critics find the decision arbitrary; this arbitrariness was acknowledged in the *Hypothesis* (Dover p. 114). Whereas the quest was to bring back Euripides, the conflict between Aeschylus and Euripides is not strictly a way of achieving that end, and indeed it results in an entirely different end, the victory of Aeschylus. Even when there are visible causal links between its phrases, the pattern is never a strictly Aristotelian-consequential sequence, if only because there is never a necessary *therefore* between the conflict and the victory. The moral conclusion is arbitrary. The grounds for the decision are not argued or even stated. 'It is neither a plausible development on the part of Dionysus nor implicit in the earlier action, and while such discontinuity is of course, *qua* discontinuity, as Aristophanic as it could possibly be – while Dionysus is as entitled as anyone to a recreative switch – in its moral assertiveness the final denunciation is simply alien.'[28]

Some other critics place *Frogs* beside the *Contest of Homer and Hesiod* as a piece of agonistically framed literary criticism. Aristophanes models on Dionysus' verdict the king Panedes' decision; his decision ultimately reveals that in a

---

27 Cf. Arist. *Rhet.* B 21 1394a21–25; Anaximenes of Lampsacus, *Ars Rhetorica* 11.1; Hermogenes, *Progymn.* 4.
28 I am indebted to Silk 2000, 264, 365–367 (with n. 31), 258–259 (with n. 7); quotation from 366–367. Cf. also Goldhill 1991, 211–219; Bowie 1993, 246–251; Walsh 1988, 80–97. For dramatic and organic sense into the decision: Sheppard 1910, 249; Segal 1961; Hooker 1980, 78–82; Biles 2015, 251; Hubbard 1991, 218–219; Lada-Richards 1999, 216–325; Riu 1999, 115–142.

contest between two great poets, any attempt to determine who is 'better' according to non-poetic criteria is doomed to be capricious. Homer loses that contest because Panedes assesses his verses out of their context (*Certamen* 205–210, Allen), applying as a criterion only whether the verses quoted were consonant with the values of his own society, and concluding that they were an endorsement of an anti-social, military ethos.[29] But the comparison is not sound. *Agon* has the same root of *agathos*: competition is inherent in the meaning of *agathos*; both of them and their connotations run alongside the Greek Literature. What is common in these works is the contest for excellence. And the final decision in both works depends on the priorities of the period and the author. Alongside the *Certamen* 'the Greeks were struck with admiration for Homer', but not in the *Frogs* for Euripides. Aristophanes from *parabasis* onwards foreshadows Aeschylus' victory.

Dionysus proclaims himself unable or unwilling twice to decide between the two poets. This is suspense, *mellesis*, a well-known Homeric technique in comic dress. The audience of Aristophanes 'might make a more reliable prediction by observing that the second speaker in an *agon* usually defeats the first speaker, and it is Euripides who goes first in every round of the contest in *Frogs*'.[30] In the politics of the *Frogs* we may have a clue to a higher, more artistic unity than can be found by the analysis of the structure. We noticed that the comedy's action is engineered not only by the initial desire of Dionysus to fetch Euripides back from Hades but also 'by chance' by the debate between the two poets in the underworld, which is re-engineered in the second part by Pluto's question (1414). Euripides is a poet δεξιός, Dionysus is looking for in the prologue. But the contest is an ἀγών σοφίας (which is the reversal) and Aeschylus is the winner. We have also noticed that the third part of the contest is comprised of the application of *parabasis* and the moral and political principles of the poet's mission (1008–10). The *parabasis* represents the *chrestoi* as silver or gold coinage that no longer functions as a medium of exchange, and the *poneroi* as the silver-plated bronze coins, which have driven the former out of circulation. Besides, in the struggle between the *poneroi* and the *chrestoi* in late fifth-century Athens, Aristophanes was in his comedies on the side of the *chrestoi*. Euripides had no chance in the contest; he was part of the political (and moral) problem Aristophanes was facing in Athens in 405.

*

---

29 Rosen 2004, 314–320. Biles 2015, 238.
30 MacDowell 1995, 292.

The *Frogs* is no doubt a political play. The poet urges the Athenians to invite Alcibiades and make him leader of the navy and in general to offer the power to politicians traditionally *agathoi* and noble. The *agon* is a substantial part of comedy. Yet, Aristophanes did not want to compose his own *Poetics*[31] (*Frogs* nonetheless foreshadows more of the subsequent critical tradition than is often realised). He argues through Euripides' mouth, that 'we admire the poets for their skill and good counsel, and because we make people better members of their communities'. Indeed, 'we make people better members of their communities', but by whose standards? *Beltious* is a comparative adjective (it means stronger), and this feature of the Greek language alone, but also the whole dialogue between Aeschylus and Euripides (1006–1076), makes it clear that Aristophanes supports the traditional moral values, the traditional *agathoi*. The vote for the noble and the καλούς τε κἀγαθούς in the *antepirrhema* leaves no doubt. Acting in a democratic way in his tragedies and by staging everyday scenes, Euripides on the one hand made all the citizens speak, including women, slaves, masters, maidens, and the old lady, and, on the other, he made lustful queens fall in love on stage (1043–1044) and his royals wear rags so that they could strike people as piteous beings (1063). For this reason, no rich man is willing to command a warship; instead, he wraps himself in rags and whines, claiming to be poor (1065–1066). This means that the bad participate in the *spoudaia* action of the noble, while the good become base and their actions appear on stage as if they belong to those of the bad. In short, the notion of the opening of the tragedy to the bad or the lower 'classes' works both ways.

Aristophanes' choice of Aeschylus is (the reverse) equivalent to Plato's banishment of the poets from his city. The common ground is the education of the young: the poets praise good men of the past, so that the young will be fired with enthusiasm to imitate them. What is not common is the rest of virtue: Aristophanes judges on the grounds of courage in war and political wisdom (not necessarily regarding Alcibiades). Plato judges on the grounds of moral virtue, which he shares with Euripides. Plato tries to define *andreia* (*La., Rep.*), but he does not dispute *andreia* itself.

I contend that the ancient quarrel between philosophy and poetry consists in fact of: (i) the infiltration of morality into fifth-century writers, especially in the second half of that century; the Greeks retained traditional values in a situation

---

[31] Halliwell 2011 entitles 'Aristophanes' *Frogs* and Failure of Criticism' his relevant chapter on Aristophanes (93–154). He cites and refutes (146, notes 90, 91) the fact that Dionysus chooses on the grounds of the political advice earlier offered by the poets.

far different from that in which the values had developed and were appropriate.³² (ii) 'From Homer onwards the chief problem of the Greek values became the need to discover a means of relating *dikaios* to *agathos*, *arete* and associated words in such a way as to make *dikaiosyne* either the whole or the part of *arete*.'³³ The values of the Homeric world in fact persist throughout the fifth century. But they do not persist unchallenged. (iii) *Arete* and other words related to virtues were being re-evaluated as co-operative values and were being interiorized; in fifth-century Athens, under the influence of democracy and the Empire, the traditional competitive values were re-evaluated into co-operative values, without the former having lapsed into oblivion. The *Old Oligarch* is eloquent on this point. In the liturgies, wealthy citizens assimilate the private virtue to public service because public service is regarded as most laudable (Lys. 21.19).³⁴ The traditional competitive virtue has been transformed into an interiorized co-operative virtue of the soul.

The re-evaluation of traditional moral values is the main idea in the ancient quarrel between philosophy and poetry. The subject of this study is the revaluation of traditional moral values, which Socrates/Plato undertakes, as it is described in early (and middle) dialogues, and Aristophanes' adherence to traditional values, as they are described in the *Frogs* and other plays. The *Frogs* necessarily belongs to this quarrel, though it opts for an opposing direction from that which Socrates/Plato and Euripides have undertaken. At the end of *Frogs*, Euripides and Socrates are seated together and talking (1491–1492). Socrates re-evaluates traditional moral values from Homeric epics down to the tragedy of the second half of the fifth century and attempts to give moral content to the old values and virtues. Euripides' *Electra*, for instance, is the most poetically and morally advanced speech before Socrates and the early Platonic dialogues. Orestes' speech 367–390 is a re-evaluation of *aretai*. Euripides rejected many other qualities in virtue of which men had hitherto been termed as *agathoi*, and claimed that *Autourgos* was the true *agathos*. The *agathos* seems to have become equal to the notion of the *dikaios*.³⁵ By depicting Electra married to Autourgos and living in a lowly cottage, while Orestes is re-evaluating these virtues, Euripides may be saying to the Athenians:³⁶ 'You believe, Athenians, that through the *Oresteia* you may bring the old values back to your life. I shall show you through my work that

---

32 Keynote of Adkins' approach; cf. Adkins 1972, 146–147.
33 Adkins 1960, 153, 259–260.
34 Adkins 1960, 212 and 1972, 124.
35 Adkins 1960, 176–178 and 1972, 115–117.
36 A revival of the *Oresteia* was probably held in the 420's.

the real problems are not of a political nature, but they are inside every individual'.[37] Aristophanes, on the other hand, pursues the maintenance of the traditional moral values and political behaviour, because Euripides' modern ideas destroy heroic Athenian society.

Homer is named as the main representative of the quarrel. Aristophanes stands as the contemporary representative of Homer and of the values of the Homeric epics and insists on the maintenance of traditional values. Euripides insists on the modernization of moral values and modernity. In Plato's early and middle dialogues, Socrates had begun a moral re-evaluation of virtues and had placed before men the ideal of moral knowledge in the sense of distinguishing traditional morals and politics from the new co-operative moral virtue. The charges against Socrates are the charges of the Athenians holding traditional moral values against the infiltration of the morality Socrates (and Plato) was introducing. This infiltration of morality constitutes part of the ancient quarrel between philosophy and poetry, as is described in the *Republic*. The Athenians adhered to traditional values and had not been persuaded by his philosophy; consequently, the majority of the jurors condemned him. Plato is interested in advancing morality and the interiorisation of virtue (*arete*). This is the subject matter, in particular aspects, of each dialogue before the *Republic*. The *Clouds* had seriously harmed Socrates while from his examination much enmity and slander had arisen against him. The *Frogs* 'condemned' him before the actual trial.[38]

Tragic poetry died with Euripides, and it died because Socrates' student made it intellectual and problematic and thereby secularized it; in the final analysis it passed away because of Socrates. The decline of tragedy is simultaneously a symptom of the decline of the *polis* itself – and it is precisely this fact that makes the *Frogs* so eminently political a comedy.[39] Socrates 'corrupts the youth', Euripides makes the Athenians *poneroi*. Both Dionysus and Meletus demand death. A decree passed after the death of Aeschylus authorized the continued production of his plays (*Vita*, Test. 1 Radt, lines 48–49). Aeschylus' posthumous career was a well-known fact among ancient scholars and authors. This means that for the audience the contest is not between a familiar style and a style known only to the oldest generation, but between two styles, which were both put to the test in the contemporary theatre.[40] Aristophanes chooses Aeschylus. By condemning Euripides, Aristophanes condemns Socrates and the re-evaluation of moral values the

---

[37] Hose's observations 2008, 95. Cf. similarly Conacher 1967, 203.
[38] Perysinakis (forthcoming).
[39] Kannicht 1988, 27; Snell 1953, 131.
[40] Dover 1993, 460; cf. Dover 1993, 36–37; Biles 2006–2007.

philosopher had undertaken. This contest is another condemnation before the trial. The *Frogs* was awarded first prize at the Lenaea in 405 and was reperformed early in 404 for political reasons.[41] The majority of Athenian society condemned Socrates, remained faithful to tradition, and condemned the emergence of modernity.

Bibliography

Adkins, A.W.H. (1960), *Merit and Responsibility*, Oxford.
Adkins, A.W.H. (1972), *Moral Values and Political Behaviour in Ancient Greece*, London.
Adkins, A.W.H. (1966), 'Aristotle and the best kind of tragedy', in: *CQ* 16, 78–102.
Allen, R.E. (ed.) (2006), *Plato, The Republic*, New Haven/London.
Allison, R.H. (1983), 'Amphibian Ambiguities: Aristophanes and his *Frogs*', in: *G&R* 30, 8–20.
Biles, Z.P. (2015), *Aristophanes and the Poetics of Competition*, Cambridge.
Biles, Z.P. (2006–2007), 'Aschylus' afterlife: reperformance by decree in 5th C. Athens', in: *ICS* 31–32, 206–242.
Bowie, A.M. (1993–1996), *Aristophanes: Myth, Comedy, and Ritual*, Cambridge.
Bremer, J. (1993), 'Aristophanes on his own Poetry', in: E. Handley *et al.* (eds.), *Aristophanes*, Vandoueuvres, 125–172.
Carey, C. (1994), 'Comic Ridicule and democracy', in: R.G. Osborne/S. Hornblower (eds.), *Ritual, Finance, Politics: Athenian Democratic Accounts Presented to David Lewis*, Oxford, 69–83.
Carter, L.B. (1986), *The Quiet Athenian*, Oxford.
Conacher, D.J. (1967), *Euripidean Drama: Myth, Theme and Structure*, Toronto.
Cornelli, G. (2016), 'He longs for him, he hates him and he wants him for himself: The Alcibiades Case between Socrates and Plato', in: G. Cornelli (ed.), *Plato's Styles and Characters. Between Literature and Philosophy*, Berlin/Boston, 281–295.
Cornford, F.M. (1966), *The Republic of Plato*, Oxford.
Donlan, W. (1980), *The Aristocratic Ideal in Ancient Greece*, Lawrence. Cf. *The Aristocratic Ideal and Selected Papers* (Wauconda Ill, 1999).
Dover, K.J. (1972), *Aristophanic Comedy*, Berkeley/Los Angeles.
Dover, K.J. (1974), *Greek Popular Morality at the Time of Plato and Aristotle*, Oxford.
Dover, K.J. (ed.) (1993), *Aristophanes, Frogs*, Oxford.
Dover, K.J. (1993), 'The contest in Aristophanes' *Frogs*', in: Sommerstein *et al.* (eds.), 445–460.
Edwards, L.C. (1990), 'Poetic values and poetic technique in Aristophanes', in: *Ramus* 19, 143–59.
Ehreberg, V. (1962), *The People of Aristophanes: A Sociology of Old Attic Comedy*, New York.
Ferrari, G.R.F. (ed.)/Griffith, T. (transl.) (2000), *Plato, The Republic*, Cambridge.
Goldhill, S. (1991), *The Poet's Voice*, Cambridge.
Gomme, A.W. (1966), 'Aristophanes and Politics', in: Segal (ed.), 29–41.

---

[41] For the second performance, cf.: Ruso 1966 and 1994, 198–219. Sommerstein 1996, 20–23; Sommerstein 1993 and 2014, 296–297; MacDowell 1995, 297–300; Dover 1993, 73–76, 373–376.

Griffith, M. (ed.) (2013), *Aristophanes' Frogs*, Oxford.
Halliwell, S. (2011), *Between Ecstasy and Truth. Interpretations of Greek Poetics from Homer to Longinus*, Oxford, Ch. 3: 'Aristophanes' Frogs and the Failure of Criticism', 93–154.
Halliwell, S. (1993), 'Comedy and publicity in the society of the polis', in: Sommerstein *et al.* (eds.), 321–340.
Handley, E.W. (1956), 'Words for 'soul', 'heart' and 'mind' in Aristophanes', in: *RhM* 99, 205–225.
Heiden, B. (1991), 'Tragedy and Comedy in the *Frogs* of Aristophanes', in: *Ramus* 20, 95–111.
Heiden, B. (1993), 'Emotion, acting and the Athenian ethos', in: Sommerstein *et al.* (eds.), *Tragedy, Comedy and the Polis*, Bari, 145–166.
Henderson, J. (ed. and transl.) (2002), *Aristophanes, Frogs, Assemblywomen, Wealth*, Cambridge MA.
Henderson, J. (1993), 'Comic hero versus political elite', in: Sommerstein *et al.* (eds.), *Tragedy, Comedy and the Polis*, Bari, 307–319.
Hooker, J.T. (1980), 'The Composition of the *Frogs*', in: *Hermes* 108, 169–182.
Hose, M. (2008), *Euripides. Der Dichter der Leidenschaften*, Munich.
Hubbard, T.K. (1991), *The Mask of Comedy: Aristophanes and the Intertextual Parabasis*, New York.
Hunter, R. (2009), *Critical Moments in Classical Literature: Studies in the Ancient View of Literature and its Uses*, Cambridge.
Hunter, R. (2014), 'Attic comedy in the rhetorical and moralizing traditions', in: M. Revermann (ed.), *The Cambridge Companion to Greek Comedy*, Cambridge, 373–386.
Kannicht, R. (1986), *The Ancient Quarrel between Philosophy and Poetry. Aspects of the Greek Conception of Literature*, The Fifth Broadhead Memorial Lecture, Michigan.
Kennedy, G.A. (ed.) (1989), *The Cambridge History of Literary Criticism*. I, *Classical Criticism*, Cambridge.
Konstan, D. (1995), *Greek Comedy and Ideology*, New York.
Lada-Richards, I. (1999), *Initiating Dionysus: Ritual and Theatre in Aristophanes' Frogs*, Oxford.
Littlefield D.J. (ed.) (1968), *Twentieth Century Interpretations of the* Frogs. *A Collection of Critical Essays*, Englewood Cliffs NJ.
Loraux, N. (1986), *The Invention of Athens: the funeral oration in the classical city* (transl. A. Sheridan), Cambridge MA/London.
MacDowell, D.M. (1995), *Aristophanes and Athens: An Introduction to the Plays*, Oxford.
MacDowell, D.M., (1993), 'Foreign birth and Athenian citizenship in Aristophanes', in: A.H. Sommerstein *et al.* (eds.), *The Comedies of Aristophanes*. IX, *Frogs*, Warminster, 359–371.
McLeish, K. (1980), *The Theatre of Aristophanes*, London.
Möllendorf, P. von (1996–1997), 'Αἰσχύλον δ'αἱρήσομαι – der 'neue Aischylos' in den Fröschen des Aristophanes', in: *WJA* 21, 129–151.
Moorton, R.F. (1988), 'Aristophanes on Alcibiades', in: *GRBS* 29, 345–359.
Moorton, R.F., (1989), 'Rites of Passage in Aristophanes' *Frogs*', in: *CJ* 84, 308–323.
Morrison, J.S. (1984), '*Hyperesia* in Naval Contexts in the Fifth and Fourth Centuries B.C.', in: *JHS* 104, 48–59.
Padilla, M. (1992), 'Theatrical and social renewal in Aristophanes' *Frogs*', in: *Arethusa* 25, 359–381.
Perysinakis, I.N. (1998²), *Ἡ ἔννοια τοῦ πλούτου στὴν Ἱστορίη τοῦ Ἡροδότου*, Ioannina.

Redfield, J. (1990), 'Drama and Community: Aristophanes and some of his rivals', in: J.J. Winkler/F. Zeitlin (eds.), *Nothing to Do with Dionysos? Athenian Drama and its Social Context*, Princeton, 314–335.
Revermann, M. (ed.) (2014), *The Cambridge Companion to Greek Comedy*, Cambridge.
Richardson, L.J.D. (1943), 'Ὑπηρέτης', in: *CQ* 37, 55–61.
Riu, Xavier (1999), *Dionysism and Comedy*, Lanham.
de Romilly, J. (1986), *La modernité d'Euripide*, Paris.
Rosen, R.M. (2004), 'Aristophanes' *Frogs* and the *Contest of Homer and Hesiod*', in: *TAPA* 134, 295–322.
Rosen, R.M. (2008), 'Badness and intentionality in Aristophanes' *Frogs*', in: I. Sluiter/R.M. Rosen (eds.), *Kakos: Badness and Anti-Value in Classical Antiquity*, Brill/Leiden/Boston, 143–168.
Rosen, R.M. (2014), 'The Greek "comic hero"', in: M. Revermann (ed.), *The Cambridge Companion to Greek Tragedy*, Cambridge, 222–240.
Rosenbloom, D. (2002), 'From *poneros* to *pharmakos*: theater, social drama, and revolution in Athens, 428–404 B.C.E.', in: *ClAnt* 21, 283–346.
Rosenbloom, D. (2004), '*Poneroi* vs *chrestoi*: the ostracism of Hyperbolus and the struggle for hegemony in Athens after the death of Perikles'. Part I, in: *TAPA* 134, 55–105; Part II, in: *TAPA* 134, 323–358.
Roselli, D. (2014), 'Social class', in: M. Revermann (ed.), *The Cambridge Companion to Greek Tragedy*, Cambridge, 241–258.
Russo, C.F. (1966), 'The Revision of Aristophanes' *Frogs*', in: *GR* 13, 1–13.
Russo, C.F. (1994), *Aristophanes: an Author for the Stage*, transl. K. Wren, London/New York.
Segal, Ch.P. (1961), 'The character and cult of Dionysus and the unity of the *Frogs*', in: *ICS* 65, 207–242.
Segal, E. (ed.) (1966), *Oxford Readings in Aristophanes*, Oxford.
Sheppard, J.T. (1910), 'Politics in the *Frogs* of Aristophanes', in: *JHS* 30, 249–259.
Ste. Croix, G.E.M. de (1966), 'The Political Outlook of Aristophanes', in: Segal (ed.) *Oxford Readings in Aristophanes*, Oxford, 42–64.
Sfyroeras, S. (2008), 'Πόθος Εὐριπίδου: reading *Andromeda* in Aristophanes', in: *AJP* 129, 299–317.
Silk, M.S. (2000), *Aristophanes and the Definition of Comedy*, Oxford.
Snell, B. (1953), *The Discovery of the Mind*, transl. T.G. Rosenmeyer, Oxford.
Sommerstein, A.H. (1974), 'Aristophanes *Frogs* 1463–5', in: *CQ* 24, 24–27.
Sommerstein, A.H. (1993), 'Kleophon and the restaging of *Frogs*', in: Sommerstein et al. (eds.), *Tragedy, Comedy and the Polis*, Bari, 461–476.
Sommerstein, A.H. et al. (eds.) (1993), *Tragedy, Comedy and the Polis*, Bari.
Sommerstein, A.H. (ed.) (1996), *The Comedies of Aristophanes*. IX, *Frogs*, Warminster.
Sommerstein, A.H. (2014), 'The politics of Greek comedy', in: Revermann (ed.) (2014), 291–305.
Stanford, W.B. (ed.) (1958), *Aristophanes, The Frogs*, London.
Stevens, P.T. (1955), 'Aristophanes, *Frogs* 788–794', in: *CR* 5, 235–237 and 16 (1966), 3.
Taplin, O. (1996), 'Fifth-Century Tragedy and Comedy', in: Segal (ed.), *Oxford Readings in Aristophanes*, Oxford, 9–28.
Tierney, M. (1935), 'The parodos in Aristophanes' *Frogs*', in: *PrRIA* Sect. C 42, 199–218.
Vickers, M. (2001), 'Aristophanes' *Frogs*: nothing to do with literature', in: *Athenaeum* 89, 187–201.

Walsh, G.B. (1988), *The Varieties of Enchantment: Early Greek Views of the Nature and Function of Poetry*, 2nd ed., Chapel Hill.
Whitman, C.H. (1964), *Aristophanes and the Comic Hero*, Cambridge.
Woodbury, L. (1976), 'Aristophanes' *Frogs* and the Athenian literacy: *Ra.* 52-53, 1114', in: *TAPA* 106, 349–357.
Woodbury, L. (1986), 'The judgement of Dionysus: books, taste, and teaching in the *Frogs*', in: M. Cropp/E. Fantham/S.E. Scully (eds.), *Greek Tragedy and its Legacy: Essays Presented to D.J. Conacher*, Calgary, 241–257.

Margarita Sotiriou
Aspects of Epinician Rhetoric and the Democratic *polis*

Bacchylides *Ep.* 10 Sn.-M.

The epinician Odes of Bacchylides (and Pindar) belong neither to the masterpieces of the narrative genre nor to the great rhetorical speeches of classical Athens. The victory Ode is, according to Kurke,[1] a 'communal drama'. Its aim is primarily to celebrate an athletic victory in order to preserve the fame of the addressee in perpetuity. The audience of the Ode consists of the future clients of the poet; therefore, the spectators of the epinician celebration must be convinced through the performance not only of the victor's value as an athlete and as a human being, but also of the poet's talent and poetic *charisma*. From this perspective we are confronted with a clear effort at persuasion. Among those scholars working in this field, Carey has already indicated that the poet's task, his diction, and the strategy he displays in order to persuade his audience, all these together provide a nexus of affinities not only with epideictic oratory but also with Attic drama. In Carey's words: '*Didaxis* and *epainos* must carry conviction'.[2]

The unique way Bacchylides invests the didactic section of his Ode 10 with an elegant rhetorical quality, using among others a famous passage from the old Athenian elegy of Solon, calls for a special method of study. I intend to do this in this essay. Of course, my aim is not to offer definite solutions. Rather, I will try to reconstruct the method Bacchylides deploys in this specific Ode to understand certain aspects of the socio-political memory he shares with his patron and his audience. Instead of narrating a mythical story from the heroic past, the poet promotes the encomiastic section of the poem by placing the epinician event of the aristocratic symposium in the contemporary socio-political context of the democratic polis. Subsequently, epinician rhetoric places the reintegrated victor back into his civic community and invites the listeners to visualize a natural and vivid link between the authority of Solonian political poetry and the lyric poet.

Aristotle (*Rh.* 1356a1ff.) divided the rhetorical means of persuasion into three categories: *logos*, *ethos* and *pathos*. Carey has already sufficiently explored two of these, *ethos* and *pathos*. My discussion will take as its starting point Carey's

---
1 Kurke 1991, 257. She follows Connor 1987, 42–47, who argues that archaic ritual and ceremony must be evaluated as types of negotiation and communication between leader and people.
2 Carey 1999, 17.

conclusions in order to cast some light on how Bacchylides, as a typical panegyrist, creates a masterful representation of the athletic success, in the context of which the element of *ethos* (moral values not only of the laudandus but also of the laudator) and specific aspects of *pistis* are combined within the performative framework of this Ode:

> Φή]μα, σὺ γ[ὰ]ρ [...] ἐπ]οιχνεῖς
> φῦ]λα, καὶ πᾶ[...
> [...]
> νασιῶτιν ἐκίνησεν λιγύφθογγον μέλισσαν,   10
> ἐγχ]ειρὲς ἵν' ἀθάνατον Μουσᾶν ἄγαλμα
> ξυνὸν ἀνθρώποισιν εἴη
> χάρμα, τεὰν ἀρετὰν
> μανῦον ἐπιχθονίοισιν,
> ὁσσά<κις> Νίκας ἕκατι   15
> ἄνθεσι ξανθὰν ἀναδησάμενος κεφαλὰν
> κῦδος εὐρείαις Ἀθάναις
> θῆκας Οἰνείδαις τε δόξαν,
> ἐν Ποσειδᾶνος περικλειτοῖς ἀέθλοις
> εὐθὺς ἐνδείξας Ἕλλασιν ποδῶν ταχεῖαν ὁρμάν·   20
> ...[.]...............οὔ]ροισιν ἔπι σταδίου
> θερμὰν ἔτι πνέων ἄελλαν
> ἔστ[..] ν δ' ἄϊξε θατήρων ἐλαίωι
> φάρε[....]ν ἐμπίτων ὅμιλον.
> τετραέλικτον ἐπεί   25
> κάμψεν δρόμον, Ἰσθμιονίκαν
> δίς νιν ἀγκάρυξαν εὐβού-
> λων [...]ων προφᾶται·
> δίς δ' ἐ[ν Νεμέ]αι Κρονίδα Ζηνὸς παρ' ἁγνόν
> βωμόν· ἁ κλεινά τε Θήβα   30
> δέκτο νιν εὐρύχορόν
>   τ' Ἄργο[ς Σικυώ]ν τε κατ' αἶσαν·
> οἵ τε Πελλάναν νέμονται,
> ἀμφί τ' Εὔβοιαν πολ[υλάϊο]ν, οἵ θ' ἱεράν
> νᾶσον Αἴγιναν. ματεύει   35
> δ' ἄλλ[ος ἀλλοί]αν κέλευθον,
> ἄντι[να στείχ]ων ἀριγνώτοιο δόξας
> τεύξεται. μυρίαι δ' ἀνδρῶν ἐπιστᾶμαι πέλονται·
> ἢ γὰρ σοφὸς ἢ Χαρίτων τιμᾶν λελογχὼς
> ἐλπίδι χρυσέᾳ τέθαλεν   40
> ἤ τινα θευπροπίαν
> εἰδώς· ἕτερος δ' ἐπὶ παισὶ
> ποικίλον τόξον τιταίνει·
> οἱ δ' ἐπ' ἔργοισίν τε καὶ ἀμφὶ βοῶν ἀγέλαις
> θυμὸν αὔξουσιν· τὸ μέλλον   45
> δ' ἀκρίτους τίκτει τελευτάς,

πᾷ τύχα βρίσει. τὸ μὲν κάλλιστον, ἐσθλὸν
ἄνδρα πολλῶν ὑπ' ἀνθρώπων πολυζήλωτον εἶμεν·
οἶδα καὶ πλούτου μεγάλαν δύνασιν,
ἃ καὶ τὸν ἀχρεῖον τί[θησ]ι   50
χρηστόν. τί μακρὰν γλῶσσαν ἰθύσας ἐλαύνω
ἐκτὸς ὁδοῦ ; πέφαται θνατοῖσι νίκας
ὕστε]ρον εὐφροσύνα
αὐλῶν [δὲ [...]

Fame, Herald of Virtue, heard through the tribes of man, riving earth's black folds you enlighten the dead with Glory's names; winners honors the world can share look with eyes serene as sea on the staid rest from games their golden triumphs earn. Now the mate of Aglaus' sister stirs this seaborne bee to build with his clear song a work for the deathless Muse, a joy in common to men that sings your skill among them, sings how triumph repeatedly wreathed your tawny head, as you planted splendor through Athens' breadth, and renown for Oeneus' race. In games of Poseidon, fine on the fields of praise you amazed the Greeks with a rushing sprint; no break and back to the ring's first mark – breath hot and short – you tensed, sprang, sprayed admirer's robes with oil, carved the roaring crowd on rounding the track's fourth lap. Isthmian victor twice proclaimed by infallible judges, twice near Nemea's altar hoy to Cronian Zeus: Famous Thebes, Argos starred with rings, and Sicyon received you grandly – joined by men of Pellene, Euboea thick with corn, and the hallowed island Aegina. Striving to reach unique success, men light out on myriad branches. Here they climb on precious hope in the lores of mind and art; here is a seer in his hour, another who strains his crafty bow at gold, still others exult in herds and harvest. Though the future bears inscrutable fruit, and fortune's scales are fickle, still finest, one among all who thrives on special skill. I know the pressure of wealth that makes the blunt seem keen – but why swerve song so far afield? Let this enlighten man: concord is the crown of conquest. Over blended reeds and lyres lift Aglaus' rising roll of glory.

(transl. R. Fagles)

Bacchylides wrotes the Ode for an Athenian victor, whose name is lost to us. Unknown also is the date of composition. We hear that the addressee was the winner of the foot race (l. 20: ποδῶν ταχεῖαν ὁρμάν) in the Isthmian games (l. 19: Ποσειδᾶνος περικλειτοῖς ἀέθλοις), and that his brother-in-law commissioned this poem (l. 9: κασιγνήτας ἀκοίτας).

A closer look at the structure of the poem allows us to follow Bacchylides' strategic choices of praise: (1) Ll. 1–9 constitute the short prooemion of the Ode. (2) From l. 10 to l. 35 the poet praises his addressee's former athletic successes. Here it is notable that Bacchylides avoids following the common epinician practice of narrating a mythical story in order to establish the necessary associations between his client and a hero of the past. On the contrary, he extends his encomiastic part by a series of gnomic statements concerning the different professions humans choose to gain δόξα. The passage forms a priamel, which reaches its climax in the statement of ll. 48–49 that 'the best for a noble man is to be widely admired among his fellow men'. The passage is duly rounded off by a reference to the power of wealth (ll. 35–51). After a typical break-off formula, the poet returns to his main theme, the praise of the victor (ll. 52–56).

Maehler[3] in his excellent commentary on Bacchylides has rebutted the established interpretation of the poem, calling attention to the close association of the 'professions-passage' of the Ode with Solon's *Elegy on the Muses* (3W):

>Μνημοσύνης καὶ Ζηνὸς Ὀλυμπίου ἀγλαὰ τέκνα,
>   Μοῦσαι Πιερίδες, κλῦτέ μοι εὐχομένῳ.
>ὄλβον μοι πρὸς θεῶν μακάρων δότε καὶ πρὸς ἁπάντων
>   ἀνθρώπων αἰεὶ δόξαν ἔχειν ἀγαθήν·
>[...]
>οὐκ ἐθέλω· πάντως ὕστερον ἦλθε Δίκη·
>πλοῦτον δ' ὃν μὲν δῶσι θεοί, παραγίγνεται ἀνδρὶ
>   ἔμπεδος ἐκ νεάτου πυθμένος ἐς κορυφήν·   10
>ὃν δ' ἄνδρες μετίωσιν ὑφ' ὕβριος, οὐ κατὰ κόσμον
>   ἔρχεται, ἀλλ' ἀδίκοις ἔργμασι πειθόμενος
>οὐκ ἐθέλων ἕπεται· ταχέως δ' ἀναμίσγεται ἄτη
>   ἀρχὴ δ' ἐξ ὀλίγου γίγνεται ὥστε πυρός
>[...]
>θνητοὶ δ' ὧδε νοεῦμεν ὁμῶς ἀγαθός τε κακός τε
>   ἢ δὴν ᾗ ταύτην δόξαν ἕκαστος ἔχει
>πρίν τι παθεῖν· τότε δ' αὖτις' ὀδύρεται· ἄχρι δὲ τούτου   35
>   χάσκοντες κούφαις ἐλπίσι τερπόμεθα,
>[...]
>σπεύδει δ' ἄλλοθεν ἄλλος· ὁ μὲν κατὰ πόντον ἀλᾶται
>   ἐν νηυσὶν χρῄζων οἴκαδε κέρδος ἄγειν
>ἰχθυόεντ', ἀνέμοισι φορεύμενος ἀργαλέοισι   45
>   φειδωλὴν ψυχῆς οὐδεμίαν θέμενος·
>ἄλλος γῆν τέμνων πολυδένδρεον εἰς ἐνιαυτὸν
>   λατρεύει, τοῖσιν καμπύλ' ἄροτρα μέλει
>ἄλλος Ἀθηναίης τε καὶ Ἡφαίστου πολυτέχνεω
>   ἔργα δαεὶς χειροῖν ξυλλέγεται βίοτον   50
>ἄλλος Ὀλυμπιάδων Μουσέων πάρα δῶρα διδαχθείς,
>   ἱμερτῆς σοφίης μέτρον ἐπιστάμενος·
>ἄλλον μάντιν ἔθηκεν ἄναξ ἑκάεργος Ἀπόλλων,
>   ἔγνω δ' ἀνδρὶ κακὸν τηλόθεν ἐρχόμενον,
>ᾧ συνομαρτήσωσι θεοί· τὰ δὲ μόρσιμα πάντως
>   οὔτε τις οἰωνὸς ῥύσεται οὔθ' ἱερά.
>ἄλλοι Παιῶνος πολυφαρμάκου ἔργον ἔχοντες
>   ἰητροί·
>[...]

---

3 Maehler 1982, 182.

Μοῖρα δέ τοι θνητοῖσι κακὸν φέρει ἠδὲ καὶ ἐσθλόν,
  δῶρα δ' ἄφυκτα θεῶν γίγνεται ἀθανάτων
πᾶσι δέ τοι κίνδυνος ἐπ' ἔργμασιν, οὐδέ τις οἶδεν   65
  πῇ μέλλει σχήσειν χρήματος ἀρχομένου,
ἀλλ' ὁ μὲν εὖ ἔρδειν πειρώμενος οὐ προνοήσας
  ἐς μεγάλην ἄτην καὶ χαλεπὴν ἔπεσεν,
τῷ δὲ κακῶς ἔρδοντι θεὸς περὶ πάντα δίδωσι
  συντυχίην ἀγαθήν, ἔκλυσιν ἀφροσύνης   70
πλούτου δ' οὐδὲν τέρμα πεφασμένον ἀνδράσι κεῖται
  οἳ γὰρ νῦν ἡμέων πλεῖστον ἔχουσι βίον,
διπλασίως σπεύδουσι· τίς ἂν κορέσειεν ἅπαντας
  κέρδεά τοι θνητοῖς ὤπασαν ἀθάνατοι
ἄτη δ ἐξ αὐτῶν ἀναφαίνεται, ἣν ὁπότε Ζεὺς   75
  πέμψῃ τεισομένην, ἄλλοτε ἄλλος ἔχει.

Splendid children of Memory and Olympian Zeus, Pierian Muses, listen to my prayer. Grant me prosperity at the hands of the Blessed Gods, and good fame ever among men [...] wealth I desire to possess but I would not have it unfairly; retribution comes always afterwards. The wealth that the Gods give to man comes to last forever, from the bottom even to the top. The wealth that the Gods give to man come to last, from the bottom even to the top of the storage jar, whereas the wealth that men honor by hybris comes not orderly but persuaded against their will by unfair deeds and quickly destruction is mingled with them. Its beginning is small as a fire [...] we mortal men, alike good and bad, are minded this way. Each of us keeps the (same) opinion he has ever had until he suffers ill and then he grieves. Till that moment, we rejoice open-mouthed in vain expectations. [...] each has his own quest. One roams in a shipboard through the fishy sea to bring home gain, tossed by grievous winds, sparing his life no whit, another is interested to plough the well-planted land with a curved ploughshare throughout the year. One gets his living by the skill of his hands in the works of Athena and Hephaestus, the master of many crafts, another through his learning of the gifts of the Olympian Muses cunning in the measure of lovely art. Another again Apollo, the far shooting Lord, makes a seer and the misfortune that comes on a man from afar is known to him, if Gods are with him, cause no augury nor offering will ever ward off what is destined to be. Others again as physicians have the task of the Healer, the master of medicines, for these men too there is no end of their labors because often comes great pain of little and a man cannot assuage it by soothing medicines, whereas he makes quickly whole someone who is confounded by evil and grievous illnesses (just) by laying his hands on him. Surely it is Fate that brings the humans both good and bad and the gifts immortal gods offer are inevitable. There is danger in every sort of business and none knows at the beginning of a matter how it will end. Cause (sometimes) someone who strives to do a good thing falls unawared into great misfortune and sore, whereas God gives good outcome in all things to one whose deeds are bad in order to be delivered from his folly. And as for the wealth there's no end which has been clearly set down. Because these (mortals) of us who have much wealth try to gain more; but who can satisfy everyone? Gods give us mortals possessions, yet a ruin is revealed in them, which whenever Zeus sends it in retribution, one man has it now another (has it) then.

Maehler placed strong emphasis on some verbal similarities or variant formulations between the two texts and on a few conceptual affinities between the two poets. In 2004 another German scholar, Stenger, attempted also to explore the intertextual dialogue between Bacchylides and Solon from another point of view. He argued that the use of the Solonian elegy as a model provides the necessary explicit signals for a contrast between the victor and 'the others' [his competitors?].

I propose to read the poem from another point of view. I shall suggest that the echo of the Solonian elegiac verses in this specific context serves as a literary model, primarily because it develops an aspect of encomiastic rhetoric determined by the 'expectations-horizon' of Bacchylides' client and because it is stimulated by the common political beliefs and ideology the poet shares with his Athenian audience. This is a particularly interesting, mainly because it allows us to detect the way Bacchylides seeks to present himself to the Athenians. Specific features of the poem enable us to determine Bacchylides' rhetorical strategy of praise.

The poem opens with the invocation of the personified Fame (Phema) who travels and visits the tribes of man (l. 1–2: φῦλα), bringing the glorious message of the athletic victory of the addressee. The phrase 'tribes of man' could allude to the panhellenic glory of this victory, as well as to the glory the athlete brings to his own tribe, Oineis, one of the ten Cleisthenic subdivisions of the Athenian democratic city (mentioned in l. 18).[4] It is worth noting here that the addressee is identified as a citizen by the name of his tribe, not by his father's name. This practice follows the main democratic features of the Cleisthenic system.[5]

The poet significantly presents himself as a 'sweet-voiced island bee' (l. 10: νασιῶτιν ἐκίνησεν λιγύφθογγον μέλισσαν). The variety of Bacchylides' metamorphoses when he, through the mouth of his chorus, emphasizes his professional role as a panegyrist is well known; he constantly prefers to use the third person, whereas Pindar employs emphatic first person statements.[6] Here the poet hastens from one theme to another, using only what is necessary or essential for his poem before moving to another theme, like a bee, which darts from one flower to another, collecting only the best part of each.[7] It is notable that Bacchylides'

---

[4] For the Cleisthenic democratic constitution, cf. Hdt. 6.131. Further, on Cleisthenes' reforms in the reorganization of the citizen-body in Athens, cf. Crawford/Whitehead 2004, 160–163.
[5] Pomeroy *et al.* 2004, 122.
[6] For a special emphasis on the subject, see Carey 1999, 18–19.
[7] Aristaios, one of the most ambiguous figures of Greek folk religion, is also the main hero of Cean mythological tradition. Pindar narrates his myth in the *Ninth Pythian Ode* (ll. 59–65). The son of Apollo and the nymphe Cyrene, Aristaios was born in Africa, at his mother's palace in

hometown Ceos is famous for its thyme honey production, just as Athens was a region which in ancient times was renowned for the quality of its thyme honey. Wearing the bee mask, Bacchylides stresses an aspect of the heritage he shares with his patron.[8]

The tone becomes unexpectedly more personal in the next few lines, when the poet turns to the victor and refers to himself in a first-person statement (ll. 13–14: τεὰν ἀρετὰν μανῦον). This rhetorical choice is charged with emotion; for it produces a sense of proximity and creates a personal bond between the speaker and his addressee. Notable also is that the speaker situates his encomiastic profession within civic space: from the general formulation of ἀνθρώποισι (l. 12 = humans) to the more specific ἐπιχθονίοισι (l. 14) which could indicate local people, the speaker's fellow citizens of Athens. The poet underlines that his addressee's athletic success is a common joy for everyone and describes his praising task (ll. 13–14: τεὰν αρετὰν μανῦον ἐπιχθονίοισιν) as a moral choice made for the public benefit (l. 12: ἐγχειρές ξυνὸν ἀνθρώποισιν). Bacchylides' rhetorical virtuosity alludes to the public aspect of epinician performance, something further developed through the perspective of (or the promise of?) a future reperformance, emphatically mirrored in l. 11: 'immortal adornment of the Muses' (ἀθάνατον Μουσᾶν ἄγαλμα).

One of the most striking features of the passage is the juxtaposition of κῦδος and δόξα.[9] Κῦδος is a well-known Homeric term, which is constantly associated with living heroes. It alludes to human confidence that is derived from gods (*Il.* Π 241, Ψ 399ff., Bacchyl. 13.59–60).[10] Kurke defines the epinician *κῦδος* as the civic adaption of its Homeric use: 'Kydos is no merely a synonym for kleos but rather signifies special power bestowed by a god that makes a hero invincible'.[11] Here the *polis* replaces the Homeric king. What is significant for the epideictic rhetoric of the epinikion is that the victor brings κῦδος to his home city, Athens, while he

---

Libya. Gaia and Hores made him immortal by nourishing him with nectar and ambrosia. From Africa, Aristaios came to Ceos, where he taught the local population the art of apiculture (A. R. 4. 1132–1133, Schol. in A. R. 2.498a–c Wendel, Schol. in Pi. *P.* 9.104, 115a–b Dr., Schol. in Ar. *Eq.* 894a–c Koster, Phylarch. fr. 16.9, Nonnus, *D.* 19.242, Schol. in Ar. fr. 511 Rose). This is the reason why he is widely considered as the founder of that art.
8 For the mythological background of this poetic metamorphosis, see Sotiriou 2012, 239–252, esp. 248–250.
9 In a hiatus as Maehler 1982, 183 also points out.
10 Benveniste 1973, 348; Fränkel 1973, 80 n. 14.
11 Kurke 1998, 131–163. Cf. also B. 1.159–160, 6.3, 12.7, Pi. *O.* 4.8–12, 3.38, 5.7, 9.19–20, 14.19, *P.* 9.73, 9.91, 11.13–14, *N.* 2.8, 3.67–70, 5.4–8, *I.* 1.10–12. Cf. also *Il.* 23.400, 406.

brings δόξα to his tribe, Oineides.[12] In the city-state δόξα as a democratic value replaces the aristocratic κλέος.[13] It is exactly what Jaeger called 'Politisierung der Ruhmesidee'.[14] Furthermore, it is worth noticing that the term δόξα is symmetrically positioned in the *polyptoton* of ll. 35ff.: each human is seeking δόξα through his profession. Δόξα is associated with the poet, as well as with the victor elsewhere in Bacchylides [text 4] (B. 9, 13.61, 13.179), something that reminds one of Solon when he asks the Muses [1. 4] to give him good repute (δόξα) among all men at all time at the beginning of his elegy.

Bacchylides invests his professions-passage with the authority of Solon, a poet and a lawgiver, whose name has been related to Athens' most substantial financial and political reforms, which led to the establishment of the Athenian πολιτεία. In both poets the review of the civic professions mirrors local Athenian society. The list is introduced by a short preface in the form of a *polyptoton* (Sol. l. 43: σπεύδει ἄλλοθεν ἄλλος – Bacchyl. l. 35–38: ματεύει ἄλλος ἀλλοίαν κέλευθον). Solon enumerates human manual professions (s.g. sea-merchant/sailor, farmer, artisan), whose main goal is financial prosperity (κέρδος, βίοτος). Such a choice is expected, since Plutarch informs us about Solon's special interest in craftsmen (*Solon* 22.1). These professions are followed by the intellectual professions (poet, soothsayer, physician), in Noussia's words, 'occupations of public relevance, the "profit" of which is never made explicit'.[15] On the contrary, in Bacchylides' priamel the intellectual professions are placed first: Bacchylides speaks about the σοφός (the wise, the skilled man), a term which is practically divided in two subcategories: the poet and the soothsayer. Then, he adds another category, that of the παιδεραστής, an activity which is socially acceptable in classical Athens and combines mental education with the training of the ephebe through physical contact. In stark contrast to his lyric predecessor, who combines the human professions with the 'hope of financial well-being',[16] the professions in Bacchylides are invested with the gain of fame (δόξα). Here, the moral evaluation of profit comes rather late in l. 49, in the conclusion of the passage about the unlimited power of wealth, which can make even the useless (ἀχρεῖον) man useful (χρηστόν). Perhaps we could associate this reference to profit with the negative aspect of the professions. Also, Solon with his familiar descriptive style casts

---

12 The Athenian phylē Oineis took its name from Oineus, illegitimate son of king Pandion. The Cleisthenic reforms concerning the formation of the Athenian phylai are discussed thoroughly in Stanton (1984).
13 Thuc. 2.43.2.
14 Jaeger 1932, 552–553. Cf. also Loraux 1981, 50–54; Dover 1994, 229; Müller 1989, 317–340.
15 Noussia 2010, 176.
16 Noussia 2010, 175.

some light on the negative aspects of wealth, when he says: 'wealthy people are dependable from top to bottom of the storage jar' (ll. 9–13).

The uncertainty of human deeds goes hand in hand with the unknown future, a connection found in both poets. In Bacchylides, we should note the verb (l. 35) ματεύω in the introductory priamel which means 'seek for'. The meaning of the verb is expanded through the moral judgment of ll. 45–47, which focus on the unpredictable future of men. One should mention here the essential role of τύχα, the human factor and the absence of God. Solon, on the other hand, rounds off his list with the element of 'risk' (κίνδυνος). All human activities are unpredictable, the conditions of human life are in fact changeable: in this regard we should note also Solon's special concern about the delusion of hope (χάσκοντες κούφαις ελπίσι = 'we take fond pleasure in our empty hopes').

When Solon speaks about μοῖρα (l. 63), which since Homer has been effectively equated to 'the inescapable destiny of death', Bacchylides replaces the term with τύχα, which indicates 'the fortune given by God', mainly because, as Noussia suggests: 'Moira is not given the role of allotting prosperity or hardship in Homer, where she or other personifications of destiny still mainly have the role of spinning the length of one's life'.[17] By contrast, from Bacchylides' non-pessimistic point of view, human beings are suffused with the light of their successes.[18]

Both Bacchylides and Solon remain conscious of their human limits in order to avoid hybris. Bacchylides is fearful about going beyond the praise of his addressee, which is why he suddenly stops the path of his song and continues with a rhetorical question at the end of the passage (ll. 51–52: 'wherefore have I turned my tongue so far out of its due course?'). The concept of 'gnoseologic measure'[19] plays a cardinal role in the ethical-political thought of Solon, where the achievement of this limit appears to be a τέλος for the poets (l. 52: σοφίης μέτρον).

*

To sum up: through Bacchylides' epinician rhetoric, Ode 10 reveals itself as a matter of 'negotiation' between the poet and the local community of Athens[20] on behalf of the victor who returns to his city, bringing glory and relishing in civic honour. It also functions as a vehicle for poetic self-presentation. Bacchylides endorses images of Athenian daily life and uses them to persuade his public in a

---

17 Noussia 2010, 189.
18 Maehler 1982, 190.
19 Noussia 2010, 185.
20 In Bacchylides' time Athens was an empire. Cf. Hornblower 2004, 247.

place where choral poetry mostly resorts to mythological exemplum. In my opinion this is a conscious poetic choice that articulates the conceptual framework located at the centre of the socio-political system.

In the Ode the poet adapts material familiar to the moral code of his audience and sets it in a new context, thereby recalibrating the mythological narrative. Bacchylides adjusts his artistic achievement to the early democratic ethos of his addressee's hometown, while he sounds the democratic feeling of his audience. His poetic persona can serve as an intermediate between the political elegy of Solon and the civic space of Attic oratory. He does not choose to narrate a local myth of Attica, a region with a rich mythological tradition, and he underscores the moral dimension of his theme in order to portray both himself and his client as idealized citizens.[21]

The professions-passage goes beyond a simple affinity with Solon as to both subject matter and diction. The incorporation of traces from the former Attic elegy reveals the potential relation Bacchylides sought to cultivate with his predecessors. It belongs to the rhetorical repertoire of the poet, which enables him to strengthen and clarify his position in accordance with the expectations of his audience. Bacchylides emphasizes his commitment to the great poets of the Athenian past, thus indicating a personal bond with his client, and the literary and political history of his motherland.[22] He captures the mood of the didactic political elegy and introduces himself as a professional in order to present the audience with his moral truth. Whether the epinician performance took place privately or served as part of a public gathering is not easy to answer. Besides, Solon also promoted his political thoughts and reforms in the context of festivals and civic rituals.

The lyric composition of Bacchylides frames the dialogue between the sympotic world of the aristocratic class of Athens and the civic space of the local Athenian society. The rhetorical repertoire invests Bacchylides' speech with authority, alluding to the coexistence of athletic success and democracy as two things deserving of political praise. From this point of view, keeping in mind the social function an epinicion fulfils, I suggest that the epinician performance of the ode (ll. 53–54: εὐφροσύνα ... αὐλῶν) should not be thought as located in a private place, e.g. at the addressee's house, but instead at a public feast or ceremony organized and funded by his phylē.

---

[21] Similarly, cf. Hornblower 2004, 258.
[22] De Jong 2004, 219.

Bibliography

Benveniste, E. (1973), *Indo-European Language and Society*, London.
Carey, C. (1999) 'Ethos and Pathos in Bacchylides', in: L.I. Pfeijffer/S.R. Slings (eds.), *One Hundred years of Bacchylides*, Amsterdam, 17–29.
Connor, R.W. (1987), 'Tribes, Festivals and Processions: civic ceremonial and political manipulation in archaic Greece', in: *JHS* 108, 40–50.
Crawford, H.M./Whitehead, D. (2004), *Archaic and Classical Greece. A Selection of ancient sources in translation*, Cambridge.
De Jong, I. (2004), 'Pindar and Bacchylides', in: I.J.F. de Jong/R. Nünlist/A. Bowie (eds.), *Narrators, Narratees, and Narratives in Ancient Greek Literature. Studies in Ancient Greek Narrative*, I, Leiden/Boston, 213–232.
Dover, K.J. (1994), *Greek popular morality in the time of Plato and Aristotle*, Indianapolis/Cambridge.
Fagles, R. (ed.) (1989), *Bacchylides, Complete Poems*, Translated with a Note to the New Edition, with a Foreword by Sir M. Bowra, Introduction and Notes by A.M. Parry, New Haven/London.
Fränkel, H. (1973), *Early Greek Poetry and Philosophy*, New York.
Hornblower, S. (2004), *Thucydides and Pindar: Historical Narrative and the World of Epinikian Poetry*, Oxford.
Jaeger, W. (1932), 'Tyrtaios. Über die wahre ἀρετή', in: *SPAW* 23, 537–568.
Kurke, L. (1991), *The Traffic in Praise. Pindar and the Poetics of Social Economy*, Ithaca/London.
Kurke, L. (1998), 'The Economy of Kudos', in: C. Dougherty/L. Kurke (eds.), *Cultural poetics in archaic Greece. Cult, performance, politics* (based on a conference at Wellesley College in October 1990), Oxford, 131–163.
Loraux, N. (1981), *L'invention d'Athènes: histoire de l'oraison funèbre dans la 'cité classique'*, Paris/New York.
Maehler, H. (1982), *Die Lieder des Bakchylides*. Erster Teil: *Die Siegeslieder*, Leiden.
Müller, W.C. (1989), 'Der schöne Tod des Polisbürgers oder "Ehrenvoll ist es, für das Vaterland zu sterben"', in: *Gymnasium* 36, 317–340.
Noussia, M. (ed.) (2010), *Solon the Athenian, The poetic fragments*, Leiden/Boston.
Pomeroy, B.S./Burstein, M.S./Donlan, W./Roberts, T.J. (2004), *A Brief History of Ancient Greece*, New York/Oxford.
Stanton, R.G. (1984), *The Tribal Reform of Kleisthenes the Alkmeonid*, Munich.
Stenger, I. (2004), *Poetische Argumentation. Die Funktion der Gnomik in den Epinikien des Bakchylides*, Berlin/New York.

Eleni Volonaki
Performing the Past in Lycurgus' Speech *Against Leocrates*

1 Performative aspects of oratory

Modern scholars, over a number of years, have thoroughly discussed the interrelation between dramatic contests and legal trials in formal aspects such as performance before an audience and judgement by democratically-selected judges.[1] They have stressed the similarities and differences between Athenian drama and forensic oratory in terms of context, subject-matter, verbal and thematic influences, structure, plot, narrative and characters, and finally the role of the audience.[2] In the oratorical texts, resemblances can be revealed with dramatic 'parts' in terms of the context in which they were performed, the relationship between litigants and judges, the cast of roles constituted by fictive identities, the physical appearance (*opsis*) of the litigants, and their behaviour and conduct (*ēthos*). These are all factors that determine the performance, not the literal meaning of the words themselves but the meaning of the words as spoken by the speaker, a performer.

In antiquity, most rhetorical theories focused on the importance of delivery in the presentation of a forensic speech. Aristotle acknowledges that the study of delivery is essential, since 'the whole business of rhetoric is concerned with appearance' (*Rhetoric* 3.1404a1–8). Aristotle (*Rhetoric* 3.1403b16), however, was also concerned with the rhetorical art of 'what to speak' (ἅ δεῖ λέγειν), i.e. content, arrangement, and style, as distinct from the art of 'how to speak' (ὡς δεῖ εἰπεῖν). Ancient rhetoricians discussed the techniques of designing a speech in such a way that the litigants would win their cases in court and would influence their audiences' decisions through a variety of arguments related to *ēthos* (their character and personality), *pathos* (arousing emotions of the judges) and *pisteis* (proofs), based on common views and rhetorical *topoi* as well as rhetorical strategies.

---
[1] Aristotle, *Rhet.* 3.1403b24–30 recognised a similarity between theatrical and rhetorical delivery.
[2] Dorjahn 1927, 85–93; Perlman, 1964 155–172; Bers 1985, 1994, 1997, 2009; Hall 1995, 2006, ch. 12; Calame 2011, 1–19; Edwards 2012, 87–115 and 2013, 56–76.

https://doi.org/10.1515/9783110629729-012

Nearly all modern scholars approach the understanding of performance as encompassing delivery – the use of gestures and vocal ploys – and the convergences and divergences between oratory and theatre. The interest of a new approach, as presented in this paper, is to offer a holistic perspective on performance and oratory. According to this perspective, oratorical performance is to be seen within an artful communication between the speaker and the audience beyond delivery. One needs to consider both direct/sensory techniques (gestural and vocal ploys) and cognitive/emotional techniques (communication between the speaker and the audience). Texts offer numerous indications of the performative dimension of the forensic speeches. In addition, the interaction of speaker and speech with the audience should be taken into consideration to make better sense of the oratorical text.

The present chapter involves the performance of the past in Lycurgus' speech *Against Leocrates*, the performative dimensions of quotations from epic, tragic and lyric poetry, going beyond *hypokrisis*, 'delivery', and focusing on the impact of the content of the speech's quotations upon the audience. There may be no indications of 'delivery', i.e. information about gestures, voice, or changes in the tone of speaking, but there are words and expressions that confirm a subtle communication between Lycurgus and his audience as he attempts to recreate a rehearsal of tragic, epic, and lyric pieces from earlier oral performance and to evoke similar emotions and views to those which had existed when such pieces were actually performed in fifth-century Athens. Lycurgus' own inclusion of poetry in his forensic speech is an element of extemporaneity that is meant to impress, entertain, move, educate, promote traditional ideals such as patriotism, and thus persuade the judges to win his *eisangelia* against Leocrates. The focus will be placed on the objectives of his use of poetry in relation with the judges and the desirable outcome of the trial.

The nostalgic view of the past appears to function effectively as a kind of legal proof, evidence, and argumentation. Finally, the orator's 'authoritative voice'[3] is transformed and strengthened through the voices of the poets, Euripides, Homer, and Tyrtaeus, and the voices of the heroes portrayed in their poems respectively, so that the speaker interacts with the judges, brings them to share in well-established traditional views from the ancestors, and effectively persuades them that the defendant has been a coward when his city was in danger.

---

[3] For Lycurgus' changing the authoritative voice, cf. Allen 2000, 5–31.

2 Poetic quotations in oratory

The use and significance of poetic quotations in oratory has preoccupied ancient rhetoricians and modern scholars. Poetry was important to the training of the ancient *rhētor*[4] and was the means of education for *rhētores* in matters of eloquence and syntax.[5] Aristotle draws from Homer and the tragic poets in his *Rhetoric*, assuming that logographers should have had a wide knowledge of poetry.

Orators praised the poets for their wisdom, their didactic authority, and influence. It is possible that the Athenian judges liked quotations from poetry. Isocrates stresses the significance of the use of tragedy as establishing models of human nature in order to entertain and please the audience (Isocrates, 2.48–49). Poetry can, thus, be effective in oratory for its didactic and entertaining purpose.

Aristotle, *Rhet.* 3.1.9.1404a speaks of the Athenians' general knowledge of mythological stories, which intensifies the enjoyment of the audience. Entertaining performances in court, such as those implied by Philocleon in Aristophanes' *Wasps* (562–570),[6] required an experienced audience rather than an educated one. Nevertheless, Aristotle is sceptical about the ability of most of the spectators in a theatre to recall even the most well-known material (*Poetics* 1451b23–26). Modern theorists, however, express different views. Revermann, for example, argues that 'Athenian audiences in the fifth and fourth centuries, despite the diversity in their perceptiveness, education, and experience of performances, were competent enough to recognise and interpret rhetorical effects at least at a basic level'.[7]

The presentation of poetic quotations in court and their performative value within a forensic context adds to the oration's overall impact upon the judges. Firstly, poetic quotations were chosen for specific purposes of persuasion and therefore appealed to the judges' common knowledge of the poetic extracts. Secondly, it is true that all the extant quotations from poetry are limited to a small number of forensic speeches delivered in public trials; the three speeches of Aeschines, *Against Timarchus* (346 BCE), *On the False Embassy* (343 BCE), and *Against Ctesiphon* (330 BCE), the speeches of Demosthenes, *On the Crown* (330 BCE) and *On the False Embassy* (343 BCE) and the speech of Lycurgus, *Against*

---

[4] e.g. *Rhet. ad Alex.* 18:1433b11–14 on the way Euripides is quoted.
[5] Perlman 1964, 160–161.
[6] For the comic exaggeration and the audience's response, cf. Carey 2000, 198–203; Hall 2006, 353.
[7] Revermann 2006, 99–124.

Leocrates (330 BCE).⁸ All these trials were held within a period of six years, between 346 and 330 BCE. ⁹ It is worth mentioning that most of the tragic quotations and surely the most extensive ones are used in forensic speeches delivered in the same year, 330, by Lycurgus and Demosthenes themselves, in two public trials that came to court almost at the same time, eight years after the defeat of the Athenians at Chaeronea. The fact that direct quotations from poetry appear quite infrequently in the extant corpus of speeches may have reflected the Athenians' prejudice towards highly-educated speakers. On the other hand, given that the surviving examples come from speeches that were delivered by the speechwriters themselves who were active politicians at their time, it may be suggested that performing tragedy in court was a challenge to inexperienced speakers or simple Athenian citizens (*idiotēs*).

There was an inherent antagonism towards experts, and therefore speakers in court usually present themselves as ignorant and sometimes inexperienced in order to dispel any allegation of rhetorical expertise and skill or professionalism.¹⁰ The role of a speaker in court would have been expected to be quite different from the role of an actor, but the limits between the two genres may have blurred. Thus, it may not be a coincidence that Aeschines, a former actor, was the first Athenian orator whom we know of to have used poetic citations in court.¹¹

In 345 BCE, in his prosecution against Timarchus, Demosthenes' political ally and fellow prosecutor, Aeschines uses poetry¹² to show how Timarchus' own sexual behaviour is shamefully distant from the examples of honourable love presented by the 'good and useful poets' (Aesch. 1.141).¹³ The practice of using poetic

---

8 It is obvious that poetic quotations in forensic oratory are all included in the speeches that involve the political rivalry between Aeschines and Demosthenes, in particular the political trials that followed their Embassy to Philip II for the peace negotiations, and indirectly Lycurgus' political agenda supporting Demosthenes at the time.
9 330 BCE relates to Lycurgus' first attempt to stabilize, protect, and preserve the works of the three tragedians, Aeschylus, Sophocles, and Euripides; cf. Hanink 2014, 9ff.
10 For the claim of amateurism in general, cf. Lys. 12.3, Dem. 54.1–2.
11 Demosthenes (18.180, 267, 19.246–247, 337) presents Aeschines as a generally weak actor when referring to his former career, and he claims that Aeschines had played poorly on stage. The specific plays he names are all by either Sophocles or Euripides; cf. Hanink 2014, 134ff.
12 Aeschines includes in his first speech five quotations from Homer (144: *Iliad* 18.324–329; 148: *Iliad* 18.333–335; 149: *Iliad* 23.77–91; 150: *Iliad* 18.95–99), three from Euripides (128: tragedy unknown; 151: *Sthenoboia* (fr. 671 N.); 152: *Phoenix* (fr. 809 N.). and one from Hesiod (129: *Works and Days* 763–764).
13 Demosthenes and Timarchus had accused Aeschines for high treason due to his inactivity during the second embassy (346 BCE), where he was sent to ratify the terms of peace. Aeschines counterattacked by claiming that Timarchus had usurped the right to speak before the Assembly

quotations in a court-trial was most probably novel but proved effective since Timarchus was after all convicted of *atimia*. Nevertheless, it took fifteen more years before two other orators adopted the same rhetorical practice, at least those we know of.[14]

3 Lycurgus *Against Leocrates*: the past and the poetry

In 330 BCE Lycurgus prosecuted Leocrates on the charge of treason. His speech is the first in the corpus of ancient oratory for its quantity of quoted poetic verse. Lycurgus deploys an unusually excessive number of historical examples and quotations from the poets in his speech *Against Leocrates*. Nothing can surpass the extravagance in the use of poetry by Lycurgus, particularly in his 55-line performance of Praxithea's great patriotic speech from Euripides' *Erechtheus* (*Leocr.* 100). It is very likely that Lycurgus used the poets in his other speeches as well, which have not been preserved to us, for Hermogenes reports that 'he digresses many times into myths and stories and poems' (*Peri ideōn* 2.389); in his speech *Against Menesaichmos*, or 'Delian speech', he seems to have taken the opportunity to recount the story of Abaris and the Hyperboreans.[15]

In his speech *Against Leocrates*, Lycurgus devotes sixty out of the speech's one hundred and fifty paragraphs to historic and poetic material, consisting of three types of arguments: (a) examples of patriotism and piety from the distant past as well as from the more recent past and the present, related to the battle at Chaeronea and the defeat of the Athenians by Phillip II (75–97); (b) poetic quotations which illustrate the patriotism both of the Athenians and the Spartans (98–110); and (c) examples of punishment in previous cases of treason and similar misconduct to that of Leocrates (111–135). Given the length of all this material, it seems unlikely that the quotations were added to the original speech delivered in court in its edited form for publication. It seems more likely that all poetic references and historical examples constitute an essential part of the orator's strategy

---

even though he was prostituting himself to many men in the port city of Piraeus. The suit succeeded and Timarchus was sentenced to *atimia* and politically destroyed, according to Demosthenes.

14 On specific evidence concerning Aeschines' use of earlier literature in a dramatic/performative context.

15 Hall 2006, 368.

and therefore must have been included in the original form of speech as performed by Lycurgus himself. There is no reference to a clerk of court reading this material, and it can thus be assumed that Lycurgus himself was also a performer.

The case, as presented by Lycurgus in his speech *Against Leocrates*, is briefly as follows: after the city of Athens had been destroyed at the battle in Chaeronea in 338 BCE, the Athenians voted on a series of strict measures to protect the city from the threat posed by Phillip II and the expansion of Macedonian power. Among these measures, it was voted that citizens should not send their families away from the city and that they themselves were committed to serve as her guardians. Leocrates, most probably, fled from Athens before these measures had been voted upon, and went first to Rhodes and afterward to Megara for trade, together with his family and all his possessions. Eight years later, when he returned to Athens, Lycurgus prosecuted him for treason via an *eisangelia* (330 BCE). Lycurgus falsely gives the impression that Leocrates had violated the decree, but on the other hand he asks the judges to act as legislators in this specific case, setting an example for cases in the future (1.9). Given the difficulty of convincing the judges that flight is equivalent to treason, and in the absence of any legal precedent, Lycurgus makes a speech of epideictic character which emphasizes one's duty toward the city as opposed to turning toward treason and desertion. The theme itself allows for a display of patriotic behaviour to contrast with the alleged treasonable action of the defendant. Morevoer, he devotes a long section of the speech (72–132), immediately after the narration of the events concerning Leocrates' flight and return and the discussion of the relevant laws, to the presentation of mythical and poetic material. Such a long section, which speakers normally devote to presenting an alleged conflict or a personal attack against their opponents, is unparalleled in Attic oratory. Hence, Lycurgus has been strictly criticised both by ancient and modern scholars for failing in his rhetorical style.[16]

The performative aspect, however, of his style has not been adequately appraised. He introduces a lively element of dramatic performance, epideictic display, and extemporaneity as an integral part of the forensic speech and an effective strategic device for persuasion. The rare application of such material in court[17] confirms the assumption that the Athenians would be expected to show prejudice against any pretentious element of a dramatic performance in court. Moreover, there are common appeals by litigants in court that the judges should

---

16 Cf. Dionysius of Halicarnassus, Hermogenes; Jebb 1893; for a review, see Allen 2000, 11; Hanink 2014, 29–31.
17 Cf. 2. 'Poetic quotations in oratory' in this article.

not be deceived by the litigants' devices, but they should only look for the truth.[18] It is remarkable how Lycurgus succeeds in the presentation of a variety of literary and epigraphic evidence to such an extent that, as we will see, he comes very close to a victory. His mastery lies not only in his authoritative voice as a very influential political figure at the time, but also in his interpretation, justification, and delivery of the literary sources he cites in court.

In the first section (1.72–97), the examples taken mainly from Athenian mythology and history, as well as a mythological episode from Sicily, are skillfully interwoven with arguments from *pathos*; Lycurgus attempts to persuade the judges that Leocrates deserves punishment for his impiety, betrayal, and ingratitude toward the city. The tone is epideictic, and the delivery resembles that of an *epitaphios logos*; Lycurgus as a prominent political figure and reformer in financial, religious, and educative issues attains the role of a distinguished orator who represents his city through his *epainos* of the ancestors and the idealisation of the past. With reference to the ancestors, he takes the opportunity to praise the democratic constitution and the ancestral customs and laws to set these as an example of fifth-century ideology and behaviour. The praise of the past includes also an advisory tone since Lycurgus needs to convince the judges to make their decision in accordance with the stereotyped standards of ancestral tradition and legislation.

The second group of examples includes quotations from poetry which reflect the moral values of patriotism, civic identity, and self-sacrifice (98–110). The orator mingles his own interpretative comments of the poets' classical ideals with the theatrical presentation of the poetic extracts to emphasise Leocrates' dishonourable conduct. Lycurgus' 'literary criticism' of Euripides, Homer, and Tyrtaeus distinguishes his role from that of a *hypocrites* ('actor'), but on the other hand acknowledges the importance of the theatrical performance that will take place in court, so that the judges pleasantly accept the poetic quotations as part of Lycurgus' proofs, while at the same time the dramatization of the poetic extracts becomes even more authoritative.

The performative dimension of the poetic quotations lies both in their delivery (*hypokrisis*) and in their effect upon the judges. Even though there are no clear indications concerning the delivery, e.g. voice, gesture, etc., these quotations encompass the oral performance of epic, dramatic, and lyric poetry of fifth-century Athens. Each quotation represents a specific genre, and it can thus be suggested that when citing tragedy, for example, one needs to cite it in such a way that the audience realise that they are attending a tragic extract; and the same goes for

---

18 On the discourse of deception in Attic oratory, cf. Kremmydas 2013, 51–89.

the other quotations as well. Thus, there must be some techniques to bring into the court the dramatic effect of Euripides' *Erechtheus* or Homer's *Iliad* upon the audience so that the judges adopt Lycurgus' commentary, which follows, concerning the importance of the heroes and their deeds.

3.1 Euripides' *Erechtheus*

Euripides' *Erechtheus* involves the mythical story of Erichthonios, who was born from the bowels of the earth after it received the seed spread by Hephaistos during his attempted seduction of Athena. As an adult, Erichthonios becomes the king of Athens with the name of Erechtheus, before being buried in the soil from which he was born, by a stroke of Poseidon's trident; he had defeated and killed the god's son, Eumolpus the king of Thrace and ally to the Eleusinian rivals. However, this victory would come only with the sacrifice of Erechtheus' daughter.[19]

Euripides presents on the Athenian stage the wisdom of the autochthonous king and founder of the city of Athens. The homonymous tragedy becomes more interesting, since it was performed between 423 and 422 BCE, towards the end of the first phase of the Peloponnesian War, and probably in connection with the beginning of the reconstruction of the temple of Athena Polias, known as Erechtheion. The historic narrative of the war, which makes Erechtheus an enemy of Eumolpus, the son of Poseidon, is dramatized during the dramatic festival of Great Dionysia, a fact that attributes a political dimension to the Euripidean tragedy.

Euripides' *Erechtheus* has reached us in a fragmentary condition, either through citations or through a papyrus which is itself incomplete. Lycurgus cites a long monologue by Praxithea, Erechtheus' wife, who accepts the sacrifice of her daughter in the name of the civic principles that ought to be observed by all Athenians. Lycurgus reflects Euripides' own dramatization of Erechtheus' myth and the values which his tragedy enhances, but also his own personality, his relation to the social and spiritual environment of his time, his political stance toward the city of Athens and its constitution.[20] Praxithea's words can be placed into the context of a narrative action dramatized on an Athenian stage before an Athenian audience that is calling Periclean ideology into question in the face of the Peloponnesian war, and as such it becomes even more intense and effective.[21]

---

[19] On the myth of Erechtheus, cf. Calame 2011, 2–3.
[20] As Hanink 2014, 28 notes, 'Lycurgus frames the lengthy passage of Euripides' *Erechtheus* in such a way that effectively rewrites literary history'.
[21] Calame 2011.

Lycurgus summarizes the plot of Euripides' *Erechtheus* before citing Praxithea's monologue in his speech *Against Leocrates* (98–99). In the beginning he calls the judges to become his audience:

[98] καίτοι σκέψασθε, ὦ ἄνδρες: οὐ γὰρ ἀποστήσομαι τῶν παλαιῶν: ἐφ' οἷς γὰρ ἐκεῖνοι ποιοῦντες ἐφιλοτιμοῦντο, ταῦτα δικαίως ἂν ὑμεῖς ἀκούσαντες ἀποδέχοισθε.

[98] Now pay close attention, men, for I am not about to turn away from the ancestors. Justice demands that you listen to the deeds for which they won respect and accept them into your heart.

In the specific passage, Lycurgus firstly calls for the judges' attention to what is to follow: καίτοι σκέψασθε, ὦ ἄνδρες. Two clauses with γὰρ justify the reasons why the judges should first pay attention and then listen to Praxagora; Lycurgus explains that he will not turn away from the ancestors, since their deeds have won respect and been taken to heart (ποιοῦντες ἐφιλοτιμοῦντο). Moreover, Lycurgus asks the judges not only to listen but also to accept the prologue from Euripides' *Erechtheus*; the phrase ταῦτα δικαίως ἂν ὑμεῖς ἀκούσαντες ἀποδέχοισθε implies that the judges will be the audience of this monologue, and this suggests the dramatisation of the scene and the creation of a special communication between the judges and the speaker. The adverb δικαίως emphasises the exemplary value and legal justification of incorporating the tragic quotation into the forensic speech. In his summary, Lycurgus focuses on the specific story of the daughter's sacrifice: when the large army of Eumolpus and the Thracians was about to invade the country, Erechtheus went to Delphi and asked the god what he should do to gain victory over the enemy; the god's prophecy was that he should sacrifice his daughter before the two armies would meet in battle and in obedience to the god. Erechtheus performed the god's command and drove the invaders from his country.

There are three significant points stressed in this narration of the story; firstly, Erechtheus was a hero of his country who wished to save it before the enemy's threat; secondly, he asked the god's instructions; and thirdly, he obeyed the god's command and willingly sacrificed his daughter to protect his country. In effect, Lycurgus praises Erechtheus as the hero who made the ultimate sacrifice for the sake of his own people; the implication, of course, is that Leocrates' action was completely the opposite and as such should be considered treason.

Lycurgus subsequently concludes that Euripides should be praised on the grounds that he is a good poet 'ἀγαθὸς ποιητής' ('good poet'), since he chose to create a tragedy with the particular myth of Erechtheus. According to Lycurgus, Euripides thought that the ancestors' deeds would be the best example for the citizens, since if the citizens paid attention and looked at them as spectators, they would learn to love their country (τὸ τὴν πατρίδα φιλεῖν).

> [100] διὸ καὶ δικαίως ἄν τις Εὐριπίδην ἐπαινέσειεν, ὅτι τά τ' ἄλλ' ὧν ἀγαθὸς ποιητὴς καὶ τοῦτον τὸν μῦθον προείλετο ποιῆσαι, ἡγούμενος κάλλιστον ἂν γενέσθαι τοῖς πολίταις παράδειγμα τὰς ἐκείνων πράξεις, πρὸς ἃς ἀποβλέποντας καὶ θεωροῦντας συνεθίζεσθαι ταῖς ψυχαῖς τὸ τὴν πατρίδα φιλεῖν. ἄξιον δ', ὦ ἄνδρες δικασταί, καὶ τῶν ἰαμβείων ἀκοῦσαι, ἃ πεποίηκε λέγουσαν τὴν μητέρα τῆς παιδός. ὄψεσθε γὰρ ἐν αὐτοῖς μεγαλοψυχίαν καὶ γενναιότητα ἀξίαν καὶ τῆς πόλεως καὶ τοῦ γενέσθαι Κηφισοῦ θυγατέρα.

> [100] Euripides therefore deserves our praise because, in addition to his other poetic virtues, he chose to make a tragedy out of this myth, considering that their deeds would serve as the best example that citizens could look to and attend as spectators and thus accustom their hearts to love their country. The iambic verses he wrote for the girl's mother are worth hearing, gentlemen of the court, for in them you will see the magnanimity and nobility that made her worthy of our city and to be Cephisus' daughter.

The present participles, 'πρὸς ἃς ἀποβλέποντας καὶ θεωροῦντας',[22] encourages the judges to become the audience by paying attention and looking at the spectacle that will obviously follow: an act, the orator's performance of Praxagora. As a result, the judges will get used to the idea of loving their country; the phrasing 'συνεθίζεσθαι ταῖς ψυχαῖς τὸ τὴν πατρίδα φιλεῖν' recalls the *catharsis* (the cleansing from harmful emotions) in the positive and educative value of obtaining a moral lesson of how to love one's country. The assumption that the judges will be the audience of the Euripidean verses, as they had been composed for Praxithea, becomes clear in the phrase, 'καὶ τῶν ἰαμβείων ἀκοῦσαι, ἃ πεποίηκε λέγουσαν τὴν μητέρα τῆς παιδός'. Moreover, the following statement, 'ὄψεσθε γὰρ ἐν αὐτοῖς μεγαλοψυχίαν καὶ γενναιότητα ἀξίαν καὶ τῆς πόλεως καὶ τοῦ γενέσθαι Κηφισοῦ θυγατέρα' seems to indicate that a performance will immediately follow, and that Lycurgus will play the role of Praxithea, he is the one who will dramatize Praxithea's monologue, while the judges will be the audience who will perceive and realize Praxithea's magnanimity and nobility. As becomes obvious, Lycurgus will attempt to set an example for education and imitation through his performance of the mother's monologue, an example like that Euripides had set in his own time through his tragedy, one aiming to shape the citizens in such a way as to love their country.

Subsequently, Praxithea's monologue is presented in a dramatized form, with iambic metre and tragic extract; and we may suggest that Lykourgos will say

---

[22] ἀποβλέπω: 'pay attention to', 'regard' (*LSJ* A.2); θεωρέω: 'look at, attend as spectator' (*LSJ* 2.II)

himself the monologue, keeping the metre and the dramatic context so that the judges will realise that for that moment they are the audience of this tragic monologue. Lycurgus has the authoritative voice of a political figure who has introduced many novelties into the public sphere, the voice of Euripides, whom he admires and praises among the classical poets, and, finally, the voice of Praxithea, whom he praises as an idealised female prototype of bravery and courage. Praxithea starts her speech with a reference to the nobility, that should be known by their favours toward the city (l. 1–3). She offers many reasons for which she has decided to give her daughter to be sacrificed; she refers to the city of Athens as the best of all and her citizens as *autochthones*, arguing that those who desert the city are no longer citizens but foreigners without a country (l. 4–15). She also explains that it is preferable for one only person to die than the many (l. 16–21). Moreover, she says that in opposition to other mothers, who cry when their children go to war, she would have sent her child, if she had a boy, to fight for his country to gain the glory, just like her daughter who will herself gain all the glory for her sacrifice (l. 22–40). Praxithea presents herself as the saviour of the city (l. 41–42) and appeals to the preservation of ancestral traditional institutions and rituals (l. 43–49). Finally, she offers her daughter while she is praising the love for country that should be shared by all (l. 50–55).

It is obvious that the specific monologue involves two essential points: first, the *autochthonia* of the Athenians, which should be defended against any threat by the enemies, and secondly the patriotism (*philopatria*), which is praised and presented as the most prominent ideal of each citizen. As Lycurgus remarks, after the specific quotation from Euripides' *Erechtheus*, Praxithea's monologue and the tragedy ensured that citizens grew to love their country and would never desert or shame it as a result (*Leocr.* 1.101):

> ταῦτα, ὦ ἄνδρες, τοὺς πατέρας ὑμῶν ἐπαίδευε. φύσει γὰρ οὐσῶν φιλοτέκνων πασῶν τῶν γυναικῶν, ταύτην ἐποίησε τὴν πατρίδα μᾶλλον τῶν παίδων φιλοῦσαν, ἐνδεικνύμενος ὅτι εἴπερ αἱ γυναῖκες τοῦτο τολμήσουσι ποιεῖν, τούς γ' ἄνδρας ἀνυπέρβλητόν τινα δεῖ τὴν εὔνοιαν ὑπὲρ τῆς πατρίδος ἔχειν, καὶ μὴ φεύγειν αὐτὴν ἐγκαταλιπόντας μηδὲ καταισχύνειν πρὸς ἅπαντας τοὺς Ἕλληνας, ὥσπερ Λεωκράτης.

> These verses, gentlemen, educated our fathers. Though all women by nature love their children, the poet portrayed this woman as loving her country more than her children, showing thus that if women will have the courage to do this, men should devote themselves to their country ahead of everything else. They should not abandon their country and flee or disgrace it in front of all the Greeks, as Leocrates did.

The key-word here is ἐπαίδευε, which reflects the view that Athenian tragedy formed the civic ideology and represented democracy.²³ In this context, the idea of education confirms the dramatisation of Praxithea's monologue that has preceded and justifies the performance of a tragic monologue in court, using it as an example and thus an argument against Leocrates, who, according to Lycurgus, not only abandoned his country but also disgraced it in front of all the Greeks. The universality of Athenian tragedy is emphatically stressed here to underline the unanimous guilt of Leocrates' treason.

Lycurgus obviously recognized in the myth of Erechtheus a prototype which had inspired and educated the ancestors of the Athenian judges. Euripides' tragedy adds validity and authority since Athenian classical tragedy has widely acquired recognition and fame by the late fourth century, particularly Euripidean tragedy.²⁴ Moreover, Euripides' version of the myth has an emphatic dramatic impact upon the audience because of the contrast created between a woman who sacrificed her own daughter for the sake of the city and supported the civic values from the classical period and a man, Leocrates, who was a coward and traitor of the city at a critical moment of danger a few years before the trial.

Lycurgus' quotation from Euripides' *Erechtheus* can be seen as an integral part of the *epitaphios* tradition, following Demosthenes' funeral oration for the dead at the Chaeronea battle, and dealing with the myth of Athenian *autochthonia*, which constitutes an essential part of the *epainos* in an *epitaphios logos*. Moreover, Erechthus – the archaic king of Athens and the founder of the *polis* – was one of the *eponymoi* heroes of Athens (thus the first Athenian tribe was named *Erechtheis*) and symbolized its ancestral history and tradition as well as its democratic constitution.

The Athenians' victory over Eumolpus is a commonplace of Athenian epideictic oratory, particularly in *epainos*,²⁵ used both by Euripides and Lycurgus in a different context in each case, dramatic and forensic respectively. Beyond the encomiastic nature of the story, in the specific trial, the mythic quotation may also be related to the recent history of the Athenians, after the battle at Chaeronea, when Alexander the Great had razed the city of Thebes, supposedly killing

---

23 Cf., for example, Hall 1991 and 2010; Goldhill/Osborne 1999.
24 In the second half of the fourth century a new vision of 'classical' tragedy was developed in such a way as to forge ideological links between the city's triumph in the fifth century and its theatrical history. Lycurgus' programme aimed at turning the city's 'golden age' into a usable past which provided thus new opportunities for innovation in political, financial, and cultural development, especially after the expansion of Macedonian power in Greece.
25 On the commonplaces of epideictic oratory, cf. Thomas 1989, 218; Ziolkowski 1981, 74–137; Loraux 1986, 241–251; Volonaki 2014, 16–33; Hanink 2014, 34–35.

6,000 of its inhabitants and enslaving another 30,000 (Diod. Sic. 17.11.1–14.1). The story of Eumolpus' invasion is also quoted by Demosthenes in the epitaphios logos that he was elected to deliver for those who died at the battle of Chaeronea in 338. The same story enhances the encomiastic tone of the epideictic arguments and historic examples that Lycurgus is using to emphasise Leocrates' guilt for treason.[26]

Lycurgus, as the performer, represents a plurality of voices: his own, Praxithea's, and Euripides'.[27] Lycurgus is justified to be the performer in this instance, since he is the one who re-evaluated the importance and value of 'classical tragedy' through his programme of rewriting, collection, and archiving tragic texts, the erection of the statues of the three tragic poets in the *agora*, and the reconstruction of the theatre itself. It is likely that Lycurgus attempts to justify the value of poetry by establishing the virtues of the poets.[28]

By virtue of his status as Eteoboutad, 'Lycurgus was in a position to embody Praxithea in a rather strong sense, and to share her solemn priestly authority'.[29] The choice of Euripides' *Erechtheus* is associated with Lycurgus' own religious background, which involved his personal involvement in the religious, theatrical, and dramatic restructure of his time. Lycurgus employs an authoritative voice through his status as Eteoboutad, a reformer of culture and religion, and as an administrator of public finances, in order to quieten down the *dicastic thorybos* that might break out due to the Athenians' prejudice against an excessive use of poetry in court or even toward the presentation of an old play of Euripides, *Erechtheus*.

On balance, the performative aspects in the presentation of Euripides' *Erechtheus* involve the dramatisation that takes place while Lykourgos delivers and reproduces Praxithea's monologue. There are no indications concerning stance, voice, gestures of delivery, but what we know from the text is that the specific tragic monologue addresses the judges in a way similar to how it had addressed the audience in the fifth-century production of the tragedy, recalls the ideals of patriotism as they are expressed in this monologue, and asks the judges to accept the female prototype of heroism and love for country. The speaker makes clear through his delivery that he is saying Praxithea's monologue as if he were playing

---

26 For the interrelation between Lycurgus 1, *Against Leocrates* and Demosthenes 60, *Epitaphios*, cf. Loraux 1986, 393 n. 40.
27 Loraux 1986, 396ff.
28 On the view that Lycurgus reclaims Greece's most popular tragedian, Euripides, for Athens and assigns tragedy to a most important place in the city's history, cf. Hanink 2014, 70–87.
29 Lambert 2015, 4–24.

this role. On the other hand, however, he cannot take the role of an actor but as an orator he addresses the judges through the medium of a dramatic text.

3.2 Homer, *Iliad*

Lycurgus goes further to recollect the virtues of those heroic times that constitute the *palaia*. He quotes the example of Hector, who encouraged the Trojans to fight for their country; he also cites a monologue where Hector displays the glory that is acquired through death in battle for the sake of protecting and saving women, children, and country. The Homeric hero is presented as a convincing model for the prosecution's case. Lycurgus praises Homer and explains that the examples of nobility and brevity illustrated in epic poetry can be more persuasive than the laws (*Leocr.* 1.102):

> [102] βούλομαι δ' ὑμῖν καὶ τὸν Ὅμηρον παρασχέσθαι ἐπαινῶν. οὕτω γὰρ ὑπέλαβον ὑμῶν οἱ πατέρες σπουδαῖον εἶναι ποιητὴν ὥστε νόμον ἔθεντο καθ' ἑκάστην πεντετηρίδα τῶν Παναθηναίων μόνου τῶν ἄλλων ποιητῶν ῥαψῳδεῖσθαι τὰ ἔπη, ἐπίδειξιν ποιούμενοι πρὸς τοὺς Ἕλληνας ὅτι τὰ κάλλιστα τῶν ἔργων προῃροῦντο. εἰκότως· οἱ μὲν γὰρ νόμοι διὰ τὴν συντομίαν οὐ διδάσκουσιν ἀλλ' ἐπιτάττουσιν ἃ δεῖ ποιεῖν, οἱ δὲ ποιηταὶ μιμούμενοι τὸν ἀνθρώπινον βίον, τὰ κάλλιστα τῶν ἔργων ἐκλεξάμενοι, μετὰ λόγου καὶ ἀποδείξεως τοὺς ἀνθρώπους συμπείθουσιν.

> [102] I wish to bring Homer also to your attention praising his poetry. Your ancestors considered him such an important poet that they established a law that every four years at the Panathenaia the rhapsodes recite the epic poems of this poet alone of all the poets, showing in this way the Greeks that they admired the noblest deeds. And rightly so, since the laws because of their brevity do not teach but merely order what one should do; the poets, on the other hand, by representing human life and selecting the noblest deeds, persuade men by using both reason and clear examples.

The phrase τὸν Ὅμηρον παρασχέσθαι[30] connotes the presentation of the Homeric citation and by implication indicates its performative value here. The praise of the poet is consistent with the praise of Euripides earlier in the speech in the sense that Lycurgus justifies the necessity for his citation while adding authority to the poet's voice in the forensic context. Moreover, Lycurgus goes on to recall the ancestors' rhapsodic competitions where the Homeric poems used to be recited; thus, he signals the oral culture in which the Homeric epics were orally delivered and therefore performed. The reminder that the ancestors had made a law for this kind of competition adds legal authority to the oral presentation and

---

30 For παρασχέσθαι meaning 'to present', cf. *LSJ* B.I.3, III.

by implication to the orator's performance of the Homeric poem. Furthermore, the phrase 'ἐπίδειξιν ποιούμενοι' suggests again the epideictic nature not only of the content but also of the application of poetic quotation in Lycurgus' speech. He chooses to cite poetry to present examples for his legal case and to praise the poets; the poems and the message he wishes to emphasise justify his rhetorical strategy in the specific speech. The adverb 'εἰκότως' is emphasised to show that the poetic quotations are far more important than the laws in his case; the performance of the Homeric poem not only teaches but offers logic and reason together with the necessary proof to establish his case. In other words, the performance of Hector's speech constitutes a reasonable argument and proof for his legal case against Leocrates. Lycurgus explains why he is using poetry in such a way so that his performance acquires authority from the poetry itself, but the poetry cited also lends significance support to his speech.

Hector's brief address to his people (only 6 lines) focuses on the praise of an honourable death in war in defence of one's country. In the same vein, Lycurgus emphasises the ancestors' virtue, which has been proven in their deeds and not only in words, since they died not only for their country but for the whole of Greece. The performative value of the epic poem is underlined by the phrase 'τούτων τῶν ἐπῶν ἀκούοντες' (104) with reference to the ancestors' oral experience, implying that the judges are now the audience for the poem. Lycurgus earlier praised the rhapsodic competition that had occurred many decades before, during the Panathenaia, and it can be suggested that he plays the role of the rhapsodist in the forensic context.

The epideictic nature of the epic recitation is stressed in the praise of the ancestors' achievements in the past, such as their victory at Marathon (104) when they repelled the barbarian invader, dying not only for their fatherland but also for the safety of all of Greece. Epic poetry is praised and exemplified to such an extent that not only the bravery and victory of the Athenians in the Persian wars is emphasised, but also their superiority over all Greece. Lycurgus has his own literary and authoritative voice in praising and interpreting Homer, on the one hand, and Hector's voice, on the other, a hero who glorifies death in battle and sets a moral example in the past and present. Obviously, there is a connection between Homer and Euripides, Hector and Praxithea, through Lycurgus' voice.

3.3 Tyrtaeus' elegy – Simonides' epigrams

Tyrtaeus was a Spartan poet who wrote of the Second Messinian War.[31] As with the other poets, Lycurgus praises Tyrtaeus for two reasons: firstly, under his command, the Greeks defeated their enemy and organized their system of training for their young men, and secondly, Tyrtaeus had composed elegiac poems which used to teach the ancestors to be courageous (106). The orality of the elegiac poems in the past and the performance in their recitation is underlined by the phrase, κατέλιπε γὰρ αὐτοῖς ἐλεγεῖα ποιήσας, ὧν ἀκούοντες παιδεύονται πρὸς ἀνδρείαν ('he left them elegies, so that they, through hearing them, are educated to become brave'); the implication is that the judges will also benefit from listening to Tyrtaeus' elegy.

Lycurgus commends how the ancestors attributed distinction to Tyrtaeus more than to any other poet; they were so enthusiastic about Tyrtaeus that they established a law that whenever they were on campaign, they must summon everyone to the tent of the king to hear the poems of Tyrtaeus, because they thought that this would encourage them to die for their country. Here we have evidence supported by a law that poetry has shaped in the past brave citizens to such an extent that it motivated the young men to sacrifice their lives for the good of their country.

Lycurgus emphasizes the usefulness of Tyrtaeus' poems so that he can justify, in this specific instance, his own performance of an elegy; he says that the judges will benefit by listening to the elegy because they will be able to understand the sort of deeds that brought men fame in their country (107: χρήσιμον δ' ἐστὶ καὶ τούτων ἀκοῦσαι τῶν ἐλεγείων, ἵν' ἐπίστησθε οἷα ποιοῦντες εὐδοκίμουν παρ' ἐκείνοις, 'it's useful to hear these elegies in order to understand by which deeds they flourished'). The phrase ἀκοῦσαι τῶν ἐλεγείων indicates that the judges will be Lycurgus' audience for his elegy. The usefulness of Lycurgus' performance is stressed within a context of temporary education regarding Athenian history. Here again, as in the earlier two instances, there is no indication that someone else, for example the court-clerk, makes the recitation, and so we can assume that Lycurgus himself recites the poem.

The elegy is one of the longest fragments of Tyrtaeus (fr. 10 West) to survive and it is preserved only because Lycurgus quotes it here. The first ideal stressed in the whole of the elegy is the noble and glorious death that may come when fighting for one's country. The poem goes on to describe all the misfortunes that

---

[31] The legend that Tyrtaeus was actually an Athenian is found in Plato *Laws* 629a but is most probably an invention of Athenian propaganda; cf. Harris 2001, 189 n. 76.

befall someone who leaves behind his city; he will be hated by all, he brings shame on his family, disgrace to his noble shape, complete dishonour and wretchedness. The phrasing portrays a *persona* to avoid and implicitly describes Leocrates' character. The poet then urges the audience to choose the opposite behaviour, since no one respects or cares for the man who flees, or for his descendants after him. Young men are encouraged to stand next to each other and fight, not to turn to shameful flight or fear, not to flee and abandon the older men.

Lycurgus criticizes the poem by emphasizing the usefulness of these words to the ancestors, who, having heard them, became so brave that they won the Persian Wars – the best and noblest victory of all (108). Here we have another example, where ancestral values are closely related to literary history; the epideictic tone of funeral speeches is predominant, and Lycurgus recalls that standard section of the *epainos*, which refers to the Greeks' victory in the Persian Wars. There are two allusions here, one to the Athenian victory over the Persians in 490 and the other to the battle at Thermopylae in 480, where a small band of Spartans held back the much larger Persian army for several days before they were overwhelmed. Lycurgus' voice is that of a poet who acts as an educator; the Homeric values of bravery and courage that are continuously prominent in the epideictic poetry of the fifth and fourth centuries BCE are here re-evaluated to enhance civic ideology not only of the city of Athens but also of the whole of Greece, obviously against the Macedonian threat.

Lycurgus closes the section of literary evidence and performance with two epigrams attributed to the poet Simonides (555–468 BCE). These poems constitute true testimonies of the Spartans' and the Athenians' courage for all the Greeks. The first one was written for the Spartans announcing that they lie there dead, after having been obedient to their laws (108). The second one is for the Athenians' ancestors after the Marathon battle, praising them for their victory over the strong and wealthy Persians.

Both epigrams praise the sacrifice, bravery, and courage of Spartans and Athenians. Lycurgus' praise of Tyrtaeus, a Spartan poet who has influenced not only the Spartans but also the Athenians and the rest of the Greeks, is emphatically reaffirmed here in the presentation of the funerary epigrams of both the Spartans' and the Athenians' ancestors.

4 Conclusion

As has been shown so far, poetry constitutes a separate and complete section in Lycurgus' speech.[32] According to Aristotle's classification of proofs cited in court, poetry is included among other *atechnai pisteis* (artless evidence), such as laws, decrees, oaths, wills, witnesses, etc. On this view, direct quotations from poetry can be taken as a form of legal evidence upon which Leocrates' conviction is being established. As Lycurgus has himself demonstrated, there is more to the performance and recitation of poetry than its legal value. Poetry supersedes any law, since it sets examples to imitate, and thus it can educate, shape civic values, and thus persuade the judges.

Lycurgus presents himself in the very beginning of the speech (*Leocr.* 1.5–6) as a disinterested prosecutor who has no personal involvement with the defendant Leocrates but is bringing this case only for the sake of the city. His method of prosecution, as he argues (*Leocr.* 1.31–32), is opposite to that of a sycophant, making himself into a symbol of the positive ethical values.[33] In this context, Lycurgus appears to be interested only in justice, appealing to the kind of punishment that used to be enforced by the ancestors in similar occasions. As a political figure, Lycurgus has proved that his main concern is the public good and the protection of the city. His political *persona* contributes to the way he addresses the judges in court, in that it creates a specific communication between him and his audience. His political *ēthos* constitutes an important performative aspect of his prosecution in court. Moreover, his use of poetic quotations, from tragedy, epic, and lyric poetry, as related to his reforms, adds dramatisation to his speech and constitutes a further performative aspect concerning his influence upon the judges' decision.

Lycurgus, as a clever politician, saw the opportunity to insert a new voice into the Athenian political arena, acting as someone who is simply voicing permanent but silenced concerns, while having erased his private voice. Lycurgus seems to think that mythical stories about the Athenians' ancestry are necessary for the contemporary cultivation of virtue among the citizens. Given that he introduces a new model of a public prosecutor and a novel approach to politics in the city, the use of myths about the ancestors can be seen as 'a necessary part of the work of re-founding'.[34]

---

[32] Dorjahn 1927, 89–90.
[33] For Lycurgus' status as a prosecutor in this speech, cf. Allen 2000.
[34] Allen 2000, 27–30.

Poetry constitutes a source of credibility and authority, as well as a source of political archetypes of behaviour for the continuity of ancient ideals in the city of Athens.[35] Lycurgus has a plurality of voices, first his own as a prominent politician who has a vision to reform the education of the *ephebes* and the cultural programme by re-evaluating classical tragedy, the three tragedians and the golden age of civic, ideological, and cultural principles they represented. Moreover, he has the voice of an Eteoboutad: he comes from a family of priests and has implemented changes in religious matters and laws while administering the public finances for twelve years. He also retains other authoritative voices, those of the poets and their personality as reflected in their work, but also the voices of the heroes presented from the mythical background.

As has been shown, there is a specific pattern in Lycurgus' use of poetic quotations and his performance of the poetic extracts from tragedy, epic, and elegy. He offers the judges a literary criticism of each poet and genre; he praises each poet, his work, his personality, and his contribution to Athenian glory and history. Lycurgus addresses the judges as an audience who will hear each poem and will benefit from it; either they will be educated, or they will understand further the importance of certain values, or they will themselves become patriots and good citizens. He is using poetry as a medium of dramatic mechanism to arouse emotions, to share ideals of patriotism and heroism with the judges, to promote specific heroic prototypes, and finally to recall the impact of literary genres of fifth-century Athens and their associated performative value into the forensic context of an *eisangelia* of late fourth-century Athens.

The text offers numerous indications of the performative dimension of Lycurgus' speech *Against Leocrates*. As stated in the beginning of this chapter, the holistic view of performance in oratory involves the development of a better understanding of the objectives of Lycurgus' speech, his mechanisms of persuasion, and the extent to which the performative aspects of his speech may have influenced the outcome of Leocrates' trial. Lycurgus interacts with his audience through the dramatic mechanisms of poetic citations, makes use of the past to influence the present trial, employs *ēthos* and *pathos* to communicate with the judges, and, as we later find out (Aesch. 3.252), succeeds in persuading almost all of them.

By connecting the past with the present and integrating the literary genres of fifth-century Athens at a trial of an *eisangelia* in the last quarter of the fourth cen-

---

[35] For the nostalgic view of tragedy, as well as the argument that a forensic speech imitates the fundamental mechanisms of tragedy, cf. Wilson 1996, 310–331.

tury Lycurgus' rhetorical strategy lies in the oral and performative value of education. In classical Athens, poetry was always performed for an audience so that the Athenians were educated with certain moral and social values, connected with excellence, freedom, and democracy. Lycurgus employs the same approach of education in his use of poetic quotations in court; he wishes to educate the judges so that they reach the best and most beneficial verdict for the city. Thus, his rare and most extensive rhetorical use of poetry can be accepted in court as performed by Lycurgus' authoritative and plural voices.

Bibliography

Allen, D.S. (2000), 'Changing the Authoritative Voice: Lycurgus' *Against Leocrates*', in: *CA* 19, 5–33.
Azoulay, V./Ismard, P. (2011), *Clisthène et Lycurgue d'Athènes*, Paris
Bers, V. (1994), 'Tragedy and rhetoric', in: I. Worthington (ed.), *Persuasion. Greek Rhetoric in Action*, London/New York, 176–95.
Bers, V. (2009), *Genos Dikanikon. Amateur and Professional Speech in the Courtrooms of Classical Athens*, Cambridge MA.
Calame, C. (2011), 'Myth and Performance on the Athenian Stage: Praxithea, Erechtheus, Their Daughters, and the Etiology of Autochthony', in: *CPh* 106, 1–19.
Carey, C. (2000) 'Observers of speech and hearers of action', in: O. Taplin (ed.), *Literature in the Greek and Roman worlds*, Oxford, 192–216.
Carey, C. (2007), 'Epideictic Oratory', in: I. Worthington (ed.), *A Companion to Greek Rhetoric*, 1st ed., London, 236–252.
Collard, C./Cropp, M.J./Lee, K.H. (eds.) (1995), *Euripides, Selected Fragmentary Plays*, I, Warminster.
Cropp, M.J. (1995), 'Erechtheus', in: C. Collard/M.J. Cropp/K.H. Lee, 148–194.
Dorjahn, A.P. (1927), 'Poetry in Athenian Courts', in: *CPh* 22, 85–93.
Fisher, N. (1976), *Social values in classical Athens*, London.
Goldhill, S./Obsorne, R. (1999), *Performance Culture and Athenian Democracy*, Cambridge.
Hall, E. (1991), *Inventing the Barbarian: Greek Self-Definition Through Tragedy*, Oxford.
Hall, E. (1995), 'Lawcourt Dramas: The Power of Performance in Greek Forensic Oratory', in: *BICS* 40, 39–58; cf. 'Lawcourt Dramas: Acting and Performance in Legal Oratory', in: E. Hall (2006), *The Theatrical Cast of Athens*, Oxford, chapter 12.
Hall, E. (2002), 'The singing actors of antiquity', in: P. Easterling/E. Hall (eds.), *Greek and Roman actors. Aspects of an Ancient Profession*, Cambridge, 3–38.
Hall, E. (2006), *The Theatrical Cast of Athens*, Oxford.
Hall, E. (2010), *Greek Tragedy: Suffering under the Sun*, Oxford.
Hanink, J. (2014), *Lycurgan Athens and the Making of Classical Tragedy*, Cambridge.
Hansen, M.H. (1975), *Eisangelia: the sovereignty of the people's court in Athens in the fourth century B.C. and the impeachment of generals and politicians*, Odense.
Harris, E.M. (2000), 'Open Texture in Athenian Law', in: *Dike* 3, 27–79.
Jebb, R.C. (1893), *The Attic Orators. From Antiphon to Isaeus*, London.

Kremmydas, C. (2013), 'The Discourse of Deception and Characterisation in Attic Oratory', in: *GRBS* 53, 51–89.
Lambert, S. (2010), 'Connecting with the past in Lykourgan Athens: an epigraphical perspective', in: L. Foxhall/H.-J. Gehrke/N. Luraghi (eds.), *Internationale Geschichte Spinning Time*, Stuttgart, 225–238.
Lambert, S. (2015), Review of Johanna Hanink (2014), *Lycurgan Athens and the Making of Classical Tragedy*, Cambridge, in: *Bryn Mawr Classical Review* 2015.04.2.
Loraux, N. (1986), *The Invention of Athens: The Funeral Oration in the Classical City*, transl. A. Sheridan, Cambridge.
Parker, R.C.T. (1996), *Athenian Religion: A History*, Oxford/New York.
Perlman, S. (1964), 'Quotations from Poetry in Attic Orators of the Fourth Century', in: *AJP* 85, 155–172.
Petrie, A. (ed.) (1922), *Lycurgus, The speech against Leocrates*, Cambridge.
Revermann, M. (2006), 'The competence of theatre audiences in fifth and fourth century Athens', in: *JHS* 126, 99–124
Schwenk, C. (1985), *Athens in the Age of Alexander the Great: The Dated Laws and Decrees of the Lykourgan Era 338–322 B.C.*, Chicago.
Sonnino, M. (ed.) (2010), *Euripidis Erechthei quae extant*, Florence.
Todd, S.C. (2007), *Lysias Commentary 1–11*, Oxford.
Thomas, R. (1989), *Oral Tradition and Written Record in Athens*, Cambridge.
Ullman, B.L. (1942), 'History and Tragedy', in: *TAPA* 72, 25–53.
Volonaki, E. (2014), 'Narratological elements in epideictic oratory', in: *Platon* 59, 16–33.
Wilson, P.J. (1996), 'Tragic Rhetoric: The Use of Tragedy and the Tragic in the Fourth Century', in: M.S. Silk (ed.) *Tragedy and the Tragic: Greek Theatre and Beyond*, Oxford, 310–331.
Worthington, I./Cooper, C.R./Harris, E.M. (2001), *The Oratory of Classical Greece*. V, *Dinarchus, Hyperides, and Lycurgus*, Austin.
Xanthakis-Karamanos, G. (1979) 'The Influence of Rhetoric on Fourth-Century Tragedy', in: *CQ* 29, 66–76.
Ziolokowski, J.E. (1981), *Thucydides and the Tradition of Funeral Speeches at Athens*, New York.

Part III: **Drama in Attic Oratory**

Evangelos Alexiou
Rhetoric, Poetry and the *agelaioi sophistai*

The Innovative Isocrates

In the *proemium* of his final speech, *Panathenaicus* (339 BCE), Isocrates protests, in an autobiographical reference, against the misfortunes and slanders in relation to his *logon paideia*, which he calls *philosophy*,[1] but also against his physical weaknesses: while he was better able to form a correct opinion about the truth of any matter than 'those who claim to have exact knowledge', he was unable to speak before an assemblage of many people (9). The lack of a strong voice and confidence before the public deprived him of an active political presence in the Assembly. However, he subsequently revels in the fact that he did not decide due to these weaknesses to remain inglorious or obscure (11). He turned to pedagogical activity and the authoring of written rhetorical speeches, dealing not with trivial suits or private contracts but with major and important cases, maintaining that the content of his speeches grants him higher honor than that bestowed to those who speak in public.[2]

Regardless of whether his disabilities were the real causes or a pretext for the turn of Isocrates to written speech, the above statements have nothing to do with the disappointment of an active person or with an antidemocratic attitude, as is sometimes argued in the literature.[3] On the contrary, they are seen to be part of a rhetorical strategy; by overemphasizing his weaknesses, Isocrates employs two rhetorical techniques known from his encomia as *chalepon* and *para to prosekon*; thereby he highlights the difficulty of a venture which does not correspond to the difficulties in order to magnify his final achievement.[4] Isocrates is exceptionally

---

1 Cf. *Antid.* 183, 271; Mikkola 1954, 201–203; Eucken 1983, 14–18; Nightingale 1995, 13–59; Schiappa 1999, 168–184; Livingstone 2007, 15–34; Too 2008, 23–26; Alexiou 2010, 80f.; Timmerman/Schiappa 2010, 43–66.
2 Cf. *Antidosis* 276.
3 Cf. Heilbrunn 1975, 157; Campbell 1984, 17–59; Steiner 1994, 187; Too 1995, 74–112. Blank 2017, 263–290 interprets the isocratic *apragmosyne* as a symbol of aristocratic intellectualism in fourth-century Athens. Cf. nevertheless Haskins 2004, 17: 'Yet unlike other literary *apragmones* of his generation, especially Plato and other Socratics, Isocrates adopts the quietist stance in order to reinvent democratic rhetoric, not to disavow its legitimacy altogether'. See also Ober 1998, 249.
4 See Arist. *Rhet.* 1367b14–17: καὶ εἰ παρὰ τὸ προσῆκον ἐπὶ δὲ τὸ βέλτιον καὶ τὸ κάλλιον, οἷον εἰ εὐτυχῶν μὲν μέτριος, ἀτυχῶν δὲ μεγαλόψυχος, ἢ μείζων γιγνόμενος βελτίων καὶ καταλλακτικώτερος. Cf. 1415a 1–3; Isocr. *Euag.* 8–11, 27; *Bus.* 3; Xenoph. *Ages.* 1.1.

ambitious, seeks social recognition within the framework of *homologoumene arete*, i.e. the popular morality which he himself professes,[5] and innovation is a fundamental factor for the interpretation of his work. What I will try to demonstrate next is how his innovation is interweaved with an elitist novel speech, which seeks in every step the competition with his fellow-craftsmen, in rhetorical art as well as political life.

*

In *Panathenaicus* 16–19 Isocrates turns against his antagonists, who, according to him, are more hostile to him than private citizens: without possessing particular didactic capabilities, they use the Isocratic discourses as their examples, comparing them with their own speeches in the worst manner possible, tearing them apart and mistreating them in every conceivable way. The culmination of this attitude is the episode that narrates what was conveyed to him by students of his (18–19) in relation to a group of three to four of the *agelaioi sophistai* – as he calls them – who were at the Lyceum just before the festivity of the Panathenaia of 342 BCE. They were discussing poetry, the poetry of Hesiod and Homer in particular, among an audience that applauded their performance, when the boldest one among them turned against Isocrates by slandering the fact that he disdains those activities and the learning and teaching of all others, except for those who attend his presentations.

Earlier research has tried to identify the recipients of isocratic criticism. Teichmüller surmises that it is Aristotle and his pupils, such as Theodectes, Theophrastus and Xenocrates or Heraclides Ponticus.[6] Gomperz recalls Zoilus from Amphipolis, the known ὁμηρομάστιξ.[7] It is a fact that the uncontrolled criticism of his contemporaries extended to Isocrates (*Against the Rhetor Isocrates*; see *Suda* ζ 130 s.v. Ζωΐλος). Aristotle indeed was occupied with Homer[8] and competed with the school of Isocrates.[9] In the catalogue of Aristotelian works (Diog. Laert. 5.22) *On Rhetoric, or Gryllus* appears fifth in a row. It is possible in this work, which was elaborated soon after 362 B.C., when the son of Xenophon Gryllus fell in the battle of Mantinea, that the young Aristotle exercised some kind of criticism

---

[5] *Antidosis* 84. See Alexiou 2007. Cf. Dover 1974.
[6] Teichmüller 1881, 260–270. Cf. Spengel 1851, 17f.
[7] Gomperz 1905–1906, 19.
[8] So Diog. Laert. 5.22: Περὶ ποιητῶν; 5.26: Ἀπορήματα Ὁμηρικά.
[9] Cf. Philod. *De rhet.* (P. Herc. 832) c. xlviii 36 (II,50 Sudhaus); Cic. *De or.* 3.141; Quint. 3.1.14; Diog. Laert. 5.3.

on Isocrates.¹⁰ The *Protrepticus* of Aristotle can also be interpreted as a reaction to *Antidosis* of Isocrates.¹¹ On the other hand, Aristotle in his *Rhetoric* derives most of his stylistic examples from the work of Isocrates, and nothing substantiates the view that he mistreated the speeches of Isocrates.¹² The polemical treatment, however, of the speeches of Isocrates is substantiated by the *Letter* of Speusippus to Philip II of Macedon.¹³ Having the Isocratean *Philippus* as a point of reference, Speusippus, a nephew of Plato and his successor as head of the Academy, accuses Isocrates of omissions while enumerating the benefactions of Philip and his ancestors in Greece, as well as for his failure in attempting to dissolve the slanders that circulated against the Macedonian king (3; 10; 13). Speusippus' polemical positions sought to limit the influence of Isocrates and his students in the Macedonian court.¹⁴ According to Diogenes Laertius (4.2), who cites earlier evidence, Speusippus was the first to publish secret teachings of Isocrates (τὰ καλούμενα ἀπόρρητα).¹⁵

In any case, chronological issues along with insufficient evidence render an identification of the antagonists of Isocrates in *Panathenaicus* extremely difficult.¹⁶ Isocrates refers to antagonists of his, probably from the Academy, who do not meet his own pedagogical criteria. The critical question of the present study is not the identification of the antagonists of Isocrates, but the content of his criticism and the image of the *agelaioi sophistai* that the rhetorician creates (*Panath.* 18):

ἐν τῷ Λυκείῳ συγκαθεζόμενοι τρεῖς ἢ τέτταρες τῶν ἀγελαίων σοφιστῶν καὶ πάντα φασκόντων εἰδέναι καὶ ταχέως πανταχοῦ γιγνομένων διαλέγοιντο περί τε τῶν ἄλλων ποιητῶν καὶ τῆς Ἡσιόδου καὶ τῆς Ὁμήρου ποιήσεως, οὐδὲν μὲν παρ' αὐτῶν λέγοντες, τὰ δ' ἐκείνων ῥαψῳδοῦντες καὶ τῶν πρότερον ἄλλοις τισὶν εἰρημένων τὰ χαριέστατα μνημονεύοντες.

Three or four of the common sophists who say they know everything and quickly appear everywhere were sitting in the Lyceum and were discussing the poets, especially the poetry

---

10 Kennedy 1963, 83f.; Chroust 1965, 576–591. Cf. Rapp 2002, I 232–235; Flashar 2006, 115, 202–203.
11 See von der Mühll 1939–1940, 259–265; Flashar 2006, 168f. Cf. Düring 1961, 20–23, 33–35; Schneeweiss 2005, 29f.
12 For a detailed discussion, see Alexiou 2016, 401–418.
13 See Natoli 2004, 111f. Cf. Wareh 2012, 134–195.
14 Such a student was e.g. Python of Byzantium, who in 344/3 B.C. represented the politics of Philip in Athens (Demosth. 18.136; *Epist.* II 10; [Demosth.] 7.20; 7.23). See Ryder 2000, 73f.; Fündling 2014, 114.
15 See Engels 2003, 179f.
16 See Roth 2003, 86–89.

of Hesiod and Homer. They were saying nothing of their own but were reciting the poets' words and repeating the best of what others had said before.

(transl. Too)

The term ἀγελαῖος means 'one belonging to a herd' and metaphorically 'one of the common herd, common, ordinary'.[17] In reality, Isocrates relegates his antagonists to the category of the illiterate, the civilians, who envy him and imitate him without originality.[18] The disdainful disposition of the orator is appositely indicated by A. Korais, who in commenting on τῶν ἀγελαίων interprets it thus: τῶν εὐτελῶν, τῶν φαύλων, τῶν χυδαίων.[19] This disdainful characterisation is opposed to the 'elitist self-confidence' (elitäres Bewußtsein, so called by Roth)[20] of the antagonists of Isocrates, who assert that they know everything, but in practice do not surpass the usual, the common. In other words, while Isocrates, despite his physical weaknesses, sets high goals and realizes them, they make big promises and pride themselves on small achievements: they ruminate upon Hesiod and Homer, along with the best commentators on those poets, without themselves discovering anything new. The phrase 'saying nothing of their own' (οὐδὲν παρ' αὐτῶν λέγοντες) is crucial: it denotes spiritual subjugation and lack of originality. In Aristotelian terms it is the definition of *chaunos* in *Nicomachean Ethics*: *megalopsychos* is whoever has high pursuits and is worthy of them (1123b 2), *chaunos* is whoever has high pursuits and is unworthy of them (1123b 8–9).

The above is consistent with the set conviction of Isocrates that the intellectual vocation must aim at big and important issues, which he himself defines as useful and politically beneficial. In his *Letter* IX 15–17 the orator attributes great cowardice and mean spiritedness to those who, while they have serious intellectual interests, they pride themselves on trivialities, envying those who are able to give advice on the most important matters. He himself on the contrary expresses such great confidence in his own ability (*mega phronein*) at eighty years of age that he sends a letter to Archidamus seeking a unified Greece against Persia. Such an issue belongs within the necessary and honorable. In the opening statements

---

[17] Probably here Isocrates suggests derogatorily the motif of the 'wandering sophist', which Plato identifies with ignorance and fraud (see *Tim.* 19e; *Euthyd.* 288b), although Isocrates referring to the wanderings of Gorgias focuses only on its economical dimension (*Antid.* 155–157). Cf. Montiglio 2005, 105–117.
[18] For 'originality' in Isocrates, cf. Behme 2004. It should be clarified, however, that the originality in Isocrates is mainly based on the innovative interpretations of the same matter, not by necessity on the original thematic of his speeches (e.g. *Png.* 10).
[19] Korais 1807, 179.
[20] Roth 2003, 87.

of the encomium *Helen,* Isocrates turns against the eristic philosophers because they are proud of the handling of an absurd and paradoxical subject (1). Supposing that absolute knowledge is feasible only in insignificant matters, it is preferable for one to have a likely conjecture about useful things than exact knowledge of small and useless things given the practical affairs of political life (4–5).[21] In a similar context, in *Againsts the Sophists* 8 and *Antidosis* 262 Isocrates uses the terms *adoleschia* (garrulity) and *mikrologia* (hairsplitting).[22] In *Helen* 9–10 Isocrates asserts that those who claim intelligence and profess to be sophists ought to surpass and be superior to private citizens not on subjects that have been ignored by others, but on those over which everyone competes (*antagonistai*)! Otherwise they resemble athletes who boast achievement in a contest where no one else cares to compete. The image from the athletic arena clearly refers to the agonistic ideal.[23] When, therefore, big promises do not correspond to their results, it is a matter of *alazoneuesthai*, which means 'to make false pretensions', in essence it is a synonym of *pseudesthai* (*Soph.* 10).[24] On the contrary, Isocrates emphasizes his own *epieikeia* (honesty), evidence of which are the sincerity and the consistency of his big promises during his life (*Antid.* 195; cf. *Png.* 14).

Therefore, the main weight of the Isocratic claim does not lie on the rejection of high pursuits, but on the justified or unjustified ambition which, unlike that of the *agelaioi sophistai*, presupposes the innovative idea and the beneficial content. Competition with his fellow-craftsmen and elitist ambition are central motives of the pedagogical and rhetorical activity of Isocrates.

These characteristics are recorded with exceptional accuracy in the encomium *Evagoras*. Isocrates criticises the lack of encomia produced for exceptional contemporary men (5: *agathoi*), while he himself takes pride in writing the first encomium of prose for a contemporary historical personality, the recently deceased king of Cyprus Evagoras I (8). It is noteworthy how Isocrates innovates compared to both of his fundamental literary sources, which he imitates creatively, namely the *Funeral Speeches* as a collective praise of the fallen heroes, and the *Epinician Odes* of the choral lyric poetry.[25] In *Evagoras* 6 the mention of the

---

21 Cf. *Ad Nic.* 39; Flacelière 1961, 20; Eucken 1983, 44–74; Alexiou 2007, 3–4.
22 Cf. Dressler 2014, 179 and 206.
23 On such athletic metaphors in Isocrates, cf. *Evag.* 79; *Ad Nic.* 11; *Phi.* 82; *Png.* 3–6; 43–44, 85; *Demon.* 12.
24 See Isocr. *Arch.* 98; *Panath.* 20, 74; *Soph.* 1, 10; *Antid.* 195. Cf. the definition of *alazon* in Aristotle *Eth. Nic.* 1127a 20–22: δοκεῖ δὴ ὁ μὲν ἀλαζὼν προσποιητικὸς τῶν ἐνδόξων εἶναι καὶ μὴ ὑπαρχόντων καὶ μειζόνων ἢ ὑπάρχει. Cf. also Xen. *Cyr.* 1.6.22; 2.2.12; *Mem.* 1.7.1; Pl. *Rep.* 490a; Aristoph. *Nu.* 102; *Ra.* 280.
25 See Alexiou 2010, 32–37.

envy of the audience continues a pattern which dominates the *proemium* of the Thucydidean *Epitaphios* (Thuc. 2.35.2).[26] Pericles expresses the common difficulty of the orator for a praise worthy of the fallen and prefers the direct relation between deeds and honor, namely a public funeral, because speech, being at a disadvantaged, is submitted to the torture of audience envy. Mankind is tolerant of the praises of others so long as each hearer thinks that he can do as well or nearly as well himself, but when the speaker rises above him, envy is aroused, and he begins to be incredulous. Isocrates (*Evag.* 6) begins also with the envy of the audience, but in contrast to Pericles, who decides to satisfy the wishes and beliefs of all who hear him, he adopts a decisive and innovative attitude: he condemns outright envy of great deeds and extols individual progress, making speech the most appropriate means of meriting glory. Envy is a disease and its only benefit is that it constitutes the greatest evil to those who feel it (*Evag.* 6; cf. *Antid.* 13; Demosth. 20.140).[27] Isocrates attributes to the orator a new, pioneering pedagogical role: he asks that he set aside the foolish and envious audience, who prefer encomia of mythical characters, and that he employ noble motives to condition the rest of them to listen to encomia of contemporary men who may have been their own benefactors. The orator is transformed into a pedagogue of his audience, is called to educate them in the praise of contemporary personalities. Only thus in rhetoric, as well as in any other art, is progress achieved:

> οὐ μὴν δουλευτέον τοὺς νοῦν ἔχοντας τοῖς οὕτω κακῶς φρονοῦσιν, ἀλλὰ τῶν μὲν τοιούτων ἀμελητέον, τοὺς δ' ἄλλους ἐθιστέον ἀκούειν, περὶ ὧν καὶ λέγειν δίκαιόν ἐστιν, ἄλλως τ' ἐπειδὴ καὶ τὰς ἐπιδόσεις ἴσμεν γιγνομένας καὶ τῶν τεχνῶν καὶ τῶν ἄλλων ἁπάντων οὐ διὰ τοὺς ἐμμένοντας τοῖς καθεστῶσιν, ἀλλὰ διὰ τοὺς ἐπανορθοῦντας καὶ τολμῶντας ἀεί τι κινεῖν τῶν μὴ καλῶς ἐχόντων.

> But sensible men must not become slaves to those with such perverse thoughts but must disregard them and accustom others to hear about those whom it is just to praise, particularly as we know that progress in the arts and in all other things is not due to those who adhere to the status quo but to those who make improvements and dare always to change things that are wrong.

(transl. Too)

---

26 See in detail Alexiou 2009 and 2016a, 55–60.

27 Isocrates complains repeatedly about the envy of his fellow-citizens: *Panath.* 21, 23; *Antid.* 4, 13, 142, 163, 259. For *phthonos* in Isocrates, see Ober 1998, 264–273; Said 2003, 217–234; Alexiou 2010, 76–77. Cf. generally Walcot 1978; Konstan 2006, 111–128; Sanders 2008; Ludwig 2009; Sanders 2014, esp. 79–99.

It is to the same innovative initiative of Isocrates that his competition with choral lyric poetry must also be attributed. Following the tradition of the great choral lyrics of the past, Pindar and Bacchylides,[28] Isocrates considers it his duty to award praise worthy of the deeds of Evagoras (*Evag.* 4).[29] But the mimesis of the poetic encomium is not passive. Indeed, in *Evagoras* (9–11) the earliest systematic literary comparison between poetry and prose is attempted.[30] Isocrates admits that poetry has an advantage over prose in that it presents the gods as interacting with people and aiding them in battle, and it can be expressed not only in conventional expressions but also with the use of many decorations and figures to impress the audience. Such devices are not permitted to prose writers; their speech is oriented towards the precise relation between words and ideas in current use.

However, the assertions of Isocrates of the differences between prose and poetic speech are purposely excessive. His statements do not derive from the desire for pure literary criticism,[31] as, for example, Dionysius of Halicarnassus would do, but from the conscious attempt of the orator to compete with poetry and to undermine its role (11: τοὺς ἀγαθοὺς ἄνδρας εὐλογεῖν μηδὲν χεῖρον τῶν ἐν ταῖς ᾠδαῖς καὶ τοῖς μέτροις ἐγκωμιαζόντων). The orator expresses the great difficulty of his undertaking in order to emphasize his innovation.[32] So, the culmination of the advantages of poetry does not end in the acquittal of Isocrates, but in competition with it, and in the creation of a new kind of prose, that of the encomium of contemporary historical personalities.[33]

It should be emphasized that Isocrates attempts simultaneously to weaken poetry in both its aesthetic effect and content. He attributes the psychological advantage to poetry, which only with metre and rhythm is superior to prose, even if it is lacking in style and content. Indeed, he expresses the assertion that if the style and content were maintained, but the metre did not exist, the well-regarded

---

28 Cf. Race 1987; Vallozza 1990, 49f.; Ford 1993, 48f.; Papillon 1998, 45f., 50f.; Vallozza 1998; Alexiou 2000; Race 2007, 515f.; Alexiou 2010, 35f., 177f.
29 Cf. Pind. *Nem.* 7.12–13; *Olymp.* 10.3; 11.4–8; *Pyth.* 3.114–115; Bacchyl. 1.181–184; 3.90–98.
30 See Alexiou 2010, 79–89. Cf. Dover 1997, 96; Graff 2005.
31 Perlman 1964, 160.
32 This technique of Isocrates is detected correctly by Anonym. *In Hermog.* 7. 906 Walz (= I 406 Mand.): ὁ μέντοι Ἰσοκράτης διὰ τὸ συμφέρον αὐτῷ μόνοις τοῖς ποιηταῖς φησι ταῦτα προσεῖναι, ἵνα ἑαυτόν, φησί, σεμνύνῃ, εἰ διὰ μόνων πολιτικῶν λέξεων ἐγκωμιάζειν Εὐαγόραν δύναται. Cf. Buchheit 1960, 67; Usener 1994, 61–63.
33 Cf. Haskins 2004, 20. For Isocrates as a creator of a new kind of prose speech, which competes with the poetic speech, see Nicolai 2004, 49–54.

poems would appear far inferior to our current opinion of them (11).³⁴ This is further implied by the expression *psychagogein*, that is that 'poetry enchants the listeners'. The concept of *psychagogia* refers initially to the invocation of the souls of the dead; its use shifted from magic ceremonies to poetry and rhetoric because it projects a desired process onto a foreign object.³⁵ One can distinguish the irony of Isocrates behind the word, as the aesthetics of poetry is not necessarily consistent with useful content but aims simply and only at the satisfaction of the audience.³⁶

In *To Nicocles* 42–49 Isocrates protests against the attitude of the listeners in regard to what is beneficial. People praise works in prose which offer advice, and the maxims of the leading poets such as Hesiod, Theognis and Phocylides; however, they enjoy listening to base comedy (*phaulotaten komodian*) rather than to the precepts of these teachers. According to Isocrates, most people do not seek the noblest and the most useful but enjoy pleasures that are in every way opposed to their own advantage. Consequently, whoever wishes to please the masses should not seek the most useful speeches, but those that are full of fictions (45).³⁷ Homeric poetry and tragedy are characteristic examples of this. Homeric poetry and the first inventors of tragedy had true insight into human nature and presented pleasant subjects to the public. Homer narrated in mythical form the contests and battles of the demigods, tragedy projected the myths onto contests and actions on stage. Such examples prove for those who wish to attract the interest of their listeners (*psychagogein*) that they must abstain from admonition and advice; on the contrary, they should say primarily whatever seems to be most delightful to crowds. The terms *polloi* and *ochlos*, which are used here by Isocrates derogatorily (*Ad Nic.* 45, 48, 49), refer to the basic distinction between the common-ordinary and the exceptional-significant, which he himself sets as an objective of the intellectual élite, for poetry as well as for rhetoric.³⁸ Indeed, he asks of the monarch Nicocles, whom with a pun he describes as not being one of the many but ruling over many (50), not to follow the opinion of many but to confront the significant issues with utility rather than pleasure as a criterion.

---

34 Cf. for this argument Gorgias (82 B11, 9 D.–K.): τὴν ποίησιν ἅπασαν καὶ νομίζω καὶ ὀνομάζω λόγον ἔχοντα μέτρον; Plat. *Gorg.* 502c; *Rep.* 393d, 601b; Dion. Hal. *De comp. verb.* 3 (p. 11 Us.-Rad.); Hermog. *De id.* 2.10 (p. 389 Rabe).
35 See Aesch. *Pers.* 687; Eurip. *Alc.* 1128; Plat. *Leg.* 909b; Plut. *De sera num. vind.* 560F; Arist. *Poet.* 1450a33–34. Cf. Hellwig 1973, 33; De Romilly 1975, 15; Yunis 1996, 201–207.
36 Olympiodorus (*In Plat. Gorg.* 33.1 Westerink), who attributes demagogic intentions to the poets, recognizes the negative meaning of *psychagogein*. Cf. Jackson/Lycos/Tarant 1998, 223 n. 621.
37 Cf. *Antid.* 133, 221; *De pac.* 109; *Demon.* 45; *Panath.* 1.
38 Cf. Azoulay 2010, 19–48.

Consequently, Isocrates seeks with his epideictic speech his superiority over his competitors on the basis of both style and content. His stylistic innovation consists of an approach to poetic and prose language, so that epideictic speech surpasses the level of the style of the judicial oratory.[39] In *Antidosis* 46–48 he distinguishes between judicial and epideictic orations and prefers the superiority of the latter, among others, because of the added grace of its poetic style.[40] In the *proemium* of *Panegyricus* (11–14) he defends the systematic and elaborate editing of the style of an epideictic speech, competing with his rivals, such as, for example, Alcidamas: simplicity is better suited to the judicial oratory, precision to the epideictic.[41] The first kind is easier, it matches everyday speech and does not require particular care and art; the second kind, on the other hand, is more difficult than the first, it surpasses the everyday speech of individuals. In § 12 the carelessness displayed in the wording (τῶν εἰκῇ λεγομένων) is a clear hint against the supporters of improvisation and, by extension, of the plainness of style.

It is evident that Isocrates, by placing the judicial speeches at a lower level in terms of rhetorical art and social benefit,[42] creates a rating hierarchy between rhetorical sub-genres, and propagates the epideictic kind and the written speech that he himself represents as the highest of the kind. He considers most beautiful those speeches that treat the greatest subjects, best demonstrate the speaker's talent, and most help those who listen to them (*Png.* 4).[43] However, the innovative thought of Isocrates does not focus its attention on the praise of the inventor of an issue, but on competition with his fellow-craftsmen and the better process of the same issue: the actions of the past are common legacy, but it is the mark of a wise person to use these events at an appropriate time, conceive fitting arguments on each of them, and set them out in good style (*Png.* 9). This intellectual superiority, which is indicated by *phronesis*, a central Isocratic value,[44] signifies the fundamental principle of Isocratic innovation (*Png.* 10):

---

39 Cf. Atkins 1952, 128.
40 Cf. Dion. Hal. *Isocr.* 2 (p. 57 Us.-Rad.): περιόδῳ ... ῥυθμοειδεῖ πάνυ καὶ οὐ πολὺ ἀπέχοντι τοῦ ποιητικοῦ μέτρου; Cic. *De or.* 3,173; *Orat.* 190; Usher 1973, 54; Too 1995, 33–34; Papillon 1998; Walker 2000, 25. For the rhythm in the Isocratic period, see Usher 2010, 82–95.
41 On precision (*akribeia*) in Isocrates, see Wersdörfer 1940, 95–96, 138; Usher 1990, 151–152; Bons 1993, 162–165; Hammerstaedt 1996, 1224–1225. Cf. also Kurz 1970, 32–34. For the juxtaposition between Alcidamas and Isocrates, see O'Sullivan 1992, 23–62; Mariss 2002, 26–55.
42 See *Antid.* 3, 38, 40, 42, 228; *Panath.* 1, 11; *Soph.* 6; *Hel.* 7; *Png.* 78.
43 Cf. Poulakos 1997, 76f.
44 See Steidle 1952, 257–296, esp. 261ff.; Mikkola 1954, 203–205; Wilms 1995, 214, 219f., 268f.; Poulakos 2004, esp. 56ff.; Depew 2004, 157–185, esp. 166ff.

ἡγοῦμαι δ' οὕτως ἂν μεγίστην ἐπίδοσιν λαμβάνειν καὶ τὰς ἄλλας τέχνας καὶ τὴν περὶ τοὺς λόγους φιλοσοφίαν, εἴ τις θαυμάζοι καὶ τιμῴη μὴ τοὺς πρώτους τῶν ἔργων ἀρχομένους, ἀλλὰ τοὺς ἄρισθ' ἕκαστον αὐτῶν ἐξεργαζομένους, μηδὲ τοὺς περὶ τούτων ζητοῦντας λέγειν, περὶ ὧν μηδεὶς πρότερον εἴρηκεν, ἀλλὰ τοὺς οὕτως ἐπισταμένους εἰπεῖν ὡς οὐδεὶς ἂν ἄλλος δύναιτο.

I think that other arts, and especially the study of discourse, would be best improved if we would admire and honor not those who first undertook these tasks but those who brought each of them to their highest level of accomplishment, and not those who are eager to speak about things no one else has addressed before but those who speak so wisely that no one else would be able to speak afterwards.

(transl. Papillon)

A series of examples proves the consistency with which Isocrates applies this principle. In *Panegyricus*, for example, having as the content of the speech his favourite topic, the peace of the Greeks and war against the Persians, he himself participates in a diachronic rhetorical struggle for the pan-Hellenic idea, in which he contends for the first prize (*Png*. 3: ἱκανὸν ἆθλον). The orator here insinuates forerunners of the pan-Hellenic idea, such as Gorgias and Lysias.[45] Homeric poetry is appraised, positively this time, in the context of the pan-Hellenic idea, while the Trojan War is interpreted by Isocrates as a prototype for a new struggle against the Persians (159).[46] Furthermore, the *Helen* of Isocrates is an encomium closely connected to Gorgias' *Encomium of Helen*. The innovation of Isocrates does not lie in the subject, for which he praises his predecessor, but in the wish to compete and amend his teacher, who authored a defence of what she did and not an encomium for her (14). The κάλλος becomes the dominant subject of the speech, while at the end, the homonymous heroine is praised, because one might attribute to her, among other events, the Trojan War, and that the Greeks were not subjugated to barbarians (67).[47]

Isocrates' attempt to compare Heracles and Theseus (*Hel*. 23–25) is placed within the same context of competition. According to Isocrates, it is about two comparable mythical heroes with common conditions: starting with similar weapons, occupations, common divine origin and related ambitions, they both became champions of human life. There is one difference: Theseus is superior to

---

45 A passage from the *Epitaphios* of Gorgias (Philostr. *Vit. soph*. 1.494 K. = 82 B5b D.–K.): τὰ μὲν κατὰ τῶν βαρβάρων τρόπαια ὕμνους ἀπαιτεῖ τὰ δὲ κατὰ τῶν Ἑλλήνων θρήνους is repeated almost word for word in the Isocratic *Panegyricus* 158. In *Olympicus* (33.3) and the *Epitaphios* of Lysias (2.54–60), innovating pan-Hellenic voices, with an influence on Isocrates are also recognised. Cf. Mathieu 1925, 23–28; Buchner 1958, 16–26; Eucken 1983, 144.
46 See in detail Alexiou 1998, 283–298.
47 See Kennedy 1958, 77–83. Cf. Braun 1982, 158–174; Papillon 1996, 377–391; Zajonz 2002, 293.

Heracles based on two central criteria, which Isocrates sets continuously as presuppositions of his innovative rhetorical speech. Firstly, Theseus constitutes an autonomous personality. He possesses both freedom and intellectual autonomy (αὐτὸς αὑτοῦ κύριος ὤν), so that he himself can choose his struggles. The labours of Heracles were imposed by Eurystheus – they were not the result of free choice.[48] Isocrates interprets this condition as a sample of ethical inferiority. Furthermore: the dangers of Heracles concerned him alone, not to the benefit of the others, while Theseus chose dangers through which he would become a benefactor of either the Greeks or his homeland.

It becomes evident that the innovation of Isocrates in the rhetorical treatment of the myth is selective and interpretative: he chooses those elements that can be linked to his pedagogical and political agenda and interprets them in such a way so that he can project his personal ideas on them. Also, his ideas are repeated persistently in the entirety of his work, independently from the individual objective of the speech. Heracles, for example, in *Philippus* (109–115) plays a different role than in *Helen*. In that speech, Isocrates urges Philip II of Macedon, famous for his ambition, to develop the role of benefactor to the Greeks,[49] in order to imitate his mythical ancestor, Heracles, who functions as an *exemplum*.[50] The originality of Isocrates is emphasised: while others praise continually the strength and the labour of Heracles, none of the poets or prose writers made any mention of the virtues of his soul.

Heracles is presented already in Euripides as a benefactor of Greece (*Her. Fur.* 1309; cf. 877, 1252), and for Lysias he was author of many benefits to all mankind (2.16). However, Kehl[51] is right to assert that the originality claimed by the systematic praise of Heracles in *Philippus* lies in the extensive and complete statement of the endowments of the soul of the hero, which are enumerated: (110) *phronesis, philotimia, dikaiosyne*, (114) *philanthropia, eunoia*. Heracles freed the Greeks from wars, civil strife, and many other evils and indicated to their descendants which cities they should have as allies and which as enemies when making war (111). This concerns the so-called first Trojan War, the conquest of

---

48 Cf. the presentation of the Athenian citizens after their liberation from Theseus in *Helen* 35. It is about high-minded citizens (*mega phronountes*) who encompass the freedom that Heracles is deprived of here, not only legally but also in terms of their whole stance. And in *Helen* 16 Zeus honors Helen more than Heracles, because Heracles accepts only might (*ischys*), whereas Helen accepts beauty (*kallos*) to be superior to might. See Alexiou 1995, 92f.
49 *Philippus* 20, 32, 36, 37, 76, 116, 140, 153. Cf. Papillon 2007, 68.
50 Cf. Papillon 1996, 11f.; 2001, 87f.; Gotteland 2001, 47; Blank 2014, 490–492.
51 Kehl 1962, 82.

Troy by Heracles,⁵² which serves as the prototype for a new expedition against the Persians. Isocrates calls upon the reconciliation of the Greeks and the expedition of Heracles against Troy as an expression of the three above-mentioned values, *phronesis* (wisdom), *philotimia* (ambition) and *dikaiosyne* (justice) of the mythical hero. The connection of *philotimia*, a pre-eminently competitive value, with two cooperative values, confirms the positive attitude of Isocrates towards an ambition that will not be exhausted in individual self-confirmation, but will be expressed through social contribution.⁵³

A corresponding innovation is observed in the prose encomium of Agamemnon in *Panathenaicus* (74–87).⁵⁴ Isocrates justifies his venture to knit the encomium of the mythical hero together with a new competition with his fellow-craftsmen: he wants to help him because of his missing out on the reputation that he should have, something that happened to Isocrates himself (75). The speeches called upon by the latter are the true and the beneficial ones (78), because people love wonders more than real benefits and false stories more than the truth. Agamemnon, when compared to Achilles, is traditionally an ambiguous mythical figure and it is a fact he does not receive a similar praise in any other rhetorical text of the fourth century BCE.⁵⁵ Agamemnon is thus represented by Isocrates as the Homeric hero par excellence, in the face of whom the national leader of a pan-Hellenic expedition is projected. Indeed, it is interesting to contrast the role of Agamemnon as Commander-in-Chief of the Greeks with the positions of Isocrates regarding his rhetorical activity. Agamemnon alone was deemed worthy to be the commander of all Greece (76: στρατηγὸς ἁπάσης τῆς Ἑλλάδος). Such is also the rhetorical activity of Isocrates as the leading proponent of discourses (13: τῶν λόγων ἡγεμόνα). Isocrates did not choose mythic discourses or those full of wonders and fictions (1: μυθώδεις, τερατείας καὶ ψευδολογίας μεστούς). Agamemnon ignored tasks that would be amazing and wondrous but of no practical use (77: τὰ περιττὰ τῶν ἔργων καὶ τερατώδη καὶ μηδὲν ὠφελοῦντα τοὺς ἄλλους). With the power he acquired, he did not harm a single Greek city. As in the case of Heracles in the *Philippus*, Isocrates contends by deploying similar arguments in the *Panathenaicus* that Agamemnon put an end to the evils of the Greeks, reconciled their

---

52 Heracles plundered the city, when Laomedon, king of Troy, deceived him in terms of the reward with his immortal horses which he had promised him if he saved his daughter Hesione from a sea-monster. See Hom. *Il.* 5.638–642, 648–651; Pind. *Isthm.* 6.24–56; Soph. *Aj.* 1299–1303; Apollod. *Bibl.* 2.103–104; 2.134–138; Gotteland 2001, 239–244.
53 See Alexiou 1995, 47–49, 125–126; 2010, 68f. Cf. generally for *philotimia* Dover 1974, 229–234; Liddel 2007, 165–182; Alexiou 2014, 738; 2018, 114–133 with further bibliography.
54 Cf. Race 1978; Roth 2003, 131–135.
55 Gotteland 2001, 244f.; Blank 2014, 533.

cities with one another, and attempted a war against the barbarians which surpassed every other contemporary or later campaign in nobility and benefit (78). Similarly, the speeches of Isocrates urge unity among the Greeks and war against the Persians as the most noble, greatest, and most beneficial acts (13–14). His supremacy in wisdom (82: *phronesis*), the par excellence value of the education of the Isocratic speeches,[56] is the main virtue with which Agamemnon achieved all that he had and managed, for ten years, to restrain heroes who were not similar to the common people but from divine lineage and each with individual antagonistic pursuits, full of anger, aggression, envy, and ambition. It is obvious that Isocrates understands hierarchies on a military as well as a rhetorical level and parallels his role as a pan-Hellenic orator with the military activity of the mythical king.[57]

*

The political dimension of the innovative speech of Isocrates is in play here and is consistent with the novelties of his rhetoric, which – contrary to Demosthenes, for example – transcends the orders of his city. This is based on the conviction of Isocrates that the system of government or institutions do not constitute the safeguards for the course of a society. For him, that job belongs to an 'aristocracy of values', which is centred on individuals who are mentally and ethically outstanding figures, not on the three types of constitution.[58] In fact, the Isocratic speeches reflect moral and political ideas which demonstrate continuity and consistency, whether it be an encomium of a monarch, as in the *Evagoras*, or advice to a monarch, such as the *To Nicocles*, or advice to a democratic audience, as in the *Panegyricus*, *Areopagiticus* or *On the Peace*.[59]

Isocrates draws the reader's attention to the unity of rhetoric and politics. In the *Philippus* 12 Isocrates is self-characterised as *philotimos*. His ambition lies in

---

56 See *Antid.* 209, 271, 293–294; *Evag.* 41, 80; *Phi.* 110; *Panath.* 127, 204.
57 Cf. Gagarin 2002, 118: 'Isocrates sees himself as belonging to the company of the great statesmen of the past and the present'; Also Too 1995, 132–140; Papillon 2004, 186 n. 53.
58 Isocrates treats this topic in *Panathenaicus* 131–133: he stresses the importance of a democracy which makes use of the rules of aristocracy. He distinguishes the three types of political systems – oligarchy, democracy and monarchy – without, however, focusing on the constitutional differences, but rather on the political leaders' collective ability and moral code, and especially on whether these leaders pursued their own interests instead of those of the polis. Cf. Morgan 2003, 189f.; Konstan 2004, 120; Forsdyke 2009, 242; Alexiou 2015, 50f.
59 Cf. Davidson 1990, 31. As Niall Livingstone has argued (1998, 271), the speeches of Isocrates have a consistent moral and intellectual tone and create a strong impression of unity.

overcoming obstacles, as far as the rhetorical result of his speech is concerned – because of age – but also in the realisation of his political and pedagogical objectives. Isocrates states that it is difficult to deliver two discourses upon the same subject adequately, especially since the *Panegyricus* has preceded a speech that even those who malign him emulate and admire even more than those who praise it excessively (*Phi.* 11). Recipients of the speech *Philippus* are the King of Macedon, but also the students of Isocrates, who are called upon to understand that the *Panegyricus* (380 BCE) was doomed to be ineffective (*Phi.* 12–13) because it was addressed to an audacious audience that favours spectacles,[60] such as the utopian laws and constitutions written by the sophists, which are useless in real political life, as opposed to actions:

> (12) ἀλλ' ὅμως ἀπάσας ἐγὼ ταύτας τὰς δυσχερείας ὑπεριδὼν οὕτως ἐπὶ γήρως γέγονα φιλότιμος ὥστ' ἠβουλήθην ἅμα τοῖς πρὸς σὲ λεγομένοις καὶ τοῖς μετ' ἐμοῦ διατρίψασιν ὑποδεῖξαι καὶ ποιῆσαι φανερὸν ὅτι τὸ μὲν ταῖς πανηγύρεσιν ἐνοχλεῖν καὶ πρὸς ἅπαντας λέγειν τοὺς συντρέχοντας ἐν αὐταῖς πρὸς οὐδένα λέγειν ἐστίν, ἀλλ' ὁμοίως οἱ τοιοῦτοι τῶν λόγων ἄκυροι τυγχάνουσιν ὄντες τοῖς νόμοις καὶ ταῖς πολιτείαις ταῖς ὑπὸ τῶν σοφιστῶν γεγραμμέναις, (13) δεῖ δὲ τοὺς βουλομένους μὴ μάτην φλυαρεῖν, ἀλλὰ προὔργου τι ποιεῖν καὶ τοὺς οἰομένους ἀγαθόν τι κοινὸν εὑρηκέναι τοὺς μὲν ἄλλους ἐᾶν πανηγυρίζειν, αὐτοὺς δ' ὧν εἰσηγοῦνται ποιήσασθαί τινα προστάτην τῶν καὶ λέγειν καὶ πράττειν δυναμένων καὶ δόξαν μεγάλην ἐχόντων, εἴπερ μέλλουσί τινες προσέξειν αὐτοῖς τὸν νοῦν.

> (12) Nonetheless, overlooking these difficulties, I have become so ambitious in my old age hat by speaking to you, I wished at the same time both to make a demonstration by example for my students and to make it clear to them that being an annoyance at panhellenic gatherings and speaking to everyone who gathers together for them is tantamount to speaking to no one. Such speeches turn out to be just as ineffective as laws and constitutions written by the sophists. (13) Those who wish to avoid trivial speech and do something of value, or who think they have found something of common interest, ought to let others give panhellenic speeches (*panegyreis*) and should instead find someone to be the spokesman for their cause – someone with a wide reputation and who is able to speak well and do what is needed – if anyone is to take it seriously.

> (transl. Papillon)

The main antithesis is observed between the μάτην φλυαρεῖν (trivial speech, empty nonsense) and the προὔργου τι ποιεῖν (to do something of value, to further some practical purpose).[61] The philosophical, utopian pursuits are placed here on

---

60 Cf. *Phi.* 129; *Panath.* 263.
61 In *Helen* 4–5, where Isocrates turns with similar argumentation against futile philosophical quests, he uses the term *terthreia* 'use of extreme subtlety, formal pedantry' (Hesych. τ 521 s.v. τερθρεία· λογομαχία. ἀπάτη. φλυαρία. φληναφία. Cf. *Souda* τ 344) and encourages the pursuit of truth, which for the orator always extends to the practical side of the daily political life.

the same level as an ineffective multitude of listeners of oratorical speeches. The aim of Isocratic education is the useful, the socially beneficial, and this requires a practical result, far and beyond the borders of the city-state. Demosthenes in his speeches repeatedly accuses the Athenians for inactivity in their struggle against a warlike Philip,[62] just as Isocrates also condemns the inactivity of his city Athens, but in the context of the pan-Hellenic idea and of the war against the Persians. And he will not hesitate to surpass his city when it will not respond to his calls, turning to Philip and exercising criticism on it as well as on the path it strays from by the ravings of the orators in the Assembly (*Phi*. 129).

Isocrates attributes to Philip uniqueness in political and military hierarchy: contrary to all others, who are under the control of cities and laws and obliged to do whatever is prescribed (ὑπὸ πόλεσι καὶ νόμοις οἰκοῦντας, καὶ οὐδὲν ἐξὸν αὐτοῖς ἄλλο πράττειν πλὴν τὸ προσταττόμενον), the release of Philip from the impositions of a city-state due to fortune, combined with his wealth and power, which guarantee the ability to compel, are the conditions for the achievement of the pan-Hellenic idea. Persuasion will be useful with the Greeks; compulsion will be advantageous against the barbarians (*Phi*. 14–16). The Isocratic Philip is not called to abandon his antagonistic ambitions, but to satisfy them in such a way that he can win, as a benefactor, the good will (*eunoia*) of the Greeks.[63] The main argument here is not the rejection of the ambition of Philip, but rather the justified or unjustified *megalophrosyne* (41).[64] The pan-Hellenic community, as if it is about the enlarged community of the city-state, constitutes the field of action of the Macedonian king. In *Philippus* 127 Isocrates calls upon the same opposition between those descendants of Heracles that are under the bonds of their constitutions and laws, and Philip, who is characterised as ἄφετος (with untrammeled freedom), free from some particular city and citizen of the whole of Greece, which he must consider his fatherland, and for the sake of which he must fight just as his mythical ancestor had.

Just as the rhetorical role of Isocrates in the *Panathenaicus* is paralleled with the military leadership of Agamemnon, so too in *Philippus* Isocrates secures for himself the superior role of the rhetorical elite. His role as a counsellor reveals

---

62 See Demosthenes 1.15; 1.17; 1.14: προΐεσθαι; 4.11: ἀμέλεια; 4.17, 6.3: ἀργῶς ἔχειν; 9.5: ῥαθυμία, ἀμέλεια; [11.22]. See also 4.25 –26; 8.5–9; 8.39; 8,58–59; 9,6–7; 9,8–14; 9,17; 10,11; 10,56; 10,60–61; Mader 2005, 11–35.

63 See *Phi*. 6, 68, 77, 79, 86, 95, 114, 127, 136, 145; 154; Dobesch 1968, 205. For the political meaning of *eunoia* in Isocrates, see De Romilly 1958, 92–101; Alexiou 1995, 129.

64 Cf. *Phi*. 71; 122. For the meaning of *megalophrosyne* and the positive or negative connotations cf. *Evag*. 27, 45, 46; *Nicocl*. 35; *Png*. 25, 170; *Phi*. 4, 71; *De pac*. 50; *Areop*. 7, 73; Alexiou 2010, 108–109 with further bibliography.

analogous parameters with those of the image of the Macedonian king. Isocrates' superiority in the intellectual field is a match for Philip's comparable supremacy in military-political action (*Phi.* 81–82):

> (81) ἐγὼ γὰρ πρὸς μὲν τὸ πολιτεύεσθαι πάντων ἀφυέστατος ἐγενόμην τῶν πολιτῶν· οὔτε γὰρ φωνὴν ἔσχον ἱκανὴν οὔτε τόλμαν δυναμένην ὄχλῳ χρῆσθαι καὶ μολύνεσθαι καὶ λοιδορεῖσθαι τοῖς ἐπὶ τοῦ βήματος καλινδουμένοις· (82) τοῦ δὲ φρονεῖν εὖ καὶ πεπαιδεῦσθαι καλῶς, εἰ καί τις ἀγροικότερον εἶναι φήσει τὸ ῥηθέν, ἀμφισβητῶ καὶ θείην ἂν ἐμαυτὸν οὐκ ἐν τοῖς ἀπολελειμμένοις ἀλλ' ἐν τοῖς προέχουσι τῶν ἄλλων. Διόπερ ἐπιχειρῶ συμβουλεύειν τὸν τρόπον τοῦτον, ὃν ἐγὼ πέφυκα καὶ δύναμαι, καὶ τῇ πόλει καὶ τοῖς Ἕλλησιν καὶ τῶν ἀνδρῶν τοῖς ἐνδοξοτάτοις.

> (81) For of all citizens, I was by nature the least suited to political activity. I did not have a strong enough voice or enough confidence to allow me to handle a crowd, to accept abuse, and to attack those who frequent the speaker's platform. (82) But as far as being intelligent and well educated, even if someone says that I am uncouth to say so, I would disagree and would place myself not in the lower ranks but among the most prominent. Therefore, I try to give advice to the city, to the Greeks, and to men of the highest renown in the way in which I am by nature best able to do.
>
> (transl. Papillon)

Isocrates defines here an evaluation scale of intellect, similar to that of politics. He repeats his known weaknesses regarding his timidity and lack of a loud voice, except that those are now accompanied by severe criticism of the populace and the common orators, patrons of politics. Isocrates changes his weaknesses into advantages. By the standards of a bad political administration he ranks himself in the lowest position, while on the intellectual scale he holds an extremely prominent position, above the others (οὐκ ἐν τοῖς ἀπολελειμμένοις ἀλλ' ἐν τοῖς προέχουσι τῶν ἄλλων).[65] This attitude emanates from the basic principle of the education of the Isocratic speeches, according to which rhetoric aims to reach the best opinion (*doxa*), with which one can succeed by his powers of conjecture to achieve most often to the best possible result (*Antid.* 271).[66]

The role of Isocrates as a counsellor refers to his having the right opinion to the utmost degree. The concepts *symboulos, symbouleuein* return systematically

---

[65] The *apoleipesthai* and *proechein* derive from the athletic and have a 'competitive' content: in the intellectual contest, Isocrates pursues the first prize of victory. In *Evagoras* 79–81 Nicocles contends in the field of education just as the runners, while Isocrates assumes the role of the active spectator.
[66] Cf. *Panath.* 30; Steidle 1952, 276; Wilms 1995, 231; Livingstone 1998, 268–269; Poulakos 2001; Papillon 2007, 61f., 70.

in the *Philippus*.⁶⁷ In *Phi*. 105 Isocrates identifies his advice with that of the ancestors of Philip, if they had had such an opportunity to advise. And in *Phi*. 113 Isocrates parallels his words with the great deeds of the ancestors of Philip, demonstrating as such with his rhetoric what the ancestors of Philip did with actions. Philip is called upon, therefore, to apply in practice what Isocrates projects with his rhetorical speech.⁶⁸ The innovator Isocrates appears as a counsellor-authority who, by addressing Philip, transcends the bonds of his democratic city and of an inconsiderate audience.

How this political dimension alludes to Isocrates's criticism of the *agelaioi sophistai* in the *proemium* of the *Panathenaicus* (18), who regurgitate passively the words of others, is further justified by the presence of the Spartan sympathizer at the end of the *Panathenaicus*. What takes place here is a conversation and questioning of the preceding speech of the teacher by one of his former students, an unknown Spartan sympathizer (200–265).⁶⁹ It is an extensive 'dialogue scene', forerunners of which are met in other speeches of the orator, but not to this extent (*Areop*. 56–59; *De pac*. 57; *Antid*. 141–149; *Phi*. 17–23). The student considers that the *Panathenaicus* includes ambiguous arguments (240: *logoi amphiboloi*): he asserts that on the surface the encomium is a praise of the peace-loving Athenians, according to the opinion of the many; essentially, however, it constitutes a praise of the warlike Spartans, in accordance with the opinion of the minority (241–242).⁷⁰

Regardless of whether the student of Isocrates is right or not in his interpretation of the speech, it is noteworthy that the speech ends in aporia: Isocrates praises the nature and the diligence of the student, he does not reveal, however, if he was right in his interpretation or not (265). The student is praised because he is ranked among the few who toil and exercise a pioneering criticism, inventing something new, in contrast to those who simply imitate or listen to others – it is the liveliest indication of what L. Collins Edwards⁷¹ defines as 'innovative imitation': an Isocratically educated student must be an imitator of Isocrates, but also an innovator. In his speech *Against the Sophists* Isocrates insists on innovation in rhetorical originality of treatment (13: *kainos echein*), as well as the exemplary role of the teacher himself, who, in addition to teaching, must constitute an

---

67 *Phi*. 9, 14, 16, 18, 55, 57, 82, 83, 88, 89, 94, 105, 136, 152, 154, 155.
68 Cf. Heilbrunn 1975.
69 Among the various suggestions about the identity of the unknown sympathizer the historian Theopompus seems to be the most likely; see Roth 2003, 219–222.
70 For the argumentation of the student, see Blank 2014, 563–587 and Alexiou 2015a, 73–90 with further bibliography.
71 Collins Edwards 2010, 383.

example of oratory for the students, because only those who are moulded by him and can imitate him will immediately appear more graceful orators than others (17–18). Contrary to the *agelaioi* opponents of Isocrates, who simply refer to or imitate the works of others with no innovation (18–19; 263), the Spartan sympathizer represents an advanced and savvy student, a critical and innovative audience.[72]

The comparison made by the student in *Panathenaicus* between the envious antagonists of Isocrates who are trying to imitate him, addressing a sleeping audience of epeidictic speeches, and the epic poets who imitate Homer, is appropriate, because it summarises the rhetorical as well as the political dimension of the orator's superiority: they pale in comparison to their role model, Isocrates, far more than the epic poets who are compared to Homer. The student urges Isocrates to publish the speech, to please the true, and not the fictitious representatives of the intellectual élite:

> (262) συμβουλεύω γάρ σοι … διδόναι τοῖς βουλομένοις λαμβάνειν, (263) εἴπερ βούλει χαρίσασθαι μὲν τοῖς ἐπιεικεστάτοις τῶν Ἑλλήνων καὶ τοῖς ὡς ἀληθῶς φιλοσοφοῦσιν, ἀλλὰ μὴ προσποιουμένοις, λυπῆσαι δὲ τοὺς θαυμάζοντας μὲν τὰ σὰ μᾶλλον τῶν ἄλλων, λοιδορουμένους δὲ τοῖς λόγοις τοῖς σοῖς ἐν τοῖς ὄχλοις τοῖς πανηγυρικοῖς, ἐν οἷς πλείους εἰσὶν οἱ καθεύδοντες τῶν ἀκροωμένων, καὶ προσδοκῶντας, ἢν παρακρούσωνται τοὺς τοιούτους, ἐναμίλλους τοὺς αὐτῶν γενήσεσθαι τοῖς ὑπὸ σοῦ γεγραμμένοις, κακῶς εἰδότες ὅτι πλέον ἀπολελειμμένοι τῶν σῶν εἰσιν ἢ τῆς Ὁμήρου δόξης οἱ περὶ τὴν αὐτὴν ἐκείνῳ ποίησιν γεγονότες.

> I advise you … to give it to those who want it, [263] if you want to bring pleasure to the best of the Greeks and to those who are truly devoted to philosophy and do not just make a pretense of it. Do it also if you want to bring pain to those who admire your works more than others but criticize them to the crowds at the panegyric festivals, where those who sleep are more numerous than those who actually listen. They expect that if they mislead this kind of audience, their own works will rival yours, for they fail to understand that their work is further behind yours than that of those who write the same kind of poetry as Homer are behind his reputation.

> (transl. Papillon)

*

From the above-mentioned it may be concluded that Isocrates attributes a central role to his rhetorical activity, which in continuous comparison with his rivals combines the innovative interpretations of an issue with a social benefit. They

---

[72] See *Panathenaicus* 263; 271; 272. Cf. Bruss 2012, 329f.

are the two qualities that his opponents, *agelaioi sophistai*, lack: the lack of originality and the passive imitation do not correspond only to their grandiose promises, which are empty of content, but also to their due role in cultural hierarchy. The elitist innovative speech of Isocrates interweaves with his hierarchy of the branches of oratory and highlights the prominent role of the intellectuals, which is fulfilled only when they focus their interest on innovative and high, and hence socially beneficial objectives. This motivation is a crucial component of Isocratic rhetoric, which promotes creative and rejects passive imitation, sets epideictic speeches above judicial ones, and seeks progress through an aristocracy of values, which in the realisation of political objectives – such as for example the panHellenic idea – transcends the bonds of the city-state. The passive imitators of Isocrates, as *agelaioi sophistai*, are placed, on the contrary, on the same lower level with a helpless, passive, and sleeping audience which is presented with oratorical speeches in panegyric festivals.

Bibliography

Alexiou, E. (1995), *Ruhm und Ehre. Studien zu Begriffen, Werten und Motivierungen bei Isokrates*, Heidelberg.

Alexiou, E. (1998), 'Η παρουσία του Ομήρου στο έργο του Ισοκράτη. Παιδεία και πολιτική προπαγάνδα', in: M. Paizi-Apostolopoulou (ed.), *ΟΜΗΡΙΚΑ. Από τα Πρακτικά του Η΄ Συνεδρίου για την Οδύσσεια*, Ithaca, 283–298.

Alexiou, E. (2000), 'Enkomion, Biographie und die "unbeweglichen Statuen": Zu Isokrates Euagoras 73–76 und Plutarch Perikles 1–2', in: *C&M* 51, 103–117.

Alexiou, E. (2007), 'Rhetorik, Philosophie und Politik: Isokrates und die homologoumene arete', in: *Rhetorica* 25, 63–87.

Alexiou, E. (2009), 'Das Proömium des isokrateischen Euagoras und die Epitaphienreden', in: *WJ* 33, 31–52.

Alexiou, E. (2010), *Der Euagoras des Isokrates. Ein Kommentar*, Berlin.

Alexiou, E. (2014), 'Die Rhetorik des 4. Jahrhunderts', in: B. Zimmermann/A. Rengakos (eds.), *Handbuch der griechischen Literatur der Antike. II. Die Literatur der klassischen und hellenistischen Zeit*, Munich, 734–859.

Alexiou, E. (2015), 'The Rhetoric of Isocrates' Evagoras: History, Ethics and Politics', in: C. Bouchet/P. Giovanelli-Jouanna (eds.), *Isocrate. Entre jeu rhetorique et enjeux politiques*, Lyon, 47–61.

Alexiou, E. (2015a), 'Die Spiegelfunktion der isokratischen Rhetorik: Der lakonisierende Schüler und die Pleonexie großen Stils', in: M. Tziatzi/M. Billerbeck/F. Montanari/K. Tsantsanoglou (eds.), *Lemmata. Beiträge zum Gedenken an Christos Theodoridis*, Berlin, 73–90.

Alexiou, E. (2016), 'Isokrateszitate in der aristotelischen Rhetorik und das Schweigen über Demosthenes', in: *Hermes* 144, 401–418.

Alexiou, E. (2016a), *Η ρητορική του 4ου αι. π.Χ. Το ελιξίριο της δημοκρατίας και η ατομικότητα*, Athens.

Alexiou, E. (2018), 'Competitive Values in Isocrates and Xenophon. Aspects of *Philotimia*', in: M. Tamiolaki (ed.), *Special Issue. Xenophon and Isocrates. Political Affinities and Literary Interaction*, Berlin, 114–133.
Atkins, J.W.H. (1952), *Literary Criticism in Antiquity*, I, London.
Azoulay, V. (2010), 'Isocrate et les élites. Cultiver la distinction', in: L. Capdetrey/Y. Lafond (eds.), *La cité et ses élites: Pratiques et représentations des formes de domination et de contrôle social dans les cités grecques*, Bordeaux, 19–48.
Behme, T. (2004), 'Isocrates on the Ethics of Authorship', in: *Rhetoric Review* 23, 197–215.
Blank, T. (2014), *Logos und Praxis. Sparta als politisches Exemplum in den Schriften des Isokrates*, Berlin.
Blank, T. (2017), 'Counsellor, Teacher, Friend. The *apragmôn* as Political Figure in Isocrates', in: A. Queyrel Bottineau/M.-R. Guelfucci (eds.), *Conseillers et ambassadeurs dans l'antiquité*, Besançon, 263–290.
Bons, J.A.E. (1993), 'ΑΜΦΙΒΟΛΙΑ. Isocrates and Written Composition', in: *Mnemosyne* 46, 160–171.
Braun, L. (1982), 'Die schöne Helena, wie Gorgias und Isokrates sie sehen', in: *Hermes* 110, 158–174.
Bruss, K. (2012) 'Searching for Boredom in Ancient Greek Rhetoric. Clues in Isocrates', in: *Ph&Rh* 45, 312–334.
Buchheit, V. (1960), *Untersuchungen zur Theorie des Genos Epideiktikon von Gorgias bis Aristoteles*, Munich.
Buchner, E. (1958), *Der Panegyrikos des Isokrates. Eine historisch-philologische Untersuchung*, Wiesbaden.
Campbell, B. (1984), 'Thought and Political Actiodn in Athenian Tradition. The Emergence of the Alienated Intellectual', in: *History of Political Thought* 5, 17–59.
Chroust, A.-H. (1965): 'Aristotle's First Literary Effort. The Gryllos, a Lost Dialogue on the Nature of Rhetoric', in: *REG* 78, 576–591 (= Chroust, Anton-Hermann [1973], *Aristotle. New Light on his Life and on Some of his Lost Works*, II, London, 29–42).
Collins Edwards, L. (2010), 'Shifting Paradigms. Mimesis in Isocrates', in: P. Mitsis/C. Tsagalis (eds.), *Allusion, Authority, and Truth. Critical Perspectives on Greek Poetic and Rhetorical Praxis*, Berlin/New York, 377–400.
Davidson, J. (1990), 'Isocrates against Imperialism. An Analysis of the De Pace', in: *Historia* 39, 20–36.
De Romilly, J. (1975), *Magic and Rhetoric in Ancient Greece*, Cambridge MA/London.
De Romilly, J. (1958), '*Eunoia* in Isocrates or the Political Importance of Creating Good Will', in: *JHS* 78, 92–101.
Depew, D. (2004), 'The Inscription of Isocrates into Aristotle's Practical Philosophy', in: T. Poulakos/D. Depew (eds.), *Isocrates and Civic Education*, Austin, 157–185.
Dover, K. (1974), *Greek Popular Morality in the Time of Plato and Aristotle*, Oxford.
Dover, K. (1997), *The Evolution of Greek Prose Style*, Oxford.
Dressler, J. (2014), *Wortverdreher, Sonderlinge, Gottlose. Kritik an Philosophie und Rhetorik im klassischen Athen*, Berlin/Boston.
Düring, I. (1961), *Aristotle's Protrepticus. An Attempt at Reconstruction*, Göteborg.
Engels, J. (2003), 'Antike Überlieferungen über die Schüler des Isokrates', in: W. Orth (ed.), *Isokrates. Neue Ansätze zur Bewertung eines politischen Schriftstellers*, Trier, 175–194.
Eucken, C. (1983), *Isokrates. Seine Positionen in der Auseinandersetzung mit den zeitgenössischen Philosophen*, Berlin/New York.

Flacelière, R. (ed.) (1961), *Isocrate, Cinq discours. Éloge d'Hélène, Busiris, Contre les Sophistes, Sur l'attelage, Contre Callimachos*, Paris.
Flashar, H. (2006): 'Dialoge, Philosophie, Rhetorik', in: H. Flashar/U. Dubielzig/B. Breitenberger (eds.), Aristoteles, *Fragmente zu Philosophie, Rhetorik, Poetik, Dichtung. Übersetzt und erläutert*, Berlin, 21–245.
Ford, A. (1993), 'The Price of Art in Isocrates. Formalism and the Escape from Politics', in: T. Poulakos (ed.), *Rethinking the History of Rhetoric. Multidisciplinary Essays in Rhetorical Tradition*, Boulder, 31–52.
Forsdyke, S. (2009), 'The Uses and Abuses of Tyranny', in: R. Balot (ed.), *A Companion to Greek and Roman Political Thought*, Chichester UK/Malden MA, 231–246.
Fündling, J. (2014), *Philipp II von Makedonien*, Darmstadt.
Gagarin, M. (2002), 'Logos as Ergon in Isocrates', in: L. Calboli Montefusco (ed.), *Papers on Rhetoric IV*, Rome, 111–119.
Gomperz, H. (1905–6), 'Isokrates und die Sokratik', in: *WS* 27, 163–207; 28, 1–42.
Gotteland, S. (2001), *Mythe et rhétorique. Les examples mythiques dans le discours politique de l'Athènes classique*, Paris.
Graff, R. (2005), 'Prose versus Poetry in Early Greek Theories of Style', in: *Rhetorica* 23, 303–335.
Hammerstaedt, J. (1996), 'Improvisation', in: *RAC* 17, 1221–1225.
Haskins, E.V. (2004), *Logos and Power in Isocrates and Aristotle*, Columbia SC.
Heilbrunn, G. (1975), 'Isocrates on Rhetoric and Power', in: *Hermes* 103, 154–178.
Hellwig, A. (1973), *Untersuchungen zur Theorie der Rhetorik bei Platon und Aristoteles*, Göttingen.
Jackson, R./Lycos, K./Tarant H. (ed.) (1998), *Olympiodorus, Commentary on Plato's Gorgias*, Leiden.
Kehl, H. (1962), *Die Monarchie im politischen Denken des Isokrates*, Bonn.
Kennedy, G.A. (1958), 'Isocrates' Encomium of Helen. A Panhellenic Document', in: *TAPhA* 89, 77–83.
Kennedy, G.A. (1963), *The Art of Persuasion in Greece*, Princeton.
Konstan, D. (2004), 'Isocrates' Republic', in: T. Poulakos/D. Depew (eds.), *Isocrates and Civic Education*, Austin, 107–124.
Konstan, D. (2006), *The Emotions of the Ancient Greeks. Studies in Aristotle and Classical Literature*, Toronto.
Korais, A. (1807), Ἰσοκράτους λόγοι καὶ ἐπιστολαὶ μετὰ σχολίων παλαιῶν, II, Paris.
Kurz, D. (1970), *AKRIBEIA. Das Ideal der Exaktheit bei den Griechen bis Aristoteles*, Göppingen.
Liddel, P. (2007), *Civic Obligation and Individual Liberty in Ancient Athens*, Oxford.
Livingstone, N. (1998), 'The Voice of Isocrates and the Dissemination of Cultural Power', in: Y.L. Too/N. Livingstone (eds.), *Pedagogy and Power. Rhetorics of Classical Learning*, Cambridge, 263–281.
Livingstone, N. (2007), 'Writing Politics. Isocrates' Rhetoric of Philosophy', in: *Rhetorica* 25, 15–34.
Ludwig, P.W. (2009), 'Anger, Eros, and Other Political Passions in Ancient Greek Thought', in: R.K. Balot (ed.), *A Companion to Greek and Roman Political Thought*, Chichester UK/Malden MA, 294–307.
Mader, G. (2005), '*Pax Duello Mixta*. Demosthenes and the Rhetoric of War and Peace', in: *CJ* 101, 11–35.

Mariss, R. (2002), *Alkidamas. Über diejenigen, die schriftliche Reden schreiben, oder über die Sophisten. Eine Sophistenrede aus dem 4. Jahrhundert v. Chr. eingeleitet und kommentiert*, Münster.
Mathieu, G. (1925), *Les idées politiques d'Isocrate*, Paris.
Mikkola, E. (1954), *Isokrates. Seine Anschauungen im Lichte seiner Schriften*, Helsinki.
Montiglio, S. (2005), *Wandering in Ancient Greek Culture*, Chicago.
Morgan, K.A. (2003), 'The Tyranny of the Audience in Plato and Isocrates', in: K.A. Morgan (ed.), *Popular Tyranny. Sovereignty and its Discontents in Ancient Greece*, Austin, 181–213.
Natoli, A.F. (ed.) (2004), *The Letter of Speusippus to Philip II. Introduction, Text, Translation and Commentary*, Stuttgart.
Nicolai, R. (2004), *Studi su Isocrate. La comunicazione letteraria nel IV sec. a.C. e i nuovi generi della prosa*, Rome.
Nightingale, A. (1995), *Genres in Dialogue. Plato and the Construct of Philosophy*, Cambridge.
O'Sullivan, N. (1992), *Alcidamas, Aristophanes, and the Beginnings of Greek Stylistic Theory*, Stuttgart.
Ober, J. (1998), *Political Dissent in Democratic Athens. Intellectual Critics of Popular Rule*, Princeton.
Papillon, T.L. (2001), 'Rhetoric, Art, and Myth. Isocrates and Busiris', in: C.W. Wooten (ed.), *The Orator in Action and Theory in Greece and Rome*, Leiden, 73–93.
Papillon, T.L. (1996), 'Isocrates on Gorgias and Helen. The Unity of the Helen', in: *CJ* 91, 377–391.
Papillon, T.L. (1998), 'Isocrates and the Greek Poetic Tradition', in: *Scholia* 7, 41–61.
Papillon, T.L. (2004), *Isocrates*, II, Austin.
Papillon, T.L. (2007), 'Isocrates', in: I. Worthington (ed.), *A Companion to Greek Rhetoric*, Malden MA/Oxford, 58–74.
Perlman, S. (1961), 'The Historical Example, Its Use and Importance as Political Propaganda in the Attic Orators', in: *SH* 7, 150–166.
Poulakos, T. (1997), *Speaking for the Polis. Isocrates' Rhetorical Education*, Columbia SC.
Poulakos, T. (2001), 'Isocrates' Use of Doxa', in: *Ph&Rh* 34, 61–78.
Poulakos, T. (2004), 'Isocrates' Civic Education and the Question of Doxa', in: T. Poulakos/D. Depew (eds.), *Isocrates and Civic Education*, Austin, 44–65.
Race, W.H. (1978), '*Panathenaicus* 74–90. The Rhetoric of Isocrates' Digression on Agamemnon', in: *TAPhA* 108, 175–185.
Race, W.H. (1987), 'Pindaric Encomium and Isocrates' *Evagoras*', in: *TAPhA* 117, 131–155.
Race, W.H. (2007), 'Rhetoric and Lyric Poetry', in: I. Worthington (ed.), *A Companion to Greek Rhetoric*, Malden MA/Oxford, 509–525.
Rapp, C. (ed.) (2002), Aristoteles, *Rhetorik. Übersetzt und erläutert*, I–II, Berlin.
Roth, P. (ed.) (2003), *Der* Panathenaikos *des Isokrates. Übersetzung und Kommentar*, München/Leipzig.
Ryder, T.T.B. (2000), 'Demosthenes and Philip II', in: I. Worthington (ed.), *Demosthenes. Statesman and Orator*, London/New York, 45–89.
Said, S. (2003), 'Envy and Emulation in Isocrates', in: D. Konstan/K. Rutter (eds.), *Envy, Spite and Jealousy: The Rivalrous Emotions in Ancient Greece*, Edinburgh, 217–234.
Sanders, E. (2008), '*Pathos Phaulon*. Aristotle and the Rhetoric of *Phthonos*', in: I. Sluiter/R. Rosen (eds.), *Kakos. Badness and Anti-Value in Classical Antiquity*, Leiden/Boston, 255–281.

Sanders, E. (2014), *Envy and Jealousy in Classical Athens. A Socio-Psychological Approach*, Oxford.
Schiappa, E. (1999), *The Beginnings of Rhetorical Theory in Classical Greece*, New Haven/London.
Schneeweiss, G. (ed.) (2005), *Aristoteles*, Protreptikos. *Hinführung zur Philosophie. Rekonstruiert, übersetzt und kommentiert*, Darmstadt.
Spengel, L. (1851), *Über die* Rhetorik *des Aristoteles*, Abh. Bayer. Akad. der Wiss., Phil.-Hist. Kl., Munich.
Steidle, W. (1952), 'Redekunst und Bildung bei Isokrates', in: *Hermes* 80, 257–296.
Steiner, D.T. (1994), *The Tyrant's Writ: Myths and Images of Writing in Ancient Greece*, Princeton.
Teichmüller, G. (1881), *Literarische Fehden im vierten Jahrhundert vor Chr.*, I, Breslau.
Timmerman, D.M./Schiappa, E. (2010), *Classical Greek Rhetorical Theory and the Disciplining of Discourse*, Cambridge.
Too, Y.L. (1995), *The Rhetoric of Identity in Isocrates. Text, Power, Pedagogy*, Cambridge.
Too, Y.L. (2008), *A Commentary on Isocrates' Antidosis*, Oxford.
Usener, S. (1994), *Isokrates, Platon und ihr Publikum. Hörer und Leser von Literatur im 4. Jahrhundert v. Chr.*, Tübingen.
Usher, S. (1973), 'The Style of Isocrates', in: *BICS* 20, 39–67.
Usher, S. (ed.) (1990), *Isocrates, Panegyricus and To Nicocles*, Warminster.
Usher, S. (2010), '*Eurhythmia* in Isocrates', in: *CQ* 60, 82–95.
Vallozza, M. (1990), 'Alcuni motivi del discorso di lode tra Pindaro e Isocrate', in: *QUCC* 64, 43–58.
Vallozza, M. (1998), 'Sui topoi della lode nell' Evagora di Isocrate (1, 11, 72 e 51–52)', in: *Rhetorica* 16, 121–130.
Von der Mühll, P. (1939–40), 'Isokrates und der Protreptikos des Aristoteles', in: *Philologus* 94, 259–265.
Walcot, P. (1978), *Envy and the Greeks. A Study of Human Behaviour*, Warminster.
Walker, J. (2000), *Rhetoric and Poetics in Antiquity*, Oxford.
Wareh, T. (2012), *The Theory and Practice of Life. Isocrates and the Philosophers*, Cambridge MA/London.
Wersdörfer, H. (1940), *Die ΦΙΛΟΣΟΦΙΑ des Isokrates im Spiegel ihrer Terminologie*, Leipzig.
Wilms, H. (1995), *Techne und Paideia bei Xenophon und Isokrates*, Stuttgart/Leipzig.
Yunis, H. (1996), *Taming Democracy. Models of Political Rhetoric in Classical Athens*, Ithaca/London.
Zajonz, S. (2002), *Isokrates' Enkomion auf Helena. Ein Kommentar*, Göttingen.

Mike Edwards
The Orators and Greek Drama

A recent avenue of productive scholarship has been the relationship between oratory and drama, especially in the area of performance. The holding of the international conference at which I delivered the original version of this paper is indicative of the importance increasingly attached to the study of that relationship, as is the Centre for Ancient Rhetoric and Drama in the Department of Philology at Kalamata, which was set up by Professor Xanthaki Karamanou, a scholar with deep interests in both fields.[1] In this paper I wish to revisit briefly two overlaps that I have written on previously – the uses of dramatic and other poetry made by the orators, and the uses of dramatic and other poetry made by Aristotle in the *Rhetoric* – and then take a look at a third, the appearance of orators in comic drama. My conclusions, which are not all entirely original,[2] are not designed to challenge the general validity of the oratory/drama relationship; nevertheless, they may make us pause a little before we finally mint drama and oratory on two sides of the same coin.[3]

Poetry, of course, long predated prose, and it is hardly surprising that the narratives of the Homeric epics are regularly punctuated by speeches, beginning in line seventeen of the *Iliad*. Early examples of legal situations include the ecphrastic trial scene on Achilles' shield (*Iliad* 18.497ff.), the dispute between Hermes and Apollo over the stealing of the latter's cattle in the Homeric *Hymn to Hermes*, and the trial of Orestes in Aeschylus' *Eumenides*; while Clytemnestra's commanding use of her rhetorical skills in persuading Agamemnon to tread on the purple tapestries (Aesch. *Ag.* 855ff.) reflects the Athenians' addiction to (usually male) rhetorical performance.[4] The links between oratory and drama were expertly explored in a ground-breaking article by Edith Hall some time ago now,[5]

---

[1] My thanks to Professor Markantonatos and to Dr Eleni Volonaki for inviting me to Kalamata for the excellent *Poet and Orator: A Symbiotic Relationship in Democratic Athens* conference.
[2] See, for example, the articles by North 1952 and Perlman 1964.
[3] In what follows I revisit my article from 2007. This is not my normal practice, but is, I think, justifiable here by the relative inaccessibility of the original.
[4] The speeches, both direct and indirect, which alternate with and enhance the narrative in historical texts, are another literary context in which oratory plays a vital role, and Pericles' *Funeral Oration* links historiography with epideictic oratory (Thucydides 2.35ff.). For a recent discussion of the rhetoric of envoys as represented in Herodotus, Thucydides and Xenophon, see Rubinstein 2016. Further on speeches in Herodotus, see Zali 2015.
[5] Hall 1995.

https://doi.org/10.1515/9783110629729-014

and all this would lead us to expect that the texts of the Attic orators would be infused with quotations from drama and poetry. But this is not actually the case.[6]

In fact, there are no poetic quotations in the extant texts of six of the ten canonical orators (Antiphon, Andocides, Isocrates, Isaeus, Hyperides, Dinarchus), and a seventh, Lysias, has only one quotation in a fragment (frg. 235 Carey), from the tragic poet Carcinus.[7] We do not know the context. There are then only a handful of quotations in the Demosthenic corpus, though there are rather more in the three speeches of Aeschines and the single extant speech of Lycurgus. Aeschines employs nine quotations in his prosecution of Demosthenes' political ally Timarchus in 346/5.[8] The main group of these is introduced by the defensive remark that his opponent speaks 'of Achilles and Patroclus and of Homer and other poets' (1.141) and is designed to underline the debased nature of Timarchus' homosexuality, one of 'those whose love is illicit, men who recognize no limits'. Nick Fisher comments that the exegesis 'is produced above all by the nature of the case, and the need to anticipate his opponent's tactics, as well as (perhaps to a lesser extent) his own natural desire to display his cultural knowledge, powers of interpretation, and recitation skills',[9] though Aeschines does not in fact recite all the lines, but has the clerk read out three of the Homeric quotations. When Demosthenes faced Aeschines in person three years later, he cleverly picked up and repeated the Hesiod (Dem. 19.243) and three lines from Euripides frg. 812 (Dem. 19.245). He supplemented these with sixteen lines from Sophocles' *Antigone* (175–90), comparing his opponent to the tyrant Creon (Dem. 19.247), and forty-two lines from Solon's elegiacs (frg. 4 West) on dishonest demagogues (Dem. 19.255), with the subtle suggestion that Aeschines should wear a soft skull-cup. These were worn by invalids to keep their heads warm, and Demosthenes had previously accused Aeschines of feigning illness (19.124), but his audience will have understood the reference to Solon's wearing a cap when he recited his poem about Salamis (Plutarch, *Solon* 8.1). It is perhaps not surprising that Demosthenes

---

6 The absence of poetic quotations in Attic oratory has frequently been noted, as by Hall 1995, 45: 'direct quotations from poetry in the extant corpus of speeches are therefore surprisingly infrequent'. In my view 'infrequent' is something of an understatement.

7 Carey in the OCT quotes Blass 1887, 373, 'Hier allein bei allen älteren Rednern wird eine Dichterstelle ... als Auctorität citirt', omitting in the ellipsis '(aus dem Tragiker Karkinos)'.

8 If we include a non-existent line from the *Iliad*, which Aeschines claims 'Homer often says' (1.128). Of the other eight, four are from the *Iliad* (18.324–329, 333–335, 23.77–91, 18.95–99), three from lost plays of Euripides (frgs 865, 672, 812 Nauck), and one from Hesiod (*Works and Days* 763–4). Cf. Aesch. 1.128–129, 144, 148–152.

9 Fisher 2001, 286.

has the clerk read out these longer quotations,¹⁰ not wanting to involve himself in a recitation contest with his rival who had been a tragic actor, but like Aeschines earlier he may also have wanted not to appear to be showing off.¹¹ Aeschines retorted by repeating the lines of Hesiod (Aesch. 2.144) and adding a second quotation from Hesiod (*Works and Days* 240–1) soon after (Aesch. 2.158). The poetic rivalry continued in the *Crown* trial of 330, with Aeschines now the prosecutor and speaking first: he picks up and extends his second quotation from the *Works and Days* (240–5, at Aesch. 3.135), and later adds four verse epigrams (Aesch. 3.184-185, 190). Demosthenes responds with the opening line of Euripides' *Hecuba* and two iambic lines of unknown origin (Dem. 18.267).¹² But it should be emphasised that the Demosthenic quotations all come in the context of his rivalry with Aeschines. There are none in the other genuine speeches of the Demosthenic corpus,¹³ though an elegiac couplet from Simonides is quoted in one of the speeches by Apollodorus ([Dem.] 59.97).

Aeschines' more extensive use of poetic quotations need not surprise us, given his background as a tragic actor, or tritagonist in Demosthenes' slur,¹⁴ but we might indeed have expected far more. Douglas MacDowell wrote that 'Aeschines' speech *Against Timarkhos* contains a remarkably large number of poetic quotations'.¹⁵ But I am not sure that eight quotations in the 196 sections of this long speech are really so remarkable, and similarly with Edward Harris' comment on Aeschines' 'extensive quotations' whereby 'he portrays himself as a cultured gentleman'.¹⁶ Aeschines may well have been proud of his education, but he is careful to pick his moments and does not risk displaying it at every opportunity.

Lastly, the orator who arguably made the most extensive use of quotations, though this judgment is based on a single surviving speech, is Lycurgus. The *Against Leocrates*, which was delivered just prior to the *Crown* trial, has seven quotations: four lines of iambics of unknown origin; fifty-five lines from Euripides'

---

10 MacDowell 2000, 312 suggested that not all of the Solon may have been read out.
11 Perlman 1964, 165–166 perceptively suggested that the fact that the clerk read them out will have given them the feel of witness statements.
12 For Yunis 2005, 98, nn. 209 and 210, the first unknown iambic line is '[a] nondescript verse that could have come from any tragedy or been made up for this context', while the second 'evokes tragedy as it begins, but it is so hackneyed that it could just as well evoke comedy'.
13 Though there is a close similarity between a sentence in 40.10 and Hom. *Iliad* 15.37–38.
14 E.g., Dem. 18.129. This is a tacit admission by Demosthenes, as are his other attacks on Aeschines' acting ability, that Aeschines *was* a successful actor, rather like the slurs against the B-movie actor who became President of the United States, Ronald Reagan.
15 MacDowell 2000, 302.
16 Harris 1995, 28.

lost *Erechtheus*; six lines from the *Iliad* (15.494-499); thirty-two lines of Tyrtaeus (frg. 10 West); two sets of two-line epigrams by Simonides; and two lines of iambics, again of unknown origin (Lyc. 1.92, 99, 103, 107, 108, 132). These all come in quick succession in the proofs section of the speech. If Hermogenes had more texts of Lycurgus to draw on than survive to us when he commented that Lycurgus 'often digresses into myths and stories and poems' (*Peri ideon* 2.389), it may be that the level of quotation in the *Against Leocrates* was not unusual and that he deserves the condemnation he has received from modern scholars for excessive use of it.[17] S. Perlman argued that Lycurgus, like Aeschines, substituted quotations for proof from laws and witnesses when he 'had to rely on moral rather than on strictly legal arguments',[18] but we should also remember that Lycurgus was a leading cultural figure in Athens, responsible for the texts of the three tragedians that have been preserved via the Alexandrian library. Background factors such as these may lie behind the greater use of poetic quotations in Lycurgus and Aeschines than was normal for speakers in the assembly and lawcourts.

It follows that we need to be wary of remarks like that of Victor Bers, that 'the speakers quite often quote tragedy for the same reason they quote or refer to Homer, Tyrtaeus or Solon: poetry represents a sort of unassailable wisdom'.[19] For this implies that quotations are more frequent and from a greater range of authors than they actually are (Aeschylus is not quoted at all, Sophocles only by Demosthenes),[20] and it also raises the question as to why there are not *more* quotations from the poets who were the fount of wisdom. Now, there are many parallels between the dramatists and orators in their employment of rhetorical strategies,[21] and the tragic tenor of the narrative in Antiphon 1 has been noted more than once.[22] Bers reasonably suggests that jurors may have found a speech too reminiscent of tragedy tasteless, but this raises further questions about parallels between the theatre and courtroom. Again, the poetic vocabulary of Antiphon has been remarked on,[23] and even Isocrates, who was determined to eradicate poetic diction from prose,[24] admits the popularity of poetic-sounding epideictic oratory (Isoc. 15.47) and recognises the importance of employing poetic examples when speaking in front of a large audience (Isoc. 2.42–44, 48–49). But our surviving

---

[17] As, e.g., by Dobson 1919, 281.
[18] Perlman 1964, 168.
[19] Bers 1994, 190.
[20] Aristophanes also does not feature.
[21] E.g., the use of *topoi*. See, for instance, Usher 1999, 16–21.
[22] As, e.g., by Bers 1994, 189–190.
[23] As, e.g., by Gagarin 1997, 27.
[24] Cf. Isoc. 9.8–11.

epideictic speeches do not contain poetic quotations. Likewise, Lysias went to extremes to avoid poetic vocabulary according to Dionysius of Halicarnassus (*On Imitation* 9, *Lysias* 3), but to my mind he would not have risked his income stream, or more charitably would not have failed his clients, by regularly omitting poetic quotations from his speeches if this was common practice. It is likely that speakers were wary of showing off,[25] and quotation when there was little evidence available may have been a factor, though this means that Antiphon missed a trick in *Against the Stepmother*, when he had no solid evidence or witnesses to call on.[26] We also need to take into account a passage of Aristophanes' *Wasps* (579–580), where Philocleon remarks, 'and if Oeagrus [a tragic actor] comes into court as a defendant, he doesn't get off until he's picked out the finest speech in *Niobe* [a tragedy of Aeschylus or Sophocles] and recited it to us'.[27] Once more, this does not sit well with the surviving forensic speeches, and does little to dispel the suspicion that the parallels between the *orchestra* and the *bema* have perhaps been overstated.

A further consideration which makes the lack of quotation all the more surprising is the apparent importance of poetry in the training of an orator, at least as far as we are led to believe by Aristotle's *Rhetoric*. Aristotle illustrates his rhetorical points far more often by quotations from poetry and drama than from the orators themselves, with thirty-one quotations from Homer and seventeen from Euripides, marking the latter's popularity in the fourth century – which may account in reverse for the mere five quotations from Sophocles and none at all from Aeschylus, with a few from comedy. Quotations from the orators, on the other hand, are extremely rare in Aristotle, and eight members of the canon do not feature at all. This includes Demosthenes, of whom there are at most three direct mentions in the *Rhetoric*: one of these (*Rhet.* 2.23.3) concerns an otherwise unknown trial and there is no quotation; a second (*Rhet.* 2.24.8) is the only certain reference to the orator, but records Demades' condemnation of his policy; and the third (*Rhet.* 3.4.3) refers to a simile which is not found in the extant works and is usually thought to refer to the fifth-century general of the same name. There are doubtless more subtle allusions to Demosthenes' works,[28] and Demosthenes' absence is readily explicable by Aristotle's family ties with the kings of Macedon.

---

25 See, e.g., Carey 1996, 411.
26 We might also recall that the defendant in Antiphon 6 was a choregus – a seemingly appropriate context for poetic quotation.
27 Transl. Sommerstein 1983.
28 E.g., at *Rhet.* 1.7.41. See Cope/Sandys 1877, *ad loc.*

This argument might lead one to expect that the Macedonian sympathiser Aeschines would feature prominently, but not so. Lysias fares only slightly better, quoted anonymously at *Rhet.* 2.23.19 and indirectly at *Rhet.* 3.10.7, in a paraphrase of the Funeral Oration (Lys. 2.60).[29] Lysias is not named in the Greek (Freese's Loeb translation is misleading here), nor is he at the very end of the *Rhetoric* (3.19.6), where the final words echo the final words of Lysias 12. That leaves Isocrates, who as the leading rhetorician of the period before Aristotle is the only orator regularly mentioned by him; and a number of other non-canonical orators and rhetoricians are also mentioned, including Gorgias and Aristotle's friend Theodectes, who wrote tragedies as well as an *Art of Rhetoric*. It is true, of course, that the canon of ten orators known to us was not yet formed in Aristotle's day, but the near-absence of two of the leading fourth-century logographers, Lysias and Demosthenes, and Aristotle's preference for using poetic quotations to illustrate rhetorical matters are striking. It then comes as no surprise that Aristotle in fact approves of the use of poetry in court (*Rhet.* 1.15.13–14), but this is more a reflection of the often theoretical, not practical, nature of the *Rhetoric*.

We come, finally, to the topic of the appearance of the orators in drama, specifically comedy. The only member of the canon who appears in the extant plays of Aristophanes directly is Antiphon. That is, if it is the orator who is being referred to at *Wasps* 1270 ('he's as hungry as Antiphon') and 1301. The identification is accepted by most modern commentators, such as MacDowell and Alan Sommerstein, who note other sources for Antiphon's alleged greed, which include Plato Comicus fr. 103, cited in Ps.-Plut. *Antiphon* 833c (here greed for money), and Xen. *Mem.* 1.6 (greed for money and food).[30] But the earlier, now rather naive-sounding dismissal of the identification by B.B. Rogers ('it is quite impossible to believe that Aristophanes is here alluding ... to the illustrious Rhamnusian, the son of Sophilus, the orator and politician whose character is given in Thucydides, viii.68')[31] long preceded the doubts expressed more recently by Emmanuela Bakola,[32] and further caution is expressed by Ian Storey,[33] by Biles and Olson in

---

[29] Salamis replaces Aegospotami in error.
[30] See MacDowell 1971, 296–297; Sommerstein 1983, 232.
[31] Rogers 1875, 195.
[32] Bakola 2005, 611 n. 15.
[33] Storey 1985, 319–322, who prefers the identification of this Antiphon with the 'base' Antiphon son of Lysidonides (cf. Cratin. frg. 212; Xen. *Hell.* 2.3.40).

their commentary on the *Wasps*,³⁴ and by Roisman and Worthington in their commentary on Ps.-Plutarch.³⁵ What speaks to me in favour of the identification is the second reference to Antiphon in line 1301, dining with 'the Phrynichus group' – again, if this Phrynichus is the son of Stratonides who was later, with Antiphon, one of the leaders of the Four Hundred.³⁶ But I would also note the remarkable coincidence that Amynias, the man who is 'as hungry as Antiphon', was dining in the company of Leogoras (line 1268), who in turn was the father of Andocides, the second member of the canon. Andocides was born about 440, and so would have been about 18 when the *Wasps* was produced in 422; hence it is no surprise that Aristophanes jokes about the father rather than the son, especially in the context of another wealthy member of Athens' aristocracy from the same generation, though Aristophanes does not portray Leogoras and Antiphon as dining together. I note further that at *Clouds* 109 Leogoras keeps pheasants, exotic birds in this period such as would be the pastime of a rich man; and the Ps.-Plutarchan *Life* (833d) says that one of Antiphon's most celebrated speeches was the one *Against Erasistratus Concerning the Peacocks*, rather more exotic birds than pheasants. The version of *Clouds* we have was produced sometime before 416, while Paul Cartledge suggests that the *Against Erasistratus* will have been written about 415.³⁷ So there is no necessary connection at all here, but small world.

Another orator whose father apparently featured in comedy was Isocrates. According to the Ps.-Plutarchan *Life* (836e) Theodorus was made fun of for his reed pipes by both Aristophanes and Strattis – and a fragment of Strattis (frg. 3) pokes fun at Isocrates 'the flute-borer' (αὐλοτρύπης) and his concubine Lagisce. But my final orator in comedy comes much later, in the plays of Timocles. As David Whitehead noted,³⁸ according to Athenaeus (341F–342A) Hyperides appears in the *Delos* and the *Icarians* (as well as in Philetaerus' *Asclepius*). In the *Delos*, produced in 323, he is described as 'Hyperides of the glib tongue' (ἐν λόγοισι δεινός), an expression bettered by Aeschines (3.215) when he calls Demosthenes a 'crafty contriver of words' or 'dreadful deviser of words' (δεινὸς δημιουργὸς λόγων). The *Delos* passage contains a list of politicians bribed by Harpalus, which includes Demosthenes. But perhaps more entertaining is the second reference, in the *Icarians*. A hundred years after Leogoras and his pheasants, the gourmet of

---

34 Biles/Olson 2015, 451–452: 'there is no real ground for choosing between them and little need to do so, given that someone else may be in question in any case'.
35 Roisman/Worthington 2015, 86–87.
36 The judgment of Biles/Olson 2015, 461, for example, is 'probably'.
37 Cartledge 1990, 58–59.
38 Whitehead 2000, 10–11.

the early 320s favoured fish: 'so you will cross the Hypereides river, which teems with fish, and in tender tones, or spluttering noisy bombast of reasoned logic, with retraced arguments frequently repeated, is prepared to meet anything when he has loosed the bolts; and ready for hire, he waters the fields of the briber' (transl. Gulick).

Bibliography

Bakola, E. (2005), 'A Missed Joke in Aristophanes' *Wasps* 1265–1274', in: *CQ* 55, 609–613.
Bers, V. (1994), 'Tragedy and rhetoric', in: I. Worthington (ed.), *Persuasion. Greek Rhetoric in Action*, London, 176–195.
Biles, Z.P/Olson, S.D. (2015), *Aristophanes, Wasps*, Oxford.
Blass, F. (1887), *Die attische Beredsamkeit*, I, 2nd ed., Leipzig.
Carey, C. (1996), 'Rhetorical means of persuasion', in: A.E. Rorty (ed.), *Essays on Aristotle's Rhetoric*, California, 399–415.
Carey, C. (ed.) (2000), *Aeschines*, Texas.
Carey, C. (ed.) (2007), *Lysiae orationes cum fragmentis*, Oxford.
Cartledge, P.A. (1990), 'Fowl Play: A Curious Lawsuit in Classical Athens', in: P.A. Cartledge/ P. Millett/S.C. Todd (eds.), *Nomos*, Cambridge, 41–61.
Cope, E.M./J.E. Sandys (1877), *The Rhetoric of Aristotle*, I, Cambridge MA.
Dobson, J.F. (1919), *The Greek Orators*, London.
Edwards, M.J. (2007), 'Rhetoric and Technique in the Attic Orators and Aristotle's *technê rhêtorikê*', in: J. Roe/M. Stanco (eds.), *Inspiration and Technique. Ancient to Modern Views on Beauty and Art*, Bern, 35–47.
Fisher, N.R.E. (2001), *Aeschines, Against Timarchos*, Oxford.
Freese, J.H. (1926), *Aristotle, Art of Rhetoric*, Cambridge MA.
Gagarin, M. (1997), *Antiphon, The Speeches*, Cambridge.
Gulick, C.B. (1930), *Athenaeus, The Deipnosophists*, IV, Cambridge MA/London.
Hall, E. (1995), 'Lawcourt dramas: the power of performance in Greek forensic oratory', in: *BICS* 40, 39–58.
Harris, E.M. (1995), *Aeschines and Athenian Politics*, Oxford.
MacDowell, D.M. (1971), *Aristophanes, Wasps*, Oxford.
MacDowell, D.M. (2000), *Demosthenes, On the False Embassy (Oration 19)*, Oxford.
North, H. (1952), 'The use of poetry in the training of the ancient orator', in: *Traditio* 8, 1–33.
Perlman, S. (1964), 'Quotation from poetry in Attic orators of the fourth century B.C.', in: *AJP* 85, 155–172.
Rogers, B.B. (1875), *The Wasps of Aristophanes*, London.
Roisman, J./Worthington, I. (2015), *Lives of the Attic Orators*, Oxford.
Rubinstein, L. (2016), 'Envoys and *ethos*: team speaking by envoys in classical Greece', in: M.J. Edwards/P. Derron (eds.), *La Rhétorique du pouvoir. Une exploration de l'art oratoire délibératif grec*, Geneva, 79–128.
Sommerstein, A.H. (1983), *Aristophanes, Wasps*, Warminster.
Storey, I.C. (1985), 'The Symposium at *Wasps* 1299 FF.', in: *Phoenix* 39, 317–333.

Usher, S. (1999), *Greek Oratory. Tradition and Originality*, Oxford.
Whitehead, D. (2000), *Hypereides*, Oxford.
Yunis, H. (2005), *Demosthenes, Speeches 18 and 19*, Texas.
Zali, V. (2015), *The Shape of Herodotean Rhetoric. A Study of the Speeches in Herodotus' Histories with Special Attention to Books 5–9*, Leiden/Boston.

László Horváth
Dramatic Elements as Rhetorical Means in Hyperides' *Timandrus*

The use of dramatic elements, dialogues and poetical expressions had been an established device of Attic oratory from the outset.[1] But these can be considered as devices of colour, serving primarily to enliven the style and entertain the listeners, aiming only secondarily to add effects strengthening the evidence. It is sufficient for my purpose to cite the example of the first two canonical Attic orators. Antiphon, in his speech on the poisoning case, calls the murderous stepmother by the name of Clytaemnestra, while in the διήγησις he uses the terminology of tragedy in narrating the fateful toast of the two good friends. In his late, monotonous defence, Andocides attempts to create a tragicomic milieu, describing his opponent's troubled private life as a pleasant source of relief.

In certain speeches of Hyperides, however, the 'dramatization' of the discourse serves a uniquely strategic purpose. In examining his speech *Against Athenogenes*, I suggested that in the history of Attic oratory it demonstrated that the indictment showed an exceptionally close resemblance to contemporary comedy in the masterly use of ἠθοποιία; moreover, the judges' thoughts were intentionally steered toward a 'relative genre', New Comedy. Hyperides inserted into his speech comic elements that could be described as ordinary, as well as striking turns of speech, and thus he elevated 'comedy-making' to an almost exclusive, strategic level of his argumentation. The Athenian judge might not even have noticed that his perspective and judgement had been influenced by the compelling choreography of comic plays. Thus the orator, in a hopeless legal situation (after all, a valid contract, even countersigned by his 'client', had to be annulled!), relied on the precisely calculated reactions from the audience: besides the confusing plethora of laws cited out of context, he recreated the comic milieu they were imbued with, while he strengthened beyond all customary (and compulsory) measure their agricultural, even αὐτόχθονες, connections, thereby painting an image of Athenogenes as an urban intriguer of alien and hostile allegiances.[2]

Although a mere 64 lines of the discourse *Against Timandrus* are extant, we can discern traces and dramatic elements which hint at a similar strategy of argument. This is, true even though the charges represented by Hyperides were, as

---

1 This study was supported by the OTKA NN 104456 project.
2 Horváth 2007.

far as it can be established, founded on more solid legal grounds. The laws pertained both to the obligatory leasing of the inheritance and to the raising of all the minors in the family, if at all possible, in one and the same place.³ In addition, Natalie Tchernetska argued on the basis of the few lines of the text published in the first edition (read from the verso): 'A possible reconstructed text of ll. 12–21 follows; these read like a New Comedy recognition scene'.⁴ With further readings and the reconstruction of the formerly missing text in hand, we can now say that 22 lines of the 64 bear a dramatic tone, while 42 pertain to the legal context and a general presentation of the situation. Thus, the dramatically informed lines not only serve to paint the ἦθος of the guardian, but also help to heighten the πάθος integral to tragedy by evoking a well-known stage setting, thereby steering the sympathy of the judges towards the accusant representing the orphans. This dramatic device is ἀναγνώρισις, the mutual recognition of long-separated brothers (chapters 3–5; 135v 18–138v 17):

> Indeed, it was in order to get the money that he did the same man's sister a wrong worthy of capital punishment. When these two brothers and two sisters were left here, the girls being orphans without a mother or a father, and all of them small children (perhaps the eldest brother Antiphilos, who died, was ten years old), this man Timandros brought up the younger sister in his own home, dragging her away and taking her to Lemnos when she was perhaps seven. And this no guardian nor any man of good will would do, not even those who hold war captives in their possession: even they sell them, as far as possible, as a family. Now, not even those slave-masters and traders who do anything outrageous for profit, when they trade in children who are siblings or when they market a mother with children or a father with children, because they sell them, with financial loss, for less, [this being] the right thing to do. For affection between people comes about by close contact and by growing up together rather than by kinship. As evidence of this: neither would all fathers be fond of their children if they were not brought up with them from infancy, if straight away someone had kidnapped them and kept hold of them, nor would children be fond of their parents if they were not brought up by them. Timandros, then, is responsible for precisely this, that the sisters could not recognise each other on sight in a street or a temple, not having seen each other for more than thirteen years, while it was their brother, my client Akademos, who recognised his own sister, but when he went to Lemnos, he did not know her when he saw her.⁵

---

3 Thür 2008a and 2008b.
4 Tchernetska 2005, 5.
5 [3] διὰ τὰ χρήματα καὶ εἰς τὴν ἀδελφὴν τουτουῒ θανάτου ἄξια ἠδίκηκεν· καταλειφθέντων γὰρ τουτωνὶ δυοῖν ἀδελφοῖν καὶ ἀδελφαῖν δυοῖν ὀρφαναῖν καὶ μητρὸς καὶ πατρὸς καὶ παιδαρίων πάντων ὄντων – ἴσως γὰρ ὁ πρεσβύτατος ἀδελφὸς Ἀντίφιλος ὁ τελευτήσας ἦν δέκα ἐτῶν – τὴν νεωτέραν αὐτῶν ἀδελφὴν ἀποσπάσας οὑτοσὶ Τίμανδρος ἔτρεφε παρ' αὑτῷ ἀποκομίσας εἰς Λῆμνον ἴσως οὖσαν ἑπτὰ ἐτῶν. καίτοι τοῦτο μὴ ὅτι ἐπίτροπος ἢ εὔνους ἂν ἄνθρωπος ποιήσαι,

The 'subject' incorporated into the speech can be seen as an excessively simplified stage scene represented to the judges, with the separation of the siblings and the lack of ἀναγνώρισις (the comic element of an encounter in the street or a public square) and then its realization: the brother finds his sister (tragic element).

Aristotle considers ἀναγνώρισις a key characteristic of complex tragic plots, in addition to περιπέτεια, of course. Without intending to offer an exhaustive list of his categories, I shall highlight some specific groups. Ἀναγνώρισις may come in three principal forms (*Poetics* 16). (1) 'the least artistic kind, which is largely used owing to incompetence – discovery by tokens';[6] (2) 'In the second place come those which are constructed by the poet and are therefore inartistic. For instance, in the Iphigeneia Orestes revealed himself. She was revealed to him through the letter, but Orestes himself says what the poet wants and not what the plot requires. So this comes near to the fault already mentioned';[7] (3) recognition that follows from memory, where a character realizes something from something he or she sees or hears. The most perfect form of recognition comes when it is concomitant with περιπέτεια: 'Now since the discovery is somebody's discovery, in some scenes one character only is revealed to another, the identity of the other being obvious; but sometimes each must discover the other. Thus Iphigeneia was discovered by Orestes through the sending of the letter, but a separate discovery was needed to make him known to Iphigeneia.'[8]

ἀλλ' οὐδ' οἱ κατὰ πόλεμον ἐγκρατεῖς γιγνόμενοι τῶν σωμάτων, ἀλλὰ καὶ κατ' οἰκίαν πωλοῦσιν ὅτι μάλιστα. [4] οἱ τοίνυν ἀνδραποδοκάπηλοι καὶ ἔμποροι κέρδους ἕνεκα πᾶν πράττοντες ἀσελγές, ἂν ἀδελφὰ παιδάρια πωλῶσιν ἢ μητέρα καὶ παιδία ἢ πατέρα καὶ παιδάρια ἑστῶσι, ζημιούμενοι ἐλάττονος ἀποδίδονται αὐτῶν τι τοῦτο τῶν δικαίων ὄν. αἱ γὰρ εὔνοιαι τοῖς ἀνθρώποις εἰσὶ διὰ τὴν συνήθειαν καὶ τὸ συντρόφους αὐτοὺς εἶναι μᾶλλον ἢ διὰ τὰς συγγενείας. τεκμήριον δὲ τούτου· οὔτε γὰρ ἂν πατέρες τοὺς αὑτῶν παῖδας ἀσπάσαιντο, εἰ μὴ ἐπ' αὐτοῖς ἐκ παιδαρίων τραφεῖησαν, εἰ εὐθύς τις αὐτῶν μικρὰ ὄντα ἀποσπάσαι, οὔτε οἱ παῖδες τοὺς γονέας εἰ μὴ ὑπ' ἐκείνων τραφείησαν. [5] Τίμανδρος τοίνυν τούτου αὐτοῦ γε αἴτιος γέγονεν, ὥστε τὰς μὲν ἀδελφὰς ἀλλήλας μὴ ἀναγνῶναι μήτε ἐν ὁδῷ μήτε ἐν ἱερῷ ἰδούσας – πλεόνων γὰρ ἐτῶν ἢ τριῶν καὶ δέκα οὐχ ἑωράκασιν ἑαυτάς – τὸν δὲ ἀδελφὸν τουτονὶ Ἀκάδημον ἀναγνωρίσαι τὴν ἑαυτοῦ ἀδελφήν, ἐλθόντα δὲ εἰς Λῆμνον μὴ γνῶναι ἰδόντα. Greek text: Horváth 2014, 184–186. Slightly emended English translation: Tchernetska *et al*. 2007.

6 Arist. *Po*. 1454b πρώτη μὲν ἡ ἀτεχνοτάτη καὶ ᾗ πλείστη χρῶνται δι' ἀπορίαν, ἡ διὰ τῶν σημείων. English translations by W.H. Fyfe.

7 Arist. *Po*. 1454b δεύτεραι δὲ αἱ πεποιημέναι ὑπὸ τοῦ ποιητοῦ, διὸ ἄτεχνοι. οἷον Ὀρέστης ἐν τῇ Ἰφιγενείᾳ ἀνεγνώρισεν ὅτι Ὀρέστης· ἐκείνη μὲν γὰρ διὰ τῆς ἐπιστολῆς, ἐκεῖνος δὲ αὐτὸς λέγει ἃ βούλεται ὁ ποιητὴς ἀλλ' οὐχ ὁ μῦθος· διὸ ἐγγύς τι τῆς εἰρημένης ἁμαρτίας ἐστίν.

8 Arist. *Po*. 1452b ἐπεὶ δὴ ἡ ἀναγνώρισις τινῶν ἐστιν ἀναγνώρισις, αἱ μέν εἰσι θατέρου πρὸς τὸν ἕτερον μόνον, ὅταν ᾖ δῆλος ἅτερός τίς ἐστιν, ὁτὲ δὲ ἀμφοτέρους δεῖ ἀναγνωρίσαι, οἷον ἡ μὲν

Several examples of the person-related ἀναγνώρισις relevant to the *Timandrus* speech are known from surviving tragedies. The most famous scene is the meeting of the siblings, Electra and Orestes, dramatized by all three major tragic playwrights. In each case, it is only the brother, Orestes, who perceives the identity of his sister, while she does not recognize him; in all three cases, sisterhood must be confirmed by objective evidence. Aeschylus, *The Libation Bearers*, 212ff.: Orestes reveals his identity to Electra. He then identifies himself by means of the veil woven by his sister. Sophocles, *Electra*, 1221ff.: the recognition of the two siblings is complemented by the introduction of the old pedagogue, whom Electra does not recognize [1348ff.]. Euripides, *Electra*, 224ff.: Orestes is not recognized by Electra. The old pedagogue [534ff.] encourages her to identify the *peplos*; in fact, she wrapped her brother into that when saving him. 560ff.: the old pedagogue recognizes Orestes from the scar above his eye-brow and reveals his identity to Electra. The various synonyms of 'seeing' and 'recognizing' appear in a multitude of different types in the Greek texts. It seems Euripides had a special predilection for the dramatic device of person-related ἀναγνώρισις. (*Helen*, 557ff.: Menelaus and Helen incredulously recognize each other in Egypt. *Ion*, 1397ff.: Creusa recognizes the cradle in which she had laid her son, thus identifying Ion as her own son.) Here, however, the recognition of siblings is important, repeatedly emphasized by Aristotle in analyzing ἀναγνώρισις (Chapters 11; 16.2; extensive discussion in 17.3). It is equally telling that *Iphigenia in Tauris* is the second most discussed play in Aristotle, surpassed only by *Oedipus Rex*. Indeed, it is a nearly perfect amalgamation of the three most important criteria of tragedy (περιπέτεια, ἀναγνώρισις, and πάθος). We might even assume that *Poetics*, written after 335 BCE, reflects the popularity of Euripides' much-examined tragedy.[9] Although the *Timandrus* speech cannot be dated on the basis of the extant text and the relevant testimonies, Hyperides' *acme* falls precisely to the second half of the 340s and the 330s. The literary environment of the 4th century BCE was imbued with Euripides. This is confirmed by inscribed monuments as well. The *didaskalia* inscriptions sporadically available from the years 341–339 BCE (their density decreases from the 330s) inform us that Euripidean reperformances triumphed at the Great Dionysia held in those three years: in 341 BCE, *Iphigenia* (presumably *in Tauris*) with the famous Neoptolemus in the lead; in 340, *Orestes*;

Ἰφιγένεια τῷ Ὀρέστῃ ἀνεγνωρίσθη ἐκ τῆς πέμψεως τῆς ἐπιστολῆς, ἐκείνου δὲ πρὸς τὴν Ἰφιγένειαν ἄλλης ἔδει ἀναγνωρίσεως. Cf. Rátvay 1907.

9 Preßler 1998, 97. On *didascalia* inscriptions, Reisch (1907) continues to be an important authority.

and in 339, again a play by Euripides (the title is lost).[10] The 4th-century popularity of *Iphigenia* is attested by some dozen vase decorations in Southern Italy.[11] In Athens, the representation of tragedies on vases had been pushed in the background.[12]

The dramatic climax of *Iphigenia in Tauris* is the mutual recognition of Orestes and Iphigenia. This dramatic peak runs to more than 300 lines (472–840), until at long last, before sacrificing his brother, Iphigenia realizes Orestes' identity. Objective evidence is present here: the homespun and object retrieved from memory (814ff.). This scene was presumably considered the textbook example of the ἀναγνώρισις of siblings; no wonder that Aristotle testified to this. Without suggesting a one-to-one correspondence, let us list the motifs shared between *Timandrus* and the play: (1) the siblings are orphaned, both parents dead; (2) they have an elder sister (Electra), but she is back home; (3) they have no more brothers, since even Pylades is only an almost-brother (Academus' brother had died at the age of 10); (4) their elder sister was separated from her brother to live in a foreign country (541: Ἰφ. ἐκεῖθέν εἰμι· παῖς ἔτ' οὖσ' ἀπωλόμην. Cf. 834ff.); (5) the sister's life was ruined by her father, though Iphigenia lays no blame at Agamemnon's door; (6) at their reunion, they do not recognize each other; (7) the brother finds his sister and returns home with her (1362ff.: Ἀγαμέμνονος παῖς, τήνδ' ἐμὴν κομίζομαι / λαβὼν ἀδελφήν, ἣν ἀπώλεσ' ἐκ δόμων).

Satyrus, the author of the Euripides debate [fr. 39. 7] claims that the renaissance of the first type of ἀναγνώρισις, based on objective evidence, was Euripides' contribution to New Comedy.[13] The fraternal recognition known from the world of comedy, as well as its delay, is the starting point of Menander's *Perikeiromene*, to name but the most famous example. Here, although Glykera knows her twin brother, Moschion, he, unaware of the truth, tries to court her, which leads to serious complications. In lines 770ff., then, family memories and objective evidence result in ἀναγνώρισις. Ἀναγνώρισις is central to *Men at Arbitration*, though it does not occur between siblings here.

---

10 Mette 1977, 91–92. Cf. *TrGF* I, 13. and Cropp 2000, 62.
11 It is worth mentioning that Aristophanes parodied Euripides' tragedy in at least two comedies. *Lemnian Women* [fr. 373 = fr. 324 Dind.] mocks the name of Thoas, king of Lemnos, parodying lines 32–33. Λῆμνος κυάμους τρέφουσα τακερούς καὶ κάλους / ἐνταῦθα δ' ἐτυράννευεν Ὑψιπύλης πατὴρ / Θόας, βραδύτατός γ' ὢν ἐν ἀνθρώποις δραμεῖν. (Edmonds: fr. 356–357). Cf. Cropp 2000, 174. Thoas was the king of Lemnos [cf. Hom. *Il.* 14.230; 23.145].
12 Allan 2001, 67–86.
13 πρὸς γυναῖκα καὶ πατρὶ πρὸς υἱὸν καὶ θεράποντι πρὸς δεσπότην, ἢ τὰ κατὰ τὰς περιπετείας, βιασμοὺς παρθένων, ὑποβολὰς παιδίων, ἀναγνωρισμοὺς διά τε δακτυλίων καὶ διὰ δεραίων, ταῦτα γάρ ἐστι δήπου τὰ συνέχοντα τὴν νεωτέραν κωμῳδίαν, ἃ πρὸς ἄκρον ἤγαγεν Εὐριπίδης.

The world of comedy is suggested by an analogy found in *Timandrus*, where the orator depicts the behaviour of slave-traders. In Plautus' comedies based on Greek examples, we often see the phenomenon of a free girl falling into the hands of a slave-trader, only to experience a fortunate turn of ἀναγνώρισις and, not least, passionate love, which help her reveal the truth and thus liberate her again (see *Poenulus, Rudens, Curculio*).[14]

Through the study of the dramatic features of the *Athenogenes* and *Timandrus* speeches, we may come to appreciate Hyperides' shining talent, admired by his contemporaries, that virtuosity and wit which Cicero summed up in one expressive word: *acumen*. For he claims, 'There are two sorts of jokes, one of which is excited by things, the other by words.'[15] And concerning the farcical wit inherent in phrasing (with *facetiae* and *ridiculum* being near synonyms), he adds, 'in words, the ridiculous is that which is excited by the point (*acumen*) of a particular expression (*verbum*) or thought (*sententia*): but all scurrilous buffoonery (*scurrilis dicacitas*) is to be studiously shunned'.[16] In Cicero's assessment, refined wit (*acumen*) is an exclusive property of Hyperides' style among the Attic orators: 'Isocrates possessed sweetness, Lysias delicacy, Hyperides pointedness, Aeschines sound, and Demosthenes energy'.[17] Hyperides had a probably unique talent for striking a balance between dramatic, now humorous and entertaining, now tragically-tinged turns of phrases in his speeches in the context of Attic courtrooms where the deployment of the vilest means of passion and hatred were the order of the day. And he did so not without considerable success.[18]

---

14 About the scene of 'selling mothers and children', suggestions have been made by Jones 2008, 19–20 on the basis of Tchernetska *et al.* 2007, 1–4. A more complete edition of the Greek text has been published: Horváth 2014, 184–188.

15 Cic. de Orat. 2.240: *Duo sunt enim genera facetiarum, quorum alterum re tractatur alterum dicto.*

16 Cic. de Orat. 2.244: *In dicto autem ridiculum est id, quod verbi aut sententiae quodam acumine movetur ... in hoc scurrilis dicacitas magno opere fugienda est.*

17 Cic. de Orat. 3.28: *suavitatem Isocrates, subtilitatem Lysias, acumen Hyperides, sonitum Aeschines, vim Demosthenes habuit*, translated by J.S. Watson. A similar characterization can be found in Quintilianus Inst. 2.15.9: *dulcis in primis et acutus Hyperides, sed minoribus causis, ut non dixerim vilioribus, magis par.*

18 Curtis 1970 has arrived at a similar conclusion while investigating the impact of Hyperides.

Bibliography

Allan, W. (2001), 'Euripides in Megale Hellas: Some Aspects of the Early Reception of Tragedy', in: *Greece & Rome* 48,1, 67–86.
Cropp, M.J. (ed.) (2000), *Euripides, Iphigenia in Tauris*, Warminster.
Curtis, T.B. (1970), *The Judicial Oratory of Hyperides*, PhD Diss., Chapell Hill NC [microfilm].
Horváth, L. (2007), 'Hypereides' Rede gegen Athenogenes und die zeitgenössische Komödie', in: *Wiener Studien* 120, 25–34.
Horváth, L. (2014), *Der neue Hypereides*, Berlin.
Jones, C. (2008), 'Hyperides and the Sale of Slave-Families', in: *ZPE* 164, 19–20.
Mette, H.J. (1977), *Urkunden Dramatischer Aufführungen in Griechenland*, Berlin/New York.
Preßler, F. (1998), 'Die "Iphigenie bei den Tauern" in der "Poetik" des Aristoteles', in: B. Zimmermann (ed.), *DRAMA: Beträge zum antiken Drama und seiner Rezeption*, Stuttgart.
Rátvay, J. (1907), *A felismerés a görög drámában [Recognition in Greek Drama]*, Újvidék [Novi Sad].
Reisch, Emil (1907), 'Urkunden dramatischer Aufführungen in Athen', in: *Zeitschrift für die Österreichischen Gymnasien*, 289–315.
Tchernetska, N. (2005), 'New Fragments of Hyperides from the Archimedes Palimpsest', in: *ZPE* 154, 1–5.
Tchernetska, N./Handley, E./Austin, C./Horváth, L. (2007), 'New Readings in the Fragment of Hyperides' *Against Timandros* from the Archimedes Palimpsest', in: *ZPE* 162, 1–4.
Thür, G. (2008a), 'Zu ΜΙΣΘΩΣΙΣ und ΦΑΣΙΣ ΟΙΚΟΥ ΟΡΦΑΝΙΚΟΥ', in: *Acta Antiqua Academiae Scientiarum Hungaricae* 48:1–2, 125–137.
Thür, G. (2008b), 'Zur phasis in der neu entdeckten Rede Hypereides' gegen Timandros', in: *ZSStRom* 125, 645–663.

Andreas Seraphim
Thespians in the Law-Court

Sincerity, Community and Persuasion in Selected Speeches of Forensic Oratory

1 Introduction

In a scene midway through William Gaddis' 1955 novel, *The Recognitions*, the struggling and immature playwright Otto, trying to seduce his ethereal poet friend Esmé, catches up with her on the streets of New York City and proclaims his undying love. 'You know I am sincere', he concludes by pleading, 'I have always been sincere with you'. Otto's pledge of sincerity reminds me of how insistently, albeit in indirect/inexplicit ways, Aeschines and Demosthenes posit their own sincerity and their opponents' trickery in the trials of 343 and 330 BCE.

Sincerity, whether in the private context of a conversation between two lovers, or in the public context of Athenian trials, is an important key to communication and persuasion. Sincerity is 'a communicative relation between one's speech and 'the Other' with whom one interacts'.[1] Whether authentic or pretended, sincerity, if used skilfully, enables the speaker to forge a rapport with the audience and reinforces his or her ability to communicate a message to the recipient and move hearers and viewers into a state of receptivity. In this chapter, using the fierce rivalry between Aeschines and Demosthenes, as displayed in Aeschines 2, 3 and Demosthenes 18, 19, I aim to offer an updated analysis of how both orators use the *rhetoric of sincerity* to win over the law-court audience.

The concern to demonstrate sincerity mirrors a deep anxiety in public discourse in ancient Athens about the potential for deception inherent in oratory.[2]

---

[1] Altes 2008, 109. Cf. Trilling 1972; Markovits 2008, 20–22.
[2] Dionysius of Halicarnassus, for example, refers to Pythias' allegation that the speeches of Demosthenes, like those of his teacher Isaeus, were the target of general suspicion of chicanery and deception 'because of their great rhetorical skill' (*Is.* 4.23–24: τῆς πολλῆς ἐπιτεχνήσεως). Aeschines also accuses Demosthenes of being a sophist, since written speeches were associated with the sophists and teachers of rhetoric, who had a reputation for deceit and trickery (1.175; 2.156 etc.). Sincerity is used, in the rhetorical context, interchangeably with truthfulness and authenticity. Anxieties about the possibility of deception can also be seen in a wide range of literary genres, from Homer to drama to philosophy. For a detailed discussion of anxiety about deception in public Athenian discourse: Hesk 1999, 201–230; Hesk 2000; Markovits 2008, 62–80.

https://doi.org/10.1515/9783110629729-016

This anxiety is redoubled by the introduction of theatrical elements, since these are unbounded by the norms of sincerity. An actor onstage is expected to fabricate and simulate, but if one places acting techniques in front of an audience in the courts, who are expecting truth, then those same techniques become hazardous and a cause for blame and invective.[3] Aeschines and Demosthenes alike seek, in parallel with their concern to demonstrate their own sincerity, to exploit the image of unreality and deception that relates to theatre as a means of undermining the other's character, public authority, and personal credibility. This zero-sum contrast serves a twofold purpose: to invite the audience to side with the speaker who (allegedly) tells the truth, and to isolate the dissembling political thespian who, as presented by his adversary, is deploying imagery, linguistic and character patterns, delivery, and other strategies that are rooted in theatrical skills, in order to deceive the audience.

The rhetoric of sincerity aims, in other words, to promote bonding and affiliation and, at the same time, distancing and division. Its fundamental purpose is what Burke in his sturdy book, *A Rhetoric of Motives*, calls *identification*: a speaker indicates that his 'properties' – in the case of Aeschines and Demosthenes, the moral duty of truth-telling and straight-talking in a public-speaking context – are in line with the demand of the audience and the public in general to listen to the truth, thereby affirming a community with the audience and forging proximity.

A speaker does not have to *actually* share motives with the audience; he may well create an appearance or image, i.e. the role or characterization that a person adopts, in order to identify with groups of people and embrace their values, while at the same time concealing his own real intentions, attitudes and beliefs. 'Consubstantiality' – the sharing of substance between two individuals – ends, according to Burke, in persuasion.[4] To put it schematically, Subject A is not identical to Subject B, but if Subject B *perceives* common interests with Subject A, then Subject B identifies with Subject A. The rhetoric of sincerity, in other words, results in the *rhetoric of community*: the conscious, psychological attachment to a group and the belief that this group has shared interests, practices, and values.

---

[3] Serafim 2017, 19: 'This is not to suggest, of course, that oratory always represents reality: there is ample space for imagination in oratorical speeches'. In the speeches that are under examination in this chapter, for example, Aeschines and Demosthenes both manipulate the depiction of themselves and their opponents by deliberately choosing, altering, and/or highlighting events of the past to project their characters in a specific way, overemphasising some of their traits and de-emphasising others, but never fully fabricating characters. For a comprehensive examination of the register of reality in oratory, see Serafim 2017, 19–20.
[4] Burke 1969, 20–23.

The rhetoric of sincerity also has the capacity to generate division or prolong hostility; it functions, by persuading the audience by setting up individuals as antithetical to its expectation to listen to the truth. The rhetoric of sincerity, therefore, functions as a means for the speaker artfully to construct the audience's frame of mind, by affiliating speaker with audience, while simultaneously estranging his opponent from the group. The social identity theory of H. Tajfel and J. Turner indicates that the activation of group attitudes and identities and inter-group relations – i.e. in-group solidarity and out-group hostility – has a huge impact upon behaviours and behaviours and attitudes in target audiences.⁵ The central hypothesis of social identity theory is that members of an in-group will seek to find negative aspects of an out-group, thus enhancing their self-image.

The association of Aeschines and Demosthenes with actors, and the attribution to them of skills rooted in theatre and acting, are powerful weapons in their opponents' arsenals, helping to denigrate of their public credibility and authority and thus creating out-group hostility. The two orators apply the rhetoric of sincerity differently in their speeches, however. Demosthenes is formidable in drawing attention to the status of Aeschines' speeches as mere performances with no reality behind them; in castigating his opponent's use of acting techniques, especially vocal ones, as a means of deceiving the audience; and in inviting the verbal or non-verbal reaction of the hearers and viewers in the law-court (θόρυβος).⁶ Demosthenes never tires of finding ways of exploiting and embroidering the audience's perception that Aeschines was a tragic actor by profession, as indicated by a variety of ancient sources.⁷ Demosthenes, for example, claims that his opponent is nothing more than a *tritagonist*, a label that amounts to 'third-rate actor'.⁸

Aeschines, in turn, given that he cannot completely dissociate himself from the theatre, attempts an alternative approach: to use his theatrical training to his advantage by portraying Demosthenes in the role of a tragic villain and to stress his opponent's own association with the specific (and specifically disturbing)

---

5 Tajfel and Turner 1979. Also Miller *et al*. 1981, 494–511; Conover 1984, 760–785; Lau 1989, 220–223; Huddy 2003, 511–558. Cf. Carey 1990, 49; Hall 2006, 388; Arena 2007, 151.
6 Bers 1985, 1–15; Thomas 2011, 175–185. For Lateiner 1995, xix, non-verbal reactions refer to 'human acts and responses capable of communication – conscious, intentional, voluntary or otherwise – and include gesture, posture, body-talk, paralinguistics, chronemics, and proxemics. Events include somatic, vocal (non-verbal), dermal, thermal, and olfactory messages, and experiences'.
7 Hermog. *Id*. 1.1.95.23–4; Phot. *Bibl*. 243.354a; *Sch. in Hermog. Stat*. 421.22–30W4.
8 Haigh 1907, 230–234; Pickard-Cambridge 1968, 134; Csapo/Slater 1994, 222–223; MacDowell 2000, 289; Hughes 2012, 12–14, 113; Serafim 2017, 18.

phenomenon of actor-politicians: actors who turned into notoriously dissembling politicians. In this regard, it should be noted that, as with Aeschines, Demosthenes is also associated with the stage by the ancient sources, which refer, for example, to how his early vocal shortcomings made him ask for the assistance of actors.[9] Aeschines tries hard to turn the tables on his opponent: seeking to undermine Demosthenes' authority and credibility by attempting to underline any potential implication of his opponent as being associated with the use of (inherently deceitful) acting practices in the (supposedly truthful) context of public speaking.

A few words of caution are necessary at this point about the status of actors in Athenian politics and the use of their skills to serve political ends. Despite Aeschines' and Demosthenes' regular scornful references to each other's (real or alleged) association with acting and actors and the use of theatrical skills to deceive the audience, it is clear that there was a symbiotic relationship between oratory and theatre in classical Athens,[10] and that actors were highly-esteemed in society in general, including in some political contexts.[11] For example, the fact that actors were sent on political and diplomatic missions 'because of [their] profession that naturally wins friends',[12] as Aeschines says in 2.15, would seem to imply that acting skills and talents were not thought of as being necessarily confined rigidly to

---

9 Plu. *Dem.* 7, 11.1, 3; *Vit. Or.* 845a–b: Demosthenes' training with the actor Andronicus is mentioned; Phot. *Bibl.* 493a41.
10 The intersection between theatrical and rhetorical performances culminates in the mock-trials staged by Bdelycleon in the latter part of Ar. *V.* The congruity between theatre and oratory involves mutual borrowing. An example is the use of *agōnes logou* in tragic plays. These contests do not just embody the idea of oratorical debate between two speakers, but they also include language that is suggestive of an oratorical debate. On the reciprocal relationship between oratory and theatre: Xanthakis-Karamanos 1979, 66–76; Scodel 1997, 489–504; Webb 1997, 339–369; Cooper 2004, 145–161; Hall 2006, 353–392; McDonald 2007, 473–489; Hubbard 2007, 490–508.
11 There is substantial evidence that actors were highly esteemed in Athens. Officials or individuals in Athens erected memorials, including both private monuments (such as marble tablets) and public monuments (such as official archives, monuments of stone near or inside the theatre of Dionysus and so forth), to honour successful actors. Secondary sources about the role of actors in fourth-century Athens include Haigh 1907, 40–48, 281–282; Csapo/ Slater 1994, 223–224; Easterling 2002, 327–341.
12 Aeschin. 2.15: διὰ τὴν γνῶσιν καὶ φιλανθρωπίαν τῆς τέχνης. The precise meaning of the term φιλανθρωπία is uncertain. Efstathiou 1999, 87 points out that this term is likely to indicate 'the popularity by which [the dramatic arts] enchant people'; cf. Paulsen 1999, 309. The translation in Carey 2000, 'they sent Aristodemus the actor as an envoy to Philip because of Philip's familiarity with and fondness for his skill (φιλανθρωπία)', which implies that Aristodemus was a member of the Athenian delegation because Philip was likely to be receptive to a message brought by

the theatre. In my book, *Attic Oratory and Performance*, I argue that 'the use of acting skills in political spaces depends on the context, the purpose and the ways in which these skills are used. The references to actors taking part in diplomatic missions possibly suggests that where actors' skills are used to cajole, mislead, or deceive foreigners, thereby securing the best interests of the city, then these skills are acceptable. This does not, however, invalidate the negative rhetoric about the use of acting abilities as a tool in the political decision-making process within Athens itself: when the actor's skill serves to mislead the people to the benefit of individuals, then acting talent may be the focus of attack and criticism'.[13]

2 Two Thespians in the Theatre of Justice

2.1 Playing a part in the law-court

Demosthenes, recognising the persuasive power of Aeschines' acting talent, launches an all-out attack against it. In Demosthenes 19, for example, Aeschines is identified with theatrical characters, such as Creon; in 19.247 we read: 'well in this play look what words these are that have been put by the poet into the mouth of Creon-Aeschines'.[14] Identification of this sort, which associates a real person

---

someone whose work he knew and enjoyed, is less convincing. It was not simply Aristodemus who participated in political missions abroad. Other actors were also sent on political delegations: Kleandros, for example, negotiated the repatriation of Theokritos after being captured during the Peloponnesian War, Ischandros appeared before the Athenians having brought political proposal from Arcadia, Neoptolemus served as an ambassador for Philip on a mission to Athens in 346 BCE, while Thettalos was a representative of Alexander to Caria; see Arnott 1991, 52–53; Harris 1995, 30–31. It is more possible, therefore, that the term φιλανθρωπία refers generally to the cachet attaching to successful actors, which allows them to move freely and makes them useful as intermediaries.

13 See Serafim 2017, 81–82.
14 The reference to Creon-Aeschines in 19.247 draws further attention to some of the qualities of his tyrannical character, aiming to elicit feelings of fear and odium towards him among the Athenians. As Aeschines himself refers to Demosthenes' attempt to liken him to Dionysius of Sicily (identification that does not figure in the extant written copy of Demosthenes 19), 'with loud cries he urged you to watch out for me' (2.10). The fear of tyranny persisted throughout the classical period and induced the Athenians to pass anti-tyrannical legislation, such as the law of Eucrates (337/6 BCE). The idea that tyranny was a significant threat also pervades Athenian literature. Dramatic and non-dramatic sources alike exploit the same recurrent negative stereo-

with the character that he enacted onstage, serves to highlight Aeschines' propensity towards acting, even when the setting does not allow him to act. Aeschines is tacitly presented here as eroding the boundaries between the public and the theatrical space. He is a professional dissimulator, someone able to pretend, to take over roles, and to manipulate the facts, to reproduce them in a false yet credible way, relocating the fiction associated with the safe space of the theatre into the context of ordinary life, where untruths can have a real impact.

A scathing reference to the association of Aeschines' profession with his public authority and his citizenry also occurs in 18.267:

> καὶ 'κακὸν κακῶς σε' μάλιστα μὲν οἱ θεοί, ἔπειθ' οὗτοι πάντες ἀπολέσειαν, πονηρὸν ὄντα καὶ πολίτην καὶ τριταγωνιστήν.

> May you, you wretch, wretchedly be destroyed, first of all, by the gods but also by all these people, since you are a miserable citizen and a miserable bit-part actor.

The quotation, highlights Demosthenes' attempts to draw a parallel between his opponent's ruinous acting profession (as the reference to τριταγωνιστής indicates) and his villainous citizenship. This parallel can be seen as a means of underlining, and incriminating in the minds of the audience, Aeschines' failure to keep to the demarcated boundaries between public and theatrical space, and his tendency to relocate the fiction associated with the safe space of the theatre into the context of politics and public speaking where untruths can have a real impact.

Aeschines, in turn, tries to apply his knowledge of theatre to portray Demosthenes in a devastating fashion. In 3.231, for example, he identified Demosthenes with Thersites.

> [A] καὶ εἰ μέν τις τῶν τραγικῶν ποιητῶν τῶν μετὰ ταῦτα ἐπεισαγόντων ποιήσειεν ἐν τραγῳδίᾳ τὸν Θερσίτην ὑπὸ τῶν Ἑλλήνων στεφανούμενον, οὐδεὶς ἂν ὑμῶν ὑπομείνειεν, ὅτι φησὶν Ὅμηρος ἄνανδρον αὐτὸν εἶναι καὶ συκοφάντην· [B] αὐτοὶ δ' ὅταν τὸν τοιοῦτον ἄνθρωπον στεφανῶτε, οὐκ οἴεσθε ἐν ταῖς τῶν Ἑλλήνων δόξαις συρίττεσθαι.

> [A] And if any of the tragic poets whose works are performed afterwards were to present Thersites being crowned by the Greeks, none of you would tolerate it, because Homer describes him as a coward and slanderer. [B] But when you yourselves crown a man like this, don't you think you are being hissed at in the minds of the Greeks?

---

types of the tyrant: violence, lust, impiety, imperiousness, high-handed and self-centred policies, and greed for absolute power are some of the standard features of literary portrayals of tyrants.

I divide this section into two parts: in part A, Aeschines invites the law-court hearers/viewers to think about their reaction to the supposed tragic scenario of Thersites, a coward and slanderer, crowned as if he was a hero. It should be remembered here that tragedy in democratic Athens was a forum for playing out dilemmas regarding political decisions and the exercise of power: the tragic stage was a safe environment to explore the kinds of decisions that the demos regularly had to make. By imagining Thersites crowned, Aeschines presents to the law-court audience a striking and shocking image that would have undoubtedly provoked a reaction had it actually happened in the theatre. In so doing, in part B of the passage, Aeschines shows how the lesson from such a tragedy would be that it should be inconceivable to crown someone such as Demosthenes. If the Athenians were to crown him, the rest of the Greeks would hiss at them. The term συρίττεσθαι relates to the theatrical experience and refers specifically to the aggressive mood of the audience when they do not like the poor acting of performers.[15] In this way, Aeschines attempts to put pressure particularly on the judges, inviting them to think about their decisions as evaluated not only by their fellow Athenians but also by the Greeks as a whole, remembering that, as claimed in 3.56, Greeks from other cities were present in the court environs.

In 3.157, Aeschines goes even further by attributing to Demosthenes the role of the villain, the man responsible for the destruction of Thebes.

> ἀλλ' ἐπειδὴ τοῖς σώμασιν οὐ παρεγένεσθε, ἀλλὰ ταῖς γε διανοίαις ἀποβλέψατ' αὐτῶν εἰς τὰς συμφοράς, καὶ νομίσαθ' ὁρᾶν ἁλισκομένην πόλιν, τειχῶν κατασκαφάς, ἐμπρήσεις οἰκιῶν, ἀγομένας γυναῖκας καὶ παῖδας εἰς δουλείαν, πρεσβύτας ἀνθρώπους, πρεσβύτιδας γυναῖκας ὀψὲ μεταμανθάνοντας τὴν ἐλευθερίαν, κλαίοντας, ἱκετεύοντας ὑμᾶς, ὀργιζομένους οὐ τοῖς τιμωρουμένοις, ἀλλὰ τοῖς τούτων αἰτίοις, ἐπισκήπτοντας μηδενὶ τρόπῳ τὸν τῆς Ἑλλάδος ἀλιτήριον στεφανοῦν, ἀλλὰ καὶ τὸν δαίμονα καὶ τὴν τύχην τὴν συμπαρακολουθοῦσαν τῷ ἀνθρώπῳ φυλάξασθαι.

> But since you were not there in person, witness their disasters with your mind's eye and imagine that you can see their city being captured, the demolition of the walls, the burning of the houses, the women and the children being led away to slavery, old men, old women learning late in life to forget their freedom, weeping, begging you, angry not at the people who were taking revenge on them but at the men responsible for these events, solemnly instructing you under no circumstances to crown the curse of Greece but to be on your guard against the evil destiny and the bad luck that dogs the man's footsteps.

---

15 Pickard-Cambridge 1968, 275; Roselli 2011, 49.

Aeschines recreates the past 'tragedy' of the Thebans in the present and exploits it to the best rhetorical effect. The wording and the colourful description are designed to draw on the experience of the Athenians as theatregoers and to conjure up the image of the capture of cities and the slaughter and subjugation of populaces. These themes were commonly staged in tragic plays, as, for example, in Euripides' *Trojan Women*. The loaded and colourful description of the destroyed physical setting with the demolished walls and burned houses, together with the presentation of people weeping and crying out on account of the catastrophic reversal of their lives also stir up the emotions of the audience. The image of the Thebans begging the Athenian judges and onlookers (ἱκετεύοντας ὑμᾶς) as if they were present in their city during the turmoil and instructing them (ἐπισκήπτοντας) not to crown the curse of Greece, purports to elicit the compassion of the hearers for the Thebans and their rage and hostility for Demosthenes, 'the curse of Greece'. The emotions attributed by Aeschines to the Thebans, which are presented so vividly, offer a model for the incitement of similar emotions in the 'here and now' of the trial.

Both speakers also reinforce the negative portrayal of their opponents by associating them with scoundrels who were actors. In Dem. 19.94, for example, Aeschines and his cronies, the actors Ctesiphon and Aristodemus,[16] are accused first of having raised false expectations (τὴν πρώτην ἔφερον τοῦ φενακισμοῦ), when they reported that Philip wanted peace, and then of assigning the completion of the deceptive part to Philocrates and Aeschines. Although the noun φέναξ and its cognates have no necessary connection with the theatre, nevertheless the term Demosthenes uses, φενακισμός, carries implications of imposture, which, in this context, given the identity of the agents, may also have associations with theatre.[17] This may be a tacit way of constructing the audience's perspective and encouraging it to see an analogy between theatrical and political space: just as actors dissimulate onstage, so Ctesiphon and Aristodemus, two actors who turned into politicians, are portrayed as playing out a deception on the public stage.

Aeschines, presumably on the principle that the best defence is a good offence, also accuses Demosthenes of being himself associated with dissembling actors who turned into politicians. Despite Demosthenes' claims that Aris-

---

16 Ctesiphon is an obscure person. He does not seem to be the same Ctesiphon who had suggested the crowning of Demosthenes.
17 A good parallel is provided by MacDowell 2000, 218: φέναξ and its cognates are used of 'a tragedian who brings a character on stage, giving a false impression that she will speak' (Ar. *Ra.* 919–921).

todemus was an accomplice of Aeschines, the latter claims that it was Demosthenes who had several times and, in many ways, supported that actor. In 2.17, Aeschines points out, for example, that it was Demosthenes who suggested the crowning of Aristodemus after he had been sent as an ambassador to Philip, in contrast to all the other Athenians, who demanded his punishment because he failed in his ambassadorial mission. In 2.19, Aeschines also points out that Demosthenes tried to help Aristodemus deal with the financial burden of taking part in the first embassy to Philip. In 2.156, meanwhile, Aeschines claims that Demosthenes was closely associated with the comic actor Satyrus.

2.2 The voice of dissimulation

Another way of highlighting an adversary's theatricality in the minds of the audience is through references to vocal excess. A wide range of sources indicate the paramount importance of voice for actors,[18] and Demosthenes, for example, frequently refers to his opponent's oral excess, as in 19.206, 208, 216, 336; connecting it with theatre and acting. In 19.336, for example, we read:

> ἂν οὕτω φυλάττητ' αὐτόν, οὐχ ἕξει τί λέγῃ, ἀλλὰ τὴν ἄλλως ἐνταῦθ' ἐπαρεῖ τὴν φωνὴν καὶ πεφωνασκηκὼς ἔσται.
>
> If you keep an eye on him in that way, he will not have anything to say; here his vociferation and his voice training will go for nothing.

A parallel is in Demosthenes 18.308–9: πεφωνασκηκὼς καὶ συνειλοχὼς ῥήματα καὶ λόγους συνείρει τούτους σαφῶς καὶ ἀπνευστεί 'one who has been training his voice and hoarding words and phrases, which he reels off clearly and without pausing for breath'. The participle πεφωνασκηκώς, which is also used in Dem. 18.308–309, refers specifically to theatrical training, as, for example, in Plu. *Vit. Or.* 844ff., where it is mentioned that Demosthenes himself paid the actor Neoptolemus to train him to deliver passages without pausing for breath (τοῦ δὲ πνεύματος αὐτῷ ἐνδέοντος Νεοπτολέμῳ τῷ ὑποκριτῇ μυρίας δοῦναι, ἵν' ὅλας

---

18 Pl. *R.* 568c3; *Lg.* 817c; Arist. *Rh.* 1403b26–33; 1413b14–28; Arist. Pr. 11.22; Demetr. *Eloc.* 193–195; D.S. 15.7, 16.42; Plu. *Vit. Or.* 848b. On the vocal ability of actors: Pickard-Cambridge 1968, 167–171; Csapo/Slater 1994, 256–258, 265–268; MacDowell 2000, 352; Hall 2002, 22–23; Cooper 2004, 145–146. For a catalogue of references to Aeschines' career as an actor in later sources: Kindstrand 1982, 93.

περιόδους ἀπνευστως λέγῃ).¹⁹ The reference to training and breath control alludes specifically to Aeschines' theatrical training and invites the law-court audience to think of his speech as being like a play with no reality behind it, and therefore to be cautious so as not to be deceived by his eloquence.

Demosthenes' self-presentation in 19.206, 208 (passages cited below in order) as being a careful and cautious speaker, in sharp contrast to Aeschines' oral excesses, merits closer examination.

> τίνα δὲ φθέγγεσθαι μέγιστον ἁπάντων καὶ σαφέστατ' ἂν εἰπεῖν ὅ τι βούλοιτο τῇ φωνῇ; Αἰσχίνην οἶδ' ὅτι τουτονί. τίνα δ' οὗτοι μὲν ἄτολμον καὶ δειλὸν πρὸς τοὺς ὄχλους φασὶν εἶναι, ἐγὼ δ' εὐλαβῆ; ἐμέ· οὐδὲν γὰρ πώποτ' οὔτ' ἠνώχλησα οὔτε μὴ βουλομένους ὑμᾶς βεβίασμαι.

> And who would you say has the loudest voice, and could say the most clearly whatever he wished? This man Aeschines, I am sure. And which man do they call timid and cowardly in the face of the crowds, but I call cautious? Me, because I have never annoyed you or browbeaten you against your will.

> τί ποτ' οὖν ἐστι τὸ αἴτιον ὅτι οἱ βδελυρώτατοι τῶν ἐν τῇ πόλει καὶ μέγιστον φθεγγόμενοι τοῦ καὶ ἀτολμοτάτου πάντων ἐμοῦ καὶ οὐδενὸς μεῖζον φθεγγομένου τοσοῦτον ἡττῶνται; (19.208)

> So what is the reason why the most obnoxious and loudest-voiced men in Athens are so completely defeated by me, the most timid of all, with a voice as quiet as anyone's?

Although several ancient sources report that Demosthenes had experienced early problems with his voice,²⁰ nevertheless, we can safely assume that he had long since corrected any vocal weaknesses with the precious assistance of actors, and that this helped him to win over the large law-court and assembly audiences.²¹ The references to his own weak voice can be seen, therefore, as an attempt to achieve an interlocking goal: to dissociate himself from the theatre, given that, as mentioned above, a loud voice was important for acting professionals, while simultaneously drawing attention to Aeschines' stentorian 'theatrical' voice, with its associated implications of the creation of an illusion for the spectators.

---

19 Cf. Pl. *Lg.* 665e: καὶ ταῦτά γ' εἰ καθάπερ οἱ περὶ νίκης χοροὶ ἀγωνιζόμενοι πεφωνασκηκότες ἰσχνοί τε καὶ ἄσιτοι ἀναγκάζοιντο ᾄδειν οἱ τοιοῦτοι [...] 'moreover, if old men like that were obliged to do as the choristers do, who go lean and fasting when training their voices for a competition [...]'; Arist. *Pr.* 901b22. On the vocal training of actors, including information about breath control: Hall 2002, 23, 33–34; Lightfoot 2002, 213.
20 Cf. n. 9.
21 Goodwin 1970, 113; Usher 1993, 234–235; Fredal 2006, 164–165.

Demosthenes' reference to his mediocre voice seems to approximate to a technique frequently used by orators: the appeal to the sympathy of the judges by stressing the speaker's inexperience in court and his incapacity to deal with his adversary, who is formidable in talking eloquently and persuasively.[22] Demosthenes cannot claim that he is inexperienced. Thus, he attempts to give a new twist to the *topos* to serve his purposes: he expresses his worries that Aeschines' theatrical skills in speaking and his loud voice can charm the audience, whereas his own weak voice would not, despite the fact that he tells the truth. Demosthenes seeks to turn the weapons of Aeschines against him: the latter's well-practised vocal eloquence, which would potentially dignify his law-court performance and charm the audience, gives the former the opportunity to turn the speech into an 'I-You' antithesis. Demosthenes' (alleged) weakness in voice represents sincerity by means of straight talking, whereas the pompous verbal eloquence of his opponent represents insincerity and trickery.

References to Aeschines' verbal exhibitionism and speechifying can also be found in Demosthenes 18. In §127, for example, Demosthenes cites lines that Aeschines uses in the peroration of his speech, in 3.260:

εἰ γὰρ Αἰακὸς ἢ Ῥαδάμανθυς ἢ Μίνως ἦν ὁ κατηγορῶν, ἀλλὰ μὴ σπερμολόγος, περίτριμμ' ἀγορᾶς, ὄλεθρος γραμματεύς οὐκ ἂν αὐτὸν οἶμαι ταῦτ' εἰπεῖν οὐδ' ἂν οὕτως ἐπαχθεῖς λόγους πορίσασθαι, ὥσπερ ἐν τραγῳδίᾳ βοῶντα 'ὦ γῆ καὶ ἥλιε καὶ ἀρετή' καὶ τὰ τοιαῦτα.

If the prosecutor was Aeacus, or Rhadamanthus, or Minos and not a sponger, a common scoundrel, a damned clerk, I do not believe he would have spoken that way or produced such repulsive expressions, bellowing as if on the tragic stage, 'O earth and sun and virtue' and such like.

Demosthenes claims that Aeschines uses a loud voice (βοῶντα), as if he was on the tragic stage (ὥσπερ ἐν τραγῳδίᾳ; cf. 18.13: ἐτραγῴδει; 19.189: τραγῳδεῖ). Carey is right to argue that 'the fact that Demosthenes feels the need to make the attack is revealing. The skills and qualities that had served Aeschines in the theatre were of equal value in the Assembly. There is abundant evidence that Aeschines had an impressive speaking voice, a fact that must have particularly unnerved Demosthenes'.[23] Sensibly, therefore, Demosthenes uses any possible means to neutralise the impact that Aeschines' vocal abilities might have upon the audience and to estrange him from the audience by inviting the judges and

---

22 Cf. Dem. 7.2, 53.13, 58.3; Antiphon 1.1–3, 5.1.4, 5.2–3, 6.2–3; Lys. 1.2, 12.3, 17.1, 19.1–2, 31.4.
23 Carey 2000, 10.

the bystanders to envisage him as simply playing a theatrical part on the dicastic rostrum.

3 As if you were in the theatre, Demos!

The clearest example of the association of Aeschines' voice with theatre is in 19.337–338, where Demosthenes claims that Aeschines played the role of Thyestes and other figures from the Trojan War in a failed performance that made the audience hiss him and almost stone him.

> [A] Καίτοι καὶ περὶ τῆς φωνῆς ἴσως εἰπεῖν ἀνάγκη· πάνυ γὰρ μέγα καὶ ἐπὶ ταύτῃ φρονεῖν αὐτὸν ἀκούω, ὡς καθυποκρινούμενον ὑμᾶς. [B] ἐμοὶ δὲ δοκεῖτ' ἀτοπώτατον ἁπάντων ἂν ποιῆσαι, εἰ, ὅτε μὲν τὰ Θυέστου καὶ τῶν ἐπὶ Τροίᾳ κάκ' ἠγωνίζετο, ἐξεβάλλετ' αὐτὸν καὶ ἐξεσυρίττετ' ἐκ τῶν θεάτρων καὶ μόνον οὐ κατελεύεθ' οὕτως ὥστε τελευτῶντα τοῦ τριταγωνιστεῖν ἀποστῆναι, ἐπειδὴ δ' οὐκ ἐπὶ τῆς σκηνῆς, ἀλλ' ἐν τοῖς κοινοῖς καὶ μεγίστοις τῆς πόλεως πράγμασι μυρί' εἴργασται κακά, τηνικαῦθ' ὡς καλὸν φθεγγομένῳ προσέχοιτε.

> [A] And in fact I perhaps need to say something about his voice; I hear he also prides himself very much on that, in the belief that he will overcome you by his acting. [B] But when he was performing the troubles of Thyestes and the men at Troy, you used to drive him away and hiss him out of the theatres and all but stone him to death, so that in the end he gave up being a tritagonist. And now that he is brought about thousands of troubles, not on the stage but in the city's most important public affairs, I think it would be a very strange thing indeed if you were to pay attention to him on this occasion as being a good speaker.

This passage above is divided into two sections, marked here as A and B, with one common addressee: the law-court audience. The first section presents Aeschines' law-court speech as a theatrical performance with no reality behind it. A remarkable feature of the first section is the use of the phrase ὡς καθυποκρινούμενον ὑμᾶς. Demosthenes seems to have coined the participle: although the formation (the κατά-compound) and syntax (ὡς followed by participle) are common,[24] this compound form, unlike other (plain or compound) forms of the verb ὑποκρίνομαι, is transitive, meaning 'he will overcome you by acting'.[25] Language here indicates the emphasis that Demosthenes places on the detrimental effect of Aeschines' political acting upon the audience.

The second section consists of a vivid description of a theatrical performance by Aeschines. Attention is paid to the reaction of the theatrical audience. The

---

[24] Smyth 1959, 473–474, §§2120–2122.
[25] The verb recurs only in later works, such as D.H. *Dem.* 53; Luc. *DDeor.* 13.2; Ph. 2.280, 2.520.

verbs ἐξεβάλλετε 'drive away' and ἐξεσυρίττετε 'hiss' present regular aspects of the response of the audience within a theatrical context, and therefore invite the law-court audience to 'see' the viewers in the theatre reacting in an aggressive way against Aeschines: this will have been their normal response to poor acting. 'The hissing of the spectators was understood to articulate their collective desire to expel a performer and reject a production'.[26] Indeed, Aeschines is presented as an unsuccessful professional, 'a third-rate actor'. The description here, I argue, is not just about a past incident. Rather, it is an attempt by Demosthenes to make the contemptuous response of the theatrical audience a model for the law-court audience in the here and now of the trial. The invited alignment of the law-court with the theatrical audience seeks to stir *thorubos* as an expression of the audience's disapproval of Aeschines. Demosthenes' attempt to stir up a reaction among the members of the audience serves his purpose to create a certain disposition in them towards his opponent, by instructing them to 'see' Aeschines in a negative way, when he takes to the rostrum.[27]

Examples of the invited alignment of the law-court with the theatrical audience also occur in Aeschines' speeches, as in 3.76, where the appearance of Demosthenes, when he invited the Macedonian envoys to go into the Theatre of Dionysus, is presented in a vivid and colourful way:

> [...] καὶ προσκεφάλαια ἔθηκε, καὶ φοινικίδας περιεπέτασε, καὶ ἅμα τῇ ἡμέρᾳ ἡγεῖτο τοῖς πρέσβεσιν εἰς τὸ θέατρον, ὥστε καὶ συρίττεσθαι διὰ τὴν ἀσχημοσύνην καὶ κολακείαν.

> And he placed cushions there and spread out rugs and at daybreak led the ambassadors into the theatre, with the result that he was hissed at for his undignified and fawning behaviour.

There is an interesting implied contrast between audiences here: Demosthenes is performing like a flatterer for the Macedonian envoys, but there is another audience in the theatre, the Athenians, who react with hostility. This vivid description of Demosthenes' attire and demeanour as a flatterer brings before the eyes of the audience the image of him entering the theatre with the Macedonians and being booed by the Athenians. Thus, the Athenians in court are subtly invited to imitate the reportedly hostile reaction of the theatrical audience, possibly to interrupt Demosthenes' speech and certainly to vote against him. There is also another dimension to the presentation of Demosthenes as being hissed at by the theatrical audience: the Athenian audience is invited to perceive the gap between Demosthenes' words and

---

[26] Roselli 2011, 49.
[27] On Dem. 19.337–338: Easterling 1999, 157–159; Serafim 2015, 96–108.

deeds. Despite his claims that he always serves the best interests of the Athenians and despite his rhetoric, especially in speech 18, that it is a source of pride for him that he has been opposed to Philip, Demosthenes is vividly presented here as ignoring the Athenians and fawning over Philip's representatives.[28]

4 Conclusion

This chapter has explored the ways in which Aeschines and Demosthenes exploit the image of unreality and deception that is associated with the theatre as a means of undermining each other's authority and credibility. Demosthenes' use of theatrical patterns and imagery is intense. A combination of the widely accepted association of Aeschines with theatre and acting, and the insistent ways in which Demosthenes exploits and embroiders this association, may have given him a significant advantage in persuading the audience that the law-court speech and performance of his opponent was an example of theatrical deception.

Aeschines, in turn, thinking that the best form of defence is attack, responds to Demosthenes' barbs both by using his acting skills with precisely the potency that Demosthenes feared, while at the same time highlighting the negative aspects of Demosthenes' own theatrical associations. Aeschines' strategy has a twofold goal: the first concerns the use of his theatrical skills to portray Demosthenes as tragic villain. The second goal is to associate Demosthenes with actors who turned into dissembling politicians, inviting the audience to think of his opponent as being of the same stock. Aeschines attempts, presumably, to invite the audience to think that whereas he himself was an actor on the theatrical stage only, his opponent was playing a part on the public stage, bringing theatre into the law-court and attempting, thereby, to deceive them.

Bibliography

Altes, L.K. (2008), 'Sincerity, Reliability and Other Ironies – Notes on Dave Eggers' *A Heartbreaking Work of Staggering Genius*', in: E. D'hoker/G. Martens (eds.), *Narrative Unreliability in the Twentieth-Century First-Person Novel*, Berlin, 107–128.
Arena, V. (2007), 'Roman Oratorical Invective', in: W. Dominik/J. Hall (eds.), *A Companion to Roman Rhetoric*, London, 149–160.

---

28 On this passage: Serafim 2015, 96–108.

Bers, V. (1985), 'Dikastic Thorubos', in: P.A. Cartledge/F.D. Harvey (eds.), *Crux: Essays Presented to G. E. M. de ste Croix on his 75th Birthday*, Devon, 1–15.
Burke, K. (1969), *A Rhetoric of Motives*, Berkeley/Los Angeles.
Carey, C. (1990), 'Structure and strategy in Lysias XXIV', in: *Greece & Rome* 37, 44–51.
Carey, C. (ed.) (2000), *Aeschines*, Austin.
Conover, P.J. (1984), 'The Influence of Group Identifications on Political Perception and Evaluation', in: *The Journal of Politics* 46, 760–785.
Cooper, C. (2004), 'Demosthenes Actor on the Political and Forensic Stage', in: C.J. Mackie (ed.), *Oral Performance and its Context*, Leiden/Boston, 145–161.
Csapo, E./Slater, W.J. (1994), *The Context of Ancient Drama*, Ann Arbor.
Easterling, P.E. (1999), 'Actors and Voices: Reading between the Lines in Aeschines and Demosthenes', in: S. Goldhill/R. Osborne (eds.), *Performance Culture and Athenian Democracy*, Cambridge, 154–166.
Efstathiou, A. (1999), *A Commentary on Aeschines' De Falsa Legatione, Chapters 1–96*, PhD Thesis, Royal Holloway, University of London.
Fredal, J. (2006), *Rhetorical Action in Ancient Athens: Persuasive Artistry from Solon to Demosthenes*, Carbondale.
Goodwin, W.W. (ed.) (1970), *Demosthenes, On the Crown*, Cambridge.
Haigh, A.E. (1907), *The Attic Theatre: A Description of the Stage and Theatre of the Athenians, and of the Dramatic Performances at Athens*, Oxford.
Hall, E. (2002), 'The Singing Actors of Antiquity', in: P. Easterling/E. Hall (eds.), *Greek and Roman Actors. Aspects of an Ancient Profession*, Cambridge, 3–38.
Hall, E. (2006), *The Theatrical Cast of Athens. Interactions between Ancient Greek Drama and Society*, Oxford.
Hesk, J. (1999), 'The Rhetoric of Anti-rhetoric in Athenian oratory', in: S. Goldhill/R. Osborne (eds.), *Performance Culture and Athenian Democracy*, Cambridge, 201–230.
Hesk, J. (2000), *Deception and Democracy in Classical Athens*, Cambridge.
Hubbard, T.K. (2007), 'Attic Comedy and the Development of Theoretical Rhetoric', in: I. Worthington (eds.), *A Companion to Greek Rhetoric*, London, 490–508.
Huddy, L. (2003), 'Group Identity and Political Cohesion', in: D.O. Sears/L. Huddy/R. Jervis (eds.), *Oxford Handbook of Political Psychology*, Oxford, 511–58.
Hughes, A. (2012), *Performing Greek Comedy*, Cambridge.
Kotlinska-Toma, A. (ed.) (2015), *Hellenistic Tragedy: Texts, Translations and a Critical Survey*, London/New Delhi/New York/Sydney.
Kindstrand, J.F. (1982), *The Stylistic Evaluation of Aeschines in Antiquity*, Stockholm.
Lateiner, D. (1995), *Sardonic Smile: Nonverbal Behaviour in Homeric Epic*, Ann Arbor.
Lau, R.R. (1989), 'Individual and Contextual Influences on Group Identification', in: *Social Psychology Quarterly* 52, 220–31.
Lightfoot, J.L. (2002), 'Nothing to do with the *Technitai* of Dionysus?', in: P. Easterling/E. Hall (eds.), *Greek and Roman Actors. Aspects of an Ancient Profession*, Cambridge, 209–24.
MacDowell, D.M. (ed.) (2000), *Demosthenes, On the False Embassy. Oration 19*, Oxford.
Markovits, E. (2008), *The Politics of Sincerity: Plato, Frank Speech, and Democratic Judgment*, Pennsylvania.
McDonald, M. (2007), 'Rhetoric and Tragedy: Weapons of Mass Persuasion', in: I. Worthington (ed.), *A Companion to Greek Rhetoric*, London, 473–489.
Miller, A.H./Gurin, P./Gurin, G./Malanchuk, O. (1981), 'Group Consciousness and Political Participation', in: *American Journal of Political Science* 25, 494–511.

Paulsen, T. (1999), *Die Parapresbeia-Reden des Demosthenes und des Aischines. Kommentar und Interpretationem zu Demosthenes, or. XIX, und Aischines, or. II*, Bochum.
Pickard-Cambridge, A. (1968), *The Dramatic Festivals of Athens*, Oxford.
Roselli, D.K. (2011), *Theatre of the People: Spectators and Society in Ancient Athens*, Austin.
Scodel, R. (1997), 'Drama and Rhetoric', in: S.E. Porter (ed.), *Handbook of Classical Rhetoric in the Hellenistic Period 330 BCE–AD 400*, Leiden/New York, 489–504.
Serafim, A. (2015), 'Making the Audience: Ekphrasis and Rhetorical Strategy in Demosthenes 18 and 19', in: *Classical Quarterly* 65, 96–108.
Serafim, A. (2017), *Attic Oratory and Performance*, New York/London.
Smyth, H.W. (1959), *Greek Grammar*, Rev. by G.M. Messing, Cambridge.
Tajfel, H./Turner, J. C. (1979), 'An integrative theory of intergroup conflict', in: W.G. Austin/S. Worchel (eds.), *The Social Psychology of Intergroup Relations*, Michigan, 33–37.
Thomas, R. (2011), 'And you, the Demos, made an uproar: performance, mass audiences, and text in the Athenian democracy', in: A.P.M.H. Lardinois/J.H. Blok/M.G.M. van der Poel (eds.), *Sacred Words: Orality, Literacy and Religion*, Leiden/Boston, 161–187.
Trilling, L. (1972), *Sincerity and Authenticity*, Cambridge.
Usher, S. (ed.) (1993), *Greek Orators. V, Demosthenes, On the Crown*, Warminster.
Webb, R. (1997), 'Poetry and Rhetoric', in: S.E. Porter (ed.), *Handbook of Classical Rhetoric in the Hellenistic Period 330 BCE–AD 400*, Leiden/New York, 339–369.
Xanthakis-Karamanos, G. (1979), 'The Influence of Rhetoric on Fourth-century Tragedy', in: *Classical Quarterly* 29, 66–76.
Yunis, H. (ed.) (2001), *Demosthenes', On the Crown*, Cambridge.

Part IV: **Society, Law and Drama**

Penelope Frangakis
The Reception of Rhetoric in Greek Drama of the Fifth Century BCE

The Use of Rhetorical Techniques in the Art of Euripides

Development of Rhetoric in Antiquity: From Epic Poetry to Attic Drama

The development of rhetoric has its origins in antiquity. The plays by Greek dramatists are among the manifestations of various kinds of texts with rhetorical elements that were produced partly as a result of simple or complex intertextual relations to literature. The authors of these texts, knowingly or inadvertently, actively or inertly[1] used texts of classical forms and themes as points of reference, and thus developed many of the techniques of rhetoric originating from traditional forms of oral discourse and poetry.[2]

The relationship of rhetoric to literature is complex and varied.[3] Far earlier than the use of rhetoric in the fifth century BCE, Greek literature had from a very early stage displayed rhetorical techniques that were eventually defined and described.[4]

Devices which were later considered to be 'rhetorical' developed in poetry and can be discovered as early as in Homer's epic poetry.[5] The *Essay on the Life and Poetry of Homer* (*De Vita et Poesi Homeri*) which can be found in Plutarch's *Moral Essays* (*Moralia*) demonstrates the contribution of Homer to literature, including the use of formal rhetorical devices. As is conveyed in this work as far as the form and content of literature is concerned, not only figures of speech, adaptations of regular grammatical usage, types of speech, but also styles of rhetoric were anticipated by Homer.[6] An analysis of Homer's rhetoric is given in chapters 161–198. An emphasis is placed on the rhetorical power of Homer's speeches and

---

[1] Morgan/Harrison 2008, 218.
[2] Mastronarde 2010, 208–209.
[3] Laird 2008, 210.
[4] Kennedy 1994, 24.
[5] Lloyd 1992, 19.
[6] Edwards 1991, 56.

his knowledge of the technique of the rhetor (chapters 161–174).[7] In the poetry of Homer the speeches that are produced are for a particular audience and a particular occasion. Such speeches are an essential tool of the epic genre.[8] Speeches in the Homeric poems display artistic unity and are divided into parts. Odysseus, for example, in the *Iliad* gives a speech (9.225–306) in which he provides a prooemium (228–231), a brief narration (232–248), and proof (249–306).[9]

The power of the logos that was conveyed through the epic poems of Homer became influential for later works. Homer's poetry would inspire rhetoricians with, for example, the debates of the *Iliad*,[10] would be used for verbatim quotations, and would be subjected to assimilations within later texts.[11]

Homer's epic poetry occupies an important position in the history of rhetoric, as it constitutes a fundamental stage of the development of the rhetorical aspect of Greek literature.[12] Homer further develops his predecessors' rhetorical techniques and in turn those techniques are expanded and further developed later as fertile grounds were created for the advancement of rhetoric.

The fifth century constitutes one of the most important stages in the history of the development of rhetoric. During the course of the fifth century, there was an emergence of a rhetorical consciousness.[13] An increasing awareness of the advanced skills of argumentation and presentation, as well as the advancement in these skills, were produced by the practice of argumentative and persuasive speech in the courts of the democratic system, but also in the assembly-meetings of the Athenian demos.[14] The individual rhetores that took a leadership role at such assembly-meetings represented the 'varying degrees of democratic or oligarchic ideology'.[15]

Democracy of the fifth century, in particular, played a significant role in the creation of a fertile ground for the development of rhetoric. As democracy developed in Athens after the Persian Wars and in Syracuse when democracy replaced tyranny, *logos* would be considered particularly important, acknowledged for its

---

7 Keany/Lamberton 1996.
8 Mastronarde 2010, 208–209.
9 Kennedy 1994, 13–14.
10 Kennedy 1989, 86.
11 Morgan/Harrison 2008, 219–220.
12 Conacher 2003, 86.
13 Kennedy 1994, 24.
14 Mastronarde 2010, 208–209.
15 Kennedy 1994, 16.

power to potentially influence a situation in which it could be applied. Techniques of oratory and Greek rhetorical theory would be cultivated within these shifting political contexts.

Among the contributors to the development of the art of rhetoric during the fifth century were the sophists. These classical rhetoricians and teachers of rhetoric recognised that rhetorical elements could be discovered in Greek literature prior to the fifth century. Their sophistic teaching was to explore 'new critical attitudes towards politics and morality, expressed in new rhetorical forms.'[16]

Rhetoric would expand during the fifth century and would have an effect on the emergence of drama. During classical Greek antiquity, in parallel with advances in the skills of argumentation and presentation,[17] the dramatic texts that will be produced were to further cultivate the art of rhetoric.

Contribution of Euripides to the Development of Rhetoric

Among the playwrights who contributed to the development of rhetoric through the genre of drama is Euripides. This unconventional dramatist[18] developed drama by producing plays which not only have aspects of continuity with the past, such as the revival of old structures,[19] existing tragic strategies,[20] established dramatic techniques that 'bring a speech, an episode, or an entire play to a formal resolution';[21] but also of innovation, such as the introduction of new structures, the development in his own technique,[22] as well as the development of rhetoric. Euripides' plays display the use of innovative rhetorical techniques[23] and provide important evidence for the development of rhetoric between 438 and 418.[24] Euripides not only develops rhetoric within his plays but also advances the use and implementation of rhetorical techniques. The rhetorical features in some of the plays of Euripides had reached an advanced development before the visit

---

16 Easterling 1989, 64–65.
17 Mastronarde 2010, 208–209.
18 Storey/Allan 2005, 131.
19 Gregory 2005, 258.
20 Goward 1999, 121.
21 Gregory 2005, 259.
22 Easterling 1989, 66.
23 Meltzer 2006, 114–115.
24 Lloyd 1992, 23.

to Athens in 427 of Gorgias, who was among the sophists who were to teach the art of rhetoric in the second half of the fifth century.[25] Euripides, concerned with the proper use of rhetoric,[26] further developed the art of rhetoric with his skill in language and argumentation.

Euripides' uses of rhetoric, most of which are distinctive,[27] indicate the pervasiveness of rhetoric in his plays. His rhetorical sophistication has been acknowledged ever since the production of these plays. He has been considered the most rhetorical of the tragedians,[28] as 'a rhetorical poet who subordinated consistency of character to verbal effect'.[29] Euripides' expertise in rhetoric was praised by later authors such as Aristophanes who, although he accuses him of making his characters argue and debate, for example in the comic play *Frogs* (89–91, 771–778, 954, 1069, 1083–1088), nevertheless shows recognition in *Peace* and *Frogs* (775) of Euripides' skill in rhetoric.[30]

Euripides would receive influence as far as rhetoric is concerned from important sources of inspiration that applied and developed rhetorical techniques in different genres, and he would develop those rhetorical elements in the genre of drama.

The rhetorical techniques applied in Euripides' plays came about to a great extent as a result of the influence of forms of classical tradition such as epic poetry. As is demonstrated in the *Essay on the Life and Poetry of Homer* in Plutarch's *Moral Essays*, the sayings of Homer influenced dramatists.[31] Among those dramatists is Euripides, who uses narrative patterns which originated in Homer's epic poetry. Similarly to Homer, he further develops the techniques that his predecessors developed[32] and acknowledges the power of *logos*. The recognition of the importance of *logos* is conveyed in his plays. In one passage of *The Suppliants* (201–204) *logos* is perceived to have a civilising function. In *The Trojan Women* it is considered a means of influencing others, as a 'defence against chaos' and as an 'alternative to action'.[33] Euripides, like Homer, not only is aware of the power of logos but also has the skill to use it artfully. As is asserted in Plutarch's *Essay on*

---

25 Mastronarde 2010, 208–209.
26 Meltzer 2006, 111.
27 Mastronarde 2010, 208.
28 Conacher 2003, 82.
29 Easterling 1989, 65–66.
30 Lloyd 1992, 19.
31 Keany/Lamberton 1996.
32 Edwards 1991, 56.
33 Gregory 1991, 159–160.

the Life and Poetry of Homer, Homer was an 'artificer of discourse'.[34] As for Euripides, he also had the skill to shape logos into artful forms.

The power of logos, its uses and effects were to also concern the sophists during the fifth century. The techniques of persuasive speech taught by these rhetoricians influenced dramatic texts such as those of Euripides. Influenced by sophistic teachings, Euripides adapted in his plays the techniques of the new rhetoric developed by sophists such as Protagoras, Gorgias, and Antiphon. Some speeches in Euripides' plays illustrate qualities which derive from the works of teachers of rhetoric. Inspired, for example, by Gorgias, these speeches make various uses of *logos* so as to achieve different purposes, including the enhancement of pity and the production of joy. Furthermore, Gorgias but also Antiphon have been considered responsible for inspiring Euripides' speeches in terms of structure, antithesis, 'adaptation of commonplaces (*topoi*) to varied content', as well as argument from probability.[35]

Among the rhetorical techniques used by the sophists, their methods of arguments prove to be particularly influential in Euripides' plays. A range of procedures of argument used by the sophists in the late fifth century BCE,[36] such as the argument from reciprocity, the argument from expedience or advantage, the argument from custom, and the argument from justice, are found in *Hecuba*. Other types of arguments are used as well, such as the argument from human nature, the argument of superior force, and the argument by analogy,[37] as is evidenced in *Hippolytus*.

The speeches and dialogues of Euripides' plays have been constructed with techniques that in most cases and to various degrees achieve a rhetorical effect.

Euripides' use of different sequences in speeches, in the argumentations of characters, such as that of the general to the particular, or the contrary, of the particular to the general, result in a combination of philosophic generalisations and particular applications. Passages of Euripidean rhetoric that display such a combination can be found, for example, in *Hippolytus* (376, 378, 386, 419–421, 428–430), where Phaedra, one of the main protagonists, makes statements that contain certain ethical generalisations with a particular application to this character's own case.[38]

---

[34] Keany/Lamberton 1996.
[35] Kennedy 1989, 91.
[36] Meltzer 2006, 114.
[37] Gregory 1991, 68–69.
[38] Conacher 2003, 88.

Euripides adopts contemporary formulations and, in comparison to Aeschylus and Sophocles, makes more explicitly self-conscious the speeches of his characters.[39] The characters used by Euripides present their cases in the organised framework of rhetoric;[40] they speak a simple language. However, their style and their reasoning are elaborate, and their sayings and contradictions have elements of rhetorical art. Odysseus, for example, in *Hecuba* adapts his words to the situation and consequently uses not only appropriate, but also effective arguments.[41]

In constructing the dialogues in his plays, Euripides draws much of his inspiration from the examples of speeches, heroic oratory, and different arguments that can be found in Homeric epic poetry. These include the scenes of conflict depicted in the *Iliad*. Further contributing to the influences received by Euripides in his synthesis of dialogues is the advancement during the fifth century of the dialogical form, which would subsequently dominate literary genres, including drama.

In developing the dialogical form in his plays, although he retains certain dialogical traditions such as metre, Euripides nevertheless creates a conversational style for his characters that is similar to normal speech. He does this through the selection of words from everyday speech, as prescribed by Aristotle (*Rhetoric* 1404b5). His dialogues are usually debates that consist of long speeches of more or less equal length, contrasted speeches, and defences against accusations. In his incorporation of debates in dramatic scenes, Euripides demonstrates an increasing skill.[42]

Euripides' use of rhetoric becomes most evident in the *agones* (debates) of his plays. The *agones* that are featured in Euripides' plays contribute immensely to forming these works into being more rhetorically powerful. Arguments and debates of the characters are most prominently depicted in the agonistic form of paired speeches.[43] In fact, the most rhetorical parts of the plays can be found in opposing set speeches of the *agon*.[44] Euripides also develops rhetoric within drama by the way in which he uses the *agon* and the dexterity with which he presents this dramatised debate. Similarly to Sophocles, he makes regular use of the *agon* to structure the episodes of his plays. The *agon* of Euripides, however, is generally more detached from the action. Contrary to Euripides' *agon* speeches,

---

39 Pelling 2005, 85.
40 Easterling 1989, 77.
41 Bollack 2010, 250.
42 Conacher 2003, 87.
43 Mastronarde 2010, 208–209.
44 Conacher 2003, 94.

the *agones* of Sophocles are lacking in proems and have nothing so formalised in their conclusions.⁴⁵

The structure that Euripides gives to the *agon* speeches draws its inspiration not only from epic poetry, for example from the *Iliad*'s structure of speeches which usually consists of prooemium, brief narration, and proof, but also from the structure consisting of prooemion, narration, proof, and epilogos to be found in classical judicial orations,⁴⁶ as well as in the works of sophists.

The structure of Euripides' *agon* speeches usually consists of beginning, internal transitions, and ending.⁴⁷ Most of Euripides' *agon* speeches have proems, distinctively rhetorical features that can also be found in speeches of his predecessors' epic poetry, history, and drama. After a proem, the speech is divided into sections that are often distinguished from each other and may provide information. The speech is concluded with an epilogue.⁴⁸ The *agones* are concluded differently depending on whether there is a third party involved in their speeches. And so the speeches of the *agones* (in plays such as *Heraclidae, Hecuba, The Trojan Women, Phoenician Women*, and *Orestes*) in which there is a third party involved have a different type of conclusion in comparison to *agones* (in earlier plays such as *Alcestis* and *Medea*) that tend to conclude with *gnomai*, which are shared between two characters with no third party involved.⁴⁹

A variety of methods of argument used in Euripides' *agon* speeches indicates his rhetorical skill in the development of techniques of argumentation, and constitutes further evidence of his application of rhetoric in the *agones*. The *reductio ad absurdum* that occurs in the *agones* of Euripides is a type of argument that is used by him in his own distinctive style.⁵⁰

The argument from probability, 'found in the political discourse of the fifth century' and not in Homeric epic poetry and 'based on the assumption of universal characteristics of human nature',⁵¹ was used in drama, including the *agon* speeches of the extant plays of Euripides. For example, we find this in *Hippolytus* (962–970, 983–1035) and *Hecuba* (1195–1207). Drawing inspiration from Protagoras, who wrote a collection of 'topics' on argument⁵² and made the weaker case

---

45 Lloyd 1992, 27–28.
46 Kennedy 1989, 86–87.
47 Gregory 2005, 259.
48 Lloyd 1992, 25.
49 Lloyd 1992, 27–28.
50 Lloyd 1992, 31–32.
51 Kennedy 1994, 24.
52 Kennedy 1994, 17.

the stronger as taught by Aristotle (*Rhetoric* 1402a23–26), Euripides uses the argument from probability so as to 'analyse possible motives' and to portray characters that try 'to make the best of a weak case'.[53]

Another variety of the argument from probability that is used frequently in Euripides' *agones* is the hypothetical syllogism. Euripides' use of formulaic expressions in rhetorical contexts indicates rhetorical influence. Euripides expresses hypothetical syllogism in phraseology very similar to that of the logographer and Attic orator Lysias, who uses the formulaic phraseology 'if ... then ...; but in fact ...'.[54]

Other methods of argument that are used in the *agon* speeches of Euripides include the argument from expediency and the argument from reciprocity. The argument from expediency appears in his earlier plays' *agones*, which focus attention on self-interest, for example, the *Medea* (271–336, 368–369) and *Hecuba* (218–331, 1132–1182).[55] The earlier plays of Euripides such as *Hecuba* and *The Suppliants* also contain agonistic passages that have a rhetorical effect through the argument of reciprocity.[56]

In conclusion, it has become apparent that Euripides, operating under several influences, further developed the techniques of rhetoric with an artistic skill that enabled him to combine old and new rhetorical techniques in his plays. By comparison to others who contributed to the development of rhetoric in their own fields of expertise, such as Homer in epic poetry and the sophists with their teachings and writings, Euripides in turn inserted and in his own way advanced rhetorical elements within drama. It is difficult to determine in particular cases the exact extent of rhetorical influence that he received in the synthesis of his plays. From the evidence hitherto provided, it can be established that Euripidean passages of rhetoric have been to various degrees inspired by a range of sources, including rhetorical devices used by Homer and the sophists. The course of development of Euripides' plays reveals that these works vary in composition, have distinguishing patterns, and prove his ability to develop not only his own technique but also the techniques of others. He develops rhetorical techniques to a greater extent than his predecessors, and in certain cases Euripides is among the dramatists that anticipate rhetorical techniques that his contemporaries and successors would come to define and describe.

---

[53] Lloyd 1992, 29.
[54] Michael 1992, 31–32.
[55] Kennedy 2001, 380.
[56] Conacher 2003, 96–98.

Bibliography

Bollack, J. (2010), 'Notes on Tragic Rhetoric in Euripides' *Hecuba*', in: P. Mitsis/C. Tsagalis (eds.), *Allusion, Authority, and Truth, Critical Perspectives on Greek Poetic and Rhetorical Praxis*, Berlin/New York, 249–262.
Conacher, D.J. (2003), 'Rhetoric and Relevance in Euripidean Drama', in: J. Mossman (ed.), *Euripides*, Oxford, 81–101.
Easterling, P.E. (1989), 'Euripides', in: P.E. Easterling/B.M.W. Knox (eds.), *The Cambridge History of Classical Literature*, I 2, *Greek Drama*, Cambridge, 64–86.
Edwards, M.W. (1991), 'The *Iliad*: A Commentary. Volume V: Books 17–20', in: G.S. Kirk (ed.), *The Iliad. A Commentary*, Cambridge.
Goward, B. (1999), *Telling Tragedy. Narrative Technique in Aeschylus, Sophocles and Euripides*, London.
Gregory, J. (2005), 'Euripidean Tragedy', in: J. Gregory (ed.), *A Companion to Greek Tragedy*, Malden/Oxford/Carlton.
Gregory, J. (1991), *Euripides and the Instruction of the Athenians*, Ann Arbor.
Gunderson, E. (ed.) (2009), *The Cambridge Companion to Ancient Rhetoric*, Cambridge.
Keany, J.J./Lamberton, R. (eds.) (1996), *Plutarch, Essay on the Life and Poetry of Homer*, Atlanta.
Kennedy, G.A. (1994), *A New History of Classical Rhetoric*, Princeton.
Kennedy, G.A. (2001), 'Focusing of Arguments in Greek Deliberative Oratory', in: G. Nagy (ed.), *Greek Literature. V, Greek Literature in the Classical Period: the Prose of Historiography and Oratory*, New York/London, 377–384.
Kennedy, G.A. (1989), 'Oratory', in: P.E. Easterling/B.M.W. Knox (eds.), *The Cambridge History of Classical Literature. I 3, Philosophy, History and Oratory*, Cambridge, 86–114.
Laird, A. (2008), 'Approaching Style and Rhetoric', in: T. Whitmarsh (ed.), *The Cambridge Companion to the Greek and Roman Novel*, Cambridge, 201–217.
Lloyd, M. (1992), *The Agon in Euripides*, Oxford.
Mastronarde, D.J. (2010), *The Art of Euripides: Dramatic Technique and Social Context*, Cambridge.
Meltzer, G. (2006), *Euripides and the Poetics of Nostalgia*, Cambridge.
Morgan, J./Harrison, S. (2008), 'Intertextuality', in: T. Whitmarsh (ed.), *The Cambridge Companion to the Greek and Roman Novel*, Cambridge, 218–236.
Pelling, C. (2005), 'Tragedy, Rhetoric, and Performance Culture', in: J. Gregory (ed.), *A Companion to Greek Tragedy*, Oxford, 83–102.
Storey, I.C./Allan, A. (2005), *A Guide to Ancient Greek Drama*, Oxford.

Brenda Griffith-Williams
Families and Family Relationships in the Speeches of Isaios and in Middle and New Comedy

Introduction

According to the pseudo-Plutarchian *Lives of the Ten Orators*, Isaios, known to us as a logographer who specialized in disputed inheritance cases in the Athenian courts, is mentioned in Theopompos's comedy *Theseus*.[1] The surviving fragments of the play provide no indication of the context, and it may seem rather surprising that Isaios is mentioned at all. We know that Demosthenes and Hypereides were quoted, and satirized, by comic poets such as Alexis, Antiphanes and Anaxandrides,[2] but Demosthenes and Hypereides – unlike Isaios – were public figures active in Athenian politics, not just writers of speeches for litigants in private cases.[3] Moreover, Isaios was at a very early stage of his career as a logographer when Theopompos wrote and produced his *Theseus*, for which he won a prize at the Lenaia in one of the years between 390 and 380 BCE.[4] Nearly all Isaios's surviving speeches are later, but one of them Is. 5, was delivered around 389.[5] This speech comes from the long-running dispute about the estate of Dikaiogenes II, a case involving an elite Athenian family whose ancestors included the tyrant-killer Harmodios, so it is tempting to think that their wealth and prominence brought the young logographer to the attention of the Athenian public, and of the comic poet. And perhaps the substance of the legal cases that Isaios dealt with – family quarrels over the property of someone who has died – also provided material for the comic stage.

In any society where private ownership of property is recognized, ancient or modern, most individuals and families will have some experience of inheritance.

---

1 μνημονεύει δ' αὐτοῦ Θεόπομπος ὁ κωμικὸς ἐν τῷ Θησεῖ. *Vita Isaei, ex Vitis X Oratorum Plutarcho Adscriptis*, in Wyse 1904, 2.
2 Webster 1970, 44–47.
3 Cf. Roisman/Worthington 2015, 174: 'Isaeus was less well known in Athens than Lysias, yet was recognizable enough for mention in a play ... Theopompus wrote comedies in the late fifth to early fourth century; the surviving fragments of his *Theseus* do not permit reconstruction of the context of Isaeus' mention'.
4 Webster 1970, 259.
5 Edwards 2007, 80.

https://doi.org/10.1515/9783110629729-018

In many cases, perhaps the majority, it will cause no problems: property passes from generation to generation, or in accordance with a testator's wishes, and there is no disagreement. But in a minority of cases, competing claims lead to bitter rivalry and jealousy, quarrels, and sometimes a complete breakdown of normal family relations. Only the most intractable of these disputes end up as contested cases in court. In the modern world, inheritance disputes, especially those involving the rich and famous, are the subject matter of gossip columns and news headlines, and they also provide rich material for novelists and dramatists. In classical Athens these disputes, and the families involved, were surely talked about in barbers' shops and private homes, and it seems reasonable to think that they may also have featured in contemporary comedy.

It would be particularly interesting to compare the experience of those Athenian citizens who both listened to Isaios's speeches in the courts and watched the comedies of poets such as Theopompos, Anaxandrides and Eubolos on stage. How did they react to the performances they witnessed in their respective capacities as dikasts and theatregoers? Was their reception of the forensic speeches influenced by what they had seen on the comic stage? And did Isaios, when he constructed his speeches, exploit their experience of comedy to the advantage of his clients? Did he, for example, consciously try to make his audience laugh? Was his presentation of the protagonists in the stories told by his clients modelled on, or at least influenced by, characters from comedy?

All these questions are, ultimately, unanswerable, because we know so little detail about the themes and plots of Middle Comedy: that is, the Athenian comedies that were written and produced in Isaios's lifetime. We do know, nevertheless, that families and family relationships were central to the plots of New Comedy, and there are certainly recognizable similarities between some of the family crises and problems described in Isaios's speeches and those in the plays of Menander, whose first work was produced some twenty years after Isaios's death. We also have some evidence that similar plots featured among the more diverse range of themes dealt with by earlier comic poets. We know, for example, that Alexis and Antiphanes each wrote a play called *Epiklēros*,[6] foreshadowing the central theme of Menander's *Aspis* and other plays of New Comedy. The title of Alexis's lost comedy *Epitropos*[7] suggests a guardian appointed to manage the estate inherited by a child, although the word can have other meanings. Another title of a lost play by Antiphanes, *Homopatrioi* ('brothers by the same father'),

---

6 Alex. *Fragmenta* (Kock: *Comicorum Atticorum fragmenta*, II), 78–80; Antiph. *Fragmenta* (Kock), 94.
7 Alex. Fragmenta (Kock: *Comicorum Atticorum fragmenta*, II), 82.

also suggests a comedy about family relations, possibly involving inheritance;[8] and there are references in fragments of Alexis and Anaxandrides to men who increase their paternal inheritance, or, in some cases, squander it[9] – an offence of which Isaios's speakers frequently accuse their opponents.[10] Moreover, some of the stock characters of New Comedy, including the scheming prostitute or courtesan, had their origins in Middle Comedy.[11]

Although it is impossible to prove that contemporary comedy had a direct influence on Isaios's speeches, it is still worthwhile to look for situations and characters that are common to his speeches and extant later comedy, and to compare their treatment in the different genres of forensic oratory and comedy. In the rest of this chapter I shall explore three crisis situations experienced by Athenian families, with examples from Isaios and Menander: first, the death of a soldier while serving abroad; secondly, conflicts between wives and mistresses (and their offspring); and finally, the exploitation of vulnerable elderly people.

Athenian families in crisis, 1: the death of a soldier abroad

One situation that must have been familiar to many Athenian families was the death of a relative abroad on military service. In many such cases the soldier would have left a legitimate son, who would have been automatically entitled to take over his father's estate. A soldier with no legitimate son would have been likely to leave a will adopting a son, with the intention of making clear his wishes about his succession,[12] but unless he adopted his next of kin there was a risk that the will would be challenged. And if he left neither a natural nor an adopted legitimate son, the scope for conflict and confusion over the disposition of his estate would be even greater.

Conflict and confusion dominate Menander's *Aspis*, where the plot centres on competing claims to an 'heiress' (*epiklēros*). In the opening scene, a slave

---

8 Antiph. *Fragmenta* (Kock), 175.
9 Anaxandr. Fragmenta (Kock), 45; Alex., Fragmenta (Kock: *Comicorum Atticorum fragmenta*, II), 105; Alex. Fragmenta (Kock: *Comicorum Atticorum fragmenta*, II), 246.
10 See, e.g., Is. 5.43, 6.61, 7.35, 10.25.
11 On the *hetaira* in Middle Comedy, see Nesselrath 1990, 318–324.
12 According to Rubinstein 1993, 23, six of the ten known fourth century Athenian testators died in war or while travelling, and another made a will before embarking on a military campaign from which he returned safely.

called Daos arrives in Athens carrying the shield of his master, Kleostratos, who has apparently died in battle, together with a valuable collection of booty. Kleostratos was unmarried, and he left a sister as the only surviving member of their father's *oikos*. She was about to be married to Khaireas, the stepson of her father's brother Khairestratos, but Smikrines, her father's miserly older brother, wants to claim her as an *epiklēros* so that he can get control of her wealth. Since this was a comedy, the audience would have expected a happy ending, and the plot is eventually resolved by the revelation that Kleostratos is not dead after all; it was simply a case of mistaken identity. Moreover, the audience at one of Menander's comedies knew, either right from the beginning or shortly afterwards, that the action they were watching resulted from confusion and misunderstanding on the part of the characters, because the Prologue (normally spoken by an omniscient deity) had told them the true facts. So they heard, in effect, two versions of the story, and their reaction to the second, enacted version was influenced by their knowledge of the first, narrated one.

The dikasts who listened to Isaios's speeches also heard two versions of the story (both narrated rather than enacted), but it was their job to decide which version was true, or at least more likely to be true than the other. Three of these speeches come from disputes about the wills of soldiers who died abroad. One is Is. 6, where Philoktemon left a will adopting a son before he set off for the campaign on which he was killed, but the will was challenged by members of his family. In Is. 9, the speaker says he came home from military service to find that his half-brother, Astyphilos, had died in Mytilene, and his estate had been taken over by a cousin who claimed that Astyphilos had adopted his son in a will. The ensuing battle over the estate involved allegations of forgery and corruption, and even hints of murder.

In Is. 4, another case involving a contested will, the speaker gives a graphic account of the reaction when news of the death of a mercenary soldier, Nikostratos, reached Athens:

Τίς γὰρ οὐκ ἀπεκείρατο ἐπειδὴ τὼ δύο τάλαντω ἑξάκις εἰσηλθέτην; Ἡ τίς οὐ μέλαν ἱμάτιον ἐφόρησεν, ὡς διὰ τὸ πένθος κληρονομήσων τῆς οὐσίας; Ἡ πόσοι συγγενεῖς καὶ ὑεῖς κατὰ δόσιν προσεποιήσαντο τῶν Νικοστράτου; Δημοσθένης μέν γε ἀδελφιδοῦς ἔφη αὐτῷ εἶναι, ἐπειδὴ δ' ἐξηλέγχθη ὑπὸ τούτων, ἀπέστη· Τήλεφος δὲ δοῦναι αὐτῷ Νικόστρατον ἅπαντα τὰ ἑαυτοῦ, καὶ οὗτος οὐ πολλῷ ὕστερον ἐπαύσατο. Ἀμεινιάδης δὲ ὑὸν αὐτῷ πρὸς τὸν ἄρχοντα ἧκεν ἄγων οὐδὲ τρί' ἔτη γεγονότα, καὶ ταῦτ' οὐκ ἐπιδεδημηκότος τοῦ Νικοστράτου ἕνδεκα ἐτῶν Ἀθήνησι. Πύρρος δὲ ὁ Λαμπτρεὺς τῇ μὲν Ἀθηνᾷ ἔφη τὰ χρήματα ὑπὸ Νικοστράτου καθιερῶσθαι, αὐτῷ δ' ὑπ' αὐτοῦ ἐκείνου δεδόσθαι. Κτησίας δ' ὁ Βησαιεὺς καὶ Κραναὸς τὸ μὲν πρῶτον δίκην ἔφασαν τοῦ Νικοστράτου ταλάντου καταδεδικάσθαι, ἐπειδὴ δ' οὐκ εἶχον τοῦτο ἀποδεῖξαι, ἀπελεύθερον αὐτὸν ἑαυτῶν προσεποιήσαντο εἶναι· καὶ οὐδ' οὕτως ἃ ἔλεγον ἀπέδειξαν. Καὶ οἱ μὲν εὐθὺς κατὰ τὰ πρῶτα ἐπὶ τὰ Νικοστράτου ᾄξαντες οὗτοί εἰσί

Who did not cut his hair when the two talents came into dispute six times? Who did not wear black, as if he would inherit the estate through mourning? How many relatives and sons pretended that Nikostratos had bequeathed them his property? Demosthenes claimed to be his nephew, but gave up when Hagnon and Hagnotheos exposed him as a fraud. Telephos said Nikostratos had bequeathed him all his property, but he, too, withdrew his claim shortly afterwards. Ameiniades came before the Archon with a boy not yet three years old who was supposedly Nikostratos's son, even though Nikostratos had not been in Athens for eleven years. Pyrrhos of Lamptra declared that the money had been dedicated to Athena by Nikostratos, who had given it to him himself. Ktesias of Besa and Kranaus first of all said that Nikostratos owed them a judgment debt of one talent, but when they were unable to prove this, they pretended that he was their freedman, but again they couldn't prove it. These were the men who at the start immediately swooped down on Nikostratos's property.

(Is. 4.7–10)[13]

Some scholars have seen this passage as an indication that the Athenian legal system was inadequate to cope with complex inheritance claims,[14] but it is possible to take it less seriously, and Edith Hall identifies it as an example of logographic humour: 'an amusing characterization of the excessive displays of bereavement evinced by litigants in a dispute over a will'.[15] But humour, as Hall points out, is 'culturally and historically relative', and it is difficult to assess the tone of a text when we have no idea how it was delivered by the original speaker. I agree, nevertheless, that the passage reads like a parody: an anecdote based on real life, but subtly exaggerated, and certainly not a serious critique of the Athenian legal system in general.[16] Making the audience laugh was not, of course, the primary aim of a logographer, but providing some occasional light relief from the sombre and sometimes even sordid details of an inheritance dispute would have been one way of engaging their attention and sympathy.

---

13 All translations from the speeches of Isaios are based on Edwards 2007, with minor adaptations. On the text of Is. 4.7, see Edwards 2002.
14 See, e.g., Cohen 1995, 169: 'Cases like that of the estate of Nicostratus, where no adult direct descendants were ready to defend their right to their patrimony, seem to have represented an open invitation to those ready to construct fictive genealogies or exaggerate the closeness of existing kin relations'.
15 Hall 2006, 389.
16 Cf. Griffith-Williams 2013, 10–12.

Athenian families in crisis, 2: wives, mistresses, and bastards

Male Athenian citizens (unlike their female kin) enjoyed considerable sexual freedom before, during and after marriage. Provided he did not seduce a fellow citizen's wife or daughter (which would have risked prosecution) or bring his *pallakē* or *hetaira* into the marital home (which would have flouted convention), an Athenian man could indulge in whatever relationships he chose without breaking the law or incurring strong social disapproval. Yet the law was strict in defining rights of inheritance and citizenship. Only legitimate children (that is, those born to a legally married wife) could inherit their father's estate; and, under Perikles's law of 451/50 BCE, only someone of Athenian parentage on both sides was an Athenian citizen. Some non-marital relationships inevitably led to the birth of illegitimate children (*nothoi*), and that in turn could result in disputes over inheritance between children of the same father by different mothers (sometimes known by modern scholars as 'amphimetric disputes').[17]

It is not surprising to find that questions of legitimate birth, the inferior status of bastards (*nothoi*), and the potential for conflict between wives and mistresses are preoccupations of both Isaios's clients and the characters of Athenian comedy.[18] Kiron's grandson, the speaker of Is. 8, reminds the dikasts that if they decide he is illegitimate, then he not only loses the right to inherit from Kiron but may also be at risk of losing his citizenship (Is. 8.43). The resolution of the plot of Menander's *Epitrepontes* – typically of 'recognition' plots in comedy – depends on the revelation that the baby rejected by Kharisios, who thinks it is his wife Pamphile's bastard, is in fact his own child, because it was he who raped Pamphile at a festival before they were married. This, then, is another example of the obligatory happy ending in comedy.[19]

Any attempt to pass off a *nothos* as legitimate would have been illegal, and (according to traditional Athenian values) morally repugnant. According to the

---

[17] Cf. Ogden 1996, 189: 'The structure that above all sowed discord in Greek families was the amphimetric one, i.e. that in which a man kept two women (ideally, but not necessarily, in tandem) and fathered lines of children from both. Inevitably, both women competed to be regarded as the 'legitimate' wife, and their respective lines of children competed for succession'.

[18] The word *nothos* occurs in a fragment of a play by Euboulos apparently as a general term of abuse rather than denoting a legal status: νόθος, ἀμφίδουλος, οὐδαμόθεν οὐδείς, κύων ('bastard, child of slaves, nobody from nowhere, dog'). Eub. *Fragmenta* (Demianczuk), 2.

[19] Cf. Hall 2006, 84: 'In the utopian world of New Comic endings, the potentially catastrophic disruption caused by unauthorized pregnancy is always contained or defused'.

speaker of Is. 6, that is what Euktemon did when he introduced a boy whose parents were former slaves to his phratry, in the face of objections from his legitimate son Philoktemon:

> Ἐπειδὴ δὲ οὔθ' ὁ υὸς αὐτῷ Φιλοκτήμων συνεχώρει οὔθ' οἱ φράτερες εἰσεδέξαντο, ἀλλ' ἀπηνέχθη τὸ κούρειον, ὀργιζόμενος ὁ Εὐκτήμων τῷ υἱεῖ καὶ ἐπηρεάζειν βουλόμενος ἐγγυᾶται γυναῖκα Δημοκράτους τοῦ Ἀφιδναίου ἀδελφήν, ὡς ἐκ ταύτης παῖδας ἀποφανῶν καὶ εἰσποιήσων εἰς τὸν οἶκον, εἰ μὴ συγχωροίη τοῦτον ἐᾶν εἰσαχθῆναι. Εἰδότες δ' οἱ ἀναγκαῖοι ὅτι ἐξ ἐκείνου μὲν οὐκ ἂν ἔτι γένοιντο παῖδες ταύτην τὴν ἡλικίαν ἔχοντος, φανήσοιντο δ' ἄλλῳ τινὶ τρόπῳ, καὶ ἐκ τούτων ἔσοιντο ἔτι μείζους διαφοραί, ἔπειθον, ὦ ἄνδρες, τὸν Φιλοκτήμονα ἐᾶσαι εἰσαγαγεῖν τοῦτον τὸν παῖδα ἐφ' οἷς ἐζήτει ὁ Εὐκτήμων, χωρίον ἓν δόντα. Καὶ ὁ Φιλοκτήμων, αἰσχυνόμενος μὲν ἐπὶ τῇ τοῦ πατρὸς ἀνοίᾳ, ἀπορῶν δ' ὅ τι χρήσαιτο τῷ παρόντι κακῷ, οὐκ ἀντέλεγεν οὐδέν.

> But when his son Philoktemon would not agree to this and the members of his phratry would not admit the boy, and the sacrificial victim was removed from the altar, Euktemon was angry with his son and wanted to insult him. So he became engaged to a sister of Demokrates of Aphidna, with the intention of recognizing her children and bringing them into his family, unless Philoktemon agreed to allow this boy to be introduced. His relatives, knowing that he would not have any more children at his time of life, but that they would appear in some other way and as a result there would be still greater disputes, persuaded Philoktemon, gentlemen, to allow the introduction of this boy on the terms Euktemon sought, giving him a single plot of land. And Philoktemon, ashamed at his father's folly but at a loss how to cope with the problem he faced, made no objection.
>
> (Is. 6.22–24)

The roles of father and son are reversed in the following dialogue from Menander's *Samia*, where it is Moschion who persuades his adoptive father, Demeas, not to reject his concubine, Chrysis, with the child she has borne in his absence:

> γαμετὴν ἑταίραν, ὡς ἔοικ', ἐλάνθανον
> ἔχων.
> {(Μο)}γαμετήν; πῶς; ἀγνοῶ <γὰρ> τὸν λόγον.
> {(Δη)} λάθ]ριό[ς τι]ς ὑ<ός>, ὡς ἔοικε, γέγονέ μοι.
> [...] ἐς κόρακας ἄπεισιν ἐκ τῆς οἰκίας
> ἤ]δη λαβ[ο]ῦσα.
> {(Μο)}μηδαμῶς.
> {(Δη)}πῶς μηδαμῶς;
> ἀλλ' ἦ με θρέψειν ἔνδον υὸν προσδοκᾶις
> νόθον; [.....]ν γ' οὐ τοῦ τρόπου τοὐμοῦ λέγεις.
> {(Μο)} τίς δ' ἐστὶν ἡμῶν γνήσιος, πρὸς τῶν θεῶν,
> ἢ τίς νόθος, γενόμενος ἄνθρωπος;
> {(Δη)}σὺ μὲν
> παίζεις.
> {(Μο)}μὰ τὸν Διόνυσον, <ἀλλ'> ἐσπούδακα
> οὐθὲν γένος γένους γὰρ οἶμαι διαφέρειν

> ἀλλ' εἰ δικαίως ἐξετάσαι τις, γνήσιος
> ὁ χρηστός ἐστιν, ὁ δὲ πονηρὸς καὶ νόθος
> καὶ δοῦλος[

> Dem. I thought I had a mistress, but I seem to have acquired a wife.
> Mosch. A wife? What do you mean? I don't understand.
> Dem. I seem to have become – quite without my knowledge and consent – the father of a son. Well, she can take him and get out of the house – to the Devil, for all I care.
> Mosch. Oh, no!
> Dem. Why not? Do you really expect me to bring up a bastard in my house, to humour someone else? That's not my line at all.
> Mosch. For heaven's sake! Who's legitimate, or who's illegitimate? We're all human, aren't we?
> Dem. You must be joking.
> Mosch. By God I'm not, I'm perfectly serious. I don't think birth means anything. If you look at the thing properly, a good man's legitimate, a bad man's both a bastard and a slave.[20]

Demeas's initial attitude – of course, he would not want to bring up an illegitimate child in his own house – is what one would expect from a conventional Athenian father; and when Moschion starts to argue that legitimacy is unimportant, Demeas responds disbelievingly, but Moschion insists that he is serious. In real life many, if not most Athenians would probably have been shocked by Moschion's unconventional views, but in the theatre they were free to laugh, because Moschion had already told them in the Prologue that Demeas's anger was based on a misunderstanding: the mother of the baby that Chrysis is nursing is not Chrysis herself, as Demeas thinks, but Plangon, and the father is Moschion, who intends to marry Plangon and so make the child legitimate.

The reason for Demeas's anger is that Chrysis, as he thinks, is trying to behave like a wife, not a *hetaira*; the words γαμετὴν ἑταίραν, at the beginning of the passage, are an oxymoron, because γαμετή properly belongs with γυνὴ – a 'married woman', or 'wedded wife'. The social role of a *hetaira* is explicitly contrasted with that of a wife by the speaker of Is. 3, *On the estate of Pyrrhos*, who claims that Pyrrhos was not legally married to Phile's mother. This passage graphically illustrates the lifestyle of a *hetaira*, which may well have been similarly portrayed by the poets of Middle Comedy.

> Ὡς μὲν ἑταίρα ἦν τῷ βουλομένῳ καὶ οὐ γυνὴ τοῦ ἡμετέρου θείου, ἣν οὗτος ἐγγυῆσαι ἐκείνῳ μεμαρτύρηκεν, ὑπὸ τῶν ἄλλων οἰκείων καὶ ὑπὸ τῶν γειτόνων τῶν ἐκείνου μεμαρτύρηται πρὸς ὑμᾶς· οἳ μάχας καὶ κώμους καὶ ἀσέλγειαν πολλήν, ὁπότε ἡ τούτου ἀδελφὴ εἴη παρ' αὐτῷ, μεμαρτυρήκασιν γίγνεσθαι περὶ αὐτῆς. Καίτοι οὐ δή πού γε ἐπὶ γαμετὰς γυναῖκας

---

20 Men. *Sam.*, 130–142 (transl. Miller 1987, with minor adaptations).

οὐδεὶς ἂν κωμάζειν τολμήσειεν·οὐδὲ αἱ γαμεταὶ γυναῖκες ἔρχονται μετὰ τῶν ἀνδρῶν ἐπὶ τὰ δεῖπνα, οὐδὲ συνδειπνεῖν ἀξιοῦσι μετὰ τῶν ἀλλοτρίων, καὶ ταῦτα μετὰ τῶν ἐπιτυχόντων.

You've heard the testimony of Pyrrhos's other friends and neighbours that the woman whom the defendant has testified he betrothed to [Pyrrhos] was a hetaira available to anybody who wanted her and was not his wife. They have testified that the defendant's sister was the subject of fights, revelry, and frequent disorder whenever she was at Pyrrhos's house. But I don't suppose that anybody would dare to sing songs about a married woman, and married women do not go with their husbands to dinner parties or see fit to dine with strangers, especially chance visitors.

(Is. 3.13–14)

Athenian families in crisis, 3: elder abuse

Throughout the centuries, inheritance disputes have often involved what an American socio-legal historian has called 'pathetic and demeaning stories about old people':[21] stories in which a rich but vulnerable old person, whose mental capacity is in decline, is (allegedly) exploited by greedy and unscrupulous 'friends' or relatives who want to get their hands on his (or her) property.

We can find two such stories in the speeches of Isaios, each of which deploys a cast of characters that could easily have featured in a comedy.[22] The first is *On the estate of Kiron* (Is. 8), where the speaker, Kiron's grandson, is responding to a speech already made by his opponent, Kiron's nephew. The nephew has claimed that Isaios's client is illegitimate, because his mother was not Kiron's legitimate daughter. Even if there are no direct parallels in extant comedy, some elements of the story told in this speech read remarkably like a comic plot. The narrative episodes could be transposed into dramatic scenes, and it is easy to imagine the characters portrayed by actors on stage. At the centre of the plot is Kiron, a rich but confused and gullible old man deceived by his scheming wife and her villainous brother, Diokles. The speaker himself plays a relatively minor role, as does his opponent, the timid and ineffectual nephew who is portrayed as a mere puppet under the control of Diokles.

Among the most memorable 'scenes' in the speech are those that occur after Kiron's death. First, the speaker goes to Kiron's house to remove the body for burial from his own home, but is prevented from doing so by Kiron's grief-stricken widow:

---

21 Friedman 2009, 89.
22 Another speech, Is. 7, is probably the response to such a story.

ἧκον γὰρ ἐγὼ κομιούμενος αὐτὸν ὡς θάψων ἐκ τῆς οἰκίας τῆς ἐμαυτοῦ, τῶν ἐμαυτοῦ οἰκείων τινὰ ἔχων, ἀνεψιὸν τοῦ πατρός· καὶ Διοκλέα μὲν οὐ κατέλαβον ἔνδον, εἰσελθὼν δὲ εἴσω κομίζειν οἷος ἦν, ἔχων τοὺς οἴσοντας. δεομένης δὲ τῆς τοῦ πάππου γυναικὸς ἐκ τῆς οἰκίας αὐτὸν ἐκείνης θάπτειν, καὶ λεγούσης ὅτι βούλοιτ' ἂν αὐτὴ τὸ σῶμα τὸ ἐκείνου συμμεταχειρίζεσθαι μεθ' ἡμῶν καὶ κοσμῆσαι, καὶ ταῦτα ἱκετευούσης καὶ κλαιούσης, ἐπείσθην, ὦ ἄνδρες ...

I came with one of my relatives, my father's cousin, to remove the body for burial from my own house. I did not find Diokles at the house, so I entered, accompanied by bearers, and was ready to remove it. But when my grandfather's widow asked me to bury him from that house, and with supplications and tears said that she said that she herself would like to help us lay out and adorn his body, I consented, gentlemen.

(Is. 8. 21–22)

That encounter marked the beginning of a power struggle between the speaker and Diokles over the conduct of Kiron's funeral, culminating at the funeral itself where the speaker publicly accused Diokles of taking Kiron's property and inducing his nephew to claim the estate. The speech does not tell the story in chronological order, and the narrative subsequently moves back in time to reveal the beginning of Diokles's machinations while Kiron was still alive. After Kiron's two sons died, as the speaker explains, Diokles was afraid that he would secure the succession by adopting one of his grandsons – as, indeed, most Athenians in his situation would probably have done. It was evidently part of the nephew's case that Kiron could not adopt one of his daughter's sons because they were illegitimate, so Isaios tells an elaborate story to explain the real reason why he did not do so. After listing Kiron's extensive property, the speaker explains, in a narrative with distinctly comic overtones (Is. 8.35–36.), that after Kiron's sons had died his wife, at the instigation of her brother Diokles, repeatedly pretended to be pregnant and to have suffered a miscarriage, so that Kiron would not adopt one of his grandsons because he still hoped to father another son of his own.[23]

Another 'pathetic and demeaning story' about an old person is to be found in Is. 6, where Isaios explains (and seeks to excuse) Euktemon's allegedly illegal introduction of a 'son' into his phratry by portraying him as the confused and gullible victim of a conspiracy to defraud him of his wealth by a greedy kinsman in collusion with the boy's mother. Euktemon, according to the speaker, lived to the age of ninety-six, outliving all his three legitimate sons; but the speaker's opponent claims that he left two younger sons by a second wife. Isaios's client puts forward an alternative story in which Euktemon, who had previously led a happy

---

[23] On the importance in Athenian drama of plots relating to pregnancy (including fake pregnancies) and childbirth, see Hall 2006, 60–97.

and prosperous life, in old age became infatuated with Alke, a former slave and prostitute who managed an apartment block for him in Kerameikos, and who had two sons reputedly by a freedman called Dion. Eventually Euktemon went to live with her permanently, abandoning his wife and family, until he was 'reduced to such a state either by drugs or disease or something else that she persuaded him to introduce the older of the two boys to the members of his phratry under his own name' (Is. 6.21).

I have written more extensively elsewhere about the theatrical and performative aspects of Is. 6,[24] but it is worth pointing out in the present context that the character of Alke may well have affinities with the scheming prostitute of Middle Comedy; and the speaker's pointed remark to the dikasts, 'I think many of you know her' (Is. 6.19) is perhaps a reminder that notorious *hetairai* were often portrayed by name in comedy.[25]

Conclusion

It is worth repeating that the speeches and comedies discussed in this chapter portray Athenian families in crisis. The stories they tell are not about normal every-day life in fourth century Athens, although they provide some occasional glimpses of it; in fact, they rely on situations that were probably quite unusual. As we have seen, family crises can provide the raw material for both a comic poet and a logographer, but they use the material in different ways and for different purposes. For the comic poet, whose aim is to amuse and entertain his audience, situations and characters that they will recognize from real life are only the starting point. Compared with the absurdist fantasies of Aristophanic Old Comedy, Menander's plays may seem firmly grounded in reality; New Comedy has been recognized as the forerunner of the modern comedy of manners, and also has affinities with the sitcoms and soap operas familiar to television audiences. Like all comic dramatists, however, Menander exaggerates and distorts reality: incidents such as the mistaken identity of the dead soldier in *Aspis*, or the confusion over the parentage of the baby in *Samia*, certainly could have happened in the Greek world of the late fourth century, but they probably did not happen all that often.

---

24 Griffith-Williams 2017.
25 Cf. Nesselrath 1997, 278: 'In Middle Comedy the hetairai mentioned and sometimes described in no little detail are very often figures from real contemporary life about whom theatregoers could hear often when they gossiped in the streets and whose services they might even be able to enjoy (if they had enough money to pay for them)'.

Indeed, their very improbability (but not impossibility) could have contributed to the comedic effect.

The primary aim of a logographer, unlike that of a comic poet, is not to entertain his audience (although it may be to his advantage if he can do so incidentally) but to win cases for his clients. It was obviously crucial to their success that the dikasts believed their stories, rather than those of their opponents, and it was up to Isaios to make those stories as plausible as possible, starting from the true (or supposedly true) information provided by the clients. He may sometimes have chosen to distort or embellish this 'truth', or even to suppress some of it, but unlike the comic poet he could not simply give free rein to his imagination because he had to make the story fit the requirements of the relevant law, and because blatant lies would be open to challenge from those who knew the true facts. Some of the dikasts who listened to stories like those about Kiron and Euktemon may have known about similar situations from their own families or neighbourhoods, but most of them, probably, did not. Some of the people and situations they heard about in court may, nevertheless, have been familiar to them from the comic stage, and, as I have argued elsewhere:

> Just as people nowadays talk about characters from soap operas and sitcoms, Athenian theatregoers would have discussed these characters with their friends and neighbours as if they were real. So their willingness to accept a story they heard in court may have been influenced by what they had seen on stage as much as by their experience of real life, and it's possible that Isaios deliberately shaped his story to meet the theatregoers' expectations.[26]

It is, of course, equally possible that some of the later comic poets, including Menander, drew the inspiration for the family relationships they describe in their plays from real life forensic speeches, but that would be a subject for a separate study.

Bibliography

Cohen, D. (1995), *Law, Violence and Community in Classical Athens*, Cambridge.
Edwards, M. (2002), 'A Note on Isaeus 4.7', in: *Mnemosyne* 55, 87–88.
Edwards, M. (ed.) (2007), *Isaeus*, Translated with Introduction and Notes, Austin.
Friedman, L. (2009), *Dead Hands: a Social History of Wills, Trusts, and Inheritance Law*, Stanford.

---

[26] Griffith-Williams 2017.

Griffith-Williams, B. (2013), *A Commentary on Selected Speeches of Isaios*, Leiden.
Griffith-Williams, B. (2017), 'Would I lie to you? Narrative and Performance in Isaios 6', in: A. Serafim/S. Papaioannou (eds.), *A Theatre of Justice*, Leiden.
Hall, E. (2006), *The Theatrical Cast of Athens*, Oxford.
Miller, N. (transl.) (1987), *Menander: Plays and Fragments*, London.
Nesselrath, H.-G. (1990), *Die Attische Mittlere Komödie: ihre Stellung in der Antiken Literaturkritik und Literaturgeschichte*, Berlin.
Nesselrath, H.-G. (1997), 'The Polis of Athens in Middle Comedy', in: G.W. Dobrov (ed.), *The City as Comedy: Society and Representation in Athenian Drama*, Chapel Hill, 271–288.
Ogden, D. (1996), *Greek Bastardy*, Oxford.
Roisman, J./Worthington, I. (eds.) (2015), *Lives of the Attic Orators: Texts from Pseudo-Plutarch, Photius, and the Suda*. Oxford.
Rubinstein, L. (1993), *Adoption in IV. Century Athens*, Copenhagen.
Webster, T.B.L. (1970), *Studies in Later Greek Comedy*, 2nd ed., Manchester.
Wyse, W. (ed.) (1904), *The Speeches of Isaeus, with Critical and Explanatory Notes*, Cambridge.

Edward M. Harris
Aeschylus' *Eumenides*
The Role of the Areopagus, the Rule of Law and Political Discourse in Attic Tragedy

The Areopagus is the most paradoxical of all Athenian political institutions. When addressing the courts of Athens, litigants describe the Areopagus as the most respected and most trusted institution in democratic Athens. In 331 BCE Lycurgus (*Leocr.* 12) called it the finest example (κάλλιστον ... παράδειγμα) of justice in all of Greece. The reputation of the Areopagus so outstrips that of other courts in Athens that even those defendants who are condemned by it agree that its verdicts are just. In his *Against Aristocrates*, Demosthenes (23.65) considers the Areopagus the most distinctive and most hallowed court of Athens. He claims that 'All men think that in such cases what they consider just is less robust than the standard of justice maintained by this court. In this tribunal alone no defendant who has been convicted or accuser who has lost has ever proved that his case wrongly decided.' Aeschines (1.92) calls it *akribestaton*, which is a hard word to translate for it combines the ideas of most precise, most accurate, and most strict. In a speech attributed to Lysias (6.14), the Areopagus is the most august (σεμνοτάτῳ) and most just court (δικαιοτάτῳ) in Athens. Demosthenes (20.157) and Lysias (26.11–12) say that the Areopagus is the court that deals with the most important cases, those involving murder (cf. Dinarchus 1.6; Aeschin. 3.20). When Socrates in Xenophon's *Memorabilia* (3.5.20) asks Pericles "Do you know any other body that tries cases and conducts its other business better or more in accordance with law, honor, and justice than the Areopagus?" the prominent democratic politician replies that this institution is beyond reproach. The reputation of the Areopagus continued for many centuries; writing in the first century BCE, Diodorus (1.75.3) listed it alongside the Council at Sparta as the best court in all of Greece.[1]

The tragedians of democratic Athens also treat the Areopagus with the utmost respect. In Euripides' *Orestes* (1650–1652) Apollo tells the matricide how the gods who preside at the Areopagus and will judge his case and deliver a most righteous vote. In Euripides' *Electra* (1258–1263) the Dioscouroi state that the vote of the Areopagus is most pious and firm (cf. *Iphigeneia among the Taurians* 943–

---

[1] The recent works of Wallace 1989 and de Bruyn 1995 do not analyze the reputation of the Areopagus and the reasons for its fame.

975). In Sophocles' *Oedipus at Colonus* (947–949) Creon calls the Council *euboulon*, a body that deliberates well or makes good decisions. And Aeschylus devoted an entire play, the *Eumenides*, the final play in the *Oresteia*, the only surviving trilogy in Greek tragedy, to the foundation of the Areopagus. At the trial of Orestes, Athena praises the court as a stronghold guarding the land.

>   ἔνθεν ἔστ' ἐπώνυμος
>   πέτρα πάγος τ' Ἄρειος. ἐν δὲ τῷ σέβας   690
>   ἀστῶν φόβος τε ξυγγενὴς τὸ μὴ ἀδικεῖν
>   σχήσει τό τ' ἦμαρ καὶ κατ' εὐφρόνην ὁμῶς,
>   αὐτῶν πολιτῶν μὴ 'πικαινούντων νόμους.
>   κακαῖς ἐπιρροαῖσι βορβόρῳ θ' ὕδωρ
>   λαμπρὸν μιαίνων οὔποθ' εὑρήσεις ποτόν.   695
>   τὸ μὴ ἄναρχον μήτε δεσποτούμενον
>   ἀστοῖς περιστέλλουσι βουλεύω σέβειν
>   τὸ μὴ τὸ δεινὸν πᾶν πόλεως ἔξω βαλεῖν.
>   τίς γὰρ δεδοικὼς μηδὲν ἔνδικος βροτῶν;
>   τοιόνδε τοι ταρβοῦντες ἐνδίκως σέβας   700
>   ἔρυμά τε χώρας καὶ πόλεως σωτήριον
>   ἔχοιτ' ἄν, οἷον οὔτις ἀνθρώπων ἔχει,
>   οὔτ' ἐν Σκύθησιν οὔτε Πέλοπος ἐν τόποις.
>   κερδῶν ἄθικτον τοῦτο βουλευτήριον,
>   αἰδοῖον, ὀξύθυμον, εὑδόντων ὕπερ   705
>   ἐγρηγορὸς φρούρημα γῆς καθίσταμαι.

> So this rock is named
> from then the Hill of Ares. Here the reverence
> of citizens, their fear and kindred do-no-wrong
> shall hold by day and in the blessing of the night alike
> all the while the people do not muddy their own laws
> with foul infusions. But if bright water you stain
> with mud, you nevermore will find it fit to drink.
> No anarchy, no rule of a single master. Thus
> I advise my citizens to govern and to grace,
> and not to cast fear utterly from your city. What
> man who fears nothing is ever righteous? Such
> be your terrors, and you may deserve and have
> salvation for your citadel, your land's defence,
> such as if nowhere else found among men, neither
> among the Scythians, nor the land that Pelops held.
> I establish this tribunal. It shall be untouched
> by money-making, grave but quick to wrath, watchful
> to protect those who sleep, a sentry on the land.
>
> (transl. R. Lattimore).

No other political institution in Athens received such an honor in Athenian tragedy.

Although the orators and the tragedians repeatedly praise the Areopagus, the historians Herodotus, Thucydides, and Xenophon in his *History of Greece* never mention it at all.[2] One can read the main sources for the history of Greece from 500 to 362 BCE and find not one reference to the Areopagus. The situation is much the same with the inscriptions: out of all the inscriptions preserved in whole or in part from the fifth century not one mentions the Areopagus, and I have found only two from the fourth century inscriptions dated to the fourth century BCE mention the Areopagus (*IG* ii^3 292 [352/1], line 19; 320 [337/6], lines 11–14, 17–19, 24–25). And Aristophanes, whose plays often ridicule the activities of the Council, the Assembly, and the other Courts and lampoon many officials and politicians, passes over the Areopagus in silence.

Perhaps the greatest paradox of the Areopagus in Aeschylus' final play in his *Oresteia* trilogy, the *Eumenides*. In the beginning of the play the audience see the Erinyes or Furies pursuing Orestes for the murder of his mother Clytemnestra (Aesch. *Eum.* 34–116). On the advice of Apollo (Aesch. *Eum.* 64–93),[3] Orestes flees from Delphi to Athens and appeals to its patron goddess Athena (Aesch. *Eum.* 235–243, 276–298). Athena comes in response to Orestes' pleas (Aesch. *Eum.* 397–414), then listens to the charges made by the Erinyes and to Orestes' defence of his actions (Aesch. *Eum.* 415–469). To try the case Athena establishes the court of the Areopagus (*Eum.* 470–489, 689–706). Athena praises the institution as incor-

---

2 Pleket 1969, 30 n. 39 observes that the Council that Herodotus (5.72.1–2) reports Cleomenes attempted to abolish only to be met with resistance could have been the Council of the Areopagus. But this could also be the old Council of 400 or the new Council of 500. Hornblower 2013, 213 thinks that 'it would be surprising' if the new system of ten tribes for selecting the members of the Council of 500 was already in operation by the time of Cleomenes' arrival (although he does not rule out the possibility), but Herodotus (5.66) clearly implies that it was. Hornblower also notes that the Areopagus would have been filled with members appointed during the tyranny, but admits that they could have changed sides after the overthrow of Hippias. On the other hand, Herodotus (9.1) does mention the Council of 500 later in his narrative but does not mention the Areopagus in any other passage, which makes it unlikely that he alludes to the Areopagus earlier in his narrative. When Herodotus (8.52.1) does mention the Areopagus, it is the place and not the court.
3 The transposition of lines 85–87 to before line 64 proposed by Sommerstein 1989, 93–94, following Burges, is unnecessary and unconvincing. Orestes has already received protection in Apollo's temple so there is no need for him to ask for assurances before Apollo speaks. Orestes asks for the firm promise after Apollo instructs him to leave the god's shrine at Apollo and travel to Athens. His request reveals his anxiety about the upcoming journey.

ruptible and the outstanding court in the Greek world. Yet according to the *Constitution of the Athenians* (25.1–4) (written in the 320s BCE), in 462, just a few years before the production of the *Oresteia* just a few years in 458,[4] Ephialtes launched a series of attacks on the Areopagus, which in 462 culminated in a reform stripping the Council of its additional powers (*ta epitheta*), through which it had exercised its protection of the constitution (τῆς πολιτείας φυλακή). The reform, or revolution of Ephialtes, as some scholars call it, put an end to a period of seventeen years when the Areopagus held a leading role in Athens. Or so we are told by the *Constitution of the Athenians* attributed to Aristotle. This is not the place to enter into the as yet unresolved controversy over the authorship of this work, but if it was not written by Aristotle himself, it was composed by someone very closely associated with his school and deeply influenced by his views because we find a similar though not identical account of the reforms of Ephialtes in Aristotle's *Politics* (2.9.3–4.1274a8–16).[5]

What is even more strange is that Aeschylus, who appears to praise the Areopagus without qualification, was earlier associated with Pericles, who had acted as his *choregos* (producer) in 472 for his successful trilogy which included the *Persians*.[6] According to the *Constitution of the Athenians* (27.1) and Plutarch (*Pericles* 9.2–4), Pericles was a close ally of Ephialtes during this period and helped him to reduce the powers of the Areopagus. In fact, Aeschylus appears to endorse Pericles' foreign policy in the *Eumenides*. Before 462 Athens had been allied with Sparta ever since the outbreak of the Persian Wars. This policy appears to have been championed by the general Cimon.[7] In 462 Pericles succeeded in reversing the policy of his rival Cimon, who was ostracized around this time, and concluded an alliance with Argos, Sparta's traditional enemy in the Peloponnese.[8] Aeschylus provides a mythological justification for this alliance in the *Eumenides* (754–777; cf. 289–291, 669–673) when he has Orestes declare after his acquittal that his

---

4 For the date of the play, see *TrGF* III: T 65.
5 On the authorship of the *Constitution of the Athenians*, see Rhodes 1981, 61–63 with references to earlier views.
6 *TGrF* III: T 55 (= *IG* ii² 2318, lines 10–11).
7 Plut. *Cim.* 16.1–4.
8 For Cimon's ostracism, see Pl. *Grg.* 516d with Brenne 2001, 193–195 and Scheidel 2002, 350–357. For the alliance between Athens and Argos, see Thuc. 1.102.4. Sommerstein 1989, 31 asserts that 'There can be no doubt that Aeschylus was personally a strong supporter of the Argive alliance and of the adventurous foreign policy pursued since 462/1'. This confident attempt to guess at Aeschylus' personal views is nothing but speculation. The alliance was official Athenian policy in 458, and Aeschylus was simply following official policy. We do not know if it was out of conviction or not.

native city of Argos will henceforth always be a faithful ally of Athens.⁹ Thus Aeschylus seems to be linked to Ephialtes through Pericles and in opposition to Cimon, yet he praises the Areopagus, the very institution these two men had supposedly attacked. And what are we to do with the passage in Xenophon's *Memorabilia* (3.5.20) ignored by modern scholars, in which Pericles says he has nothing to criticize about the Areopagus?

The question of Aeschylus' political stance in the *Eumenides* has been the subject of heated debate ever since the publication of Aristotle's *Constitution of the Athenians* exactly a hundred years ago in 1893 and shows no signs of abating.¹⁰ The issue appears insoluble. What I would like to suggest is not so much a new answer as a new approach. When a question in classical scholarship begets so much fruitless debate, the means of resolving the debate is often not to offer a new answer, but to re-examine the nature of the question, the evidence on which the old answers are based, and the methods by which scholars have approached it. This issue has wide ramifications because it raises questions about the relationship of tragedy to political discourse and oratory in Classical Athens. Goldhill has asserted that tragedy questions (or problematizes) democratic ideology; Rhodes has rightly questioned this approach and observed that the political views of Attic tragedy are those of the Greek *polis* in general, not just democratic Athens.¹¹ But what was this ideology and what were its main tenets? Rhodes leaves us in the dark.

What I will show in the next part of my paper is that the supposed facts on which many modern views are built are not facts at all. Many modern scholars, both historians and literary critics alike, have accepted much of the information found in chapters 23 to 27 of the *Athenaion Politeia* as reliable despite some obvious problems.¹² According to this work, the Areopagus gained ascendancy

---

9 For discussion of the alliance and its relationship to this passage, see Dover 1957.
10 For discussion of the relationship between the alleged reforms of Ephialtes and the *Eumenides*, see Podlecki 1966, 74–100; Dover 1957; Sommerstein 1989, 29–32 and 2010, 281–288. As this essay shows, all of these studies aim to solve a non-existent problem.
11 Goldhill 1987; Rhodes 2003. The arguments of Wilson 2009, 23–27 are undermined by his reliance on the document inserted into the text of Andocides 1.96–98, which has now been shown to be a forgery. See Canevaro/Harris 2012 and Harris 2013/2104, which refutes in detail the flawed attempt of Sommerstein 2014 to defend document's authenticity.
12 Though differing in their interpretations of the evidence, the following scholars accept the main features of the account in [Arist.] *Ath. Pol.* 23–28 and believe that Ephialtes brought about major changes affecting the Areopagus: Wallace 1974; O'Sullivan 2001; Rihll 1995; Poddighe 2014, 248–258. For scepticism about the importance of the so-called reforms of Ephialtes, see Day and Chambers 1962, 127 (the risk of 'exaggerating the reforms of Ephialtes into the destruction of a *politeia*') and especially Mann 2007, 71 and Zaccarini 2018.

through no actual decision but by its leadership during the period before the battle of Salamis when the generals were at a loss (*Ath. Pol.* 23.1). The constitution then remained under the leadership of the Areopagus for seventeen years after the Persian Wars (*Ath. Pol.* 25.1). Then Ephialtes stripped away the powers of Areopagus and gave them to the Council of Five Hundred, the Assembly and to the courts (*Ath. Pol.* 25.2). If there are good reasons to question the view that the Areopagus enjoyed a period of ascendancy from 480 to 462, then there is no reason to believe that the reforms of Ephialtes brought an end to this ascendancy and must have concerned other matters. If the account of the *Athenaion Politeia* is mistaken in connecting the reforms of Ephialtes with the Areopagus, the link between these reforms and the *Eumenides* is broken, and a new approach to the politics of the play is required, one that can provide a more satisfying account of the relationship between the poet Aeschylus and the Attic orators in their comments about the Areopagus, a topic all but completely ignored by literary critics.

First, we must examine what the *Athenaion Politeia* states about the origin of the ascendancy of the Areopagus (*Ath. Pol.* 23.1). This work states that before the battle of Salamis, the generals were in despair and gave the order *sauve qui peut*. In this crisis the Areopagus distributed eight drachmas to each person and got them to man the ships. This statement is contradicted by all the sources for the events leading up to the battle of Salamis. Herodotus (7.140) informs us that as the Persians approached, the Athenians consulted Apollo at Delphi and received two oracles, the second advising them to seek the protection of the wooden walls (Hdt. 7.140–142). In a debate in the Assembly Themistocles persuaded the Athenians that this meant they should man their ships and set up a base at Salamis (Hdt. 7.143.1–2). In his account of the evacuation of Attica, Herodotus (8.40.2–41.2) does not so much as mention the Areopagus and contradicts the account of the *Athenaion Politeia* by placing the evacuation under the control of authorities other than the Areopagus. There is no mention of any distribution of funds. One may not wish to place too much weight on the decree of Themistocles found at Troezen and erected around 300 BCE, but if we admit (as most scholars nowadays do) that it is a forgery, it might have been based on earlier accounts of the Persian Wars.[13] The decree contains orders to man the fleet and does not mention the Areopagus. After the evacuation, the decisions about the campaign were made by a council of Greek allies (Hdt. 8.57), and it was Themistocles again who was respon-

---

13 For the original publication, see Jameson 1960 and for early doubts about its authenticity, see Habicht 1961. Scholars have recently tended to reject the document's authenticity. See Johansson 2001; Johansson 2003, 2004a and 2004b; Knoepfler 2010.

sible for the ruse that for forced the Greek fleet to fight in the straits between Salamis and Attica (Hdt. 8.74.1–83.2). One might object that Herodotus wrote at least a generation after the events. But Aeschylus in his *Persians* (355–371), performed in 472, just eight years later, by and large confirms Herodotus' account on this point and does not mention the Areopagus at all. If the Areopagus played a central role before the battle of Salamis, why does Aeschylus, who has Athena praise the Areopagus in the *Eumenides*, not mention it in the *Persians*? It is also suspicious that the *Athenaion Politeia* states that the Areopagus controlled such a large fund that it could give eight drachmas to each citizen, that is, about 160,000 drachmas or over twenty-six talents, to about twenty thousand citizens at the time, when none of the sources for the fifth century and for the fourth century ever state that the Areopagus managed large public funds.

Despite the assertion of the *Athenaion Politeia* that the Areopagus was the leading force in Athens after the Persian Wars, Thucydides (Thuc. 1.89–108) gives it no role in the key events after the battle of Plataea. Thucydides is likewise silent about the Areopagus in his account of the early years of the Athenian empire. Again it is again Themistocles who masterminds the building of the walls around Athens (Thuc. 1.89.3–93), and the Athenians collectively establish the main institutions of the Delian League to pay tribute (Thuc. 1.96). The leading military figure in this period is Cimon who gained prestige through his victories at Eion (Thuc. 1.98), Skyros (Thuc. 1.98), and Eurymedon (1.100.1).

One might claim that the Areopagus exerted its control in this period through its judicial powers, in particular, its powers over the legal procedure of *euthynai*.[14] According to this view, the Areopagos tried important cases and could influence events by favouring the prosecution of politicians opposed to its policies. This attempt to defend the *Athenaion Politeia* fails for want of evidence and is contradicted by the sources. All the trials attested in the period between 495 and 462 are tried either in the Assembly or in the regular courts. Herodotus (6.21.2) reports that the Athenians punished Phrynichus, how produced a play about the capture of Miletus, for reminding them of their own misfortunes with a fine of 1,000 drachmas and ordered that no one should ever produce the play again. It is not clear whether the Athenians imposed this fine at a trial in court or in the Assembly, but there is no reason to see the Areopagus playing a role. Herodotus (6.104) also reports Miltiades was 'greeted' by his enemies upon his return to Athens with

---

14 See Sealey 1964; Rhodes 1981, 316–318; Jones 1987, 59; Carawan 1987. Sommerstein 1989, 14 follows these scholars but notes that 'No source explicitly states that the Areopagos was ever responsible for εὔθυναι.' Sommerstein does not examine the evidence for trials in the period before 362 BCE and therefore does not see how the sources contradict this assumption.

an accusation of holding a tyranny in the Chersonese and brought to court (δικαστήριον), but acquitted (ἀποφυγών). This trial must be dated shortly before his election as general before Marathon in 490 BCE. Here Herodotus is more specific and states that the trial took place in a court.[15] Herodotus (6.136) reports another trial of Miltiades in 489 BCE after his return from Paros. Xanthippus, the son of Ariphron, charged him with 'deceiving the Athenians' (τῆς Ἀθηναίων ἀπάτης εἵνεκεν).[16] The people took his side to the extent that they did not condemn him to death, but imposed a fine of fifty talents for his offence. In this case, the trial took place in the Assembly and in this respect resembled the trial of the generals in 406 BCE. Here it is quite clear that the Areopagus was not responsible.[17]

There are three other trials from the period before 462 BCE, but the evidence for these trials comes from late sources and may not be reliable. According to Crateros (*FGrHist* 342 F 11 = Plutarch *Aristides* 26), there was an indictment (*eisangelia*) brought against Themistocles after his ostracism, but Plutarch (*Themistocles* 23.1) says that the accuser brought a public charge for treason (γραψάμενος προδοσίας). It is hard to reconcile this information with the account of Themistocles' exile in Thucydides (1.135–138, especially 1.135.3), which does not mention a trial.[18] But such a trial might explain why Thucydides (1.138.6) says that Themistocles could not be buried in Attica because he had been exiled for treason, which could not refer to his ostracism. Yet this punishment could have been imposed by a vote of the Assembly, not by a court. Finally, Diodorus (11.54–55) states that Themistocles was accused of treason before his ostracism and acquitted. When he was at Argos after his ostracism, the Spartans wanted to have Themistocles tried before a court of the Greeks, but he fled to the court of Admetus

---

15 Cf. Hansen 1975, 69: 'There is no indication that Miltiades was brought before the Council of the Areopagos'. Cf. *ibid*. 19; 52. Hansen believes that this may have been 'the first known example of the application of' *eisangelia*, but nothing in the account of Herodotus indicates any similarity to this procedure. The use of the term may have been anachronistic.
16 Cf. Plutarch *Cimon* 4; Cornelius Nepos *Milt*. 7.5–6 (*proditionis*).
17 Hansen 1975, 69 asserts that 'The trial must be classified as an *eisangelia* since the case is heard by the Assembly'. There is no reason to believe this assertion, which relies on the assumption that all trials held in the Assembly were cases of *eisangelia*.
18 For discussion of the evidence, see Frost 1980, 186–194, who dates the trial in absentia in 471. For a refutation of Forrest 1960, who argued that Themistocles was received by the *douloi* who took control of Argos after Sepeia (Hdt. 6.77–81, 83) but driven out when the aristocrats regained power, see Wörrle 1964, 120–123.

(cf. Thuc. 1.136–137). All the sources for the trial contradict each other, which undermines the credibility of each. Whatever happened, however, none of the accounts for the alleged trial of Themistocles mentions the Areopagus.

The *Constitution of the Athenians* (27.1) mentions Pericles' accusation of Cimon when he was general at his *euthynai* but does not give a precise date or context. According to Plutarch (*Pericles* 10.5. Cf. *Cimon* 14.4), Pericles was elected by the people as one of the prosecutors for the trial of Cimon on a charge of treason, but, possibly under the influence of Elpinice, gave only one speech and did the defendant little harm. These two sources appear to contradict each other, but neither grants a role to the Areopagus.[19] At the trial of Leocrates in 331 BCE, Lycurgus (*Leocr.* 117–118) mentions a trial of Hipparchus for treason in the Assembly. The *Constitution of the Athenians* (22.3–4) reports that Hipparchus was ostracized in 488/7, and it is possible that Lycurgus has transformed the ostracism into a trial. What is important is that Lycurgus thought that the trial was held in the Assembly and not at the Areopagus.[20] Thus, we have evidence for several trials before 462, and not a single one of these sources names the Areopagus as the court before which these trials took place. Finally, one should observe that the *Constitution of the Athenians* (25.1) states that Ephialtes attacked the Council and 'destroyed' (ἀνεῖλεν) many of the members of the Areopagus by bringing them to trial (ἀγῶνας) about the funds that they had administered (περὶ τῶν διῳκημένων). This points to trials at their *euthynai*, which must have been conducted by the regular courts because Ephialtes would not have prosecuted members of the Areopagus before the Areopagus with such success. As we will see, this section of the *Constitution of the Athenians* is very unreliable, but it assumes that it in this period, cases for *euthynai* were not heard by the Areopagus. The attempt to explain the alleged prominence of the Areopagus during the period 480–462 BCE finds no support in the ancient sources, which state that trials in this period took place either in the Assembly or in a court. As M. Ostwald (1986, 345) has observed, 'the Areopagos receives no mention in any of the six cases and that all point to trial by some kind of popular court'.

---

[19] Hansen 1975, 71 claims that this trial must have been an *eisangelia* in the Assembly, but this is contradicted by the *Constitution of the Athenians*, which calls the trial part of Cimon's *euthynai*. There is also no example of the Assembly electing a group of prosecutors for an *eisangelia*. Note also that Plutarch (*Cimon* 14.4) says that the trial took place before 'judges' (πρὸς τοὺς δικαστάς). Hansen implausibly attempts to evade this objection by claiming 'we cannot be sure that Plutarch uses the word δικαστής in its technical sense'. What else would the word mean? What is the non-technical sense of the word?

[20] Hansen 1975, 69–70 claims that this trial must have been an *eisangelia* because it was heard in the Assembly, but nothing compels us to accept this conclusion.

But there are other problems that completely undermine the credibility of chapters 23–27 of the Aristotelian *Constitution of the Athenians*. In chapter 24.1 we read that Aristides in the period after the Persian Wars convinced the Athenians to leave the countryside and come to live in the city where there would be food for everyone. This is flatly contradicted by what Thucydides (2.14.1), a contemporary witness, tells us about the Athenians on the eve of the Peloponnesian War, namely, that most still lived in the countryside. The evidence of Thucydides finds confirmation in recent field surveys, which show that the Attic countryside was densely inhabited throughout the fifth century BCE.[21] In the account of the reforms of Ephialtes, dated by this work to 462, there is another amusing howler ([Arist.] *Ath. Pol* 25.2–4): we learn that Ephialtes collaborated with Themistocles in attacking the Areopagus. The author of this work appears to have overlooked the fact that Themistocles was ostracized around 470, did not return to Athens and died in Asia.[22] If this part of the account of Ephialtes' reforms is untenable, how reliable is the rest of the information in this chapter? One cannot cherry-pick statements from this account of Athenian politics from 480 to 450: if much of the information is found to be false or incorrect, that should cast doubt on the remaining information found in the account. And later on in its account of Athenian history, the *Constitution of the Athenians* (35.2) states that the Thirty removed the laws of Ephialtes and Archestratus about the Areopagites. But if the laws of Ephialtes and Archestratus removed the powers of the Areopagus, the abolition of these laws should have led to a resurgence of their power. But instead of finding the Areopagus playing a major role in the accounts of the Thirty found in the Aristotelian *Athenaion Politeia* (34.3–38.4), Xenophon (*Hell*. 2.3.1–2.4.3), Lysias (12 and 13 *passim*), and Diodorus (14.3.7–14.6.1), the Areopagus is conspicuous by its absence. In fact, Lysias (12.69) states that the Areopagus fought against Theramenes, who was among those responsible for setting up the regime of the Thirty.

The next chapter contains another amusing blunder: here the *Constitution of the Athenians* (26.1) states that in the years after the measures of Ephialtes in 462 BCEE, the more reputable people (*epieikesterous*) lacked a leader because their main representative Cimon was rather young and had only recently entered politics.[23] This is utterly false: Cimon appears to have been active in politics before

---

21 For the evidence of field surveys, see Lohmann 1993 and Fachard/Knodell/Banou 2015.
22 For the sources, see Thuc. 1.135.2–3; Pl. *Grg*. 516d; Dem. 23.204–2–5; Plu. *Them*. 21.5 and D.S. 11.55.103 with Brenne in Siewert 2002, 247–257.
23 Rhodes 1981, 326 lists several attempts to emend the word at *Ath. Pol*. 26.1, but these emendations rest on the assumption that the author of this work could not have made a serious mistake. But, as we have seen, the author makes several serious errors in this section. Because he

480 because his name turns up on ostraka for the previous decade, and Davies has placed his birth around 510 BCE, which would make him around fifty years old in 460 BCE.[24] Cimon also led expeditions as early as 478, sixteen years before Ephialtes' alleged reforms; he forced Pausanias to yield control of Byzantium in 478/77 (Pl. *Cim.* 6.5–6; Thuc. 1.95.1–96.1), captured Eion from the Persians in 477/76 (Plu. *Cim.* 7.1–2; Thuc. 1.98.1. Cf. Hdt. 7.107), captured Scyros shortly afterwards (Pl. *Cim.* 8.3–4; Thuc. 1.98.2), and around 468 defeated the Persian fleet at Eurymedon (Thuc. 1.101.1; Plu. *Cim.* 12.4–6). Cimon was clearly the most prominent general in this period, but despite the abundant evidence for his military activity from 478 to 465 BCE the *Constitution of the Athenians* (23.3) states that during the period after the Persian Wars there were two main leaders in Athens, Aristides and Themistocles, with one devoted to military affairs, the other to political matters. But there is no evidence for Themistocles' military activity after he extorted money from the islanders (Hdt. 8.111–112), and the *Constitution of the Athenians* passes over the well-attested military activity of Cimon in silence. On the other hand, if Cimon was not able to lead the upper class against the demagogues, it was because he was ostracized around 462, something the author of the *Athenaion Politeia* appears to have overlooked, though other sources are well aware of the ostracism, which is confirmed by ostraka.[25] The *Constitution of the Athenians* (26.1) also states that the army was commanded by men selected for their family connections and not military experience, battle casualties were extremely high, decimating the ranks of the respectable people both among the rich and among the people. Rhodes, who normally leaps to the defence of this work, admits 'we have no reason to suppose that the men elected were either more or less experienced in the earlier period than in the later'.[26]

As for the claim that the older families lost control of public affairs, once again the evidence points the other way. Several members of several major old families being active in politics in the period from 462 to 430. Pericles came from the Alcmeonid family, which traced its roots back to the sixth century BCE. His father Xanthippus had been active during the Persian Wars.[27] Pyrilampes was

---

makes a serious error about the Cimon's start in politics, he could also have made one about his age.
24 For the date of Cimon's birth, see Davies 1971, 302, followed by Rhodes 1981, 325–326.
25 For the evidence for Cimon's ostracism, see Pl. *Grg.* 516d with Brenne 2001, 193–195 and Scheidel 2002, 373–387.
26 Rhodes 1981, 328.
27 See Davies 1971, 455–460 for the family of Pericles.

also descended from a family that was powerful in the sixth century BCE.²⁸ Thucydides the son of Melesias was a member of the Philaid family and was a powerful influence in Athenian politics until his ostracism.²⁹ Callias, who negotiated the famous peace that bears his name in 449, was a member of the *Kerykes*, a famous *genos*.³⁰ Andocides, who served as general in the campaign against Megara in 446 (*IG* i³ 1353; Thuc. 1.114; D. S. 12.5.2) and again at Samos in 441 (Androtion *FGrHist* 324 F38) and at Corcyra in 433 (Thuc. 1.51), traced his lineage back to the sixth century BCE.³¹ Even though Cimon was ostracized around 462 and dies fighting on Cyprus around 450, his son Lacedaemonius was a general in 433/2 BCE (*IG* i³ 364, lines 8–9; Thuc. 1.45). That makes six upper class families providing leadership and holding positions of responsibility in this period and decisively refutes the statement of the *Athenaion Politeia*.³²

But the blunders continue: the *Constitution of the Athenians* (27.1) states that one reads that Pericles stripped the powers of the Areopagus and turned the Athenians toward naval power. But as anyone who has read Herodotus (7.144.1–2) knows, it was Themistocles who convinced the Athenians to build a large fleet in 483, something that the *Constitution of the Athenians* (23.7) mentions a few chapters before.³³ In this same chapter the *Constitution of the Athenians* (27.3) recounts that Pericles introduced pay for judges in the courts because he was less wealthy than Cimon and could not compete with his generosity, but Davies has rightly shown that there is no reason to believe that Pericles' wealth was any less than that of Cimon.³⁴

In this section the author of the *Athenaion Politeia* (23–27) was clearly influenced by Aristotelian ideas about radical democracy, which led to several distortions of Athenian history during the period 480 to 460 BCE. In the *Politics* (*Pol.* 4.4.3–4.1292a3–13) Aristotle describes what he considers to be the main features of radical democracy:

---

28 See Davies 1971, 322–335 for the family of Pyrilampes.
29 See Davies 1971, 230–237 for the family of Thucydides the son of Melesias. For his ostracism, see Scheidel 2002, 373–387.
30 For the family of Callias, see Davies 1971, 254–270.
31 For the family of Andocides, see Davies 1971, 27–32.
32 Cf. Mann 2007, 98–123.
33 Rhodes 1981, 336 expresses perplexity: 'It is not clear what Pericles' own contribution was supposed to be'. Rhodes collects passages in which Pericles is said to have stressed the importance of naval power, but is unwilling to admit that the author of the *Constitution of the Athenians* has made yet another error.
34 See Davies 1971, 459–460 on Pericles' wealth.

> Another kind of democracy is where all the other regulations are the same, but the multitude is sovereign and not the law; and this comes about when the decrees of the assembly over-ride the law. This state of affairs is brought about by demagogues; for in the state under democratic government guided by law a demagogue does not arise, but the best classes of citizens are in the most prominent position; but where the laws are not sovereign, then demagogues arise; for the common people become a single composite monarch, since the many are sovereign not as individuals but collectively.

The parallels between the analysis of the *Politics* and the narrative of the *Constitution of the Athenians* are striking.[35] First, the *Constitution of the Athenians* claims that after Ephialtes the constitution became more 'slack' (ἀνίεσθαι μᾶλλον) because of eager demagogues. Second, the more respectable people were not in control, and the Areopagus had lost its powers. Third, as a result, the leaders managed affairs with less attention to the laws (τοῖς νόμοις προσέχοντες) than they had previously (οὐχ ὁμοίως καὶ πρότερον). In his summary of the various constitutional changes during the fifth century, the *Constitution of the Athenians* (41.2) also describes the period after Ephialtes as one during which many mistakes were made because of the demagogues (διὰ τοὺς δημαγωγούς).

There is a similar account of Athenian politics in the period 480 to 45 BCE to the one found in the *Constitution of the Athenians* found in another part of Aristotle's *Politics* (2.9.3–4.1274a6–16), which shares much in common with this analysis of extreme democracy. Aristotle traces the growth of Athenian democracy to Solon's measure to allow all citizens to serve in the courts.

> For as the law-court grew strong, men courted favour with the people as a tyrant, and so brought the constitution to the present democracy; and Ephialtes and Pericles docked the power of the Council on the Areopagus, while Pericles instituted pay for serving in the law-courts, and in this manner finally the successive leaders of the people led them on by growing stages to the present democracy. But this does not seem to have come about in accordance with the intention of Solon, but rather as a result of accident (for the common people having been the cause of naval victory at the time of the Persian invasion became proud and adopted bad men as popular leaders when the respectable classes opposed their policy).

Later in the *Politics* (5.3.5.1304a5–24) states that the reputation of the Areopagus rose during the Persian Wars, but the naval victory at Salamis ultimately made the democracy stronger.[36] There are some minor differences between the account

---

[35] Rhodes 1981, 329 cites several passages from Aristotle but does not note how they have shaped the narrative in the *Constitution of the Athenians*.
[36] For ideas about the relationship between naval power and the growth of democracy as an ideological construct without historical foundation, see Ceccarelli 1993.

in *Constitution of the Athenians* and in Aristotle's *Politics*, but there are also broad similarities. The *Politics* does not state that the power of the Areopagus was the result of its distribution of funds before the battle of Salamis and does not mention Aristides and Themistocles as leaders in the period after the victory at Salamis. The *Politics* also attributes the change in politics to the decisive role played by the people in the fleet during the Persian Wars, a view that is not found in the *Constitution of the Athenians*. But there is the same contrast between a period when the Areopagus had more power and a period after the measures of Ephialtes and Pericles, which removed the powers of the Areopagus and gave rise to a period when demagogues held power.[37] To form a contrast with the dissolute period of the demagogues that followed the so-called reforms of Ephialtes, the *Constitution of the Athenians*, like Aristotle in the *Politics*, had therefore to invent a period of good government under the leadership of the Areopagus. The account of Athenian politics in these chapters of the *Constitution of the Athenians* was therefore not based on careful research (as the numerous errors reveal) but on certain philosophical views about democracy, the rule of law, and successful government. The author freely invented facts and re-arranged historical events to fit a pre-conceived pattern. And just as Aristotle and the Aristotelian *Constitution of the Athenians* invented a period of ascendancy for the Areopagus, they also fabricated a reduction of the Council's powers by Ephialtes.

The view that there was a change in Athenian politics sometime in the middle of the fifth century BCE goes back to the last decades of this century. After the Athenian defeat at Syracuse, there began an intense debate about the *patrios politeia*, the ancestral constitution. In 411 there was a decision to search out the laws of Cleisthenes passed by Clitophon in the belief that they were more aristocratic than the present constitution (*Ath. Pol.* 29.3). This belief was probably mistaken, but it is valuable insofar as it reveals that already in 411 some thought that there had been a democratic reform sometime between 508 and 411 that was responsible for the setback the Athenians suffered in the Peloponnesian War. After the final defeat in 404 the search for scapegoats intensified. A handful of politicians including Anytus and Meletus identified Socrates as one of the main causes (cf. Aeschin. 1.173 for Socrates teaching Critias, the leader of the Thirty). The philosophers struck back replied in kind and blamed the politicians. The most devastating attack was made by Plato (*Gorgias* 515e): 'For I am told Pericles made the Athenians idle and cowardly and talkative and covetous, because he was the first to establish pay for service among them'. In the same dialogue Plato (*Grg.* 519a)

---

37 It is interesting to note that the *Constitution of the Athenians* (26.1: ἐπιεικεστέρους; ἐπιεικεῖς) and the *Politics* (2.9.4.1274a16; ἐπιεικῶν) use similar terms for the upper classes.

blames Themistocles, Cimon, and Pericles for Athens' misfortunes. This would place the origin of Athenian decline earlier than the point at which the *Constitution of the Athenians* places it, but still locates the start of the problems in the period after Cleisthenes. There is another version of the idea in the *Laws*, but in this work Plato (*Lg.* 698a–699b) describes a Golden Age before and during the Persian Wars when the Athenians cultivated 'reverence' (*aidos*) and the rule of law. This gave way to a period of decadence and license when the old style of music was abandoned and new styles introduced, which had a corrosive effect on the Athenian character (Pl. *Lg.* 700a–701b). Isocrates in his *Areopagiticus* (7.20) also speaks of a Golden Age, which he says was the product of the laws of Solon and Cleisthenes, which shaped Athenian character. During this Golden Age, Isocrates (7.37–42) the Areopagus supervised the youth and enforced moral discipline. This was followed by a period of indulgence and laxity, which the Areopagus had restrained (Isocr. 7.54–55), but Isocrates does not specify the date when the Areopagus lost its powers. The author of the *Athenaion Politeia* and Aristotle in the *Politics* appear to have combined these various ideas (a turn to the worse after the Persian Wars, the introduction of pay for judges by Pericles as the source of indiscipline, and the rule of the Areopagus as a Golden Age, the introduction of more democracy as a result of naval warfare) and added some details to produce a tendentious account of Athenian politics between the Persian Wars and the outbreak of the Peloponnesian War in 431, a period in which there were relatively few sources to obstruct or restrain their ideological assumptions.[38]

A closer examination of the reliable sources for the period from 480 down to the start of the Peloponnesian War in 431 reveals that there was no major change in the way politics was conducted in Athens.[39] As we have seen, there was broad continuity in one respect: members of the leading families in Athens continued to play a leading role in the Assembly and in the military from the Persian Wars until the outbreak of the Peloponnesian War.[40] There were a few *novi homines* in

---

38 Cf. Rhodes 1981, 287, who tries unsuccessfully to explain how the Areopagus could have exerted power, then admits: 'most probably the tradition of a period of Areopagite supremacy arose later to explain why Ephialtes had had to attack the Areopagus to bring in fuller democracy'. But if the period of Areopagite supremacy was a later invention, then Ephialtes' attacks on the Areopagus should also be a later invention. Rhodes sees the right solution to the problems, but then contradicts himself.
39 This section draws on Harris 2013a, 308–313 and Mann 2007, 45–190, esp. 71: 'Hinsichtlich der Kommunikation zwischen den Demagogen und dem Volk gibt es keine Indizien, daß die Situation vor 462/61 eine signifikant andere gewesen wäre als danach'. Mann decisively refutes the assumptions of Rhodes 1981, 287.
40 See Harris 2013a, 308–313 and Mann 2007, 124–142.

the years after Ephialtes, but Aristides and Themistocles, who played a major role in politics before Ephialtes, did not come from powerful families.[41] Both before and after Ephialtes, prominent leaders gained influence by serving as generals and won popular support by their generosity in performing liturgies or other public benefactions.[42] Before and after Ephialtes ambitious politicians advanced their careers by marriages with wealthy and influential families.[43] And both before and after Ephialtes leading politicians tend to have avoided prosecuting their opponents in court and used ostracism to eliminate their enemies.[44]

That the author of this work allowed his own political preconceptions to colour his interpretation of historical events is not cause for amazement. In several other passages he allows his preconceptions to shape his view of events. For instance, Herodotus (1.59.3) says that when Croesus was king of Lydia, there were three factions in Attica: the men of the plain headed by Lycurgus, the son of Aristolaides, the men of the coast headed by Megacles, the son of Alcmeon, and the men from the hills or 'beyond the hills' (*hyperakrioi*) headed by Peisistratus. According to Herodotus, the three groups were regional and did not promote different political agendas. According to the *Constitution of the Athenians* (13.4), however, Megacles championed a moderate constitution, Lycurgus promoted oligarchy, and Peisistratus was the most 'populist' (*demotikotatos*) of the three. As many scholars have noted, this account applies anachronistic labels to the three groups.[45] The ideal of the mixed constitution does not appear until the late fifth century (Thuc. 8.97.2) and was popular in the works of Plato and Aristotle. The distinction between democracy and oligarchy also did not arise until the late fifth century BCE and is not found in the Archaic period.[46] In a similar fashion, the *Constitution of*

---

[41] For the family of Themistocles, see Davies 1971, 211–220. For the family of Aristides, see Davies 1971, 48–53.
[42] For the importance of military activity, see Harris 2013, 309–311, a factor not discussed by Mann 2007. For public benefactions, see Harris 2013a, 311–312 and more extensively Mann 2007, 142–164. Mann 2007, 165–183 also stresses the importance of *paideia*.
[43] Harris 2013a, 312 and Mann 2007, 98–123.
[44] For the use of ostracism and the avoidance of the courts, see Harris 2013a, 312–313.
[45] Rhodes 1981, 185–186: 'the ideological interpretation as formulated by *A.P.* and Plutarch must arouse suspicion. The μέση (*A.P.*) or μεμειγμέν(η) (Pl. *Sol.* 13iii) was a philosopher's ideal and particularly an Aristotelian ideal (e.g. Arist. *Pol.* IV.1295b34–1296a21; cf. also Is. XII. *Panath.* 133, Plato *Lg.* IV 712d2–e5), wholly out of place in the early sixth century; and the labels 'oligarchic' and 'democratic' thought less obviously inapplicable, are likewise the product of later thought about how cities ought to be governed'. See also Sealey 1960 = Sealey 1967, 9–38; Hopper 1961.
[46] For the origins of the terms democracy and oligarchy in the late fifth century at Athens, see Harris 2016.

the Athenians interprets Solon's claim that he pulled up the *horoi* to mean that Solon carried out a cancellation of debts, a view that rests on an anachronistic interpretation of the term *horos* as a security-marker.[47]

The question naturally arises, what did Ephialtes reform? The most likely answer is that Ephialtes expanded and reorganized the regular courts to cope with the increasing amount of litigation generated by imperial administration. The *Constitution of the Athenians* (35.2) in fact states that abolishing the laws of Ephialtes destroyed the power of the regular courts (τὸ κῦρος ὃ ἐν τοῖς δικασταῖς κατέλυσαν), which is confirmed by the accounts of the regime of the Thirty, during which the regular courts did not operate. One should also note that shortly after the reforms Pericles introduced pay for those serving on the courts ([Arist] *Ath. Pol* 27.3; Plut. *Pericles* 9.2).[48] This would indicate that the volume of legal business and the number of trials had grown so large that it was no longer possible to rely on those who were willing to volunteer and serve without pay. In fact, Aristophanes (*Wasps* 661–663) believed that there was so much judicial business in 422 BCE that cases kept six thousand judges busy for three hundred days a year. The Old Oligarch, writing in the early 420s, described the enormous amount of judicial business the courts were required to transact ([X.] *Ath. Pol.* 3.2). Much of this litigation arose from matters concerning the allies ([X.] *Ath. Pol.* 1.14, 16–18 [Cf. Thuc. 1.77.1]; 3.5) and the fleet ([X.] *Ath. Pol.* 3.4). Inscriptions confirm this picture by providing much evidence for judicial business arising from the administration of relations with the allies. For instance, the regulations about Chalcis, which were probably dated to around 446, also imposed on other allies, provide for cases where the penalty is death, exile or confiscation to be heard again in Athens (*IG* i³ 40, lines 71–76). The decree regulating the reassessment of the tribute in 426 provides for the prosecution of all those who failed to implement the decrees provisions and probably repeats procedures from earlier assessments (*IG* i² 63, lines 13–16). A similar provision for prosecution in Athenian courts is found in the regulations for the payment of tribute, which is probably to be dated around 448/7 (*IG* i³ 34, lines 31–41) and another dated to 426/5 (*IG* i³ 68, lines 43–47). The decree about weights, measures and coinage standards contains also contains such a provision for prosecution against those who attempt to rescind or alter the terms of the decree (*IG* i³ 1453C, lines 18–22). An honorary decree dated

---

47 See Harris 1997. Though scholars still differ about the nature of the *seisachtheia*, there is now a general consensus that the term *horos* in Solon's poem cannot mean security-marker.
48 The sources do not date the introduction of pay for service in the courts, but appear to place it after the measures of Ephialtes.

to 450/49 contains privileges granted to Acheloion, one of which is to have his case brought before the Polemarch (*IG* i³ 19, lines 1–5).

But the main point for our understanding of the 'politics' of the *Eumenides* is that there is no reason to believe that the Areopagus enjoyed a period of leadership between 480 and 462 so there is no reason to think that the reforms of Ephialtes put an end to this period of leadership.

This brings us back to Aeschylus' *Eumenides*. We have broken the link between the play and Ephialtes' reform because there is no reason to think that the reforms had anything to do with the Areopagus, and Aeschylus' *Eumenides* consequently had nothing to do with Ephialtes' reforms. Yet the search for the political meaning of the *Eumenides* should not be adjourned. One still can ask the question why Aeschylus chose to write a play about the Areopagus and why he chose to do so in 458/57.

To understand why Aeschylus wrote a play about the Areopagus we need to know more about the Areopagos and its role in Athenian life. As a preliminary we need to review briefly the Athenian view of the different parts of government. For us government can be divided into three branches: the Executive, the Legislative, and the Judicial. The Athenians tended to divide up the parts of government differently into the deliberative, the judicial, and the magistracies. The fullest exposition of this tripartite system is found in Aristotle, but it is taken for granted in Pericles' praise Athenian political institutions in his *Funeral Oration*.⁴⁹ The deliberative consists of the council and assembly and is concerned with *ta koina*, that is, public affairs that are the common concern of the entire community ([Arist.] *Ath. Pol.* 43.2–49). The prime function of the courts is to resolve *ta idia diaphora* – private disputes, that is, disagreement between individuals in accordance with law ([Arist.] *Ath. Pol.* 63–69). The magistrates are concerned with the administration of public affairs ([Arist.] *Ath. Pol.* 50–62).

The Areopagus is referred to as the Council of the Areopagus (ἡ βουλὴ ἡ ἐξ Ἀρείου πάγου), but the title is misleading since its main function appears to have been judicial. Indeed in the *Eumenides* Athena when establishing the Areopagus says she has selected *dikastai*, a term that means judges not jurors, who will judge (483). In fact, *The Constitution of the Athenians* (57.3) in the account of the democracy of his day lists the Areopagus alongside the courts at the Palladion and the Delphinon as a court concerned with homicide and wounding. It is significant that in his discussion of deliberative part of democracy, the *Constitution of the Athenians* (42.1–49.5) nowhere mentions the activities of the Areopagus, which would appear to indicate that it had no deliberative functions, but belonged

---

49 See Thuc. 2.37.1 with Harris 2006, 29–39.

mainly to the judicial sphere. It is therefore significant that when describing the new court, Athena uses words that are associated with justice and punishment. First, she calls the Areopagus *aidoios*, full of *aidos* 'reverence'. In the myth in Plato's *Protagoras* (323c–d) links *dike* and *aidos* as the necessary virtues to provide peace and stability in the community. In the *Laws* (698b) Plato says that under the old constitution *aidos* (reverence) was their master, which caused them to wish to live as slaves to the law. The word *aidos* tends not to appear in forensic oratory, but accusers often accuse defendants who violate the law with *anaideia* (shamelessness) or being *anaides* (shameless), that is, lacking *aidos*.[50] Athena also calls the Areopagus 'quick to anger'. To modern ears, this might make the members of the Areopagus sound emotional, if not irrational. But for the Athenians anger was the correct response to violating the law.[51] Although anger was considered to be out of place in the Assembly (Thuc. 3.44), accusers often encourage the judges in court to feel anger toward defendants who are guilty, and this anger will lead them to impose the harsh punishments that criminals deserve. The following passages from Demosthenes illustrate the point:

> Dem. 19.302 – It is reasonable for you (the judges) to be angry with traitors and you should be angry with no one more than Aeschines.
> Dem. 21.2 – The Assembly was angry at the injustices I suffered at the hands of Meidias.
> Dem. 21.46 – Outrage (hybris) deserves your (i.e., the judges') anger.
> Dem. 23.168 – You (the Athenians) were angry when you removed Cephisodotus from office.
> Dem. 24.218 – Because of all I have said you should be angry and punish the defendant.
> Dem. 40.5 – You, the judges, should be angry with my opponent.
> Dem. 57.49 – The entire deme was angry at those who illegally forced their way in.
> Dem. 58.31 – The judges were angry with my father when they convicted him.

The status of the Areopagus as a court helps to explain why the Areopagus is found in certain literary genres and not in others. The historians Herodotus, Thucydides, and Xenophon, who wrote histories about public events of Athens – in Greek terms *ta koina* as opposed *ta idia* to private matters – never mention the Areopagus. The historians are interested only in the activities of the deliberative part of government and the magistracies; they record the decisions and debates of the Council and the Assembly and recount the actions of magistrates concerned with *ta koina*. The only trials that receive mention are public cases or other public procedures such as *euthynai* such trials of generals in 424 after the expedition to Sicily in Thucydides (4.65) or the trial of the generals in the Assembly

---

50 See for examples of *anaideia* Dem. 18.22; 19.72; 21.62, 109, 194; 22.8, 27; 23.101, 144; 24.65, 111. For examples of *anaides*, see Dem. 19.16, 175; 21.107, 151, 185, 201; 22.59, 65, 75; 23.99; 24.183.
51 For the role of anger in forensic oratory, see Rubinstein 2004.

after Arginousai in 406 in Xenophon's *History of Greece* (1.7.4–24). The Areopagus was never responsible for public policy, and the Council therefore never appears in the accounts of the historians, whose concern was the collective achievements of the Athenians. By contrast, as noted in the introduction to this paper, the Areopagos is often mentioned in forensic oratory; Aeschines, Demosthenes, Lycurgus, Lysias, and Dinarchus all mention its activities in court speeches and praise its excellence.

But the Areopagus was not just one of several courts. It is the most respected and the best court in Athens. The opinion was justified. The members of the Areopagus were all ex-archons, men who had been selected by lot and had passed a rigorous *dokimasia*, then served as magistrates with responsibilities for administering the courts. In fact, the *thesmothetai* were required to pass a double examination, first before the Council, second before the court (Dem. 20.90; *Ath. Pol.* 55.2–3).[52] The archons also passed an equally strict *euthynai* at the end of their terms of office before they could become members of the Areopagus.[53] Not all Athenians could be archons; shortly before 457/56 a candidate had to be from the top two property classes, the *pentakosiodimnoi* and the *hippeis* and afterwards he could not be a thete, a member of the lowest property class, that probably made up half of the citizen body ([Arist.] *Ath. Pol.* 26.2). In the *Eumenides*, Athena alludes to this property qualification and the rigorous selection process: when choosing the judges for the Areopagus she says: "selecting the very best of my citizens" (487: κρίνασα δ' ἀστῶν τῶν ἐμῶν τὰ βέλτιστα).[54] The members of the Areopagus were thus unlike the members of the other courts for whom there was no property qualification, who did not have to pass a double *dokimasia*, had no experience administering judicial business, and were not examined at *euthynai* in an office before serving on the courts.

In addition the Areopagus kept strict internal discipline and dismissed member for even minor infractions as Dinarchus (1.56) informs us. The Council's accounts were regularly examined (Aeschin. 3.20). No similar procedures are attested for the regular *dikastai*. The careful regulations were necessary for the Areopagus because its members served for life, a privilege unparalleled for all other public offices in Athens. The members of the Areopagus thus possessed more expertise than any other office. For this reason, the Areopagus was often

---

52 On the *dokimasia* of archons and the Areopagites, see Rhodes 1981, 614–621 and especially Feyel 2009, 171–184.
53 For the *euthynai*, see [Arist.] *Ath. Pol.* with Efstathiou 2007.
54 Sommerstein 1989, 170 fails to see the allusion to the rigorous selection procedures for the Areopagus.

consulted in the fourth century and could be instructed to conduct investigations. When Aeschines was appointed to represent the Athenians in a dispute over the temple at Delos, the Athenians invited the Areopagus to review the appointment.[55] The Assembly might also order the Areopagus to make a report, which might contain a recommendation.[56] When Harpalus was suspected of giving bribes to several leading politicians, the Assembly entrusted the Areopagus with the task of making an investigation and presenting its finding in a report.[57] Some scholars believe that this activity of the Areopagus represented a conservative turn in Athenian politics after 350 BCE, but this view is mistaken. The Areopagus only served in an advisory role in this period, and the final decision always lay in the Assembly or in the courts (e.g. Din. 1.58–60). Athens after 350 BCE was no less democratic after 350 BCE than it was before 350 BCE.[58] The Areopagus also had a reputation for justice in its verdicts. One should not make the mistake of thinking that the Areopagus had a stricter standard of relevance in judging case than the regular courts, which had a broader standard. Both types of courts were bound by the same procedural rules, but the Areopagus had a reputation for living up to the ideals shared by all the courts because of its expertise and strict internal discipline.[59] In fact, Aeschines and Lycurgus think that the court served as an example for the regular courts. And the respect for the expertise of the Areopagus shows that the Athenians were not hostile to legal expertise as some scholars have claimed without good evidence.[60]

Even though Aristotle wanted to transform the Areopagus into an oligarchic or aristocratic body in accordance with his ideas about the guardianship of the laws and about the mixed constitution,[61] the Areopagus met all the criteria: the members were selected by lot, there was a low property qualification after 457,

---

55 Dem. 18.134–136 with Harris 1995, 121–122, 205. For other sources and discussion, see de Bruyn 1995 149–151, but her date of 344 for the incident is not convincing.
56 On the role of the Areopagus in making reports (*apophaseis*), see Din. 1.50 and de Bruyn 1995, 117–146, whose account is more reliable than that of Wallace 1989, 115–119.
57 For the sources and references to earlier treatments, see Harris 2013a, 46–47.
58 See Harris 2016a.
59 View that the Areopagus had a different standard of relevance than the regular courts: Lanni 2006, 75–114. Evidence demonstrating that the Areopagus and the regular courts did not have a different standard of relevance: Harris 2009–2010, 327–328.
60 On the respect for legal expertise, see Harris 1991 (*pace* Todd 1996).
61 For the view that the Areopagus represented an aristocratic element, see Aristotle *Politics* 2.9.2.1273b36–41.

their conduct was subject to review by democratic institutions.[62] There is no need to think that life-long tenure made them into an oligarchic institution.[63]

But the Areopagus was more than a court. It was also held an important symbolic role that scholars have failed to grasp. This is the paradox of the Areopagus: it looms very large in the imagination of the Athenians, yet is absent from its political history, the actual decisions of policy. The Areopagus represented the stability of law amid the turbulence and flux of democratic politics. One must bear in mind that the final stage of development of democratic institutions in Athens was the work of Cleisthenes shortly after the overthrow of the Peisistratid tyranny. The institutions he created were aimed in large part at preventing a recurrence of tyranny, that is the concentration of power in the hands of one man.[64] Power was thus radically decentralized: there were dozens of magistrates, five hundred members of the council, large courts of *dikastai*. There was no longer just one Polemarch, but ten generals ([Arist.] *Ath. Pol.* 22.2). To prevent even these magistrates from perpetuating their hold on power, terms were limited to a single year, often with no possibility of re-appointment: nine new archons, five hundred new members of the council every year.[65] Generals might be re-elected, but they still had to stand for election once every year and could be removed from office anytime during their term for misconduct. Witness the fate of Pericles during the plague (Thuc. 2.65).

In the midst of this democratic flux, there was a need for stability and continuity. This is true for any community. For instance, in Great Britain the Queen provides the nation with a symbol of stability and continuity – even though her children's marriages are not models of stability. The Queen stands above politics: she is not supposed to intervene in elections nor to take sides in debates. She never intervenes in the formulation of policy. The Queen has almost no power but symbolic role is enormous so much so that the British are willing to spend many pounds on maintaining the symbol. For a brilliant analysis of her role one should read the relevant pages of Walter Bagehot's in his work on the *English Constitution*.

---

[62] For a low property qualification as consistent with democracy, see Aristotle, *Politics* 2.9.2.1274b39–41.

[63] The Areopagus was accused of being oligarchic for its emergency powers in late 338 (Lyc. *Leocr.* 52), but this was a criticism of a temporary measure, not an objection to the nature of the Council. See Harris 2016, 79.

[64] For the aim of preventing tyranny in the laws of the Archaic period, see Harris 2006, 3–28.

[65] Members of the Council might be appointed again, but only after an interval. For members serving twice, see Rhodes 1984 with the bibliography cited there.

In Athens it was the laws that provided the order and stability amidst democratic flux – public speakers and generals might come and go, but the laws abided. In fact, when the Ephebes swore their oath of loyalty, they promised to uphold not the democracy or to support the Council and Assembly but to obey the established laws and the officials who were ruling prudently, that is, in accordance with the laws (Rhodes/Osborne 2003, n. 88, lines 12–14). Since the laws provided Athenians with their sense of continuity and stability, the Athenians believed that the laws should not be changed. For instance, Herodotus (1.29.1) tells us that after Solon produced his law code, he left Athens for ten years so that he would not be forced to modify his legislation. Before he left he had bound the Athenians by strong oaths not to change their laws.[66] There was a general feeling that one should respect the established laws and not repeal nor legislate in defiance of them. In fact, Demosthenes in his *Against Timocrates* (24.139–42) praises the Locrians for making politicians propose new laws with a noose around their neck. If the proposal was voted down, the noose was tightened and the politician strangled. A speaker who delivered a speech written by Antiphon (5.14) praises the laws about homicide, which were administered primarily by the Areopagus, for remaining the same: 'I think that all would agree that the laws which are established about these matters are the best framed of all the laws and the most holy. For it is their nature to be the oldest laws in this land since they are the same about the same things, which is the greatest indication of laws being well framed.' In the fifth century, the Athenians often tried to prevent changes in important statutes by including entrenchment clauses, which threatened severe penalties for those who proposed changes or repeal.[67] The emphasis on the importance of keeping the law stable was not just a democratic view, but an ideal shared by most Greek city-states.[68]

We find this idea about the importance of keeping the laws stable expressed by Athena in *Eumenides* (693–695). Athena links the Areopagus' ability to maintain peace and order with the citizens' willingness to maintain the laws unchanged. She is appealing to a general belief about the rule of law, not alluding to any specific laws passed in the previous decade.

Because the Areopagus was responsible for the most important trials, those involving deliberate homicide, because the court took its task so seriously, and because its reputation was so awe-inspiring, it was considered improper to laugh

---

66 [Arist.] *Ath. Pol.* 7.2; Plutarch *Solon* 25.6–28.1.
67 On entrenchment clauses, see Lewis 1997, 136–149. For their role, see Harris 2006, 23–25.
68 For entrenchment clauses in other *poleis*, see Sickinger 2008.

in the presence of members of the Areopagus as we are told in an anecdote recounted by Aeschines (1.81–84). According to Aeschines, the Areopagus was invited to give its advice about a proposal by Timarchus about houses on the Pnyx. The member of the Areopagus who addressed the Assembly was Autolycus, a man who had lived a virtuous and pious life worthy of the Council. During his speech, he said that Timarchus was better acquainted with the area in question than the Council of the Areopagus. The people in the Assembly applauded this part of the speech, but Autolycus did not understand why. He told the Assembly that the Areopagus does not accuse or defend, but could make allowance for Timarchus thinking that the place was quiet, and said that the project would incur a small expense for the people. These words provoked even more laughter. When Autolycus spoke about 'sites for houses' and 'tanks', the Assembly thought that this was some kind of *double entendre* and an allusion to Timarchus' lewd activities. At this point Pyrrhander came forward and scolded the people for laughing in front of the Council of the Areopagus. The people drove Pyrrhander off the speaker's platform and said: 'We know that we should not laugh in front of the Council, but because everyone knows the truth about Timarchus, we cannot control ourselves'. Because the court had such a reputation for probity and piety and was entrusted with such important responsibilities, it was thought improper to laugh in its presence. This is why the court is never mentioned in Aristophanes and Old Comedy: its task and reputation were so serious that such flippant behaviour was not considered appropriate. Unlike the Council, regular courts, Assembly and the magistrates, the Areopagus was not a joke. The Areopagus was respected and venerable, which is why it was considered an appropriate subject for tragedy.[69] In her charter of the Areopagus, Athena twice refers to the 'august' nature of the court (690 and 700: σέβας).[70] This was appropriate because the Areopagus judged the most serious cases, those pertaining to homicide.

But why did Aeschylus write a drama about the foundation of the Areopagus to be produced in the spring of 458? If one is going to link the play to contemporary developments, it should be to the recent reform that allowed the third property class, the zeugites, to become archons, which would have qualified them to become members of the Areopagus ([Arist.] *Ath Pol.* 26.2). The first member of this class to become an archon took office in 457/8, which means that the reform must

---

[69] For the differences between the serious genre of tragedy and the ridiculous genre of comedy, see Taplin 1986.
[70] The attempt of Sommerstein 1989, 215–216 to read deliberate ambiguity into lines 690–692 is far-fetched and relies on the assumption that the account of Ephialtes' attacks on the Areopagus is reliable.

have taken place a year or two before. This was an important development because a large segment of the population now needed to be reminded of the responsibilities of this body and to gain respect for its role and reputation.

To instruct these citizens who will now be eligible to serve as archons for the first time, Aeschylus provides a model trial as a way of teaching them about their new duties. The trial of Orestes follows the same basic pattern that all litigation conformed to, falling into two parts, the first part before the magistrate, and the second part the trial itself before a group of *dikastai,* judges, who listened to both sides then cast their votes in favour of the plaintiff or the defendant. Scholars like Sommerstein have concentrated on the legal features of the trial, but have missed the way that Aeschylus has portrayed the first part of the trial. This would have been especially relevant to the new men qualified to be archons, because one of their main roles was to receive the charges brought by accusers and to conduct the *anakrisis* before the trial.

One of the main tasks of the archon was to draw up the *engklema,* perhaps the most important document in Athenian litigation.[71] To compose this document, the magistrate asked the accuser his name, patronymic and residence or status. This was important because if the accuser was an Athenian, the case would go to one court, if a foreigner or metic, it would go to another court. The accuser then had to state the charges following the language of the substantive part of a written statute and show how the defendant had violated a specific written statute. If he did not, the official would reject the charge.[72] The official might then ask if there were any relevant accompanying circumstances. Once the accuser provided this information, the official turned to the defendant and elicited the same information: name, patronymic, and status or place of residence. The defendant was then asked to give his reply to the charges (*antigraphe*).

When the Erinyes and Orestes come before Athena, the goddess follows the main steps of the preliminary stages for an Athenian trial. First, she asks the accusers who they are (Aesch. *Eum.* 408), and the Erinyes give their name, their parent, and their place of residence (Aesch. *Eum.* 416–417): 'We are the gloomy children of the night. Curses they call us in our homes beneath the ground'. They also give their status (Aesch. *Eum.* 419, 421): 'We drive from home those who have shed the blood of men'. The Erinyes then present their charge (Aesch. *Eum.* 425): 'He murdered his mother by deliberate choice'. Athena then asks if there are any extenuating circumstances (Aesch. *Eum.* 426): 'By random force or in fear of someone's wrath?' The Erinyes deny that any extenuating circumstances exist

---

[71] On this document, see Harris 2013b.
[72] See for example Lys. 13.85–87 with Harris 2013a, 124–125.

(Aesch. *Eum.* 427): 'Where is the spur to justify man's matricide?' Here Athena attempts to determine what kind of homicide the defendant is charged with just as the *basileus* attempted to determine whether the accusation was deliberate homicide (*phonos ek pronoias*), involuntary homicide (*phonos akousios*), or just homicide (*phonos dikaios*) so he could assign the case to the right court ([Arist.] *Ath. Pol.* 57.2–3). When the Erinyes deny that there are any extenuating circumstances, she also reminds them that she must hear both sides (Aesch. *Eum.* 428): 'Here are two sides, and only half the argument'. This statement echoes the pledge in the Judicial Oath that bound all the judges to listen to both sides equally and without favour or hostility to either party (Aeschin. 2.1; Dem. 18.2; Isoc. 15.21).

After getting all the information she needs from the accusers, she turns to the defendant Orestes and asks him for the same information and for his version of the facts (Aesch. *Eum.* 436–441): 'Your turn, stranger. What will you say in answer? Speak, tell me your country and your birth, what has befallen you, then defend yourself against the anger of these; if it was confidence in the right that made you sit to keep this image near my hearth, a supplicant in the tradition of Ixion, sancrosanct' (transl. Lattimore). Orestes prefaces his answer by assuring Athena that he is not polluted (Aesch. *Eum.* 445–453), which is equivalent to saying that he is innocent: Orestes complies by giving his place of residence and his father's name (Aesch. *Eum.* 455–459): 'Learn next with no delay where I am from. I am of Argos and it is to my honor that you ask the name of my father, Agamemnon, lord of seafarers, and your companion when you made the Trojan city of Ilium no city any more' (transl. Lattimore). Orestes then presents his case and asks her to judge it (Aesch. *Eum.* 459–69):

> It was my mother
> of the dark heart, who entangled him in subtle gvyes
> and cut him down. The bath is witness to his death.
> I was an exile in the time before this. I came back
> and killed the woman who gave me birth, and will not deny it.
> My father was dear, and this was the vengeance for his blood.
> Apollo shares responsibility for this.
> He counterspurred my heart and told me of pains to come
> if I should fail to act against the guilt ones.
> This is my case. Decide if it be right or wrong.
> I am in your hands. Where my fate falls, I shall accept.
>
> (transl. Lattimore)

Like the *basileus*, Athena does not presume to make a decision in the dispute (Aesch. *Eum.* 470–472): 'The matter is too big for any mortal man who thinks he can judge it. Even I have not the right to analyze cases of murder where wrath's edge is sharp, and all the more since you have come, and clung a clean and innocent supplicant against my doors' (transl. Lattimore). Despite her belief in his innocence, she does not presume to decide the case. Just as she recognized that Orestes had a right to reply to the charges, she knows that the Erinyes also have the right to present their case to the court (Aesch. *Eum*. 427): 'Yet these, too, have their work. We cannot brush them aside' (transl. Lattimore). Just as the *basileus* handed over the case to a court to try, Athena entrusts the decision to judges. Just as Athenian judges swore an oath before hearing a case and were often reminded of that oath by litigants, the judges whom Athena selects will also swear an oath Aesch. *Eum*. 481–484):

> Then, since
> the burden of the case is here, and rests on me,
> I shall select judges of manslaughter, and swear
> them in, establish a court for all time to come.[73]

(transl. Lattimore)

To conclude. The *Eumenides* of Aeschylus is concerned with the political and legal views of the Athenians. Like all Attic tragedies, the *Eumenides* is not concerned with the personalities of individual leaders (I do not find the allegorical approach of Vickers convincing), but with politics in the deeper more profound sense: those shared values and beliefs that helped to maintain justice and order in Athens, a view well expressed by Oliver Taplin.[74] Prominent among these values was the rule of law and respect for the procedures that attempted to put that ideal into practice: trial by impartial judges pledged to vote according to the law, use of the secret ballot, the right of the defendant to hear and reply to the charges and to present evidence, the belief in equality before the law (expressed very eloquently in Euripides *Suppliant Women* 433–434, 437), free access to written statutes, accountability of all officials, and the opposition to tyranny, which was the rule of one man unrestrained by law.[75] These are values that are much more relevant for our understanding of Attic drama than democratic ideology. After all, the word *demokratia* is not attested until after 435 BCE at Athens, and in Attic tragedy the word *demos* occurs far less frequently than words like *nomos*, *dike*, and

---

[73] I see no reason to accept the transposition of line 475 to after line 482 proposed by Lobel and followed by Sommerstein.
[74] Taplin 1986.
[75] Rhodes 2003 writes vaguely of 'constitutional government', but this is too general and misses the specific features of the rule of law.

dikaios.⁷⁶ They were also values shared by the Greeks who attended the Dionysia at Athens and who watched Athenian tragedies when they were produced in foreign cities.⁷⁷ We should also remember that the deep respect for the Areopagus, which symbolized the rule of law, outlived the democracy. When St. Paul came to Athens, he chose to address not the Assembly, not the Council, both of which were still meeting, nor the magistrates, but the Areopagus. And the Areopagus remains in contemporary Greece the name of the highest court, an eloquent testimony to the view that democracy and the rule of law go hand in hand today as they did almost 2,500 years ago.

Bibliography

TrGF = Snell/Kannicht/Radt (1971–2004).
Brenne, S. (2001), *Ostrakismos und Prominenz in Athen*, Vienna.
Cairns, D./Knox, R.A. (eds.) (2004), *Law, rhetoric, and comedy in classical Athens: Essays in honour of Douglas M. MacDowell*, Swansea.
Carawan, E. (1987), '*Eisangelia* and *Euthyna*: The Trials of Miltiades, Themistocles, and Cimon', in: *GRBS* 28, 167–208.
Ceccarelli, P. (1993), 'Sans thalassocratie, pas de démocratie? Le rapport entre thalassocratie et démocratie à Athènes dans la discussion du Ve et IVe siècle av. J.-C.', in: *Historia* 42.4, 444–470.
Clapperton, B. (forthcoming). 'Relevance in the Areopagus and in the Regular Courts of Athens', Paper delivered at the Classical Association, Edinburgh, 2016.
Davies, J.K. (1971). *Athenian Propertied Families, 600–300 B.C.*, Oxford.
de Bruyn, O. (1995), *La compétence de l'Aréopage en matière de procès publics dès origines de la Polis à la conquête romaine de la Grèce (vers 700–146 avant J.C.)*, Stuttgart.
Dover, K.J. (1957), 'The Political Aspect of Aeschylus' *Eumenides*', in: *JHS* 77, 230–237.
Efstathiou, A. (2007), '*Euthyna* procedure in the 4th C. Athens and the Case *On the False Embassy*', in: *Dike* 10, 113–135.
Fachard, S./Knodell, A.R./Banou, E. (2015), 'The 2104 Mazi Archaeological Project (Attica)', in: *Antike Kunst* 58, 178–186.
Faraguna, M. (ed.) (2013), *Archives and Archival Documents in Ancient Societies*, Trieste.
Forrest, W.G. (1960), 'Themistokles and Argos', in: *CQ* 10, 221–241.
Foxhall, L./Lewis, A.D.E. (eds.) (1996), *Greek Law in its Political Setting*, Oxford.
Frost, F.J. (1980), *Plutarch's Themistocles: A Historical Commentary*, Princeton.

---

76 For words meaning 'law' and 'justice' in Aeschylus and Sophocles, see Harris *et al.* 2010, 16–18.
77 For production of Attic drama outside Athens, see Vahtikari 2014. One of the drawbacks of the approach of Goldhill is that it fails to explain how Attic drama could be popular outside of Athens.

Gagarin, M. (ed.) (1991), *Symposion 1990. Vorträge zur griechischen und hellenistischen Rechtsgeschichte*, Cologne/Weimar/Vienna.

Goldhill, S. (1987), 'The Great Dionysia and Civic Ideology', in: *JHS* 107, 58–76.

Goldhill, S. (2004), *Language, Sexuality, Narrative: The Oresteia*, Cambridge.

Habicht, C. (1961), 'Falsche Urkunden zur Geschichte Athens im Zeitalter der Perserkriege', in: *Hermes* 89, 1–35.

Hansen, M.H. (1975), *Eisangelia: The Sovereignty of the People's Court in Athens in the Fourth Century B.C. and the Impeachment of Generals and Politicians*, Odense.

Harris, E.M. (1991), 'Response to Trevor Saunders', in: Gagarin (ed.), 133–138.

Harris, E.M. (1997), 'A New Solution to the Riddle of the *Seisactheia*', in: Mitchell/Rhodes, 103–112.

Harris, E.M. (2006), *Democracy and the Rule of Law in Classical Athens: Essays on Law, Society and Politics*, Cambridge.

Harris, E.M. (2009–2010), Review of Lanni (2006), in: *Dike* 12/13, 323–331.

Harris, E.M. (2013a), *The Rule of Law in Action in Democratic Athens*, Oxford.

Harris, E.M. (2013b), 'The Plaint in Athenian Law and Legal Procedure', in: Faraguna (ed.), 143–162.

Harris, E. M. (2013–2014), 'The Authenticity of the Document at Andocides *On the Mysteries* 96–98', in: *Τεκμήρια* 12, 121–153.

Harris, E.M. (2016a), 'From Democracy to the Rule of Law? Constitutional Change in Athens during the Fifth and Fourth Centuries BCE', in: Tiersch (ed.), 71–84.

Harris, E.M. (2016b), 'The Flawed Origins of Athenian Democracy', in: Havlíček/Horn/Jinek (eds.), 43–55.

Harris, E.M. (2017), 'How to 'Act' in an Athenian Court: Emotions and Forensic Performance', in: A. Serafim (ed.).

Harris, E.M. (forthcoming). 'The Athenian View of an Athenian Trial', in: C. Carey/B. Griffith-Williams/I. Giannadaki (eds.), *The Use and Abuse of Law*.

Harris, E.M./Thür, G. (eds.) (2008), *Symposion 2007: Gesellschaft für griechische und hellenistische Rechtsgeschichte*, Vienna.

Harris, E.M./Leão, D./Rhodes, P.J. (eds.) (2010), *Law and Drama in Ancient Greece*, London.

Havlíček, A./Horn, C./Jinek, J. (eds.) (2016), *Nous, Polis, Nomos. Festschrift Francisco L. Lisi*, St. Augustin.

Hopper, R.J. (1961), "'Plain', 'Shore,' and 'Hill' in early Athens', in: *ABSA* 56, 189–219.

Hornblower, S. (ed.) (2013), *Herodotus, Histories Book V*, Cambridge.

Jameson, M. (1960), 'A Decree of Themistokles from Troizen', in: *Hesperia* 29, 198–223.

Johansson, M. (2001), 'The Inscription from Troizen: A Decree of Themistocles?', in: *ZPE*, 69–92.

Johansson, M. (2003), 'Thucydides on the Evacuation of Athens in 480 B.C.', in: *MH* 60, 1–5.

Johansson, M. (2004a), 'Plutarch, Aelius Aristides and the Inscription from Troizen', in: *RM* 147, 343–354.

Johansson, M. (2004b), 'Some Notes on μεθίστημι in the Inscription from Troizen', in: *CQ*^{2} 54, 283–285.

Jones, L.A. (1987), 'The Role of Ephialtes in the Rise of Athenian Democracy', in: *Classical Antiquity* 6, 53–76.

Knoepfler, D. (2010), 'Les Vieillards relégués à Salamine survivront-ils au jubilé de la publication du décret de Thémistocle trouvé à Trézène?', in: *CRAI* 2010, 1181–1233.

Lanni, A. (2006), *Law and Justice in Courts of Classical Athens*, Cambridge.

Leão, D. (2010), 'The Legal Horizon of the *Oresteia*: The Crime of Homicide and the Founding of the Areopagus', in: Harris/Leão/Rhodes, 39–60.
Lohmann, H. (1993), *Atene. Forschungen zur Siedlungs' und Wirtschaftsstruktur des klassischen Attika*, I–II, Cologne.
Mann, C. (2007), *Die Demagogen und das Volk: Zur politischen Kommunikation in Athen des 5. Jahrhunderts v. Chr*, Berlin.
Ostwald, M. (1986), *From Popular Sovereignty to the Sovereignty of Law: Law, Society and Politics in Fifth-Century Athens*, Berkeley.
O'Sullivan, L. (2001), 'Philochorus, Pollux and the νομοφύλακες of Demetrius of Phalerum', in: *JHS* 121, 51–62.
Pleket, H. (1969), 'The archaic *tyrannis*', in: *Talanta* 1, 19–61.
Poddighe, E. (2014), *Aristotele, Atene, e le metamorfosi dell'idea democratica: da Solone a Pericle (594–451 a.C.)*, Rome.
Podlecki, A.J. (1986), *The Political Background of Aeschylean Tragedy*, Ann Arbor.
Raaflaub, K.A./Ober, J./Wallace, R.W. (2007), *Origins of Democracy in Ancient Greece*, Berkeley.
Rhodes, P.J. (1981), *A Commentary on the Aristotelian Athenaion Politeia*, Oxford.
Rhodes, P.J. (1984), 'Members Serving Twice the Athenian Boule and the Population of Athens Again', in: *ZPE* 57, 200–202.
Rhodes, P.J. (2003), ''Nothing to do with Democracy': Athenian Drama and the Polis', in: *JHS* 123, 104–119.
Rhodes, P.J./Lewis, D.M. (1997), *The Decrees of the Greek States*, Oxford.
Rihll, T.E. (1995), 'Democracy denied: why Ephialtes attacked the Areiopagus', in: *JHS* 115, 87–98.
Rubinstein, L. (2004), 'Stirring up Dikastic Anger', in: D. Cairns/R.A. Knox (eds.), *Law, rhetoric, and comedy in classical Athens: Essays in honour of Douglas M. MacDowell*, Swansea, 187–203.
Sealey, B.R.I. (1956), 'The Entry of Pericles into History', in: *Hermes* 84, 234–247.
Sealey, B.R.I. (1958), 'On Penalizing Areopagites', in: *AJP* 79.1, 71–73.
Sealey, B.R.I. (1960), 'Regionalism in archaic Athens', in: *Historia* 9, 155–180.
Sealey, B.R.I. (1967), *Essays in Greek Politics*, New York.
Sickinger, J.P. (2008), 'Indeterminacy in Greek Law: Statutory Gaps and Conflicts', in: E.M. Harris/G. Thür (eds.), *Symposion 2007: Gesellschaft für griechische und hellenistische Rechtsgeschichte*, Vienna, 99–112.
Siewert, P. (ed.) (2002), *Ostrakismos-Testamonien*, I, Stuttgart.
Snell, B./Kannicht, R./Radt, S.L. (1971–2004), *Tragicorum Graecorum Fragmenta*, Göttingen.
Sommerstein, A. (ed.) (1989), *Aeschylus, Eumenides*, Cambridge.
Sommerstein, A. (2010), 'Orestes' Trial and Athenian Homicide Procedure', in: E.M. Harris/D. Leao/P.J. Rhodes, 25–38.
Sommerstein, A. (2014), 'The Authenticity of the Demophantus Decree', in: *CQ* 64.1, 49–57.
Taplin, O. (1986), 'Fifth century Tragedy and Comedy: A *Synkrisis*', in: *JHS* 106, 163–174.
Tiersch, C. (ed.) (2016), *Die athenische Demokratie im 4. Jhr. – Zwischen Modernisierung und Tradition*, Berlin.
Todd, S.C. (1996), 'Lysias Against Nicomachus: The Fate of the Expert in Athenian Law', in: L. Foxhall/A.D.E. Lewis (eds.), *Greek Law in its Political Setting*, Oxford, 101–132.
Vahtikari, V. (2014), *Tragedy performances outside Athens in the late fifth and the fourth centuries BCE*, Helsinki.

Wallace, R.W. (1974), 'Ephialtes and the Areopagos', in: *GRBS* 15, 259–269.
Wallace, R.W. (1989), *The Areopagos Council, to 307 B.C.*, Baltimore/London.
Wilamowitz-Möllendorf, U. von (1893), *Aristotle und Athen*, Berlin.
Wilson, P. (2009), 'Tragic Honours and Democracy: Neglected Evidence for the Politics of the Athenian Dionysia', in: *CQ* 59, 8–29.
Wörrle, M. (1964), *Untersuchungen zur Verfassungsgeschichte von Argos im 5. Jahrhundert*, PhD Diss. University of Erlangen.
Zaccarini, M. (2018), 'The Fate of the Lawgiver: The Invention of the Reforms of Ephialtes and the Patrios Politeia', in: *Historia* 67, 495–512.

List of Contributors

Evangelos Alexiou is Professor of Ancient Greek Literature at the Department of Philology in the Aristotle University of Thessaloniki. Since 1999 he has also been working with the Hellenic Open University. His research interests include: Rhetoric, Plutarch and Biography, Second Sophistic, Ethics and History of Ideas in Antiquity. His publications include: *Ruhm und Ehre. Studien zu Begriffen, Werten und Motivierungen bei Isokrates* (Heidelberg, 1995), *Πλουτάρχου Παράλληλοι Βίοι. Η προβληματική των θετικών και αρνητικών παραδειγμάτων* [*The Parallel Lives of Plutarch: The Issue of Positive and Negative Examples*] (Thessaloniki, 2007), *Der Euagoras des Isokrates. Ein Kommentar* (Berlin, 2010). Further, he is the author of 'Die Rhetorik des 4. Jahrhunderts', in: B. Zimmermann/A. Rengakos (eds.) (2014), *Handbuch der griechischen Literatur der Antike*, II, Munich, 734–859 and *Η ρητορική του 4ου αι. π.Χ. Το ελιξίριο της δημοκρατίας και η ατομικότητα* [*The Rhetoric of Fourth Century BCE: The Elixir of Democracy and Individuality*] (Athens, 2016). He has also published articles on Thucydides, Isocrates, Lysias, Xenophon, Plutarch, Dio Chrysostom and Julian.

Guido Avezzù is Professor of Greek Literature at the University of Verona. His main areas of research are Athenian oratory (critical editions of Lysias' speeches 1, 2, and 12: 1985 and 1991, and of Alcidamas' speeches and fragments: 1982), and Greek tragedy and its reception. His publications on this subject include the critical editions of Sophocles' *Philoctetes* and *Oedipus at Colonus* (Milan, 2003 and 2008) and monographs on the relation between myth and tragedy (*Il mito sulla scena. La tragedia ad Atene*, Venice, 2003) and on the staging of the story of Philoctetes (*Il ferimento e il rito. La storia di Filottete sulla scena ateniese*, Bari, 1988). His latest works include the English translation of Friedrich Schiller's *Über den Gebrauch des Chors in der Tragödie* (with an Introduction by S. Halliwell), in: *Skenè* 1:1, 2015: 140–166; essays on Sophocles: 'Commiato da Edipo e da Sofocle', in: F. Citti/A. Iannucci (eds.) (2012), *Edipo classico e contemporaneo*, Hildesheim, 31–46; 'Text and Transmission', in: A. Markantonatos (ed.) (2012), *Brill's Companion to Sophocles*, Leiden/Boston, 39–57; 'Considerazioni sui drammi satireschi di Sofocle, in: G. Bastianini/A. Casanova (eds.) (2013), in: *I papiri di Eschilo e di Sofocle. Atti del convegno internazionale di studi*, Florence, 53–64; on Aeschylus: 'Scena e politica in Eschilo', in: J. Jouanna/F. Montanari (eds.) (2009), *Eschyle à l'aube du théâtre occidental*, Fondation Hardt, 165–203; 'Reticence and *phobos* in Aeschylus's *Agamemnon*', in: *Comparative Drama* 52/1–2, 2018: 23–53; on Euripides: '"It is not a small thing to defeat a king". The Servant/Messenger's Tale in Euripides' *Electra*', in: *Skenè* 2:2, 2016: 63–86; 'Collaborating with Euripides: Actors and Scholars Improve the Drama Text', in: *Skenè* 4:1, 2018: 15–37; on classical tragic paradigms in Shakespeare's drama: 'Classical Paradigms of Tragic Choice in Civic Stories of Love and Death', in: S. Bigliazzi/L. Calvi (eds.) (2016), *Shakespeare, Romeo and Juliet, and Civic Life. The Boundaries of Civic Space*, New York/London, 45–65.

Chris Carey is Emeritus Professor of Greek at UCL. He has published on Greek epic, lyric, drama, historiography, oratory and law.

Michael Edwards is an Honorary Research Fellow at Royal Holloway, University of London, and an Honorary Professor at the Department of Philology in the University of the Peloponnese,

Kalamata. He has published widely on Greek oratory, including commentaries on Antiphon, Andocides and Lysias, and a translation of the speeches of Isaeus. He was formerly Director of the Institute of Classical Studies in London, and President of the International Society for the History of Rhetoric.

Andreas Fountoulakis is Associate Professor of Greek Literature and Drama and Director of the Drama and Visual Arts Laboratory of the University of Crete. His research interests include Greek tragedy and comedy, ancient popular theatre, Hellenistic poetry, the Second Sophistic, and the reception of antiquity in Modern Greek literature. He is the author of *Violence and Theatricality: Studies on Violence as a Dramatic Element in Classical and Post-Classical Greek Tragedy* (1995) and *In Search of the Didactic Menander: An Approach to Menander's Comedy and an Exploration of the Samia* (2004) [in Greek]. He is co-editor of *Thoughtful Adaptations: Cross-Cultural and Didactic Aspects of Cavafy's Poetry* (2007) [in Greek] and and *Theatre World: Critical Perspectives on Greek Tragedy and Comedy* (2017). He is also the author of numerous articles published in refereed journals, edited volumes, and conference proceedings. He is currently working on gender and genre in Lucian's *Dialogues of the Courtesans*.

Penelope Frangakis is a postdoctoral researcher at the Department of Philology in the University of the Peloponnese.

Brenda Griffith-Williams is an Honorary Research Associate in the Department of Greek and Latin at University College London. Her main research field is Athenian inheritance law. She has published *A commentary on selected speeches of Isaios*, and several articles on Athenian law and rhetoric.

Edward M. Harris is Emeritus Professor of Ancient History at Durham University and Honorary Professorial Fellow at the University of Edinburgh. He is the author of *Democracy and the Rule of Law in Classical Athens* (CUP 2006) and *The Rule of Law in Action in Democratic Athens* (OUP). He has translated Demosthenes 20–22 and 23–26 (Texas) and co-edited *The Law and the Courts in Ancient Greece, Law and Drama in Ancient Greece,* and *The Ancient Greek Economy: Markets, Households, and City-States*.

László Horváth is Associate Professor with habilitation at the Greek Department of ELTE Budapest; Director of Eötvös József Collegium, the Hungarian partner institution of the École Normale Supérieure; and Head of the Byzantium Centre. He has earned world-wide acclaim through the critical edition of the text of the Hyperides Palimpsest.

Ioanna Karamanou is Associate Professor of Ancient Greek Literature at the Department of Classics (School of Philology) of Aristotle University of Thessaloniki. Her research interests focus on Greek tragedy and its reception, dramatic fragments, papyrology and ancient literary criticism. She is the author of *Euripides: Danae and Dictys* (Munich/Leipzig 2006, De Gruyter), *Euripides: Alexandros* (Berlin/Boston 2017, De Gruyter) and *Refiguring Tragedy: Studies in Plays Preserved in Fragments and their Reception* (Berlin/Boston 2019, De Gruyter). She has published a number of articles in international peer-reviewed journals and collective volumes. She is currently preparing a commentary on the fragments of Diphilus as part of the *KomFrag* project.

List of Contributors —— **423**

Marcel Lysgaard Lech earned his PhD in classical studies from the University of Copenhagen, Denmark, in 2011 and is Associate Professor in Classics at the University of Southern Denmark. He has written on Greek drama and theater and translated works by Aeschylus, Sophocles, Euripides, Aristophanes and Plato into Danish.

Andreas Markantonatos is Professor of Greek at the Department of Philology in the University of the Peloponnese, Director of the Centre for Ancient Rhetoric and Drama (CARD), and Vice-President of the Olympic Centre for Philosophy and Culture (OCPC). He is the author, among others, of *Tragic Narrative: A Narratological Study of Sophocles' Oedipus at Colonus* (2002), *Oedipus at Colonus: Sophocles, Athens, and the World* (2007), *Euripides' Alcestis: Narrative, Myth, and Religion* (2013), *The Voice of the Past: Critical Perspectives on Attic Drama* (2019) [in Modern Greek], and *Euripides' Heracles: Mortal Bodies and Immortal Memory* (2020). He has edited several multi-authored volumes, including *Crisis on Stage: Tragedy and Comedy in Late Fifth-Century Athens* (2012, together with Bernhard Zimmermann), *Brill's Companion to Sophocles* (2012) and *Brill's Companion to Euripides* (2019), and has published widely on Greek drama and modern literary theory. He is currently working on an annotated edition of Sophocles' *Oedipus at Colonus* for Liverpool University Press.

Ioannis N. Perysinakis is Emeritus Professor of Ancient Greek Literature at the Department of Philology in the University of Ioannina. His teaching and research interests focus on ancient Greek Literature with an emphasis on moral values and political behaviour from Homer to the fifth century BCE, as well as on the development and revaluation of moral values in Plato and Aristotle, and the reception of ancient Greek in Modern Greek Literature. He has written extensively on Homer, Hesiod, lyric poetry, Greek tragedy, Plato and Modern Greek Literature. His publications (after the completion of his PhD Diss. *Wealth and Society in Early Greek Literature*, King's College, London, 1982) include: Ἡ ἔννοια τοῦ πλούτου στὴν Ἱστορίη τοῦ Ἡροδότου (*Dodone*, Supplement 31, Ioannina, 1998²); *Pindar's Imagery of Poetry: The Nemean Odes* (*Dodone*, Philology, 1997/1998); Ἀρχαϊκὴ Λυρικὴ Ποίηση (Athens, 2012), which offers an extensive running commentary on moral values and political behaviour in archaic lyric poetry. He is currently working on the ancient quarrel between philosophy and poetry.

Andrea Rodighiero is Associate Professor of Greek Language and Literature at the University of Verona. He is the author of several articles relating to Greek literature, Attic drama and its tradition. His books include commentaries on Sophocles' *Oedipus at Colonus* (1998) and on *Women of Trachis* (2004), *Una serata a Colono: Fortuna del secondo Edipo* (2007), *Generi lirico-corali nella produzione drammatica di Sofocle* (2012), and *La tragedia greca* (2013).

Adele Scafuro is Professor of Classics in the Dept. of Classics at Brown University (Providence, RI, USA) where she has taught since 1983. She is the author of *The Forensic Stage, Settling Disputes in Graeco-Roman Comedy* (CUP 1997, 2000, 2004), co-editor of *The Oxford Handbook of Greek and Roman Comedy*, and Series Editor (Greek side) of *Brill Studies in Greek and Roman Epigraphy*.

Andreas Serafim is a specialist in Greek rhetoric and performance criticism, with a Ph.D. from University College London (2013). He is a Postdoctoral Fellow in Classics at the University of Cyprus. He is a specialist in Greek oratory/rhetoric and performance, with a wide range of other research interests, including ancient Greek religion, reception, linguistics, sex/gender theories, and other interdisciplinary theories (such as humour theories and persuasion).

Margarita Sotiriou is Assistant Professor of Ancient Greek Literature. She is the author of *Pindarus Homericus* (Göttingen, 1998). Her publications focus on archaic lyric poetry, mainly choral song, its poetics, performance and reperformance, as well as its reception and intertextuality. She is currently working on an annotated edition of the Epinician Odes of Bacchylides.

Eleni Volonaki is Assistant Professor of Ancient Greek Literature in the Department of Philology, University of Peloponnese. She has published on Athenian Law, forensic, deliberative and epideictic oratory and rhetoric, Hellenistic poetry, Epic poetry and social values. She is the author of a commentary on two speeches of Lysias 13 (*Against Agoratos*) and 30 (*Against Nikomachos*). She is currently working on the annotated editions of Apollodoros' *Against Evergos and Mnesiboulos* and Lykourgos' *Against Leokrates*.

General Index

Achilleis 181
achoreutos 24
Acropolis 107, 249
Admetus 128–132, 134–135, 137–138, 140–145, 156, 396
adoleschia 309
advocate 136, 161, 210
adynaton 135, 141, 173
Aeschines 189, 283–284, 332, 344, 349–350, 352, 354–356, 360, 408, 412
Aeschylus 20, 30, 105, 108, 147–148, 150, 153, 167, 177, 181–182, 186, 188–189, 191–192, 228, 248, 251–254, 256–262, 264, 284, 329, 332–333, 342, 370, 373, 389–395, 397, 399, 401, 403, 405–407, 409, 411–413, 415–419, 421, 423
Agamemnon 4, 14, 20–21, 27, 85, 158, 185, 188–190, 192, 195–199, 201, 211, 227, 316–317, 319, 329, 343, 414
agathos 239, 250, 253, 254, 255, 262–263, 309
agelaioi sophistai 305–307, 309, 311, 313, 315, 317, 319, 321
agnoêma 40
agon 71–72, 84–90, 85, 88, 92, 96–98, 128, 166, 261, 370–372
agora 72, 81, 108, 111, 251, 253, 293
Agorakritos 72, 81
aidoios 407
aidos 403, 407
alazoneuesthai 309
Alcestis 123, 127–130, 132–134, 137–138, 143, 145–146, 156, 174, 371
Alcibiades 250–251, 257–258, 262
Alexandros 83–90, 92–96
Alexis' *Epiklēros* 376
Alope 87–88
amynia 106
anachronism 235
anaideia, anaides 407
anakrisis 413
anapaests 22, 24–26, 106
Anaxandrides' *Io* 46

ancient quarrel 249, 251, 253, 255–257, 259, 261–267, 423
Andromache 84, 90, 202–204, 207, 212, 225
angelia 21
anhosiotaton 11
antepirrhema 113, 115, 118, 249, 262
antilogiai 84
Antiope 87, 90–92, 95
Antiphanes' *Epiklēros* 376
Antiphanes' *Homopatrioi* 376
Antiphon 10, 90–91, 93–94, 173, 181, 184, 207, 209–214, 330, 332–335, 339, 357, 369, 411
antiquity 60, 64, 68, 72, 151, 179, 181, 248, 267, 281, 300, 324, 326–327, 361, 365, 367, 417, 421–422
Aphrodite 4, 17, 19, 45, 204
Apollo 59, 128, 130–135, 137–138, 172, 183, 190, 200, 256, 273–274, 329, 389, 391, 394, 414
Archeptolemus 184
Archedamian War 102, 104, 109, 114
Areopagus 169, 171, 182–183, 186, 389–398, 400–403, 406–412, 416
arete 106, 251, 254, 263–264, 306
Argive Assembly 182, 184, 188, 200, 205
Argos 183–184, 188, 234, 240, 242, 271, 392–393, 396, 414, 416
aristocracy 101, 103, 111–112, 116–117, 317, 323, 335
aristocrat 102, 107, 110–111, 117
Aristophanes 3, 17, 34, 46, 60, 65, 71–73, 75, 77, 79–81, 101–102, 104–107, 112, 115–118, 123, 125, 176, 216–217, 242–246, 249, 251–257, 260–264, 283, 332–335, 343, 368, 391, 405, 412
Aristophanes of Byzantium 65
Aristotle 7–8, 11, 21, 30–31, 43, 54, 61, 67–68, 74, 95–97, 126, 148, 151, 153–155, 158–159, 161, 172, 174, 177, 254–255, 260, 265, 269, 279, 281, 283, 298, 306–307, 309, 324–326, 329, 333–

334, 336, 341–343, 370, 372, 392–393, 400–404, 406, 409–410, 419, 421–423
Aristotle's *Constitution of the Athenians* (*Athenaion Politeia*) 392–393, 397–406
arthra 23
artless proofs 21
Assembly 71–72, 74, 79, 123, 187, 234, 243–246, 284, 305, 319, 357, 391, 394–397, 403, 407, 409, 411–412, 416
asyndeton 28, 74–75
ate 24, 113
Athena 15, 23, 103, 107, 118, 273, 288, 379, 390–391, 395, 406–408, 411–415
Athena Polias 288
Athenian Boule 186
Athenian families 73, 377, 380, 383, 385
Athenian justice 184
Athens 19, 35, 41–42, 48, 55, 58, 61–64, 71, 81, 101–107, 109, 112, 116–117, 125, 146, 153, 159, 164, 167, 169, 176, 182–184, 186, 188–190, 207, 215, 218, 220, 234–235, 237–239, 242–245, 250–251, 253–254, 258–259, 261, 263, 271, 274–278, 282, 286–288, 291–293, 297, 299, 305, 307, 319, 329, 332, 335, 343, 347, 350–351, 353, 356, 366, 368, 375–376, 378–379, 385–386, 389, 391–393, 395, 398–399, 403–405, 407–411, 415–416
Attic law 90
atykhēma 40
audience 3, 5–6, 8, 12, 23–24, 26, 33–35, 54, 56, 58, 61, 63–64, 80–81, 84, 105, 111–112, 114–117, 123, 126, 138, 144, 154–155, 158, 161, 164, 166, 169, 174, 176, 181, 186, 206, 213–214, 217, 233–246, 249–250, 253, 256, 261, 264, 269, 274, 278, 281–283, 287–293, 295–299, 306, 310–312, 317–318, 321–322, 330, 332, 339, 347–350, 352–360, 366, 376, 378–379, 385–386, 391
autochthones, autochthonia 63, 291–292
axiotes 106

Bacchylides' *Ode* 10 269, 277
bad (κακός) 37, 44, 54, 67, 74, 161, 171, 176, 203–204, 241, 249–250, 255–259, 262, 273, 320, 353, 382, 401
Bakchylides 241
basanos (examination under torture) 210
basileus 414–415
bastardy 387
Battle of Marathon 253–254
Bdelycleon 73, 245
Berlage, J. 126
Brown, P. 49, 63
Buxton, R.G.A. 96

captatio benevolentiae 7–8, 18, 89–90
Cartledge, P. 72, 335
Cassandra 19, 83
catharsis 290
cavalry 101–102, 104–107, 109–110, 114–118
Chabrias 54
Chaeronea 284–286, 292–293
chalepon 305
characterization 3, 5, 18, 23, 25, 54, 74, 176, 308, 344, 348, 379
chaunos 308
Chorus 15, 17, 22, 25–26, 72, 77–80, 83, 85, 87–88, 95, 101–105, 107, 109–118, 138, 143, 159, 166, 170, 238, 245, 249, 274
chrestoi 250–251, 253–254, 257, 261, 267
Chrysis 37–40, 42–45, 49–57, 59–60, 381–382
Cimon 102, 108, 110, 114, 118, 392–393, 395–400, 403, 416
citizenship 35, 43–44, 53, 55, 57, 63–64, 352, 380
City Dionysia 233, 238
Cleaenetus 103, 110–111, 117
Cleon 71–81, 101–102, 105, 110–112, 116–118, 164
Clytemnestra 3, 157, 183–185, 190, 192, 195–199, 211, 214, 329, 391
Collard, C. 3, 6–14, 16–22, 27, 83–86
comedy 33–36, 41–43, 45–46, 48–50, 54, 59–65, 71–72, 81, 101, 106, 123,

181, 191, 204, 233, 236, 240–246, 252–254, 261–262, 264, 312, 331, 333–335, 339–340, 343–344, 375–378, 380, 382–383, 385, 412, 416
comic poets 246, 375–376, 386
communis opinio 124
community 10, 38, 60, 62, 65, 85, 93, 96, 154, 167, 185, 252, 256, 262, 269, 277, 319, 347–348, 386, 406–407, 410
Conacher, D. 84, 126–127, 153, 156–157, 264, 366, 368–370, 372
constitutiones 128
Corinth 44, 113–116, 118, 197
Corinthians 104, 115
Coryphaius 105
Creon 155–173, 175–176, 194, 197–198, 206, 330, 351, 390
Cusset, C. 47–48
Cyclops 117, 130–131

Dale, A. M. 26, 174
Danaos 234
Daos 378
defence 18, 28, 38, 101, 106, 109, 112, 114, 158, 164, 168–169, 173, 190, 193, 195, 206, 208, 256, 295, 314, 339, 354, 360, 368, 370, 390–391, 399
Deiphobos 83–86
Dekeleia 249
delivery 72–73, 281–282, 287, 293, 348
demagogue 71–72, 79, 81, 102, 240–242, 254, 330, 399, 401–402
deme of Cydathenaeum 72
Demeas 35–40, 42–45, 47, 50–61, 381–382
democracy 63–65, 81, 104, 110–112, 116–118, 123, 176, 184, 188, 233, 235–237, 239–246, 251, 263, 278, 292, 317, 366, 400–404, 406, 410–411, 416
democratic ideology 64, 101, 126, 393, 415
dēmos 72
Demosthenes 72, 74–75, 153, 164, 166, 174, 189, 220, 283–285, 292–293, 317, 319, 330–335, 344, 347–360, 375, 379, 389, 407–408, 411
Desiderius Erasmus of Rotterdam 125

diabolē 54
didaskalia 342
diegesis 5, 8–9
Dik, H. 89, 170
dikaios 263, 414, 416
dikaiosyne 263, 315–316
dikastai (see *judges*) 406, 408, 410, 413
dike 187, 407, 415–416
dike phonou 187
Diocles 187
Diogenianus of Pergamon 33
Dionysus 249, 251–252, 255, 257–262, 264, 350, 359
discourse 3, 35, 55, 64–65, 84, 93, 96, 102, 104, 153, 155, 162–163, 176, 218, 245, 287, 306, 314, 316, 318, 339, 347, 365, 369, 371, 389, 393
distichomythia 5–6, 28
Dobrov, G. W. 117
Draco 184, 186–188, 220
drama 1, 3, 6, 29–31, 66, 69, 71, 84, 86, 96, 98–99, 123–124, 127–128, 131, 133, 147–151, 153–155, 172, 174, 176–179, 182–183, 188, 206, 216, 229–230, 233, 235–237, 239, 241, 243, 245–248, 256, 265, 267, 269, 281, 303, 329–331, 333–335, 337, 345, 347, 361–363, 365, 367–373, 384, 387, 412, 415–418, 421–423
drama of *logos* 84
dramatic elements 339, 341, 343
dramatic performance 124, 237, 286
dramatis personae 124, 127
Dubischar, M. 85, 126–127, 165
Duchemin, J. 88–89, 126–127, 171

Easterling, P. E. 124, 156, 163, 165, 350, 359, 367–368, 370
Edwards, L. C. 252, 321
eisangelia (impeachment) 187
Ekklesia 72
ekphrasis 4
Canetti, E. 24
emotional proximity 19
emotions 37, 46, 48–50, 54, 58, 61, 65, 124, 166, 171, 200, 281–282, 290, 299, 354
engklema 413

envy 52, 106, 112, 251, 308, 310, 317
epainos 106, 269, 287, 292, 297
ephebes 238, 299, 411
epic 46, 53, 108, 191, 233–235, 282, 287, 294–295, 298–299, 322, 361, 365–366, 368, 370–372, 421, 424
epideictic display 286
epieikeia 309
Epinician Odes 269, 309
epinician rhetoric 269, 271, 273, 275, 277
epirrhematic syzygy 103, 118
epirrhemes 103
epitaphios logos 243, 287, 292–293
Erechtheion 288
Erinyes 188, 391, 413–415
erôs 41–42, 45–46, 58–59
erotic epigram 46
erôtos anangkais 40
Eubulus' *Danae, Lacones, Leda* 46
eulogy 106–107, 113–114, 117, 137
Eumolpus 288–289, 292–293
eunoia 315, 319
Euripides 3, 15, 18, 20, 24–26, 34, 46–47, 61, 83–84, 86, 88–92, 96, 123, 125–129, 145–146, 154–157, 165–167, 173–174, 181–182, 186–189, 191, 194, 197, 199–201, 204, 212, 215, 220, 234, 238–242, 244, 249, 251–264, 282–285, 287–295, 315, 330–331, 333, 342–343, 354, 365, 367–372, 389, 415
euthynai 395, 397, 407–408, 416
exarchos 87
exordium 7, 17, 89, 141, 144, 157
extemporaneity 282, 286

fathers 49, 103, 106–107, 109–111, 113–115, 117, 144, 157, 160, 183, 185, 198, 201, 291, 340
female characters 3
figura etymologica 142, 169
fleet 104, 116, 190, 259, 394–395, 399–400, 402, 405
forensic oratory 9, 85, 160–161, 175, 281, 284, 347, 377, 407–408
Fortune 13–16, 18, 23, 256, 258, 271, 277, 319
Funeral oration 101–103, 106–108, 253, 292, 297, 309, 329, 334, 406

Gaddis, W. 347
gametê 57
gestures 15, 282, 293
glossa 21
gnômê 90, 142–143
gnômês bouleumasin 40
Goldhill, S. 35, 63, 84, 124, 127, 156, 164, 238, 242, 260, 292, 393, 416
Gorgias' *Helen* 39–40
graphe asebeias 252
Great Dionysia 127, 237, 288, 342
Greek Anthology 46
Greek Epigram 46
Greek magical papyri 47
Greek tragedy 4, 96, 123–125, 127, 129, 131, 133, 135, 137, 139–141, 143, 145–146, 153–154, 163, 171, 174–175, 390
Griffin, J. 235
gruzein 72

Hades 128, 130, 135, 137–138, 196, 249, 252, 257, 261
Halliwell, S. 127, 153, 158, 160–161, 164–166, 171, 244, 259, 262
hamartia 35
Hecuba 3–5, 7, 9, 11, 13, 15, 17, 19–23, 25–27, 29–31, 83–86, 95–96, 150, 192, 197, 199, 206–207, 212, 331, 369–373
heiress (*epiklēros*) 377–378
Helen 7, 10, 34, 38–40, 42, 53, 85, 183–184, 197–199, 204, 208, 211, 218, 309, 314–315, 318, 342
Hellenistic kingdoms 65
helping friends and harming enemies 177, 259
Heracles 30, 78, 96, 129, 137, 146, 149, 314–316, 319, 423
Heraclidae 118, 207, 371
Hermeneus 21
Hermione 183, 202–204
Herms, mutilation of the 215
Herodotus 10, 177, 194, 223, 227, 230, 258, 329, 337, 391, 394–396, 400, 404, 407, 411, 417

heroic world 233–234
heroism 145, 244, 250, 293, 299
hetairai 33, 42, 53–56, 184, 385
historical narrative 106
Höhne, C. 126
Homer 45, 108, 146, 155, 163, 174, 204, 239, 252–253, 255–256, 260–261, 263–264, 277, 282–284, 287–288, 294–295, 306, 308, 312, 322, 330, 332–333, 347, 352, 366, 368–369, 372
homicide law 12, 184, 188
homologoumene arete 306
hoplites 104, 106–107, 110–111, 115–116
horizein 12
hosion 11
hybris 54, 273, 277, 407
hyperbaton 89, 96, 170
hypocrites 287
hypokrisis 282, 287
hypophora 77
hypostasis 142
hypotheticals 191–192, 194–195, 200, 205–207, 209–214, 216, 218, 220–221, 225, 230

Ibycus 46
idiotēs 284
Ilium 25, 414
imaginary lawcourts 181, 218, 220
imitation 167, 290, 321, 323, 333
inheritance law 386, 422
innovation 61, 292, 306, 311, 313–316, 321–322, 367
interiorization of virtue 264
intertextuality 181–182
Iphigeneia 181
Iphigeneia, the sacrifice of 189
isocola 76
Isocrates 90, 174, 283, 305–322, 330, 332, 334–335, 344, 403

judges 39, 54–55, 190, 211, 217, 219, 244, 246, 262, 271, 281–283, 286–296, 298–299, 339–341, 353–354, 357, 397, 400, 403, 405–408, 413–415

kataboê 72
Khaireas 378
Kleisthenes 233
Kleostratos 378
Knights 71–81, 101–102, 105–109, 112–113, 117, 242–246, 254
kolakeuein 75
Kratinus' *Dionysalexandros* 243
kraugē, krazein 72

lalein 72
Lamian War 233
Lape, S. 35, 63
larungizein 72
laudandi 114, 117
Lenaia 233, 375
Leocrates 281–287, 289, 291–293, 295, 297–299, 331–332, 397
Life of Sophocles 163
Lloyd, M. 84–85, 88–90, 94, 126–127, 165–166, 193–194, 212, 215, 365, 367–368, 371–372
logographers 283, 334
logon paideia 305
logos 26, 84, 243, 254, 269, 287, 292–293, 366, 368–369
loidoria 54
lyricism 26

MacIntosh, F. 245
Marathon 106–107, 115–116, 253–254, 295, 297, 396
marriage 33–34, 41, 48, 50, 55, 58–65, 73, 168, 192–193, 195, 197–198, 203, 220, 380, 404, 410
martyres (witnesses) 210
Mastronarde, D. J. 5–6, 28, 84–85, 90, 124, 165, 365–368, 370
megalophōnia 72
megalophrosyne 319
megalopsychos 308
mellesis 261
Melos 26, 240, 242
Menander 33–37, 39, 41, 43, 45–51, 53, 55–57, 59–65, 204, 343, 376–378, 380–381, 385–386

Menelaus 7, 85, 95, 158, 163, 174, 182–185, 196–199, 201–202, 204, 211, 218, 227, 342
Menestheus 108, 118
merit 91, 96, 106–107, 110, 142, 144, 356
metabole 15–16, 19, 22
metapoetic 24–25
metatheatrical 25
metatheatrics 181
Middle Comedy 34, 42, 46, 376–377, 382, 385
mikrologia 309
Miller, Th. 126
mimesis 255–256, 311
Minos 193, 206, 357
mistresses 377, 380
mochtheroi 253–254
moral values 96, 143, 249, 262–264, 270, 287
morality 34, 37, 45, 47, 53–55, 58, 67, 97, 177, 262, 264–265, 279, 306, 324, 367
Moschion 34–45, 47, 49–51, 53–61, 343, 381–382
Mossman, J. 3
murder 5, 9, 52–54, 62–63, 172–173, 181–183, 185, 187–191, 193–207, 209, 211, 213–215, 217–221, 223, 225, 227, 378, 389, 391, 414
Muse 24, 271, 273, 275–276
Myrmidons 181
Mysteries, profanation of the 251
Mytilenean debate 76

Nagy, G. 124, 239
narratio 137, 141–142, 144
Naupactus 105
Nemesis 72
New Comedy 34–36, 41, 43, 45–46, 48–50, 59, 61, 204, 339–340, 343, 375–377, 385
Nicias 72, 74, 116, 239
Nikai 118
Nikeratos 36, 54–62
nomos 4, 9–13, 185–186, 189, 252, 415
nosêma 40
nothos (bastards) 380

Oedipus 149, 153, 155, 157–167, 169–173, 175–179, 194–195, 201–202, 206, 229, 342, 390, 421, 423
oikos 34, 43–44, 50, 53–57, 59–62, 64–65, 93, 95, 378
Old Attic Comedy 101, 106
Olympians 103, 130, 132, 137, 217
Onomacles 184
opsis 23, 281
oratio recta 72, 75, 205, 215
oratory 9, 26, 35, 51, 54, 64, 71–72, 85, 90, 123–125, 127, 129, 131, 133, 135, 137, 139, 141, 143, 145–146, 155, 160–161, 163–164, 167, 169, 172, 175, 191–192, 194, 207–208, 214–215, 218, 220, 245, 253, 269, 278, 281–287, 292, 299, 303, 313, 322, 329–330, 332, 339, 347–348, 350–351, 367, 370, 377, 393, 407–408
Orestes 21, 154, 181–192, 198–202, 204–205, 207, 211, 215, 217–218, 222, 239–243, 263, 329, 341–343, 371, 389–392, 413–415
Orphic myth 46
ostrakophoria 251

paideia 34, 305, 404
palaistra 110–111
Palamedes 83, 85, 90, 96, 208–209
pallakê 43, 50, 55–57
palliatae 33
Panathenaicus 305–307, 316–317, 319, 321–322
Panhellenic values 128
Paphlagon 72, 74–81, 102, 106, 110–111, 116, 118
para to prosēkon 305
parabasis 101, 103, 105–106, 112, 117–118, 245, 249, 251, 253, 257–258, 261
parakatalogē 153
Parthenon Frieze 101, 112
Pasiphae 193, 206, 213, 224
past 13, 15–16, 22, 25, 101, 103, 105, 107, 109–111, 113, 115, 117, 135, 141, 163, 172, 183, 188, 192, 194, 206, 218, 235, 241, 255–256, 262, 269, 271, 278, 281–

283, 285, 287, 289, 291–293, 295–297, 299, 311, 313, 317, 348, 354, 359, 367
pathos 20, 26, 269, 281, 287, 299
patrios politeia (ancestral constitution) 402
Peitho 4, 19–21, 96
Peloponnesian War 102, 192, 218, 259, 288, 351, 398, 402–403
peplos 107, 342
performance 3–4, 7, 26, 28, 35, 61, 64, 71, 73, 75, 77–79, 81, 123–124, 128, 153–154, 165, 170, 174, 181, 233, 235, 237–238, 250, 269, 275, 278, 281–283, 285–287, 290, 292, 295–299, 306, 329, 349–351, 357–358, 360, 376
Pericles 55, 63, 107, 110, 112, 114, 259, 310, 329, 389, 392–393, 397, 399–403, 405–406, 410
peroratio 9, 144
personae loquentes 174
persuasion 3–4, 17–19, 21, 39, 51, 91, 96, 158, 160, 165–166, 174, 269, 283, 286, 299, 319, 347–348
pharmakos 250–251
Pheres 128–129, 131, 135, 138, 141–145
philanthropia 315
philia 19, 41, 137
Phillip II 285–286
philosophy 191, 249, 251, 253, 255–257, 259, 261–264, 305, 322, 347
philotimia 315–316
phōnē miarē 72
Phormio 105, 110, 116–118
phronesis 313, 315–317
Phrygians 181
Phrynichus 184, 187–188, 335, 395
Phrynichus' *Capture of Miletos* 244
phtonos 106
Pindar 12, 136, 241, 269, 274, 311
pisteis 21, 158, 281, 298
pisteis atechnoi 21
Plangon 34–38, 40–41, 49–51, 53, 55, 57–61, 382
Plato *Phaedrus* 46
Plato *Symposium* 46

Plutarch 33–35, 62, 108, 174, 238–239, 276, 330, 335, 368, 392, 396–397, 404, 411, 416
Pnyx 72, 79–81, 412
poetic quotations 283–287, 295, 298–299, 330–334
poetry 46, 123, 126, 153–155, 163, 168, 175, 191, 233, 249, 251–257, 259–264, 269, 278, 282–285, 287, 293–299, 305–307, 309, 311–315, 317, 319, 321–322, 329–330, 332–334, 366, 368–372
polis 35, 44, 53, 55, 57, 61, 63–65, 95, 101, 184, 233, 235, 238, 243, 245–246, 254, 257, 264, 269, 271, 273, 275, 277, 292, 317, 393, 416
political behaviour 96, 249, 258, 264
politicians 81, 111, 118, 237, 243–246, 262, 284, 335, 350, 354, 360, 391, 395, 402, 404, 409, 411
politics 46, 67, 71–73, 81–82, 118–120, 146–147, 178, 181, 231, 235, 238, 241, 243, 245–248, 250, 253–254, 261, 264–265, 267, 279, 298, 307, 317, 320, 323, 325, 336, 350, 352, 361, 367, 375, 392, 394, 398–404, 406, 409–410, 415, 417–419
polysyndeton 141
Polydorus 199
Polymestor 4, 6, 8–9, 11, 18–19, 192, 199, 212
Polyxena 9, 196, 199
poneroi 250–251, 253–254, 261, 264, 267
Poseidon 15, 22–23, 78, 103, 107, 113, 116–118, 271, 288
praise 33, 101, 103, 105–107, 109, 111, 113–117, 159, 163, 167, 169, 256, 260, 262, 271–272, 274, 277–278, 287, 289–291, 294–297, 299, 309–316, 318, 321, 390–393, 395, 406, 408, 411
Praxagora 289–290
Praxithea 191, 198, 226, 285, 288–293, 295
Priam 22, 25, 83–85, 87–89, 92–95
probationes artificiales 140
prodosia 235
progonoi 106, 115

prohedria 110
prokatalepsis 6, 142
prooimion 7–8, 18
prosklēsis (challenge) 210
prostates tou demou 251
prothesis 5, 7, 90
psychagogein 312
Pylos 73, 102, 116–118

quaestiones 128
quarrel 44, 86, 131, 137, 249, 251, 253, 255–257, 259, 261–267, 423

real women 3
reception 61, 181, 215, 239, 345, 365, 367, 369, 371, 373, 376, 421–424
reductio ad absurdum 141–143, 215, 371
reperformance 228, 265, 275, 424
representative democracy 64–65
revaluation 263, 423
revenge 8–9, 181–183, 185, 187, 189–197, 199–201, 203–207, 209, 211, 213, 215, 217, 219, 221, 223, 225, 227, 353
reversal 199, 210, 252, 261, 354
rhēsis 88
rhētor 283
rhetoric 1, 3–5, 7, 9, 11, 13, 15, 17, 19–21, 23, 25–27, 29–31, 33, 35, 37, 39, 41, 43, 45, 47, 49, 51, 53–55, 57, 59–61, 63, 65–69, 71–72, 74, 81, 83–85, 87, 89–99, 120, 125, 141, 147–151, 153–155, 157–158, 161, 163, 165–166, 171, 174–179, 182, 189–190, 199, 207, 215–216, 230–231, 260, 269, 271, 273–275, 277, 279, 281, 283, 300–301, 305–307, 309–313, 315, 317, 319–321, 323–327, 329, 333–334, 336–337, 347–349, 351, 360–362, 365–373, 416, 418, 421–424
rhetoric of sincerity 347–349
rhetorical aporia 89–90
rhetorical drama 84
rhetorical means 96, 129, 269, 339, 341, 343
rhetorical performances 73, 174, 350
rhetorical techniques 125, 305, 366–369, 372
rhetorical *topoi* 186, 281

Rhodes, P. 125, 235–236, 238, 246, 392–393, 395, 398–401, 403–404, 408, 410–411, 415
romantic character 48
romantic love 35, 48, 50
Rudd, N. 35, 48–50
rule of law 389, 402–403, 411, 415–417, 422

Salamis 106–107, 115–116, 330, 334, 394–395, 401–402
Sansone, D. 6, 17, 91, 125–127, 155, 164, 167, 172, 189, 220
satire 101, 116, 118, 243
Sausage-seller 72, 74, 76–81, 106, 111
schemata sensum 129
Schultz, P. 117–118
Second Messinian War 296
self-presentation 15, 26, 277, 356
sēmeion 94
senex amator 43
Seriphians 243
sincerity 309, 347–349, 357, 360
Sisyphos 83
slander 89–90, 171, 217, 264, 305, 307
Solon 43, 164, 169, 178, 260, 269, 272, 274, 276–279, 330–332, 361, 401, 403, 405, 411
Solygeia 104, 109, 115–116
sophia 92, 260
Sophilus' *Tyndareos* or *Leda* 46
sophisticated 176, 194, 249, 260
Sophocles 61, 97, 146–150, 153, 155–156, 159, 161, 163, 165–167, 170–171, 173–179, 181, 194, 201, 220, 229–230, 284, 330, 332–333, 342, 370–371, 373, 390, 416, 421, 423
Sostratus 48–49
Sparta 116, 176, 389, 392
speaker 4, 8, 22, 27, 71, 76, 79, 84–85, 89–91, 93, 95, 129, 141–142, 144, 146, 155–156, 158, 160, 165–166, 174–175, 194, 204, 208, 210–214, 217–219, 240–241, 245, 252, 260–261, 275, 281–282, 284, 286, 289, 293, 310, 313, 320, 332–333, 347–350, 354, 356–358, 377–385, 411–412

spectators 26, 50, 59, 64, 74, 112, 117,
    164, 269, 283, 290, 356, 359
spoudaia 255, 262
stēlē 186
sthenos 11
stichomythia 9, 13, 27–28, 76, 80
Stoa Poikile 186
strategoi 110, 118
symbouleuein 320
symboulos 320

tekhnês paraskeuais 40
tekmērion 93
Terence 37
Thanatos 128, 132, 135, 137
theatre 31, 48, 69, 81, 84, 99, 105, 110,
    151, 165, 167, 178, 183, 229, 233–238,
    242–248, 264, 266, 282–283, 293,
    301, 332, 348–362, 382, 387, 422
Theocritus' *Idylls* 46
theology 118
Theoric fund 236
Theorus 113, 118
Thermopylae 297
Theseus 19, 108, 155, 158–159, 162–165,
    167–168, 175–176, 193, 206, 314–315,
    375
Thirty 213–214, 251, 332–333, 398, 402,
    405
Thomson, D. 124, 126
thōpeuein 75
thorubos 71, 359
thrulein 72
Thucydides 71–73, 76, 93, 104, 110, 114–
    115, 164, 188, 192, 218, 242–243, 245,
    258, 260, 329, 334, 391, 395–396, 398,
    400, 407
topography 20

topos 40, 90, 107, 109, 112, 171, 214, 357
tragedy 3–4, 14, 22, 30, 48, 61, 84, 86,
    96–99, 119, 123–129, 131, 133, 135, 137,
    139–141, 143, 145–151, 153–155, 161,
    163–165, 171, 173–179, 181, 183, 191–
    192, 194, 205, 207–208, 214–215, 218,
    220, 228–229, 233, 235–236, 238–239,
    241–244, 246–248, 252, 255, 257, 262–
    268, 283–284, 287–293, 298–301, 312,
    331–333, 336, 339–340, 342–343, 345,
    353–354, 361–362, 373, 389–391, 393,
    412, 415, 418, 421–423
tragic women 3
trial–debate 83–85, 88, 90, 93, 95–96
tricolon 15, 95
Trojan Women 3–4, 7, 16, 18, 22, 25–26,
    83, 85, 87, 96, 240, 242, 354, 368, 371
Troy 15, 20, 22–23, 39, 83, 93, 108, 184,
    203, 208, 316, 358
Tyche 15, 183
tykhês agreumasin 40
Tyndareus 183–187, 191, 201–202, 204,
    217
Typho 117
Tyrtaeus 282, 287, 296–297, 332

vengeance 7–8, 131, 202, 414

Warham, W. 125
Wasps 73–74, 102, 242, 245, 254, 283,
    333–335, 405
Wilson, P. 237–238, 393
wives 33, 43–44, 52, 62, 215, 377, 380

Zeitlin, F. 14, 182, 243
Zeus 78, 130–132, 135–136, 146, 191,
    271, 273, 315

Index Locorum

Aelianus
Varia Historia
2.8 — 3, 83

Aeschines
Against Timarchus
30–31 — 94
141 — 284
173 — 402
81–84 — 412
On the False Embassy
1 — 414
Against Ctesiphon
154 — 237
184–185, 190 — 331

Aeschylus
Oresteia — 181, 189, 191, 263, 390–392
Agamemnon
109–157 — 97
184–227 — 197
855ff. — 329
916 — 164
1039 — 95
1501–1502 — 214
Choephoroi
543–550 — 192
994–996 — 192
212ff. — 342
Eumenides
34–116 — 391
64–93 — 391
81–82 — 190
235–243 — 391
276–298 — 391
289–291 — 392
397–414 — 391
408 — 413
415–469 — 391
416–417 — 413
419 — 413
421 — 413
425 — 413
426 — 413
427 — 414–415
427 — 414–415
428 — 414
436–441 — 414
445–453 — 414
447 — 94
455–459 — 414
459–69 — 414
470–472 — 414
470–489 — 391
481–484 — 415
485 — 94
585 — 164
657–666 — 190
662 — 94
669–673 — 392
689–706 — 391
754–777 — 392
Persians — 05, 153, 392, 395, 355–371, 395
951–952 — 105
Seven Against Thebes
1 — 163

Alexis
Agonis — 34
fr. 2 — 34
Apokoptomenos — 34
fr. 20 — 34
Epiklēros — 376
Alex. Fragmenta — 376–377
Epitropos
Alex. Fragmenta — 376–377
Isostasion — 54
fr. 103 — 54, 334
Syntrechontes — 34
fr. 217 — 34
Traumatias — 34
fr. 236 — 34

Anaxilas
Neottis — 42, 54
frr. 21–22 — 54

Anaximenes
36.44   214

Anaximenes Lamps.
Rhetoric ad Alexandrum
18 (1432b11–14)   6

Andocides
On the Mysteries   215, 417
119   216
48–53   215
50   215
51   215
53   215

Anonymous
Life of Sophocles   163
Vita Aristophanes
XVIII.50–58   61
Greek Anthology   46

Antiphanes
Homopatrioi   376
Antiph. Fragmenta   376–377
Hydria   42, 54
fr. 210   54

Antiphon
Against the
Stepmother   207, 333
fr. 44(a)   10
1, 9   209
2   90
2, 13   209
3, 2   209
7   209
11   209–210
11–12   209
Tetralogies
Anonymous Prosecution for Murder
2.1–6   173
2.2.12   207
2.2, 4–5   209
2.3.11   209, 211
2.4,6   209

The Second Tetralogy:
Prosecution for Accidental Homicide
3.2.1   90
3.1   93
3.1,4   202
3.1.6   214
3.1,6; 3.2,3–4; 3.2,6; 3.4,2   209
3.2.2   212
3.3   93
On the Murder of Herodes
14   411
32   209
52   209
61.1   94
74   209
74–75   210–211
84   93, 209
93   209
On the Choreutes   207, 209–211
7   90
27   210–211
47   93
48   209

Antiphon the Sophist
DK87 B97   91

Apollonius
Argonautica   46

Archias
7.191.5   91
7.641.2   91
9.439.2   91
16.153   91

Aristophanes
Acharnians   71, 118, 243–245, 247, 253
67   244
134ff.   118
184, 236, 295, 341–346   101
377–382, 502–503   245
593–622   111
633   106
676–677   106
696–697   104

Babylonians	243, 245	577	109, 112
Birds		579	110
348	101	595–610	113
364	101	654–656	78
Clouds	3, 103, 254, 260, 264, 335	741–742	110
		748–749	80
31	109	766	110–111
534–562	117	781	104
575–576	106	788	111
689–692	109	817–819	110
985–986	104	836–840	91
991	103	855	102
1366	260	985–996	79
1397–1398	91	1000–1050	80
Ecclesiazusae	46, 71	1265–1266	114
877–1111	46	1300–1315	110, 112
1055–1056	214	1334	104
Frogs	107, 123, 244, 247, 249–250, 255–256, 259–266, 368	1369–1372	104
		fr. 47	110
		Kokalos	34, 60
689	247	Lemnian Women	343
774–776	92	fr. 373 = fr. 324 Dind.	343
1006–1012	123	Lysistrata	46, 243, 249
1026–1027	107–108	Peace	125, 242–243, 368
1455–1456	94	533–534	125
Knights	71–74, 76–78, 80–81, 101–102, 105–109, 112–113, 117, 242–247, 254	738	106
		752–760	242
		910–921	94
		Testimonia	33
46–52	111	1	61
47–49	74	Thesmophoriazusae	
50–51	75	832	94
52–57	110	Wasps	
58–60	111	54–66	117
67–68	75	74–75	109
213–218	111	225–226	101
255–257	76	383	109
344–352	76	420	101
368–374	77	466	109
395–396	77	562–570	283
415–416	74	579–580	333
428	77	661–663	405
429–431	77	684–685	107
475–479	78	711	104
511	112	923–926	102
540	110	1016	106
565–580	103	1029–1037	242

1062	101	1252a.24–1253b.23	95
1075	101	1252b9–16	61
		1253b1–1260b24	61
Aristotle		1255b30–40	95
Athenaion Politeia	393–395, 398–400, 403, 418	1273b36–41	409
		1274a6–16	401
7.2	411	1274a8–16	392
13.4	404	1274a16	402
22.2	410	1277a5–11	95
22.3–4	397	1278b–1279a	95
23–27	400	1292a3–13	400
23–28	393	1295b34–1296a21	404
23.1	394	1304a5–24	401
23.7	400	*Protrepticus*	307, 324
25.1	392, 394, 397	*On Rhetoric*	54, 74, 154, 260, 281, 283, 307, 333–334, 370, 372
25.2	394		
25.2–4	398		
26.1	398–399, 402	1354a 11ff.	54
26.2	408	1355b35–38	158
27.1	392, 397, 400	1356a1ff.	269
27.3	400, 405	1356a1–4	158
28.3	242	1356a1–13	174
29.3	402	1357b4–17	94
34.3–38.4	398	1367b14–17	305
35.2	398, 405	1375b33–1376a8	334
41.2	401	1386a17–24	159
42.1–49.5	406	1386b28–29	159
43.2–49	406	1397a31–1397b14	333
55.2–3	408	1399b16–22	334
57.2–3	414	1400b9	223
57.3	406	1401b41–46	333
63–69	406	1402a3–28	172
Nicomachean Ethics	308	1402a23–26	372
1123b 2	308	1403b16	281
1123b 8–9	308	1403b24–30	281
1127a 20–22	309	1403b26–33	355
1134b18–21	11	1403b34–35	7
1156b 1–6	43	1404a	283
Poetics	21, 126, 153, 283, 341–342	1404a1–8	281
		1404b5	370
1449a23–28	153	1406b24–1407a13	333
1450b7–8	126	1408b9–10	161
1451b23–26	283	1408b30–31	154
1452b	341	1408b33–35	153
1454b	341	1411a1–1411b20	334
Politics	81–82, 392, 400–403, 409–410	1413b14–28	355
		1413b31–1414a8	74

1415a24–25	7	243	330
1415a35s	8	245	330
Rhetoric to Alexander		247	330
29	89	255	330
		302	407

Athenaeus

8.347e	253	*Against Leptines*	
		10.3	94
		90	408

Bacchylides

Epinician Odes	269, 309	*Against Meidias*	
l. 35–38	276	2	407
9, 13.61, 13.179	276	46	407
10	269	150	167
		62	407
		107	407

Cicero

De Inventione		109	407
1.16.21	89	151	407
De Oratore		185	407
1.119	89	194	407
2.240	344	201	407
2.244	344	*Against Androtion*	
3.28	344	1–2	219
Rhetorica ad Herennium		2–3	219
1.4.6	89	8	407
		27	407
		59	407

Democritus

68 B53a	93	65	407
		68	236
		75	407

Demosthenes

Olynthiac 2		*Against Aristocrates*	389
12	164	65	389
On the Crown		99	407
2	414	101	407
22	407	144	407
190	94	168	407
267	331	207.1	94
308–309	355	*Against Timocrates*	411
On the False Embassy		7–8	219
16	407	65	407
72	407	111	407
94	354	139–42	411
175	407	183	407
184.2–4	160	218	407
206	355, 356	*Against Aristogeiton 1*	
208	355	25–26	201
216	355	*Against Boeotus 1*	
336	355	7–8	203

Against Boeotus 2
5	407
24	73

Against Macartatus
57	220

Against Eubulides
49	407

Against Theocrines
31	407

Against Neaera
33–34	54
97	331
110–111	55
112	55
122	43, 56, 62

The Funeral Speech
1–3	106
4–7	12, 106
6–11	106
7	106
9	106
10–13	106
15	106
23	106
30	103, 106
31	106
33	106
34	106

Desiderius Erasmus Roterodamus
Opus Epistolarum
188.30–31	126

Dio Chrysostom
7	63

Diodorus Siculus
12.53	207
17.11.1–14.1	293

Eubulus
Danae	46, 94
fr. 322.3	94
fr. inc. 898.5–6	94
Eub. Fragmenta	380
Kampylion	42, 54
frr. 40–41	54

Sfingokarion	91
fr. 106.1, 7	91

Eunicus
Anteia	42

Eupolis
Autolykos	92, 94
fr. 282.23–25	92
fr. 282.23–28	94
Dēmoi	
fr. 129	94
Marikas	243

Euripides
Alcestis
1–27	130
28–76	128, 133
611–612	86
614–628	138
629–672	138
673–674	143
675–705	143
790	159

Alexandros
fr. 48	84, 94
fr. 48.3–4	92
fr. 50	84, 88
fr. 55	86
fr. 60	84, 92–93
fr. 62a.9–10	86
fr. 62b.33–34	86
fr. 62i	94
frr. 49, 51, 59	85
frr. 56, 61	84

Andromache
30	89
147–273	84
183–185	90
186–191	90
334–335	212
334–351	203, 225
433–434	95
545–546	86
547–746	84
706	94
590	250

Index Locorum — **441**

Andromeda	61, 249	267–270	206, 224
52–53	249	726–727	61
Antiope	87, 90–92, 95	736–737	22
fr. 189	92	736–786	4–5, 29
fr. 200	92	736–845	4, 26
fr. 202	92	756–759	4, 26–28
fr. 206.4	90–91	806–813	22
fr. 206.4–6	90	1132–1182	372
fr. 216	95	1187	89–90
Archelaus		1187–1191	90
fr. 253	90	1195–1207	371
fr. 261	89	1217–1233	192, 212, 224
Bacchae	97	1232–1233	95
266–271	90	P. Oxy. 4557 (388.400 MP3, 2nd c.)	26
268	91	P. Oxy. 4558 (389.010 MP3, 6th c.)	26
270–271	160	P. Oxy. 4559 (389.100 MP3, 4th c.)	26
Cretans		*Helen*	10, 34, 342
438	181	55	89
fr. 472e	192	185	24
472e, 7–11	193, 206, 224	557ff.	342
472e 46–49	193	1630	89
Electra		1640	89
224ff.	342	*Heracleidae*	207, 371
415–413	181	398–419	198, 206, 215, 226
422–417	181	*Heracles*	
560ff.	342	1–5	94
899	89	134–287	87
1024–1029	197, 198, 206, 213, 215, 221	181	89
		504	89
1041–1045	198, 201, 211, 218, 221	*Hippolytus*	
		58	83, 87
1093–1096	202	176ff.	47
1201	159	376	369
1221ff.	342	378	369
1258–1263	389	386	369
Erechtheus		419–421	369
422	181	428	181
fr. 360	215	428–430	369
fr. 360.13	92	486–489	90
fr. 360.13–21, 32–41	198, 206	503	90
fr. 360.32–41	226	612	259
fr. 360.38	191	921	161
Hecuba		932–933	90
107–143	154	962–970	371
218–331	372	983–1035	193, 371
244	89	986	157
258–70	227	986–991	90

988–989	157	*Meleagros*	
1007–1012	193	fr. inc. 928b	90–91
1008–1020	173	fr. 528.2	90
1021–1024	193, 206, 224	*Orestes*	
1038–1040	90	48–50	184
1041–1044	193, 199, 206, 210, 223	283–293	200, 222
		287	92
1151–1152	86	356–455	184
Hippolytus Calyptomenos		408	181
fr. 439	90–91	440	184
fr. 439.2	91	447	184
fr. 439.3	91	467–469	184
Ion		491–541	184
837f.	89	500–503	185
Iphigenia in Aulis		507–517	201, 217, 222
313	95	512–519	185
333	90	523–525	185
378	164	526–533	184
400	164	534–541	185
405–400 (*posthumous*)	181	544–550	90
481–495	227	552–554	191
528–537	227	560	95
829	163	566–571	204, 215, 222
1115–1116	90	622	95
Iphigenia in Tauris		755–758	184
146	24	852–956	154
472–840	343	884–887	184
541	343	902ff.	241
814ff.	343	903	160
834ff.	343	934–337	205
943–975	389–390	943–945	240
1091	24	946–949	182
1362ff.	343	1102	183
		1134–1137	183
Medea		1140–1142	183
271–336	372	1152	183
368–369	372	1191–1203	183
374–375	197	1204	183
387	203	1486	183
431	181	1598	183
486–491	197, 225	1610	183
490–491	213	1613	183
548–549	94	1617	183
576–578	90	1621–1624	183
582	91	1648–1652	183
586–587	226	1650–1652	389
1323	159	1653	183

Palamedes		**Gellius**	
583–585	85	6.14.7	174
frr. 580–581	85		
fr. 583	90	**Gorgias**	
Phaethon	87	*Defence of Palamedes*	208
411	181	*Encomium of Helen*	208, 314, 325
499–500	90	6	39
526–527	90	19	40, 42
568	95	*Epitaphios*	293, 314
fr. 781.218	87	82 A27, B6, B11a.35	93
fr. 781.227–244	87		
1259–1260	92	**Herodotus**	
Phoenician Women		*The Histories*	
469–472	163	1.29.1	411
962–976	198	1.59.3	404
Phoenix	284	3.119	194, 223, 227
fr. 809	284	3.38	10
Sisyphos	83	6.21.2	245, 395
Sthenoboia	284	6.104	395
fr. 671	284	6.136	396
Suppliants	18, 234, 368, 372	7.107	399
201–204	368	7.140	394
349–358	234	7.144.1–2	400
365–369	234	7.140–142	394
381–597	87	7.143.1–2	394
399–462	167	8.40.2–41.2	394
415–416	90	8.57	394
426	90	8.74.1–83.2	395
433–434	415	8.111–112	399
437	415		
517–518	18	**Hesiod**	
600–624	154	*Theogony*	
601–609	188	120–122	45
604	188	*Works and Days*	
903	161	240–245	331
Trojan Women		240–2411	331
97	15	763–764	284, 330
98–196	22		
100	15	**Hesychius**	
153	15	α 626	91
860–1059	85	τ 521	318
914–915	7		
916–917	18	**Homer**	
967–968	90	*Homeric Hymns*	
970	94	*To Hermes*	329
1033–1035	95	4.265–274	172

Iliad

2.554	108
3.399–406	204
9.225–306	366
9.228–231	366
9.232–248	366
9.249–306	366
13.412	45
15.37–38	331
15.494–499	332
18.95–99	284, 330
18.324–329, 333–335	330
18.324–329; 148	284
18.333–335; 149	284
18.497ff.	329
23.77–91	330
23.77–91; 150	284
23.346	117

Odyssey

4.244–246	8
14.69	45
18.212 and 238	45

Hyginus

fab. 187	88

Hypereides

Against Athenogenes	40, 339
Against Timandrus	339

Inscriptions

IG I² 63, lines 13–16	405
IG I³ 102.38–47	188
IG I³ 104	186
IG I³ 1453C, lines 18–22	405
IG I³ 19, lines 1–5	406
IG I³ 34, lines 31–41	405
IG I³ 364, lines 8–9	400
IG I³ 40, lines 71–76	405
IG I³ 52B	207
IG I³ 68, lines 43–47	405
IG I³104.13–20	220
IG II² 2318, lines 10–11	392
IG II³ 292 [352/1], line 19; 320 [337/6], lines 11–14, 17–19, 24–25	391

Isaeus

On the estate of Pyrrhos	382
3.13–14	383
On the estate of Kiron	383
8. 21–22	384
8.35–36	384

Isocrates

To Nicocles	312, 317
35	93
38	93
42–44	332
42–49	312
44	93
45	312
48	312
48–49	332
49	312
Panegyricus	313–314, 317–318
3	309, 314
4	313
3–6	309
9	313
10	308, 313
11–14	313
14	309
25	319
43–44	309
78	313
85	309
158	314
170	319
To Philip	307, 315–319, 321
6	319
9	321
11	318
12–13	318
14	321
14–16	319
16	321
17–23	321
18	321
20	315
32	315
36	315
37	315
55	321

57	321	*Helen*	314
68	319	23–25	314
71	319	*Panathenaicus*	305–307, 316–317,
76	315		319, 321–322
77	319	1	312, 313
79	319	11	313
81–82	320	16–19	306
82	321	18	307, 321
83	321	20	309
86	319	21	310
88	321	22	90
89	321	23	310
94	321	30	320
95	319	74	309
105	321	74–87	316
109–115	315	127	317
110	317	204	317
113	321	131–133	317
114	319	133	404
116	315	240	321
122	319	263	318, 322
127	319	271	322
129	318–319	272	322
136	319, 321	*Against the Sophists*	309
140	315	*Antidosis*	305–307, 309, 313
145	319, 321	18	90
152	321	21	414
153	315	46–48	313
154	319, 321	47	332
155	321	84	306
Areopagiticus	317, 403	141–149	321
20	403	155–157	308
37–42	403	195	309
54–55	403	209	317
56–59	321	230–236	91
On the Peace		262	309
82	237	271	317, 320
Evagoras	309, 311, 317, 320	276	305
4	311	293–294	317
6	310	*Aegineticus*	
9–11	311	51.1	94
27, 45, 46	319	*Against Euthynus*	
41	317	11.1	94
45	319		
46	319	**Longus**	
79–81	320	1.13–14	47
80	317		

Lycurgus
Against Leocrates 281–282, 285–286, 289, 293, 299, 331–332

5–6	298
12	389
31–32	298
52	410
92	332
98	289
99	289, 332
100	285
101	291
102	294
103	332
107	332
108	332
112	188
113	187
117–118	397
132	332

Against Menesaichmus 285

Lysias
On the Murder of Eratosthenes

8–13	52
24–26	52
26	52, 214
30–34	62
33	52
36	205, 215
37–38	212
47	53
47–48	205

Funeral Oration

1	334
3–66	106
6	106
17	106
17.2	167
19	11
20	106
23	106
26	106
32	106
50	106
60	334
61	106
62	106
63	106
69	106
80	106

Against Andocides

6	207, 213

Defense in the Matter of the Olive Stump

19	213
20–21	213
22	213
23	213
24	213
32	213
36	213
37	213
43	18

Accusation of Calumny

2	90

Against Theomnestus 1

2–3	214
21	219

Against Eratosthenes

3	284
28–30	213
32	213–214
34	213
47	213
48	213
52	213
98	213

Against Agoratus

16	213
20.2	94
22	213
36	213
53	213
71	188
85	213
85–87	413
90	213

Against Alcibiades 1

7	104
11–12	104
14–15	104

In Defense of Mantitheus

13	104

On The Property Of Eraton		Georgos	34, 36–37
1	90, 357	15–16	37
On The Property Of The Brother Of Nicias: Peroration		Heros	34
		Kitharistes	36
23	39	Men at Arbitration	343
On the Property of Aristophanes		92	34
1	90, 357	104	33
1–2	357	107	34
25.1	94	Perikeiromene	56, 61, 343
34	217	770ff.	343
For Polystratus		1013–1014	61
4	213	Phasma	36, 47
19	213	9–28	47
27	213	82–85	47
31	39	Plokion	34, 36
Defence Against A Charge Of Taking Bribes		Samia	33–36, 40, 42, 44–45, 47–49, 51, 53, 56–59, 61, 63–64, 66, 381, 385
5	213		
15	39		
17	213	3	58
Defense Against a Charge of Subverting the Democracy		13–18	58
		30–50	49
5	213	35–56	35
12–13	39	47–48	58
Against Nicomachus		47–53	36
15	213	50–53	58–59
17	213	80–83	44, 51
Against Diogeiton		130–142	382
1	213	272–274	58
4–18	9	344	58
Against The Subversion of the Ancestral Constitution		507–514	54
		508	55
34	218	725ff.	61

Menander

		Musonius Rufus	
Aspis	34, 61, 376–377, 385	13–14	62
540–544	61		
		Ovid	
Dyskolos	34, 48–49, 61, 65	Tristia	
494	204	2.369	34
786–790	65	P. Antinoopolis	
842–844	61	15 62	
Epitrepontes	36–37, 62, 380	P. Didot I	62
878–900	47		
Fabula Incerta	36	**Pausanias**	
1.23–24	36	Attica	
		1.2	108

22.3	19	679b	61
Arcadia		698a–699b	403
25.5	117	698b	407
43.6	19	700a–701b	403
		712d2–e5	404

PGM [Papyri Graecae Magicae]

IV.1426ff.	47	778a	95
IV.1510ff.	47	*Meno*	61
IV.2444	47	73a–b	61
IV.356ff	47	*Phaedrus*	46–47
P. Geneva 155	37	251e	47
P. Stras. 2342–44	83	273a–c	172
P.Oxy. 3650, col. I	83	*Protagoras*	407
P.Oxy. 3650, col. i, 13–14	88	318e	252
P.Oxy. 3650, col. i, 15–17	87	323c–d	407
P.Oxy. 3650, col. i, 15–21	84	325e–26a	255
P.Oxy. 3650, col. i, 15.16	86	*Republic*	254–256, 259, 264
XII.14–95	47	369c	61
XXXVI.134–160	47	377b–378e	254
		378d–e	256
		383b	256

Philetairus

Korinthiastes	42, 54	392b	256
fr. 5	54	433d–e	259
Kynagis	54	443d–e	259
fr. 8	54	607b5	255
		Symposium	46, 62

Pindar

Olympian 1 For Hieron of Syracuse Single Horse Race 476 B. C.

Plato–poet

1.18	114	Cleophon	243, 267

Plautus

Third Pythian Ode	136	*Menaechmi*	
54–59	136	239a–246b	106
Ninth Pythian Ode	274	241b	106
59–65	274	241b–c	106
		244b	106

Plato

Euthyphro		283b	103

Plutarch

4d–e	219–220	*Aristides*	396
6a–c	254	FGrHist 342 F 11 =	
Gorgias	127, 402	Plutarch *Aristides* 26	396
453a2	127	*Cimon*	238, 396–397
502d2–3	165	7.1–2	399
515e	402	7.4–6	108
516d	392, 398–399	7.5	114
519a	402	8.7–9	238
Laws		12.4–6	399
629a	296		

14.4	397	**Socrates**		
De profectibus in virtute		*Apology*		
79B5	174	18e.5–19a.2	90	
Essay on the Life and Poetry of Homer (De Vita et Poesi Homeri)		**Solon**		
2.164, ll. 2015–2017	163	*Elegy on the Muses*	272	
Life of Nicias		fr. 11.7–8	164	
29.2–3	239	fr. 36.1–2 W.2	169	
Moral Essays (Moralia) 365, 368				
144 c–d	62	**Sophilus**		
Moral Essays (Amatoriae narrationes)		*Leda*	46	
796f.	62			
Moral Essays (Amatorius)		*Tyndareos*	46	
697c–771d	62			
Moral Essays (Coniugalia praecepta)		**Sophocles**		
142 e–143a	62	*Ajax*		
Moral Essays (Quaestiones Conviviales)		121–124	159	
7.8.712 c–d	33	1136	158	
Pericles		1242–1243	158	
9.2	405	*Antigone*	220, 235, 239, 330	
9.2–4	392	175–90	330	
10.5	397	442 or 440	181	
Solon		471–472	161	
25.6–28.1	411	478–479	95	
Themistocles		661–662	94	
21.5	398	904ff.	194	
23.1	396	905–912	194, 206, 223, 227	
		Electra	181–182, 189, 195, 207, 342	
Plutarch–Ps.				
Lives of the Ten Orators 375		420–410	181	
833d	335	528	196, 214, 221	
836e	335	528–532	196, 221	
Antiphon		528–540	206	
833c	334	528–546	212	
		534–546	196, 221, 227	
Quintilian		548	173	
Institutio Oratoria		566–574	197	
4.1	89	1221ff.	342	
		1348ff.	342	
Sappho		*Oedipus at Colonus*		
fr. 130	46	31–32	163	
		254–255	159	
Seneca		292	155	
De Consolatione ad Marciam		396–400	160	
24	63	401 (posthumous)	181	
		461	159	
		556	159	

728	153, 159	944–945	159
728–1043	153	947–949	390
734	159	948	169
735	158, 160	949	169, 390
736	160	951	169
737–738	158	952	169
739	159	953	169
741	158	955	169
741–752	158	956	169
743–744	156, 159	958	169
744	159	959	169
745–753	159	964	171–172
746	159	977	171
750	159	981	161
751	160	986	157, 161
753–754	160	987	171
756	160	988–999	194–195, 201, 206, 223
757	160		
762	161	991–999	172
774	161	992–994	206
776	170	1000–1001	161
782	161	1016	164
783–788	162	1199	155
787	161	1348	158
789–790	170	*Oedipus Tyrannus*	
794	161	370–371	162
806	161	436–433	181
808–9	164	548	173
814	165	583–602	173
817–886	165	807–809	173
826	165	851–854	202, 226
838	166	*Philoctetes*	164, 166, 176
871	166	98–99	289
872	166	407–409	160
874–875	166	523	160
881	166	631	159
913–914	167	806	159
929–931	167	1243	158
937–1015	164	1257–1258	158
939	168, 169	1294	158
939–959	168	*Trachiniae*	
940	158, 169	1060	91
941	169–170		
942	170	**Stobaeus**	
942–943	170	*Florilegium*	
943	169	4.20a 34	34
944	159, 169	21–22	62

Index Locorum — **451**

Suda
α 271   91
α 1982   61
ζ 130   306

Syrianus
On Hermogenes de Statibus
1 (= *Test*. 83 K.–A.),   65

Terence
Adelphoe
333ff.   37
470ff.   37

Theocritus
Idylls   46

Theodectes
Art of Rhetoric   334

Theognis
Elegiac Poems
1.979–982   93

Thucydides
Epitaphios   310
2.35.2   310
The Peloponnesian War
1.9.4   192
1.34.3   94
1.41.4   259
1.45   400
1.51   400
1.77.1   405
1.89.3–93   395
1.89–108   395
1.95.1–96.1   399
1.96   395
1.98   395, 399
1.98.1   399
1.98.2   399
1.100.1   395
1.101.1   399
1.114   400
1.135.2–3   398
1.138.3   260
1.140–144   259

2.13.2   259
2.14.2   259
2.19   114
2.20–22   110
2.22   114
2.35   93, 106, 310
2.35ff.   329
2.35.1   93
2.35.2   106
2.36.1   106
2.36.2   106
2.36.4   106
2.36.6   72
2.37   94, 167, 406
2.37.1   94, 406
2.39.2   94
2.40.1–3   93
2.41   107, 112
2.41.2   93
2.41.4   93
2.41.5   112
2.42.2   93
2.43.1   93
2.43.2.   276
2.46.1   93
2.56   115
2.56.1   115
2.58   115
2.59–65   110
2.65   93, 242, 245, 410
2.65.10   245
2.65.9–10   93
2.79   115
3.1   114
3.19.1   207
3.36.6   242
3.37   76, 115
3.37–38   76
3.38   76, 164
3.38.7   81
3.44   407
3.49.4   240
3.66.1   94
4.21–22   242
4.42   251
4.44   104
5.116.3–4   242

5.3	240	2.3.40	334
5.32	240	*History of Greece*	391, 408
5.60.6	188	1.7.4–24	408
6.16.1–3	251	*Memorabilia*	
6.31	115	1.6	334
6.35–41	242	3.5.20	389, 393
8.73.3	251	*Oeconomicus*	
8.92	188	5.5–25	61
8.97.2	404	6.17	43
		7.7–13	43

Tragicorum Graecorum Fragmenta

TrGF II F 323	161	9.14–15	61
TrGF IV T 1.21.90–91	163	*Symposium*	
TrGF IV T 100.4	174	8.3	62, 64
TrGF I 70 Carcinus II F 1e (Medea)	223		

Xenophon–Ps.
Athenaion Politeia

Various authors
Little Iliad

		1.14	405
fr.3	235	1.16–18	405
		3.2	405
		3.4	405

Xenophon
Hellenica

2.3.1–2.4.3	398

Index of Greek Words

ἀγαθός 250–251, 272, 289–290
ἀγαθός ποιητής 289–290
ἄγγελος 154
ἀγελαῖος 308
ἀγλωσσία 89, 90, 91
ἄγλωσσος 91
ἀγών 259, 261
ἀγὼν λόγων 127
ἀγὼν σοφίας 252, 259, 261
ἀκούσιος φόνος 171
ἀλάστωρ 161–162, 215
ἅμιλλα λόγων 127–128
ἀναγνώρισις 340–344
ἀνάγω 87
ἄναξ 26, 89, 189, 272
ἀνόσιον στόμα 161
ἀσθενεῖς 11
ἄφετος 319
ἀχρεῖον 271, 276

βίοτος 276

γενναῖος 250
γνώμη 260

δεξιός 260–261
δεσποτῶν 88
διαβολή 90, 171, 217
δίκαιον 11, 161, 172–173, 185, 210, 213
δίκη φόνου 186
δόμον 139, 142, 225
δόξα 271, 275–276
δούλων 88

ἔντεχναι πίστεις 129, 144
ἐπίδικα 128
ἐπιθυμίαν 43–44, 50
εὐβουλία 259
εὐγενεῖς 250
εὐγλωσσία 91
εὔγλωσσος 91
ἠθοποιία 339
ἦθος 155–156, 158, 161, 163, 174, 340
ἧσσον φέρει 91

θελκτήριοι μῦθοι 190
θυμός 102, 109, 112, 166

κακηγορία 171, 214
κακός 144, 159–160, 194, 198, 223–226, 240, 250, 272
κακῶς 7, 9–10, 37–38, 44, 144–145, 227, 241, 273, 310, 322, 352
καλός τε κἀγαθός 251
κέρδος 272, 276
κίνδυνος 273, 277
κῦδος 270, 275

λογογράφος 156, 174–175

ματεύω 277
μέγας 77, 89, 225
μοῖρα 273, 277
μοχθηρός 252

νομικόν 11
νόμων γραφαί 12

ὄλεθρος 53, 357
ὁμηρομάστιξ 306
ὄνησις 92–93, 225

πάθος 142, 340, 342
πάσχειν 9, 22, 210
πειθοῦς δημιουργός 127
πόθος 23, 40–41, 58–59, 196, 221
ποιητής 105, 252, 289–290, 341
πονηρός 118, 250, 252, 254, 256, 382

σθένουσι 10–11
σοφία 93, 252, 259
σοφός 90–92, 260

στάσεις 128

τεθνάναι 252
ὑπηρετεῖν 258
ὑπηρέτης 258
ὑπόβλητον στόμα 161

φυσικόν 11
χαμαιτύπη 53

χρηστός 93, 94, 105, 214, 250, 254, 271, 276, 382

www.ingramcontent.com/pod-product-compliance
Lightning Source LLC
Chambersburg PA
CBHW031409230426
43668CB00007B/256